D1083885

Critical Essays on William Faulkner: The Compson Family

Critical Essays on William Faulkner: The Compson Family

Arthur F. Kinney

G. K. Hall & Co. • Boston, Massachusetts

Library of Congress Cataloging in Publication Data
Main entry under title:

Critical essays on William Faulkner.

   (Critical essays on American literature)
   Includes index.
   Contents: 1. The Compson family—
   1. Faulkner, William, 1897–1962. Sound and the fury.
I. Kinney, Arthur F.,   II. Series.
PS3511.A86Z777   813'.52   82-3111
ISBN 0-8161-8464-X   AACR2

This publication is printed on permanent/durable acid-free paper
MANUFACTURED IN THE UNITED STATES OF AMERICA

CRITICAL ESSAYS ON AMERICAN LITERATURE

This series seeks to publish the most important reprinted criticism on writers and topics in American literature along with, in various volumes, original essays, interviews, bibliographies, letters, manuscript sections, and other materials brought to public attention for the first time. This volume on William Faulkner's Compson family, edited by Arthur F. Kinney, Professor of English at the University of Massachusetts, Amherst, is in many ways a remarkable book. It gathers all of Faulkner's experiments with the Compsons before the publication of *The Sound and the Fury* along with his own introductions and commentary. It also contains the major reactions to that novel in the United States, England, and France as well as the most historically significant criticism on the Compson fiction from 1929 to the present. Also included are a novella, *Candace*, by Alan Cheuse that projects the future of Caddy, the first critical essay on Faulkner by the novelist Joan Williams, and important new essays by John W. Hunt, Donald M. Kartiganer, and Professor Kinney. We are confident that this collection will make a permanent and significant contribution to American literary study.

James Nagel, GENERAL EDITOR

Northeastern University

For the Lamont Family:
Pauline, Danny, Laurie, David, Raphael,
and in memory of Walter Lamont

and for
Katherine T. Andrews,
with grateful memories of a long still
hot weary rewarding May afternoon

So I began to write, without much purpose, until I realized that to make it truly evocative it must be personal, in order to not only preserve my own interest in the writing, but to preserve my belief in the savour of the bread-and-salt. . . . So I got some people, some I invented, others I created out of tales I learned of nigger cooks and stable boys . . . in the long drowsy afternoons. Created I say, because they are composed partly from what they were in actual life and partly from what they should have been and were not: thus I improved on God who, dramatic though He be, has no sense, no feeling for, theatre.

—Fragment of Faulkner autograph manuscript
in Yale University Library, circa 1931

El artista, quieralo o no, descubre con el tiempo que ha llegado a dedicarse a seguir un solo camino, un solo objetivo, del cual no puede desviarse. / The artist, whether or not he wishes it, discovers with the passage of time that he has come to pursue a single path, a single objective, from which he cannot deviate.

—From Faulkner's Speech of Acceptance for
the Andres Bellow Award, Caracas, 1961

CONTENTS

INTRODUCTION

Arthur F. Kinney*

    " 'Brethren and sisteren . . . . I got the recollection and the blood of the Lamb! . . . Brethren . . . Breddren en sistuhn! . . . I got de ricklickshun en de blood of de Lamb!" (p. 368)[1]: the Reverend Shegog's vivid and personal testimony joining the Old Testament's sacrifice of Isaac with the New Testament's Crucifixion of Christ erupts into tongues in Nigger Hollow on Easter Sunday 1928 and transforms the celebration of the miraculous Resurrection of ages past into an ongoing, miraculous Pentecost of the present. This "undersized" visitor "in a shabby alpaca coat" with his "wizened black face like a small, aged monkey" who sits "dwarfed and countrified by the minister's imposing bulk," this stranger from St. Louis who has just come to Jefferson, Yoknapatawpha County, Mississippi, speaks at first in a "level and cold voice" that "sounded like a white man" (pp. 365–66). But not for long. The separate congregations of black men and black women, summoned by two separate bells, sit as one looking at the preacher under a Christmas bell of twisted paper. "They began to watch him as they would a man on a tight rope. They even forgot his insignificant appearance in the virtuosity with which he ran and poised and swooped upon the cold inflectionless wire of his voice, so that at last, when with a sort of swooping glide he came to rest again beside the reading desk with one arm resting upon it at shoulder height and his monkey body as reft of all motion as a mummy or an emptied vessel, the congregation sighed as if it waked from a collective dream and moved a little in its seats" (p. 366). This "meagre figure" (p. 367) at first seems consumed by his own voice—pure sound and fury, but the force and assurance translate him into "a serene, tortured crucifix that transcended its shabbiness and insignificance and made it of no moment" (p. 368). A second Christ, at a second Calvary, the intensity of his faith transfigures him once more, out of flesh again and into the balm of the Holy Spirit. Before him, Benjy Compson sits, "rapt in his sweet blue gaze" (p. 370). Before him, Dilsey Gibson sits, "crying rigidly and quietly in the annealment and the blood of the remembered Lamb" (p. 371). Frony no longer complains. " 'Yes, Jesus,' " the worshippers respond (p. 368), seeing Christ in the Reverend Shegog and becoming likenesses with him,

*A portion of this essay, in a slightly different form, was delivered as a lecture at LeMoyne College on October 24, 1981. It is printed here for the first time.

with Him. "The congregation seemed to watch with its own eyes while the voice consumed him, until he was nothing and they were nothing and there was not even a voice but instead their hearts were speaking to one another in chanting measures beyond the need for words" (p. 367). Communally they are all annealed, made one by being washed clean in the blood of the One Who saves. It is an extraordinarily memorable event in American fiction that, with a readily acknowledged power and poignancy, brings to a climax the agony and ecstasy of *The Sound and the Fury*, William Faulkner's most personal novel and his basic chronicle of the Compson family.

Faulkner's effect here, of course, is as calculated as Shegog's is. Both reach back to the roots of black oral tradition that can be seen—and has been—as drawing on the rhetorical resources of bardic poetry.[2]

> Brethren and sisteren
> I got the recollection and the blood of the Lamb
> Brethren
> Breddren en sistuhn!
> 5 I got de ricklickshun en de blood of de Lamb
> When de long, cold
> Oh, I tells you, breddren, when de long, cold
> I sees de light en I sees de word, po sinner
> Dey passed away in Egypt, de swingin chariots
> 10 De generations passed away
> Wus a rich man
> Whar he now
> O breddren?
> Was a po man
> 15 Whar he now
> O sistuhn?
> Oh I tells you
> Ef you aint got de milk en de dew of de old salvation
>   when de long, cold years rolls away!
> I tells you, breddren, en I tells you, sistuhn, dey'll
>   come a time
> 20 Po sinner saying Let me lay down wid de Lawd
> Lemme lay down my load
> Den what Jesus gwine say, O breddren?
> O sistuhn?
> Is you got de ricklickshun en de Blood of de Lamb?
> 25 Case I aint gwine load down heaven!
> Breddren!
> Look at dem little chillen settin dar
> Jesus wus like dat once
> He mammy suffered de glory en de pangs
> 30 Sometime maybe she helt him at de nightfall
> Whilst de angels singin him to sleep

Maybe she look out de do' en see de Roman po-lice passin
Listen, breddren!
I sees de day
35 Ma'y settin in de do' wid Jesus on her lap
De little Jesus
Like dem chillen dar
De little Jesus
I hears de angels singin de peaceful songs en de glory
40 I sees de closin eyes
Sees Mary jump up
Sees de sojer face
We gwine to kill
We gwine to kill
45 We gwine to kill yo little Jesus!
I hears de weepin en de lamentation of de po mammy
widout de salvation en de word of God!
I sees hit, breddren!
I sees hit!
Sees de blastin, blindin sight!
50 I sees Calvary, wid de sacred trees
Sees de thief en de murderer en de least of dese
I hears de boastin en de braggin
Ef you be Jesus, lif up yo tree en walk!
I hears de wailin of women en de evenin lamentations
55 I hears de weepin en de cryin en de turnt-away face
of God
Dey done kilt Jesus
Dey done kilt my Son!
O blind sinner!
Breddren, I tells you
60 Sistuhn, I says to you
When de Lawd did turn His mighty face, say,
Aint gwine overload heaven
I can see de widowed God shet His do'
I sees de whelmin flood roll between
65 I sees de darkness en de death everlastin upon de
generations
Den, lo! Breddren!
Yes, breddren!
Whut I see?
Whut I see, O sinner?
70 I sees de resurrection en de light!
Sees de meek Jesus saying Dey kilt Me dat ye shall live
again
I died dat dem whut sees en believes shall never die
Breddren
O breddren!
75 I sees de doom crack en hears de golden horns shoutin
down de glory

> En de arisen dead whut got de blood en de ricklickshun
> of de Lamb!

The striking rhythms, with their directness, brevity, and clarity, have the capacity to awaken and convince. Their repetition, their relentless narrative logic, is, moreover, haunting, incantatory. It insinuates the chant-response which is awakened in the Nigger Hollow congregation. It wills them into *being* that community which it urges as its fundamental message.

For behind the spellbinding magic of the Reverend Shegog's sermon there is a scriptural message, a theological interpretation of the Holy Word of God and of the Easter service that is realized by the occasion and delivery of his address. By *getting* (present) the *recollection* (past) of the blood of the Lamb (line 2), he *sees* (present) "de resurrection en de light" of the future (line 70). His understanding of Biblical history leads him to prophecy. Like his congregation, he stands at midpoint, able to learn, being tested, needing to choose. There, in the two-dimensional "painted church" where "the whole scene was as flat and without perspective as a painted cardboard set upon the ultimate edge of the flat earth, against the windy sunlight of space and April and a midmorning filled with bells" (p.364), he introduces the third dimension of depth (that is, conceptual understanding) and the fourth, of time (that is, of eternity). Prior to Dilsey, he teaches about the beginning and the end, the first and the last, in the Alpha and Omega of Easter when man and God are made one. The swinging chariots of Egypt, the dying generations of the past, even the poverty of then and now, he tells the faithful flock before him, are washed clean by Christ's blood and are eradicated in an annealment by which doom cracks (line 75) and the whole community of believers take their own chariots past the golden horns of angels to the glory of heaven and life everlasting (lines 75–76). Logic, rhetoric, and performance are likewise annealed in this single, plainspoken message.

Such a hortatory introduction and conclusion is an ancient tradition of oral sermon. By the same tradition, concepts enclose a concrete narrative that proves and illustrates them. True to form, Shegog provides such a narrative; in keeping with his triad of time melting into eternity, he juxtaposes three iconic pictures of Christ: the Babe threatened by Herod ("We gwine to kill yo little Jesus!," line 45); the man killed by Pilate ("Dey done kilt Jesus/Dey done kilt my Son!", lines 56–57); the triumphant Lord who supplied salvation ("de meek Jesus saying Dey kilt Me dat ye shall live again," line 71). Shegog's synoptic viewpoint locates the significance of Christ's life at those moments that are bloodiest; his view of them, like Christ's blood, *anneals*. But Shegog is also syncretic; the blood of Christ recollects the blood of Isaac, the blood of worship, sacrifice, communion, and salvation. In this way, even the poor are made rich (lines 12–18) and the "little chillen" (line 27), physical entities in the "painted church," become brothers and sisters in the spirit of the Lord. "Cold years rolls away" (line 18) when lamentations are instructed by belief. Only then does the recollection of blood become the annealing source of glory.

This understanding of the bleeding of Christ is crucially instructive for the very next scene, in which Jason Compson IV's possible bleeding is self-induced, self-pitying, and futile. " 'Am I bleeding much?' he said. 'The back of my head. Am I bleeding?' . . . . 'He hit me,' Jason said. 'Am I bleeding?' (p. 388). Such thoughts here are hollow parodies, like the apostolic non-acts of T. S. Eliot's contemporary hollow men in the wasteland Faulkner knew. There is no attempt by Jason to surrender, to give, or to anneal; and there is no possibility of a tortured crucifixion, even the sort that Shegog embodies at the pulpit. " 'You sure he didn't hit me?' " Jason asks "the man" who drags him away (p. 389), asking him why he would try, in such quiet desperation, to " 'commit suicide' " (p. 388), to act void of hope and faith. " 'There would have been blood if I hadn't got there when I did,' " he says, taking Jason from the little old man with the hatchet whom he has gratuitously insulted and terrorized. " 'I thought I was bleeding,' " Jason says, limply; " 'You hit your head on the rail,' " is the reply. And then, " 'You better go on. They aint here' " (p. 389). The young Quentin IV and her carnival friend with the red tie have escaped, although they too, Faulkner implies, fail to find anneal- ment in the blood of the Lamb, fail to be reborn except into a self- indulgent freedom. But then, Caroline Bascomb Compson, Jason's mother and Quentin's grandmother, has prophesied this in the preceding scene with Jason, the scene just before the Nigger Hollow service. She knows Quentin IV will disappear. " 'It's in the blood,' " she tells her son. " 'Like uncle, like niece. Or mother. I dont know which would be worse, I dont seem to care' " (p. 374). The uncle (Quentin III) and the mother (Caddy) are her own son and daughter—her own flesh and blood—but there is no sense of salvational healing for Caroline. There is no sense of kinship either. The blood is tainted; her disposition has soured. Rather than a new faith, Easter brings to Caroline and Jason Compson only self- pity and resignation. Their thinning blood, like their attenuated spirit, shows no promise of renewal.

The Sound and the Fury is pointedly and persistently a novel about blood, about blood lines. When Luster misbehaves, his grandmother Dilsey tells him that he has " 'jes es much Compson devilment . . . . es any of em' " (p. 344). When Caroline wishes to praise Jason she can do so only by eradicating his Compson blood, by making him a Bascomb. When Benjy proves to be mentally retarded, she changes his name, from that of her brother Maury to that of Benjamin; transferring nominal blood con- nections frees her of guilt. Jason's chapter of *The Sound and the Fury*, especially, insists on this blood division. It is here that Caroline Compson talks repeatedly "about how her own flesh and blood rose up to curse her" in the demise of her family through her unfortunate marriage (p. 224). " 'Remember,' " she tells Jason, Quentin IV is " 'your own flesh and blood' . . . . 'Sure,' I says, 'that's just what I'm thinking of —flesh. And a little blood, too, if I had my way' " (p. 224). What is for Caddy the vital assumption on which she bases her daughter's whole future with Jason—" 'You'll have to promise to take care of her, too—She's kin to you; your own flesh and blood' " (p. 260)—is for Jason the living symbol of her as a burden to him, of her damned and wicked nature. "Me, without any hat, in the middle of the afternoon, having to chase up and down alleys because of my mother's good name. Like I say you cant do anything with a woman like that, if she's got it in her. If it's in her blood, you can't do anything with her" (pp. 289–90). "Like I say blood always tells. If you've got blood like that in you, you'll do anything" (p. 297). "Because like I say blood is blood and you cant get around it" (p. 303). Such biological determinism expands to take in the suicidal Quentin, the idiot Benjy. "Blood, I says, governors and generals. It's a damn good thing we never had any kings and presidents; we'd all be down there at Jackson chasing butterflies" (p. 286). Blood is synonymous with the Compson line, and bad blood with the Compson name. Quentin IV's blood rises to a passionate will for survival, while Jason's passions buckle beneath him, "with my legs not using so much blood, it all would go into my head like it would explode any minute" (p. 300); "With the sun and all in my eyes and my blood going so I kept thinking every time my head would go on and burst and get it over with" (p. 301). The bad blood of the Compsons leads Jason to a kind of sardonic, nihilistic despair, a willed self-punishment that borders dangerously on self-destruction.

For Quentin III, the thought of "this Compson blood" (p. 128) also leads to despair. The "sort of blood obligation noblesse oblige" (p. 130) of a Mrs. Bland, swathed in apricot silk with the haughty pride of the nouveau riche, takes little of Quentin's attention because for him it is of little value. It is the nihilistic fatalism of his father that concerns him more deeply—so much so that in trying to escape the mechanistic time his father employs to illustrate a basis for a kind of existentialist despair he deliberately attempts to destroy his watch; he cuts himself; and he bleeds (p. 99). This, like the pounding blood in Jason's head and the bruise from the rail, parodies the annealing blood that transfixes Reverend Shegog, Benjy, Dilsey, and Frony. And it is the other kind of blood, too, the beating blood of passionate sexuality, that causes Quentin to suffer and perish. The memory of the "blood horse" (p. 138) and the scattered acts of self-mutilation ("the jerked skein of blood backward not looping," p. 143, that Versh tells him about) lead, in Quentin's consciousness, directly to memories of his bloody punishment of Caddy for sexual misconduct ("*My red hand coming up out of her face*," p. 166), of his excitement with his sister after his encounter with Natalie ("*my blood or her blood*"; "*Oh her blood or my blood Oh*," p. 167), of Caddy's own excitement over Dalton

Ames ("it was on her face and throat like paint her blood pounded against my hand," p. 188; "I felt the first surge of blood there it surged in strong accelerating beats," p. 200; "her blood surged steadily beating and beating against my hand," p. 203) merging with his ("the cut place on my finger was smarting again," p. 203) anticipating his own parodic voyeurism ("Just by imagining the clump it seemed to me that I could hear whispers secret surges smell the beating of hot blood under wild unsecret flesh watching against red eyelids the swine untethered in pairs rushing coupled into the sea," p. 219). The cut finger at Harvard and the bloodied fights with Dalton Ames (p. 200) and with Gerald Bland (pp. 204–07; 214) that stain his reputation and, finally, the vest of the formal suit he puts on for his incestuous, suicidal marriage with Caddy—his own formal ceremony responding to the formal invitation to her wedding which he has, laid out like a coffin, in his room (p. 222). As with Jason, blood signifies demise for Quentin, not rebirth. There is no annealment for either of them, as there is none for their sister Caddy, their niece Quentin IV, or their parents Caroline and Jason III.

"I feel sorry for the Compsons," Faulkner remarked in Charlottesville thirty years after *The Sound and the Fury*, in May of 1959. "That was blood which was good and brave once, but has thinned and faded all the way out."[3] "The men like Compson and Sutpen," Faulkner said on another occasion at Charlottesville, "who had the desire to be heroic—they failed through lack of character or absence of things in their character which [should] have been there but at least they tried."[4] What their blood, and their bloodline, their heredity, lacked was the realization of grace in the Christian's inherited recollection of the blood of the Lamb. What they substitute is the terror of blood and what it holds in store. Not only climactic here, it is also climactic in *Absalom, Absalom!* as Quentin's roommate Shreve leads him to find another paradigm of himself and his family in Henry Sutpen and the Sutpen dynasty. That too perished on the rocks of tainted blood and its threat.

> *Henry looks at the pistol; now he is not only panting, he is trembling; when he speaks now his voice is not even the exhalation, it is the suffused and suffocating inbreath itself:*
> —*You are my brother.*
> —*No I'm not. I'm the nigger that's going to sleep with your sister. Unless you stop me, Henry* (pp. 357–58).[5]

Here the memory triggers recollection of a visit to Henry at Sutpen's Hundred, rather than a wedding announcement. The language is revealing. Quentin

> went in, entered the bare, stale room whose shutters were closed too, where a second lamp burned dimly on a crude table; waking or sleeping it was the same; the bed, the yellow sheets and pillow, the wasted yellow face with closed, almost transparent eyelids on the pillow, the wasted

hands crossed on the breast as if he were already a corpse; waking or
sleeping it was the same and would be the same forever as long as he lived
(p. 373).

Henry Sutpen, aware of the sins of blood passion, lies like a corpse too.
His portrait, as Quentin tells it, is essentially blood*less*.

In its explicit concerns with blood and lineage, *The Sound and the Fury*
figures the whole Compson saga in minature. "More perhaps than the
chronicler of a mythic corner of Mississippi, Faulkner is the premier
American novelist of family," Donald M. Kartiganer writes;[6] he is, Edwin Berry Burgum tells us, "captivated by the family pattern."[7] The
tainted blood which the Compsons share leads to a common failure to
communicate—to listen, to speak, to relate freely with one another. Their
wills intrude. This is true no matter where we find them; to the vexed
question on whether the Quentin Compson in *The Sound and the Fury*
was the Quentin Compson of *Absalom, Absalom!* Faulkner was clear and
consistent. Working on *Absalom* in February 1934, he wrote his publisher
Harrison Smith,

> Quentin Compson, of the Sound & Fury, tells it, or ties it together; he is
> the protagonist so that it is not complete apocrypha. I use him because it is
> just before he is to commit suicide because of his sister, and I use his bit-
> terness which he has projected on the South in the form of hatred of it and
> its people to get more out of the story itself than a historical novel would
> be. To keep the hoop skirts and plug hats out, you might say.[8]

In 1958 he was telling a graduate course at the University of Virginia,

> To me he's consistent. That he approached the Sutpen family with the
> same ophthalmia that he approached his own troubles, that he probably
> never saw anything very clearly, that his was just one of the thirteen ways
> to look at Sutpen, and his may have been the—one of the most erroneous.
> Probably his friend McCannon had a much truer picture of Sutpen from
> what Quentin told him than Quentin himself did.
>   Q. But it's still Sutpen's story. It's not Quentin's story.
>   A. No its Sutpen's story. But then, every time any character gets into a
> book, no matter how minor, he's actually telling his biography—that's all
> anyone ever does, he tells his own biography, talking about himself, in a
> thousand different terms, but himself. Quentin was still trying to get God
> to tell him why, in *Absalom, Absalom!* as he was in *The Sound and the
> Fury*.[9]

By the same token, Quentin's percipience coupled with idealism color his
narration of "A Justice" and "Lion," while his recounting of "That
Evening Sun" is limited to point of view; there the absent Benjy is
represented in the syntax and diction which are more like the first chapter
of *The Sound and the Fury* than the second. The willed ignorance of Nancy's danger which Mr. Compson demonstrates in "That Evening Sun"

heralds his refusal to believe Quentin will commit suicide in *The Sound and the Fury* and his failure to understand in what ways Sutpen's rapid success in *Absalom, Absalom!* parodies the Compsons and presages their decline.

That each of these stories was a portion of the larger family study was clarified in 1945 when Faulkner wrote *The Sound and the Fury* a fifth time, an attempt he should have written earlier, he tells Malcom Cowley.[10] This "Appendix," titled simply, but tellingly, "COMPSON: 1699–1945," then became for Faulkner the foreword, not the afterword, of *The Sound and the Fury*. On this point he was decisive with his editor Robert N. Linscott.

> When you reprint THE SOUND AND THE FURY, I have a new section to go with it. I should have written this new section when I wrote the book itself, but I never thought of it until Malcolm Cowley let me help him getting together his portable Faulkner volume that Viking has.
>
> By all means include this in the reprint. When you read it, you will see how it is the key to the whole book, and after reading it, the 4 sections as they stand now fall into clarity and place. He has the only clean copy of this new section. I will write him today to have a copy of it made and sent to you. When you issue the book, print the sections in this order, print this appendix first, and title it APPENDIX. This will be anachronistic but no more so than the other sections:
>
> > 1st section: APPENDIX
> > Compson
>
> Then continue with the sections as they now are. I dont have a copy of the book and cant cite correctly, but they follow:
>
> > Benjy's section
> > APRIL 5 (I think)
> > Quentin's section
> > June 2, 1910
> > Jason's section
> > APRIL 6
> > Author's section
> > APRIL 7
>
> Be sure and print the appendix *first*, but call it as I titled it:
>
> > APPENDIX
> > COMPSON[11]

"Compson" begins not with the white Scottish line, but with the Indian chief Ikkemotubbe. Although he calls himself "L'Homme," later "Doom," he corrupts more than his name since he uses intimidation and exploitation to rule his Chickasaw people. As a result, he becomes in time "A dispossessed American King" (p. 403). His brief biographical sketch is that of a gambler whose greed finally causes his defeat (in exile); in this way he anticipates several Compsons. His life story is followed by a sketch of Andrew Jackson, pictured as sentimental, idealistic, naive. His innocence is the other side of Ikkemotubbe's craftiness, as it foreshadows the other sort of Compson. Then come the Compsons themselves—a gallery of the dispossessed—who alternate between the naive idealist (Quentin Maclachan, or Quentin I, who rebels against the King of England; Charles Stuart, who rebels against the United States; Jason II, or General Compson, who suffers the Confederates' defeat at Shiloh and Resaca; Jason III, Mr. Compson, who fails as a lawyer and father; and his son Quentin III) and the corrupt gambler (Jason Lycurgus, or Jason I, the Old Governor, who trades a racehorse for the Compson Domain, a square mile of the best land in Jefferson; Jason IV, who extorts his niece and sister and steals from his mother). The long lists of public accomplishments and gestures of heroism in "Compson" limn a long line of men internally helpless or corrupt. Together, they people a decadent aristocracy, one weakened by nature as well as by activity (or inactivity). The family history thus writ large remains a history of sound and fury signifying very little.

Doubtless Faulkner could write his "Appendix" largely by memory because the Compsons had formed the backbone of much of Yoknapatawpha; they appear in *The Sound and the Fury*, *Absalom, Absalom!*, *The Unvanquished*, *Go Down, Moses*, *Requiem for a Nun*, *The Town*, and *The Mansion*; in "That Evening Sun," "A Justice," "Lion," "Skirmish at Sartoris," "My Grandmother Millard," "Vendée," "Retreat," "Raid," "A Bear Hunt," "The Old People," "The Bear," and "Delta Autumn." Most of these appearances over several decades, moreover, coalesce, reinforcing the portraits in the "Appendix" in which a series of ineffectual and idealistic men characterized by inept efforts at honor and heroism are enclosed by Jason I and Jason IV, two speculators swift to sense an opportunity and ruthless in turning it to their own benefit. It is their rapacity from which the Compsons descend, and toward which they move—blood begetting blood, despite the half-hearted attempts of intervening teachers, lawyers, and students to transform their family line. The first Compson in Yoknapatawpha, Jason I,

> had come to the settlement a few years ago with a race-horse, which he swapped to Ikkemotubbe, Issetibbeha's successor in the chiefship, for a square mile of what was to be the most valuable land in the future town of Jefferson, who, legend said, drew a pistol and held the ravishers at bay until the bandits could be got into the jail and the auger holes bored and someone sent to fetch old Alec Holston's lock,[12]

guaranteeing his leadership in the community by averting attention from his own brigandage to those unlucky bandits "captured by chance by an incidental band of civilian more-or-less militia and brought in to the Jefferson jail because it was the nearest one" (*RN*, p. 5). Compson has only just arrived. He is not one of the first three white settlers of these Chickasaw lands (Doctor Habersham, Alexander Holston, Louis

Grenier), but of the second generation, preceding by only a year or two the Sartorises, Stevenses, McCaslins, Sutpens, and Coldfields—but he holds the thieves at gunpoint (*RN*, p. 12), displaces Holston by presiding over the meeting called to determine how to respond to their jailbreak (*RN*, p. 13), gets the lock from Holston but manages to arrange for others to pay for it (*RN*, pp. 17–19) and is defeated, finally, only by the morality of Thomas Jefferson Pettigrew: " 'Hell,' Compson said. 'Everybody knows what's wrong with him. It's ethics. He's a damned moralist' " (*RN*, p. 23).

In succeeding the nascent white civilization on Chickasaw land with the founding of Jefferson, Compson also succeeds the original triumvirate of Habersham, Holston, and Grenier as the head of the second (Compson, Peabody, and Ratcliffe, *RN*, p. 24). And it is Compson, "the gnat, the thorn, the catalyst" (*RN*, p. 29), who sells them land from the Compson Domain for the courthouse (and *at his own price!*, *RN*, p. 185), who conscripts Sutpen's French architect and sets up a workcrew on his pasture and, anticipating by generations Benjy's weekly visit to the center of Jefferson, supervises building

> a Square, the courthouse in its grove the center; quadrangular around it, the stores, two-storey, the offices of the lawyers and doctors and dentists, the lodge-rooms and auditoriums, above them; school and church and the tavern and bank and jail each in its ordered place (*RN*, p. 34).

So successful is he that he alone among the six founders of Jefferson joins the esteemed

> roster of Mississippi names:
> Claiborne. Humphries. Dickson. McLaurin. Barksdale. Lamar. Prentiss. Davis. Sartoris. Compson (*RN*, p. 97).

Having first established himself—who knows how?—by owning "the Indian accounts for tobacco and calico and jeans pants and cooking-pots on Ratcliffe's books" (*RN*, p. 188), by the time we leave him he has sold on credit to the white settlers all their necessities and luxuries out of Ratcliffe's store (*RN*, p. 189). He has become Flem Snopes to Ratcliffe's Will Varner. While his children and grandchildren honor his name for the chivalric sound of it—from the Scotland of Sir Walter Scott—Jason I has already permanently undermined family and community.

Yet in light of his success we have some sympathy for his own son's failures. Jason II, pointedly called "General" Compson, loses two battles of the Confederacy before joining the carpetbagger Redmond in building a railroad—and then selling out to him (*RN*, p. 205). A far lesser man in his old age, he is seen sitting before a pot of Brunswick stew with Major De Spain during the bear hunts,[13] giving his compass up to Ike (who, using it, does not see Old Ben)[14] and, later, his hunting horn (only to have it passed on to a mulatto McCaslin in Chicago),[15] while deeding his gun to

Boon Hogganbeck, the county's worst marksman,[16] who destroys it in a moment of rage and madness.[17] Even Lucius Priest knows General Compson as one who

> had commanded troops not too unsuccessfully as a colonel at Shiloh, and again not too unsuccessfully as a brigadier during Johnston's retreat on Atlanta, [but] was a little short in terrain, topography, and would promptly get lost ten minutes after he left camp (the mule he preferred to ride would have brought him back at any time but, not only a paroled Confederate general but a Compson too, he declined to accept counsel or advice from a mule), so as soon as the last hunter was in from the morning's drive, everyone would take turns blowing a horn until General Compson at last got in. Which was satisfactory, anyway served, until General Compson's hearing began to fail too. Until finally one afternoon Walter Ewell and Sam Fathers, who was half Negro and half Chickasaw Indian, had to track him down and camp in the woods with him all night, facing Major de Spain with the alternative of either forbidding him to leave the tent or expelling him from the club.[18]

Such decrepitude is not pathetic nor comic so much as a fit reward for a misguided life

> —the Brigadier Jason Lycurgus II who failed at Shiloh in '62 and failed again though not so badly at Resaca in '64, who put the first mortgage on the still intact square mile to a New England carpetbagger in '66, after the old town had been burned by the Federal General Smith and the new little town, in time to be populated mainly by the descendants not of Compsons but of Snopeses, had begun to encroach and then nibble at and into it as the failed brigadier spent the next forty years selling fragments of it off to keep up the mortgage on the remainder.[19]

Like father, like son: Jason III will sell off Benjy's pasture to pay for Caddy's wedding (which ends in divorce within a year) and Quentin's first year at Harvard (which ends in suicide). Jason III's myopic, flatulent philosophy and his foolish mismanagement of the Compson legacy only creates in Quentin III, his eldest son, a defensive idealism. Quentin's mismanagement shows in his vision of things. "We all believed that he [Grandfather] did fine things, that his waking life passed from one fine (if faintly grandiose) picture to another," he tells us in "A Justice,"[20] while in "That Evening Sun" he appears unmoved, as older narrator or young participant, to note of Nancy that "The jailer cut her down and revived her; then he beat her, whipped her."[21] The attitude is at one with his treatment of Deacon and the black on the railroad tracks at Christmas in *The Sound and the Fury*, but such strict limitations of sympathy are firm indications that his pity, like Jason's, is mainly self-dictated. Ever the chivalric aristocrat, the Quentin who narrates "That Evening Sun" dismisses Caddy's sharp commands while bemoaning the loss of a happier world of old that has given way to a newly mechanized world of laundries symbolic of

Jason's world of commerce.[22] For it is Jason IV who, surprisingly but suggestively, is the real avatar of their Jefferson founder. "He is the one Compson and Sartoris who met Snopes on his own ground and in a fashion held his own," Faulkner writes, with a trace of joy and pride, to Malcolm Cowley on August 16, 1945;[23] in *The Town*, Jason rents his mother's building to Montgomery Ward Snopes for his atelier of pornography, while in *The Mansion* he takes on Flem himself until Benjy returns home from the asylum, burns the Compson house to the ground (killing himself), and Flem is finally outwitted by the bachelor Orestes Snopes.[24] All of these events, from all their scattered sources in Faulkner's fiction, letters, and public comments, are contained, too, in the "Appendix" called "Compson" in Jason's assumed burden "of the rotting family in the rotting house" (p. 421).

To repeat: *The Sound and the Fury* stands as metonomy for the chronicle of the Compsons, and for the chronicle of Yoknapatawpha at its farthest reaches. The first date in Yoknapatawpha history is that of 1699 with the birth, in Scotland, of Quentin Maclachan Compson; his grandson, Jason I, is the fourth settler of the county (or what becomes the county) and the first town aristocrat, antedating the Sartorises, Sutpens, and MaCaslins; and his great-great-great grandson, Jason IV, outlives them all. The Sartorises are all dead except for Benbow by 1920; Thomas Sutpen dies in 1869 and his son Henry in 1910; Ike McCaslin is a dying seventy in 1940; Mink kills Flem around 1946. But Jason IV, like Dilsey, endures. Knowing him alone, she can say she has seen the first and the last, the beginning and end of those without grace.

The Sound and the Fury is "the damndest book I ever read," Faulkner wrote in elation to his Aunt Bama when finishing it about October 1928;[25] to his agent Ben Wasson, he remarked, "Read this, Bud. It's a real son-of-a-bitch."[26] Four years later, he could tell Bennett Cerf, his publisher, "I too have a soft spot for the book."[27] Biographers show us why in part. "I have never known anyone who identified with his writings more than Bill did," his brother John Faulkner has commented; "Sometimes it was hard to tell which was which, which one Bill was, himself or the one in the story. And yet you knew somehow that the two of them were the same, they were one and inseparable."[28] Like the Compsons Faulkner traced his ancestry back to Scotland—to Inverness—and like the Compson children Faulkner must have had vivid memories of his own "Damuddy's" death in 1907, her religiosity and stoicism finally giving way to a malingering cancer[29] that sent the Falkner youngsters from their house on Buchanan and South 11th Streets in Oxford until it could be fumigated. Indeed, Faulkner and his brothers, Joseph Blotner informs us,

> could sit for the Compsons. The shared experiences of childhood were
> there in vivid memory: Billy, Johncy, Jack, and Sallie Murry riding in the

Colonel's carriage and then splashing or trying to catch fish in Davidson's Bottom or Burney Branch. There were grim memories, like those of Damuddy's lingering illness, and lively ones such as climbing out a window of The Big Place and down a tree. And there was Oxford lore absorbed in childhood. In "That Evening Sun Go Down," wrote John Cullen, Faulkner was writing about something that actually happened. A Negro named Dave Bowdry cut his wife's throat and threw her behind their bed. "There is a ditch like the one Nancy had to cross behind the place where the Falkners use to live," Cullen noted. "Dave committed the murder a short distance from the Falkner home."[30]

In "A Justice" Quentin listens to Sam Fathers; as a boy, Faulkner used to listen to the Negro blacksmith John Henry on his grandfather's farm.[31] There was also a model (or a composite model) for Caddy.

There had been no lack of little girls to admire in his life. Sallie Murry had been almost as close as a sister—a plucky good sport of a girl, brought up without a father in the sad home where her mother kept house for her own widowed father. And just one house away had been Estelle Oldham—the oldest of the children in a family every bit as proud of its status and lineage as the Compsons. The images began to fuse in a powerful and unexpected way: the funeral, the children's ignorance, and Caddy.[32]

In creating this sister he never had, moreover, William Faulkner may well have drawn on the outspoken, independent Helen Baird whom he was courting in Pascagoula shortly before starting *The Sound and the Fury*. In addition,

Faulkner revealingly gave Jason some of his father's characteristics, his verbal idiom, his temper, his lifelong sense of having been deprived of a job that he wanted badly, and a gruffness that is as lacerating as Faulkner undoubtedly once perceived his father's to be. Faulkner's mother readily admitted Jason's many similarities to Murry Falkner. "He talks just like my husband did. My husband had a hardware store uptown at one time. His way of talking was just like Jason's, same words and same style. All those 'you know's.' He also had an old 'nigrah' named Jobus, just like the character Job in the story." Moreover, Jason is as inadequate a "father" to the girl Quentin as Murry was to his son William.[33]

Faulkner's brother Jack likewise describes their Mammy, Callie Barr, in terms resonant of Dilsey.

The "Mammys" of that time were women who, with everlasting devotion and loyalty, became second mothers to white children and in so doing became intimate and loved members of the households where they were employed. Of them surely none gave more of her affection and varied talents and was loved more in return than Mammy Callie. Like our mother she was small in size, and, also like our mother, big in will power and a sense of right and wrong. It was understood that, while Mother always had the last say, we were never to disobey Mammy Callie. And we never did—at least not for long.[34]

"The Compson family," then, David Minter sums, "mirrors Faulkner's sense of [his own] family's story" and "as a story of declension."[35]

But hardly the Faulkners alone. Typical in the broadest sense of many settlers of Oxford and Lafayette County, Mississippi, the Compsons may also take part of their story—as surely they do their name—from the Jacob Thompsons whose spacious twenty-room antebellum mansion, located across from the Shegog house which Faulkner would soon purchase, was featured in "Beautiful Homes of Mississippi" and thought by many the best house in the state. Jacob Thompson, son of Nicholas Thompson and Lucretia Van Hook, a graduate of the University of North Carolina, has in common with Jason Compson I his early emigration to Oxford (1835), his position as a town dignitary, and his interest in politics (he was a member of Congress from Mississippi from 1839 to 1853). Like General Compson, Jason II, Jacob Thompson fought in the battle of Shiloh (as well as the battle of Corinth); and he was like both Compsons the most powerful, popular, and successful of the Thompsons in northern Mississippi. After Thompson's service in Congress, President Buchanan made him Secretary of the Interior from 1857 to 1861, when he resigned upon the secession of Mississippi; he served as Confidential Agent of the Confederate States to Canada from 1864–65, conducting secret missions for President Jefferson Davis and, learning his life was threatened because he was erroneously thought to be implicated in Lincoln's assassination, he went to Europe for two years at the close of the War Between the States before returning to Oxford and then moving on to Memphis where he died.[36] He is, like the Compsons, the basis of much local legend.[37]

But, as James G. Watson has recently demonstrated, *The Sound and the Fury* is as much a work about place as about people: the Compson house keeps Benjy fenced in, traps Jason, and causes Quentin to feel strangely isolated and dislocated: it is a house haunted by sickness and death where three of the four bedrooms are characterized by Mrs. Compson's use of camphor, Damuddy's death, the children's measles, and Quentin IV's incarceration.[38] Indeed, place, Eudora Welty contends,

has surface, which will take the imprint of man—his hand, his foot, his mind; it can be tamed, domesticized. It has shape, size, boundaries; man can measure himself against them. It has atmosphere and temperature, change of light and show of season, qualities to which man spontaneously responds. Place has always nursed, nourished, and instructed man; he in turn can rule it and ruin it, take it and lose it, suffer if he is exiled from it, and after living on it he goes to it in his grave. Of course it is the stuff of fiction, as close to our living lives as the earth we can pick up and rub between our fingers, something we can feel and smell.[39]

Like the place Jefferson, hollowed from Indian forest when Mississippi was admitted to the Union in 1817, all of northern Mississippi was Chickasaw land; not until the Treaty of Pontotoc in 1832 did these Indians cede their rights. This cession was the last of a series by the Chocktaws (Treaty of Mount Dexter, 1805; Treaty of Doak's Stand, 1820; Treaty of Dancing Rabbit Creek, 1830), the Chickasaws (Treaties of 1816), and others (in the Treaty of Fort Adams, 1801; the Treaty of Hoe Buckintoopa, 1803). This slow but certain diminishment, this creeping dispossession, is what is figured in Ikkemotubbe as Habersham, Holston, and Grenier figure John Craig, John Chisholm, and John Martin, three early white traders who purchased Oxford from the Indians on June 12, 1836—purchased, in fact, just over 640 acres, just over a square mile.

Melville writes in *Moby-Dick* that real places are not to be found on maps, yet these early white frontiersmen—another was named Shegog, like the Reverend—created Lafayette County by 1836 and by June 22 they were building on the site of a Chickasaw trading post their own courthouse, to govern land equidistant to the Tallahatchie River on the north and the Yocany River, spelled and called at the time "Yocanapatafa," on the south. And another real place—real in both the historical and Melvillian senses—was the home of John D. Martin, on the original Mile, purchased for $300 in March 1855 by William Thompson, brother to Jacob.[40] This home, sited where the Compson house is on the map of Jefferson (or at the corner of what is presently Buchanan and South 13th Streets), is one of the other four antebellum mansions of Oxford. It has ten rooms, including four bedrooms, large white pillars, and now even a rotting portico; to one side is a barn, to the rear the old kitchen and, quite probably, the slave quarters. Like Jacob Thompson's house, William Thompson's house was also threatened in 1861 by Grant's burning of Oxford, and only an early warning allowed the Thompsons to bury their family jewelry and silver in the back of the property. Although the Oxford courthouse and Jacob Thompson's house were destroyed by fire, William Thompson's house was spared; he lost only seven of his eight magnolia plants—brought as seeds in a shoebox from North Carolina—and his prized box hedge. After Grant's departure, William Thompson retrieved the iron fence that surrounded the courthouse and used it to surround his own land, a fence resembling the one that keeps Benjy Compson barred from a larger world.

The story of the Martin land and Thompson house, like the history of the Compson land and house, is one of property attenuated in time, sold off bit by bit, as in the deed of June 5, 1869.

> Know all men by these presents that I William Thompson have bargained and sold, and by these presents, do bargain and sell to William H. Marshall for and consideration of Five Hundred dollars to me in hand paid, the receipt whereof is hereby acknowledged certain Lots or parcels of land lying and being in the Town of Oxford, State of Mississippi, known and

ISSETIBBEHA'S

Hunting & fishing camp where Wash Jones killed Sutpen. Later owned by Major De Spain

TALLAHATCHIE RIVER

GO DOWN, MOSES

McCaslin Edmonds

WAS

WASH
THE BEAR
A JUSTICE
RED LEAVES

Sutpen's Hundred

John Sartoris' Railroad

CHICKASAW

ABSALOM, ABSALOM!

THE UNVANQUISHED

Where by 1820 his people had learned to call it "The Plantation" just like the white man did

Sartoris

RAID

AN ODOR OF VERBENA

A ROSE FOR EMILY

SANCTUARY

PATENT

Grierson

Where Lee Goodwin was jailed, tried & lynched

THE SOUND

Burden

Compson's Mile

AND THE FURY

PERCY GRIMM

THAT EVENING SUN

for which Jason I swapped Ikkemotubbe a race horse & the last fragment of which Jason IV sold in order to become free

LIGHT IN AUGUST

Airport

DEATH DRAG

JEFFERSON
and
YOKNAPATAWPHA
COUNTY
Mississippi
1945

THE
HAMLET

SPOTTED HORSES

Varner's Crossroads

Old Frenchman Place

where Popeye murdered Tawmmy

YOKNAPATAWPHA RIVER

OLD MAN

Here was born the convict & grew a man & sinned & was transported for the rest of his life to pay for it

William Faulkner's own hand-drawn map of Yoknapatawpha County, Mississippi, loosely based on Lafayette County. Compson's Square Mile, marking the founding of Jefferson (based on Oxford), is shown at the center. From *The Portable Faulkner*, edited by Malcolm Cowley. Copyright 1946, renewed © 1974 by The Viking Press, Inc. Reprinted by permission of Viking Penguin Inc.

Chisholm Craig & Martin
Sec 28 T8 R3 West
Conveyed by Eanahyea

The State of Mississippi
Lafayette County
13th 1836 & Recorded Decr 9 1836

This Indenture Made and entered into the Eighth day of December eighteen hundred and thirty six between Eanahyea of the Chickasaw in the State of Mississippi of the one part and John Chisholm John Craig & John W Martin of the other part Witnesseth that the said Eanahyea for and in consideration of the sum of Eight hundred dollars to him in hand paid the Receipt whereof is hereby acknowledged hath bargained sold and conveyed and by these presents doth bargain sell and convey unto the said John Chisholm John S Craig & John W Martin a Section of land situate lying and being in the County of Lafayette & State of Mississippi To wit Section Number Eight in Township No Eight in Range No three west of the basis Meridian It being the land to which the said Eanahyea is entitled to under the treaty of the 20 May eighteen hundred and thirty four between the Chickasaw tribe of Indians & the United States To have and to hold the aforesaid land and bargained premises in fee simple to the only proper use and behoof of the said John Chisholm John S Craig & John W Martin heirs and assigns forever And the said Eanahyea covenants to and with the said Chisholm Craig & Martin that the before mentioned land and bargained premises he will warrant and forever defend against the claim or claims of all and every person or persons whatsoever In Testimony whereof the said Eanahyea hath hereunto set his hand and affixed his seal the day and date first above written

Attest   his
             Eanah yea X (seal)
                                                   mark

We the undersigned Chiefs do hereby certify that Eanahyea the claimant named and set forth in the foregoing deed to John Chisholm is capable to manage and take care of his own affairs Given under our hands this 9th Decr 1835
                                                his
                                   Isle ah to pa hay X
                                                mark
                                        Benj Love

I Benjamin Reynolds Agent for the Chickasaw Nation do hereby certify that from the best of my knowledge & information the facts set forth in the foregoing Certificate of the chiefs is true And that the sum of Eight Hundred dollars is a fair consideration and has been paid by said Chisholm Martin & Craig to the said Eanahyea land described in the foregoing deed 9th Decr eighteen hundred thirty six
             Pontotoc December 10th 1835
                                        Benj
Approved Wm Carroll Examining Agent

UNITED STATES OF AMERICA
TO: DEED
E-AN-NA-YEA.   THE UNITED STATES OF AMERICA.   E/283

TO ALL TO WHOM THESE PRESENTS SHALL COME, GREETING:
Whereas under the sixth Article of the Treaty made at the CITY OF WASHINGTON, on the
twenty fourth day of May, in the year of our Lord one thousand eight hundred and thirty
four, between the UNITED STATES, by their Commissioner JOHN H. EATON, and the Chickasaw
Indians, E-an-na-yea became entitled out of the lands ceeded to the UNITED STATES by
the Treaty concluded at Pontotoc Creek, on the twentieth day of October, one thousand
eight hundred and thirty two, with the Chickasaw Nations, to one Section of Land, and
WHEREAS THE PRESIDENT OF THE UNITED STATES having approved on the twenty ninth of October 1836, of the location of Section Twenty eight, in Township Eight of Range Three
West, containing six hundred and forty one acres and forty four hundredths of an acre,
in the District of Lands subject to sale at Pontotoc, Mississippi, entered as number
282 in the abstract of Reservations under the Sixth Article of the aforesaid treaty, of
the 24th May, 1834.
       NOW KNOW YE, That the UNITED STATES OF AMERICA, in consideration of the pre-
mises, and in conformity with the provisions of the said Treaty of 1834, HAVE GIVEN AND
GRANTED, and by these presents DO GIVE AND GRANT, unto the said E-an-na-yea and to his
heirs, the said tract above described: TO HAVE AND TO HOLD the same, together with all
rights, privileges, immunities, and appurtenances of whatsoever nature, thereunto belonging, unto the said E-an-na-yea and to his heirs and assigns forever.

              IN TESTIMONY WHEREOF, I, John Tyler, PRESIDENT OF THE UNITED STATES OF
AMERICA, have caused these Letters to be made PATENT, and the SEAL of the GENERAL LAND
OFFICE to be hereunto affixed.
              GIVEN under my hand of the CITY OF WASHINGTON, the ninth day of November
in the Year of our Lord one thousand eight hundred and forty two and of the INDEPENDENCE
OF THE UNITED STATES the Sixty seventh

                        BY THE PRESIDENT: John Tyler

                              By   R. Tyler. Sec'y.
                        J. Williamson   RECORDER OF THE GENERAL LAND OFFICE.
L.S. 746743

(Above) Patent dated November 9, 1842, granting 640 acres to E-Ah-Nah-Yea for the Chickasaw tribe from the United States of America subsequent to the Indian cession of lands by the Treaty of Pontotoc Creek (see Introduction). This typed statement over President Tyler's signature but dated 1929 is the only record of this transaction extant. *Photograph by Jack Cofield.*

(Left) Deed acknowledging the sale of the same 640 acres (or one square mile) by the Chickasaw Indian E-Ah-Nah-Yea to John Chisholm, John Craig, and John D. Martin, the first white settlers of Oxford and Lafayette County, Mississippi, dated December 8, 1836. The deed is analogous to that acknowledging the square mile traded by the Chickasaw chief Ik-kemotubbe to Jason Lycurgus Compson (Jason I) for a racehorse; the settlers are analogous to Doctor Habersham, Alexander Holston, and Louis Grenier in Yoknapatawphan history (see Introduction). *Photograph by Jack Cofield.*

Part of the 640 acres today, located at the center of Oxford, Mississippi. This view, from the Lafayette County Courthouse, looks past the statue of a Confederate soldier south down South Lamar Street; on the map of Jefferson, the Compson House is two blocks up South Lamar and two blocks east (left). The Jefferson cemetery, if analogous to the Oxford Cemetery, is one block north and two blocks east of this intersection. *Photograph by Arthur F. Kinney.*

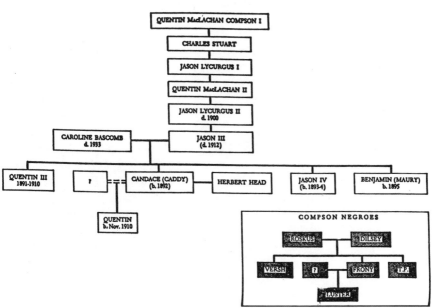

COMPSON GENEALOGY

QUENTIN MacLACHAN COMPSON I

CHARLES STUART

JASON LYCURGUS I

QUENTIN MacLACHAN II

JASON LYCURGUS II
d. 1900

CAROLINE BASCOMB
d. 1933

JASON III
(d. 1912)

QUENTIN III
1891-1910

?

CANDACE (CADDY)
(b. 1892)

HERBERT HEAD

JASON IV
(b. 1893-4)

BENJAMIN (MAURY)
b. 1895

QUENTIN
b. Nov. 1910

COMPSON NEGROES

ROSKUS

DILSEY

VERSH

?

FRONY

T.P.

LUSTER

The Compson Genealogy; dates in parentheses are conjectural. From *A Reader's Guide to William Faulkner* by Edmond Volpe. Copyright © 1964 by Edmond Volpe. Reprinted by permission of Farrar, Straus and Giroux, Inc.

(Above) The Thompson-Chandler house, corner of Buchanan and South 13th Streets, Oxford, two blocks south and east of the Lafayette County Courthouse and the Courthouse Square. One of four antebellum houses in Oxford, this is the probable model for the Compson house (see Introduction). The parlor with the fireplace where Edwin Chandler was fatally burned is to the right of the front door.

(Left, counterclockwise from top) Distant front view of the Thompson-Chandler house, showing the iron fence (now moved to Vicksburg) that distinguished the house when Faulkner was writing *The Sound and the Fury*. The black slave quarters behind the Thompson-Chandler house. Two views of Callie Barr's cabin, Rowan Oak, Oxford. Callie Barr was the model for Dilsey and her cabin is adjacent to Bailey's Woods where Faulkner played as a boy. (Faulkner purchased Rowan Oak shortly after publishing *The Sound and the Fury*.) *Photographs by Arthur F. Kinney.*

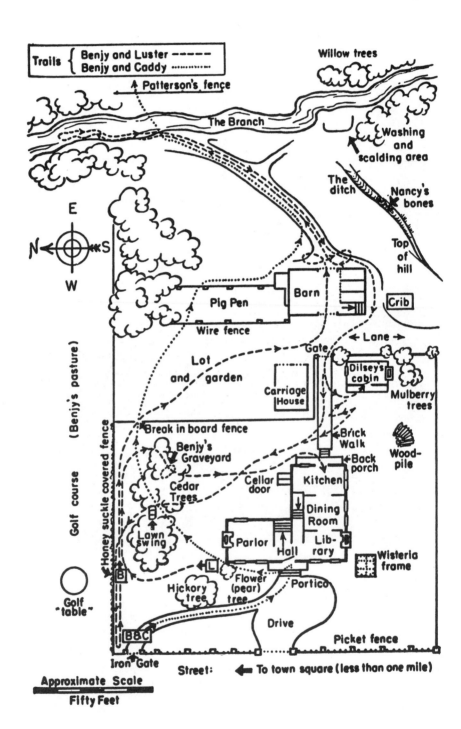

Trails { Benjy and Luster -----
         Benjy and Caddy ········

Willow trees

↑ Patterson's fence

The Branch

Washing and scalding area

The ditch

Nancy's bones

Top of hill

Crib

E
N ←—«S
W

Pig Pen

Barn

Wire fence

← Lane →

Lot and garden

Gate

Dilsey's cabin

Mulberry trees

Carriage House

Break in board fence

Brick Walk

Back porch

Wood-pile

Benjy's Graveyard

Cedar Trees

Cellar door

Kitchen

Dining Room

Golf course   (Benjy's pasture)

Honey suckle covered fence

Lawn swing

Parlor

Hall

Lib-rary

Wisteria frame

B

Hickory tree

Flower (pear) tree

Portico

Golf "table"

B&C

Iron Gate

Street: ← To town square (less than one mile)

Drive

Picket fence

Approximate Scale
Fifty Feet

(Left) Hypothetical drawing of the Compson property by George R. Stewart and Joseph M. Backus; the detail possibly suggests how vividly and concretely Faulkner describes the Compson estate. (Above) A bridge crossing the Charles River, Cambridge, Massachusetts. The lack of realistic details concerning this location, where Quentin Compson commits suicide, suggests how Faulkner based his descriptions on reports about Harvard he heard while rooming in New Haven, Connecticut, in 1918. Drawing from " 'Each in Its Ordered Place': Structure and Narrative in 'Benjy's Section,' " *American Literature*, 29, No. 4 (January, 1958), 445, reprinted with permission of *American Literature* and Joseph M. Backus. *Photograph of Cambridge by Arthur F. Kinney.*

Probable settings for the final section of *The Sound and the Fury*. (Above) The Church of God in a congested hollow of land adjacent to the northeast boundaries of the Thompson-Chandler property suggestive of Nigger Hollow. (Below) One of many houses in the hollow bordering the church and the Chandler property. (Right) The town center and houses in Water Valley, Mississippi, nearly twenty miles south of Oxford on State Route 7, where Faulkner places Mottstown on the map of Yoknapatawpha County. This small town, centered around a cotton gin, has a railroad siding (top and center) similar to that where Jason quarrels with the man from the circus. *Photographs by Arthur F. Kinney.*

The closing episode of *The Sound and the Fury*. (Left) The Courthouse Square of Oxford, with the Confederate Soldier facing south; there is one-way traffic counter-clockwise around the courthouse. (Above, left) Sneed's Ace Hardware store, at the northwest corner of the square, existed when Faulkner wrote the novel, and is the probable model for Jason's store; Luster and Benjy would be nearly half-way around the square, going against traffic, when they reached this store. In the foreground, along the north side of the courthouse, is a field of narcissus, such as the one Benjy is holding; the picture was taken in early April. (Above, right) The chief monument in St. Peter's Episcopal (now Oxford) Cemetery is that of William Thompson; it is under a cedar grove reserved for the city's oldest and most distinguished families, and probably served as the model for the Compson monument which Benjy visits each Sunday. The Thompson name can be seen on the main monument. *Photographs by Arthur F. Kinney.*

The Sound and the Fury

April Seventh, 1928

Through the fence, between the curling flower spaces, I could see them hitting. They were coming toward where the flag was and I went along the fence. Luster was hunting in the grass by the flower tree. They took the flag out, and they were hitting. Then they put the flag back and they went to the table, and he hit and the other hit. Then they went on, and I went along the fence. Luster came away from the flower tree and we went along the fence and they stopped and we stopped and I looked through the fence while Luster was hunting in the grass.

"Here, caddie." He hit. They went away across the pasture. I held to the fence and watched them going away.

"Listen at you, now." Luster said. "Aint you something, thirty three years old, going on that way. After I done went all the way to town to buy you that cake. Hush up that moaning. Aint you going to help me find that quarter so I can go to the show tonight."

They were hitting little, across the pasture. I went back along the fence to where the flag was. It flapped on the bright grass and the trees.

"Come on." Luster said. "We done looked there. They aint no more coming right now. Lets go down to the branch and find that quarter before them niggers finds it."

It was red, flapping on the pasture. Then there was a bird slanting and tilting on it. Luster threw. The flag flapped on the bright grass and the trees. I held to the fence.

"Shut up that moaning." Luster said. "I cant make them come if they aint coming, can I. If you dont hush up, mammy aint going to have no birthday for you. If you dont hush, you know what I going to do. I going to eat that cake all up. Eat them candles, too. Eat all them thirty three candles. Come on, lets go down to the branch. I got to find my quarter. Maybe we can find one of they balls. Here. Here they is. Way over yonder. See." He came to the fence and pointed his arm. "See them. They aint coming back here no more. Come on."

We went along the fence and came to the garden fence, where our shadows were. My shadow was higher than Luster's on the fence. We came to the broken place and went through it.

"Wait a minute." Luster said. "You snagged on that nail again. Cant you never crawl through here without snagging on that nail."

Caddy uncaught me and we crawled through. Uncle Maury said to not let anybody see us, so we better stoop over, Caddy said. Stoop over, Benjy. Like this, see. We stooped over and crossed the garden, where the flowers rasped and rattled against us. The ground was hard. We climbed the fence, where the pigs were grunting and snuffing. I expect they sorry because one of them got killed today, Caddy said. The ground was hard, churned and knotted. Keep your hands in your pockets, Caddy said. Or they'll get froze. You dont want your hands froze on Christmas, do you.

"It's too cold out there." Versh said. "You dont want to go out doors."

"What is it now." Mother said.

Faulkner first gave the manuscript of *The Sound and the Fury* to Joan Williams; then, for safekeeping, he placed it in the safe of his publisher, Random House. When the first page was found missing, he made this copy; the last line (above) reads, "I rewrote these two pages this day 4th August 1952 for Joan Williams"; later the missing page was found. These two pages are in Miss William's possession and are reprinted with her permission; the original manuscript of the novel is presently at the Alderman Library, University of Virginia at Charlottesville.

described on plan of said Town as lot fourteen (14) and forty (40) off of
the South side of Lot fifteen (15) in section twenty eight Town 8, and
Range 3 west. To have and to hold to him & his heirs forever, and I do
covenant to warrant and defend the title against all persons whosoever. In
testimony whereof I have hereunto set my hand and seal the last day of
December 1868: W. Thompson[41]

Historical places can be suggestive, even if real places lie in the geography
of the imagination: in 1891 the elderly Mr. Thompson deeded the property to his daughter Mrs. Marion L. Chandler "In Consideration of love and
Affection and the Sum of one dollar," "reserving to My Self a home on
Said premises during My life and also a home for My Daughter Kate, during her life time, or if she should Marry then until She Marries."[42] It was
the Chandler house that William Faulkner knew in his boyhood and during the writing of *The Sound and the Fury*, where his schoolteacher Anna
Thompson lived with her sister Lulu Marie Lucretia Thompson.[43] Likely,
too, in a city which traded then as now on local history and local families,
he knew the children of Lucretia Thompson Chandler, William Thompson's eldest daughter, and Dr. Thomas Chandler, a physician from
Caswell County, Mississippi. These included Thomas Wiley Chandler,
who like Quentin died in college; Lulu May, who like Caddy left as a
young girl (for North Carolina); Wiley Chandler who like Jason never
married but lived and died in Oxford; and Edwin Chandler who like Benjy had in his thirties the mind of a three-year-old. It was the retarded Edwin toward whom William Faulkner took a special fondness well before
the composition of *The Sound and the Fury*; later, Dean Wells Faulkner
recalls, "Pappy" would take his daughter Jill and his niece Dean to visit
Edwin every two weeks or so.[44] She recalls that he would sit in the corner
cutting various shapes out of paper; at other times, the townspeople of
Oxford recall him running up and down behind the iron fence moaning.
Edwin Chandler died by falling into a fire, much as Benjy Compson
dies.[45]

The Compson family drew its shape and form from many directions,
just as their chief chronicle does. "In the richness of its characterization,
the complexity of its interior monologues, the incremental and expansive
nature of its structure, and the resonance of its themes," Judith Bryant
Wittenberg writes, "*The Sound and the Fury* is a powerful and mature
work of fiction that presents the squalor but also the splendor of humanity
in defeat" (p. 87). Written with apparent secrecy[46] but at a white heat
through the very seasons of Lent, Easter, and Pentecost 1928 that are its
subjects, Faulkner concentrates on what Irving Howe has called "the
ordeal and collapse of the homeland"[47] in the ordeal and collapse of the
home, and of the Compsons. All these tragedies run counter to the
Reverend Shegog's sermon, the service in Nigger Hollow, and a common
black hymn that proclaims,

May the circle be unbroken By and by, Lord, by and by,
There's a better home awaitin' In the sky, Lord, in the sky.
I was standin' by the window On that cold and rainy day
When I heard that chariot comin' For to carry my mama
    away.
I said driver, I said driver, Won't you drive your wagon slow,
Cuz that body that you're carryin', Lord, I hate to see her go.
Yes I followed close behind her, Tried to hold up and be
    brave,
But I could not hide my sorrow, When they laid her in the
    grave.
I went home, my home was lonely, Now my mother, she is
    gone,
All my brothers, my sister cryin', What a home, so sad and
    alone.
Now my father, he was broken, Yes his mind, it wasn't right,
But his spirit kept on shinin' On through the darkest night.
Well not long, he followed after, Went on to his final home;
Now I sit here, my heart is breakin', Wonderin' if I'm all
    alone.
But if I want to find them, I don't have to die this young,
Cuz I feel their spirit growin', Lord, it's growin' in our love.

This song of glory like the Compson threnody of dissolution, fuses a sense of life that is both *historie*—chronological, statistical reality—and *geschichte*—something more than the simple sum of its events. "He was born of it and his bones will sleep in it," Faulkner muses, much the same way, about himself and his countrymen in his late essay "Mississippi," "Loving all of it even while he had to hate some of it because he knows now that you dont love because: you love despite; not for the virtues, but despite the faults."[48] The steady secret is love.

    The critical reception of William Faulkner is a well-known story, often told. Despite early support by Sherwood Anderson (who helped him to publish his first two novels, *Soldiers' Pay* and *Mosquitoes,* and advised him to return to Mississippi for his third, *Flags in the Dust/Sartoris*), most of his early recognition came from journalists and book reviewers. Often they were bothered by the obscurity of his experimentation and what appeared to be the morbidity of his concern; with *Sanctuary* (1931) he was enlisted by Henry Seidel Canby in the school of cruelty. Throughout the 1930s, when Faulkner was writing and publishing nearly all of his most significant work, he was more admired in England (by Richard Hughes and Arnold Bennett) and France (by André Malraux and Jean-Paul Sartre) than in his own country. In the United States critical recognition came first in any important way in 1939, in the twin essays of Conrad Aiken ("William Faulkner: The Novel as Form") and George Marion

O'Donnell ("Faulkner's Mythology"). That year saw his election to the National Institute of Arts and Letters, but he still found no wide readership and in 1946, when Malcolm Cowley finally convinced Viking to publish a collection of his fiction arranged so as to show the development of the Yoknapatawpha chronicle, all but one of Faulkner's books was out of print. It was Cowley's anthology—coupled with the 1949 Nobel Prize for Literature (awarded in 1950, the year of the *Collected Stories* which then won the National Book Award)—that led the way to Faulkner's widespread popularity with readers, students, and critics. In the past few years, critical work on Faulkner has exceeded that of any other author in English save Shakespeare. Detailed examinations of the public response to Faulkner's work from his earliest days have been conducted, in differing perspectives, by Frederick J. Hoffman, Robert Penn Warren, John Bassett, O. B. Emerson, and Thomas L. McHaney and need not be rehearsed here.[49] There are also excellent bibliographies of his work and work on Faulkner's fiction.[50]

The Sound and the Fury was composed during the spring and summer of 1928; Joseph Blotner, in his biography of Faulkner, traces the development of the novel from early holograph outline through the several rearrangements of the Quentin section to the completion of the manuscript in September (1: 566–79). Then, in the New York apartments of Lyle Saxon and Ben Wasson Faulkner revised extensively. These changes, David Minter tells us, "reflect a clear effort to enhance the novel's accessibility, to make it less exclusively his own. He increased the number of italicized passages indicating jumps in time; he added passages that clarified episodes; he made links and associations more explicit" (p. 104). In the spring of 1929 he found a publisher in Cape and Smith of New York, but he had to insist that they keep the italics as he had written them. The book finally appeared in the autumn of 1929, alongside Ernest Hemingway's *A Farewell to Arms* and Thomas Wolfe's *Look Homeward, Angel*. *The Sound and the Fury* was issued with a separate pamphlet by Evelyn Scott, author of the literary success *The Waves* earlier that year, praising Faulkner's novel. In a comprehensive essay on the textual history of *The Sound and the Fury*, James B. Meriwether notes that

> All in all, Cape and Smith were to be congratulated on the way they brought out a novel which represented a considerable gamble for a new firm. It was published 7 Oct. 1929, an autumn for greater optimism concerning America's literary than financial condition [—Jason's falling stock market anticipates Black Thursday—], and received very good reviews, upon the whole: but it did not sell. The first printing, only 1,789 copies, sufficed until the publication of *Sanctuary* in February 1931. In that month a small second printing of 518 copies was made, and the following November a third printing, of 1,000 copies, was made from a copy of the second impression.[51]

The British edition was published in London by Chatto and Windus in April, 1931, in a printing of 2,000 copies with an introduction by the novelist Richard Hughes, author of *A High Wind in Jamaica*; the French translation, by Maurice Edgar Coindreau, *Le Bruit et la fureur*, was not published by Gallimard in Paris until 1938, nearly a decade after its initial publication in America. By 1940, the novel had done better in both those countries than in the United States.

The present compilation on the Compsons shows how, like so much of the American South, Faulkner was attracted to a study of family lineage as a way of examining the historical, religious, social, economic, and moral forces in his regional culture. Yet even while the Compsons serve as an index for assessing and measuring the past century and a half, they remain before us as nearly palpable persons, torn by their own discordant desires, needs, and apprehensions. "The Kingdom of God," published in the New Orleans *Times-Picayune* for April 26, 1925, is Faulkner's first portrait of an idiot; here this "mad cow's" bellowing and his broken narcissus look forward to *The Sound and the Fury*; he likewise shares with Benjy (by his insinuating presence) the need for warmth and understanding. His eyes, of cornflower blue, are like Benjy's "heart-shaking" and he and Benjy have in common the function of moral reference. "The Kingdom of God" shares with *The Sound and the Fury* the themes of family and brotherhood and an understanding of the sometimes desperate need to defend one's own blood, while its conclusion foreshadows the conclusion of the novel. "The Kid Learns," from the *Times-Picayune* for May 31, 1925, is Faulkner's first extended prose in the voice of Jason Compson. The opening scene joins "competition" with "money"—and both with women (like Caddy and Caroline) and business; "competition makes the world go round." In the perspective urged by this brief tale, success shows goodness, as goodness leads to (and is rewarded by) success—a valuable insight into Jason's code. Johnny's competition with the Wop has from the beginning the kind of cockiness that masks both self-assurance and self-doubt; what the subsequent false sense of well-being leads to is Faulkner's first published reference to Little Sister Death (derived from St. Francis of Assisi's "Canticle of the Creatures").[52] In retrospect, "The Kid Learns" shows Jason's tragedy—he never had a sister but only a mother—in the recognition that he had no one he cherished sufficiently to protect. Jason's tragedy would seem to be endurance without significance. *Mayday*, handlettered for Helen Baird and dated Oxford, 27 January 1926, anticipates the later portrait of Quentin III; the adolescent philosophizing of Sir Galwyn of Arthgyl (" 'It occurs to me,' young Sir Galwyn continued profoundly, 'that it is not the thing itself that man wants, so much as the wanting of it' ") resonates in the sort of abstractions that characterize Quentin's thoughts at Harvard. In a setting so charged with poetic power as to be self-mocking and with a magical metamorphosis that transforms the romance into mock-heroic, Faulkner nevertheless shows the seductive and threatening powers of water which will play so forceful a part in the later novel, and also implies a correlation among hunger and pain, fortitude, ambition, women, the self, and death. This unproven knight, with his blank face and blank shield, is self-mirroring, a nonentity whose callowness makes him naught despite the mad swirl of thoughts, images, and actions; in this too he resembles Quentin. Sir Galwyn's voyeurism with Iseult echoes Quentin III's with Caddy; the temptations resemble those posed by Caddy and Natalie before both are displaced by Little Sister Death. What saves the much more stylized *Mayday*, however, is Faulkner's ability to laugh at his hero as broadly comic in his fickleness and extreme seriousness. Faulkner's two introductions to an unpublished limited edition of *The Sound and the Fury* in 1933 are unusually personal but strikingly different from each other. Both are more revealing, and more serious, than the jocular introduction he wrote (but which remained unpublished) for his appendix on the Compsons. Faulkner's many scattered public comments on *The Sound and the Fury*, made in interviews and in classrooms, are conveniently gathered by Michael H. Cowan,[53] and so are not included here.

The second section of this book illustrates the range of immediate critical response to *The Sound and the Fury* in America, England, and France. The reaction in Faulkner's own South was mixed. The *Virginia Quarterly Review* found the work to have "the odor of dry rot [transmuted] into wonder and awe and high despair" (6, No. 1 [1930], 141), while Abbott Martin, writing for the *Sewanee Review*, found "poverty, madness, decay" but also "that beauty which hath terror in it" (38, No. 1 [1930], 116). In *The Hound and the Horn* Dudley Fitts claimed that "The prose owes a great deal to Joyce—possibly too much; but the individual impetus of Mr. Faulkner's own ability is unmistakable" (3, No. 3 [1930], 447). In England, the fiction writer Frank Swinnerton wrote in the *Evening News* (London) that

> The dialogue in this book is racy and overwhelmingly convincing. All sounds, sights and memories are so wonderfully indicated that they electrify the reader into attentive belief. The fantastic adventure of the young suicide and the little girl with the loaf is glorious. Clearly the difficult technique is not a smoke-cloud to hide poverty of any kind. But the book is a teaser, and I fear that, in spite of all its qualities, it may delay general appreciation of a talent which I believe to be outstanding in our time (May 15, 1931, p. 8).

In *The Spectator* I. A. G. Strong, borrowing from Richard Hughes' introduction, noted that "Reading *The Sound and the Fury* is like learning a new job or a new language" (April 25, 1931, p. 674). In a less reverent vein, Brigid Brophy, Michael Levey, and Charles Osborne list *The Sound and the Fury* as one of the *Fifty Works of English and American Literature We Could Do Without* (London, 1967, pp. 145–46). In being asked "What French Readers Find in William Faulkner's Fiction"—the usual answers were violence and existentialist concepts of time similar to Proust's—the French novelist Marcel Aymé answered "divine reflection" through "so much gloom, incurable misery, horror and distress" (*New York Times Book Review*, December 17, 1950; Section 7, p. 4).

My greatest regret is the lack of space for historically important and critically substantial commentary that could not be included here. George Marion O'Donnell's "Faulkner's Mythology" (*Kenyon Review*, 1, No. 3) was the first major recognition of Faulkner's broad opposition of the old aristocracy and the new merchant; Oscar Cargill, in *Intellectual America* (1941), was the first to deal with the novel as "the decay of the Compson family" (p. 374); and the first extended treatments were Harry M. Campbell's "Experiment and Achievement: *As I Lay Dying* and *The Sound and the Fury*" (*The Sewanee Review*, 51) in 1943 and Sumner C. Powell's "William Faulkner Celebrates Easter, 1928" (*Perspective*, 2, No. 4) in 1949. In the November 1951 issue of *The Explicator* A.C. Hoffman first linked *The Sound and the Fury* with *Absalom, Absalom!* (#12). In 1953 Leonard H. Frey published the first analysis of "That Evening Sun" (*Faulkner Studies*, 2:35–39) while *English Institute Essays 1952* (1954) published a gathering of seminal studies on primitivism by Cleanth Brooks, interior monologues by Carvel Collins, concepts of time by Perrin Lowrey, and mirror analogues by Lawrance Thompson. Edwy B. Lee's note on narrative and dream in the novel (*Faulkner Studies* 3:38) is still useful as is Irene C. Edmonds' study of blacks in Faulkner (especially Dilsey and Joe Christmas); this latter is in Louis D. Rubin and Robert Jacobs' *Southern Renascence* (1953), pp. 192–206. Olga Vickery published a landmark study in 1959 titled *The Novels of William Faulkner: A Critical Interpretation*, revised 1954; Chapter 3 deals with epistemology in *The Sound and the Fury*.

Worthwhile studies of the Compsons increased during the 1960s. Leon Edel approached the novel through "That Evening Sun Go Down" in *Varieties of Literary Experience* edited by Stanley Burnshaw (1962), pp. 254–55; Robert M. Slabey linked "Evening Sun" to "A Justice," *Absalom, Absalom!* and *The Sound and the Fury* in 1964 (*Studies in Short Fiction*, 1:3), and in the same year Edmond Volpe published his comprehensive and sensitive analysis and paraphrase in his *Reader's Guide to William Faulkner*. Three years later, James Guetti studied Faulkner's method in *The Limits of Metaphor*, while in 1968, ten years after Frederick L. Gwynn's seminal note on "Faulkner's Raskolnikov" in *Modern Fiction Studies* (4:169–72, pertaining to Quentin III), Jean Weisgerber published his *Faulkner et Dostoievski: confluence et influence* (translated 1974) showing in detail the relationship between *The Sound and the Fury* and *Crime and Punishment*.

The 1970s have produced extremely useful studies of *The Sound and the Fury* in the biographies of Joseph Blotner (1974), Judith Bryant Wittenberg (1979), and David Minter (1980). Among general book-length studies, attention should be paid to Chapter 4 of Joseph W. Reed, Jr.'s *Faulkner Narrative (1973)*, the first study in reader-response; Panthea Reid Broughton's *William Faulkner: The Abstract and the Actual* (1974), dealing with the use of speculative abstraction; John T. Irwin's "speculative reading" of *The Sound and the Fury* and *Absalom, Absalom!* in *Doubling and Incest/Repetition and Revenge* (1975); David Williams' *Faulkner's Women* (1977), a mythopoetic study; and Gary Lee Stonum's *Faulkner's Career* (1979), showing *The Sound and the Fury* as a stage in a dialectical process of development. Barbara H. Fried's *The Spider in the Cup: Yoknapatawpha County's Fall into the Unknowable* (1978), the LeBarron Russel Briggs Prize Honors Essay in English for 1977 at Harvard, deals mostly with *The Sound and the Fury*; it is an eloquent monograph on the Compsons at the edge of the abyss, representing the chaos of the present century where faith is undermined by the scientific and the mechanical. Lois Gordon's monograph, "Meaning and Myth in *The Sound and the Fury* and *The Waste Land*," published in *The Twenties*, edited by Warren French (1975) compares Faulkner's and Eliot's use of myth. Finally, Lyall H. Powers, in *Faulkner's Yoknapatawpha Comedy* (1980) sees the novel as one of Faulkner's many treatments of the Second Chance preventing the final collapse of the Compson family (Chapter II). Helpful specialized studies of Caddy include Eileen Gregory, "Caddy Compson's World," *Merrill Studies in "The Sound and the Fury"* (1975); Gladys Milliner, "The Third Eve" in *Midwest Quarterly*, 16 (1975), 268–75; Douglas B. Hill, Jr., "Faulkner's Caddy" in *Canadian Review of American Studies*, 7 (1976), 26–38; and Sally R. Page, *Faulkner's Women* (1972), pp. 47ff. Specialized studies of Quentin are best represented by Mark Spilka, "Quentin Compson's Universal Grief,"*Contemporary Literature*, 11, No. 4; Charles D. Peavy, " 'If I'd Just Had a Mother,' "*Literature and Psychology*, 23, No. 3; James C. Cowan's "Dream-Work in the Quentin Section," *Literature and Psychology*, 24, No. 3 (the best Freudian criticism of the novel); Lynn Gartrell Levins, *Faulkner's Heroic Design* (1974) on Quentin as chivalric knight, pp. 128ff.; May Cameron Brown and Esta Seaton, "William Faulkner's Unlikely Detective," *Essays in Arts and Science*, 8:27–33; and John V. Hagopian, "Black Insight in *Absalom, Absalom!*," *Faulkner Studies*, 1, (1980), 29–37. Recent work on Jason includes his strongest defense, Linda Welshimer Wagner's "Jason Compson: The Demands of Honor" in *Sewanee Review*, 79, No. 4 (1971) and David Aiken, "The 'Sojer Face' Defiance of Jason Compson," *Thought*, 52, No. 205 (1977), an impressive analysis of Kierkegaardian despair. "That Evening Sun" has received valuable treatment at the hands of Leo M. Manglaviti in *American Literature*, 43:649–54, Kenneth G. Johnston in *American Literature*, 46, No. 1 (1974), Joseph M. Garrison, Jr. in *Studies in Short Fiction*, 13:371–73, and Philip Momberger, *The Southern Literary Jour-*

nal, 11, No. 1 (1978). M.E. Bradford has published a recent study of "A Justice" in *Modern Age*, 18, No. 3 (1974). Any such listing is rapidly outdated, however, and readers are advised to consult annual bibliographies and checklists. Special attention should also be given the annual (summer) Faulkner issues of *The Mississippi Quarterly*, edited by Peyton Williams, Jr. and James Meriwether, which over the years have been an important repository of work by and on Faulkner, and the new and promising annual *Faulkner Studies*, edited by Barnett Guttenberg.

In this volume: citations to journals follow the MLA style, but not necessarily the forms used by the publications themselves.

Notes

1. References are to the 1929 text photographically reprinted in Modern Library (New York, 1967) and Vintage (New York, 1966).

2. The re-arrangement was first proposed by Bruce A. Rosenberg in "The Oral Quality of Rev. Shegog's Sermon in William Faulkner's *The Sound and the Fury*," *Literatur in Wissenschaft und Unterricht*, 2, No. 2 (1969), 73–88; the text here is from pp. 78–80. Many of the following observations stem from this instructive essay. For a larger context, see Gene Bluestein, "The Blues as a Literary Theme," *Massachusetts Review*, 8 (Autumn 1967), 600ff.

3. *Faulkner in the University*, ed. Frederick L. Gwynn and Joseph L. Blotner (Charlottesville, Va.: University of Virginia Press, 1959), p. 197.

4. *Faulkner in the University*, p. 204.

5. References are to the Vintage edition (New York: Random House, 1972).

6. In "Quentin Compson and Faulkner's Drama of the Generations" published in this collection, pp. 381–401.

7. *The Novel and the World's Dilemma* (New York: Oxford University Press, 1947), p. 215.

8. *Selected Letters of William Faulkner*, ed. Joseph Blotner (New York: Random House, 1977), p. 79.

9. *Faulkner in the University*, pp. 274–75.

10. *Selected Letters*, p. 205.

11. *Selected Letters*, pp. 220–21.

12. *Requiem for a Nun*, Vintage edition (New York: Random House, 1975), p. 12. All references are to this edition, indicated by *RN*.

13. "The Bear" (*Saturday Evening Post* version), rep. *Bear, Man, and God*, ed. Francis Lee Utley, Lynn Z. Bloom, and Arthur F. Kinney (New York: Random House, 1964 ed.), pp. 155–56.

14. "The Bear," p. 156.

15. "Delta Autumn," rep. *Bear, Man, and God*, p. 382.

16. *The Reivers*, Vintage edition (New York: Random House, n.d.), p. 23.

17. "The Bear" (final version), in *Bear, Man, and God*, p. 112.

18. *The Reivers*, pp. 21–22.

19. "Appendix" in *The Sound and the Fury*, pp. 408–09.

20. *Collected Stories*, Vintage edition (New York: Random House, 1977), p. 360.

21. *Collected Stories*, p. 291.

22. *Collected Stories*, p. 289.

23. *Selected Letters*, p. 197.

24. *The Mansion*, Vintage ed. (New York: Random House, n.d.), p. 328.

25. *Selected Letters*, p. 41.

26. Quoted by David Minter, *William Faulkner: His Life and Work* (Baltimore: The Johns Hopkins Press, 1980), p. 105.

27. *Selected Letters*, p. 68.

28. *My Brother Bill: An Affectionate Reminiscence* (New York, Trident, 1963), p. 275.

29. Murry C. Falkner, *The Falkners of Mississippi: A Memoir* (Baton Rouge: Louisiana State University Press, 1967), p. 9.

30. *Faulkner: A Biography* (New York: Random House, 1974), 1:566.

31. Blotner, 1: 566.

32. Blotner, 1: 568.

33. Judith Bryant Wittenberg, *Faulkner: The Transfiguration of Biography* (Lincoln, Neb.: University of Nebraska Press, 1979), pp. 84–85.

34. Murry C. Falkner, p. 13.

35. Minter, p. 94.

36. There is perhaps still another connection: the Biblical Jacob has a son named Benoni (Hebrew for "son of my sorrow"); the name is later changed to Benjamin (Hebrew for "son of the right hand" or "Son of the South"). The name *Candace* may also be Biblical in origin (Acts 8:26–40).

37. Much of the material here on the Thompson and Chandler families is drawn from Chandler family records kindly loaned me by Mrs. L. C. Andrews.

38. James G. Watson, "Faulkner: The House of Fiction," in *Fifty Years of Yoknapatawpha: Faulkner and Yoknapatawpha*, ed. Doreen Fowler and Ann J. Abadie (Jackson: University Press of Mississippi, 1980), 146–54.

39. "Some Notes on Time in Fiction," *Mississippi Quarterly*, 26, No. 4 (Fall 1973), 483.

40. The actual deed is in Book 16 filed at the Lafayette County Courthouse, where I was graciously permitted to search the ownership of the Martin property from the beginning. In 1842—after the first assignment of land to Martin—President Tyler acknowledged a treaty with E-An-Na-Yea, representing the Chickasaws, for deeding the land to the United States Government, citing the Treaty of Pontotoc, but the date of filing this agreement appears to be 1929. Faulkner alludes to the treatment of Indians by white settlers in *Requiem for a Nun* and *Go Down, Moses* and may have known something about the coincident records of Lafayette County.

41. Registry of Deeds, Book 1, p. 172.

42. Registry of Deeds, Book 2, pp. 304–05.

43. A. I. Bezzerides, *William Faulkner: A Life on Paper* (Jackson: University Press of Mississippi, 1980), p. 64.

44. Interview with Dean Faulkner Wells at her home in Oxford, Mississippi, May 23, 1981.

45. *The Mansion*, p. 322.

46. Minter, p. 94.

47. Irving Howe, *William Faulkner: A Critical Study*, 3rd ed., rev. (Chicago: University of Chicago Press, 1975), p. 46.

48. Faulkner, *Essays, Speeches & Public Letters*, ed. James B. Meriwether (New York: Random House, 1965), pp. 36; 42–43.

49. Frederick J. Hoffman, "William Faulkner: An Introduction," in Hoffman and Olga W. Vickery, *William Faulkner: Two Decades of Criticism* (East Lansing: Michigan State

College Press, 1951), pp. 1–31; Hoffman in Hoffman and Vickery, *William Faulkner: Three Decades of Criticism* (East Lansing: Michigan State University Press, 1960), pp. 1–50; Robert Penn Warren, "Introduction: Faulkner: Past and Present," in *Faulkner: A Collection of Critical Essays*, ed. Robert Penn Warren (Englewood Cliffs, N.J.: Prentice-Hall, Inc., 1966), pp. 1–22; John Bassett, "Introduction" to *William Faulkner: The Critical Heritage* (London: Routledge & Kegan Paul, 1975), pp. 1–46; O. B. Emerson, *William Faulkner's Literary Reputation in America*, unpublished PhD thesis, Vanderbilt University, 1962; and Thomas L. McHaney, "Watching for the Dixie Limited: Faulkner's Impact upon the Creative Writer," in *Fifty Years of Yoknapatawpha*, pp. 226–47.

50. John Bassett, *William Faulkner: An Annotated Checklist of Criticism* (New York: David Lewis, 1972) and McHaney, *William Faulkner: A Reference Guide* (Boston: G. K. Hall and Co., 1976). (Earlier, and somewhat outdated, is Irene Lynn Sleeth, *William Faulkner: A Bibliography of Criticism* [Denver: Alan Swallow, 1962]).

51. "Notes on the Textual History of *The Sound and the Fury*," *The Papers of the Bibliographical Society of America*, 56 (1962), 299.

52. The canticle is most easily accessible (with commentary on *The Sound and the Fury*) in Edmond L. Volpe, *A Reader's Guide to William Faulkner* (New York: Farrar, Straus, & Giroux, Inc., 1964), p. 98.

53. In *Twentieth Century Interpretations of "The Sound and the Fury": A Collection of Critical Essays* (Englewood Cliffs, N.J.: Prentice Hall, Inc. 1968), pp. 14–24.

I INTRODUCING THE COMPSONS

The Kingdom of God

The car came swiftly down Decatur street and turning into the alleyway, stopped. Two men alighted, but the other remained in his seat. The face of the sitting man was vague and dull and loose-lipped, and his eyes were clear and blue as cornflowers, and utterly vacant of thought; he sat a shapeless, dirty lump, life without mind, an organism without intellect. Yet always in his slobbering, vacuous face were his two eyes of a heart-shaking blue, and gripped tightly in one fist was a narcissus.

The two who had got out of the car leaned within it and went swiftly to work. Soon they straightened up, and a burlap bundle rested on the door of the car. A door in the wall near at hand opened, a face appeared briefly and withdrew.

"Come on, let's get this stuff out of here," said one of the men. "I ain't scared, but there ain't no luck in making a delivery with a loony along."

"Right you are," replied the other. "Let's get done here: we got two more trips to make."

"You ain't going to take him along, are you?" asked the first speaker, motioning with his head toward the one lumped oblivious in the car.

"Sure. He won't hurt nothing. He's a kind of luck piece, anyway."

"Not for me he ain't. I been in this business a long time and I ain't been caught yet, but it ain't because I been taking no squirrel chasers for luck pieces."

"I know how you feel about him—you said so often enough. But like it was, what could I do? He never had no flower, he lost it somewheres last night, so I couldn't leave him to Jake's, going on like he was for another one; and after I got him one today I couldn't of put him out nowheres. He'd of stayed all right, till I come for him, but some bull might of got him."

"And a———good thing," swore the other. "Dam'f I see why you lug him around when they's good homes for his kind everywheres."

*From *William Faulkner: New Orleans Sketches*, ed. Carvel Collins (New York: Random House, 1958), pp. 55–60. Copyright © 1958 by Carvel Collins. Reprinted by permission of Random House, Inc. First published by New Orleans *Times-Picayune* April 26, 1925.

"Listen. He's my brother, see? And it's my business what I do with him. And I don't need no———that wears hair to tell me, neither."

"Ah, come on, come on. I wasn't trying to take him away from you. I'm just superstitious about fooling with 'em, that's all."

"Well, don't say nothing about it, then. If you don't wanta work with me, say so."

"All right, all right, keep your shirt on." He looked at the blind doorway. "Cheest, what's the matter with them birds today? Hell, we can't wait here like this: be better to drive on. Whatcher say?" As he spoke the door opened again and a voice said: "All right, boys."

The other gripped his arm, cursing. At the corner two blocks away a policeman appeared, stood a moment, then sauntered down the street toward them. "———here comes a bull. Make it snappy now; get one of them fellows inside to help you and I'll head him off and keep him till you get unloaded." The speaker hurried off and the other, glancing hurriedly about, grasped the sack resting upon the door of the car and carried it swiftly through the doorway. He returned and leaned over the side of the car, trying to lift up the other sack onto the door. The policeman and his companion had met and were talking.

Sweat broke out on his face as he struggled with the awkward bundle, trying to disengage it from the floor of the car. It moved, but hung again despite his utmost efforts, while the body of the car thrust against his lower chest, threatened to stop his breathing. He cast another glance toward the officer. "What luck, what rotten luck!" he panted, grasping the sack again. He released one hand and grasped the idiot's shoulder. "Here, bub," he whispered, "turn around here and lend a hand, quick!" The other whimpered at his touch, and the man hauled him half about so that his vacant, pendulous face hung over the back seat. "Come on, come on, for God's sake," he repeated in a frenzy, "catch hold here and lift up, see?"

The heavenly blue eyes gazed at him without intent, drops of moisture from the drooling mouth fell upon the back of his hand. The idiot only raised his narcissus closer to his face. "Listen!" the man was near screaming, "do you wanna go to jail? Catch hold here, for God's sake!" But the idiot only stared at him in solemn detachment, and the man raised up and struck him terribly in the face. The narcissus, caught between fist and cheek, broke and hung limply over the creature's fist. He screamed, a hoarse, inarticulate bellow which his brother, standing beside the officer, heard and came leaping toward him.

The other man's rage left him and he stood in vacant and frozen despair, when vengeance struck him. The brother leaped, shrieking and cursing, upon him and they both went to the pavement. The idiot howled unceasingly, filling the street with dreadful sound.

"Hit my brother, would you, you———," panted the man. The other, after the surprise of the assault, fought back until the policeman leaped upon them, clubbing and cursing impartially. "What in hell is this?" he demanded when they were erect and dishevelled, glaring and breathless.

"He hit my brother, the————."

"Somebody certainly done something to him," snapped the officer. "For Pete's sake, make him stop that racket," he roared above the deafening sound. Another policeman thrust through the gathering crowd. "What you got here? Mad cow?" The idiot's voice rose and fell on waves of unbelievable sound and the second policeman, stepping to the car, shook him.

"Here, here," he began, when the brother, breaking from the grasp of his captor, leaped upon his back. They crashed against the car, and the first officer, releasing the other captive, sprang to his aid. The other man stood in amazement, bereft of power to flee, while the two officers swayed and wrestled with the brother, stretching the man, screaming and kicking, between them until he wore himself out. The second policeman had two long scratches on his cheek. "Phew!" he puffed, mopping his jaw with his handkerchief, "what a wildcat! Has the whole zoo broke out today? What's the trouble?" he roared above the magnificent sorrow of the idiot.

"I dunno exactly," his partner shouted back. "I hear that one in the car bellow out, and look around and here's these two clawing in the gutter. This one says the other one hit his brother. How about it?" he ended, shaking his captive.

The man raised his head. "Hit my brother, he did. I'll kill him for this!" he shouted in a recurrence of rage, trying to cast himself on the other prisoner, who crouched behind the other policeman. The officer struggled with him. "Come on, come on; want me to beat some sense into you? Come on, make that fellow in the car stop the howling."

The man looked at his brother for the first time. "His flower is broken, see?" he explained, "that's what he's crying about."

" 'Flower?' " repeated the law. "Say, what is this, anyway? Is your brother sick, or dead, that he's got to have a flower?"

"He ain't dead," interjected the other policeman, "and he don't sound sick to me. What is this, a show? What's going on here?" He peered into the car again and found the burlap sack. "Aha," he said. He turned swiftly. "Where's the other one? Get him quick! They've got liquor in here." He sprang toward the second man, who had not moved. "Station house for yours, boys." His companion was again struggling with the brother, and he quickly handcuffed his captive to the car, and sprang to the other's aid.

"I ain't trying to get away," the brother was shrieking. "I just want to fix his flower for him. Lemmego, I tell you!"

"Will he quit that bellowing if you fix his flower?"

"Yeh, sure; that's what he's crying for."

"Then for God's sake fix it for him."

The idiot still clutched his broken narcissus, weeping bitterly; and while the officer held his wrist the brother hunted about and found a small sliver of wood. String was volunteered by a spectator, who fetched it from a nearby shop; and under the interested eyes of the two policemen and the gathering crowd, the flower stalk was splinted. Again the poor damaged thing held its head erect, and the loud sorrow went at once from the idiot's soul. His eyes were like two scraps of April sky after a rain, and his drooling face was moonlike in ecstasy.

"Beat it, now," and the officers broke up the crowd of bystanders. "Show's all over for the day. Move on, now."

By ones and twos the crowd drifted away. And with an officer on each fender the car drew away from the curb and on down the street, and so from sight, the ineffable blue eyes of the idiot dreaming above his narcissus clenched tightly in his dirty hand.

The Kid Learns

*William Faulkner**

Competition is everywhere: competition makes the world go round. Not love, as some say. Who would want a woman nobody else wanted? Not me. And not you. And not Johnny. Same way about money. If nobody wanted the stuff, it wouldn't be worth fighting for. But more than this is being good in your own line, whether it is selling aluminum or ladies' underwear or running whiskey, or what. Be good, or die.

"Listen," said Johnny, tilted back against the wall in his chair, "a man ain't only good in our business because he'd get his otherwise, he's good because he wants to be a little better than the best, see?"

"Sure," said his friend Otto, sitting beside him, not moving.

"Anybody can keep from getting bumped off. All you gotta do is get took on a street gang or as a soda squirt. What counts is being good as you can—being good as any of 'em. Getting yours or not getting yours just shows how good you are or how good you ought to of been."

"Sure," agreed his friend Otto, tilting forward his brief derby and spitting.

"Listen, I ain't got nothing against the Wop, see; but he sets hisself up as being good and I sets myself up as being good, and some day we got to prove between us which is the best."

"Yeh," said Otto, rolling a slender cigarette and flicking a match on his thumb nail, "but take your time. You're young, see; and he's an old head at this. Take your time. Get some age onto you and I'm playing you on the nose at any odds. They wasn't no one ever done a better job in town than the way you taken that stuff away from him last week, but get some age onto you before you brace him, see? I'm for you: you know damn well."

"Sure," said Johnny in his turn, "I ain't no fool. Gimme five years, though, and it'll be Johnny Gray, with not even the bulls to remember the Wop. Five years, see?"

"That's the kid. They ain't nothing to complain, the way we done

*From *William Faulkner: New Orleans Sketches*, ed. Carvel Collins. (New York: Random House, 1958), pp. 86–91. Copyright © 1958 by Carvel Collins. Reprinted by permission of Random House, Inc. First published in New Orleans *Times-Picayune* May 31, 1925.

49

lately. Let her ride as she lays, and when the time comes we'll clean 'em all."

"And he's right," thought Johnny, walking down the street. "Take time, and get yourself good. They ain't nobody good from the jump: you got to learn to be good. I ain't no fool, I got sense enough to lay off the Wop until the time comes. And when it does—good-night."

He looked up and his entrails became briefly cold—not with fear, but with the passionate knowledge of what was some day to be. Here was the Wop in an identical belted coat and Johnny felt a sharp envy in spite of himself. They passed; Johnny nodded, but the other only jerked a casual, patronizing finger at him. Too proud to look back, he could see in his mind the swagger of the other's revealed shoulders and the suggestion of a bulge over his hip. Some day! Johnny swore beneath his breath, and he ached for that day.

Then he saw her.

Down the street she came, swinging her flat young body with all the awkward grace of youth, swinging her thin young arms; beneath her hat he saw hair neither brown nor gold, and gray eyes. Clean as a colt she swung past him, and turning to follow her with his eyes and all the vague longing of his own youth, he saw the Wop step gracefully out and accost her.

Saw her recoil, and saw the Wop put his hand on her arm. And Johnny knew that that thing he had wanted to wait for until his goodness was better had already come. The Wop had prisoned both her arms when he thrust between them, but he released his grasp in sheer surprise on recognizing Johnny.

"Beat it," commanded Johnny coldly.

"Why, you poor fish, whatayou mean? You talking to me?"

"Beat it, I said," Johnny repeated.

"You little——— ——— ———," and the older man's eyes grew suddenly red, like a rat's. "Don't you know who I am?" He thrust Johnny suddenly aside and again grasped the girl's arm. The back of her hand was pressed against her mouth and she was immovable with fear. When he touched her she screamed, Johnny leaped and struck the Wop on his unguarded jaw, and she fled down the street, wailing. Johnny's pistol was out and he stood over the felled man as Otto ran up.

"My God!" Otto shouted, "you've done it now!" He dragged a weighed bit of leather from his pocket. "I don't dast croak him here. I'll put him out good, and you beat it, get out of town, quick!" He tapped the still groggy man lightly and ran. "Beat it quick, for God's sake!" he cried over his shoulder. But Johnny had already gone after the girl, and a policeman, running heavily, appeared.

Before a darkened alleyway he overtook her. She had stopped, leaning against the wall with her face in the crook of her arm, gasping and crying. When he touched her she screamed again, whirling and falling. He caught and supported her.

"It ain't him, it's me," he told her obscurely. "There, there; it's all right. I laid him out."

She clung to him, sobbing; and poor Johnny gazed about him, trapped. Cheest, what did you do with a weeping girl?

"Now, now, baby," he repeated, patting her back awkwardly, as you would a dog's, "it's all right. He won't bother you. Tell me where you live, and I'll take you home."

"O-o-o-oh, he sc-scared me s-o," she wailed, clinging to him. Poor kid, she didn't know that he was the one to be scared, that his was the life that was about to take a dark and unknown corner, for better or worse, only the gods knew. There is still time to get out of town, though, caution told him. Otto is right; he knows best. Leave her and beat it, you fool! Leave her, and him back yonder? Youth replied. Not by your grandmother's false teeth, I won't.

He felt her pliant young body shudder with fear and her choked weeping.

"There, there, kid," he repeated inanely. He didn't know what to say to 'em, even. But he must get her away from here. The Wop would be about recovering now, and he'd be looking for him. He held her closer and her trembling gradually died away; and looking about him he almost shouted with relief. Here was old Ryan the cop's house, that had known him boy and lad for fifteen years. The very place.

"Why, say, here's the very place. Mrs. Ryan knows me, she'll look after you until I come back for you."

She clasped him sharply in her thin arms. "No, no, don't leave me! I'm so scared!"

"Why, just for a minute, honey," he reassured her, "just until I find where he went, see? We don't wanta stumble on him again."

"No, no, no, he'll hurt you!" Her wet salty face was against his. "You mustn't! You mustn't!"

"Sure, just a while, baby. I won't be no time." She moaned against Johnny's face and he kissed her cold mouth, and it was as though dawn had come among the trees where the birds were singing. They looked at each other a moment.

"Must you?" she said in a changed voice, and she allowed herself to be led to the dark door; and they clung to each other until footsteps came along the passage within the house. She put her arms around Johnny's neck again.

"Hurry back," she whispered, "and oh, be careful. I'm so afraid!"

"Baby!"

"Sweetheart!"

The door opened upon Mrs. Ryan, there was a brief explanation, and with her damp kiss yet on his face, Johnny ducked quickly from the alleyway.

Here were flying remote stars above, but below were flashing lights and paved streets, and all the city smells that he loved. He could go away for a while, and then come back, and things—lights and streets and smells—would be the same. "No!" he swore. "I've got a girl now. I ruther be bumped off than have her know I run." But ah, if this could have been put off a while! How sweet she is! Is this love, I wonder? he thought, or is it being afraid, makes me want to run back to her and risk letting things work themselves out instead of doing it myself? Anyway, I done it for her: I wasn't double-crossing the boys. I had to do it: anyone can see that.

"Well, I ain't as good as I wanted, but I can be as good as I can." He looked again at the flying stars, his pistol loose in his pocket, and smelled again the smells of food and gasoline that he loved; and one stepped quickly from out a doorway.

Why, say, here she was again beside him, with her young body all shining and her hair that wasn't brown and wasn't gold and her eyes the color of sleep; but she was somehow different at the same time.

"Mary?" said Johnny, tentatively.

"Little sister Death," corrected the shining one, taking his hand.

Mayday

William Faulkner*

And the tale tells how at last one came to him. Dawn had already come without, flushing up the high small window so that this high small window which had been throughout the night only a frame for slow and scornful stars became now as a rose unfolding on the dark wall of the chapel. The song of birds came up on the dawn, and the young spring waking freshly, golden and white and troubling: flowers were birdcries about meadows unseen and birdcries were flowers necklaced about the trees. Then the sun like a swordblade touched his own stainless long sword, his morion and hauberk and greaves, and his spurs like twin golden lightnings where they rested beneath the calm sorrowful gaze of the Young Compassionate One, touching his own young face where he had knelt all night on a stone floor, waiting for day.

And it was as though he had passed through a valley between shelving vague hills where the air was gray and smelled of spring, and had come at last upon a dark hurrying stream which, as he watched, became filled suddenly with atoms of color like darting small fish, and the water was no longer dark.

"What does this signify?" he asked of a small green design with a hundred prehensile mouths which stood at his right hand, and the small green design was called Hunger.

"Wait," replied Hunger. And the darting small fish began to coalesce and to assume familiar forms. First the dark ones segregated and the light ones segregated and became stabilized and began to follow each other in measured regular succession.

"What does this signify?" he asked of a small red design with a hundred restless hands, which stood at his left hand, and the small red design was called Pain.

"Wait," replied Pain. And in the water there appeared a face which

*Reprinted, with permission, from *Mayday* (Notre Dame: University of Notre Dame Press, 1978), pp. 47–87. Copyright © Jill Faulkner Summers. Printed by hand as a presentation gift to Helen Baird and dated "Oxford, Mississippi, 27 January, 1926." The University of Notre Dame Press edition includes an extended critical commentary.

was vaguely familiar, as the green design on his right hand and the red design at his left were familiar, and then other faces; and he leaned nearer above the waters and Hunger and Pain drew closer and he knew that he was not ever to lose them. The stream was now like an endless tapestry unfolding before him. All the faces he had known and loved and hated were there, impersonal now and dispassionate; and familiar places—cottages and castles, battlements and walled towers; and forests and meads, all familiar but small, much smaller than he had remembered.

"What does this signify?" he repeated, and Hunger and Pain drew subtly nearer and said together:

"Wait."

The tapestry unrolled endlessly. It now seemed on the point of assuming a definite pattern, what he did not know, but Hunger and Pain drew subtly nearer. Here was now in the dark hurrying water a stark thin face more beautiful than death, and it was Fortitude; and a tall bright one like a pillar of silver fire, and this one was Ambition; and knights in gold and silver armour and armour of steel, bearing lances with scarlet pennons passed remote and slow and majestic as clouds across a sunset that was as blown trumpets at evening. Himself appeared at last, tiny in mock battle with quarter staff and blunt lance and sword, and Hunger lay in his belly like fire and Pain lay in all his limbs. Then Hunger touched him and said Look! and there in the hurrying dark waters was a face all young and red and white, and with long shining hair like a column of fair sunny water; and he thought of young hyacinths in the spring, and honey and sunlight. He looked upon the face for a long while, and the hundred prehensile mouths of Hunger and the hundred restless hands of Pain were upon him.

Near the stream was a tree covered with bright never-still leaves of a thousand unimaginable colors, and the tree spoke and when the tree spoke the leaves whirled into the air and spun about it. The tree was an old man with a long shining beard like a silver cuirass and the leaves were birds of a thousand kinds and colors. And he replied to the tree, saying: "What sayest thou, good Saint Francis?"

But the good Saint Francis answered only: "Wait, it is not yet time."

Then Pain touched him and he looked again into the waters. The face in the waters was the face of a girl, and Pain and Hunger lay in all his limbs and body so that he burned like fire. And the girl in the dark hurrying stream raised her white arms to him and he would have gone to her, but Pain drew him one way and Hunger drew him another way so that he could not move as she sank away from him into the dark stream that was filled with darting fragments of sound and color. Soon these too became indistinct and then the water was once more opaque and silent and hurrying, filling the world about him until he was as one kneeling on a stone floor in a dark place, waiting for day.

And the tale tells how, in a while, one came to him, saying: "Rise, Sir Galwyn, be faithful, fortunate and brave." So he rose up and put on his polished armour and the golden spurs like twin lightnings, and his bright hair was like a sun hidden by the cloudy silver of his plumed helm, and he took up his bright unscarred shield and his stainless long sword and young Sir Galwyn went out therefrom.

His horse was caparisoned in scarlet and cloth of gold and he mounted and rode forth. Trumpets saluted him, and pennons flapped out on a breeze like liquid silver, beneath a golden morning like the first morning of the world, and young Sir Galwyn's charger marched slow and stately with pride, and young Sir Galwyn looked not back whence he had come.

In a while they came to a forest. This was a certain enchanted forest and the trees in this forest were more ancient than any could remember; for it was beneath these trees that, in the olden time, one Sir Morvidus, Earl Warwick, had slain a giant which had assaulted Sir Morvidus with the trunk of a tree torn bodily from the earth; and Sir Morvidus to commemorate this encounter assumed the ragged staff for the cognizance which his descendants still bear. The trees of this forest were not as ordinary trees, for each bough bore a living eye and these eyes stared without winking at young Sir Galwyn as he rode beneath them. These boughs were never still, but writhed always as though in agony, and where one bough touched another they made desolate moaning. But young Sir Galwyn minded them not. His bright smooth face whereon naught was as yet written, shone serene beneath his plumed morion, and his beautiful blank shield whereon naught was as yet written, swung flashing from his saddlebow, while his stainless long sword made a martial clashing against his greaves and his golden spurs like twin lightnings. And Hunger and Pain rode always at his right hand and his left hand, and his shadow circled tireless before and beneath and behind him.

For seven days they rode through this forest where enchantments were as thick as mayflowers, and as they rode young Sir Galwyn conversed with Pain and Hunger, and because he was young he gained from them much information but no wisdom. On the seventh day, having pursued and slain a small dragon of an inferior and cowardly type which had evidently strayed prematurely from its den (so that this encounter is scarcely worth recording—indeed, as Hunger later reminded him, he had much better have slain a fallow deer) young Sir Galwyn and his two companions came upon a small ivycovered stone dwelling, upon the door of which young Sir Galwyn thundered stoutly with his axe helve. One appeared in reply to this summons and stood regarding young Sir Galwyn contemplatively, tickling its nose with a feather, and sneezing at intervals.

"Give you god-den, young master," said this one civilly.

Now this was civil enough, and sensible; but young Sir Galwyn was young and hasty, and being somewhat new at the trade of errantry and having expected a giant, or at least a dragon to answer his summons, knew not exactly what was expected of him here, the regulations of knighthood having no formula covering such a situation. Whereupon young Sir Galwyn, in righteous displeasure and with admirable presence of mind, thundered in return:

"What, varlet? what, minion! Would'st address a belted knight as young master? Hast no manners, knave?"

"Why now, as for that," replies the other gravely, "during all the years I have served the people it has ever been my policy to address all men as they would be addressed, king and cook, poet and hind. But, sir belted knight, before craving pardon of you I wish to remind you that we philosophers who, so to speak, live lives of retirement, cannot be expected to keep abreast of the latest quirks and fantasies of fashion regarding the approach by a stranger of a private dwelling and so forth; an we both be but as the other judge him, then by 'r lady, there are two of us here without manners."

"Ah, yes: you refer to these two staring gentlemen riding beside me. But they are friends: I vouch for them both."

"Ay, I know them," replied the other, smiling a little, "I have seen both these gaudy staring gentlemen before. In fact, but for them no one would ever ride into this enchanted wood."

Young Sir Galwyn looked doubtful and a trifle bewildered at this, then his stainless long sword clashed against his greaves and reminded him that he was Sir Galwyn. So young Sir Galwyn said:

"But enough of this: we are wasting time."

"On the contrary," rejoins the other courteously, "I assure you that you are causing me no inconvenience whatever. In fact, and I do not say it to flatter you, I find our conversation most salutary."

"I am afraid, friend," says young Sir Galwyn haughtily, "that I do not follow you."

"Why, you just remarked that you were wasting time, and I do assure you that I am suffering no inconvenience whatever from this rencontre."

Then says young Sir Galwyn: "There is something wrong here: one of the two of us is laboring under a delusion. I have been led by those who should know to believe that Time is an old gentleman with a long white beard; and now you who are not old and who certainly have no long white beard, set yourself up to be Time. How can this be?"

"Well," replies the other, "as for my personal appearance: in this enlightened day when, as any standard magazine will inform you, one's appearance depends purely on one's inclination or disinclination to change it, what reason could I possibly have for wishing to look older than I feel? Then my wife (who, I am desolated to inform you, is away for the weekend, visiting her parents) my wife thinks that it does not look well for a man in my business to resemble a doddering centenarian, particularly as my new system of doing business eliminates the middle man from all dealings with my customers."

"Ah," says young Sir Galwyn, "you also have reorganized your business then? This was done recently?"

"Fairly so," agrees the other. "Yesterday it was. Though translated into your temporal currency it boils up into quite an imposing mess. Let me see—something like two million years, though I cannot give the exact date off hand."

"Oh . . . ." Young Sir Galwyn ponders briefly while Pain and Hunger sat their steeds sedately on his right hand and his left hand. Then young Sir Galwyn says: "Certainly this is spoken glibly enough, but how can I know that you are really Time?"

The other shrugged. "You materialists! You are like crows, with a single cry for all occasions: 'Proof! Proof!' Well, then; take for example the proverb Time and tide wait for no man. Do you believe in the soundness of this proverb?"

"Surely: I have demonstrated this truth to my complete satisfaction. And it seems to me that you who, by your own account, have spent your life serving mankind in this wood, convict yourself."

"Very well. Let us begin by asking these two gentlemen who have ridden with you for some time and who should know, what you are." He turned to young Sir Galwyn's two companions and said: "Sir Green Design and Sir Red Design, what is this thing calling itself Sir Galwyn of Arthgyl?"

Whereupon the green design called Hunger and the red design called Pain answered together: "He is but a handful of damp clay which we draw hither and yon at will until the moisture is gone completely out of him, as two adverse winds toy with a feather; and when the moisture is all gone out of him he will be as any other pinch of dust, and we will not be concerned with him any longer."

"Why, really," says young Sir Galwyn, somewhat taken aback, "I had no idea that two travellers with whom one has shared hunger and hardship could have such an uncomplimentary opinion of one, let alone expressing it in such a bald manner. But, heigh ho, gentlemen! I see that I am but wasting my youth talking with two shadows and a doddering fool who would convince me that I am not even a shadow—a thing which I, who am Sir Galwyn of Arthgyl, know to be false just as I know that beyond the boundaries of this enchanted wood Fame awaits me with a little pain and some bloodshed, and at last much pleasure. For there I shall find and deliver from captivity a young princess whom I have seen in a dream and who reminds me of young hyacinths in spring. And which of you, who are two shadows and a doddering imbecile, can know or tell me differently?"

The green design which was called Hunger and the red design called Pain sat quietly in the intermittent shadows of young leaves, but the other raised his sad dark eyes and gazed upon young Sir Galwyn's bright empty face with envious admiration. "Ah, Sir Galwyn, Sir Galwyn," said this one, "what would I not give to be also young and heedless, yet with your sublime faith in your ability to control that destiny which some invisible and rather unimaginative practical joker has devised for you! Ah, but I too would then find this mad world an uncomplex place of light and shadow and good earth on which to disport me. Still, everyone to his taste. And certainly the taking of prodigious pains to overtake a fate which it is already written will inevitably find me, is not mine. So there is naught left but for each to follow that path which seems—no, not good: rather let us say, less evil—to him; and I who am immortal find it in my heart to envy you who are mortal and who inherited with the doubtful privilege of breathing a legacy of pain and sorrow and, at last, oblivion. Therefore, young Sir Galwyn of Arthgyl, in what way can I serve you?"

"Why, in what way save by directing me to the castle where a certain princess whose hair is like a column of fair sunny water is held captive?"

"Now your description, I am sure, is most comprehensive, and it is impossible that it fit any other princess than she who reminds you, as you have previously told me, of young hyacinths in spring. But has it not occurred to you that every young knight who rides into this enchanted wood seeks a maiden whose hair is like bright water and who reminds him of young hyacinths, or perhaps of narcissi, or of cherry bloom? So I repeat, though your description of her is most happily conceived, I must ask you to bear in mind the fact that I am an old man and that it has been many a day since a girl has clung in my heart as unforgettable as a branch of apple bloom (though my wife, I do assure you, is a matchless woman and I would not for the world have it thought that I do not appreciate her) so I fear it will be necessary for me to have something a bit more tangible than an emotional reaction to understand just what captive princess you refer to."

"Is this particular wood," says young Sir Galwyn, "so full of captive princesses that you cannot tell me which one I seek?"

"Now I do not intimate that every turret you are likely to see contains a sighing virgin playing the lute and languishing for deliverance and honorable wedlock; but certainly there are enough of them whose rank and beauty will please the most exacting taste. For instance, to the westward, not far from where the sun lies down at evening there languishes in a castle of green stone the Princess Elys, daughter of Sethynnen ap Seydnn Seidi called the Drunkard, King of Wales, and her shining sleek head is the evening star in the sky above the sunset. Or to the eastward, where the sun rises from the yellow morning, there languishes in a castle of yellow stone the Princess Aelia daughter of Aelian, prince among the Merovingians and Crown Marshall of Arles, and her shining sleek head is the morning star above the dawn. Now which of these two ladies most appeals to you? You cannot go wrong (though 'tis said the Princess Elys is rather given to tears and that the Princess Aelia being of a—well, lively disposition, left some talk behind her in Provence, not all of which was flattering. In fact, one hears that old Aelian himself had more to do with his daughter's deplorable capture than people generally know. But that is all as may be: is beside the point) Which ever one you choose, these two princes are well able to set a son-in-law up in any business he wishes."

"Ah, I do not know," says young Sir Galwyn. "How can I know which of these maidens is her whom I saw in a dream? Who is there who can tell me, since you admit that you cannot? Though I am sorry that these two princesses should pine in captivity, I cannot spend my youth chasing here and there, releasing captive maidens who for all I know are much happier in durance than they would be freed again and who might object to my meddling, for I must seek her who reminds me of honey and sunlight; and so—" young Sir Galwyn turns politely to the green design called Hunger and the red design called Pain "—and so, if you gentlemen are ready, we had better take leave of this puzzling incomprehensible stranger and get onward."

And the tale tells how young Sir Galwyn of Arthgyl rode on through this enchanted forest with Hunger at his right hand and Pain at his left hand while the hermit stood staring after young Sir Galwyn's retreating back with envious admiration. Then he shook his head and turned, and entered his hut again.

The border of the wood broke suddenly before him as a wave breaks, shattering into a froth of sunlight. Beyond him, up to the horizon and beyond it until his eyes felt like two falcons straining in their sockets, down and heath flowed in a long swooping flight to a rumourous blue haze. This was the sea.

A river cut the center of this plain, and young Sir Galwyn bore toward it. The stream was hidden beyond twinkling aspen and alder, and slender white birches like poised dancing girls; and one with a spear rose from the path, saying "Halt!"

Young Sir Galwyn regarded this green jerkined yeoman haughtily. "Stand aside, knave, and let me pass."

But the man-at-arms held his ground. "In the King's name, Lord, stop ye; else I must thrust my spear into this goodly steed, for none must pass hither on pain of my life."

"In the name of what king do you cry halt to a traveller on the public road, and to a belted knight at that? Stand aside: dost think to provoke my stainless long sword against thy scurvy carcase?"

"In the name of my master, Mark, King of Cornwall, do I bid all travellers halt at this point, for in yonder stream the princess Yseult is bathing; and no man, be he knight or varlet, may look upon the naked body of the bride of a king."

"Now, certainly," says young Sir Galwyn, "this is most strange. Who is your master, that he sends his bride gallivanting about the country, bathing in rivers, in charge of a man-at-arms?"

"It is not I who am in charge of this princess: it is King Mark's nephew, Tristram, whom you will find (were I to let you pass) lying in yonder shade and writhing with love for the maiden whom he has sworn a knightly oath to bring untarnished to the bed of his uncle. And it is my opinion that the sooner this maiden is delivered to King Mark the better for us all, for I do not like the look of this expedition. I am a family man and must take care of the appearance of things."

So young Sir Galwyn, without a backward glance at that thing which had been a Cornish man-at-arms, rode on down a shaded path toward a muted rumourous flashing of hidden water. One clad in armour rose and barred his way. "Halt, or die!" spoke this one in a terrible voice.

"Who bids Sir Galwyn of Arthgyl to halt?" rejoins young Sir Galwyn in cold displeasure, as they paused eyeing each other like two young wolf hounds. They were so much alike, from their bright young faces (though to be sure the other's face was not empty, being terrible with jealousy and passion) to their mailed feet, that it was not strange that they should hate each other on sight.

"It is Tristram of Lyonness, by the grace of God and Uther Pendragon, knight; and he who would dispute this passage will be unshriven carrion beneath this sunset."

Now certainly, thinks young Sir Galwyn, I shall waste no time arguing with this unmannerly brute whose face is the color of thunder. And a would-be adulterer, also! Faith, and his vow of knighthood rests but lightly upon him who would make a Menelaus of his own uncle. But minstrels do sing of this Yseult, telling that she is as the morning star, and before her unguarded bosom's rich surprise men are maddened and their faces grow sharp as the spears of an assault. I am inclined to think it would be part of wisdom to see this paragon of a maid while I have the opportunity, if only to tell my grandchildren of it in the years. "Ho, friend," he spake, "cannot one draw near enough to look upon this ward of thine?"

Without a word the other drew his sword and furiously attacked young Sir Galwyn, so young Sir Galwyn slew this one, and tethered his horse to a near-by tree. At the end of the glade was a screen of willow and aspen; beyond this screen, young Sir Galwyn knew, would be water. So young Sir Galwyn drew near and parted the slender willows and the tire- and waiting-women of the Princess Yseult scurried with shrill cries, like plump partridges. And the Princess Yseult, who stood like a young birch tree in the water, screamed delicately, putting her two hands before her eyes.

"Ah, Tristram, Tristram!" says she, "wouldst violate thine own uncle's bed? Mother Mary, protect me from this ravisher!" then spreading her fingers a little more: "Why, this is not Sir Tristram! Who is this strange young man who dares approach the bride of a king in her bath? Help, wenches: protect me!"

"No, lady," replies young Sir Galwyn, "I am Galwyn of Arthgyl, knight at the hand of the Constable du Boisgeclin, who, having heard the beauty of the Princess Yseult sung by many a minstrel in many a banquetting hall, must needs dare all things to see her; and who, now that he has gazed upon her, finds that all his life before this moment was a stale thing, and that all the beautiful faces upon which he has looked are as leaves in a wind; and that you who are like honey and sunlight and young hyacinths have robbed him of peace and contentment as a gale strips the leaves from a tree; and because you are the promised bride of a king there is no help for it anywhere."

Well, really, thinks the princess on hearing these words, such a nice–spoken young man would hardly have the courage to harm anyone. . . . . I am afraid. Then aloud: "Who are you, and how have you managed to pass Sir Tristram, who swore that none should draw near?"

"Ah, lady," rejoins young Sir Galwyn, "what boots it who I am, who have now found all beauty and despair and all delight in an inaccessible place to which living I can never attain and which dead I can never forget? As for your Sir Tristram of Lyonness: I do not know him, unless he be one I have recently slain in yonder glade."

"Do you really think I am beautiful?" says the Princess Yseult in pleased surprise, "You say it so convincingly that I must believe you have said it before—I am sure you have said that to other girls. Now, haven't you? But I am sorry you saw me with my hair done this way. It does not suit me at all. . . . . So you have killed that impossible Sir Tristram. Really I am not at all sorry: I have stood in this cold water until, as you can see—" blushing delightfully "—that my skin is completely covered with goose bumps, and I made that stupid young man promise three times that none should approach me. It is a shame that one as handsome as he should be so impossibly dull. . . . . I am distressed you should have seen me with my hair done like this, but then you know what maids are in these degenerate days."

And the tale tells how the Princess Yseult came naked out of the water and she and young Sir Galwyn sojourned in the shade of a tree discussing various things, and how young Sir Galwyn's glib tongue wove such a magic that the Princess Yseult purred like a kitten. And afterwards they talked some more and the Princess Yseult told young Sir Galwyn all about herself and Sir Tristram and King Mark, and so forth and so on. But after a while young Sir Galwyn began to be restlessly aware that young hyacinths were no longer fresh, once you had picked them. So breaking into the middle of the plans the Princess Yseult was comfortably making for hers and young Sir Galwyn's future, young Sir Galwyn said:

"Lady, though the sound of your voice is as that of lute strings touched sweetly among tapers in a windless dusk and therefore I will never tire of hearing it, and though your body is as a narrow pool of fair water in this twilight, do you not think—" diffidently "—that it would be wise to call your women and put something on it beside the green veils of this twilight? You know how difficult a spring cold can be."

"Why, how thoughtful of you, Galwyn! But, really now, there is no hurry, is there? Surely we cannot go anywhere this late. But then, perhaps you are right about my getting into some clothes: someone might drop in. I blush to think of it, but for some reason—though it is not at all like myself—I feel no sense of immodesty whatever in being naked with you, for you are different from other men: you really understand me. However, perhaps you are right. Do you wait here quietly for me: I shall not be long. Now, promise not to follow me, not to move."

So young Sir Galwyn promised and the Princess Yseult kissed him and closed his eyes with her finger tips and kissed his eyelids and made him promise not to open them until she was out of sight, and retired. Young Sir Galwyn was too much of a gentleman to open them or to tell the Princess Yseult that he preferred seeing her back to her front, naked or otherwise, so he sat until the Princess Yseult had had ample time to collect her women, whereupon young Sir Galwyn rose and with furtive non-chalance betook him to the tree where his horse was tethered, and where the green design called Hunger and the red design called Pain waited him courteously; and they mounted and rode away from that place. And young Sir Galwyn at last drew a deep breath.

"By my faith, sir," spoke Hunger, "that was surely no sigh of a lover reft recently of his mistress? It struck me as being rather more a sigh of relief."

"To be frank with you, friend, I do not know myself exactly what that exhalation signified. Surely, one cannot find in this world one fairer than her whom I have recently left, and it seemed to me that all life must halt while I gazed upon her body like a young birch tree in the dusk, or felt the texture of her hair like a column of sunny water; still. . . . ."

"—still, this maid who is fairer than a man may hope to find more than once in a lifetime, must fain interpose between you that less fair but more tireless virtue which lives behind her little white teeth," the green design called Hunger completed for him.

"Exactly. And I now know that she is no different from all the other girls I have known, be they plain or be they beautiful. It occurs to me," young Sir Galwyn continued profoundly, that it is not the thing itself that man wants, so much as the wanting of it. But ah, it is sharper than swords to know that she who is fairer than music could not content me for even a day."

"But that, Sir Galwyn, is what life is: a ceaseless fretting to gain shadows to which there is no substance. To my notion man is a buzzing fly blundering through a strange world, seeking something he can neither name nor recognize and probably will not want. Still, you are young and you have a certain number of years to get through some how, so better luck next time."

So they rode on beneath squadrons of high pale stars, westward where the sky was like transparent oiled green silk upon a full and glowing breast, and a single star like a silver rose pinned to it. There was a faint greenish glow about them, and fireflies were like blown sparks from invisible fires. Suddenly a milk white doe bounded into the glade before them and kneeling before young Sir Galwyn, begged him to pierce her with his sword. Young Sir Galwyn did so, and lo! there knelt before him Elys, daughter of the King of Wales. She wore a green robe and a silver girdle studded with sapphires and she took young Sir Galwyn by the hand and led him deeper into the forest to a tent of lilac colored silk and ivory poles, and a bed of rushes. And young Sir Galwyn looked into the west and he saw that the evening star was no longer there.

And the tale tells how after a while young Sir Galwyn waked and raised himself to his elbow. The Princess Elys yet slept and young Sir Galwyn looked upon her in a vague sadness, and he kissed her sleeping mouth with a feeling of pity for her and of no particular pride in himself, and he rose quietly and passed without the tent. So he mounted his horse again.

The east was becoming light: high above him the morning star swam immaculately in a river of space. He heard faint horns triumphant as flung banners, and the horns grew louder. Then all at once he was surrounded by heralds with trumpets, and sarabands of dancing girls circled about him: their breasts were stained with gold and lipped with vermilion, and pages in scarlet lept among them. Then came a chariot of gold with a canopy of amythest on scarlet poles; nine white dolphins drew the chariot and in the chariot was the Princess Aelia, daughter of Aelius the Merovingian, dressed in a yellow robe and a girdle of sapphires, and the Princess Aelia stopped and leaned toward him.

"Come, Sir Galwyn of Arthgyl. I have long awaited you."

"Ah, lady," says young Sir Galwyn, "I am as one who has thirsted in a desert, and who sees before him in a dream a region of all beauty and despair and of all delight."

The Princess Aelia was pleased at this. "What a charming speech! I have heard of you, Sir Galwyn, but I had not thought to find such a nice spoken young man, or one so handsome. So come, and please to enter my chariot, and let us be going."

So young Sir Galwyn entered, and the trumpets flourished, and the nine white dolphins which drew the chariot moved like the wind. And looking upward young Sir Galwyn saw that the morning star was gone.

"Now then," says the Princess Aelia, "we can talk comfortably. So tell me about yourself."

"What can he tell you, Princess," replies young Sir Galwyn, "who has sought the whole earth over for one he has seen in a dream, who reminds him of honey and sunlight and young hyacinths; and who at last finds her in the person of an immortal whom he may only cry after as an infant in darkness, and whom he dare not touch? And because she is fairer than the song of birds at dawn or the feet of the Loves that make light in the air like doves' wings, he may never get her out of his heart, and because she is an immortal and a princess, there is no help for it anywhere."

"Why, do you really think that I am beautiful?" says the Princess Aelia in pleased surprise. "I am sorry you saw me in this rag. I hate yellow: it makes me look—oh—fat, and I am not fat. But you say that rather glibly—" giving him a glance of bright suspicion "—how many girls have you told that to, Sir Galwyn?"

"Well," says young Sir Galwyn, slightly ill at ease, "there was a certain Yseult, going to wed with the King of Cornwall, whom I paused out of curiosity to watch bathing in a pool and who insisted on my stopping to talk with her (which I could not refuse out of sheer politeness) I think I said something of this nature to her; and there was the Princess Elys who stopped me in a forest and who insisted that I accompany her to her tent to pass the night, and this too politeness forbade my refusing. And I may have said something like this to her."

"If that isn't just like a man!" exclaimed the Princess Aelia incomprehensibly. Then she stared at young Sir Galwyn with curiosity and some respect. "But I really must say, you are certainly a fast worker, as well as a discreet young man . . . . the Princess Elys! that yellow haired hussy! Heavens, what abysmal taste! Oh, men are such children: any toy for the moment. Really, I cannot see how you could have the nerve to repeat to me the same speeches you have made to a girl who roams forests at night and accosts strange young men. She is very evidently no better than she should be." The Princess Aelia stared away into space for a while. The chariot had left earth far behind and was now rushing through the sky, crashing through silver clouds like a swift ship among breakers, while falcons on planing rigid wings and with eyes like red and yellow jewels whirled about it, screaming.

The Princess Aelia continued. "To leave a creature like that, and come to me! With the same words on your lips! Ah, you have no respect for me," she wailed, "associating my name with a creature like that!" She burst into tears. "No, no, dont try to justify yourself! To think that I have come off alone with a man like you! What will my good name be worth now? How can I hold my head up ever again? Oh, I hate you, I hate you!"

"Now certainly, lady," says young Sir Galwyn, "you cannot blame me for this situation: it was on your invitation that I first entered this golden chariot."

This was sound logic, and had its usual result. "Dont talk to me!" wept the Princess Aelia, "it is just as I expected from a man like you: to injure me irreparably, and then try to justify yourself in my eyes."

"Well, this may be remedied by taking me back to earth. I am sure that I had no intention of doing anyone an injury. In fact, I cannot see that I have accomplished any hurt to you."

"But how can taking you back to earth remedy things? You will sit around low taverns and simply tear my reputation to shreds. Oh, I know you men! What am I to do?"

"Then," says young Sir Galwyn, "if you wont take me back to earth, I'll go back alone." And young Sir Galwyn threw his leg over the side of the chariot.

The Princess Aelia shrieked and threw her arms about him. "No, no! you'll be killed!"

"Then will you promise to stop crying and blaming me for something I have not done?"

"Yes." So young Sir Galwyn drew in his leg and the Princess Aelia dried her eyes on her sleeve. "Really, Galwyn, you are too stupid for words. But it did hurt me to find that, after all the nice things you said to me, or led me to believe, that I am no more to you than that—" and the Princess Aelia used a shocking word.

Young Sir Galwyn was properly shocked. "Really, Princess, I must object to such terms being applied to my friends. Besides, a lady would never know such a word, let alone repeat it."

"Oh, your ladies and your friends! Pooh, what do I care for either? But, tell me truly," clinging to him, "dont you think I am better looking than she?"

"Why, now," begins young Sir Galwyn lamely.

"Oh, you brute, I hate you! Why did I ever come away with such a beast! I wish I were dead!"

"Yes, yes!" young Sir Galwyn almost shouted, "anything if you wont cry again!"

"Ah, Galwyn, Galwyn, why are you so abysmally truthful? If you knew anything about women, you'd have learned better. But how can you have learned anything about women, poor dear, having been so successful with them? Anyway, you shouldn't have taken up with that nasty little Elys. But I'll show you what love is, Sir Galwyn; ah, I'll show you something you'll not soon forget!"

She spoke to the nine white dolphins in a strange tongue, and they turned earthward and flew at a dizzying speed. Young Sir Galwyn would have screamed with fear but the Princess Aelia's mouth was on his and young Sir Galwyn could not scream; and time and eternity swirled up and vortexed about the rush of their falling and the earth was but a spinning bit of dust in a maelstrom of blue space. The falcons planed plummetting beside the chariot and the wind screamed through the feathers of their wings, and the red and yellow jewels of their eyes were like coals of fire fanned to a heat unbearable. Young Sir Galwyn was no longer afraid: never had his heart known such ecstasy! he was a god and a falling star, consuming the whole world in a single long swooping rush through measureless regions of horror and delight down down, leaving behind him no change of light nor any sound.

And the tale tells how, in a while, young Sir Galwyn waked in a forest. Near him was his tethered steed browsing on the tender leaves of a young poplar, and beside it on two more horses sat the green design that was called Hunger and the red design called Pain, gravely and sedately waiting. So young Sir Galwyn rose and mounted, and the three of them rode away from that place. And young Sir Galwyn drew a deep breath.

"By my faith, sir," quoth Hunger, "that was surely no sigh of a lover reft recently of his mistress? It struck me as being rather more a sigh of relief."

"To be frank with you, friend, I do not myself know exactly what that exhalation signified. Surely, a man is not to find in this world three fairer ladies than I have found in as many days; and yet. . . ."

"Ay, Sir Galwyn, and yet and yet. You have known the bride of a king before ever her husband looked upon her, you have possessed, in the persons of the daughters of the two most important minor princes in Christendom, the morning and the evening stars, and yet you have gained nothing save a hunger which gives you no ease. I remember to have remarked once that man is a buzzing insect blundering through a strange world, seeking something he can neither name nor recognize, and probably will not want. I think now that I shall refine this aphorism to: Man is a buzzing fly beneath the inverted glass tumbler of his illusions." Hunger fell silent and the three of them paced steadily on amid the dappled intermittent shadows. Flowers were about the glades merrily, and birds sang every where, and the sun shone full on young Sir Galwyn's face on which was at last something written although it was not a thing of which young Sir Galwyn was especially proud, and his shield swung from his saddlebow and it did not flash quite as brightly as it once did, for there was something written on it also that young Sir Galwyn was not particularly proud of, and young Sir Galwyn's long sword had stained through its scabbard and so young Sir Galwyn drew the skirt of his cloak over his sword.

Hunger spoke again in a while: "There is still one more girl I may show you, and I guarantee that she will smoothe that look of hunger from your face. What say you, young Sir Galwyn? Shall we seek this maid?"

And young Sir Galwyn said: "Who is this maid who can smoothe all hunger and remembering from my face?"

And the other replied: "It is my sister."

And young Sir Galwyn said: "Lead on."

So the three of them rode onward into the west from which the last light was ebbing as from a smooth beach.

This place, too, was familiar. That is, it seemed to young Sir Galwyn that soon there would appear something that he had seen and known long since, that here would be reenacted a scene that he had once looked upon or taken part in. So they rode on through a valley between shelving vague hills where the air was gray and smelled of spring. At last, at young Sir Galwyn's feet lay a dark hurrying stream and beside the stream stood a tree covered with leaves of a thousand different colors, and near the tree was a paunchy little man neither standing nor lying, with a beautiful white high brow and eyes of no particular color, resembling nothing so much as water wherein a great many things had been drowned. And young Sir Galwyn stopped at the brink of the stream and Hunger and Pain paused obediently near him, and as he gazed into the dark hurrying waters he knew that he had stood here before, and he wondered if his restless seeking through the world had been only a devious unnecessary way of returning to a place he need never have left.

In a while he of the calm beautiful brow drew near to young Sir Galwyn and he made a gesture with his long pale hand. Whereupon Hunger and Pain withdrew, and they were in a desolate place. And he with the high white brow said to young Sir Galwyn:

"Choose."

And young Sir Galwyn asked: "What shall I choose?"

But the other only replied: "Look, and see."

So they stood side by side, staring into the dark waters. And as they watched the waters were no longer dark but were filled with formless fragments of color and sound like darting small fish which, as young Sir Galwyn watched, began to coalesce into a regular measured succession of light and dark.

"Now," said the paunchy little man who looked as though standing up was very uncomfortable for him, "you, who have crossed this stream once without being wetted, must now choose one of two things. In this hurrying dark flood will appear the various phases of all life, from the beginning of time down to this moment, left in this stream by those who have preceded you here and whose memories have been washed clean and blank and smooth as a marble surface after rain. And now, having completed the cycle I have allowed you, you may choose any one of these phases to live over again. And though you will be but a shadow among shades it will seem to you that this which is now transpiring was but a dark dream which you had dreamed and that you are a palpable thing directing your destiny in a palpable world.

"Or you may choose to be submerged in these waters. Then you will remember nothing, not even this conversation or this choosing; and all your petty victories, your loving and hating, all the actions you have achieved will be washed from your mind to linger in these hurrying dark waters like darting small fish for those who are to come here after you to gaze upon; and this is Fame. But once these waters have closed above you, your memory will be as a smooth surface after rain, and you will remember nothing at all."

"What, then," says young Sir Galwyn, "will I be?"

"You will not be anything."

"Not even a shadow?"

"Not even a shadow."

"And if I choose to cross this stream, how may I do so without being wetted?"

The other moved his pale smooth hand and there appeared from out the mist beyond the dark hurrying water a gray man in a gray boat without oars. The boat touched the shore at their feet and the gray man stood with his head bent, staring into the water, and his gray garment hung from his lean figure in formal motionless folds.

"And if I choose to cross this stream?" repeated young Sir Galwyn.

"As I have already told you, you will be a shadow subject to all shadowy ills—hunger and pain and bodily discomforts, and love and hate and hope and despair. And you will know no better how to combat them than you did on your last journey through the world, for my emigration laws prohibit Experience leaving my domains. And besides, man should beware of Experience as he should beware of all women, for with her or without her he will be miserable, but without her he will not be dangerous."

"Then I will no longer be that thing men call Sir Galwyn of Arthgyl?"

"You will no longer be that thing men call Sir Galwyn of Arthgyl."

"But, if I am a shadow, how can I know hunger and pain?"

The other raised his head. His eyes were the color of sleep and he regarded young Sir Galwyn wearily. "Have not Hunger and Pain been beside you since before you could remember? have they not ridden at your right hand and your left hand in all your journeys and battles? were they not closer to you than the young Yseult and Elys and Aelia could ever attain, or any of them who reminded you of honey and sunlight and young hyacinths in spring?"

"Yes, that is true. . . ." young Sir Galwyn admitted slowly. "But," he said suddenly, "I was not a shadow then."

"How do you know you were not a shadow?"

Young Sir Galwyn thought a while, and it was as though a cold wind had blown upon him. Then he said: "Who are you, who bids me choose one of two alternatives, neither of which is particularly pleasing to me?"

"I am the Lord of Sleep."

And young Sir Galwyn regarded the paunchy little man with the beautiful high brow and eyes the color of sleep, and young Sir Galwyn was silent. In a while the other said:

"Look."

And young Sir Galwyn looked as he was bid, and in the hurrying dark waters were three faces. The Princess Yseult, now Queen of Cornwall, returned his gaze, haughty with power and offended pride, and passed on; the face of the Princess Elys, daughter of the King of Wales, whom he had abandoned in the enchanted forest looked at him in reproach and sorrow. Her face was blurred as with weeping, and she raised her delicate young arms to him as she sank away into the dark stream. The third was the glittering passionate face of Aelia, princess of the Merovingians; she gave him a fierce glance and her mouth was a thin red scorn and she too passed onward with the other glittering wreckage in the water, and Pain and Hunger drawing near again said together:

"Look."

And Hunger and Pain drew subtly nearer, and there in the water was one all young and white, and with long shining hair like a column of fair sunny water, and young Sir Galwyn thought of young hyacinths in spring, and honey and sunlight. Young Sir Galwyn looked upon this face and he was as one sinking from a fever into a soft and bottomless sleep; and he stepped forward into the water and Hunger and Pain went away from him, and as the water touched him it seemed to him that he knelt in a dark room waiting for day and that one like a quiet soft shining came to him, saying: "Rise, Sir Galwyn; be faithful, fortunate, and brave."

And the tree covered with leaves of a thousand different colours spoke, and all the leaves whirled up into the air and spun about it; and the tree was an old man with a shining white beard like a silver cuirass, and the leaves were birds.

What sayest thou, good Saint Francis?

"Little sister Death," said the good Saint Francis.

Thus it was in the old days.

An Introduction to *The Sound and the Fury* [I]

William Faulkner*

Art is no part of southern life. In the North it seems to be different. It is the hardest minor stone in Manhattan's foundation. It is a part of the glitter or shabbiness of the streets. The arrowing buildings rise out of it and because of it, to be torn down and arrow again. There will be people leading small bourgeois lives (those countless and almost invisible bones of its articulation, lacking any one of which the whole skeleton might collapse) whose bread will derive from it—polyglot boys and girls progressing from tenement schools to editorial rooms and art galleries; men with grey hair and paunches who run linotype machines and take up tickets at concerts and then go sedately home to Brooklyn and suburban stations where children and grandchildren await them—long after the descendents of Irish politicians and Neapolitan racketeers are as forgotten as the wild Indians and the pigeon.

And of Chicago too: of that rhythm not always with harmony or tune; lusty, loudvoiced, always changing and always young; drawing from a river basin which is almost a continent young men and women into its living unrest and then spewing them forth again to write Chicago in New England and Virginia and Europe. But in the South art, to become visible at all, must become a ceremony, a spectacle; something between a gypsy encampment and a church bazaar given by a handful of alien mummers who must waste themselves in protest and active self-defense until there is nothing left with which to speak—a single week, say, of furious endeavor for a show to be held on Friday night and then struck and vanished, leaving only a paint-stiffened smock or a worn out typewriter ribbon in the corner and perhaps a small bill for cheesecloth or bunting in the hands of an astonished and bewildered tradesman.

Perhaps this is because the South (I speak in the sense of the indigenous dream of any given collection of men having something in com-

*Reprinted, with permission, from *A Faulkner Miscellany*, ed. James B. Meriwether (Jackson: University Press of Mississippi, 1974), pp. 156–61. Copyright © 1973 by Mrs. Jill Faulkner Summers, Executrix, for the Estate of William Faulkner. Probably an early draft of an introduction written for the (unpublished) 1933 Random House edition, with emendations of obvious typing or spelling errors by Meriwether.

mon, be it only geography and climate, which shape their economic and spiritual aspirations into cities, into a pattern of houses or behavior) is old since dead. New York, whatever it may believe of itself, is young since alive; it is still a logical and unbroken progression from the Dutch: And Chicago even boasts of being young. But the South, as Chicago is the Middlewest and New York the East, is dead, killed by the Civil War. There is a thing known whimsically as the New South to be sure, but it is not the south. It is a land of Immigrants who are rebuilding the towns and cities into replicas of towns and cities in Kansas and Iowa and Illinois, with skyscrapers and striped canvas awnings instead of wooden balconies, and teaching the young men who sell the gasoline and the waitresses in the restaurants to say O yeah? and to speak with hard r's, and hanging over the intersections of quiet and shaded streets where no one save Northern tourists in Cadillacs and Lincolns ever pass at a gait faster than a horse trots, changing red-to-green lights and savage and peremptory bells.

Yet this art, which has no place in southern life, is almost the sum total of the Southern artist. It is his breath, blood, flesh, all. Not so much that it is forced back upon him or that he is forced bodily into it by the circumstance; forced to choose, lady and tiger fashion, between being an artist and being a man. He does it deliberately; he wishes it so. This has always been true of him and of him alone. Only Southerners have taken horsewhips and pistols to editors about the treatment or maltreatment of their manuscript. This—the actual pistols—was in the old days, of course, we no longer succumb to the impulse. But it is still there, still within us.

Because it is himself that the Southerner is writing about, not about his environment: who has, figuratively speaking, taken the artist in him in one hand and his milieu in the other and thrust the one into the other like a clawing and spitting cat into a croker sack. And he writes. We have never got and probably will never get, anywhere with music or the plastic forms. We need to talk, to tell, since oratory is our heritage. We seem to try in the simple furious breathing (or writing) span of the individual to draw a savage indictment of the contemporary scene or to escape from it into a makebelieve region of swords and magnolias and mockingbirds which perhaps never existed anywhere. Both of the courses are rooted in sentiment; perhaps the ones who write savagely and bitterly of the incest in clayfloored cabins are the most sentimental. Anyway, each course is a matter of violent partizanship, in which the writer unconsciously writes into every line and phrase his violent despairs and rages and frustrations or his violent prophesies of still more violent hopes. That cold intellect which can write with calm and complete detachment and gusto of its contemporary scene is not among us; I do not believe there lives the Southern writer who can say without lying that writing is any fun to him. Perhaps we do not want it to be.

I seem to have tried both of the courses. I have tried to escape and I have tried to indict. After five years I look back at *The Sound and The Fury* and see that that was the turning point: in this book I did both at one time. When I began the book, I had no plan at all. I wasn't even writing a book. Previous to it I had written three novels, with progressively decreasing ease and pleasure, and reward or emolument. The third one was shopped about for three [actually one—Ed.] years during which I sent it from publisher to publisher with a kind of stubborn and fading hope of at least justifying the paper I had used and the time I had spent writing it. This hope must have died at last, because one day it suddenly seemed as if a door had clapped silently and forever to between me and all publishers' addresses and booklists and I said to myself, Now I can write. Now I can just write. Whereupon I, who had three brothers and no sisters and was destined to lose my first daughter in infancy, began to write about a little girl.

I did not realise then that I was trying to manufacture the sister which I did not have and the daughter which I was to lose, though the former might have been apparent from the fact that Caddy had three brothers almost before I wrote her name on paper. I just began to write about a brother and a sister splashing one another in the brook and the sister fell and wet her clothing and the smallest brother cried, thinking that the sister was conquered or perhaps hurt. Or perhaps he knew that he was the baby and that she would quit whatever water battles to comfort him. When she did so, when she quit the water fight and stooped in her wet garments above him, the entire story, which is all told by that same little brother in the first section, seemed to explode on the paper before me.

I saw that peaceful glinting of that branch was to become the dark, harsh flowing of time sweeping her to where she could not return to comfort him, but that just separation, division, would not be enough, not far enough. It must sweep her into dishonor and shame too. And that Benjy must never grow beyond this moment; that for him all knowing must begin and end with that fierce, panting, paused and stooping wet figure which smelled like trees. That he must never grow up to where the grief of bereavement could be leavened with understanding and hence the alleviation of rage as in the case of Jason, and of oblivion as in the case of Quentin.

I saw that they had been sent to the pasture to spend the afternoon to get them away from the house during the grandmother's funeral in order that the three brothers and the nigger children could look up at the muddy seat of Caddy's drawers as she climbed the tree to look in the window at the funeral, without then realising the symbology of the soiled drawers, for here again hers was the courage which was to face later with honor the shame which she was to engender, which Quentin and Jason could not face: the one taking refuge in suicide, the other in vindictive rage which drove him to rob his bastard niece of the meagre sums which Caddy could send her. For I had already gone on to night and the bedroom and Dilsey with the mudstained drawers scrubbing the naked backside of that doomed little girl—trying to cleanse with the sorry byblow of its soiling that body, flesh, whose shame they symbolised and prophesied, as though she already saw the dark future and the part she was to play in it trying to hold that crumbling household together.

Then the story was complete, finished. There was Dilsey to be the future, to stand above the fallen ruins of the family like a ruined chimney, gaunt, patient and indomitable; and Benjy to be the past. He had to be an idiot so that, like Dilsey, he could be impervious to the future, though unlike her by refusing to accept it at all. Without thought or comprehension; shapeless, neuter, like something eyeless and voiceless which might have lived, existed merely because of its ability to suffer, in the beginning of life; half fluid, groping: a pallid and helpless mass of all mindless agony under sun, in time yet not of it save that he could nightly carry with him that fierce, courageous being who was to him but a touch and a sound that may be heard on any golf links and a smell like trees, into the slow bright shapes of sleep.

The story is all there, in the first section as Benjy told it. I did not try deliberately to make it obscure; when I realised that the story might be printed, I took three more sections, all longer than Benjy's, to try to clarify it. But when I wrote Benjy's section, I was not writing it to be printed. If I were to do it over now I would do it differently, because the writing of it as it now stands taught me both how to write and how to read, and even more: It taught me what I had already read, because on completing it I discovered, in a series of repercussions like summer thunder, the Flauberts and Conrads and Turgenievs which as much as ten years before I had consumed whole and without assimilating at all, as a moth or a goat might. I have read nothing since; I have not had to. And I have learned but one thing since about writing. That is, that the emotion definite and physical and yet nebulous to describe which the writing of Benjy's section of *The Sound and The Fury* gave me—that ecstasy, that eager and joyous faith and anticipation of surprise which the yet un-marred sheets beneath my hand held inviolate and unfailing—will not return. The unreluctance to begin, the cold satisfaction in work well and arduously done, is there and will continue to be there as long as I can do it well. But that other will not return. I shall never know it again.

So I wrote Quentin's and Jason's sections, trying to clarify Benjy's. But I saw that I was merely temporising; That I should have to get completely out of the book. I realised that there would be compensations, that in a sense I could then give a final turn to the screw and extract some ultimate distillation. Yet it took me better than a month to take pen and write *The day dawned bleak and chill* before I did so. There is a story somewhere about an old Roman who kept at his bedside a Tyrrhenian vase which he loved and the rim of which he wore slowly away with kissing it. I had made myself a vase, but I suppose I knew all the time that I could not live forever inside of it, that perhaps to have it so that I too could lie in bed and look at it would be better; surely so when that day should come when not only the ecstasy of writing would be gone, but the unreluctance and the something worth saying too. It's fine to think that you will leave something behind you when you die, but it's better to have made something you can die with. Much better the muddy bottom of a little doomed girl climbing a blooming pear tree in April to look in the window at the funeral.

Oxford.
    19 August, 1933.

An Introduction to *The Sound and the Fury* [II]

William Faulkner*

I wrote this book and learned to read. I had learned a little about writing from Soldiers' Pay—how to approach language, words: not with seriousness so much, as an essayist does, but with a kind of alert respect, as you approach dynamite; even with joy, as you approach women: perhaps with the same secretly unscrupulous intentions. But when I finished The Sound and The Fury I discovered that there is actually something to which the shabby term Art not only can, but must, be applied. I discovered then that I had gone through all that I had ever read, from Henry James through Henty to newspaper murders, without making any distinction or digesting any of it, as a moth or a goat might. After The Sound and The Fury and without heeding to open another book and in a series of delayed repercussions like summer thunder, I discovered the Flauberts and Dostoievskys and Conrads whose books I had read ten years ago. With The Sound and The Fury I learned to read and quit reading, since I have read nothing since.

Nor do I seem to have learned anything since. While writing Sanctuary, the next novel to The Sound and The Fury, that part of me which learned as I wrote, which perhaps is the very force which drives a writer to the travail of invention and the drudgery of putting seventy-five or a hundred thousand words on paper, was absent because I was still reading by repercussion the books which I had swallowed whole ten years and more ago. I learned only from the writing of Sanctuary that there was something missing; something which The Sound and The Fury gave me and Sanctuary did not. When I began As I Lay Dying I had discovered what it was and knew that it would be also missing in this case because this would be a deliberate book. I set out deliberately to write a tour-de-force. Before I ever put pen to paper and set down the first word, I knew what the last word would be and almost where the last period would fall. Before I began I said, I am going to write a book by which, at a pinch, I

*Reprinted, with permission, from the *Southern Review*, N.S. 8 (October 1972), 708–10. Copyright © 1972 by the Estate of William Faulkner. Probably a final or near-final draft of an introduction written for the (unpublished) 1933 Random House edition, with emendations of obvious typing or spelling errors by James B. Meriwether.

can stand or fall if I never touch ink again. So when I finished it the cold satisfaction was there, as I had expected, but as I had also expected that other quality which The Sound and The Fury had given me was absent: that emotion definite and physical and yet nebulous to describe: that ecstasy, that eager and joyous faith and anticipation of surprise which the yet unmarred sheet beneath my hand held inviolate and unfailing, waiting for release. It was not there in As I Lay Dying. I said, It is because I knew too much about this book before I began to write it. I said, More than likely I shall never again have to know this much about a book before I begin to write it, and next time it will return. I waited almost two years, then I began Light in August, knowing no more about it than a young woman, pregnant, walking along a strange country road. I thought, I will recapture it now, since I know no more about this book than I did about The Sound and The Fury when I sat down before the first blank page.

It did not return. The written pages grew in number. The story was going pretty well: I would sit down to it each morning without reluctance yet still without that anticipation and that joy which alone ever made writing pleasure to me. The book was almost finished before I acquiesced to the fact that it would not recur, since I was now aware before each word was written down just what the people would do, since now I was deliberately choosing among possibilities and probabilities of behavior and weighing and measuring each choice by the scale of the Jameses and Conrads and Balzacs. I knew that I had read too much, that I had reached that stage which all young writers must pass through, in which he believes that he has learned too much about his trade. I received a copy of the printed book and I found that I didn't even want to see what kind of jacket Smith had put on it. I seemed to have a vision of it and the other ones subsequent to The Sound and The Fury ranked in order upon a shelf while I looked at the titled backs of them with a flagging attention which was almost distaste, and upon which each succeeding title registered less and less, until at last Attention itself seemed to say, Thank God I shall never need to open any one of them again. I believed that I knew then why I had not recaptured that first ecstasy, and that I should never again recapture it; that whatever novels I should write in the future would be written without reluctance, but also without anticipation or joy: that in the Sound and The Fury I had already put perhaps the only thing in literature which would ever move me very much: Caddy climbing the pear tree to look in the window at her grandmother's funeral while Quentin and Jason and Benjy and the negroes looked up at the muddy seat of her drawers.

This is the only one of the seven novels which I wrote without any accompanying feeling of drive or effort, or any following feeling of exhaustion or relief or distaste. When I began it I had no plan at all. I wasn't even writing a book. I was thinking of books, publication, only in the reverse, in saying to myself, I wont have to worry about publishers liking or not liking this at all. Four years before I had written Soldiers' Pay. It didn't take long to write and it got published quickly and made me about five hundred dollars. I said, Writing novels is easy. You dont make much doing it, but it is easy. I wrote Mosquitoes. It wasn't quite so easy to write and it didn't get published quite as quickly and it made me about four hundred dollars. I said, Apparently there is more to writing novels, being a novelist, than I thought. I wrote Sartoris. It took much longer, and the publisher refused it at once. But I continued to shop it about for three years with a stubborn and fading hope, perhaps to justify the time which I had spent writing it. This hope died slowly, though it didn't hurt at all. One day I seemed to shut a door between me and all publishers' addresses and book lists. I said to myself, Now I can write. Now I can make myself a vase like that which the old Roman kept at his bedside and wore the rim slowly away with kissing it. So I, who had never had a sister and was fated to lose my daughter in infancy, set out to make myself a beautiful and tragic little girl.

A Prefatory Note for "Appendix: Compson, 1699–1945"

William Faulkner

When Faulkner wrote THE SOUND AND THE FURY in 1928, he failed to finish it for anybody. In 1946, when Malcolm Cowley reached TSATF in gathering and collating material for his portable Faulkner, Faulkner discovered that the book was not even finished for himself. Possibly he realised this in 1946 only because he was incapable of finishing it until 1946; that in 1928 and 1938 he still didn't know enough about people to finish out his own, and so the book was actually not unconsciously willfull tour de force in obfuscation but rather the homemade, the experimental, the first moving picture projector—warped lens, poor light, undependable mechanism and even a bad screen—which had to wait until 1946 for the lens to clear, the light to steady, the gears to run smooth. It was too late then though. The book was done. It was last year's maidenhead now. All Faulkner could do was try and make a key. He thought a page or two pages would do it. It ran near twenty. Here it is.

*Reprinted, with permission, from *American Literature*, 43:2 (May 1971), 283–84. Copyright © 1971 by Estate of William Faulkner. James B. Meriwether comments "When he says that he 'failed to finish' *The Sound and the Fury* in 1928, and that the 1946 Appendix is a necessary 'key' to it, Faulkner may be telling us less about any weakness in the conception and execution of the novel, than he is about the strength of his own continuing interest in its characters" (p. 283). Apparently drafted (but unpublished) in 1946 for the Modern Library double edition of *"The Sound and the Fury" and "As I Lay Dying"* (1946).

II RECEIVING THE COMPSONS
United States
England
France

United States

A Family Breaks Up

Lyle Saxon*

This is the fourth novel by William Faulkner. He has gained in power with each one, and in "The Sound and the Fury" he has achieved a novel of extraordinary effect.

The story concerns the breaking up of a family; it is as merciless as anything that I know which has come out of Russia. I find myself wishing for someone with whom to compare William Faulkner, but to compare this writer from Mississippi with James Joyce or Marcel Proust or Chekov or Dostoevsky gets one nowhere, for Faulkner is definitely American. The tragedy concerns a family in a small Mississippi town; yet, like all great stories, it is universal. I use the word "great" with intention, for I believe this to be a novel of the first rank.

The story concerns the fall of the house of Compson, and the title is taken from Shakespeare's line, "Life is a tale told by an idiot, full of sound and fury, signifying nothing." The Compsons are a family run to seed, disintegrating; they are obsessed with futility; madness is in the brain of each of them. The story centers around an imbecile, Benjy, a man of thirty-three but with the mind of a small child; Benjy's eternal whimpering is felt through every page. The girl, Quentin, the youngest member of the family, indulges in promiscuous matings with traveling salesmen. Her uncle, Jason, the "normal" member of the family, is maddened with the disgrace which the young girl has brought upon them all. He works in a country store and cheats his relations of their money in order to take trips to the city to visit a prostitute, who seems to him straightforward and natural, as compared with his neurotic family. At home he cruelly nags the young girl, torments the Negro servants and browbeats his weak and futile mother.

The book is divided into four parts and the reader sees the Compson family from four points of view, first through the mind of the idiot, Benjy, in writing which is chaotic but pitifully moving. Benjy lives in a world of sounds and sights and smells; he is watched over by Luster, a Negro boy who teases him by depriving him of his treasures—a flower, a mirror, a

*Reprinted, with permission, from the *New York Herald Tribune*, October 13, 1929, 12:3.

satin slipper. Vaguely, through Benjy's eyes, the reader gets glimpses of the tragedy of the household.

Part two shifts to the mind of the man who is going mad and who is obsessed with his sister's shame; he knows that she is to have an illegitimate child and he longs to shield her from the disgrace. In his darkening mind he fancies that he is responsible for her condition. The breaking down of another mentality is shown in all its horror.

Part three shifts again, this time to the mind of Jason, the "normal" member of the family. Some of Mr. Faulkner's most extraordinary writing is in this part of the book. Jason is a fiend; he jeers at himself, at his idiot brother, at his mother. He follows the girl in order to trap her in one of her commonplace lapses. Jason takes delight in torture, both of himself and of those near him. His mind is alert. Here the story crystallizes into hard, bright clarity.

The last portion of the novel is told in the third person by the author. The reader sees the characters as they really appear. Here we have a day in the Compson household, beginning with old Dilsey, the Negro cook, who has been shown through different eyes in earlier portions of the book; now she becomes a magnificent figure in her own right. We encounter the weak, complaining mother who calls repeatedly "without inflection or emphasis or haste, as though she were not listening for a reply at all." We see the idiot, Benjy, before the kitchen stove, crying "with a slow bellowing sound, meaningless and sustained," because the stove door has been closed and the bright fire is lost to him. We see Jason in a passion which rises to madness when he discovers that the girl, Quentin, has run away with an actor and that she is beyond further torture at his hands. Jason, insane with rage, goes after her.

In order to keep Benjy quiet, old Dilsey takes him with her to a Negro church, and later lets Luster, the Negro boy, take him for a drive in the carriage. The idiot resents any change in the accustomed order of his life; the carriage must travel the same route every day or the world is awry. The Negro boy turns the horse to the left instead of to the right. The idiot begins to bellow; Jason, returning from the futile pursuit of Quentin, meets the carriage and the bellowing idiot. In a fury Jason strikes the Negro and turns the carriage around. The idiot is quieted and his "eyes were empty and blue and serene again as cornice and facade flowed smoothly once more from left to right; post and tree, window and doorway, and signboard, each in its ordered place."

It will be interesting to see what readers and critics think of this novel by William Faulkner. Many, I am sure will call the author mad. But if Faulkner is mad, then James Joyce is equally so; if Faulkner is obsessed with futility and insanity, so is Fyodor Dostoevsky. It is true that "The Sound and the Fury" is insane and monstrous and terrible, but so is the life that it mirrors. It is difficult to read, but I could not put it down. I believe, simply and sincerely, that this is a great book.

[Modernist Manner over Matter]

Winfield Townley Scott*

The Sound and the Fury is a novel about a Southern family of descending social position. There is a father with considerable polish, a mother of far less education, a son who is a business man and another who is a Harvard student, two daughters who go wrong and a son who is a deaf and dumb idiot. There is little attempted on the part of the author beyond expression of these characters; the plot element is slight. It is the method in which the story is told that chiefly concerns us.

The narrative is divided into four sections. Three of these four are done in the manner of James Joyce, *Blue Voyage*, and Gertrude Stein. That is as near as one might approximate it. The story, in short, is told through the thoughts—jumbled, confused and wandering—of three different characters, with the exception of the last section which is written in quite conservative prose. Rambling, often capital-less or periodless or puncture-less, the prose strains on for 330 pages in no very definite manner, although the manner is what concerns the author. And when one ascertains that the first section is through the mind of the idiot, one begins to appreciate the complications.

Max Eastman recently wrote an essay on the modernistic school of writers—Joyce, Cummings, Stein, *et al.*—in which he contended that the purpose of literature, primarily, is to communicate. Of course. And the chief indictment against the modernists is their utmost complete lack of communication. Under this indictment young Mr. Faulkner must fall. His novel tells us nothing. In one or two cases only does his method justify itself by a certain dramatic vividness. On the whole, his novel, over which Evelyn Scott has waxed so enthusiastic, is downright tiresome. It is so much sound and fury—signifying nothing.

*Reprinted, with permission, from *Providence (Rhode Island) Sunday Journal*, October 20, 1929, p. 27.

Decayed Gentility

Anonymous*

When "Soldiers Pay" was written a few years ago, critics found the author a young man who had a rather uncertain style, sometimes original, sometimes imitative of the school of James Joyce, but who was undeniably worth watching. In his subsequent writing the style became no more settled, but no less promising. What manner of man is this who can use incoherence so effectively on one page and on the next write a most beautifully single-minded narrative? Has he a style or hasn't he? In this novel he has given himself opportunity to try each of his methods in a story that is told in the first person by three separate characters, with a final summing up of the family history in the third person.

"The Sound and the Fury" is the story of the decaying gentility of a Southern family. Benjy, one son, is 35 years old, with the mind of a child of 3. Caddy brings disgrace by her free ways with men. Quentin is overly sensitive and commits suicide. Only Jason is a comfort to his mother; but of all the characters he is the least acceptable to the reader, who knows him for a liar and a cheat. The mother is a whining hypochondriac and the father is a drunkard.

With this array of characters, which bids fair to out-Russian the Russians, the author weaves the story of Caddy and her unfortunate marriage, the adoption of her daughter, Quentin, into the household over which Jason has become master, and the complete disintegration of the family, which is only held together as long as it is through the efforts of the negro servants, a peculiarly sane chorus to the insane tragedy.

The first part of the book takes part in the mind of Benjy, the idiot. It is told in the first person, with the utmost objectivity. Benjy cannot talk; he must be fed. He has not the intelligence to interpret either the words or the actions of the people who make up his world. He can see and he can hear, and what he thus senses makes up his part of the story, which jumps back and forth across the years with no regard to chronology, the turn of a thought indicated in italics.

The second part is told by the son Quentin when he is a freshman at

*Reprinted, with permission, from the *New York Times Book Review*, November 10. 1929, p. 28.

Harvard and his sister Caddy is being married. He is going to drown himself, and the story of what he does on the day of the suicide adds further to the history of the family.

The third part is told by Jason, who justifies his actions in his own mind, but who reveals through his words and thoughts the most contemptible nature, also verging on the insane.

In the last part the family is at its lowest ebb. Only the mother, Jason and Benjy remain, together with the aging negro servants.

The author has chosen an unusual medium for his story in not one but four styles. Yet the four are welded together in perfect unity. The objective quality of the novel saves it from complete morbidity.

[Provincialism and Mr. Faulkner]

H[enry Nash] S[mith]*

William Faulkner's novel calls for a re-examination of our premises. It raises at least two perplexing questions: first, does an unmistakably provincial locale make a book a provincial piece of writing? and secondly, what evidences of provincialism might one expect in the style of a novel written by a man who has, in the trite phrase, sunk his roots into the soil?

The first question suggests some consideration of a new Southwestern book, *Dobe Walls*. Stanley Vestal's novel, for all its wealth of frontier incident and description, is perfectly conventional in its plot, its technique, and its heroine; only in some of the men (Bob Thatcher for instance) does the influence of the Frontier on character become evident. *Dobe Walls* escapes from the here and now of life; it is a historical tale with unusually authentic information about the period and the region it treats. In this respect it is vastly different from *The Sound and the Fury*, which is concerned with a regional tradition only as it appears in the present, and from Mr. Faulkner's earlier novels, which often lean toward satire. Yet both novels have a regional setting, and both authors are residents of the provinces. Are both books to be related to the "new provincialism"?

The question of a provincial style is even more involved. One may always be suspicious when talk grows as theoretical as discussions of the "rhythm of a landscape" or "the spacious gesture of the frontier" tend to become. It seems entirely possible that some of us have been misled by an analogy, and have wandered a little into realms of speculation. Upholders of the idea of universal standards not dependent upon a genius of the age or a genius of the place have always been uneasy in the presence of such theories; and perhaps they are nearer right than we. Or maybe we are both right, but have not yet found the reconciling "nevertheless".

Let me, therefore, deliver myself from both points of view on the subject of *The Sound and the Fury*. No matter how universal the standard, there are certain pages in this novel which are very near great literature. I refer, for instance, to the character of Jason Compson, Senior, in which the typical cynicism of a decadent aristocracy is merged with—perhaps grows out of—an intensely individual delineation. They

*Reprinted, with permission, from *Southwest Review*, 15, No. 1 (Autumn 1929), iii–iv.

praise Chaucer for taking a stock character like Criseyda and, without losing typical traits, making her a person; for writing that half-allegory, half-comedy, the *Nonne Preestes Tale*, in which a remarkable verisimilitude alternates with the complete fantasy of the beast fable as colors play back and forth with the shifting light on changeable silk. In both of these respects *The Sound and the Fury* will easily bear comparison with the verses of the fat customs officer himself.

From another "universal" standpoint—the traditional definition of tragedy—Faulkner's achievement is also remarkable. Pity and fear are not often more poignantly aroused than they are in the scene where Candace Compson stands cursing her brother for the devil he is. The subject, too, is of an imposing magnitude; for as the story spreads its fragments before the reader there emerges the spectacle of a civilization uprooted and left to die. Scope such as this is not usual in American novels.

Faulkner's handling of the tradition of the Old South, nevertheless, is distinctly related to provincialism. He has realized minutely and understandingly a given milieu and a given tradition—to all intents and purposes, the milieu of Oxford, Mississippi, where the author has lived most of his life, and the tradition of the ante-bellum aristocracy. He has avoided the mere sophistication which sometimes is evident in his earlier novels, and is certainly at the farthest remove from a metropolitan smartness. That he has borrowed the stream-of-consciousness technique from Europe seems to me of minor importance: to say the least, he has modified it to his own use and has refused to be tyrannized by conventions, even the conventions of revolt.

In short, by the only definition that means very much, Mr. Faulkner is a provincial writer. He belongs to the South, if not to the Southwest. Though he is not a folklorist, though he is more concerned with life than with regionalism, his book has shown unguessed possibilities in the treatment of provincial life without loss of universality.

Told by an Idiot

R.N.L.*

In this pitiless story of a family disastrously rotting away in a Mississippi town, Mr. Faulkner reaches a pinnacle of gloom unequalled even by the Russians. A disciple (but not an imitator) of James Joyce, he uses the stream of consciousness method with uncompromising integrity, setting his scenes successively within the mind of an idiot, a neurotic adolescent, and a cruel degenerate. If he could have learned from his master the art of lightening, occasionally, the unmitigated horror of his theme by the use of contrast, if he could have remembered that a great novel needs earth and air and cannot reach its full growth within a brain or even within three brains, he might have achieved an enduring work of art instead of an extraordinary feat of virtuosity.

The book opens into chaos. Gradually the reader discovers that he is looking through the eyes of an idiot, Benjy, to whom time is non-existent and past and present are fused into a single continuous succession of memories and sensory impressions. From the darkness, shadow figures emerge and take shape: a drunken father, a whining invalid mother, four children, Quentin, Caddy, Jason, Benjy, and the negro servants who alone are untainted. All this is far away in the memories of the past. Now the stables are empty, the house is falling to ruin, the father is dead, Caddy has run away leaving her illegitimate child behind; Quentin, who loved her, has expiated by suicide his fancied share in her ruin; and Jason, now master of the house, is revenging himself upon the absent Caddy by torturing her daughter. Only the querulous whine of the mother and the comforting voice of Dilsey, the negro cook, remain unchanged, while Benjy, now a man of thirty-three, shambles cow-like along the fence, slobbering, moaning, bellowing; searching for his lost Caddy who has gone and will not return.

Piece by piece, the author lets fall the bits of actuality that fit together at last into this pattern. By permitting us to see the tragedy of degeneration through the eyes of each brother and exactly as each would have seen it, he achieves an effect as monstrously misshapen as an ape in

*Reprinted, with permission, from *Scribner's*, 86, No. 6 (December 1929), 42, 46.

moonlight and yet hauntingly real. Mr. Faulkner makes no more conces-
sion to his reader than life itself. His book is neither pleasant nor easy
reading but it misses greatness only by inches.

Tragic Frustration

Basil Davenport*

This is an original and impressive book. In manner it is a new departure in the stream-of-consciousness school. It is in four parts, the first a day as it passes through the mind of an idiot, a man of thirty-three with the intelligence of a three-year-old child; at any casual reminder, a place or a name, he is carried back to something similar that happened long before, giving hints of uncomprehended events that stir the imagination like a half-remembered nightmare. The second part, eighteen years earlier, reaches one through the mind of his brother, a boy whose mind has been strained to the breaking-point by what has happened, and who has resolved to drown himself; his thoughts give the tragic occurrences more clearly. The third part, in 1928 again, is in the mind of a third brother, and shows what the life of the family is like, now that the catastrophe is past, and they are living on with the effects as best they can. The fourth part, the next day, is told in the third person. It will be seen that there is a plainer architecture than in most books of this kind, a steady progression from fantasy to fact, and a steady movement toward externality and away from emotion.

That is to say, the tragedy constantly deepens; for the book is a tragedy of the kind that has appeared in literature almost within the memory of man, that of frustration, futility, imprisoned monotony, of

> Tomorrow and tomorrow and tomorrow and tomorrow,
> There's this little street and this little house.

The story is concerned with the decay of a great Southern family, *racé* and fine to the point of fatal weakness. Only the last of the men of the family, Jason, the *I* of Part III (and he, though coarse enough for anything) is embittered by his helpless and pitiless struggle against the wellbred weakness of the others; he systematically robs his niece and cheats his mother, and succeeds only in over-reaching himself. These people's tragedy is not in the seduction, the suicide, or their other great calamities, but in the existence that is finally left them, on a shrunken

*Reprinted, with permission, from the *Saturday Review of Literature*, 6, No. 23 (December 28, 1929), 601–02.

plantation, with half a dozen shiftless negroes, in a round of deadly monotony centered in the idiot son, Benjy.

Benjy is one of those idiots of whom some psychologist has guessed that they would regard pain, if they could feel it, as a welcome surprise. Once during the day he watches his finger stray to the fire and sees it start away, without any idea that he has hurt himself. That is symbolic of the mortal stupor by which, in one way or another, every character is prevented from really suffering from events. Quentin, the suicide, comes nearest it, and is happiest, but when we see it he has already resolved upon drowning himself, and is upon the very verge of sanity; he breaks his watch to put himself outside time, and has almost put himself outside ordinary emotions as well; he is fey. Jason is a normal brute enough, but deadened by a harsh cynicism that speaks of Benjy as the Great American Gelding and jokes about Quentin's death. The others have their drugs: mother religion, father witty, useless philosophy, Uncle Maury drink. If only one of them could feel sharp pain at anything, there would be hope or at least exaltation; but there is only a dull resentment of the life narrowing and hardening around them. The last incident is trivial but terrifying: Benjy is taken for his usual drive, but because they pass the monument on the right instead of the left, he bellows in wordless rage till they go back and take the unalterable way.

In his writing Mr. Faulkner shows a remarkable knack of opening a vista of horror with a single sentence, as when Quentin thinks of Benjy "rolling his head in the cradle till he rolled the back flat—they said the reason Uncle Maury never did any work was that he used to roll his head." His power is shown almost as much by what he does without as what he uses. There is deliciousness in the figure of Gerald, the self-conscious aristocrat, the complete Man Who Does the Right Thing; there is an exquisite tenderness in Quentin's thoughts, at Harvard, of the negroes at home; but for the most part Mr. Faulkner rigorously denies himself humor and tenderness; here they would be in his way. This is a man to watch.

Hardly Worth While

Clifton P. Fadiman*

Probably someone has already remarked that the perfect enjoyment of great literature involves two factors. The reader should make an analysis of the methods employed by the artist to produce a given effect; and at the same time he should experience a synthetic appreciation of that effect in its emotional totality. The analysis must be almost instantaneous, almost unconscious. Otherwise the reader may become enmeshed in a tangle of aesthetic judgments, and experience difficulty in feeling the work of art as a whole.

Here, perhaps, lies the problem of comprehending the present-day revolutionary novelist. Frequently the intelligent reader can grasp the newer literary anarchies only by an effort of analytical attention so strained that it fatigues and dulls his emotional perception. He is so occupied in being a detective that by the time he has to his own satisfaction clarified the artist's intentions and technique he is too worn out to feel anything further. This is why the Joycean method of discontinuity has been entirely successful only when applied to materials of Joycean proportions. For it is obvious that if the theme is sufficiently profound, the characters sufficiently extraordinary, the plot sufficiently powerful, the reader is bound to absorb some of all this despite the strain on his attention. But if, after an interval of puzzle-solving, it dawns upon him that the action and characters are minuscular, he is likely to throw the book away in irritation. The analysis has taken too long for the synthesis to be worth the trouble.

This seems to me to be the case with "The Sound and the Fury," a novel by an extremely talented young writer dealing with the mental and physical disintegration of a Southern family. Mr. Faulkner's work has been magnificently praised by Evelyn Scott and other critics for whose opinions one must have respect. It is in all humility, therefore, that I record the feeling that the theme and the characters are trivial, unworthy of the enormous and complex craftmanship expended on them. I do not see, for example, that Dilsey is more than a faithful old Negress; she is not, for me at least, "stoic as some immemorial carving of heroism," nor

*Reprinted, with permission, from the *Nation*, 130, No. 3367 (January 15, 1930), 74–75.

" They endured "

does she "recover for us the spirit of tragedy which the patter of cynicism has often made seem lost." I admit that the idiocy of the thirty-three-year-old Benjy is admirably grasped by Mr. Faulkner, but one hundred pages of an imbecile's simplified sense perceptions and monosyllabic gibberings, no matter how accurately recorded, are too much of a good thing. Similarly, Quentin and Jason are not sufficiently interesting, not large enough, in a symbolic sense, to make it worth while to follow painfully the ramifications of their minds and memories.

One has the feeling that Mr. Faulkner's experiments in the breaking-up of consciousness, in the abolition of chronology and psychological continuity, are both ingenious and sincere, but they are not absolutely necessary to his story. The fact that his material includes imbecility, incest, paranoia, and sadism does not mean that his tale is therefore complicated or obscure and in need of oblique and bizarre treatment. The relationships between his characters are a trifle unhealthy, one must admit, but must the prose in which they are described therefore be feverish? After one has penetrated the mad, echoing labyrinth of Mr. Faulkner's style one finds a rather banal Poe-esque plot, a set of degenerate whites whose disintegration is irritating rather than appalling, and two or three Negro characters who, if they were reproduced in straight prose, would appear as fairly conventional types. Sound and fury indeed. Signifying (the witticism is cheap, but inevitable) almost nothing.

England

Introduction to *The Sound and the Fury*

Richard Hughes*

There is a story told of a celebrated Russian dancer, who was asked by someone what she meant by a certain dance. She answered with some exasperation, 'If I could say it in so many words, do you think I should take the very great trouble of dancing it?'

It is an important story, because it is the valid explanation of obscurity in art. A method involving apparent obscurity is surely justified when it is the clearest, the simplest, the only method possible of saying in full what the writer has to say.

This is the case with *The Sound and the Fury*. I shall not attempt to give either a summary or an explanation of it: for if I could say in three pages what takes Mr. Faulkner three hundred there would obviously be no need for the book. All I propose to do is to offer a few introductory, and desultory, comments, my chief purpose being to encourage the reader. For the general reader is quite rightly a little shy of apparently difficult writing. Too often it is used, not because of its intrinsic necessity, but to drape the poverty of the writer: too often the reader, after drilling an arduous passage through the strata of the mountain, finds only the mouse, and has little profit but his exercise.

As a result of several such fiascos I myself share this initial prejudice. Yet I have read *The Sound and the Fury* three times now, and that not in the least for exercise, but for pure pleasure.

Mr. Faulkner's method in this book is successful, but it is none the less curious. The first seventy pages are told by a congenital imbecile, a man of thirty-three whose development has not advanced beyond babyhood. Benjy has not sense of time: his only thought-process is associative: the event of the day, then, and what it reminds him of in the past are all one to him: the whole of his thirty-three years are present to him in one uninterrupted and streamless flood. This enables the author to begin by giving a general and confused picture of his whole subject. He offers a certain amount of help to the understanding, it is true, in that he changes from roman to italic type whenever there is a change in time: but

*Reprinted, with permission, from *The Sound and the Fury* (London: Chatto & Windus, 1931), pp. vii–ix.

95

even then I defy an ordinary reader to disentangle the people and events concerned at a first reading. But the beauty of it is this: there is no need to disentangle anything. If one ceases to make the effort, one soon finds that this strange rigmarole holds one's attention on its own merits. Vague forms of people and events, apparently unrelated, loom out of the fog and disappear again. One is seeing the world through the eyes of an idiot: but so clever is Mr. Faulkner that, for the time being at least, one is content to do so.

With the second part the fog begins to clear. The narrator now is one of these vague figures, a brother Quentin, who committed suicide at Harvard in 1910: and he describes with a beautiful sense of ironical tragedy and ironical farce his last day alive. With the third and fourth parts, which return to the present day, the fog rolls away altogether, the formless, sizeless, positionless shapes looming through it condense to living people: the story quickens. It is here this curious method is finally justified: for one finds, in a flash, that one knows all about them, that one has understood more of Benjy's sound and fury than one had realized: the whole story becomes actual to one at a single moment. It is impossible to describe the effect produced, because it is unparalleled; the thoughtful reader must find it for himself.

It will be seen to be a natural corollary that one can read this book a second time at least. The essential quality of a book that can be read again and again, it seems to me, is that it shall appear different at every reading—that it shall, in short, be a new book. (Poetry has this quality, particularly.) When one comes to read Benjy's tale a second time, knowing the story, knowing the family; knowing that the name Quentin covers two people, uncle and niece; knowing Benjy's passionate animal devotion to his sister Caddy, which makes him haunt the golf-course in the hope of hearing the word which is her name, and haunt the gate from which he can see the children coming home from school, in the hope she will be among them again—it is then one begins to realize with what consummate contrapuntal skill these drivellings have been composed, with what exquisite care their pattern fits together.

[A Study in Madness]

Derek Patmore*

Mr. Faulkner's next novel, *The Sound and the Fury*, is a *tour-de-force*. It is a study of madness. The first part of the book, a description of life seen through the eyes of the idiot son of a decaying Southern family, is an amazing piece of creative writing—one's only criticism being that the author gives one no clue at the beginning of the novel that this is what he is attempting to describe. The story goes on to tell of the gradual disintegration of a frayed genteel family dominated by its ever-threatening heritage of imbecility. Already in the family there is the feeble-minded uncle, Maury, and the dumb idiot son of thirty-three, Benjy. Slowly, with the deliberateness of Greek tragedy, the dark menace of insanity engulfs the lives of all the characters in destruction. This is not a pleasant book. But it has tremendous power. It resembles Dostoevsky, but the characters are distinctly American in their brutality and senseless *naïveté*. It is difficult to read in certain passages—the writing is frequently over impressionistic, and parts are written in the 'stream-of-consciousness' manner,' but the book compels attention. It is an original and vital experiment in writing.

*Reprinted, with permission, from *Nineteenth Century and After*, 109 (January 1931), 114.

[Pathological Delinquency]

Anonymous*

Mr. Richard Hughes, in his introduction to Mr. William Faulkner's novel THE SOUND AND THE FURY (Chatto and Windus, 7s. 6d. net), does his best to reconcile the reader to the obvious fact that it is a very difficult book to understand, at all events at the first reading. He avers that he has read the book through three times for pure pleasure; and it is clear that he, another creative writer, has been interested and exhilarated by the skill shown by Mr. Faulkner in constructing a jigsaw puzzle in four parts concerning the tragic and troubled happenings in a certain afflicted family. It is not to be denied that the skill is there, but it is hard to agree that the method is successful in any but a limited sense.

The first seventy pages are supposed to represent the mental workings of a congenital imbecile, aged thirty-three in body and only three in mind, who is being led about beside a golf links by a negro boy, and who bellows whenever he hears the word "Caddy," because his sister Candace was so called and he had loved her with a queer animal attachment. Benjy, the idiot, is always hoping to see Caddy come back again, with the schoolgirls, to the gate of the house; but she never comes, for she married eighteen years ago and was unfaithful to her husband. Her husband cast her off and she bore an illegitimate child called Quentin, which was the name, also, of Benjy's brother who drowned himself at Harvard because of Caddy's immorality with Dalton Ames, whom he meant to shoot but hadn't the pluck. The second part of the novel, in fact, represents the feverish workings and memories of the boy Quentin's mind eighteen years earlier on the last day of his life, which was full of ironic incongruities on the surface and, underneath, an inferno of recollections, mainly recollections of his intense love for Caddy, of his efforts to keep her from the courses to which her tainted blood compelled her, and of his fruitless attempt to get her away from contact with the world by accusing himself of her coming child's paternity. This chapter, which is both brilliant and extremely painful, is particularly remarkable for its interweaving of a portrait of Jason Compson, the too philosophical father of this trio of doomed children. The two latter parts relate to the day before and the day after

*Reprinted, with permission, from the *Times Literary Supplement*, May 14, 1931, p. 386.

the events of the opening chapter. They describe, and compose into a more or less visible picture, the interior of the household where the younger son, Jason, a miserly, jealous and embittered man, lives with his invalid, selfish and intolerable mother, the idiot Benjy, and Quentin the girl, Caddy's child, who has inherited her mother's sexual characteristics. This is another inferno, the negro inhabitants of which seem less repulsive than the white.

For those who feel an attraction in the portrayal of pathological delinquency or find some really tragic effect in the negation, through a hereditary taint, of all the fine and kind elements in young minds no doubt the horrors of this picture will seem poetical: to others, however, they will appear to be of a kind to which no skill can add compensating merit.

[A Disturbing Beauty]

G. W. Stonier*

The Sound and the Fury is a difficult book. I have conscientiously read every word of it, partly because I know Mr. Faulkner to be a good writer, and partly because his obscurity seems to be essential to the genuine original beauty of his work. This novel is divided into four parts, each describing a day in 1910 and 1928. The first day (1928) is seen through the eyes of a deaf-mute imbecile of thirty-three whose perceptions are those of a child unrelated by reason or sense of time. The second day (1910) describes the last actions and thoughts of a brother who committed suicide as an undergraduate at Harvard. The third and fourth days are back in 1928 and give a clear picture of this unfortunate family, a girl who is driven on to the streets by bullying, a self-pitying mother, and the negroes in the kitchen. Thus the book gradually clears as you read more of it; the thought-streams of the earlier pages are replaced by pin-sharp pictures of all these characters who previously have loomed in the fog; and it ends after a hundred pages of magnificent straightforward writing, leaving one with the sense that after all the weather has cleared. I cannot do justice in a short space to the beauty which Mr. Faulkner has been able to find in these lives of imbeciles, criminals, and unfortunates. The beauty is there, original, and rather disturbing. It is a book which should be read more than once; and yet I hesitate to read it again.

*Reprinted, with permission, from the *Fortnightly Review*, NS 129, No. 774 (June 1931), 842–43.

[Tainted Blood]

Anonymous*

*The Sound and the Fury, by William Faulkner. (Chatto & Windus.
7s. 6d.)* This is a truly horrible book, conveying a frightening sense of
disintegration. It is, moreover, an example of the literature of experiment, and in spite of Mr. Richard Hughes's eulogistic introduction, I do
not feel that it is uniformly successful. The obscenities are such that it will
be unreadable for most people. The first seventy pages consist of the reactions and ravings of a congenital imbecile whose body is thirty-three but
whose mind has not advanced beyond babyhood. He frequents a golf
course, and slobbers and bellows when he hears the name 'Caddy', for it
reminds him of his sister Candace (called Caddy), for whom he cherishes
an animal attachment. The staccato style wearies one's sensibilities with
sickening blows. The rest concerns Candace's unfaithfulness to her husband, an illegitimate child, and her brother Quentin's suicide on her account at Harvard. The child grows up into a nymphomaniac. The invalid
mother is throughout selfish, neurasthenic, and impossible. It will be seen
that the novel deals with a family whose blood is tainted, and embodies
the worst traits in human nature. Skillful in parts it undoubtedly is, but it
belongs more properly to the realm of pathology than to art.

*Reprinted, with permission, from *Life and Letters*, 7 (July 1931), 67–68.

[Nothing Very Pleasant]

Orgill Mackenzie*

The sound and the fury does signify—but nothing very pleasant. There is much cleverness but no comfort of beauty in it. It is the story of a family, told from four points of view, on four days: it is constructed in fragments, scientifically broken, which dovetail when brought together, and the result is, in spite of the incredible first part, that the characters stand out as solid people, unpleasantly real, real to keep one awake at night.

There is, annoyingly, a preface by Mr. Richard Hughes. If the book is all he says of it, a preface is not only superfluous but mischievous. If, as seems obvious, it is the author's will to let the idiot's disjointed story be the first lightning flashes on the characters which, later, have steadier light on them, then it is not easy to understand why, except for advertisement purposes, he permitted any preface.

"Benjy", Mr. Hughes tells us, "has no sense of time . . . the whole of his thirty-three years are present to him in one uninterrupted and streamless flood. . . . Vague forms of people and events, apparently unrelated, loom out of the fog and disappear again. One is seeing the world through the eyes of an idiot."

The trouble is the forms are not vague enough. Even from an ideal idiot, to whom Mr. Faulkner is ready to supply effective memories we cannot accept metaphor and simile—"the bright shapes went smooth and steady on both sides, the shadows of them flowing across Queenie's back. They went on like the bright tops of wheels." People talk in character through his dumb mouth and penless fingers. He quotes his father, "He is invaluable to my own sense of racial superiority", and "Et ego in Arcadia I have forgotten the Latin for hay", and his sister, "Get up Mau——I mean Benjy." The significance of the remark is that his name had been changed from Maury to Benjy. Not the most phenomenal of memories could hold a blur of words that could have had no possible meaning at the time of their utterance. And some of the memories date back to his fifth year.

The second part is told by a brother on the day before he commits suicide. His mind runs on in this sort of way in a two-page passage

*Reprinted, with permission, from the *Adelphi*, 2, No. 5 (August 1931), 365–66.

without a full stop or a capital letter—"and i yes sir dont you and he every man is the arbiter of his own virtues". It is true that his thoughts have no capital letters, but then they have no letters at all, and, since some must be used, why on earth not use all?

The third part, told by another brother, is brutally real. The last part, told impersonally, is about people we know.

Nobody will read this book without strong feelings of some sort.

France

Preface to *The Sound and the Fury*

Maurice Edgar Coindreau*

"This novel began as a short story," William Faulkner once said to me. "It struck me that it would be interesting to imagine the thoughts of a group of children who were sent away from the house the day of their grandmother's funeral, their curiosity about the activity in the house, their efforts to find out what was going on, and the notions that would come into their minds. Then, to complicate the picture, I had the idea of someone who would be more than just a child, who in trying to find the answer, would not even have a normal brain to use—that is, an idiot. So Benjy was born. After that, the same thing happened to me that happens to many writers—I fell in love with one of my characters, Caddy. I loved her so much I couldn't decide to give her life just for the duration of a short story. She deserved more than that. So my novel was created, almost in spite of myself. It had no title until one day the familiar words 'the sound and the fury' came to me out of my unconscious. I adopted them immediately, without considering then that the rest of the Shakespearean quotation was as well suited, and maybe better, to my dark story of madness and hatred."[1]

Indeed we find in *Macbeth*, act 5, scene 5, this definition of life: "It is a tale told by an idiot, full of sound and fury, signifying nothing." The first part of William Faulkner's novel is likewise told by an idiot; the entire book vibrates with sound and fury and will seem devoid of significance to those who hold that a man of letters, each time he takes up his pen, must deliver a message or serve some noble cause. Mr. Faulkner is content to open the Gates of Hell. He does not force anyone to accompany him, but those who trust him have no cause for regrets.

The drama takes place in Mississippi among the members of an old Southern family, once proud and prosperous but today sunk in wretchedness and humiliation. In this setting three generations tear one another apart: Jason Compson and his wife Caroline, née Bascomb; their daughter Candace (or Caddy) and their three sons, Quentin, Jason, and

*Reprinted, with permission, from *Le Bruit et la fureur* (Paris: Gallimard, 1938). Copyright Editions Gallimard 1938. Trans. George McMillan Reeves, from *Mississippi Quarterly* 19:3 (Summer 1966); copyright © Mississippi State University and reprinted by permission of the editors.

Maury (who is later called Benjamin, or Benjy, so that he will not sully the name of his uncle Maury Bascomb); and finally Quentin the daughter of Caddy. Thus there are two Jasons (father and son) and two Quentins (uncle and niece). Attached to all these are three generations of Negroes: Dilsey and her husband, Roskus; their children, Versh, T. P., and Frony; and then Luster, son of Frony.

Caddy, willful and sensual, has taken a lover, Dalton Ames. When she discovers that she is pregnant, she accompanies her mother to French Lick, a thermal springs resort in Indiana, to find a husband. On April 25, 1910, she marries Sidney Herbert Head.

Quentin, who is morbidly linked to his sister by an incestuous (although Platonic) fondness, kills himself out of jealousy on June 2, 1910, at Harvard, where he has come to study. A year later Caddy, cast off by her husband, abandons to her parents the baby girl to whom she has recently given birth and whom, in memory of her brother, she has named Quentin.

Then comes the death of the father, who founders in alcoholism, leaving his destitute wife with their two surviving sons, Jason and Benjamin, and the baby that Caddy no longer has permission even to see. Jason is a monster of deceit and sadism; Benjamin is an idiot. One day, having escaped from the yard, he attempted to violate a young girl. To prevent further such incidents, he was castrated. Completely harmless ever since, he wanders like an animal and expresses himself only with cries.

Quentin, Caddy's daughter, has grown up. When *The Sound and the Fury* begins, she is seventeen and, like her mother before her, already gives herself to the young men of the town. Her uncle Jason besets her with his hatred, and that is really the whole subject of the book, the hatred of Jason during the three days of April 6, 7, and 8, 1928.

Readers familiar with Faulkner's usual technique will suspect already that the author is going to shuffle the chronology to some extent. And in fact the first part takes place on April 7, 1928; the second, eighteen years earlier, on June 2, 1910; the third, on April 6, 1928; and the fourth, two days later, on April 8. As for the events, present or past, they reach us through interior monologues, the last part alone being a direct narrative in which, accordingly, there are physical descriptions of the characters (Caroline Compson, Jason, Dilsey, Benjy) whose natures have been revealed to us little by little in the course of the monologues of the three preceding parts.

To make this complex work easily accessible to the reader, I would now like to analyze in some detail Mr. Faulkner's methods of writing and to show, by bringing them into relief, how the principal difficulties can be approached and resolved. Reading William Faulkner is in itself a little science.

The structure of *The Sound and the Fury* is essentially musical. Like a composer, Faulkner uses the system of themes. There is not, as in a fugue, a simple theme which develops and undergoes transformations; there are multiple themes which start out, vanish, and reappear to disappear again until the moment they sound forth in all their richness. One thinks of impressionist compositions, mysterious and chaotic on first hearing, but firmly structured beneath their confused appearance. *The Sound and the Fury* is a novel of atmosphere which suggests more than it says, a sort of *Night on Bald Mountain* penetrated by a diabolical wind in which damned souls are whirling, a cruel poem of hatred with each movement precisely characterized.

First movement—April 7, 1928. *Moderato*: "Life is a tale told by an idiot." It is through the atrophied brain of Benjy that Faulkner takes us into his hell. On his birthday Benjy is in the yard accompanied by his guardian, Luster, a young Negro of seventeen who has lost a quarter and is searching for it so that he can attend a tent show to be put on by a traveling company that evening. Benjy is thirty-three. For him nothing exists except animal sensations. Of these he has made himself a world in which he moves about without ever feeling restricted by notions of space and time. It is not by logic that he goes from one idea to another but by the random progression of his sensations which, unless they are direct (burning his hand, for example), are joined together by the process of association that may be set off by a gesture, a sound, or an odor. Thus the word *caddy*, spoken by some golf players, reawakens his memories of his lost sister and causes him to howl in agony. In the same way, when he snags his clothing on a fence nail, he suddenly plunges into the past to the day when, as a mere child, he got caught in a similar manner as he and Caddy were carrying a love note from Maury, their uncle, to Mrs. Patterson. By means of such retrospective soundings, two series of events materialize little by little: the grandmother's funeral, when Caddy was seven; and Caddy's wedding (April 25, 1910). Thus, in the wake of Benjy, Mr. Faulkner conducts three lines of action simultaneously.

Moreover, this tinseling of ideas free of all subservience to logic provides William Faulkner with the most suitable means of introducing the themes which will run through his symphony from one end to the other (visits to the cemetery, castration, Caddy's misconduct, the father's drunkenness, Jason's brutality, Quentin's rendezvous and her escape out the window, etc.). Embryonic in this first part, and rightly so since they are conceived in the brain of an idiot, these themes are stated precisely later on, although some of them do not reach full clarity until the last pages. At times they are presaged by a few enigmatic, one could say furtive, words. One must remember these words and wait until they reappear in sentences that give them an exact meaning. William Faulkner offers us many riddles, but he never forgets to provide the solution to them. At most, readers in a hurry will find that he makes them wait too long, and bad sportsmen will grow angry.

Second movement—June 2, 1910. This is the painful *Adagio*, the interior monologue of Quentin Compson on the day of his suicide at Harvard. Here it is no longer idiocy that disturbs the harmonious balance of thought, but the half-madness of a brain obsessed by ideas of incest and of suicide, by unbearable jealousy, by hatred for schoolmates such as Gerald Bland, a snob and a rake whom Quentin envies because love is for him a source of joy rather than an instrument of torture. The themes appear, likewise formless at first, for they are hideous thoughts held in terror by the brain that conceives them and stifles them at birth (the marriage of his too-beloved sister, the flatirons that Quentin will fasten to his feet to assure his death, the inexorable march of time which he attempts to avert by smashing his watch, and the attraction of the water which seems to lie in wait for him everywhere during the course of his last walk).

Third movement—April 6, 1928. *Allegro:* The interior monologue of Jason who, having discovered that his niece, Quentin, has arranged a rendezvous with one of the actors of the traveling company, attempts to confine her and thus drives her to the nocturnal flight that Luster and Benjy witnessed in the first part. Through the hateful mind of Jason a whole segment of the past becomes clear: the father's death, bankruptcy of the family, Caddy's misconduct and the harshness of her own people toward her, Benjy's attempt at rape which brought about his castration—all this mingled with the events of the day in the hardware store where Jason earns his living against his will.

Fourth movement—April 8, 1928. This time the narrative has become direct and objective. It begins with an *Allegro furioso.* Quentin, when she fled, carried off three thousand dollars that her uncle had appropriated for himself—hence the distraught pursuit which is abruptly interrupted by Jason's migraine and by the blow that he receives on the head. Contrastingly, next comes the *Andante religioso*, the service in the Negro church on Easter Sunday, followed, almost without transition, by an *Allegro barbaro* which ends in the calm of a *Lento:* "The broken flower drooped over Ben's fist and his eyes were empty and blue and serene again as cornice and façade flowed smoothly once more from left to right; post and tree, window and doorway, and signboard, each in its ordered place."

Such is the structural pattern of this demoniac symphony which lacks only the gaiety of a scherzo, and which achieves unity through the help of two elements of equal effectiveness—the cries of Benjy and the noble figure of Dilsey. The cries, which range from wailing to bellowing, play, in Mr. Faulkner's orchestra, the role of percussion instruments with an obsessive rhythm. This is the sonant climate of the novel. The backdrop is the Negroes, resigned witnesses of the extravagances of the whites. Among them Dilsey, black sister of Flaubert's Félicité, is the "simple heart" in all its beauty. Her animal devotion to masters whom she does not judge and her primitive good sense make it possible for her still to hold in her old hand the tiller of this drifting ship which is the Compson house. Negroes abound in contemporary novels of the South, but none attain the moving grandeur of this woman who, not in the least idealized, is, I believe, Mr. Faulkner's most successful creation.

The structure of *The Sound and the Fury* would in itself be enough to discourage the lazy reader.[2] Yet this is not the greatest of the difficulties. William Faulkner knows all the secrets of verbal alchemy. Did not Arnold Bennett say that he wrote like an angel? He knows also the power of the unexpressed. Consequently his style is full of snares. I will mention simply his very curious use of pronouns for which he only rarely gives antecedents (it is always *he* or *she*, without further specification), his use of symbols, and the boldness of his ellipses.

It is particularly in connection with Benjy that symbolism appears. For Benjy, who is more like an animal than a man, nothing exists other than sensation. Endowed with prescience, like dogs that howl in the presence of death or birds that fly before an approaching storm, he "feels" the events that take place around him and that he does not otherwise understand. Incapable of conceiving abstractions, he transcribes them into sensual images. Caddy, still a virgin, "smells like trees." After she has given herself to Dalton Ames, she no longer smells like trees, and Benjy cries, for anything that changes his habits frightens him (hence his bellowing when, on the way to the cemetery, Luster leads him to the left of the monument whereas T. P. habitually has taken him to the right). And on Caddy's wedding day he pushes her to the bathroom and forces her to enter, for that is where the lustral water flows from which she would emerge in her aboreal freshness. And Caddy, who understands, hides her face in her arms.

When Benjy is happy he speaks to us of luminous circles which whirl more or less rapidly according to the intensity of his happiness. This is what happens when he sees fire, when he chases little girls, and, at Caddy's wedding, when he has drunk too much champagne. Mr. Faulkner is careful not to clarify these symbols, for he intends them to be somewhat indistinct like the impressions that they translate, and he does not want his readers to understand too easily a character who does not understand himself.

As for the ellipses, they are either sentence fragments which reproduce photographically, if I may put it thus, the flashing play of thought, or ideas in juxtaposition with no indication of the transitions which normally would link them together. The reader will find an excellent example of the first type on page 174. Quentin, a victim of insomnia, has gone in the darkness to the bathroom to drink a glass of water. Here is how this passage should be read: "*my* hands can see, *my* fingers *are* cooled by the invisible swan-throat where Moses' rod is not needed *to make the water spring forth. Where is* the glass? *I will have to* feel for it. Careful not *to knock it off the shelf. . . .*"[3]

Now let us take an example of the second type. Annoyed by swarming sparrows, Jason says that they ought to be poisoned: "If they'd just put a little poison out there in the square, they'd get rid of them in a day, because if a merchant cant keep his stock from running around the square, he'd better try to deal in something besides chickens, something that dont eat. . . ."[4] Here Jason, after expressing an idea, answers an objection that an interlocutor might have thought of but that remains understood (in poisoning the sparrows, they would run the risk of poisoning also the animals that were brought to the square on market days).

Numerous difficulties of this type present themselves and demand the sustained attention of the reader, who must, moreover, become accustomed to the inversion of dates and the confusion of similar names (the two Jasons and the two Quentins). I do not hesitate, nevertheless, to affirm that it is not at all necessary to understand every phrase completely in order to savor *The Sound and the Fury*. I would compare this novel to landscapes that improve when seen through an enveloping haze. Its tragic beauty is increased, and its mysteriousness casts a veil over horrors that would lose some of their power if seen in too much direct light. The mind that is contemplative enough to grasp, on a first reading, the meaning of all the enigmas that Faulkner offers us would undoubtedly not experience the impression of conjuration which gives this unique work its greatest charm and its genuine originality.

*   *   *   *   *   *

Written when the author was beset with personal problems,[5] *The Sound and the Fury* was published in 1929. This date marks the beginning of William Faulkner's reputation in America. I mean his reputation in the intellectual milieux, for it was not until the appearance of *Sanctuary* (1931) that the general public stirred from its torpor. *The Sound and the Fury* cannot fail to arouse objections. Some minds like easy pleasures. But I believe that this novel is unanimously regarded as Mr. Faulkner's masterwork—first, because of its intrinsic value, but also because of its radiant energy. It seems that sparks fly from it unceasingly to light new fires. In *These Thirteen* (1931) one of the stories, "That Evening Sun,"[6] is composed of an episode of the childhood of Caddy and her brothers. *Absalom, Absalom!* is partly narrated by Jason Compson and by his son Quentin, who confides in Shreve, his friend and roommate at Harvard. *The Sound and the Fury*, then, seems to be the matrix of that "human comedy" on which Mr. Faulkner is laboring diligently. To accommodate this work he has already created towns which he has mapped on the last page of *Absalom, Absalom!*

Although perfectly conscious of the inevitable imperfection in the translation of such a perilous work, I believe I can assure the French public that this is truly a translation which I offer them and not a more or less free adaptation. I have scrupulously respected the design of the original and have not, to my knowledge, added in any way to the obscurity. On the contrary, the precision of the French language has often led me, in spite of myself, to clarify the text. Having had the pleasure of listening to Mr. Faulkner give me his own comments on the most obscure points of his novel, I have not shied away from any obstacle. I have, however, resolutely set aside all efforts to carry over into my text the flavor of Negro dialect. A solution to that problem is, in my opinion, as clearly impossible as it would be for a translator working in English to reproduce the dialect of Marseille. This sacrifice granted, I hope that I have retained, in the present version, everything that contributes to the perplexing enchantment and the power of a book which has already become a landmark in the history of American literature.

Notes

1. This quotation from Faulkner was never written down in English; the version given here is an attempt to approximate his idiom.

2. In his latest novel, *Eyeless in Gaza* (published in French under the title *La Paix des profondeurs*), Aldous Huxley goes even farther than Faulkner in the overthrow of chronology; and he does not even offer his reader the aid of associative processes. M.E.C.

3. Faulkner's exact words: "*. . . hands can see cooling fingers invisible swan-throat where less than Moses rod the glass touch tentative not to . . . .*" *The Sound and the Fury* (New York: Jonathan Cape and Harrison Smith, 1929), p. 216.

4. *The Sound and the Fury*, pp. 309–10.

5. Profound emotional shocks are a powerful factor in William Faulkner's inspiration. It was after the death of one of his children that he wrote *Light in August*, and *Absalom, Absalom!* was composed during the weeks following the death of one of his brothers in an airplane accident. M.E.C.

6. A French translation of this short story was published under my name in *Europe* (January 15, 1935). M.E.C.

III UNDERSTANDING THE COMPSONS

On William Faulkner's *The Sound and the Fury*

Evelyn Scott*

I want to write something about *The Sound and the Fury* before the fanfare in print can greet even the ears of the author. There will be many, I am sure, who, without this assistance, will make the discovery of the book as an important contribution to the permanent literature of fiction. I shall be pleased, however, if some others, lacking the opportunity for investigating individually the hundred claims to greatness which America makes every year in the name of art, may be led, through these comments, to a perusal of this unique and distinguished novel. The publishers, who are so much to be congratulated for presenting a little known writer with the dignity of recognition which his talent deserves, call this book "overwhelmingly powerful and even monstrous." Powerful it is; and it may even be described as "monstrous" in all its implications of tragedy; but such tragedy has a noble essence.

The question has been put by a contemporary critic, a genuine philosopher reviewing the arts, as to whether there exists for this age of disillusion with religion, dedication to the objective program of scientific inventiveness and general rejection of the teleology which placed man emotionally at the center of his universe, the spirit of which great tragedy is the expression. *The Sound and the Fury* seems to me to offer a reply. Indeed I feel that however sophistical the argument of theology, man remains, in his heart, in that important position. What he seeks now is a fresh justification for the presumption of his emotions; and his present tragedy is in a realization of the futility, up to date, of his search for another, intellectually appropriate embodiment of the god that lives on, however contradicted by "reason."

William Faulkner, the author of this tragedy, which has all the spacious proportions of Greek art, may not consider his book in the least expressive of the general dilemma to which I refer, but that quality in his writings which the emotionally timid will call "morbid," seems to be reflected from the impression, made on a sensitive and normally egoistic nature, of what is in the air. Too proud to solve the human problem

*Reprinted, with permission, from *On William Faulkner's "The Sound and the Fury"* (New York: Jonathan Cape and Harrison Smith, Inc., 1929). Copyright 1929 by Evelyn Scott.

evasively through any of the sleight-of-hand of puerile surface optimism, he embraces, to represent life, figures that do indeed symbolize a kind of despair; but not the despair that depresses or frustrates. His pessimism as to fact, and his acceptance of all the morally inimical possibilities of human nature, is unwavering. The result is, nonetheless, the reassertion of humanity in defeat that is, in the subjective sense, a triumph. This is no Pyrrhic victory made in debate with those powers of intelligence that may be used to destroy. It is the conquest of nature by art. Or rather, the refutation, by means of a work of art, of the belittling of the materialists; and the work itself is in that category of facts which popular scientific thinking has made an ultimate. Here is beauty sprung from the perfect *realization* of what a more limiting morality would describe as ugliness. Here is a humanity stripped of most of what was claimed for it by the Victorians, and the spectacle is moving as no sugar-coated drama ever could be. The result for the reader, if he is like myself, is an exaltation of faith in mankind. It is faith without, as yet, an argument; but it is the same faith which has always lived in the most ultimate expression of human spirit.

The Sound and the Fury is the story of the fall of a house, the collapse of a provincial aristocracy in a final debacle of insanity, recklessness, psychological perversion. The method of presentation is, as far as I know, unique. Book I is a statement of the tragedy as seen through the eyes of a thirty-three-year-old idiot son of the house, Benjy. Benjy is beautiful, as beautiful as one of the helpless angels, and the more so for the slightly repellent earthiness that is his. He is a better idiot than Dostoyevsky's because his simplicity is more convincingly united with the basic animal simplicity of creatures untried by the standards of a conscious and calculating humanity. It is as if, indeed, Blake's Tiger had been framed before us by the same Hand that made the Lamb, and, in opposition to Blake's conception, endowed with the same soul. Innocence is terrible as well as pathetic—and Benjy is terrible, sometimes terrifying. He is a Christ symbol, yet not, even in the way of the old orthodoxies, Christly. A Jesus asks for conviction of sin and a confession before redemption. He acknowledges this as in his own history, tempting by the Devil the prelude to his renunciation. In every subtle sense, sin is the desire to sin, the awareness of sin, an assertion in innuendo that, by the very statement of virtue, sin *is*. Benjy is no saint with a wounded ego his own gesture can console. His is not anything—nothing with a name. He is alive. He can suffer. The simplicity of his suffering, the absence, for him, of any compensating sense of drama, leave him as naked of self-flattery as was the first man. Benjy is like Adam, with all he remembers in the garden and one foot in hell on earth. This was where knowledge began, and for Benjy time is too early for any spurious profiting by knowledge. It is a little as if the story of Hans Anderson's Little Mermaid had been taken away from the nursery and sentiment and made rather diabolically to grow up. Here is the Little Mermaid on the way to find her soul in an uncouth and incontinent body—but there is no happy ending. Benjy, born male and made neuter, doesn't want a soul. It is being thrust upon him, but only like a horrid bauble which he does not recognize. He holds in his hands—in his heart, exposed to the reader—something frightening, un-named—*pain!* Benjy lives deeply in the senses. For the remainder of what he sees as life, he lives as crudely as in allegory, vicariously, through un-critical perception of his adored sister (she smells to him like "leaves") and, in such emotional absolutism, traces for us her broken marriage, her departure forever from an unlovely home, her return by proxy in the per-son of her illegitimate daughter, Quentin, who, for Benjy, takes the mother's place.

Book II of the novel deals with another—the original Quentin, for whom the baby girl of later events is named. This section, inferior, I think, to the Benjy motive, though fine in part, describes in the terms of free association with which Mr. Joyce is recreating vocabularies, the final day in this life of Quentin, First, who is contemplating suicide. Quentin is a student at Harvard at the time, the last wealth of the family—some property that has been nominally Benjy's—having been sold to provide him with an education. Quentin is oversensitive, introvert, pathologically devoted to his sister, and his determination to commit suicide is his protest against her disgrace.

In Book III we see the world in terms of the petty, sadistic lunacy of Jason; Jason, the last son of the family, the stay-at-home, the failure, clerking in a country store, for whom no Harvard education was pro-vided. William Faulkner has that general perspective in viewing par-ticular events which lifts the specific incident to the dignity of catholic significance, while all the vividness of an unduplicable personal drama is retained. He senses the characteristic compulsions to action that make a fate. Jason is a devil. Yet, since the author has compelled you to the vision of the gods, he is a devil whom you compassionate. Younger than the other brothers, Jason, in his twenties, is tyrannically compensating for the sufferings of jealousy by persecution of his young niece, Caddie's daughter, Quentin, by petty thievery, by deception practiced against his weak mother, by meanest torment of that marvellously accurately con-ceived young negro, Luster, keeper, against all his idle, pleasure-loving inclinations, of the witless Benjy. Jason is going mad. He knows it—not as an intellectual conclusion, for he holds up all the emotional barriers against reflection and self-investigation. Jason knows madness as Benjy knows the world and the smell of leaves and the leap of the fire in the grate and the sounds of himself, his own howls, when Luster teases him. Madness for Jason is a blank, immediate state of soul, which he feels en-croaching on his meager, objectively considered universe. He is in an agony of inexplicable anticipation of disaster for which his cruelties afford him no relief.

The last Book is told in the third person by the author. In its pages we are to see this small world of failure in its relative aspect. Especial privilege, we are allowed to meet face to face, Dilsey, the old colored woman, who provides the beauty of coherence against the background of struggling choice. Dilsey isn't searching for a soul. She *is* the soul. She is the conscious human accepting the limitations of herself, the iron boundaries of circumstance, and still, to the best of her ability, achieving a holy compromise for aspiration.

People seem very frequently to ask of a book a "moral." There is no moral statement in *The Sound and the Fury*, but moral conclusions can be drawn from it as surely as from "life," because, as fine art, it is life organized to make revelation fuller. Jason is, in fair measure, the young South, scornful of outworn tradition, scornful indeed of all tradition, as of the ideal which has betrayed previous generations to the hope of perfection. He, Jason, would tell you, as so many others do today, that he sees things "as they are." There is no "foolishness" about him, no "bunk." A spade is a spade, as unsuggestive as things must be in an age which prizes radios and motor cars not as means, but as ends for existence. You have "got to show him." Where there is no proof in dollars and cents, or what they can buy, there is nothing. Misconceiving even biology, Jason would probably regard individualism of a crass order as according to nature. Jason is a martyr. He is a completely rational being. There is something exquisitely stupid in this degree of commonsense which cannot grasp the fact that ratiocination cannot proceed without presumptions made on the emotional acceptance of a state antedating reason. Jason argues, as it were, from nothing to nothing. In this *reductio ad absurdum* he annihilates himself, even his vanity. And he runs amok, with his conclusion that one gesture is as good as another, that there is only drivelling self deception to juxtapose to his tin-pot Nietzscheanism—actually the most romantic attitude of all.

But there is Dilsey, without so much as a theory to controvert theory, stoic as some immemorial carving of heroism, going on, doing the best she can, guided only by instinct and affection and the self-respect she will not relinquish—the ideal of herself to which she conforms irrationally, which makes of her life something whole, while her "white folks" accept their fragmentary state, disintegrate. And she recovers for us the spirit of tragedy which the patter of cynicism has often made seem lost.

[Yoknapatawpha from a Historical Perspective]

Irving Howe*

The Sound and the Fury records the fall of a house and the death of a society. Here, as nowhere else in his work, Faulkner regards Yoknapatawpha from a historical perspective, yet there is little history either told or shown—not nearly so much as in *Absalom, Absalom!* or the rhapsodic interludes of *Requiem for a Nun*. Perhaps the most remarkable fact about this remarkable novel is that its rich sense of history comes from a story rigidly confined to a single family, a story almost claustrophobic in its concentration on a narrow sequence of events. Faulkner has said that *The Sound and the Fury* had its origins in "the impression of a little girl playing in a branch and getting her panties wet." That impression is to be central in the book, as a moment completely felt and seen, and from it will follow a series of actions ranging in significance far beyond the little girl with the wet panties, her family, or her homeland. In *The Sound and the Fury* Faulkner persuades us, as never before, to accept Yoknapatawpha as an emblem of a larger world beyond, and its moral death as an acting-out of the disorder of our time. But he remains in and of this local place, his feeling toward Yoknapatawpha a fluid mixture of affection and disgust. The material is seen from a perspective which in times of social decline is most useful to a writer: that simultaneous involvement with and estrangement from a native scene which allows for both a tragic and an ironic response.

Each character is unique—an entity. All of them together represent the sum of the loss which Faulkner measures in the history of Yoknapatawpha. In their squalor and pathos, the Compsons are the Southern patriciate *in extremis*. Stripped of whatever is contingent in their experience, they come to suggest a dominant quality of modern life. They are of the South, signifying its decay and its shame, but the decay is universal and, therefore, the shame should also be universal. To confine the meaning of their story to a segment of Southern life is sheer provincialism, as fatuous as an attempt to isolate a plague by drawing a line on

---

*Reprinted, with permission, from *William Faulkner: A Critical Study*, 3d ed., rev. (Chicago: The University of Chicago Press, 1951, 1975), pp. 46–52, 174.

the map. This book is a lament for the passing of a world, not merely the world of Yoknapatawpha and not merely the South.

The sense of diminution and loss is intensified by Faulkner's setting the action on Good Friday, Saturday, and Easter Sunday, so that the values of the Christian order provide a muted backdrop to the conduct of the Compsons. These Christian references are handled with delicacy and modesty, a triumph of tact Faulkner does not always repeat in his later work. They rarely break past the surface of the story to call attention to themselves and tempt us into the error of allegory; they never deflect us from the behavior and emotions of the represented figures at the center of the book.[1] Toward the end there is a scene in a Negro church, in which all that has happened is brought to a coda by the marvelous sermon of a Negro preacher—"I got de ricklickshun en 'de blood of de Lamb!' "—and the simple kindliness of some Negro figures. Here the foreground action and the Christian references seem to draw closer, not in order to score any religious point or provide critics with occasions for piety, but to allow the language of the Christian drama, as it has been preserved by the Negroes, to enforce a tacit judgement on the ending of the Compsons.

For the Compsons the family is less a tie of blood than a chafe of guilt. Love can exist only as memory of childhood, and memory only as a gall. Morality becomes a conscience-spur to the wish for death. Money is the universal solvent, replacing affection, integrity, and every other sentiment beyond calculation. All this, of course, is notoriously morbid and excessive, as literature so often is; but morbidity and excess apart, the world of the Compsons should not be too difficult for us to acknowledge.

Among the Compsons the past lives in the broken images that crowd the mind of Benjy, the idiot son, to whom the past is indistinguishable from the present. The past is sensation: the excitement of the Compson children when their "Damuddy" dies, the pleasure of sister Caddy crawling into bed with him while Dilsey scolds that a boy of thirteen is too big to "sleep with folks," the exhilaration of drinking "sassparilluh" at his sister's wedding. These are memories Benjy cannot wholly retrieve, but the limited number that he does retrieve is pure. He is affection barely qualified, and like other great idiots of literature provides a standard by which to measure sanity. Only in an idiot can love and loyalty survive. To this traditional hyperbole Faulkner adds the bitter footnote that these virtues survive in Benjy because he lacks the capacity to reject them.

That which Benjy knows—his sister smelling like trees, the pasture near his home, the fire burning cleanly, the jimsom weeds he carries as his private graveyard for the dead Compsons—he cherishes without stint or reservation. Because he loves; because the sound of Caddy's name makes him moan over her loss; because the funeral of grandmother and the wedding of sister blend in memory, with dirge and epithalamium becoming one; because even now, at thirty-three, he is again the fifteen-year-old straining at the gate and looking for Caddy after she has left with her banker-husband—*"You cant do no good holding to the gate and crying,"* his Negro keeper tells him, *"She cant hear you"*—because his sense of smell is a finer instrument that the moral sense of the other Compsons; because he cannot conceive of disloyalty, let alone commit a disloyal act; since in him the passage of time neither abates affection nor assuages woe; because of all this, Benjy is clearly an idiot. He must be.

Quentin Compson is Faulkner's image of a man aware of his dispossession, but unable to endure or transcend it. Living at an extreme of exacerbated consciousness, Quentin cannot dispose of the problems thrown up by that consciousness. Without an ordering code of belief, he is left entirely to the mercy of his perceptions, and these bring him little but chaos and pain. The "fine, dead sounds" he has heard throughout his youth, the words that form his heritage, he can neither abandon nor quicken into life.

Quentin feels that a familiar sin, because it would be there, undeniable and gross, is preferable to the routine of drift. He tries to persuade himself that he has had incestuous relations with Caddy. His story of incest is fictitious, but not merely a fantasy: " 'yes,' says Caddy, "I'll do anything you want me to, anything.' " When he turns to his father for help, the elder Compson can offer him only the stale ends of country-store skepticism. His father is lost in a sterile affection for the classics, his mother in absurd pretensions to gentility. What reason, she whines, did Quentin have for committing suicide? "It can't simply be to flout and hurt me. Whoever God is, He would not permit that. I'm a lady."

Beyond everything, Quentin yearns for death—the "clean flame" that will burn out consciousness and guilt—for he can exist neither in the the realm of the senses, which he fears, nor in the realm of the intellect, where he stumbles. Unable to forge the conscience of his race, he ends as a wanderer in an alien city; the lost son of Jefferson, Mississippi finds death in the Charles River of Massachusetts.

One Compson survives his family: Jason, the sub-moral man, rid of all supererogatory virtues, stripped to economic function and a modest, controlled physical appetite. He scorns the very notion that one human being can willingly assume and discharge obligations to another. He lives rigorously, even pedantically by the letter of his bargains. It is not that he is unkind, it is simply that he has no use for and does not believe in kindness. When the Negro boy Luster cannot produce a nickel to pay for a circus ticket, Jason prefers to burn it—with the diseased sardonic pleasure of a man turned cruel from consistency.

Like those quasi-intellectuals who abandon old allegiances to become the spokesmen of a rising new class, Jason formulates the values of Snopesism with a cleverness and vengeance which no Snopes could express. His motivating principle is never to be taken in, never to be distracted by sentiment or claims to selflessness; he knows better. Benjy he calls the "great American Gelding." Caddy he characterizes, "once a bitch, always a bitch." When the Negro servants leave for church and his mother whimpers "I know you will blame me" for the dinner being cold, Jason replies with invincible logic, "For what? . . . You never resurrected Christ, did you?" He and Mrs. Compson are the only members of the family who retain some tie at the end of the novel, he cynically using her and she fatuously deceived by him. The relationship is apt, a sign of the union between the decadent old and vicious new, with the gentility of the former veiling the rapacity of the latter. In the final passage of the section devoted to Jason, Faulkner brilliantly evokes his *Weltanschauung* as a blend of frustrated greed, coarseness, and the two most important forms of American prejudice. Dreaming of a stock-market coup, Jason says: "And just let me have twenty-four hours without any damn New York Jew to advise me what it's going to do. . . . I just want an even chance to get my money back. And once I've done that they can bring all Beale Street and all bedlam in here and two of them can sleep in my bed and another one can have my place at the table too."

To these figures of disorder and corruption, the remaining Compsons are secondary: Caddy, for whom sex is a fate rather than a temptation; Mr. Compson, who knowingly retreats from responsibility; and Mrs. Compson, always a lady and never a mother. In contrast to them stands the Negro servant Dilsey, strong, whole, uncorrupted—a voice of judgment over the Compsons and their world: "I've seed de first an de last." As she brings Mrs. Compson her hot-water bottle, as she warns her grandson not to "projeck" with Benjy's graveyard, as she blocks the thrusts of Jason's spite, she towers over the puny Compsons like some immense hieratic figure of integrity. At the end, when Dilsey brings Benjy to the Negro church, they stand alone in a landscape of ruins: the meek and the oppressed, the insulted and injured.

> In the midst of the voices and the hands Ben sat, rapt in his sweet blue gaze. Dilsey sat bolt upright beside, crying rigidly and quietly in the annealment and the blood of the remembered Lamb. . . .

To speak of greatness with regard to one's contemporaries is dangerous. But if there are any American novels of the present century which may be called great, which bear serious comparison with the achievements of twentieth-century European literature, then surely *The Sound and the Fury* is among them. It is one of the three or four American works of prose fiction written since the turn of the century in which the impact of tragedy is felt and sustained. Seized by his materials, Faulkner keeps, for once, within his esthetic means. *The Sound and the Fury* is the one novel in which his vision and technique are almost in complete harmony, and the vision itself whole and major. Whether taken as a study of the potential for human self-destruction, or as a rendering of the social disorder particular to our time, the novel projects a radical image of man against the wall.

Note

1. The following exchange comes from a recorded interview with Faulkner at the University of Virginia:

"Q. . . . . . did you make any conscious attempt in *The Sound and the Fury* to use Christian references, as a number of critics have suggested?"

"A. No. I was just trying to tell a story of Caddy, the little girl who had muddied her drawers. . . ."

[*The Sound and the Fury*: The Tragedy of the Lack of Love]

Carvel Collins*

The Sound and the Fury seems to some critics to be a sociological account of the decay of a family of the once-landed Southern aristocracy confronted by the rising commercialism. Possibly this is true. But *The Sound and the Fury*, like other good works of literary art, probably has no one "meaning." It seems to me that it also presents an idea larger and more generally applicable. I think this novel, like so many in our century, speaks of the tragedy which accompanies lack of love—love in its largest sense.

The three monologues clearly show the reader the effect which the failures of the Compson parents have on the Compson sons, whether the three sons are regarded on a realistic level as individuals or on a symbolic level as parts of the personality of one symbolic child. All three of the sons (or all three parts of the symbolic composite son, if you will permit)[1] are injured by lack of love. Quentin says that Mr. Compson's lack of love for Mrs. Compson and what she interprets as his contempt for her family have hurt her. Whether the contempt existed and was justified or not, the damage was there: *"Done in Mother's mind though. Finished. Finished. Then we were all poisoned."* This novel of "poisoning" shows Mrs. Compson to be "cold" and completely without love for her children. Quentin's monologue speaks often of the children's lack of a mother. Very near the end of his monologue Quentin is explicit about the failure of both parents.

> When I was little there was picture in one of our books, a dark place into which a single weak ray of light came slanting upon two faces lifted out of the shadow. *You know what I'd do if I were King?* [Candace] never was a queen or a fairy she was always a king or a giant or a general *I'd break that place open and drag them out and I'd whip them good* It was torn out, jagged out. I was glad. I'd have to turn back to it until the dungeon was Mother herself she and Father upward into weak light holding hands and us lost somewhere below even them without even a ray of light.

*Reprinted, with permission, from "The Interior Monologues of *The Sound and the Fury*" in *English Institute Essays 1952*, ed. Alan S. Downer (New York: Columbia University Press, 1954), pp. 53–56.

As a result of the lack of support from their cold, hypochondriac mother and their much warmer, but cynical and alcoholic, father all three sons are hurt in ways which fit the psychological roles which I think they play. As remarked above, the monologues show that each of the brothers is obsessed by their sister Candace. It is in this connection chiefly that we see them suffering for their parents' failings. Benjamin loves Candace and wants her near him, but she has been driven away forever. Quentin both loves and hates Candace, and because of the parents' failure he cannot cope normally with his ambivalent feelings. He acts according to Freudian theory in seeking punishment from his father by falsely claiming to have actually committed incest. When his father will not give either help or punishment, Quentin moves to carry out punishment on himself, first considering castration, but finally deciding upon complete self-destruction by drowning. Jason is in opposition to his sister, but because of his parents' inadequacy his opposition is frenzied hatred.

The final section of the novel, which follows the three monologues, emphasizes the warm, loving nature of the Compson's negro servant Dilsey. She works, whereas the Compsons do not; she is effectively orderly, while the Compsons are compulsively so; she is in touch with reality and has no interest in making false pretensions. In a score of ways her presence lets us see the Compson tragedy more clearly, bearing out what Quentin had said of her earlier: "They come into white people's lives . . . in sudden sharp black trickles that isolate white facts for an instant in unarguable truth like under a microscope."

In this section of the novel we are shown a sample of the love which has been missing in the Compsons. When Dilsey takes the idiot to her church on Easter the minister speaks of love.

> And the congregation seemed to watch with its own eyes while the voice consumed him, until he was nothing and they were nothing and there was not even a voice but instead their hearts were speaking to one another in chanting measures beyond the need for words.

When Dilsey and Benjamin sit in the congregation and Faulkner suggests their similarity to Mary and Jesus, about whom the minister is speaking, we sense a kind of love which the Compsons as a family have not known. The articles on Freudian psychology in the *Encyclopedia Britannica* of 1926 said:

> The maternal "life reaction" as expressively symbolized by the Madonna and Child, is unfulfilled and incomplete in the majority of women . . . the complete fulfillment . . . is to love, to be loved, to give birth to children and to nourish and cherish them.

The tragedy of the Compsons appears in bold relief in the final scene of the novel. On the last two pages of the book Jason and Benjamin confront each other most violently in an episode which seems to owe its terms and structure to a combination of the Macbeth passage discussed at the start of this paper and the Freudian roles which the two brothers play according to the interpretation of the novel which I have been making. It is a scene of "sound and fury" and illustrates that for these two warped personalities or parts of a personality life is "signifying nothing." Benjamin's bellows are described as sound, "agony eyeless, tongueless; just sound." And fury, in Jason, appears at its peak as we see him "hurling" Luster aside, "slashing" the mare into a plunging gallop as he swings her around, hitting Luster "over the head with his fist," striking Benjamin, "breaking the flower stalk," ordering Benjamin to "Shut up!" and telling Luster, "If you ever cross that gate with him again, I'll kill you." Then, when Jason's furious attack subsides and the carriage is again in familiar motion, Benjamin becomes quiet. And his eyes are "empty."

Note

1. Earlier in this essay, the author has argued that Benjy can be seen as an example of the Freudian *id*, Quentin as *superego*, and Jason as *ego*, the three making together a single composite son (Ed. Note).

[The Breakup of the Compsons]

Cleanth Brooks*

The Sound and the Fury has on occasion been read as another Faulknerian document describing the fall of the Old South. Perhaps it is, but what it most clearly records is the downfall of a particular family, and the case seems rather special. The basic cause of the breakup of the Compson family—let the more general cultural causes be what they may—is the cold and self-centered mother who is sensitive about the social status of her own family, the Bascombs, who feels the birth of an idiot son as a kind of personal affront, who spoils and corrupts her favorite son, and who withholds any real love and affection from her other children and her husband. Caroline Compson is not so much an actively wicked and evil person as a cold weight of negativity which paralyzes the normal family relationships. She is certainly at the root of Quentin's lack of confidence in himself and his inverted pride. She is at least the immediate cause of her husband's breakdown into alcoholic cynicism, and doubtless she is ultimately responsible for Caddy's promiscuity. There is some evidence that Caddy's conduct was obsessive and compulsive, a flight from her family. She tells her brother Quentin: "There was something terrible in me sometimes at night I could see it grinning at me I could see it through [my lovers] grinning at me through their faces" (p. 131).

In Faulkner's story "That Evening Sun," the events of which apparently occur in 1898, the earlier family relationships of the Compsons are revealingly portrayed. When Nancy, their Negro servant, is terrified of going home because she fears that her common-law husband is coming there to cut her throat, Mr. Compson is sympathetic and tries to be helpful. He obviously finds it difficult to take with full seriousness Nancy's irrational conviction that her man is lurking about ready to kill her, but Mr. Compson does take with great seriousness her abject terror, and he tries to find some solution that will calm her—having her stay with a friend, or putting the case before the police. But his wife, in notable contrast, is far too self-centered to view Nancy's plight with any sympathy.

*Reprinted, with permission, from *William Faulkner: The Yoknapatawpha Country* (New Haven, Conn.: Yale University Press, 1963), pp. 334–48.

Nancy's terror is to Mrs. Compson simply a nuisance, and the sooner Nancy is got out of the house the better.

In that story the Compson children have already assumed the personality patterns that we shall find later. Though they are too young to comprehend fully Nancy's desperation, Caddy and Quentin at least respond to the Negro woman's terror with concerned curiosity and, insofar as they are capable, sympathy. Jason is already a wretched little complainer, interested neither in Nancy nor in his brother and sister except as he may get his way by constantly threatening to "tell on" them.

Mr. Compson by 1910 was a defeated man. Perhaps he had always been a weak man, not endowed with the fighting spirit necessary to save his family. But there are plenty of indications that he was a man possessed of love and compassion. Benjy remembers a scene in which Caddy and Father and Jason were in Mother's chair. Jason had been crying, and his father was evidently comforting him. Caddy's head, Benjy remembers, was on Father's shoulder. And when Benjy himself went over to the chair, "Father lifted me into the chair too, and Caddy held me" (p. 91). Long after Mr. Compson's death, Dilsey remembers him as a force for order in the household and reproaches Jason with the words: "if Mr. Jason was still here hit ud be different" (p. 225). And when Caddy pleads with her cold-hearted brother to be allowed to see her baby, she says to him: "You have Father's name: do you think I'd have to ask him twice? once, even?" (p. 227). The attentive reader will have noticed that even in his drinking, Mr. Compson has evidently gone from better to worse. Caddy tells Quentin: "Father will be dead in a year they say if he doesn't stop drinking and he wont stop he cant stop since I since last summer" (p. 143). Evidently, the knowledge of his daughter's wantonness had hit Mr. Compson hard, and his parade of cynicism about women and virginity, so much of which Quentin recalls on the day of his death, must have been in part an attempt to soften the blow for Quentin and perhaps for himself. We miss the point badly if we take it that Mr. Compson, comfortable in his cynicism, simply didn't care what his daughter did.

Quentin was apparently very close to his father and the influence of his father on him was obviously very powerful. The whole of the Quentin section is saturated with what "Father said" and with references to comparisons that Father used and observations about life that Father made. Though his father seems to have counseled acquiescence in the meaninglessness of existence, it is plain that it was from him that Quentin derived his high notion of the claims of honor. Quentin has not the slightest doubt as to what he ought to do: he ought to drive Caddy's seducer out of town, and if the seducer refuses to go, he ought to shoot him. But Quentin is not up to the heroic role. He tries, but he cannot even hurt Ames, much less kill him. Caddy sees Quentin as simply meddling in her affairs, the quixotic little brother who is to be pitied but not feared or respected.

Since *Absalom, Absalom!* was written years after *The Sound and the Fury*, we must exercise caution in using the Quentin of the later novel to throw light upon the Quentin of the earlier. But Faulkner, in choosing the character Quentin for service in *Absalom, Absalom!*, must have deemed the choice a sound one. He must have felt that the experience that Quentin was to undergo in talking with his father about the Sutpens and on his journey out to Sutpen's Hundred would be compatible with, and relevant to, what he had Quentin undergo in *The Sound and the Fury.* The Quentin of *The Sound and the Fury* would indeed have been terribly impressed by Henry Sutpen's acceptance of the heroic and tragic role thrust upon him by circumstance, and the more humiliated to have to acknowledge his own pitiful inadequacy when it became necessary to protect his own sister's honor. (Presumably Quentin's encounter with Dalton Ames occurred in the summer before he saw Henry Sutpen—that is, just before he went off to Harvard in September—rather than after he saw Henry. But the two experiences could not have been widely separated in time, and the sight of Henry, who had assumed the heroic role and wrecked his life for it, would have deepened Quentin's sense of failure with Caddy's seducer, Ames.)

Quentin is emotionally committed to the code of honor, but for him the code has lost its connection with reality: it is abstract, rigidified, even "literary." Quentin's suicide results from the fact that he can neither repudiate nor fulfill the claims of the code. The idiot Benjy, of course, has no code at all. His is an inarticulate love, a love that is as direct and wordless as an odor ("Caddy smelled like trees"). Nevertheless, Benjy's love is recognizably human in that it asks something of the loved one. Benjy can sense Caddy's betrayal of honor: he screams in horror when he smells the perfume that she has worn for her lover, and is not appeased until she has washed it off.

The third brother, Jason, has repudiated the code of honor. He has adopted for himself a purely practical formula for conduct. Money is what counts. He wants none of Quentin's nonsense nor of the other kinds of nonsense in which people believe—or in which they pretend to believe. But though Jason's ostensible code is purely practical, reducing every action to its cash value, his conduct has in fact its nonpractical aspect. For Jason harbors a great deal of nonpractical and irrational bitterness, even sadism. When, in order to see the disappointment upon Luster's face, Jason deliberately drops the passes to the minstrel show into the fire, he is satisfying his perverted emotion even though he pretends to be merely throwing away what cannot be sold. His stealing systematically the money that Caddy is sending for the benefit of her daughter answers to his mercantilism, but Jason is not content to steal Quentin's allowance. He also wants the enjoyment of teasing and hurting the girl.

In his appendix on the Compsons, Faulkner declares that Jason was "the first sane Compson since before Culloden" (p. 16). In view of the quixotic Compsons, with their zest for spending themselves on foolish enterprises and their impossible notions of honor, one sees the ironic justification of the term *sane* as applied to Jason. But sanity as Jason exemplifies it is something inhuman. Jason does not love even his mother, Faulkner tells us, for he is "a sane man always," and love always involves a contradiction of such sanity. Benjy's idiocy and Quentin's quixotic madness are finally less inhuman than Jason's sanity. To be truly human one must transcend one's mere intellect with some overflow of generosity and love. Faulkner tells us that Jason is able to compete with, and even hold his own with, the Snopeses. This is the highest accolade that Faulkner can bestow on Jason, and of course, the worst damnation that he can utter. When a Compson turns Snopes, then the family has indeed run out, and the end of an order has come.

The section devoted to Jason has in it some of the most brilliant writing that Faulkner ever did. Jason is a brutal and cold-hearted man, but he does have a certain wit and a brittle logic which allows him to cap any remark made to him by his defiant niece or his ailing mother or one of his business associates. Jason is rarely at a loss, and he is so self-righteous in his bitterness that many of his comments carry a kind of nasty conviction. For example, here is Jason feeling sorry for himself: "Well, Jason likes work. I says no I never had university advantages because at Harvard they teach you how to go for a swim at night without knowing how to swim and at Sewanee they dont even teach you what water is. I says you might send me to the state University; maybe I'll learn how to stop my clock with a nose spray and then you can send Ben to the Navy I says or to the cavalry anyway, they use geldings in the cavalry" (p. 213).

Jason is typically sardonic in his description of his father's funeral. His ineffective and sycophantic Uncle Maury has braced himself for the ordeal with a few drinks and has tried to disguise the fact by chewing cloves. The tell-tale smell, however, gives him away to Jason, who observes: "I reckon [Uncle Maury] thought that the least he could do at Father's funeral [was to take a drink] or maybe the sideboard thought it was still Father and tripped him up when he passed. Like I say, if [Father] had to sell something to send Quentin to Harvard we'd all been a damn sight better off if he'd sold that sideboard and bought himself a one-armed straight jacket with part of the money" (p. 215).

Jason's usual mode is a rather ponderous sarcasm. The opening paragraph of his section of the novel is typical: "Once a bitch always a bitch, what I say. I says you're lucky if her playing out of school is all that worries you. I says she ought to be down there in that kitchen right now, instead of up there in her room, gobbing paint on her face and waiting for six niggers that cant even stand up out of a chair unless they've got a pan full of bread and meat to balance them, to fix breakfast for her" (p. 198).

For some eighty pages, in a coldly furious monologue, Jason pitilessly exposes himself. Indeed, Faulkner does more in these eighty pages to indict the shabby small-town businessman's view of life than Sinclair Lewis was able to achieve in several novels on the subject. Jason takes his place as one of the half-dozen of Faulkner's most accomplished villains. Faulkner's resourcefulness and his imaginative power keep his villains from conforming to a stereotype. Anse, Flem, Popeye, Thomas Sutpen, Percy Grimm, and Jason Compson—how different they are in personality and appearance and manner! All but Jason come largely of poor-white stock, but they have to yield nothing in meanness to this déclassé aristocrat—or is Jason's mother right in regarding him as pure Bascomb? Jason has more vitality than Anse Bundren, less maniacal fury than Percy Grimm, and far less staying power than one finds in Flem Snopes' cold rapacity. Jason does not match either the courage or the quality of perverse magnificence that attaches itself to Thomas Sutpen. Even so, in this company of prime villains Jason is among his peers, and Jason's treatment of his sister, his idiot brother, and his niece shows studied cruelty that is unmatched by any of Faulkner's other villains.

A common trait in Faulkner's villains is the lack of any capacity for love. Their lack of love shows itself in two ways, two ways that come eventually to the same thing: their attitudes toward nature and toward women. They do not respond to nature—they may very well violate nature. In quite the same way, they have no interest in women, or use them as means to their own ends. They are impotent like Flem and Popeye, or they are strong-willed abstemious men like Thomas Sutpen. Jason Compson, with no interest in nature, or in women except as objects to be manipulated, is of this breed.

The disintegration that took place in the Compson family after Jason became its head is revealed most clearly and terribly in the character of Candace's daughter, Quentin. The child is nearly everything that Jason bitterly accuses her of being: she is a cheap little wanton, offering herself to almost any man who puts in an appearance, and in her wantonness she resembles her mother. But the daughter lacks certain virtues that her mother possessed: graciousness, pity, and disinterested love. Quentin despises Benjy, the unfortunate to whom Caddy gave her love, and this is not hard to understand, remembering that she has always seen Benjy as an adult-sized all-but-mindless being and never as the little brother—the relationship in which her mother knew him. But it still is hard to forgive the callousness she shows to Dilsey. Though at times she has to appeal to Dilsey for protection from her cruel uncle, and though Dilsey always tries to mother her, Quentin shows her little love or consideration. When Dilsey remonstrates with Jason and goes on to reassure Quentin with the words "Now, now, I aint gwine let him tech you," and puts her hand on Quentin, Quentin knocks it down, blurting out: "You damn old nigger" (p. 203).

What has happened to the girl Quentin is what might have been expected. Reared in a loveless home, lacking even what her mother had had in the way of family companionship, she shows the effect of the pressures that have been exerted upon her all her life. She is cheap and thoughtless, and she has absorbed from her uncle something of his cruelty. It is very difficult for people to be good when they are frustrated and dreadfully unhappy, and Quentin is indeed dreadfully unhappy. She exclaims: "I don't see why I was ever born," and when Jason reproaches her for her loss of reputation in the town, she answers him by saying: "I dont care. I'm bad and I'm going to hell, and I dont care. I'd rather be in hell than anywhere where you are" (p. 207).

In a way the girl senses what has misshaped her. At one point she appeals, in her desperation, to Mrs. Compson, saying: "Why does [Jason] treat me like this, Grandmother? I never hurt him" (p. 276). And when her grandmother tells her that Jason "is the nearest thing to a father you've ever had. It's his bread you and I eat. It's only right that he should expect obedience from you," the girl jumps up and says to Jason: "Whatever I do, it's your fault. If I'm bad, it's because I had to be. You made me. I wish I was dead. I wish we were all dead" (p. 277).

The girl's plight is very much that of Joe Christmas, who was warped by his feeling that the fanatic old Doc Hines was always watching him with hatred. Faulkner, to be sure, does not sentimentalize Quentin. He does not minimize her shortcomings or imply that she was the mere victim of her environment, but his bitterest judgment upon Jason and what Jason's cruelty entailed is in his presentation of what Jason has caused Caddy's baby to become.

The downfall of the house of Compson is the kind of degeneration which can occur, and has occurred, anywhere at any time. William Butler Yeats' play *Purgatory* is a moving dramatization of the end of a great house in Ireland. The play ends with the last member of the family, a murderous-minded old tinker, standing outside the ruins of the ancestral house; but the burning of that house and the decay of the family have no special connection with the troubles of Ireland. According to the author, the disaster resulted from a bad marriage! The real significance of the Southern setting in *The Sound and the Fury* resides, as so often elsewhere in Faulkner, in the fact that the breakdown of a family can be exhibited more poignantly and significantly in a society which is old-fashioned and in which the family is still at the center. The dissolution of the family as an institution has probably gone further in the suburban areas of California and Connecticut than it has in the small towns of Mississippi. For that very reason, what happens to the Compsons might make less noise and cause less comment, and even bring less pain to the individuals concerned, if the Compsons lived in a more progressive and liberal environment. Because the Compsons have been committed to old-fashioned ideals—close family loyalty, home care for defective children, and the virginity of unmarried daughters—the breakup of the family registers with greater impact.

The decay of the Compsons can be viewed, however, not merely with reference to the Southern past but to the contemporary American scene. It is tempting to read it as a parable of the disintegration of modern man. Individuals no longer sustained by familial and cultural unity are alienated and lost in private worlds. One thinks here not merely of Caddy, homeless, the sexual adventuress adrift in the world, or of Quentin, out of touch with reality and moving inevitably to his death, but also and even primarily of Jason, for whom the breakup of the family means an active rejection of claims and responsibilities and, with it, a sense of liberation. Jason resolves to be himself and to be self-sufficient. He says: "Besides, like I say I guess I dont need any man's help to get along I can stand on my own feet like I always have" (p. 224). Jason prides himself in managing matters by himself and—since this is the other side of the same coin—refuses to heed the claims of anyone but himself. In his appendix Faulkner says that Jason thinks "nothing whatever of God one way or the other" but simply tries to keep clear of "the police" and fears and respects "only the Negro woman" (p. 16), Dilsey. Jason is done with religion in every way, including its etymological sense as a "binding back." Jason is bound back to nothing. He repudiates any traditional tie. He means to be on his own and he rejects every community. The fact shows plainly in the way he conducts himself not only in his own household but also in the town of Jefferson.

The one member of the Compson household who represents a unifying and sustaining force is the Negro servant Dilsey. She tries to take care of Benjy and to give the girl Quentin the mothering she needs. In contrast to Mrs. Compson's vanity and whining self-pity, Dilsey exhibits charity and rugged good sense. She is warned by her daughter Frony that taking Benjy to church with her will provoke comments from the neighbors. "Folks talkin," Frony says; to which Dilsey answers: "Whut folks? . . . And I know whut kind of folks. Trash white folks. Dat's who it is. Thinks he aint good enough fer white church, but nigger church aint good enough fer him" (p. 306). Frony remarks that folks talk just the same, but Dilsey has her answer: "Den you send um to me. Tell um de good Lawd dont keer whether he smart er not. Dont nobody but white trash keer dat." All of which amounts to sound manners and to sound theology as well.

Faulkner does not present Dilsey as a black fairy-godmother or as a kind of middle-aged Pollyanna full of the spirit of cheerful optimism. Even his physical description of her looks in another direction. We are told that she had once been a big woman, but now the unpadded skin is loosely draped upon "the indomitable skeleton" which is left "rising like a ruin or a landmark above the somnolent and impervious guts, and above that the collapsed face that gave the impression of the bones themselves being outside the flesh, lifted into the driving day with an expression at once fatalistic and of a child's astonished disappointment" (p. 282). What the expression means is best interpreted by what she says and does in the novel, but the description clearly points to something other than mindless cheeriness. Dilsey's essential hopefulness has not been obliterated; she is not an embittered woman, but her optimism has been chastened by hurt and disappointment.

Faulkner does not make the mistake of accounting for Dilsey's virtues through some mystique of race in which good primitive black folk stand over against corrupt wicked white folk. Dilsey herself has no such notions. When her son Luster remarks of the Compson household: "Dese is funny folks. Glad I aint none of em," she says: "Lemme tell you somethin, nigger boy, you got jes es much Compson devilment in you es any of em" (p. 292). She believes in something like original sin: men are not "naturally" good but require discipline and grace.

Dilsey, then, is no noble savage and no *schöne Seele*. Her view of the world and mankind is thoroughly Christian, simple and limited as her theological expression of her faith would have to be. On the other hand, Dilsey is no plaster saint. She is not easy on her own children. ("Dont stand dar in de rain, fool," she tells Luster.) She does not always offer the soft answer that turneth away wrath. She rebukes Mrs. Compson with "I dont see how you expect anybody to sleep, wid you standin in de hall, holl'in at folks fum de crack of dawn," and she refuses Mrs. Compson's hypocritical offer to fix breakfast, saying: "En who gwine eat yo messin? Tell me dat" (p. 287). Dilsey's goodness is no mere goodness by, and of, nature, if one means by this a goodness that justifies a faith in man as man. Dilsey does not believe in man; she believes in God.

Dilsey's poverty and her status as a member of a deprived race do not, then, assure her nobility, but they may have had something to do with her remaining close to a concrete world of values so that she is less perverted by abstraction and more honest than are most white people in recognizing what is essential and basic. In general, Faulkner's Negro characters show less false pride, less false idealism, and more seasoned discipline in human relationships. Dilsey's race has also had something to do with keeping her close to a world still informed by religion. These matters are important: just how important they are is revealed by the emphasis Faulkner gives to the Easter service that Dilsey attends.

The Compson family—whatever may be true of the white community at large in the Jefferson of 1910—has lost its religion. Quentin's sad reveries are filled with references to Jesus and Saint Francis, but it is plain that he has retreated into some kind of Stoicism, a version which is reflected in his father's advice to him: "We must just stay awake and see evil done for a little." Quentin's reply is that "it doesn't have to be even that long for a man of courage" (p. 195), and the act of courage in the Roman style takes Quentin into the river. Mrs. Compson, when she finds that the girl Quentin has eloped, asks Dilsey to bring her the Bible, but obviously Mrs. Compson knows nothing about either sin or redemption. Her deepest concern is with gentility and social position. And Jason, as we have seen, worships only the almighty dollar.

The first three sections of the book do little to carry forward the story of what happened at the Compsons' on the Easter weekend. Benjy's section obviously does not do so, and it is only in the light of a reading of the rest of the book and a careful re-reading of his section that the references to the present occasion emerge. Quentin's section dates from eighteen years before, and though what passes through Quentin's agonized spirit on the 2d of June, 1910, has its ultimate bearing on the events that occur in the Compson household on Easter day, 1928, the connection is not direct. Even the third section, that narrated by Jason, is not very directly related to the hectic events of Easter Sunday. For one thing, Jason's is set back one day earlier than Benjy's section: that is, Jason's tirade on the subject of bitches and of what is happening to the Compsons is uttered on Good Friday, whereas Benjy's section gives us the events of Holy Saturday. In a general way Jason's section does prepare us for what the girl Quentin is going to do, but much of it is simply typical of almost any day in the Compson household for the last year. All three sections, then, bend the bow or coil the spring for an action that will discharge itself only in the last section of the novel. None of the three—not even the third—has much narrative drive, and the first two, in general structure, resemble mood pieces, even mood poems, rather than narrative transactions. This is not, to be sure, said by way of disparagement: such action as occurs in *The Sound and the Fury* is quite sufficient for the purposes of a powerful novel.

Easter Sunday breaks bleak and chill and gray. It begins appropriately with Mrs. Compson's complaining and Dilsey's getting the fire started and the household tasks going, but once it is discovered that Quentin is not in her room, events accelerate. All of Jason's frenetic activity comes to a head when he makes the horrified discovery that his victim has found out where he has hidden the money that he has stolen from her and has escaped with it. But we do not immediately follow Jason on his frantic pursuit of his niece. Instead, once Jason is out of the house on his way to the sheriff's, we follow Dilsey and Benjy to church for the Easter service, and this service, in which Dilsey finds her exaltation, is counterpointed against Jason's attempt to find his niece and retrieve the money.

The eloquent sermon to which Dilsey listens sitting "bolt upright" and with tears sliding "down her fallen cheeks" (p. 311) describes Mary's sorrow and the crucifixion of Jesus, but ends with the promise of resurrection and of ultimate glory in which all the arisen dead "whut got de blood en de ricklickshun of de Lamb" (p. 313) shall participate. It is a vision of eternity which gives meaning to time and will wipe away all tears in a final vindication of goodness and in a full consolation of those who mourn. Beside Dilsey, Benjy sits, "rapt in his sweet blue gaze," as if he, too, understood. As Dilsey continues to weep on her way home, her daughter Frony tries to make her stop crying, pointing out that people are looking and that they will be passing white folks soon. But Dilsey does not care what people think and, caught up in her own vision, says to Frony: "I've seed de first en de last." And when Frony asks "First en last whut?" Dilsey tells her: "Never you mind. I seed de beginnin, en now I sees de endin" (p. 313). With the girl Quentin's departure, the sad story of the Compson family is now at an end. All are dead or departed except the whining hypochondriac Mrs. Compson, the cold and sterile bachelor Jason, and the uncomprehending Benjy.

Easter morning brings to Dilsey a vision that gives meaning to human events, but the Mrs. Compson to whom she returns is still full of uncomprehending reproaches. Mrs. Compson cannot understand why this latest disaster has befallen her. "It cant be simply to hurt and flout me. Whoever God is, He would not permit that. I'm a lady. You might not believe that from my offspring, but I am" (p. 315). In the meantime, Jason is off on his vain pursuit.

Jason's conversation with the sheriff reveals that the sheriff has a very clear idea of what has been going on and how Jason has mistreated his niece. The sheriff understands that the girl's act of "stealing" the money from Jason is essentially a recovery of her own property and that a rough kind of justice has been done. He tells Jason, "You drove that girl into running off" (p. 320). He refuses to act in any way to help Jason recover the money, and Jason goes away in a cold fury to pursue Quentin himself. Too wrought up even to drive his car properly, Jason heads for Mottstown, where the show is playing and where Jason expects to find Quentin and the young showman with whom she has eloped.

We are told that Jason did not think at all of his niece or of "the arbitrary valuation of the money" that she had taken. "Neither of them had had entity or individuality for him for ten years; together they merely symbolized the job in the bank of which he had been deprived before he ever got it" (p. 321). So the man who has become a kind of personified yearning for money sets out to recover not an errant girl and an actual sum of money but an abstract symbol.

Jason, who had boasted that he could get along without anyone, gets no help from anyone in his pursuit of Quentin. When he tries to make his way into the railway car belonging to the show people, he nearly gets himself killed. In his frenzy to get an answer out of the little man he finds in the car, he strikes him on the head, and the little man, in retaliating, almost succeeds in sinking a rusty hatchet in his head before someone comes to pull him off. Finally, with his raging headache—for Jason cannot stand the smell of gasoline—he is reduced to crazy-headed impotence and forced to hire a Negro man to drive him back to Jefferson. He is quite incapable of driving himself. At the end the cold-hearted Jason sits marooned on his rock of self-sufficiency.

Faulkner's titles are often whimsical, containing some meaning private to himself which never becomes completely clear in the novel. The title of *The Sound and the Fury*, however, provides a true key, for the novel has to do with the discovery that life has no meaning. Shakespeare's lines from *Macbeth*, "[Life] is a tale/Told by an idiot, full of sound and fury,/Signifying nothing," quite aptly apply to the first section of the novel. Benjy's section, a tale told by an idiot, is not a tale told at all, but a kind of fuguelike arrangement and rearrangement of sights, smells, sounds, and actions, many of them meaningless in themselves, but tied together by some crisscross of association.

Quentin's section, too, echoes the title. Quentin has learned all too well his father's despairing philosophy, which sees human beings as merely dolls filled with sawdust. What spills from the side of such a doll can never be the healing blood of a Savior, with its promise of redemption. Quentin's own phrasing is: "dolls stuffed with sawdust swept up from the trash heaps where all previous dolls had been thrown away the sawdust flowing from what wound in what side that not for me died not" (p. 194).

Jason hopes to find meaning in life by discarding all idealisms, illusions, and emotional ties, and reducing life to its inexorable brass tacks. He manages to come out with a meaning of a sort, but it is a very thin and impoverished one. At the end of the novel he has scarcely made good his boast that he is a free man able to stand on his own feet with no help from anybody. He has indeed finally succeeded, with his brittle rationalism, in outsmarting himself.

For Dilsey life does have meaning, though many of her betters would dismiss what she takes to be its meaning as illusion, the opium dispensed to a poor and illiterate people. Faulkner makes no claim for Dilsey's version of Christianity one way or the other. His presentation of it is moving and credible, but moving and credible as an aspect of Dilsey's own mental and emotional life. At any rate, it does not avail for those who will not avail themselves of it. Mrs. Compson is much too tightly locked up in her own egotism and self-pity to derive any help from it, and Jason has consciously disavowed it long ago.

Faulkner closes his novel with a final confrontation of the two remaining Compson brothers, the one who believes he can live by pure reason alone and the other who is bereft of reason, neither of whom is, therefore, fully human. Meaning for Benjy is succession in due order, driving around the courthouse square to the right of the monument rather than the left. When Luster, bored and mischievous, whips up the mare and swings her to the left of the monument, Benjy finds himself confronted by nightmare and screams his outrage—the store fronts and buildings of Jefferson are all moving in insane reverse from the order in which he knows he ought to find them. Hearing Benjy's outcry, the maddened Jason, now back from the fruitless chase after his niece, snatches the reins and, cursing, turns the old horse into the accustomed route. Whereupon Benjy ceases his bellowing as his world moves again into accustomed order, "as cornice and façade flowed smoothly once more from left to right; post and tree, window and doorway, and signboard, each in its ordered place" (p. 336). This is about as much meaning as experience can have for Benjy. For his frenzied "sane" brother, experience has hardly this much.

[The Compson Legacy]

Wendell V. Harris*

The fascination of the five-fold narrative through which Faulkner presents the history of the Compson family in *The Sound and the Fury* has tended to obscure the secondary patterns of the novel's structure. One of these is the adaption of the traditional device of fragmentation for the portrayal of the dominant traits of the Compson line. The father, Jason III, is in the direct line of descent from the Quentin Maclachan Compson who fled Culloden Moor, as Faulkner's later "appendix" to the novel informs us, and his character represents by extension the essential qualities of the declining family. Each of the major attributes of his shadowy figure can be seen serving as the ruling characteristic of one of his children.

Quentin's peculiar inheritance is the abstract, speculative turn of his father's mind; like his father, Quentin is never content simply to acknowledge the existence of phenomena, but desires always the explanation behind the fact. But his father's speculation had borne fruit in a loose philosophy which, however caustic, provided a view of life adequate to the elder Jason. Quentin's idealistic mind, finding no adequate answers, returns always to his father's mordantly expressed insights. Thus many of the father's remarks floating in Quentin's consciousness are "explanations" introduced by the significant word "because": "Because women so delicate so mysterious Father said"; "Because no battle is ever won he said"; "Because it means less to women, Father said." The father had rejoiced in the ability to express his vision of life in the sharp epigrammatic forms which had made so deep an impression on Quentin. Lacking the sense of having been granted conclusive insights, Quentin's ability to manipulate language remains largely inchoate, manifesting itself only in the form of an occasional poetic image.

The petulantly cynical tone of Jason IV is, as has not been sufficiently noted, also a natural inheritance from his father. At least two of the father's comments on Uncle Maury reveal a bitterness parallel to that of the second son's. Through Benjy's mind flits the echo of his father's "I admire Maury. He is invaluable to my own sense of racial superiority. I wouldn't swap Maury for a matched team." And Quentin recalls "but

*Reprinted, with permission, from the *Explicator*, 21, No. 7 (March 1963), #54.

father said why should Uncle Maury work if he [father] could support five or six niggers that did nothing at all but sit with their feet in the oven he certainly could board and lodge Uncle Maury now and then. . . ." In Jason IV this flippancy has degenerated into acrid cynicism.

That tempering quality of love and affection which is occasionally to be glimpsed in the father's personality finds its reflection only in Caddy. She loves Benjy, and Quentin, and her father; and even her affair with Dalton Ames, precipitating the final destruction of the family, is motivated by a love of more sincerity than Quentin or Jason or the daughter to be born of that affair would have been capable of.

The instability of Quentin, Jason, and Caddy may be traced to the mastery of each of their personalities by a dominant trait. As though such aberrations were not sufficient, the streak of insanity which runs through the family receives its final objectification in Benjy. This last-born son is, in addition, the ultimate reduction of the helplessness of the mother's side of the family. Despite the mother's claims, it is not Jason IV who represents the Bascomb personality; Benjy's helpless idiocy is the radical exemplification of the parasitical nature of both the querulous mother and her irresponsible brother Maury. Thus are the inherent traits of the decaying families anatomized.

Order and Disorder in *The Sound and the Fury*

H. P. Absalom*

It is helpful to approach this novel in the light of a paradox suggested by two statements Faulkner made about his creative activity when he was interviewed on two separate occasions. He remarked to Jean Stein: 'the writer knows probably every single word right to the end before he puts the first one down.' To H. Nash-Smith he said: 'When I started to write *The Sound and the Fury* I had no idea of writing the book it finally became; it simply grew from day to day.'

Faulkner himself has suggested that his remarks at any interview are not to be taken too seriously. As he remarks in his interview with Stein: 'If the same question is asked tomorrow the answer may be different.' However, these two contradictory statements have an important relevancy to the form and matter of *The Sound and the Fury*.

The observations that follow will be mainly concerned with the first section of the novel 'April Seventh, 1928', so that it is perhaps desirable to offer a brief outline of the book with special concern to emphasize those features which may assist the reader to share in Faulkner's synoptic vision.

The novel is concerned with a decadent Southern family, the Compsons, who are presented in the first three sections of the book through the perceptions of the three brothers, Benjy, an idiot, Quentin, a suicide, and Jason, who suffers from persecution mania. Events occurring during one day in the life of each character become, through a 'stream of consciousness' technique, an evocation of the past life, not only of the three brothers, but of the whole Compson family. The last section of the book, written in the third person, continues the narrative from the point in time at which the third section ends, and describes the events of another day in the life of the family. The date titles given to these four days—April Seventh 1928, June Second 1910, April Sixth 1928, and April Eighth 1928—suggest that Faulkner wishes the reader's interpretation of the novel to derive support from alignment with the Gospel Passion and Resurrection narrative, since we can identify April Seventh 1928 with

*Reprinted, with permission of the editor, from *Durham University Journal*, 58, No. 1 (NS 27, No. 1), (December, 1965), 30–39.

Holy Saturday, June Second 1910 with Maundy Thursday, April Sixth 1928 with Good Friday, and April Eighth 1928 with Easter Day, if we refer to a calendar for these years.

The general scheme of the novel, then, bears out Faulkner's remark that it must be approached as an integrated whole. Even at a first reading the closely woven texture of the book reveals itself. In the first section—April Seventh 1928—many scenes and statements from the characters concerned are comprehended only through a later unfolding of their meaning. An illustration of this interdependence is Benjy's recollections of Caddy's wedding, and of the funerals of Quentin and Mr. Compson, the elucidation of which appears in the later sections. The implication of the Biblical dates as section titles awaits the clarification it receives in the last chapter, which is controlled, in the selection of its material, by the Death and Resurrection theme. A number of events in the first section become comprehensible in the light of parallel incidents that occur later in the narrative. Examples that come to mind are those situations in which Quentin fights, Benjy approaches the swing, Caddy confronts Jason at her father's funeral, and Benjy attempts to escape from the Compson family confines. The reader is forced to switch from one event to the other in order to recognize their mutual implications, and so concludes that the complete design of the author impregnates almost every event and regulates the growing comprehensibility of the narrative.

There is however quite a different aspect of the reader's experience to be considered. The important place of the technique of 'stream of consciousness' in the novel has already been mentioned. This is a stream that moves with much turbulence and many an eddy, and the tangled state of mind that Benjy's recollections reveal is an outstanding example of its apparent disorder. It is consideration of this aspect of the novel that inclines the reader to concur with Faulkner's other opinion that the book simply grew from day to day with little sign of an integrated pattern to control its direction.

There is here then a problem confronting the reader. On examination, how far can he conclude that *The Sound and the Fury* reconciles the seemingly conflicting principles of order and disorder, of freedom and discipline, in the vision it offers of the Compson family?

This inquiry will probably gain in brevity if not in clarity if an attempt is made to limit it primarily to the Benjy section, although the nature of the task will demand frequent references to the book as a whole.

Although the most exciting impression one gets from this first section derives from the seemingly chaotic memories which constitute Benjy's past, and which continually suffer interruption from intrusion by the more recent events that make up April Seventh 1928, the reader will be able to recognize, after some scrutiny, a linear progression of incidents which although broken by the refraction of Benjy's awareness, still retains a quality of inevitable movement from dawn to dusk. This sense of continuity is supported by numerous allusions to the passing of time on that particular day.

This passage of time is recorded in forms suitable to Benjy's awareness, so that in spite of his conscious ignorance of time, Benjy is involved as a witness that such temporal continuity really exists. There are various references to shadows, high, short, elongated. The sun shines on the grass. Later it gleams on the showman's red tie, and slants on the grass. The moon is up when Benjy sees Quentin his niece in the swing and the light is turned on in the library. There are references to supper after Jason has returned from his day's work. Benjy sits in the dark of an empty room. He is undressed for bed, and in the dusk watches the faint outline of his niece escaping from her bedroom. However oblivious Benjy may appear to be of the time sequence in the realm of memory, this progression of time obtrudes a persistent presence through the welter of his experiences. The disconnected way in which sunlight, moonlight, twilight and dark thread his more remote past only discloses more clearly Benjy's involvement in the 'mechanical progression of time' of which his brother Quentin is so intensely aware. However rebellious the main characters in *The Sound and the Fury* are to the time sequence, it remains a potent symbol of the author's ability to control his material in its most elusive and amorphous condition.

Benjy's revival of his past loses none of its chaotic features when we recognize the random and variable nature of the stimuli that set it in motion. Sometimes a word is enough, or a phrase, sometimes an object, sometimes a person; at other times the overtone of a previous memory. But closer and more extensive examination disclose that the majority of these recollections are organized around a few thematic centres which dominate the contents of Benjy's mind. These nodal centres can be recognized as (a) affection for Caddy, (b) awareness of death (c) experience of sex. It is consistent both with the fluid nature of Benjy's consciousness, and with the purposive cast of Faulkner's creativeness that these themes, however distinguishable, continually intertwine with each other, and strengthen the reader's awareness of pattern within Benjy's mental confusion.

Benjy's affection for Caddy embraces a wide field of his experience. When he is introduced to the reader, Benjy is searching for his sister and associates her with the golfer calling 'Caddy'. He is reminded of his walk with her in cold weather; he recalls their excursions to the stream, his visit with her to Mrs. Patterson, his traumatic experience of seeing her with Charlie in the swing, his mistaking his niece for her, his visit to and from Mrs. Compson's bed where Caddy quietens him when upset by his mother's tactlessness. He remembers his drunkenness at his sister's wedding. He recalls his obsession with the slipper. He retains a clear memory of Caddy disobediently climbing the tree to watch the mourners. The last incident recorded in this section is Benjy recalling how he fell asleep in Caddy's arms.

The existence of death occupies a large place in Benjy's recollections on this April day. One of Luster's frequent attempts to tantalize Benjy is the disorganization of Benjy's graveyard which, Dilsey suggests, is especially associated with Benjy's way of spending time. One of the rare occasions on which there is, ironically, a normal relationship between mother and son is their visit together in the old family surrey to the Compson cemetery, a visit which, as Jason later in the story reveals, is no isolated incident but part of Benjy's routine. Death, in the form of the decease of Damuddy, Quentin, and Mr. Compson, affects Benjy through his most powerful channel of communication—his sense of smell. In the light of later episodes in the novel, Benjy's references to rain, perfume, marriage, and the stream, all contain an undertone of death, and contribute to the complexity of the death-theme as it works through and controls Benjy's evocation of the past. The title of the first section, with its reference to Christ's burial is an additional reminder of the relevance of this theme of death to Benjy's mode of consciousness.

The theme of sex too has a variety of ramifications which involve Benjy's concern for his sister. His unease at finding Caddy and Charlie by the swing conditions his response to his niece when later he finds her in the same condition. His discomfort, when confronted with sexual relations is partly responsible for the upset he feels at Caddy's marriage, and is symbolized by the suffering of his drunken state on that occasion. The theme of sex is further associated for Benjy with a state of disturbance in the incident in which Benjy bungles the function of go-between when he carries a letter from Uncle Maury to Mrs. Patterson, and becomes frightened. Concern for his sister explains Benjy's so-called attack on the school girl whom he identifies with Caddy, and for which he suffers castration. Other experiences of Benjy can be seen coloured by a sexual significance when their relation to other events in the book are detected.

For example, the muddy clothes of Quentin and Caddy point to the later sexual relation between brother and sister during which the earlier experience in the stream is specifically mentioned. Benjy notices the later incident of Luster and his niece Quentin playing in the dirt, which recalls some of the same features in Quentin's and Caddy's behaviour. The burning of Benjy's hand in the stove fire has certain tenuous links with the sexual behaviour of Quentin and Caddy, since fire has for Benjy a close association with Caddy who brought him to Mrs. Compson's bedroom where the fire engrossed his attention. He later compared Caddy's hair with fire. Fire was also an important element in Quentin's dream of his incestuous relation with Caddy since he envisaged them consequently existing in 'the clean flame' of hell. The drunkenness of Benjy at the wedding of his sister, if detached, as the fragmentary nature of its inclusion allows, and linked to the equally fragmentary later references by Quentin and Jason to associations of strong drink and sex, becomes another thread in the fibrous structure of the sexual theme that gives coherence to Benjy's memories.

Faulkner's use of these three themes as controls over Benjy's consciousness shows how successfully he demonstrates in this first section the resolution of the principles of freedom and discipline, order and chaos. He has ingeniously circumvented the danger of formlessness to which he is exposed by his choice of an idiot as main character, and his use of the 'stream of consciousness' technique. The moulding influence of the thematic organizations of affection, death, and sex, in the Benjy section of *The Sound and Fury*, when extended as it is to the later sections of the book saves the author's material from the ever-present threat of incoherence that accompanies any treatment of direct human consciousness in the novel.

The 'drivellings' as Richard Hughes describes it of Benjy's mind are provided with a wider dimension when the reader becomes aware of the sort of family to which Benjy belongs. The impression that the Compson family is a deeply divided, disorganized group of people is strengthened by the additional perspective with which the distinctive forms of the consciousness of Benjy, Quentin, and Jason provide the reader. Their distinctive style of expression contributes strongly to the sense of alienation within the family. It is on this level of reading experience that the novel bears out Faulkner's dictum about its growing from day to day.

Yet while the reader is intensely aware of divisive factors at work within the Compson family, and never more so than when he contemplates in Benjy one whose congenital nature appears to condemn him to the extreme degree of disassociation, he also discovers that this centre of division is paradoxically an extremely integrated unit. Members of the family may be divided, but the Compsons present a family consciousness of certain codes and attitudes in which each member shares and which becomes more clearly defined with the growing process of family disintegration. It is by his treatment of the material of this family tradition that Faulkner again offers evidence of his ability to preserve a balance between individual autonomy and corporate identity.

He achieves this result in the first section by presenting Benjy, not only as an idiot, but as a Compson idiot whose reactions are very largely a reflection of Compson mentality. Luster draws attention to the fact when he remonstrates with Dilsey about his relationship to Benjy—'He ain't none of my uncle', and reminds the reader that there is involved here a blood-relationship with the Compson family. E. B. Burgam in his book, *William Faulkner—Patterns of American Decadence* expresses this point succinctly when he writes,—'Benjy's state of mind is only a distortion of the frame of mind of the rest of them.'

Benjy belongs to a family who believe it part of family pride that they should be responsible for the care and protection of their own members, especially if one is an imbecile. The evidence of this novel suggests that the family's concern for Benjy forms part of their moral conscience, and that he disturbs the deepest layers of family concern. Mrs. Compson regards the affliction of Benjy as a judgement upon her for the sin of pride. Caddy's attachment to Benjy is partly explained by his ability to make her aware of the moral implication of her love affairs. She shows that responsibility for Benjy's welfare weighs heavily upon her at the time of her marriage, and it is reasonable to assume that this concern is conditioned by her own sense of moral deficiency which she acknowledges when Quentin refers to it. Quentin is aware that he is kept at Harvard because the family has caused Benjy to suffer the injustice of the misappropriation of his pasture, and the thought of this family indifference to Benjy's welfare reinforces Quentin's decision to commit suicide. Jason's sense of family pride is outraged when he recalls Benjy running round the yard before the public gaze, and his vehement threat that Benjy will be sent to Jackson asylum draws some of its venom from an awareness that in wishing this to happen he is breaking with an established family tradition.

Faulkner solicits the reader's support for the view that Benjy is closely involved in the family by placing the idiot in the role of catalyst to the rest of the Compsons who are judged by their attitude towards Benjy. Caddy's character is largely redeemed by her protective attitude towards her brother. Part of Quentin's ineffectualness lies in his inability to fulfil Caddy's plea to look after Benjy. Jason's failure to establish any real personal relations is high-lighted by his brutal references to his brother and by his repeated threat to send Benjy to the asylum. Mrs. Compson's selfishness is nowhere more apparent than when she disassociates Benjy from her family by changing his name, and (at moments of distress when he needs a mother's attention) treats him merely as a nuisance, and leaves him to the inefficient charge of the negro servants. Mr. Compson's bonhomie towards his son is fitful and unsacrificial, corresponding with his general cynicism. The reader's sympathy which Quentin the niece arouses by her condition, starved of family affection, is alienated by her callousness towards her uncle.

Faulkner uses the time dimension in the novel to relate Benjy's life in the family to the growing declension of the Compson fortunes. The physical and moral deterioration of the family is marked by the passage of time, and Benjy functions as a kind of psychological time-piece which registers the pace of this decline. For example, Mrs. Compson refuses to face the reality of Benjy's condition and continues to treat him as a baby when he is physically as large as the fullgrown negro T.P. The reference to Benjy's size emphasizes Mrs. Compson's reluctance to face harsh facts. At five years, Benjy is too heavy to be carried, and Mrs. Compson's protest at Caddy's attempt to do this discloses the false conception of gentility that the Compsons represent. At thirteen, Benjy has to sleep in Uncle

Maury's room, an indication that with the departure from the house of the poor relative, there is a further breaking up of family life. At fifteen Benjy is referred to by the negro servant Roskus as a sign of the family's ill-starred destiny since both Quentin and Mr. Compson have recently died in pathetic circumstances. Benjy's adolescence is marred by his attack on the schoolgirl, and his consequent castration, a measure that in the light of subsequent comments upon it by Quentin and Jason symbolically draws attention to the family's diminished humanity.

The frequent references to Benjy's thirty-third birthday which coincides with Holy Saturday suggest the tomb-like existence of the family, which is symbolized throughout the novel by Mrs. Compson's darkened bedroom, by the dungeon in which Quentin imagines his family, by Mr. Compson's definition of time as a mausoleum and by Jason's headache which causes him temporary amnesia. The description of Benjy at the supper table 'as if even eagerness were muscle-bound in him too, and hunger inarticulate, not knowing it is hunger,' accords with the entombment of the Compson condition which offers its most pathetic example in the locked bedroom of the niece.

The decadence of the Compson family reveals its presence in the sense of doom that influences the conduct of all the members, and involves even Benjy, although unlike the others he is unaware of its nature. Mrs. Compson regards it simply in terms of inherited bad blood, and fears her favourite Jason may show early signs of infection from it. Mr. Compson generalizes it to include human nature under the image of the Diceman with the loaded dice. Quentin even from childhood regards his sister and himself as under a curse. Caddy and her daughter believe their nature is irretrievably bad, and Jason fears he may succumb to a family inheritance of abnormality which may affect even his putative marriage partner for as he says 'blood is blood, and you can't get around it.' The family doom when transferred to Benjy is recognized primarily through his role as victim. The reader is invited to see in this condition the essence of Benjy's nature, by the way in which Benjy is represented in archetypal terms. Quentin and Caddy remind the reader of the Biblical associations of his name—'Benjy came out of the Bible' Caddy said. 'Benjy the child of mine old age held hostage into Egypt. O Benjamin', recalls Quentin. Jason's references to 'geldings', to the Great American Gelding, to 'the star freshman' of 'the state asylum' to show his disgust with Benjy, emphasize a quality of monstrosity in his brother that, taken together with Mrs. Compson's belief that Benjy is a sign of divine judgement upon her, enlarges the concept of victim, so that Benjy becomes the very symbol of victimisation, and his wailing as Faulkner describes it 'might have been all time and injustice and sorrow' and 'the grave hopeless sound of all voiceless misery under the sun.'

However necessary Faulkner finds the need to symbolize Benjy's condition, he provides also the ever present concrete illustration of Benjy as victim through the relationship between him and Luster. Benjy's enforced dependence upon the whims of the negro receives an ironic twist of significance, when Luster inverts the true situation between him and Benjy by justifying his behaviour to Dilsey with the words, 'Don't I always does what he wants.' The truth about Benjy's status as victim is clearly seen when Luster appeals to Benjy as an equal partner in his misdemeanours, and so intensifies the reader's awareness of Benjy's incapacity to enjoy a normal relationship. Benjy's failure to achieve this discloses the same failure in human relationships that the Compson family exₓₚerience with each other. For most part of his existence, Benjy remains the passive recipient of Compson direction. He suffers the sadistic bouts of Luster who blows out his candles, disarranges his graveyard flowers, and alters his accustomed route to the cemetery. At his sister's wedding he is rendered drunk by the negro boys, and is led from pillar to post by a number of protectors in the family circle.

The Compsons are inclined to regard the world as a hostile place. Mrs. Compson is always promising to leave it by dying. Mr. Compson believes the power behind the universe has loaded the dice against man. Quentin arrives at a state of mind which experiences life as 'without relevance inherent . . . with the denial of significance it should have affirmed' and fears he may lose his sense of identity. Jason has a temporary hallucination in which the powers of heaven and hell, and Omnipotence Himself, are arraigned against him.

Benjy, too, shares in the Compson experience of hostility, but this hostility is encountered in a way consistent with his imbecility. It is the world of objects that opposes Benjy. In his drunken state 'the box jumped away and hit me on the back of the head.' Objects like fire, flowers, and candles have a life of their own. Their appearance and disappearance seem to be part of a design to distress Benjy.

A more subtle treatment of this theme of victim is involved in the use of the technique that Faulkner chooses in the section devoted to Benjy. Although the memories of Benjy are presented as the contents of an idiot's mind, and reflect the objective cast of Benjy's perception, they are not allowed to remain untouched in this form. To give them the desired significance which Benjy's limited mentality cannot provide, the author carries on where Benjy has to leave off. He relates events and characters to a time dimension. Because Benjy sees everything as present, he cannot visualize his experiences in terms of cause and effect, and does not recognize the relations between different events which a time sequence permits. So his memories have to be worked over by Faulkner before they surrender their real significance in the novel. This demands a wider context than that of an idiot's recollection. By retaining the contents of Benjy's mind the author draws out implications of which Benjy is unaware. One of the consequences of this treatment of material is that Benjy records situations and statements which become the media through which his own character is evaluated. This result is possible because Benjy has no self-awareness. He sometimes gives direct evidence of this incapacity, as when he regarded the movements of his body as though it operated apart from any centre of self-consciousness and was merely a part of the objective external world. When he burnt his hand this is how he describes the experience. 'My voice went louder then, and my hand tried to go back to my mouth but Dilsey held it.' Benjy introduces the topic of rain but is unaware of the implications it has for the family. For Quentin rain is associated with Caddy's promiscuity and his death wish. Jason regards rain as one of the many forms of frustration he has to endure. Rain at Mr. Compson's funeral provided Jason with a symbol of the general indifference of the family towards him. Quentin's remembrance of a saying of Dilsey that rain never hurt young folk suggests that rain is one of several moral gauges that marks the path of the Compson neurotic decline. Because Benjy is unable to reveal the nature of his own character, the author has to depend upon the observations of other characters to a far greater extent than the normal technique of a novel allows. As a result one is forced to conclude that by a technical sleight of hand, Benjy is put into the position of bearing witness against himself, since most of the remarks made about him are derogatory. The treatment of the victim theme, therefore, reaches a more profound level by the use of a technique where the first person narrator is deprived of any capacity for self-revelation although paradoxically he is presented by means of that most revealing of literary techniques, the stream of consciousness.

W. M. Frohock in *The Novel of Violence* points out that 'Faulknerian characters who narrate are under an unholy amount of stress . . . their constant apprehension over what is imminent constituting what amounts to a third temporal dimension'.

The Compson family exhibit this tension in a notable way. Mrs. Compson's outburst to Mr. Compson at Caddy's unladylike behaviour and her fear that the Compson blood is contagious, Quentin's last soliloquy as he is aware of his approaching suicide, Jason's feverish state of mind during his hunt for his niece who has gone for a jaunt in a car,—these are all states of mind in which tension is built up through a concern for the future. But this concern is not the only cause of such a tension. The characters mentioned are equally aware of a condition of family defection. Mrs. Compson recognizes in Caddy's conduct and her husband's indifference, the corrupting contagion of Compson blood. Quentin's last hours prompt the recall of Caddy's lust, his father's moral apathy, and the irony of Compson gentility. Jason feeds his sense of frustration on references to an endangered family reputation and to other sources of irritation with his family.

Benjy shares this family familiarity with tension, but in his own way. He indicates its presence by the use of his voice. His whole existence is punctuated by signals of distress, and marked by a rhythm of silence and sound. But his sensation of anxiety does not depend upon a foreboding of the future. However his reaction of unease is frequently aroused by events which contain the seed of future trouble. For example, Benjy is troubled by events like Caddy's absence, her love affair with Dalton Ames, her wedding, his niece's assignation with the showman of the red tie. In the context of the whole novel, these situations presage future trouble, and also mark stages in the family's decline. Benjy does not recognize the future consequences of these events or these implications for family decline. What he clearly recognizes, however, is the presence in an immediate situation of a disturbing element. He reacts to the full immediacy of an experience as though its future implications are sensed within its present context. Moreover, while he is unaware of decline, the consequences of decline, moral or physical disturb him. The loss of his pasture increases his desire to get away from the fenced garden. The removal of the wall mirror in which he found much consolation causes him to moan, and arouses in him so great a sense of loss that even a fetish object like Caddy's slipper fails to comfort him. He notices the emptiness of the dark room to which he retires with the slipper, now empty of the furniture that has been sold to pay Quentin's expenses at Harvard, and he will not be comforted. Although incapable of distinguishing between the natural and the unnatural in the deaths of Damuddy, Quentin, and Mr. Compson, he shows by his sharp protest at each that he has an intuitive grasp of the inevitability and future recurrence of death. As Roskus says of him 'He knowed they time was coming like that pointer done. He could tell when his'n coming, if he could talk. Or yours. Or mine.' With no comprehension of the future Benjy instinctively grasped the nature of Caddy's moral lapse and the consequences of distress implicit in it, by being able to apprehend its full impact through immediacy of experience. This exposure to the whole potential of an event is the source of Benjy's special kind of tension, and enables Faulkner to link Benjy's concern with what other Compsons feel when the same incident is later recalled by them.

Faulkner's treatment of Benjy's castration is an illustration of this. As Benjy relates the event that led to it and the effect of it the reader deduces that it symbolizes frustration ('I tried to get out') and the disorder of change, ('They're gone') for Benjy. When Quentin recalls an act of self-mutilation, he does so because he wishes to indulge in the fantasy of sexlessness to avoid the discomfort Caddy's loss of virginity has caused him; Jason recalls Benjy's castration, to marvel at the irrationality of Benjy's sense of frustration, and to suggest a way by which his brother would have been oblivious of the change. The recollection of Benjy's experience comes to both brothers in a context of deep dissatisfaction with women members of the family. Faulkner's understanding of Benjy's experience in terms of immediacy and latency enables him to use the very limitations of Benjy's perception and the consequent isolation of his condition to reveal the degree of the idiot's involvement in the tension-stricken sensitivity of the Compson family.

Another characteristic of the Compson mentality is that they declare their uneasiness about the growing dissolution of their family life by taking refuge in the realm of fantasy. Mrs. Compson withdraws into a world of faded gentility and hypochondriac seclusion whenever the real world intrudes too harshly.

Mr. Compson's cynicism creates a world of sawdust humanity, and personal insignificance in which ethical standards are reduced to a moral solipsism, and existence in such a world demands the support of the whisky bottle. Quentin dwells in a dream of romantic idealism which subjects him to a series of traumatic shocks when he faces the fact of sexual behaviour. Jason suffers from persecution mania which convinces him that the whole structure of the universe is organized against him when he goes in search of his niece. Caddy and her daughter Quentin escape from the lovelessness of their family into a world dominated by sex, where marriage becomes a necessity for Caddy and her school-girl daughter frantically tries to give herself an identity by 'crude and hopeless efforts to feminize' her bedroom.

One of the consequences of this family retreat into a world of make-believe is their inability to understand each other. Mr. Compson's indifference to moral values deludes him into believing that his son Quentin will not commit suicide. His trust in Caddy's maturity receives a shock when her pregnancy causes her husband to cast her off. Mrs. Compson showed herself incapable of understanding Benjy. She drove her daughter from home through failure to gain her confidence. She allowed Herbert her son-in-law to delude her about Jason's job in the bank, and she failed to realize that her favourite son was deceiving her.

Quentin suffered delusions about the intention of his schoolmate. He misunderstood Caddy's attitude towards virginity; he was confused about the identity of the Italian girl, and mixed up Gerald Bland with Dalton Ames. Jason was incapable of understanding his niece. He misconstrued the compassion of his employer, and the reactions of the sheriff, and misread the intention of the caravan dweller. He imagined that the church people were organized to frustrate him.

Benjy, too, inhabits a highly idiosyncratic world and experiences the consequent difficulty of achieving communication to which his congenital deaf and dumb condition, even if it is not so radical as Luster asserts, is an additional impediment. His vision involves a world of moving shapes that seem indistinguishable and of equal significance, whether they are encountered in a drunken condition, or as a result of a blow on the head, or become part of the scenery viewed from a moving carriage. Benjy appears to visualize the external world in a flat dimension in which people are reduced to objects of identical significance. For example, the passage in which Benjy watches Roskus milking at the barn is narrated in a toneless fashion which equates Roskus, birds, cows, T.P., horses and calf as mere components of a flat picture. Each element evokes the same lack of emotional response. Persons become significant by their association with natural environment—Versh smells like rain, Caddy smells like trees. Benjy also tends to confuse objects with their effects, as fire with firelight, sickness with impregnated cloth, fire with its mirrored reflection; impersonal objects are also given personality—'her rings were jumping,' 'wire came across my shoulder. It went to the door, and then the fire went away,' 'the cellar door and the moonlight jumped away and something hit me.' This distorted view of the objective world corresponds with Benjy's difficulty in achieving any real personal contact with others, a failure that Luster and Jason recognize when they downgrade Benjy to the animal level by calling him 'mule head' or 'gelding'. Benjy fails to distinguish between his niece at the swing, and Caddy in the same situation, although Caddy's reaction of affection is clearly different from the hostility Benjy's presence arouses in his niece. He confuses Caddy with the school girl outside the fence. He cannot distinguish between marriage and death, or between the three representatives of the separate Compson generations at their funerals. His response on each occasion is the same. That Faulkner wishes the reader to include Benjy in the family endowment of perverse vision is evident when we recognize that Quentin showed the same confusion between funeral and marriage (Shreve's remark about 'wedding or a wake' indicates this), and that he regarded negroes not as persons but as a form of behaviour, or when Jason is described as experiencing a situation through the same medium as Benjy—'he could almost smell it', and, like Benjy, finds the presage of impending disaster in the immediate experience.

Benjy's seemingly random perceptions, then, are rigorously controlled by their identification with the outlook of the Compson family, and in this way Faulkner attempts to resolve the paradox of freedom and control which his two dicta mentioned above pose for the reader of *The Sound and the Fury.*

In support of this resolution Faulkner calls in the aid of the novel's special technique. While he appears to restrict the viewpoint from which the reader may encounter the Compson family by making the introduction depend upon the limitations inherent in an idiot's perception, Benjy's inability to comprehend his experiences provides the characters who emerge from his recollection with an opportunity to present a wide variety of comment, and so to release the reader from the restrictions of Benjy's awareness. An example of the way in which even in a matter of subsidiary material, Faulkner overcomes this self-imposed confinement and can offer a many-angled vision is his treatment of the episode between Uncle Maury and Mrs. Patterson. Faulkner so arranges the material that the reader is enabled to follow the event from as many as six different points of view—Benjy's, Caddy's, Mr. Compson's, Mrs. Patterson's, Mr. Patterson's, and Uncle Maury's.

The 'stream of consciousness' technique employed in this novel by Faulkner, offers little initiative to characters introduced through this medium to contribute to the development of the narrative. While one cannot agree with Sartre's contention in his article 'Time in Faulkner' (*La nouvelle revue française*, June-July 1939) that there is no action in the novel—'nothing happens, everything has happened'—one recognizes that characters tend to appear and disappear from the story unexpectedly and at the whim of the narrator's train of associations. It is, indeed, this kind of activity that contributes so effectively to the reader's impression of a pervasive sound and fury in the novel. Yet at the same time, under these same fluid conditions, certain characters do recur with a sort of obsessional frequency. Caddy dominates the Benjy section and, if with diminishing force, the following sections. Benjy moves in and out of sight even in his own narration, and is certainly an object of concern throughout the Quentin and Jason sections. However limited Benjy's actions and experiences are throughout the book, he seems to nose his way through the awareness of the Compsons with disconcerting awkwardness. He provokes their attention, and as we have noticed, they are defined to a large extent by their reaction to his presence. In the early section Quentin and Jason are both endowed with a purposive role that comes to light only in the later sections of the book. Mrs. Compson's flitting through the narrative is an essential contribution to the weird atmosphere and tone of the Compson family. Mr. Compson's somewhat remote influence affects the attitudes of almost all the characters from Quentin's confused reliance, to Jason's sneering reminiscences.

By using the built-in pattern of repetition which the stream of consciousness technique supplies, Faulkner is able to give his characters a range of activity and influence which the restrictive nature of the technique would seem to rule out. At the same time Faulkner is providing one more thread by which to bind the loose amalgam of Compson memories.

Part of Faulkner's technique in this novel depends, as the context of the title suggests, upon his interest in the treatment of Time, a treatment which is deeply influenced by the paradox we have been considering. One explanation for the characters' surprising and often frenetic conduct is their peculiar attitude to Time. Benjy's unawareness of Time, except as the hearing of sound allows him to jumble events and people together in a quite arbitrary way. Quentin's struggles to forget Time give his narrative its spasmodic and desperate tone. Jason treats Time as part of life's general hostility towards him, and tries to combat it by excited rhetoric and restless activity. Mrs. Compson attempts to withdraw from it, and Mr. Compson turns it into an abstraction about which to philosophize.

The Compson symbol of Time is the one-handed kitchen clock which is always three hours slow and serves as a token of the irrational and temperamental attitude to life that a family ruled by impulse adopts.

While the reader is thus confronted with the unpredictable and somewhat anarchic behaviour of the Compsons, he is not allowed to forget the irrevocable and irresistible movement of Time within which the Compson destiny pursues its feverish way. The titles of each section make us aware of this. So do the frequent references to clocks and bells. There is a latent awareness in many of the characters that Time is an important factor with which to reckon. We become aware, behind the kaleidoscope of Benjy's impressions, that a particular day is moving from dawn to dusk with the sun registering, almost unnoticed, the passage of time. Then there are the seasonal changes to which the reader's attention is drawn, even though it be through the disorganized and erratic memory of the Compsons. All these details convey a sense of the inevitable direction in which the family is moving, from light to gloom, in spite of the uncoordinated efforts of the individual members, who in their search for identity and autonomy merely disturb the surface of the Compson destiny.

We conclude that even Time has been pressed into the author's service to aid him in continuing within artistic bounds the fluid material of human consciousness. The criterion of his success in this task is surely that the discipline of his control never destroys either the vitality or the volatile immediacy of the experience of his characters.

[The Composition of *The Sound and the Fury*]

Michael Millgate*

Perhaps the single most arresting fact about the manuscript of *The Sound and the Fury* is that the first page bears the undeleted title "Twilight."[1] Clearly the title was no more than tentative: it may, indeed, have been the title of the original short story from which the novel grew, and it is worth noting in this respect its closeness to "That Evening Sun Go Down," the quotation from W. C. Handy's "St. Louis Blues" used as the title of another story of the Compson children on its first publication. But it is interesting to speculate whether the title was intended to apply to the one section or to the work as a whole and on its possible breadth of reference in either case. As a title for the first section alone, "Twilight" would presumably refer to the half-world of Benjy himself, held in a state of timeless suspension between the light and the dark, comprehension and imcomprehension, between the human and the animal. As a title for the whole book, the word immediately suggests the decay of the Compson family caught at the moment when the dimmed glory of its eminent past is about to fade into ultimate extinction.

In Quentin's section, in particular, twilight, as a condition of light and a moment in time, takes on very considerable importance. In his most agonising recollections of Caddy, he sees her at twilight, sitting in the cleansing waters of the branch and surrounded by the scent of honeysuckle, and these three elements of the scene—the twilight, the water and the honeysuckle—take on an obsessive significance for Quentin himself and operate as recurrent symbols throughout this section of the novel. As water is associated with cleansing, redemption, peace and death, and the honeysuckle with warm Southern nights and Caddy's passionate sexuality, so twilight, "that quality of light as if time really had stopped for a while," becomes inextricably confused in Quentin's mind with the scents of water and of honeysuckle until "the whole thing came to symbolise night and unrest." Quentin continues:

> I seemed to be lying neither asleep nor awake looking down a long corridor of grey halflight where all stable things had become shadowy

*Reprinted, with permission, from *The Achievement of William Faulkner* (London: Constable, 1965), pp. 86–103, 313–14.

paradoxical all I had done shadows all I had felt suffered taking visible form antic and perverse mocking without relevance inherent themselves with the denial of the significance they should have affirmed thinking I was I was not who was not was not who.[2]

This passage would seem to be central to the meaning both of the particular section and of the book as a whole. There has just been a momentary anticipation of Quentin's carefully planned final release through death by water—travelling back into Cambridge he becomes aware of "the road going on under the twilight, into twilight and the sense of water peaceful and swift beyond"—and we realise that Quentin himself is at this moment not merely mid-way between sanity and madness but precisely poised between waking and sleeping, between life and death.[3] His world has become in fact "shadowy paradoxical"—we have just seen his actual fight with Gerald Bland overlaid in his consciousness by his remembered fight with Dalton Ames—and, for all the apparent orderliness of his actions, he has finally lost his sense of personal identity ("thinking I was I was not who was not was not who"). The passage, in this respect, seems also to relate directly to the passage in *Macbeth* from which Faulkner took his final title for the book, and specifically to its descriptions of life as "a walking shadow," a tale "signifying nothing."

The phrase about "all stable things" becoming "shadowy paradoxical" aptly defines the hallucinatory world of the Quentin section, but it is also relevant to the treatment of "fact," of "truth," throughout the novel. Like *Absalom, Absalom!*, *The Sound and the Fury* is in part concerned with the elusiveness, the multivalence, of truth, or at least with man's persistent and perhaps necessary tendency to make of truth a personal thing: each man, apprehending some fragment of the truth, seizes upon that fragment as though it were the whole truth and elaborates it into a total vision of the world, rigidly exclusive and hence utterly fallacious. This forms an essential part of the conception which Faulkner dramatised through the interior monologues of the first three sections of *The Sound and the Fury*, and the novel might thus be considered as in some sense a development, much richer than anything of which Anderson himself was capable, of the "theory of the grotesque" propounded at the beginning of *Winesburg, Ohio*:

> The old man has listed hundreds of the truths in his book. . . . There was the truth of virginity and the truth of passion, the truth of wealth and of poverty, of thrift and of profligacy, of carelessness and abandon. Hundreds and hundreds were the truths and they were all beautiful.
>
> And then the people came along. Each as he appeared snatched up one of the truths and some who were quite strong snatched up a dozen of them.
>
> It was the truths that made the people grotesques. The old man had quite an elaborate theory concerning the matter. It was his notion that the moment one of the people took one of the truths to himself, called it his

truth, and tried to live his life by it, he became a grotesque and the truth he embraced became a falsehood.[4]

Faulkner admired *Winesburg, Ohio*, and there is a discernible similarity between Anderson's conception of Winesburg and Faulkner's creation of Jefferson, the town which he had begun somewhat painstakingly to lay out in *Sartoris* and which in *The Sound and the Fury* is for the first time integrated into the structure and action of the novel. In 1925 Faulkner especially praised *Winesburg, Ohio* for its "ground of fecund earth and corn in the green spring and the slow, full hot summer and the rigorous masculine winter that hurts it not, but makes it stronger";[5] he praised it, that is to say, for just that recurrent evocation of the land and the moving seasons which he himself achieved in *Soldiers' Pay* and *Sartoris* and which is also present, though less pesistently and much less obviously, in *The Sound and the Fury*. Some of the time-levels in the Benjy section can be identified by their allusions to the cold, the rain, and so on, while Quentin, in his section, is intensely aware, with the heightened sensitivity of a man about to die, of the countryside through which he walks:

> In the orchard the bees sounded like a wind getting up, a sound caught by a spell just under crescendo and sustained. The lane went along the wall, arched over, shattered with bloom, dissolving into trees. Sunlight slanted into it, sparse and eager. Yellow butterflies flickered along the shade like flecks of sun. (p. 151)

Jason, as might be expected, shows no such sensitivity, but in the final section both the settings of the action and the changing weather of that particular day are very precisely described, and throughout the novel such evocations of place, of climate, of seasonal change are among the many elements which anchor action and meaning firmly to the human level.

The notation of manners in the novel is not especially rich, nor is any particular attention given to the detailed creation of scene and setting, but in the third and fourth sections, at least, there exists a sense of a social and physical environment that is more than adequate to counteract the metaphysical elements in the novel's thematic material, to prevent its explorations of human grotesquerie from wandering into the fantastic, as so often happens in the work of Carson McCullers, Flannery O'Connor and other Southern writers. No account of *The Sound and the Fury* can afford to undervalue those elements for which, primarily, we read the book and which seem clearly to have been most important to Faulkner himself—its powerful image of a family in disunion and decay, its presentation of the tragedy of "two lost women," of Caddy and her daughter. "Art is simpler than people think," wrote Faulkner to Cowley[6] and, highly sophisticated literary craftsman though he was, he never lost sight of the essential fact that technique alone is meaningless, that it achieves value only insofar as it serves to evoke, define and illuminate the human situation.

It was at the Nagano Seminar in 1955 that Faulkner gave his fullest account of how *The Sound and the Fury* came to be written:

> That began as a short story, it was a story without plot, of some children being sent away from the house during the grandmother's funeral. They were too young to be told what was going on and they saw things only incidentally to the childish games they were playing, which was the lugubrious matter of removing the corpse from the house, etc., and then the idea struck me to see how much more I could have got out of the idea of the blind, self-centeredness of innocence, typified by children, if one of those children had been truly innocent, that is, an idiot. So the idiot was born and then I became interested in the relationship of the idiot to the world that he was in but would never be able to cope with and just where could he get the tenderness, the help, to shield him in his innocence. I mean 'innocence' in the sense that God had stricken him blind at birth, that is, mindless at birth, there was nothing he could ever do about it. And so the character of his sister began to emerge, then the brother, who, that Jason (who to me represented complete evil. He's the most vicious character in my opinion I ever thought of), then he appeared. Then it needs the protagonist, someone to tell the story, so Quentin appeared. By that time I found out I couldn't possibly tell that in a short story. And so I told the idiot's experience of that day, and that was incomprehensible, even I could not have told what was going on then, so I had to write another chapter. Then I decided to let Quentin tell his version of that same day, or that same occasion, so he told it. Then there had to be the counterpoint, which was the other brother, Jason. By that time it was completely confusing. I knew that it was not anywhere near finished and then I had to write another section from the outside with an outsider, which was the writer, to tell what had happened on that particular day. And that's how the book grew. That is, I wrote that same story four times. None of them were right, but I had anguished so much that I could not throw any of it away and start over, so I printed it in the four sections. That was not a deliberate *tour de force* at all, the book just grew that way. That I was still trying to tell one story which moved me very much and each time I failed, but I had put so much anguish into it that I couldn't throw it away, like the mother that had four bad children, that she would have been better off if they all had been eliminated, but she couldn't relinquish any of them. And that's the reason I have the most tenderness for that book, because it failed four times.[7]

A number of points here demand discussion. In the first place, there is a good deal of evidence to support Faulkner's statement that the novel began as a short story. Maurice Coindreau recalls Faulkner telling him:

> "Ce roman, à l'origine, ne devait être qu'une nouvelle, me dit, un jour, William Faulkner. J'avais songé qu'il serait intéressant d'imaginer les pensées d'un groupe d'enfants, le jour de l'enterrement de leur grand'mère dont on leur a caché la mort, leur curiosité devant l'agitation de la maison, leurs efforts pour percer le mystère, les suppositions qui leur viennent à l'esprit."[8]

It was to be a story, therefore, similar in conception to "That Evening Sun," in which the Compson children are again placed in a situation whose adult significance they do not fully comprehend; Faulkner published the story in March 1931, and he had written it, at the very latest, by October 1930.[9] With this in mind we can quite readily disentangle from the opening section of *The Sound and the Fury*, where they occur in chronological and logical sequence, the sometimes quite widely separated fragments of a short story, "without plot," describing the experiences of the Compson children on the night of their grandmother's funeral; it is in the course of this material, moreover, that we first meet the image of Caddy's muddy drawers—seen from below as she clambers up the tree outside the Compson house in order to see what is happening inside—which, on other occasions, Faulkner spoke of as the basic image from which the whole book originated.

Faulkner told his Japanese audience that he used no notes in writing *The Sound and the Fury*, and certainly none seem to have survived. It is astounding that the complexities of the Benjy section should have been accomplished without recourse to notes, but Faulkner was clearly capable of such feats: the whole of *As I Lay Dying*, for instance, was apparently written without notes and with little subsequent revision, the whole thing completely pre-conceived and then written out in a single creative burst, while the appearance in *Sartoris* of embryonic versions of many scenes and episodes not fully developed, so far as we can tell, until many years afterwards, is sufficient evidence of the clarity and ambitiousness of Faulkner's conceptualising powers. The Benjy section, however, seems to have been evolved under creative pressure, not conceived beforehand. All Faulkner's accounts of the creation of *The Sound and the Fury* agree in stressing the extent to which the novel grew as his imagination worked upon it, its scope and meaning expanding irresistibly outwards, and the degree to which he allowed it to develop—giving no thought to its commercial prospects—in the directions which the themes and the material seemed to demand. Faulkner was hardly accurate in speaking of Quentin as telling "his version of that day, or that same occasion," but there is some overlapping of the events which Benjy and Quentin experience or recall, and their interior monologues certainly illuminate the same fundamental situation—the plight of the Compson family, with its vigorous past, its pathetically inadequate present, and its manifest lack of any future.

The pattern established by Faulkner's disposition of the novel's four sections can be viewed in a number of different ways, and they have been seen, for example, as exemplifying different levels of consciousness, different modes of apprehension or cognition, contrasted states of innocence and experience; M. Coindreau speaks of them as four movements of a symphony.[10] All these elements are present, and there is an overall movement outwards from Benjy's intensely private world to the fully public and social world of the fourth section. The pattern, however, is not solely progressive: despite the superficial affinities between the first and second sections on the one hand and the third and fourth sections on the other, the most fundamental relationships would seem to be those between the first and last sections, which offer a high degree of objectivity, and between the second and third, which are both intensely subjective. Benjy is a first-person narrator, as are Quentin and Jason, but his observations do not pass through an intelligence which is capable of ordering, and hence distorting, them; he reports the events of which he is a spectator, and even those in which he is himself a participator, with a camera-like fidelity. His view of Caddy, it is true, is highly personal, but we infer this view from the scenes which his camera-mind records; Benjy does not himself interpret this or other situations and events; still less does he attempt to impose a biassed interpretation upon the reader, as, in effect, do Quentin and Jason. Nor does he himself judge people, although he becomes the instrument by which the other characters are judged, their behaviour towards him serving as a touchstone of their humanity.

Faulkner seems to have worked gradually towards the convention of pure objectivity which he follows in the Benjy section, and it is interesting to see the trend of his revisions, between manuscript and published work, to the well-known scene in which Benjy burns his hand. The incident begins in the manuscript as follows:

> "Ow, mammy," Luster said. "Ow, mammy." I put my hand out to the firedoor.
> "Don't let him!" Dilsey said, "Catch him back." My hand jerked back and I put it in my mouth, and Dilsey caught me. I could still hear the clock between the times when my voice was going. Dilsey reached back and hit Luster on the head.
> "Git that soda," she said. She took my hand out of my mouth. My voice went louder then. I tried to put it back, but Dilsey held it. She sprinkled soda on it. "Look in the pantry . . ."[11]

The published text reads as follows:

> "Ow, mammy." Luster said. "Ow, mammy."
> I put my hand out to where the fire had been.
> "Catch him." Dilsey said. "Catch him back."
> My hand jerked back and I put it in my mouth and Dilsey caught me. I could still hear the clock between my voice. Dilsey reached back and hit Luster on the head. My voice was going loud every time.
> "Get that soda." Dilsey said. She took my hand out of my mouth. My voice went louder then and my hand tried to go back to my mouth, but Dilsey held it. My voice went loud. She sprinkled soda on my hand.
> "Look in the pantry . . ." (p. 72)

A similar process of revision can be seen in the last paragraph of the section, which opens on page 33 of the manuscript as follows:

> Father went to the door and stood with his hand on the light button. He
> looked at us again, and the light went off and he turned black in the door.
> Then the door turned black. Caddy held me . . .

Benjy would scarcely have been capable of the linking of cause and effect
implicit in "light button," and in the book this passage becomes:

> Father went to the door and looked at us again. Then the dark came
> back, and he stood black in the door, and then the door turned black
> again. Caddy held me . . . (p. 22)

Such changes, though interesting, are of a minor kind, and they are
typical in this of many of the revisions which Faulkner made to the
original manuscript version of the first section.

Some of the revisions are more substantial, however, and it will be
useful to look more closely at the changes made between the manuscript
of the novel and the bound carbon typescript, both now in the Alderman
Library at the University of Virginia. Several of the discrepancies between
these two versions reveal Faulkner working towards what was to prove at
once an elaboration and a simplification of his technique in the opening
section of the book. Thus the first page of the manuscript lacks all the
references to Luster's hunting in the grass for his lost quarter and to the
fact that the day is Benjy's birthday which appear in the typescript and on
pages 1 and 2 of the published text, and in the manuscript version as a
whole there is an almost total absence of material relating to Luster's
search for the quarter, to his desire to go to the show, to Benjy's birthday
or to Benjy's age. Faulkner presumably realised before or during the process of reworking the first section that the allusions to Benjy's birthday
and, still more, to Luster's search for the missing quarter, could be made
to serve as a kind of motif or signal of present time in the section and thus
assist the reader in keeping his bearings among the shifting and merging
time-planes. At a later stage still, in correcting the proofs of the book,
Faulkner attempted to provide another kind of assistance to the reader by
the addition of further italicisation to indicate points at which a shift of
scene was taking place.

In both manuscript and typescript Faulkner had indicated by means
of underlining that he wished the breaks in time sequence within the
Benjy section to be suggested by changes back and forth between roman
and italic type: it seems not to have been his intention that all such breaks
should be accompanied by a type change, but rather that occasional
italicisation should alert the reader to the kind of process going on in
Benjy's mind.[12] In his admirable article on the textual history of the
novel, James B. Meriwether has shown that when Faulkner received the
galley proofs from Cape and Smith he found that considerable editorial
changes had been made in the first section, apparently by his friend and
literary agent, Ben Wasson, whom Cape and Smith had recently appointed as an assistant editor. In particular, the device of italicisation had

been abandoned and replaced by the insertion of breaks in the text (i.e. wider spaces between lines) at points where breaks in the time sequence occurred.[13] Wasson had presumably defended his action on the grounds that italicisation permitted the differentiation of only two dates, whereas at least four distinct times were actually involved. Faulkner replied, rejecting these arguments and explaining why he had restored the italics as they had appeared in his typescript and even added a few more in order to avoid obscurity; his letter, forcefully phrased, reveals beyond all question the absolute self-confidence and intellectual clarity with which he regarded the finished novel and the technical experimentation which it embodied:

> I received the proof. It seemed pretty tough to me, so I corrected it as written, adding a few more italics where the original seemed obscure on second reading. Your reason for the change, i.e., that with italics only 2 different dates were indicated I do not think sound for 2 reasons. First, I do not see that the use of breaks clarifies it any more; Second, there are more than 4 dates involved. The ones I recall off-hand are:—Damuddy dies. Benjy is 3. (2) His name is changed. He is 5. (3) Caddy's wedding. He is 14. (4) He tries to rape a young girl and is castrated. 15. (5) Quentin's death. (6) His father's death. (7) A visit to the cemetary [sic] at 18 (7). [sic] The day of the anecdote, he is 33. These are just a few I recall, so your reason explodes itself.
>
> But the main reason is, a break indicates an objective change in tempo, while the objective picture here should be a continuous whole, since the thought transference is subjective; i.e., in Ben's mind and not in the reader's eye. I think italics are necessary to establish for the reader Benjy's confusion; that unbroken-surfaced confusion of an idiot which is outwardly a dynamic and logical coherence. To gain this, by using breaks it will be necessary to write an induction for each tranference. I wish publishing was advanced enough to use colored ink for such, as I argued with you and Hal [Harrison Smith] in the speak-easy that day. But the form in which you now have it is pretty tough. It presents a most dull and poorly articulated picture to my eye. If something must be done, it were better to re-write this whole section objectively, like the 4th section. I think it is rotten, as is. But if you wont have it so, I'll just have to save the idea until publishing grows up to it. Anyway, change all the italics. You overlooked one of them. Also, the parts written in italics will all have to be punctuated again. You'd better see to that, since you're all for coherence. And dont make any more additions to the script, bud. I know you mean well, but so do I. I effaced the 2 or 3 you made.

*   *   *

> I hope you will think better of this. Your reason above disproves itself. I purposely used italics for both actual scenes and remembered scenes for the reason, not to indicate the different dates of happenings, but merely to permit the reader to anticipate a thought-transference, letting the recollection postulate its own date. Surely you see this.[14]

In reworking the manuscript version of the second section Faulkner made far more extensive additions and revisions than in the preceding section. This becomes immediately clear from a comparison between the opening paragraph of the manuscript and the corresponding passage in the published book. The manuscript reads:

> The shadow of the sash fell across the curtains between 7 and 8 oclock, and then I was hearing the watch [sic] again, and I lay there looking at the sinister bar across the rosy and motionless curtains, listening to the watch. Hearing it, that is. I dont suppose anybody deliberately listens to a watch or a clock. You dont have to. You can be oblivious to the sound for a long while, then in a second of ticking it can create in the mind unbroken the long diminishing parade of time you did not hear. Where up the long and lonely arrowing of light rays you might see Jesus walking, like. The true Son of Man: he had no sister. Nazarene and Roman and Virginian, they had no sister one minute she was
>
> Beyond the wall Shreve's bedsprings complained thinly, . . .[15]

Here for comparison, are the opening paragraphs of section two in the published book:

> When the shadow of the sash appeared on the curtains it was between seven and eight oclock and then I was in time again, hearing the watch. It was Grandfather's and when Father gave it to me he said, Quentin, I give you the mausoleum of all hope and desire; it's rather excrutiating-ly apt that you will use it to gain the reducto absurdum of all human experience which can fit your individual needs no better than it fitted his or his father's. I give it to you not that you may remember time, but that you might forget it now and then for a moment and not spend all your breath trying to conquer it. Because no battle is ever won he said. They are not even fought. The field only reveals to man his own folly and despair, and victory is an illusion of philosophers and fools.
>
> It was propped against the collar box and I lay listening to it. Hearing it, that is. I dont suppose anybody ever deliberately listens to a watch or a clock. You dont have to. You can be oblivious to the sound for a long while, then in a second of ticking it can create in the mind unbroken the long diminishing parade of time you didn't hear. Like Father said down the long and lonely light-rays you might see Jesus walking, like. And the good Saint Francis that said Little Sister Death, that never had a sister.
>
> Through the wall I heard Shreve's bed-springs . . . (pp. 93–94)

Faulkner's alterations achieve certain improvements in phrasing and elaborate the insistence on time, but perhaps the most interesting of the new elements are the references to Mr. Compson. Throughout the section, as revised in the carbon typescript and the published book, Quentin's mind runs on his father almost as much as it does on Caddy. Quentin is, of course, very much like his father in many ways, and in his obsession with family tradition and honour it is understandable that he should refer to his father, the head of the family, as a transmitter of that tradition and as a source of authority and advice. The irony of this situation, however, and a major cause of Quentin's tragedy, is that just as his mother has failed him as a source of love so his father fails him utterly in all his roles of progenitor, confessor and counsellor. He has become, indeed, Quentin's principal enemy, his cold and even cynical logic persistently undermining the very basis of all those idealistic concepts to which Quentin so passionately holds. Throughout the section there is a battle in progress between Quentin's romantic idealism and Mr. Compson's somewhat cynical realism, a battle which is not finally resolved in *The Sound and the Fury* and which is resumed on an even larger scale in *Absalom, Absalom!*. Indeed, if we are to understand that the discussion between Quentin and his father at the end of the section is purely a figment of Quentin's imagination and never actually took place, then it has to be said that in *The Sound and the Fury* the battle is never properly joined—as, according to Mr. Compson himself, no battle ever is—and that it is, rather, a series of skirmishes in which Quentin suffers a progressive erosion of his position and a steady depletion of his reserves. Father and son are, in any case, too much alike in their fondness for words, for abstractions, and in choosing to evade life—the one in drink, the other in suicide—rather than actively confront it.

Whenever Quentin acts, his concern is for the act's significance as a gesture rather than for its practical efficacy. He seeks pertinaciously for occasions to fight in defence of his sister's honour, knowing in advance that he will be beaten and concerned in retrospect only that he has performed the act in its ritualistic and symbolic aspects. It is the fight with Gerald Bland which reveals most clearly the degree to which Quentin's obsessions have divorced him from actuality since throughout the struggle it is the remembered fight with Dalton Ames which remains for Quentin the superior reality. Throughout a whole day of quite extraordinary incident—with two fights, an arrest, a court hearing, much movement and many encounters—Quentin's mind remains preoccupied with the past. It is almost as though Faulkner were playing on the idea that a drowning man sees his whole life pass before him, and we come to realise that this last day of Quentin's is a kind of suspended moment before death.

Quentin's own obsession with time derives primarily from his recognition of it as the dimension in which change occurs and in which Caddy's actions have efficacy and significance. His search is for a means of arresting time at a moment of achieved perfection, a moment when he and Caddy could be eternally together in the simplicity of their childhood relationship; his idea of announcing that he and Caddy had committed incest was, paradoxically, a scheme for regaining lost innocence:

> it was to isolate her out of the loud world so that it would have to flee us of necessity and then the sound of it would be as though it had never

been . . . if i could tell you we did it would have been so and then the
others wouldnt be so and then the world would roar away . . . (p. 220)

The similarity between this conception and the image of motion in stasis
which haunted Faulkner throughout his life, expecially as embodied in
Keats's "Ode on a Grecian Urn," suggests—as do the echoes of Joyce—that
Quentin is in some measure a version of the artist, or at least the aesthete,
as hero. But Quentin's conception is artificial, rigid, life-denying: as Mr.
Compson observes, "Purity is a negative state and therefore contrary to
nature. It's nature is hurting you not Caddy . . ." (p. 143) The inadequacy of Quentin's position is exposed in terms of Caddy and her vitality
and humanity. In the Benjy section we recognise Caddy as the principal
sustainer of such family unity as survives: we glimpse her as the liveliest
spirit among the children and their natural leader, as the protector and
comforter of Benjy, and even as the pacifier of her mother, and it is highly
significant for us as well as for Benjy that she is persistently associated
with such elemental things as the fire, the pasture, the smell of trees, and
sleep. Her sexual freedom appears as the expression of a natural rebellion
against the repressive, contradictory, and essentially self-centred
demands made upon her by the different members of her family; it certainly seems spontaneous and affirmative by the side of Quentin's
fastidious or even impotent avoidance of sexual experience—we note, for
example, his revulsion at his childish experiments with Natalie and the
fact that he is known at Harvard for his indifference to women—or
Jason's rigid compartmentalisation of his sexual life and strict subordina-
tion of it to his financial interests.

Caddy finds an outlet from family repression in sexual activity, but
she is also both a principle and a symbol of social disruption. Her assertion
of individuality is much less positive and urgent than that of such a
character as Ursula Brangwen in D. H. Lawrence's *The Rainbow*; even
so, she is brought, like Ursula, to break with traditional patterns and, in
so doing, to demonstrate just how moribund those patterns have become,
how irrelevant both to modern conditions and to the needs of the human
psyche. It is possible to feel, however, that although Caddy is the core of
the book she is not herself a wholly successful creation. Faulkner often
spoke of Caddy, outside the novel, with an intensely passionate devotion:
"To me she was the beautiful one," he said at the University of Virginia,
"she was my heart's darling. That's what I wrote the book about and I
used the tools which seemed to me the proper tools to try to tell, try to
draw the picture of Caddy."[16] The original image of the little girl with the
muddy drawers grew into the rich and complex conception of Caddy,
beautiful and tragic both as child and as woman, but although this conception is already present in the first section of the novel it is evoked,
necessarily, in somewhat fragmentary fashion, as we glimpse Caddy in
various family situations, as we sense how much she means to Benjy, as

e to associate her, through Benjy, with images of brightness, com-
d loss. In the second section Caddy is more clearly visible, and
    are passages of remembered dialogue as revealing of Caddy's
character as of Quentin's, but the world of Quentin's section is so
unstable, so hallucinatory, that the figure of Caddy, like so much else, is
enveloped in uncertainty. In Jason's section Caddy's agony is most mov-
ingly evoked, but only briefly so, while in the final section of the book she
is no more than a memory.

It was an essential element in Faulkner's overall conception of the
novel that Caddy never be seen directly but only through the eyes of her
three brothers, each with his own self-centred demands to make upon her,
each with his own limitations and obsessions. Asked at Virginia why he
did not give a section to Caddy herself, Faulkner replied that it seemed
more "passionate" to do it through her brothers, and one is reminded of
his remarks at Nagano about the beauty of description by understatement
and indirection: "Remember, all Tolstoy said about Anna Karenina was
that she was beautiful and could see in the dark like a cat. That's all he
ever said to describe her. And every man has a different idea of what's
beautiful. And it's best to take the gesture, the shadow of the branch, and
let the mind create the tree."[17] It certainly seems likely that to have made
Caddy a "voice" in the novel would have diminished her importance as a
central, focal figure. As the book stands, however, Caddy emerges im-
completely from the first two sections, and in the last two attention shifts
progressively from her to her daughter, Quentin. The different limitations in the viewpoints of Benjy, Quentin and Jason make unavoidable the
shadowiness, the imprecision, of Caddy's presentation: because the mind
of each is so closed upon its own obsessions it is scarcely true to speak of
their interior monologues as throwing light upon Caddy from a variety of
angles; it is rather as though a series of photographs in differing focus
were superimposed one upon the other, blurring all clarity of outline or
detail. The novel revolves upon Caddy, but Caddy herself escapes
satisfactory definition, and her daughter's tragedy, simply because it is
more directly presented, is in some ways more moving.

It is characteristic that Jason should be the only member of the
Compson family who is able to cope with the practical and social implications of Caddy's defection. Where Mrs. Compson can only moistly complain, Benjy bellow his incomprehending grief, Quentin commit suicide,
Jason can adjust himself to the situation and turn it to his own advantage
and profit. Jason—the one Compson who was capable of meeting Snopes
on his own ground, as Faulkner wrote to Malcolm Cowley[18]—becomes in
this way the representative of the new commercial South, and his section
strikes a specifically contemporary note in its evocation of the petty
business man, with Jason himself appearing, in this role, as a typical
figure, sharing the fundamental characteristics of a legion of other small
businessmen in North and South alike. It is perhaps for this reason that

Jason's seems much the least "Southern" of the sections. If it also seems the most readily detachable section—it was the one which Faulkner first suggested for inclusion in *The Portable Faulkner*[19]—that is a measure of the degree to which Jason's singleminded and ruthless pursuit of material self-interest serves to isolate him not only from his family but from the community as a whole. The attitude of Jefferson towards Jason is sufficiently revealed through the reactions of such characters as Earl, Job, and, in the final section, the sheriff, while Jason's opinion of Jefferson is amply expressed in statements such as the following: "Like I say if all the business in a town are run like country businesses, you're going to have a country town." His contempt for the town is only exceeded by his contempt for his own family, its history and its pretensions:

> Blood, I says, governors and generals. It's a damn good thing we never had any kings and presidents; we'd all be down there at Jackson chasing butterflies. (p. 286)[20]

Since Jason's instincts are commercial and materialistic, they are also anti-rural and anti-traditional: his is a willed deracination from the community in which he continues to live. As we have seen, however, it is this very materialism and deracination which makes Jason the one male Compson with any practical competence.

The progression from Benjy's section through Quentin's to Jason's is accompanied by an increasing sense of social reality: Benjy is remote in his idiocy and innocence, Quentin moves from the isolation of his half-mad idealism into the total withdrawal of suicide, but Jason is wholly in the world, acutely sensitive to social values, swimming with the contemporary commercial current. The action of the novel is thus presented increasingly in terms of social, economic and political perspectives; it is Jason who first refers, however ironically, to the family's more distinguished past, and it is not until the last section of the novel that we are first given an image of the Compson house in all it decrepitude. To interpret *The Sound and the Fury* simply as a socio-economic study of the decline of a Southern family is obviously inadequate; what can be said is that this is one of the novel's many aspects, and one which becomes increasingly important as the book proceeds. It seems possible that Faulkner felt that he had created the social context of the action in insufficient detail, that the book did not clearly evoke the patterns of manners and customs within which his characters moved: the Compson "Appendix" he wrote for *The Portable Faulkner* is devoted partly to clarifying the meaning of the novel at certain points but primarily to the elaboration of the Compsons' family history and to the further definition of their place in the social and economic life of Jefferson. It is in the Appendix, too, that we find the abundantly particularised description of the farmers' suppy store which Jason now owns and which Miss Melissa Meek valiantly enters, striding on through that gloomy cavern which only men ever entered—a cavern cluttered and walled and stalagmite-hung with plows and discs and loops of tracechain and singletrees and mule-collars and sidemeat and cheap shoes and horse liniment and flour and molasses, gloomy because the goods it contained were not shown but hidden rather since those who supplied Mississippi farmers, or at least Negro Mississippi farmers, for a share of the crop did not wish, until that crop was made and its value approximately computable, to show them what they could learn to want, but only to supply them on specific demand with what they could not help but need—and strode on back to Jason's particular domain in the rear: a railed enclosure cluttered with shelves and pigeon-holes bearing spiked dust-and-lint-gathering gin receipts and ledgers and cotton samples and rank with the blended smell of cheese and kerosene and harness oil and the tremendous iron stove against which chewed tobacco had been spat for almost a hundred years, . . .[21]

This was the kind of thing which Faulkner had done superbly in *The Hamlet* and *Go Down, Moses*, and it is possible to think that *The Sound and the Fury* would have been strengthened by some such stiffening, by a richer notation of setting and social context. Faulkner wrote the book from within the comprehensive conception of the world of Jefferson which he had already achieved and amply demonstrated in *Sartoris*, and he may have underestimated the extent to which it was desirable to recreate this world for the reader of *The Sound and the Fury*. It is noteworthy, at any rate, that in subsequent novels such as *As I Lay Dying, Light in August, Absalom, Absalom!, The Hamlet*, and *Go Down, Moses*, Faulkner seems quite deliberately to create setting and context, in both physical and social terms, at a very early stage of the book, evoking and defining the situation almost in the manner of Balzac or Hardy before proceeding to the main action.

It must be admitted that each of the first three sections of *The Sound and the Fury* has about it some suggestion of the *tour de force:* the Quentin section seems a deliberate exercise in the Joycean mode, while the Jason section raises to the level of art the self-revelatory interior monologue of the unimaginative man which Sinclair Lewis had developed in *Babbitt* and *The Man Who Knew Coolidge*, published in 1922 and 1928 respectively. The Benjy section seems to have been more exclusively Faulker's invention, a deliberate attempt to extend the boundaries of the novel beyond the point to which Joyce had already pushed them. Yet Faulkner never regarded the book as a *tour de force*; unlike *As I Lay Dying, The Sound and the Fury* was a book which grew and developed as he worked upon it, and his adoption in the final section of the point of view of the omniscient author seems to have been forced upon him not by the demands of a deliberate design but by the more immediate pressures stemming from an urgent need for self-expression.

In various accounts of the writing of *The Sound and the Fury*

Faulkner says that having failed in three attempts to tell the story, to rid himself of the "dream," he had tried in the final section to pull the whole novel together, retelling the central story more directly and clearly.[22] In fact, the section contributes relatively little to our understanding of the narrative events touched upon in earlier sections; rather it forces us to view some aspects of those earlier sections in a radically different way. Simply by giving us for the first time detailed physical descriptions of Dilsey, Benjy, Jason and Mrs. Compson, Faulkner—playing on some of the most fundamental of human responses to storytelling—effectively modifies our feelings towards them. Simply by recreating in such detail the routine of Dilsey's day, evoking the qualities demanded in performing such duties in a household such as that of the Compsons', Faulkner allows her to emerge for the first time both as a fully-drawn character and as a powerful positive presence. When the action shifts to Jason and his vain pursuit of Quentin we notice that many of his experiences have something in common with Quentin's experiences during the last day of his life—there are, for example, the journeyings back and forth, the moments of violence, the unsatisfactory brushes with the representatives of the law—and we come finally to recognise that, for all the differences between them, both brothers display a similar obsessiveness and fundamental irrationality.

We read the fourth section in the emotional, as well as thematic and narrative, context of its three predecessors. The last of these, Jason's section, has been sustained on a scarcely varied note of savage bitterness, and imbedded within it have been some of the most painful incidents in the book, notably those in which Jason frustrates Caddy's frantic attempts to see her child; only the flashes of brilliantly sardonic humour have prevented its final effect from being one of total negation. It is therefore tempting, in the final section, to see in the immensely positive figure of Dilsey, and the importance given to her, a certain overall reassurance and even serenity; but although the section does contain positives which to some extent off-set the negations of the previous sections it would be too much to say that the novel closes on a note of unqualified affirmation. Dilsey "endures," but her endurance is tested not in acts of spectacular heroism but in her submission to the tedious, trivial and wilfully inconsiderate demands made upon her by the Compson family, as when Mrs. Compson allows her to make her painful way upstairs to tend to Benjy before telling her that he is not yet awake:

> Mrs. Compson stood watching her as she mounted, steadying herself against the wall with one hand, holding her skirts up with the other.
> "Are you going to wake him up just to dress him?" she said.
> Dilsey stopped. With her foot lifted to the next step she stood there, her hand against the wall and the grey splash of the window behind her, motionless and shapeless she loomed.
> "He aint awake den?" she said.

"He wasn't when I looked in," Mrs. Compson said. "But it's past his time. He never does sleep after half past seven. You know he doesn't."

Dilsey said nothing. She made no further move, but though she could not see her save as a blobby shape without depth, Mrs. Compson knew that she had lowered her face a little and that she stood now like a cow in the rain, as she held the empty water bottle by its neck.

"You're not the one who has to bear it," Mrs. Compson said. "It's not your responsibility. You can go away. You dont have to bear the brunt of it day in and day out. You owe nothing to them, to Mr. Compson's memory. I know you have never had any tenderness for Jason. You've never tried to conceal it."

Dilsey said nothing. She turned slowly and descended, lowering her body from step to step, as a small child does, her hand against the wall. "You go on and let him alone," she said. "Dont go in dar no mo, now. I'll send Luster up soon as I find him. Let him alone, now." (pp. 338–339)

The Easter Sunday service in the Negro church is immensely moving, an apotheosis of simplicity, innocence, and love, with Dilsey and Benjy as the central figures:

In the midst of the voices and the hands Ben sat, rapt in his sweet blue gaze. Dilsey sat bolt upright beside, crying rigidly and quietly in the annealment and the blood of the remembered Lamb. (pp. 370–371)

But the moment passes; the sense of human communion rapidly dissolves as they move into the world of "white folks" (p. 371) and return to the Compson house, described now for the first time and seen as a symbol of decay:

They reached the gate and entered. Immediately Ben began to whimper again, and for a while all of them looked up the drive at the square, paintless house with its rotting portico. (p. 372)

It is clear, however, that Faulkner does not intend any simple moral division between the Negroes and their white employers. Luster in particular has been less impressed by the service than by the performance on the musical saw he had witnessed the previous night, and in his treatment of Benjy he displays a streak of mischievous cruelty. Dilsey tries to comfort Ben, but she is forced to rely upon the treacherous Luster to take him to the cemetery and it is with a note of pathetic resignation that she says, "I does de bes I kin." (p. 396) On the final pages of the novel it is pride, the sin which has been the downfall of the Compson family, which induces Luster to drive to the left at the monument instead of to the right, and if the final restoration of Benjy's sense of order seems at first to offer a positive conclusion to the novel we must also remember that the order thus invoked is one purely of habit, entirely lacking in inherent justification, and that it is restored by Jason, whose concern is not with humanity or morality or justice but only with social appearances. As so often in this novel, such meaning as at first sight the incidents appear to possess proves on closer inspection to dissolve into uncertainty and paradox.

In Shakespeare's play, Macbeth's "sound and fury" soliloquy is spoken as death approaches, and by the end of Faulkner's novel the doom of the Compson family seems about to be finally accomplished. In *Macbeth* the forces of good, embodied in Malcolm and Macduff, are gathering strength and it is perhaps characteristic of the desperate mood of *The Sound and the Fury* that the forces of good are not so readily identifiable, nor seen as ultimately triumphant. Yet in *Macbeth* the forces of good are external to Macbeth and Lady Macbeth, whereas in *The Sound and the Fury* some of the elements making for life do appear within the Compson family group, most notably in Dilsey but also in Caddy and her daughter. It is Quentin who gives Luster the quarter he so desires, it is Quentin who struggles in the last section to maintain at least some semblance of family harmony and order but who finally breaks down under Jason's verbal torture, and it is perhaps to be taken as a sign of hope—especially in view of the resurrection images which some critics have perceived in the description of her empty room—that Quentin finally makes good her escape and that, unlike her mother, she leaves no hostage behind. In the Compson genealogy Faulkner speaks of Quentin in pessimistic terms, yet the suggestion that Faulkner wanted to write a novel about Quentin after her departure from Jefferson[23] at least indicates that he felt the Compsons were not yet finished with, that there was more to be said—or perhaps only more to be suffered.

Notes

1. The deposit of the Massey Collection in the Alderman Library has happily reunited the original first page of the manuscript of *The Sound and the Fury* with the remainder; page 5 is still missing (see James B. Meriwether, *The Literary Career of William Faulkner* [Princeton, 1961] , p. 65).

2. Quentin's experience seems strongly reminiscent, in certain respects, of the "weird seizures" suffered by the Prince in Tennyson's *The Princess*: see, for example, III. 167–173; see also the Prince's injury, VI. 1–3, and especially VII. 30–35, in which the word "twilight" twice occurs.

3. See *A Green Bough*, X, entitled "Twilight" on its first publication in *Contempo*, I (February 1, 1932), 1.

4. Anderson, *Winesburg, Ohio* (New York, n.d.), pp. 4–5.

5. Faulkner's *Dallas Morning News* article on Anderson, in *Princeton University Library Chronicle* (Faulkner number), p. 90. See William L. Phillips, "Sherwood Anderson's Two Prize Pupils," *University of Chicago Magazine*, XLVII (January 1955), 12.

6. Faulkner to Cowley, 4 in Faulkner-Cowley correspondence, Yale University.

7. *Faulkner at Nagano*, pp. 103–105, ed. Robert A. Jelliffe (Tokyo, 1956).

8. Coindreau, Preface to *Le bruit et la fureur*, p. 7; cf. *My Brother Bill*, pp. 69, 125; above, pp. 105–111.

9. *Literary Career*, p. 175.

10. Coindreau, op. cit., pp. 9–12; above, pp. 105–111.

11. Manuscript, Alderman Library, p. 26.

12. See George R. Stewart and Joseph M. Backus, " 'Each in Its Ordered Place': Structure and Narrative in 'Benjy's Section' of *The Sound and the Fury*," *American Literature*, XXIX (January 1958), 440–456; their conclusion, after discovering that "a change in type does not always indicate a break between units and that a new unit can be introduced without a change in type," is that Faulkner's device becomes "worthless" (p. 446).

13. James B. Meriwether, "Notes on the Textual History of *The Sound and the Fury*," *Papers of the Bibliographical Society of America*, 56 (1962), pp. 294–299.

14. Faulkner to Wasson, undated, in Massey Collection.

15. Manuscript, Alderman Library, p. 34 (reproduced as Fig. 10 of *Literary Career*).

16. *Faulkner in the University*, ed. Frederick L. Gwynn and Joseph L. Blotner (Charlottesville, Va., 1959), p. 6.

17. *Faulkner at Nagano*, p. 72.

18. Faulkner to Cowley, 7.

19. Faulkner to Cowley, 7.

20. Cf. Scott, *Quentin Durward* (London, n.d.), p. 63. When Quentin first introduces himself he is asked whether Durward is "a gentleman's name":

> "By fifteen descents in our family," said the young man; "and that makes me reluctant to follow any other trade than arms."
> "A true Scot! Plenty of blood, plenty of pride, and right great scarcity of ducats, I warrant thee."

21. *Portable Faulkner* (New York, 1954), pp. 745–746.

22. E.g., *Writers at Work*, ed. Malcolm Cowley (New York, 1958), p. 130.

23. Linscott, "Faulkner Without Fanfare," *Esquire*, 60, No. 1 (1963), p. 38.

The Ordeal of Consciousness:
Psychological Aspects of Evil in
The Sound and the Fury

Michel Gresset*

Like *As I Lay Dying*, but in a much less linear, more elaborate and complex fashion, *The Sound and the Fury* can be described as a novel about an ordeal. This ordeal can be found to unfold itself simultaneously upon three levels. The first is individual: the four protagonists who successively hold the center of the stage, undergo it of course; but also the character who has been Faulkner's clue to the novel, Caddy, and all the others: father and mother and uncle and granddaughter and Luster and Dilsey, like the characters in *As I Lay Dying*, are all involved in one great trial, and the tangled plot of the book follows the consequences, both psychological and moral, of these multiple confrontations. However, the sum of these individual "agons" is not simply algebraic: it is human, that is to say, living and complex; it constitutes a common ordeal, that of the Compson family and of the Negroes, and therefore acquires a social and historical value. Lastly, on a third and deeper level, there is in *The Sound and the Fury* that opening which is characteristic of the symbolistic novel, where the shadows of the poor players fretting their hour in life are cast upon a wider, metaphysical scale of reference.

THE DOUBLE TEST

What is the nature of this ordeal? From the very beginning, Faulkner's characters are put through a double test. On the one hand, they are up against what Faulkner recurrently called "environment"; the reader is supposed to judge them by the yardstick of their ability to insert or integrate themselves in the community and in reality at large. Thus, each of the great Faulknerian heroes embodies, sometimes victoriously but more often pathetically (as Quentin says, "tragedy is second-hand"), the romantic conflict, Solitude versus Society. Their failure always stems from their being unable to turn into redemptive, or at least workable dialectic, this fundamental hiatus between the individual human being and the world.

*Reprinted, with permission, from *Mississippi Quarterly*, 19, No. 3 (Summer 1966), 143–53. The original title restored by the present editor.

On the other hand, and on a deeper, even more secret level, the characters undergo the test of their own identity. This is a quest, neither mystical nor cultural nor imposed upon them by exterior, worldly standards, but born out of their very being, through one of those interior necessities that are so characteristic of Faulkner's sense of the human predicament: one of those "compulsions" that account for the opaque, either dumb or very prolix, sometimes even blind behaviour of characters like Quentin or Darl.

I do not feel that it is a gross simplification thus to reduce both the situation and the movement of *The Sound and the Fury* to this double test of identity (i.e., the discovery of harmony with one's own self and with the world), for it is precisely the organic center from which stem and to which converge all the psychological and even psychic complications which make the novel such a dense, compact and entangled whole, any more than it is a simplification to reduce a ball of string to one thread.

CADDY

It is only natural, in order to unravel the threads of the plot from this point of view, to take up first the character of whom her creator said again and again that it had been his Ariadne's clue: Caddy, woman and essence of woman, a being with whom Faulkner felt in such a close relationship that she could only be described through an aura of epithets, associations, shiftings of registers and symbols: a presence above all, since she is more action than words, more intuition than reasoning, and is not allowed a section like her brother; but a honeysuckle-intoxicating, full-bodied, triumphant presence. There is no break in her existence, once it is established primarily on the level of sensuality, except for her real, sincere tenderness for Benjy and Quentin: this she does not allow to grow into a fixation, as she easily fills the possible affective gap by transference and natural compensation. She is at once submitted (and wholly submissive) to the eternal laws of femininity and draws from it her superlative, magnificent physical aura. It does not take her long to solve the only problem with which she is confronted: that of "environment." Within the social unit of the family, integration soon (even precociously) proves impossible: therefore, with no harm done to her conscience nor any obstacle set to her consciousness, she will exclude herself from it, like a foreign body expelled. But her flights, soon followed by her departure, start a disorder within the family not commensurate with the consciousness she had of its consequence. And her relative lack of awareness entails a proportionate lack of responsibility.

The whole family is involved in her failure to emerge "normally" from it, and Quentin, unlike Hemingway's character in *A Farewell to Arms*, will not be left "stronger at the broken place." Moreover, according to the ironical laws of Faulkner's tragic time, heredity will weigh upon her own daughter when she is confronted with the same choice, that is, open conflict or harmony with the family. And Miss Quentin will be even more precocious than her mother.

Thus it can be seen how, in Faulkner's world, nobody can ever say "back to normalcy." Although apparently unconcerned with moral problems as such (a careful parallel with Hawthorne's Pearl might prove of interest), the unsophisticated (in nature) Caddy works evil within the family because she objectively starts a process that will eventually prevent all members from living together on good terms ever again.

In other words, there is no "good savage" solution possible in Faulkner's world. Wild nature, as will be seen with Eula in *The Hamlet*, is no more workable from the community's point of view than over-sophistication, psychological complexities and/or moral niceties.

Just as there is about the Southern land "a kind of still and violent fecundity" that is both tantalizing and agonizing, the blunt intrusion of nature, of instinct, and especially of sex in the unsteady balance of the family order proves to be no better alternative than the Hamlet-like waverings of Quentin's consciousness. At the beginning, this balance was already precarious: but having lived through two extreme spiritual experiences—one could sum them up under the headings Eros (Caddy) and Thanatos (Quentin)—the family is left shattered beyond repair.

Caddy's failure on the family level is due to such a quality of identity as inevitably tears to pieces the frame that has formed her. She is responsible after all, but only with due respect to that excess of nature with which, as a Faulknerian woman, she is endowed, and which drives her away from the community. Her portrait is a magnificent artistic projection of that quality in woman which always fascinated Faulkner: the tremendous, dumb, secret, brooding, irreducible urge of instinct. Caddy was his favorite child in more than one sense; in his gallery of characters, she is the first achievement of his vision of Eve before the Fall.

BENJY

The idiot of course remains throughout below these problems but he is not left outside the test altogether. For if he is incapable of grasping, as concepts, the two conflicting realities whose clash expels or eliminates his sister and brother (the ego and the community), his mind is constantly shot through by blundering inchoate intuitions of their relationship. The fact of being alive in the world is not problematic for him, for he is on a level with the world (which is ironical enough; but of course there is no "good idiot" solution suggested by Faulkner either): thus his sentimental life (he has one, especially in his relation with his sister—who, apart from Jason, would not fall in love with her?) establishes itself on the level of sensations, immediately translated into tears or well-being, without it ever going beyond. Instead of being, like Quentin, the place where good (the insertion in the real and the conquest of identity) and evil (the incapacity to achieve both simultaneously without letting the irremediable effects of time sneak in between) are at war, he is only the victim of the conflict. A cross for his family, he himself only carries one insofar as, through affective backlashes, he shares in his family's reactions to the common test: Caddy's flight, Quentin's and his father's deaths, Jason's fury. Aesthetically unworthy of a tragic destiny he can only have that of a living "reductio ad absurdum of all human experience": merely pathetic. A human being for all that in him is sub-human (his remaining outside awareness, for instance), he does not escape the common curse: man's propensity to evil. He will try to rape the passing girls and set the house on fire. But the very fact that he does not reach awareness leaves him outside evil; irresponsible, without any consciousness of liberty and therefore without liberty, he cannot possibly be punished; his crimes have no existence beyond fact, mere objective fact. His castration therefore is no punishment: it affects no more than his body. He and Darl embody two extreme positions, both tangential to evil. As human beings, they are steeped in evil but do not partake of it.

QUENTIN

With Quentin the test becomes crucial, in the literal sense. In him the evil of consciousness waylaid, baffled, disengaged from reality is most tragically incarnated. From the start, he owns more conventional assets than either his sister or any of his brothers: the sale of a meadow pays for his studies at Harvard where, ironically, his experience of the world amounts to new traumas that protract and exasperate his idea of an initial fault, his so-called incest with his sister; this growing into a destructive obsession, gradually takes on the dreadful aspect of original sin.

All of Quentin's self-knowledge organizes itself around the image, or the concept, of his sister, of this triumphant feminine entity which changes his own, while she irresistibly attracts and shocks or even outrages him. Thus Quentin, in the crucial time of adolescence, lets his consciousness be invaded and blocked by her, in all the time seeing her mainly and even blindly as a she, who is, and whom is not; no wonder, then that he misses the first test altogether and remains outside the promised land of identity. Some time before his suicide, he is found repeating those obsessive phrases "I was," "I am not," "I'll not be." These indeed constitute a very lucid outline of his own psychological story. Before his supposed "fall" with Caddy, he was Quentin Compson, a boy with prospects of living up to his ancestors' standard. His traumatic experience with Caddy leaves him on the edge of identity, and he gradually realizes that, with his ego falling beneath the sheer psychic and moral weight of this experience, life would become intolerable: why not then abolish the whole unbearable tangle of trauma, fault, and feminine water—thus surrendering himself to the very opacity that his consciousness cannot live with, let alone outlive?

As could be expected with a young man so sensitively involved, his failure in the test of identity entails the same in that of integration. He does not belong in Harvard. His vision of himself in the world tends to become a mere accumulation of refusals until one solution imposes itself upon his mind: that of failure carried, like a cross, to its ultimate consequences: suicide.

Obviously, the process is not as simple as this; the faltering of a knowledge striving after articulation is not without an intricate connection with the failure of a communication with his sister which, he so eagerly hoped, might be total (and of course, as a puritan, he chooses not to resolve the fundamental ambiguity of the means to realize this end). In proportion as she retreats, betraying the demanding bond that he forces upon her, submitting to the natural call for otherness, for anything else but the narrow, exacting "Compson honor" which is both her brother's obsession and alibi, he too retreats now no longer from the honor of his family but from reality and finally from life: he carries "the symbol of his frustration into eternity."

Quentin's monologue, a masterpiece of insight and sympathy, displays the inexorable movement of a mind, shut in its own, self-constituted vicious circle, toward the assumption of its death-wish.

JASON

Jason undergoes the test simply and effectively; he finds no difficulty whatever in quickly establishing both his identity and his integration: money is the common denominator. In fact he finds them at the lowest possible level: meanness is his main psychological trait. It would remain such, however, were it not repeatedly provoked by his brother, by his sister, and by her daughter: then his meanness takes on a diabolical quality that turns him into an almost archetypal villain. There is irony in the fact that while he has completely renounced the spiritual values of the Compsons, he is the one to provide for their material needs. But there is even more irony when he is ruined by the most tainted, the most "identical" upshoot of the family: the young and sexually precocious Quentin who is Caddy's daughter.

These ironical strokes are not gratuitous. They are the signs of a profoundly organic—neither scientific, nor aesthetic—vision of History (as represented by the story of the Compsons) as evincing a twofold movement: linear, of decadence, and cyclic, of fatality. In *The Sound and the Fury* the two combine in a highly effective way, as will now be seen more clearly in the study of the relationship between children and parents.

THE FATHER

The latter offer a very poor example of harmony indeed, unless it be the entirely negative harmony of incapacity and failure. The uncle is a mere parasite: Benjy, who is a nuisance to the community at large, had first received his uncle's name. The father is a failure on any other level than those of words and alcohol; he is the perfect spokesman for the famous Faulknerian rhetoric, which falls with verbal arabesques the emptiness which is at the core of the being, just as the baroque aesthetics filled the dreaded void with curves. Himself incapable of living in any other present but the golden and dusty time of his ancestors, he hands over Quentin, with the watch, his superb but vain piece of advice: "I give you the mausoleum of all hope and desire."

His death leaves no real gap in the family: his absence is only felt as that of a decorative link in the chain of the Compson memory (which probably explains the surreptitious presence of Caddy at his burial). As a father, he is of course an utter failure.

THE MOTHER

Even worse is the model offered by the mother. She is completely alienated from her part, from her place in and of the family. Instead of taking on her responsibilities, she lets Dilsey, Luster, or Jason shoulder them. Morever, what makes her odious is her constant desire to fill with words the void, the absence, the failure that she is and that she is fully aware of being. Her recurrent, wailing auto-criticism makes her one of the rare thoroughly unlikable feminine characters in Faulkner's work: a worthy mother of Jason the villain. Her only merit—and her useful function—is to get the key problem in the common ordeal: that of identity which, as a woman, she approaches through heredity and names: Jason can cope with reality: therefore he is not a Compson but a Bascomb. And of course she is right in a way: though not a rational explanation, this serves as a clue to our understanding of the book. And what she wishes for her granddaugher is terrible, indeed, but very significant: that she may have neither a father nor a name. We know that Quentin, just before his suicide, had uttered this very telling regret: "a mother!"

THE NAME

The mother's reproach to Caddy is no less significant: "let alone a woman who cant even name the father of her child." On a purely verbal level, she wishes for her grandchildren what her own children seek with their muscles and even with their lives: an identity. She does not contradict herself when she says "I have known it would happen as soon as they named her Quentin." This of course is only an onlooker's comment;

but she does put her finger upon what she calls the "curse," the incidence of time on the consciousness, from which stems the problem of identity. She hints at the terrible legacy of splendor and shame (and time has melted the former while increasing the latter) bequeathed to contemporaries by their ancestors in those clans where evil spread and proliferated through physical, mental, and moral in-breeding: there have been objective reasons for the cyclic recurrence of taints too. Again and again, Faulkner shows the effects of Time to be not only linear, but cyclic. Miss Quentin, named after her uncle, who had no mother, follows and even worsens the pattern set by her mother who "cannot name her child's father."

It is clearer now how this poem of evil is orchestrated: irony conducts. Structurally, the book seems to leave no other way of "triumphing over circumstances" but idiocy, suicide, mammonism, and prostitution.

THE NEGROES

Admirably coherent as it is, Faulkner's profound and searching analysis of the working of evil within and between the consciousnesses is further reinforced by the counterpoint supplied by the Negroes. Here we enter a world that seems to have nothing in common with the other, and whose only link with it is the stubborn adhesion of the Negroes to a family even until its complete disintegration.

For Roskus, who dies in harness; for Frony; for T. P.; for Luster, so precociously manly and yet so childish; and above all for Dilsey, who is both a superb major creation and the living embodiment of so many of the virtues extolled by Faulkner at Stockholm, there is no problem that is not solved daily, in and by the very flow of life. The Negroes' time is horizontal, while the Compsons' is vertical with a downward and whirling movement. Instead of being led to "end them" by vainly trying to oppose their troubles with their puny weapons, like the whites, the Negroes "suffer the slings and arrows of outrageous fortune." In calmness and dignity (two of the rare virtues that Faulkner and Hemingway both admire), they cope with a world in which the Compsons are failures. This success is obvious in Dilsey, and even in Luster, but it is not simple: for on the one hand, through one of those ironies that Faulkner, like a playwright, has so well shown to lie in the Southern tragedy, the Negroes are at least partially robbed of their sense of identity because so much depends on age-old customs, going back to slavery (e.g. Jason's attitude, who constantly sets the Negroes "in their place"); on the other they do not have this legacy of glory and fault weighing so heavily upon them. Their community is not even looked upon by whites as a possible pattern of salvation.

By comparison with the harsh, jarring, pessimistic picture of evil in the consciousness of the white people, one may find this vision of a stereotyped Negro who is neither a drinker nor a thief nor a fornicator rather idealized. There is, no doubt, a note of personal gratitude and affection in Dilsey's portrait, as, thirteen years later, Faulkner was to make clear in the dedication of *Go Down Moses*:

> "To Mammy Caroline Barr, Mississippi (1840–1940), Who was born in slavery and gave to my family a fidelity without stint or calculation of recompense and to my childhood an immeasurable devotion and love."

But it is clear, and will certainly be made clearer by further studies, how much the work owes to the biography—not so much to factual, or anecdotal, biography as to a kind of affective and spiritual autobiography. This, far from reducing Faulkner's stature, will on the contrary throw into relief and enhance his tremendous power as a creator, quite unique in twentieth century American literature.

METHOD

The main point of this critical sketch has been to suggest a modest reading of Faulkner's work that, contrary to all ambitious "exterior" approaches (Christian, existentialist, Marxist, psychoanalytic, etc.), focuses primarily not on the ideas behind the writing, but on what actually takes place in the course of the story: both on the structure and on the texture of the work.

This is particularly important as regards the problem of evil. Any critic who approaches Faulkner's work with a preconceived idea of what he will find there is bound to harvest what *he*, not Faulkner, has sown. In such a complex and elaborate work of art as *The Sound and the Fury* especially, it seems better—more responsible and also more modest—to begin with as careful a consideration as possible of the *working* of evil within the consciousness. After all, it may be hard to decide whether Faulkner was above all a metaphysician or a novelist, besides being, as we all know from his repeating it so often, a story teller; but he certainly was more than slightly interested in psychology. First because this was the "camino real" to his people's souls; second because the deeper he probed into them, the more exciting the challenge became to his technique as a craftsman.

Moreover, his work is grounded on solid realities like family and community, not on ideas, and even less on theories, be they sociological or psychoanalytical. He never, even in *A Fable*, had a thesis as his purpose. He just stole from every possible source, confessed to it unabashedly, and of course was right from beginning to end. If he had needed a sponsor, Balzac was there, and Dickens too. His greatest plunder was the South.

What is a family, or a community, or even a population, but a gathering of individuals, therefore of consciousnesses, brought and held together by all sorts of links? Faulkner was not a philosopher; evil, to him, was not an abstraction, but a part of reality, immanent, pervasive, tangible, and permanent, like time. Now both the structure and the style of *The Sound and the Fury* show (1) evil to be woven into the working of the consciousness as well as brooding and lurking over and around it, like Southern storms, and (2) irony to lie in the cyclic recurrence of the same impact of time upon the consciousness. The study of Evil inevitably leads one to that of Time and its effect upon the human "psyche," with Irony as the great lesson to be drawn. Irony is the sign both of God's sneering indifference (as in Thomas Hardy) and of Man's utter impotence (as in more contemporary novelists like Samuel Beckett).

That Faulkner used the Bible—and he did, of course: just as he *used* the South; everything in him was devoted to his literary creation—is no reason why one could not read the old concepts of damnation and redemption in the characters' minds, with the old key of psychology. Identity, integration: the other critical step consists in seeing what happens to the characters or rather how they come out: do they survive? do they perish? There are no such things as "commercial endings" in Faulkner's fiction. The way he wanted his stories to end is a main clue to our understanding of his general intention.

Well, there is not much hope left for the family at the end of this book. In spite of Dilsey and the superb passage about the Great Negro Easter Sunday (one of the finest musical pieces in modern literature), *The Sound and the Fury* ends with Benjy's voice "roaring and roaring" before hushing as everything takes "its ordered place" again; but only through an idiot's sense of order can it be said that Good and Evil resume their position; and he is below the level of choice. For the family, "what is done cannot be undone," and evil has passed repair. There is no hope left because the consciousnesses, apart from Jason's or the villain's, have given way. In Faulkner's work the order of the world is conservative; it rests on the individual and on the family and on the community, in a progressive opening up to the cosmos. In this, Faulkner is the last link in the great chain of Anglo-American symbolistic writers: in France, the only equivalence is to be found in poetry.

Besides being, since Melville's *Moby-Dick*, one of the few truly Shakespearian books of the last century, *The Sound and the Fury* is both Faulkner's *Waste Land* and his *Saison en Enfer*.

The Eyes of Innocence: Faulkner's "The Kingdom of God"

Charles D. Peavy*

Faulkner's sketch "The Kingdom of God" appeared in the New Orleans *Times-Picayune* on April 26, 1925. The idiot in the sketch served as a model for Benjy in *The Sound and the Fury*, published four years later.[1] That Faulkner had a religious theme in mind when he wrote the early story is suggested by its title. Just what that theme is, however, is not immediately apparent. "The Kingdom of God" describes the abortive attempt of two bootleggers to unload some liquor in an alleyway in New Orleans. Their efforts are foiled, however, by the presence of the idiot brother of one of the men. The idiot, whose eyes are "clear and blue as cornflowers," has a narcissus gripped tightly in one fist. While the idiot's brother is trying to distract a policeman, the other bootlegger, in a fit of frustration, cruelly strikes the idiot and breaks the stem of the narcissus. The idiot screams—"a horse, inarticulate bellow"—which attracts a crowd and draws the police to the scene. The two bootleggers are arrested, and the idiot continues to bellow until the narcissus is splintered with a sliver of wood and a bit of string. Then, with a police officer on each fender, "the car drew away from the curb and on down the street, the ineffable blue eyes of the idiot dreaming above his narcissus clenched tightly in his dirty hand." The "cornflower blue" eyes of the idiot, the narcissus clutched in his hand, the breaking of the narcissus, the splinting of the broken stalk, and the final tranquillity that descends upon the idiot and is reflected in his eyes, are used four years later in the final section of *The Sound and the Fury*.

The most striking parallel between the two works is in the description of the idiot's eyes—both pairs are cornflower blue. Cornflower is one of the regional or common names for any of the various species of *Houstonia*, particularly the *Houstonia coerulea*, or common bluet. Significantly, another common name for the flower is Innocence. I suggest that the depiction of the idiot's eyes, which are also described as "ineffable" and "heavenly blue," contains the key to the meaning of the sketch and to the theme of the novel.

*Reprinted, with permission, from *Papers on Language and Literature*, 2, No. 2 (Spring 1966), 178–82.

The eye-color of the two idiots, the color of Innocence, should be taken symbolically, for an idiot is "innocent" in many senses of the word: (1) free from any moral wrong, not tainted with sin or evil; (2) free from blame or guilt; (3) lacking in worldly knowledge, naive: an innocent child; (4) deficient in sense or intelligence, half-witted, a simpleton or idiot. Doubtless Faulkner was conscious of the multiple meanings of the word "innocent"[2] and intended the idiot himself to be a symbol of innocence. Faulkner once said that "Benjy is incapable of good and evil because he had no knowledge of good and evil."[3] The title of the sketch, then, is not mere whimsy, but is a statement of a theme which Faulkner was to develop more fully in *The Sound and the Fury*.

"The Kingdom of God" is probably a reference to Mark 10: 14–15, or to Luke 18:17, where Christ says that whoever does not receive the kingdom of God like a child shall not enter it, or to Matthew 18:3, where Christ says that unless people become like children, they will never enter the kingdom of heaven. The passages in Mark and Luke are usually taken to mean that one cannot receive the kingdom of God if he is proud and self-righteous, and that children manifest the attitude of simple and unquestioning trust that God requires of those who will enter His kingdom. Mark 10:14 relates how Jesus was angry at the Pharisees because of their loveless indifference to human needs ("But when Jesus saw it, he was much displeased, and said unto them, suffer the little children to come unto me, and forbid them not; for of such is the kingdom of God").

In Faulkner's sketch the idiot is loved by his brother, who tries to protect him from harm. The other bootlegger, however, who refers to the idiot as "loony" and "squirrel chaser," has often expressed his dislike for him ("I know how you feel about him," says the brother, "you said so often enough"); and one of the policemen calls the idiot "mad cow" and shakes him. In both the sketch and the novel Faulkner uses people's reaction to the idiot to illustrate pride, hostility, and inhumanity. In the novel, the idiot Benjy is despised by his older brother Jason, who has himself appointed Benjy's guardian and then has Benjy castrated. In both works people view the idiot as a nuisance that should be put away in an asylum. In the sketch the bootlegger complains, "Dam'f I see why you lug him around when they's good homes for his kind everywheres," but is answered by his companion, "Listen. He's my brother, see?" In the novel, Jason urges his father to send Benjy to the state asylum ("I reckon you'll send him to Jackson, now"), and Benjy's niece Quentin insists, "He needs to be sent to Jackson." In the final scene of the novel Jason strikes Benjy and breaks the stem of the narcissus, an unfeeling and inhumane action that closely parallels that of the bootlegger in "The Kingdom of God."

The biblical Pharisees were shut off from the kingdom of God because of their self-righteousness and spiritual arrogance. Christ's indignation at such action is echoed in "The Kingdom of God" and in the concluding section of *The Sound and the Fury*, both of which contain

Faulkner's parabolical warning against modern pharisaism. This idea is fully developed in the novel, when Frony objects to Dilsey's bringing the idiot to the Negro church on Easter Sunday.[4]

> "I wish you wouldn't keep on bringin him to church, mammy," Frony said. "Folks talkin."
> "Whut folks?" Dilsey said.
> "I hears em," Frony said.
> "And I knows whut kind of folks," Dilsey said, "Trash white folks. Dat's who it is. Thinks he aint good enough fer white church, but nigger church aint good enough fer him."
> "Dey talks, jes de same," Frony said.
> "Den you send um to me," Dilsey said. "Tell um de good Lawd dont keer whether he smart er not. Dont nobody but white trash keer dat."

Dilsey's "white trash" are the modern Pharisees, whose self-righteous hypocrisy prevents them from accepting Benjy and thus excludes them from the kingdom of heaven. Dilsey alone seems to understand the meaning of the Easter sermon, which is filled with references to children ("Look at dem little chillen settin dar. Jesus wus like dat once. . . . Ma'y settin in de do' wid Jesus on her lap, de little Jesus. Like dem chillen dar, de little Jesus"), pride and arrogance ("I hears de boasting en de braggin"), and humility ("de meek Jesus"). Dilsey, in her simple faith and enduring humility, says to Benjy, "You's de Lawd's chile, anyway. En I be His'n too, fo long, praise Jesus."

The destructive pride and self-love of the modern world are symbolized by the narcissus[5] which is clutched by the idiot in both the sketch and the novel; in *The Sound and the Fury* the narcissus represents the self-love of Mrs. Compson and her sons Jason and Quentin.[6] Traditionally, the narcissus has symbolized egotism and conceit, but it is also the plant of nemesis.[7] In the classic myth, Hera ordered Nemesis, the deity of vengeance, to punish Narcissus for his egotism, and Nemesis changed him into the narcissus flower. Also, the Fates wore wreaths of narcissus flowers, the scent of which was so painfully sweet as to cause madness, a reminder that narcissism, the symbol of egotism and conceit, will be ultimately punished.[8]

Faulkner's sketch, "The Kingdom of God," thus not only contains the model for Benjy in *The Sound and the Fury* but also the idea that was to be developed in the concluding chapter of what Faulkner considered his finest novel. The idiot and his narcissus serve as both a symbol of innocence and a warning against overweening self-love. Acceptance of the idiot—an extension of Christian charity and humaneness to the "innocents" of the world—prepares one for entrance into the kingdom of God; a failure to do this through spiritual arrogance (symbolized by the narcissus) will result in destruction, "de darkness en de death everlastin upon de generations."[9]

Notes

1. Carvel Collins, in his edition of *New Orleans Sketches*, was the first to note that the idiot in "The Kingdom of God" anticipated the character Benjy in *The Sound and the Fury*; see *New Orleans Sketches* (New Brunswick, N.J., 1958), p. 27. Quotations from "The Kingdom of God" are from this text; [the story is also rep. above, pp. 45–48—Ed's Note].

2. Faulkner's interest in language is attested by his brother John: "Bill always claimed the English language didn't have enough words in it. I guess, so far as he was concerned, he was right about that. He certainly used just about every one there was and sometimes some most of us didn't even know we had. Every now and then I would think Bill had made up one but I'd look in the dictionary and there it would be. That's one thing Bill did for us. He made us become familiar with our dictionaries": *My Brother Bill; An Affectionate Reminiscence*, (New York, 1963), p. 264. Faulkner's ability to find the *mot juste* should be remembered when he describes the idiot's "heavenly blue" eyes as "ineffable." One of the meanings of ineffable is "too sacred to be spoken, celestial, divine."

3. Malcolm Cowley, ed., *Writers at Work, The Paris Review Interviews* (New York, 1958), pp. 131–32.

4. *The Sound and the Fury*, p. 306. All references to the novel in this note are from the Modern Library Edition.

5. Lawrence E. Bowling, in "Faulkner and the Theme of Innocence," *Kenyon Review*, XX (Summer 1958), 485, argues that "the narcissus has also a Christian tradition, for it is the flower which in the Bible is called 'the rose' and is identified with Jesus. Thus Benjy's narcissus, like Benjy himself, symbolizes not only the world's selfishness but also its need for love." Bowling refers to Isaiah 35:1 and to the Song of Songs, 2:1.

6. In *Sartoris*, Narcissa receives anonymous, and obscene, love letters. In the short story, "There Was a Queen," Narcissa gives her body to the blackmailer in order to get them back, preferring to sleep with the man rather than risk someone reading the letters and *thinking* that she is not virtuous. In *Sanctuary* a perverted sense of respectability causes Narcissa to betray her brother Horace and to have Ruby Goodwin driven from town.

7. See "The Language of Flowers," in Ernest and Johanna Lehner, *Folklore and Symbolism of Flowers, Plants, and Trees* (New York, 1960), p. 122.

8. Lehner, p. 73.

9. *The Sound and the Fury*, p. 312.

"The Beautiful One": Caddy Compson as Heroine of *The Sound and the Fury*

Catherine B. Baum*

William Faulkner's statement that *The Sound and the Fury* is "a tragedy of two lost women: Caddy and her daughter"[1] indicates that he intended Caddy Compson to be both a central and a tragic figure in the novel. None of the critics, however, emphasizes the role of Caddy as much as Faulkner does, and even those who do consider her life a unifying force in the novel have not thought of the novel as her tragedy. Lawrence Bowling points out that Caddy is "the essential center of the main action . . . the primary obsession with Benjy and Quentin and Jason throughout the first three sections of the book,"[2] yet he treats her life as but one aspect of the "theme of innocence"[3] he finds in the novel, thus ignoring her role as tragic heroine. Similarly, Olga Vickery sees Caddy as a center of action, but she thinks Caddy's importance is primarily technical, rather than thematic: "Within the novel as a whole it is Caddy's surrender to Dalton Ames which serves both as the source of dramatic tension and as the focal point for the various perspectives."[4] Caddy's function, [Mrs.] Vickery believes, is to provide an opportunity for each of the brothers to react to her and thereby to reveal his own character. In view of Faulkner's remarks, however, it seems just as likely that the reverse is true—that the main function of the other characters is to reveal something about Caddy.

Because no one of the Compsons has a complete and unbiased view of Caddy, there is an obscurity surrounding her character, but it is not an impenetrable obscurity. In fact, a main aim of the novel is to allow the reader to piece together information and derive for himself a true picture of Caddy. Faulkner's technique in *The Sound and the Fury* is very much like that he used in *Absalom, Absalom!*, of which he said: "It was . . . thirteen ways of looking at a blackbird. But . . . when the reader has read all these thirteen different ways of looking at the blackbird, the reader has his own fourteenth image of that blackbird which I would like to think is the truth."[5] Similarly, the reader can see several distorted ways of looking

*Reprinted, with permission, from *Modern Fiction Studies*, 13, No. 1 (Spring 1967), 33–44. *Modern Fiction Studies*, © 1967 by Purdue Research Foundation, West Lafayette, Indiana 47907.

at Caddy, but through careful reading and discernment, he will be able to derive that fourteenth image, the truest picture of Caddy.

That Caddy's life is a cohesive force in the novel can easily be seen. She is the central concern of each brother, and the telling of her story is the common purpose of each section. She causes the other characters to speak out. She is the only human factor in Benjy's life which gives it meaning, for the other things he loves are inanimate objects—the fire, the pasture, the red and yellow cushion, the blue bottle, and the jimson weed. Caddy is also the main interest of her brother Quentin. His thoughts turn ceaselessly from the present—his trip on the bus, his walk on the bridge, his adventure with the Italian girl—to the past, and the past for Quentin *is* Caddy. His thoughts revolve around her pregnancy, her wedding, and the question of honor, which to him is inextricably bound up with Caddy. She likewise is important to Jason, her antagonist, as the ruination of his plans for the future.

Many explanations have been offered for the arrangement of the four sections of the novel, but no one has noticed the most simple and probable one: a logical and traditional ordering based on the chronology of Caddy's life, her childhood, adolescence, and maturity. Because the past is as immediate to Benjy as the present, he reveals Caddy's personality as a child, and his section logically comes first. With an ever-present concern about chastity and honor, Quentin is best suited to tell of Caddy's adolescence and loss of innocence. His section therefore follows Benjy's. Since Jason is interested not in morals, but in money, he is concerned about Caddy only as she affects his financial welfare; for this reason, she impinges on his consciousness only after her divorce from Herbert, which costs Jason his promised job. She is again of interest to him when he can appropriate to himself the money she sends Quentin. Jason then, fittingly enough, tells the story of Caddy's adulthood, her divorce and her relationship with her daughter. The climax of the novel is Caddy's defeat at the hands of Jason, who leaves her stammering, helpless, and broken, as she acknowledges, " 'I have nothing at stake. . . . Nuh-nuh-nothing. . . .' "[6]

The final section of the novel comments on life without Caddy and the love she represents. As Dilsey says, " 'I seed de beginnin, en now I sees de endin' " (p. 313). The events of this day, as Quentin, "the extension of Caddy,"[7] runs away, mark the disintegration and the "endin" of the Compson family. Without the warmth of Caddy's love, everything seems cold and dying. The house is "decaying" (p. 301) and "rotting" (p. 313), and the word "cold" is used repeatedly to describe the weather, the house, the meals, Jason, and Mrs. Compson. Benjy's sorrowful moans have the effect of a Greek chorus crying "woe." As "the grave hopeless sound of all voiceless misery under the sun" (p. 332), these cries furnish an appropriate dirge for the loss of Caddy.

All that remains of Caddy is her "white satin slipper . . . yellow now, and cracked and soiled" (p. 332). This slipper is a touching and effective symbol of Caddy's life, which once was clean and shining too, but now is spoiled and dirty like the slipper.

In addition to its structural significance, Caddy's life also thematically represents love, compassion, pity, and sacrifice in a family which is destroying itself through its lack of these qualities. This most important role is also the most neglected by the critics. Before one can understand Caddy's unselfish love, he must understand her character, and it is here that many critics seem to have gone astray, apparently accepting at face value Jason's and Quentin's evaluations. To Charles Anderson, Caddy is only a promiscuous nymphomaniac,[8] to Carvel Collins, she represents the libido, and ". . . her development as charted in the novel is a twisting of the libido's normal development toward full sexuality";[9] to Bowling, ". . . Caddy is essentially like Jason in that she is a naturalist and never rises above her natural state."[10] Powell speaks of "the darkness of her soul,"[11] and Foster describes her as "a sensitive, beautiful girl, but given to bitchery from her early teens."[12] Certainly there is some basis for these feelings. Caddy has affairs with several men, becomes pregnant and marries a man she does not love in order to give her unborn child a father.

To judge her solely on the basis of these facts, however, is to distort her character completely. Faulkner in 1957 remembered her as "the beautiful one, she was my heart's darling. That's what I wrote the book about and I used the tools which seemed to me the proper tools to try to tell, try to draw the picture of Caddy."[13] And he adds, " '. . . Caddy was still to me too beautiful and too moving to reduce her to telling what was going on. . . .' "[14] Thus to Faulkner, Caddy is not only central, but also beautiful and moving.

Caddy's most important and distinctive quality is unselfish love. She is the only Compson who loves without thought for self and with a genuine desire for the happiness of others, especially for her two innocent brothers, Benjy and Quentin. Caddy offers the care that Benjy needs, "the tenderness," Faulkner says, "to shield him in his innocence."[15] She gets into bed with him to help him go to sleep, she is concerned about him when his hands are cold, and she tries to make him happy by telling him about Christmas: " 'Santy Claus, Benjy. Santy Claus' " (p.27). She has the ability to sense what he wants and the initiative to get it for him: " 'You want to carry the letter.' Caddy said. 'You can carry it' " (p.32); " 'He wants your lightning bugs, T.P. Let him hold it a while' " (p. 55). She knows that Benjy likes the red and yellow cushion and that " 'if you'll hold him, he'll stop [crying]' " (p. 82). These are things the other members of the family either do not know or do not care about.

The beauty of Caddy's love becomes especially prominent when seen against the background of the other characters' lack of concern for Benjy's happiness. Quentin never hurts Benjy, but neither does he show any affection for him. Jason pesters and teases Benjy by cutting up his paper dolls; Luster impishly whispers "Caddy" in his ear to make him cry (p. 74); Mrs. Compson's words to Benjy are usually sharp and chilled—" 'You, Benjamin' " (p. 60)—or they are admonitions to the rest of the household to keep him quiet. Mr. Compson and Dilsey both seem to care about Benjy, but they are either too busy or too preoccupied to do anything for him. Mr. Compson's " 'Well, Benjy. . . . Have you been a good boy today' " (p. 83) shows some distracted interest, but he does not play an active role in Benjy's life. Dilsey tries to protect Benjy from Luster's teasings (p. 74), but she is kept too busy by her work around the house and the whining demands of Mrs. Compson. Only Caddy is actively interested in his welfare.

The reaction of Caddy's daughter, Quentin, to Benjy heightens the effect of Caddy's tenderness by contrast. Quentin feels only disgust and repugnance for Benjy and his repulsive table manners (p. 89), whereas Caddy had solicitously and patiently fed him. When Benjy was distressed at finding Caddy and Charlie in the swing, Caddy ran to comfort Benjy and gave up Charlie (p. 67). On the other hand, when Benjy finds Quentin with her boyfriend in the swing, Quentin calls him an *"old crazy loon"* (p. 67) and runs to the house, not to comfort Benjy, but to complain to Dilsey.

Caddy has other qualities as admirable as her selfless love. In the first section of the novel she is an active and curious little girl. She is the one who asks many questions about Damuddy's funeral and who finds an ingenious way of getting around her father's orders that the children go to bed immediately after supper:

'Your pa say for you to come right on up stairs when you et supper. You heard him.'
'He said to mind me.' Caddy said. (p. 46)

While Jason tags along saying " 'I'm going to tell . . .' " (p. 46) and while Quentin obediently stays behind on the kitchen steps (p. 47), Caddy leads the way to the tree outside the parlor window so that she can see what's going on inside. She is the one, as Faulkner put it, "brave enough to climb that tree to look in the forbidden window."[16] Although Caddy disobeys her father's instructions, still her behavior is better than Quentin's excessive obedience which keeps him from participating in life, and it is an indication of her independence and spirit.

Only Caddy knows her brother Jason for what he is. When he makes one of his numerous threats to "tell," Caddy defies him: " 'Let him tell . . . . I dont give a cuss' " (p. 39). When Jason destroys Benjy's dolls, Caddy's fierce protectiveness reveals the intensity of her love:

'He cut up all Benjy's dolls.' Caddy said. 'I'll slit his gizzle.'
'Candace.' Father said.
'I will.' Caddy said. 'I will.' She fought. Father held her. She kicked at Jason. He rolled into the corner, out of the mirror. (p. 84)

Caddy's tone here suggests her youthful confidence that she can handle anything. The poignancy of the scene, however, is that Jason cannot be destroyed so easily.

The qualities Caddy evinces before her loss of innocence—her self-reliance, courage, independence, and especially her love—are attributes that certainly make her "beautiful and moving,"[17] and Benjy's section of the novel serves largely to reveal these traits. That Caddy loses these qualities is her tragedy, and the remainder of the novel depicts the tragic changes as the world finally destroys her courage and her love.

Caddy is doomed, Lawrence Bowling points out, by "the general state of lovelessness into which all the Compson children were born without any choice on their part."[18] The lack of guidance from her father, the coldness of her mother, the vengefulness of Jason—all contribute to her downfall. More than this, she is doomed by society itself for violating its mores and by the attitude of men like Dalton who consider women only "bitches" (p. 179).

One cannot however, place all the blame on circumstances or the Compson family. A large part of the reason for Caddy's damnation is found in herself. Ironically enough, those qualities in her character that are admirable are the ones which lead to her fall: her complete selflessness, which leads her to be indifferent to her virginity and to what happens to her; her willingness to put the other person's interests first; and her great desire to communicate love. She is too selfless for the world she is in, because all that the world, in the form of Jason and Dalton, knows how to do is take advantage of that selflessness. What Cash said of Darl in *As I Lay Dying* is applicable also to Caddy: "this world is not his world; this life his life."[19] This world is not "the right place for love"[20] for Caddy. In a family which needs tenderness and compassion as urgently as do the Compsons, the destruction of such a capacity for love is a terrifying waste.

By the end of *The Sound and the Fury*, Caddy has changed from a loving, innocent girl to a feverish, anxious woman who, as Jason said, looked "like some kind of a toy that's wound up too tight and about to burst all to pieces" (p. 227). In the novel's appendix, published in 1946, it is evident that she has changed even more: she has become the mistress of a German staff general, and she has become "ageless and beautiful, cold serene and damned" (p. 12). Now, as the librarian Melissa Meek believes, ". . . *Caddy doesn't want to be saved hasn't anything anymore worth being saved for nothing worth being lost that she can lose*" (p. 16). If the older Caddy is impervious now to harm from the world, she is also completely and irrevocably damned. Quentin believes "temporary" is the saddest word (p. 197), but for Caddy the saddest thing is the permanence of her doom.

Caddy's constant and selfless love for others makes it momentarily difficult to understand her coldness when she is with the Nazi. Yet the change has been prepared for in the novel, and her coldness years later is only the logical culmination of forces working against her earlier. The dramatic alteration of her character can be traced in stages through her relationships with the seven men important in her life: Benjy, Charlie, Dalton, Quentin, Herbert, Jason, and the Nazi general. Mr. Compson can be omitted because he does not delineate any particular segment of her life; his influence on her is a more general one.

In her childhood relations with Benjy, Caddy is self-confident, warm, and innocent. Then the beginning of Caddy's sexual experience and her loss of innocence is marked by the episode with Charlie in the swing. But she is still in control of her feelings and is able to give up Charlie for Benjy's sake. When she meets Dalton, however, she loses her mastery over herself:

> he's crossed all the oceans all around the world
> then she talked about him clasping her wet knees her face tilted back in
> the grey light the smell of honeysuckle. . . . (p. 169)

She is a childlike Desdemona in her wonder at knowing someone who has seen "all the oceans." She seems still innocent mentally and spiritually, if not physically.

When Quentin asks Caddy if she loves Dalton, she does not declare her love in words:

> . . . Caddy you hate him dont you dont you
> she held my hand against her chest her heart thudding I turned and
> caught her arm
> Caddy you hate him dont you
> she moved my hand up against her throat her heart was hammering
> there. (p. 169)

Her pounding heart should prove her love more than words could, but Quentin cannot understand. "Incapable of love" (p. 10), he must hear the word to comprehend it. To Quentin, love is just a word, as Addie Bundren puts it, "a shape to fill a lack."[21] To Caddy, who knows the meaning of love and who has loved, the word is not necessary.

Caddy's interest in men is a natural part of growing up, like her playing with the perfume and the hat. Since she should not remain as much a child as Benjy, it is wrong to condemn her interest in Dalton. What one could censure her for, however, and what the world *does* censure her for, is that she gives herself completely and without reserve to Dalton. She loves Dalton and wishes to communicate her love, and the lack of love in the Compson household drives her to seek it outside the family. Robert Penn Warren writes that the only real villains in Faulkner are "those who deny the human bond"[22]—like Jason, Quentin, and Mrs. Compson. Caddy fights to assert the human bond. Her love for Dalton is not passive, but active; she did not "*let*" him kiss her, she "*made*" him (p. 152).

Caddy's giving herself to Dalton reveals not only her love, but also her selflessness. Love to her is more important than morality, and she has been taught no good reason for preserving her chastity. All her mother cares about is the appearance of virtue and Caddy places no value on her maidenhood, which means "no more than a hangnail" (p. 10) to her. What does matter to her is the communication of love. Mr. Compson perhaps best expresses Caddy's attitude toward virginity when he says it is "contrary to nature" (p. 135), or, as Olga Vickery says, it is "an artificial isolation of the woman."[23] Virginity, therefore, is just one of the "high dead words."[24]

Caddy's loss of mental and spiritual innocence comes towards the end of her affair with Dalton. Thinking Dalton has hurt Quentin, she tells him to go away. Then she realizes Quentin is not hurt, and she is anxious to go to Dalton. Her words indicate her growing awareness of his true feeling toward her:

> let me go Ive got to catch him and ask his let me go Quentin please let me go let me go
> all at once she quit her wrists went lax
> yes I can tell him I can make him believe anytime I can make him . . . anytime he will believe me. (pp. 181–2)

The repetition of "let me go" and "anytime I can make him believe me" seems to indicate an increasing desperation on Caddy's part and a fearful realization that she might not be able to make Dalton believe her. Caddy does not say what it is she can make him believe, but a probable answer is that she is afraid she is pregnant and is apprehensive about whether or not he will believe he is the father. She seems to know that Dalton is not as close to her as she would like to think.

In her relationship to Quentin after her affair with Dalton, Caddy's sense of despair is evident in her willingness for Quentin to kill her or commit incest with her (pp. 170–171). It makes no difference to her which alternative he chooses: "yes Ill do anything you want me to anything yes" (p. 175). Her own well-being is a matter of no concern to her, and her independence seems to have disappeared. Her affair with Dalton, she knows, hurts both Quentin and Benjy. Quentin she pities because he cannot understand what it is to love: "poor Quentin . . . youve never done that have you" (p. 170). The sad thing for Quentin is that he has never done anything. As T. S. Eliot has pointed out, ". . . it is better, in a paradoxical way, to do evil than to do nothing; at least exist."[25] In these terms, Caddy's fall is better than Quentin's innocence.

That Benjy is hurt by Caddy's actions is evident in his bellowings and pulling at her dress when she comes in after having been with Dalton (pp. 87–88). Quentin notices that when Caddy is near Benjy now, her eyes are "like cornered rats" (p. 168). Torn as she is between her love for Benjy and her new love for Dalton, she has good cause to feel despair.

The men in Caddy's life after Dalton appear only vaguely in *The Sound and the Fury*, and one can only speculate about Caddy's motives in going with them. There is no evidence that she loved them as she had Dalton, but her indifferent attitude toward virginity and her need to give and receive love may explain her giving herself to them.

Just before her marriage to Herbert, Caddy tells Quentin, "... *I died last year I told you I had but I didnt know then what I meant I didnt know what I was saying. ... But now I know I'm dead I tell you*" (pp. 142–143). Even with Dalton she had half suspected that he would not "believe" her and might betray her. Since then, she has evidently learned that she can trust no one. When she becomes pregnant and is forced to face the consequences of her actions, she knows that she is dead.

In her marriage to Herbert, Caddy is willing to assume responsibility for her actions. She cares nothing for Herbert, but her concern for Benjy and her father has convinced her that marrying Herbert is the only thing she can do. When Quentin says, "... *we can go away you and Benjy and me where nobody knows us where* . . . ," Caddy's answer shows both her realism and her ever-present concern for Benjy: "*On what on your school money the money they sold the pasture for so you could go to Harvard dont you see you've got to finish now if you dont finish he'll have nothing*" (p. 143). When Quentin tells Caddy to think of Benjy and her father and not to marry Herbert, Caddy's interest in the welfare of others is still predominant: "*What else can I think about what else have I thought about . . . Father will be dead in a year they say if he doesnt stop drinking and he wont stop he cant stop since I since last summer and then they'll send Benjy to Jackson I cant cry I cant even cry* . . ." (pp. 142–143). Her love for her father is also revealed in the broken, rushed way she speaks of him. By marrying Herbert, Caddy hopes she will enable her father to stop worrying about her and to stop drinking. Then he will not die in a year, and Benjy will not have to be sent to Jackson. So, although Slatoff castigates Caddy for "abandon[ing] Benjy,"[26] the marriage is really one of her most selfless acts; it will, she hopes, benefit Benjy in the long run.

Caddy's compassion for Benjy and reluctance to leave him are seen on her wedding day. When she hears Benjy crying, she rushes out to him and hugs him (pp. 59, 101). She has not stopped loving Quentin either, for as Herbert tells Quentin, "... *Candace talked about you all the time up there at the Licks . . . she couldnt have talked about you any more if you'd been the only man in the world* . . ." (pp. 126–127). In her eagerness to have Quentin promise to take care of Benjy and Mr. Compson, she not only expresses her heart-felt concern for them but also seeks to divert Quentin's mind from the shattering fact of her pregnancy. Although he tenaciously tries to find out about her pregnancy, her own situation is of such slight importance to her and the well-being of Benjy and her father are of such major importance that she brushes off his questions in order to extract his promise:

Have there been very many Caddy
I dont know too many will you look after Benjy and Father
You dont know whose it is then does he know
Dont touch me will you look after Benjy and Father. (p. 134)

After her marriage and subsequent divorce from Herbert, Caddy sends her daughter back to Jefferson with Mr. Compson. At first, this act seems heartless, but it is almost the only thing she could do. In entrusting Quentin to her father, Caddy probably hoped that things would turn out well for her, and at any rate, as Jason pointed out later to her, Caddy had no way to provide for her. When Mrs. Compson coldly refused to let Caddy come home in spite of Mr. Compson's pleas that she be allowed to do so (p. 228), she practically determined Caddy's fate. Thrown entirely on her own, Caddy could do little but become a mistress or a prostitute, and she did not want her daughter to become part of such a life.

Caddy did not forget her daughter, however, and Jason remarks that she would come back once or twice a year to see her (p. 228). The first time she came back, Jason allowed her only a passing glimpse of Quentin, and he noticed that ". . . Caddy saw her and sort of jumped forward" (p. 223). The involuntary movement shows love for Quentin and eagerness to have her back. The only way Jason can keep her from going out to see Quentin is by attacking her in her most vulnerable spot, her love for Benjy: "So the next time I told her that if she tried Dilsey again, Mother was going to fire Dilsey and send Ben to Jackson and take Quentin and go away" (pp. 225–226). This threat seems to have been effective, for there is no evidence of Caddy's again trying to go to the house.

Slatoff criticizes Caddy for her attitude toward Quentin: "We learn that she is concerned about her daughter Quentin's welfare, but not concerned enough to do anything serious about it."[27] What Slatoff ignores is that Caddy is so hamstrung by the maneuverings of Jason and the unforgivingness of Mrs. Compson that she is powerless to do anything more for Quentin than send her money. Caddy is cut off almost entirely from communication with the Compson household: Jason censors her letters to Quentin (p. 208), she learns of her father's death only by accident (p. 220), and Jason tells her, " 'We dont even know your name at that house' " (p. 221).

The most important reason for Caddy's not taking Quentin away is again her love. She does not want Quentin to become a mistress or a prostitute, and Jason knows it. When she offers Jason a thousand dollars to let her have Quentin back, he mocks her:

> 'And I know how you'll get it,' I says, 'You'll get it the same way you got her. And when she gets big enough—' Then I thought she really was going to hit at me. . . .
> 'Oh, I'm crazy,' she says, 'I'm insane. I can't take her. Keep her. What am I thinking of.' (p.227)

Now like a wound-up toy (p. 227), Caddy is completely frustrated and broken down by her lifelong antagonist, Jason. He notes that "her hands were hot as fever" and that she is making a strange noise: ". . . she begun to laugh and to try to hold it back all at the same time. 'No. I have nothing at stake,' she says, making that noise, putting her hands to her mouth, 'Nuh-nuh-nothing,' she says" (p. 227). This is a terrifying picture of the collapse of her spirit.

Still, Caddy is anxious about Quentin; even though she realizes that Jason has not " 'a drop of warm blood' " in him (p. 226), she pleads with him to take care of Quentin. Her broken and incoherent sentences indicate her highly emotional state and her sense of helplessness: " 'Just promise that she'll—that she—You can do that. Things for her. Be kind to her. Little things that I cant, they wont let . . .' " (p. 226). By this time Caddy has lost her self-confidence and her innocence; she is reduced to pleading with the brother she knows will not help her. The only quality Caddy has not lost is her love, for she still cares about Quentin.

But in Faulkner's appendix to the novel, when Caddy is seen with the Nazi, even the love is gone, and destruction is complete. Yet even though Caddy's final position with the Nazi represents spiritual damnation, it seems to be, ironically enough, one of worldly success. The picture of Caddy which the librarian finds is "filled with luxury and money and sunlight—a Cannebière backdrop of mountains and palms and cypresses and the sea, an open powerful expensive chromiumtrimmed sports car, the woman's face hatless between a rich scarf and a seal coat, ageless and beautiful, cold serene and damned . . ." (p. 12).

The description of Caddy here resembles that of Eula Varner riding out of Frenchman's Bend with her impotent bridegroom: "The beautiful face did not even turn as the surrey drew abreast of the store. It passed in profile, calm, oblivious, incurious. It was not a tragic face: it was just damned."[28] The coldness and serenity isolate and protect the two women from the world. Yet there is an important difference between Caddy and Eula. Eula's face is not tragic, just damned: she had had nothing to lose; Caddy had much to lose, and her face is both tragic and damned. Although she gains the "luxury and money and sunlight" (p. 12), she loses "anything . . . worth being saved for," as the librarian Melissa Meek pointed out, and she now has "nothing worth being lost that she can lose" (p. 16). Caddy is damned because she has become cold, empty-eyed, and passionless like Eula Varner. She has lost her capacity for love, and Dilsey's comment "What a sinful waste . . ." (p. 109) is the most apt summary of her tragedy. Even selfless love can result in the destruction of the person who practices it. The wasteful loss of Caddy's great capacity for compassion and sacrifice makes her fate the most unbearable and tragic doom in *The Sound and the Fury*.

Notes

1. Jean Stein, "William Faulkner," *Writers at Work, The* Paris Review *Interviews*, ed. Malcolm Cowley (New York, 1958), p. 130.

2. Lawrence Bowling, "Faulkner and the Theme of Innocence," *Kenyon Review*, XX (1958), 475.

3. Bowling, p. 466.

4. Olga Vickery, *"The Sound and the Fury:* A Study in Perspective," *Publications of the Modern Language Association*, LXIX (1954), 1017.

5. Frederick L. Gwynn and Joseph L. Blotner, eds., *Faulkner in the University* (Charlottesville, Virginia, 1959), p. 274.

6. William Faulkner, *The Sound and the Fury* (New York, 1946), p. 227. Subsequent references, which appear in the text, are to this edition.

7. Bowling, p. 475.

8. Charles Anderson, "Faulkner's Moral Center," *Etudes Anglaises*, VII (1954), 57.

9. Carvel Collins, "A Conscious Literary Use of Freud?" *Literature and Psychology*, III, iii (1953), 3.

10. Bowling, p. 476.

11. Sumner C. Powell, "William Faulkner Celebrates Easter, 1928," *Perspective*, II (1949), 208.

12. Ruel E. Foster, "Dream as Symbolic Act in Faulkner," *Perspective*, II (1949), 181.

13. Gwynn and Blotner, p. 6.

14. Gwynn and Blotner, p. 1.

15. Robert A. Jellife, *Faulkner at Nagano* (Tokyo, 1956), p. 104.

16. Gwynn and Blotner, p. 31.

17. Gwynn and Blotner, p. 1.

18. Bowling, p. 479.

19. William Faulkner, *As I Lay Dying* (New York, 1946), p. 532.

20. Robert Frost, "Birches," *The Poems of Robert Frost* (New York, 1946), p. 128.

21. Faulkner, *As I Lay Dying*, p. 464.

22. Robert Penn Warren, *William Faulkner and His South*, The First Peter Rushton Seminar in Contemporary Prose and Poetry, No. 16 (unpublished essay, Univ. of Virginia, Charlottesville, Virginia, 1951), p. 14.

23. Vickery, p. 1026.

24. Faulkner, *As I Lay Dying*, p. 467.

25. T. S. Eliot, "Baudelaire (1930)," *Selected Essays 1917–1932* (New York, 1932), p. 344.

26. Walter J. Slatoff, *Quest for Failure: A Study of William Faulkner* (New York, 1960), p. 151.

27. Slatoff, p. 151.

28. William Faulkner, *The Hamlet* (New York, 1940), p. 270.

Nihilism in Faulkner's *The Sound and the Fury*

John V. Hagopian*

Immediately upon the publication of *The Sound and the Fury* in 1929, Evelyn Scott asserted that Dilsey, the compassionate and enduring Negro servant of the degenerate Compson family, was to be taken as the moral norm of the novel. "Dilsey," she said, "provides the beauty of coherence against the background of struggling choice. She recovers for us the spirit of tragedy which the patter of cynicism has often made seem lost."[1] Twenty years later Sumner C. Powell called attention to the Christian dimensions of Dilsey's values, citing Faulkner's "use of the Christian order as a dramatic contrast to the disorder of the Compsons and as a judgment on them."[2] Soon after that, Faulkner's Nobel Prize Speech of 1950 stimulated a decade of critiques which interpret Dilsey as the moral norm, thereby making *The Sound and the Fury* a novel which embodies some positive moral vision, often denoted as Christian.[3] That view remained almost without serious challenge until Cleanth Brooks recently asserted that "the title of *The Sound and the Fury* . . . provides a true key, for the novel has to do with the discovery that life has no meaning." Brooks conceded that "for Dilsey life does have meaning . . . [but] Faulkner makes no claim for Dilsey's version of Christianity one way or the other. His presentation of it is moving and credible, but moving and credible as an aspect of Dilsey's own mental and emotional life."[4] However, if Brooks is correct that the title *is* an accurate indication that "the novel has to do with the discovery that life has no meaning," then Faulkner does make a claim against Dilsey's version of Christianity—for the novel itself denies it. Furthermore, Brooks does not show how the structure, especially that of the so-called Dilsey section, supports the notion that the title is indeed an accurate guide to the meaning. It is the burden of this paper to demonstrate that a structural analysis of the closing chapter of *The Sound and the Fury* does, in fact, reveal nihilism as the meaning of the whole.

More than fifteen years ago Mark Schorer explained that technique is

*Reprinted, with permission, from *Modern Fiction Studies*, 13, No. 1 (Spring 1967), 45–55. *Modern Fiction Studies*, © 1967 by Purdue Research Foundation, West Lafayette, Indiana 47907.

the only means that a writer has of "discovering, exploring, and developing his subject, of conveying its meaning, and, finally, of evaluating it."[5] *The Sound and the Fury* has, unfortunately, been too often discussed in terms of readers' responses to various individual characters, or of Faulkner's latter-day reminiscences and philosophizing, or of the morality of Southern Protestantism, rather than in terms of technique. One of the most crucial elements of technique is closure, namely, the means by which the action is rounded off and rendered whole and the meaning finally embodied;[6] and an analysis of closure is one of the most economical ways of reaching an understanding of the total form of a work. What has hitherto not been observed of the final chapter of *The Sound and the Fury* is that it has four parts: a prologue, and three distinct actions which develop motifs that are first struck in the prologue. Furthermore, each of the final three movements recapitulates themes and motifs of the first three chapters—the Quentin, Jason, and Benjy sections, respectively—and each ends on a semblance of closure. However, the first two of these closures are merely tentative. They are false conclusions, and in proceeding beyond them Faulkner is, in effect, repudiating the terms by which they would have determined the total form-content. The final closure encapsules everything that precedes it and shapes the ultimate meaning of the novel.

Perhaps two schematic summaries will serve to clarify these general ideas before they are explored in detail.

I.
STRUCTURE OF THE FINAL CHAPTER
Prologue
Dawn to 9:30 a.m.
All remaining Compsons and Gibsons
at home; three movements
toward closure foreshadowed

1.	2.
Movement to	*Movement to*
Tragic-Christian Closure	*Socio-Economic Closure*
9:30 a.m. to 1:30 p.m.	9:30 a.m. to 1:30 p.m.
Dilsey's stately walk to church and return—a recapitulation of the theme of Quentin section	Jason's furious drive to the carnival in pursuit of Miss Quentin—a recapitulation of the theme of Jason section

3.
Movement to Nihilistic Closure
1:30 to about 3 p.m.
Benjy and Luster's erratic trip by horse and buggy to monument—
a recapitulation of the theme of the Benjy section

II.
RELATION OF THE THREE CLOSURES TO THE
ENTIRE NOVEL

Chapter 1:	*Chapter 2:*	*Chapter 3:*
Benjy Nihilism	Quentin Christian Morality [Bracketed by Mr. Compson's nihilistic philosophy]	Jason Socio-Economic values

Chapter 4:

First Closure
casts novel in
Tragic-Christian terms

Second Closure
casts novel in
Socio-economic terms

Third Closure
casts novel in
Nihilistic Existential terms

I. STRUCTURE OF THE FINAL CHAPTER

Prologue: Dawn to 9:30 a.m. (pp. 281–303)[7]

In moving from ritual to rage to irrationality, the opening section of the last chapter focuses first on Dilsey (281–293), then on Jason (293–300), and finally on Benjy and Luster (300–303) in a thematic progression that foreshadows the three closure movements which follow. That Dilsey's values cannot prevail is seen immediately in the symbolism that marks her first emergence from the cabin. Dilsey appears dressed in "colour regal and *moribund*," the theological purple of her silk dress covered by the royal maroon of her velvet cape. But that cape has a "border of mangy and anonymous fur" which significantly undermines the symbolic power of those colors. Indeed, Faulkner tells us that "the days or the years had consumed" Dilsey's strength, leaving only a "ruin." As Dilsey completes her stately ritual of emergence and withdrawal, "a pair of jaybirds came up from nowhere, . . . swung in raucous tilt and recover, screaming into the wind that ripped their harsh cries . . ." (282). That their cries are a sardonic mockery of all Dilsey stands for is suggested shortly afterward when Luster throws a rock at the jaybirds, shouting, "Git on back to hell, whar you belong at. 'Taint Monday yit" (285). Thus hellish forces invade the peace and calm of a cold Easter morning, signifying that Christian values cannot appease or redeem the meaningless violence of the Compsons. Then when Dilsey, dressed in blue gingham (the Virgin's color) re-emerges from her cabin and enters the house, she hears the whining of Mrs. Compson, who is dressed in "a dressing gown of quilted black satin" (Satan's color). Dilsey can patiently endure the Compsons, but cannot prevail over them. Arbitrarily summoned by Mrs. Compson's demand that she dress Benjy and then halted half-way up the stairs by the contradictory demand thàt she immediately prepare Jason's breakfast, Dilsey stops "with her foot lifted to the next step . . . her hand against the wall . . . motionless and shapeless" (287–288). Dilsey's gesture of appeasement is paralyzed and she returns to her kitchen. Restored to her proper domain, Dilsey resumes singing as she works, "something without particular tune or words, repetitive, mournful and plaintive, austere" (286). Indeed, she is the only character in the novel who orders and expresses her experience in song, but it is not a song of triumph and no one listens or learns from her. When the kitchen clock strikes five times, Dilsey can confidently announce that it is eight o'clock, but she cannot set the Compson clock in order. And, as she listens, there is "no sound save the clock *and the fire*" (290). Finally, in control of the instruments of ritual order, she rings "a small clear bell" summoning the Compsons to breakfast; but when Jason arrives, he introduces the second motif of the prologue—disorder and, in his behavior to follow, a mockery of the rituals of Easter.

It is now Jason, and not Dilsey, who dominates the scene with his fury at the broken window in his room and at Miss Quentin's absence from the breakfast table. He commands Dilsey to summon her—a command Dilsey cannot fulfill. Mrs. Compson apologizes to Jason for having given the Negroes permission to attend church, and Jason deliberately misunderstands her to mean the carnival. This is only one of a series of gratuitous insults to Christian institutions, and a foreshadowing of the church and carnival episodes which immediately follow the prologue. Upon his discovery that Miss Quentin has run off with the money, Jason becomes a Snopesish "man in motion," accompanied by the swirl of jaybirds shrieking past the house. His frantic gestures are in strong contrast with the ritual dignity and grace of Dilsey at the opening of the prologue.

With Jason gone, the focus shifts to Benjy and Luster, and the emphasis is on the motif of Benjy's "slow bellowing sound, *meaningless and sustained*" (301). It is the subsequent development of this motif that finally closes the novel. Before taking Benjy to the pasture, Luster comically underlines the fact that Benjy is a manifestation of meaninglessness when he protests to Dilsey, "I aint lying. Ask Benjy ef I is" (302). Benjy can never affirm or deny anything; he can only be, and his being is nothingness.

The First Two Movements Toward Tentative Closures 9:30 a.m. to 1:30 p.m.

1. *Dilsey to and from the Church* (pp. 303–317)

2. *Jason to and from the Carnival* (pp. 317–329)

These two actions function as a kind of dissonant counterpoint. The morning bells of the church mark Dilsey's second stately emergence from her cabin, dressed once again in the symbolic theological and royal colors (303), and the same bells also mark Jason's frenzied drive to the sheriff's house (317). Both are mocked by Benjy's "hopeless and prolonged" wail, "all time and injustice and sorrow become vocal for an instant by a conjunction of planets" (303–4). That wail suggests the futility both of Dilsey's rituals to order the chaos of the universe and of Jason's attempts to recover his money. As she moves through a wasteland landscape toward church, Dilsey exchanges ritual greetings with the other communicants—"Sis' Gibson! How you dis mawnin?" / "I'm well. Is you well?" / "I'm right well, I thank you" (307); at the same time Jason rejects the sheriff's greeting with a peremptory "You ready to go now?" (317). The Negroes move toward church "with slow sabbath deliberation" (308), while Jason drives "on out of the bells and out of town" thinking "every damn one of them will be at church" (321). The members of the Negro congregation are attuned to their God and drawn "to one another in chanting measures beyond the need for words" (310), but Jason imagines himself (like Satan in *Paradise Lost*, VI: 135) "dragging Omnipotence down from His throne, if necessary; of the embattled legions of both hell and heaven through which he tore his way and put his hands at last on his fleeing niece" (322). As Reverend Shegog greets his "breddren en sistuhn" (311), Jason erupts into the pullman car of the carnival with an imperious "Where are they? . . . Quick, now" (324) and becomes involved in a furious battle with the indignant carnival hands (325–26). At that very moment the minister is preaching about "de angels singin de peaceful songs en de glory" (312). As the sermon closes with a reference to "de arisen dead whut got de blood en de ricklickshun of de Lamb" (313), Jason is "falling, thinking So this is how it'll end, and he believed that he was about to die" (326). On the next page is a drawing of the electric eye of Mottson looking down on Jason, an eye surely derived from the degenerate technological god manifested by Fitzgerald's Dr. T. J. Eckleburg in *The Great Gatsby*. By 12:30 both the church service and Jason's pursuit are ended. Back in the house, Dilsey enters a "pervading reek of camphor" in Mrs. Compson's room (314), just as Jason in terrible pain from his headache thinks "I can get something [camphor] for it at Jefferson" (329). At one o'clock, having summoned Luster and Benjy to dinner, Dilsey repeats, "Jason aint comin home" (316, 317) at the same moment that Jason "wasn't thinking of home, where Ben and Luster were eating cold dinner at the kitchen table. Something . . . permitted him to forget Jefferson as any place which he had ever seen before, where his life must resume itself" (329).

Although these two extended passages are stretched over exactly the same time period and embody a thematic contrast in a considerable number of details, each independently constitutes a different movement toward closure. The focus on Dilsey comes first and presents only the first of three possible conclusions for the novel as a whole. "I've seed de first en de last," says Dilsey—and "I seed de beginnin, en now I sees de endin" (313). These pronouncements, together with the return from church to the "square, paintless house with its rotting portico," would have terminated the novel in such a way as to make of the Reverend Shegog's sermon an appropriate epigraph for the entire novel. The completed action would then be seen from a Christian perspective, for, indeed, "de generations passed away," and the Compson line, which "aint got de milk en de dew of de old salvation" (311), has come to an end.

The idea that Christian values cannot redeem the Compsons was already dramatized in Chapter II when Quentin, unable to prove false his father's nihilistic pronouncements, committed suicide. In the first closure of the last chapter the same idea is recapitulated by Dilsey, who realizes that the Compson line comes to an end without salvation. Just as surely as Quentin's watch without hands, Dilsey's broken kitchen clock confirms Mr. Compson's observation that "Christ was not crucified: he was worn away by a minute clicking of little wheels" (96). The irony of Dilsey's faith in the Christian message of Reverend Shegog—just like the irony of her certainty that she can see through the disorder of time—was foreshadowed in the Quentin section when Quentin recalled that a brothel full of Negroes in Memphis "went into a religious trance ran naked into the street. It took three policemen to subdue one of them. Yes Jesus O good man Jesus O that good man" (189). At Dilsey's Easter service a member of the congregation had chanted, "I sees, O Jesus! Oh I sees!" (312).

But Faulkner abandons this Christian motif and for the second ending shifts the focus to Jason's futile pursuit of his niece and his money. This recapitulates Chapter III, "April 6, 1928," when once before Jason pursued his niece in a pain-wracked drive through the countryside around Jefferson. It is significant, too, that his departure and return in a power-driven machine, symbolic of the money-drives of the industrial age, contrasts with the slow, deliberate pace of the Negroes moving on foot to church and back. Accompanying this contrast is a contrast in tone between the tragic and the sardonic-comic. Jason is almost reduced to the level of a Tom and Jerry cartoon and the action closes with the frustrated Jason hoist with his own petard as the Negro charges him four dollars to drive him back to Jefferson. Here, too, the novel might have ended without the least suggestion of seeming incomplete. The final perspective would then have been a socio-economic one, evoking the "thirty pieces of silver" rather than the milk and the dew of the old salvation. Had that been the case *The Sound and the Fury* would have required consideration as an exposé of the anti-Christian materialism of the New South, similar to that of the comic Snopes trilogy.

Final Conclusion: 1:30 to about 3 p.m.

3. *Luster and Benjy's Abortive Progress* (329–336)

As Faulkner moves beyond the two closures described above, he shifts perspective to the action of Luster and Benjy. This thematically takes us back full circle to the opening of the novel, where neither God nor Mammon prevails—merely chaos and meaninglessness. Once again Benjy moans before his stalk of jimson weed; once again he howls at the golfers' calls for "Caddy"; and once again he finds only temporary solace in Dilsey's compassion for him.

It becomes clear to Dilsey that Benjy cannot remain quiet until four o'clock when T. P. is to drive him to the cemetery, and she reluctantly lets Luster take him. This time the movement away from the house is neither on foot or by machine—it is by animal. The aged mare Queenie is hitched to a broken-down surrey; her gait is slow, but hardly dignified—"resembling a prolonged and suspended fall." Moving in the direction of *death* (i.e., the cemetery), Benjy's eyes are as empty as those of the statue of the Confederate soldier, until his purely meaningless sense of order is violated when Luster swings the horse to the left of the monument. Then "bellow on bellow" Benjy's voice mounts, until Jason leaps on the surrey, strikes both Luster and Benjy, and whips the horse into a plunging gallop homeward. "Benjy, fer God's sake!" shouts Luster, invoking the Deity for the first time—and in vain. Finally, "his [Ben's] eyes were empty and blue and serene again as cornice and façade flowed smoothly once more from left to right; post and tree, window and doorway, and signboard, each in its ordered place" (336).

Thus the novel reaches its final closure in heavily ironic terms: Jason, his paradise lost, vents his violence not to drag Omnipotence down from His throne, but for purely selfish motives to restore a meaningless sense of order. It is reminiscent of the end of Chapter I when after another very hard day for Benjy, "the dark began to go in smooth, bright shapes, like it always does, even when Caddy says that I have been asleep" (94). At the end, for the first time in the novel, Faulkner does not bring the action from dawn to darkness; instead he thematically bends the novel back to its beginning. The terms of closure are neither Christian nor socio-economic; they are nihilistic. It is the *reducto absurdum* of the experience of Easter Sunday and the Easter week-end.

II. RELATION OF CLOSURE TO THE BODY OF THE NOVEL

Faulkner himself has said that in the last chapter he "tried to gather the pieces together and fill in the gaps by making [himself] the spokesman."[8] The first three chapters are presented from the perspective of the three Compson brothers, each with his own peculiarly distorted sense of time. Benjy's view is that of the eternal present. He has no awareness of the past as past; fragments of past events occur to him in an achronological sequence, all as if they were occurring on April 7, 1928. Quentin, on the other hand, is past-oriented—even past-obsessed. He associates almost all present events with episodes of the past, or sees the present itself as inevitably becoming the past. In committing suicide, he enacts his father's dictum that "its not even time until it was" (197). Jason, however, is a "man in motion" constantly projecting himself into the future, scrambling out of the past and the present as fast as he can into future wealth, power, and status: "Just let me have twenty-four hours without any damn New York jew to advise me. . . . Once I've done that they can bring all Beale Street and all bedlam in here" (280). None of the Compson brothers lives in harmony with an orderly rhythm of time. Nevertheless, all their time-perspectives have in common that necessary attribute of any stream-of-consciousness—the experiencing of all present events in an irreversible, one-directional flow. Each of the first three chapters moves inexorably from morning to night, however much that movement is broken by flash-forwards, flash-backs, or memories.[9]

However, when Faulkner shifts in the last chapter from the subjective points-of-view of his characters to an objective narrator's perspective, he is no longer bound to any one character's sense of time. Hence, it is inaccurate to say, as Cleanth Brooks does, that "it is only in the fourth section of the book, the one dominated by Dilsey, that we enter into a proper notion of time."[10] To be sure, the flow of present time is not interrupted by any recapitulation of events from the past, yet neither does it move in an irreversible, one-directional flow. Nor is the focus solely on Dilsey. As we have seen, the prologue shifts from character to character before the narrator temporarily fixes on Dilsey's progression to and from the Easter services—an action that moves from 9:30 to 1:30. But then, for the first time in the novel, the forward motion of time is broken off and those same four hours are presented in terms of Jason's actions. When the time sequence again reaches 1:30, the narrator focuses attention on Benjy and Luster until the climatic events at the Confederate monument in mid-afternoon. Since there are, after the prologue, three time sequences each focused on a different character or characters, it is simply false to assert that the last chapter embodies either Dilsey's point-of-view or her notion of time.

Although the objective narrator manipulates the time-flow of the last chapter, he does so to deal with themes that were presented from the purely subjective points-of-view of the earlier chapters. And thus he makes objective and authorial the futility of Christian values to order the Compson experience in terms of sin and redemption. Faulkner's chorus figure is Quentin's father, Jason Compson III. The father's nihilistic pronouncements open and close the Quentin section. At the beginning Quentin recalls him saying, "[in this watch] I give you the mausoleum of all hope and desire . . . the reducto absurdum of all human experience. . . . Because no battle is ever won. . . . They are not even fought. The field only reveals to man his own folly and despair, and victory is an illusion of philosophers and fools. . . . / . . . nothing is even worth the changing of it" (95, 97). At the end he is remembered saying, "a love or a sorrow is a bond purchased without design. . . . / [temporary] was the saddest word of all there is nothing else in the world its not despair until time its not even time until it was" (196–97). The action of his three sons and of the novel as a whole confirms Mr. Compson. It is because Quentin realizes that his father is right, that it is futile to look to Jesus and St. Francis for any meaningful guide to action in a time-bound world, that he commits suicide. But before completing his deathward movement, Quentin meticulously arranges his effects in perfect—and meaningless—order. Jason, too, furiously pursues a selfish order which will allow all bedlam to enter the Compson world. The futility of secular-materialistic values as an ordering of the Compson experience is revealed when the fluctuations of the stock market (the news of which never reaches him in time) and the flight of Miss Quentin mock his quest. At the end Benjy is, of course, unaware of the futility of his more primitive kind of order in the face of existential nothingness; but the chaos he experiences and responds to with moanings and howlings, and the false order that ironically soothes him, dramatically frame the entire novel in the same way that Mr. Compson's sophisticated commentary frames the Quentin section. It is therefore Mr. Compson, and not Dilsey, whose values finally prevail. Time is demonstrated to be indeed the *reducto absurdum* of all human experience.

R. W. Flint said a decade ago that "Faulkner's fiction, made up as it is of a great many interesting styles and techniques, deserves to be called thoroughly composed, *durchkomponiert,* as the Germans say of music, not only in what it presents, but in what it suggests."[11] Nowhere is the *Durchkomponierung* more brilliantly manifested than in *The Sound and the Fury*.

Notes

1. Quoted with apparent approval by William van O'Connor, *The Tangled Fire of William Faulkner* (Minneapolis, 1954), p. 44.

2. "William Faulkner Celebrates Easter, 1928," *Perspective*, II (1949), 215.

3. A sampling of opinions in the full-length studies confirms this. Irving Howe: "Dilsey is strong, whole, uncorrupted. She is the voice of judgment over the Compsons and their

world." *William Faulkner: A Critical Study* (New York, 1952), p. 41; Hyatt Waggoner: "Dilsey is a kind of foster-mother of Christ, the enabling agent of revelation at once spiritual and aesthetic." *William Faulkner: From Jefferson to the World* (Lexington, 1959), p. 46; Walter J. Slatoff: "[The final scene of Benjy and Luster] does not negate the moderate affirmation of the Dilsey episode, nor does it really qualify it. Rather it stands in equal suspension with it as a commentary of equal force." *Quest for Failure* (Ithaca, 1960), p. 158; Olga Vickery: "Dilsey . . . becomes through her actions alone the embodiment of the truth of the heart which is synonymous with morality. . . . In a sense, Dilsey represents a final perspective directed toward the past and the Compsons, but it is also the reader's perspective for which Dilsey merely provides the vantage point. . . . / There is no doubt but that Dilsey is meant to represent the ethical norm, the realizing and acting out of one's humanity." *The Novels of William Faulkner* (Baton Rouge, 1959), pp. 32, 47; Michael Millgate: "Faulkner's main concern in this [final] section is apparently to establish firm images of order, stability, and trust to set over against the images of disorder, decay, selfishness, and deceit which have dominated the earlier sections." *Faulkner* (Edinburgh, 1961), p. 32; Frederick J. Hoffman: "Faulkner associates her [Dilsey's] dignity and power of endurance with universal truths and values, which will become the final means of judging the Compsons. . . . / From these several objective portraits [in the last chapter] it becomes obvious that the one of Dilsey will dominate and that in its terms Faulkner intends a final perspective upon the Compson story." *William Faulkner* (New York, 1961), pp. 58–59.

4. *William Faulkner: The Yoknapatawpha Country* (New Haven, 1963), pp. 347, 348; see above, p. 137.

5. "Technique and Discovery," originally published in *Hudson Review*, I (Spring, 1948) and widely reprinted.

6. Students of Gestalt psychology will recognize that I am using a variation of a technical term in that discipline. *Closure* is, of course, not a synonym of *conclusion*. *Closure* is determined by the internally unifying force or set of vector forces that structure an object and render it as a meaningful, discreet, and perceptible whole. However, such a whole—even a work of literature—need not have a conclusion to be "closed;" *vide* a circle or Joyce's *Finnegans Wake*. Although *The Sound and the Fury* shares with *Finnegans Wake* the feature of having the ending lead in some way back to the opening, it does not as literally make a circle of the work. Only thematically does Faulkner's ending recapitulate the opening. *The Sound and the Fury* does have a conclusion, and as in most novels its conclusion provides important elements of closure.

7. Page references cited in parentheses throughout the text are to the Modern Library edition of *The Sound and the Fury* (New York, 1946). All italics are mine.

8. Malcolm Cowley, ed., *Writers at Work: The Paris Review Interviews* (New York, 1959), p. 130.

9. A flashback may be defined as an interruption of present events with a past event which is consciously experienced by the character as *past;* but a flash-forward is an interruption of present events by a past event which is consciously experienced by the character as a *present* event.

10. Brooks, p. 328.

11. "Faulkner as Elegist," *Hudson Review*, VII (Summer, 1954), 257

The Recollection and the Blood: Jason's Role in *The Sound and the Fury*

Duncan Aswell*

The Sound and the Fury has attracted widespread critical attention largely because of the technical brilliance and difficulty of the Benjy and Quentin sections and the moving Easter service that Dilsey attends near the end of the novel. Considerably less emphasis has been placed upon the depiction of Jason, one of Faulkner's most vivid, convincing, and humorous portraits. Jason's monologue serves as an ironic commentary on the major themes of the novel, extending their significance in ways Jason is largely unaware of. His conception of himself as a man of the world allows him to assert his total unlikeness to Benjy and Quentin, neither of whom is able to cope with the world at all. Yet Faulkner shows Jason to be not only incompetent in practical, worldly affairs, but driven by the same compulsions and forced to act out the same obsessions as his unfortunate brothers.[1]

The Reverend Shegog articulates a central theme of the novel when he addresses his "breddren en sistuhn" in the audience on the subject of "the recollection and the blood of the Lamb." The preacher speaks to all mankind as his brethren and to an extent the search of the Compsons for some significant truth or meaning in life is the dilemma faced by every human being. But the preacher's emphasis on "the recollection and the blood" is specially relevant to the three Compson brothers in their relationships to their sister Caddy. Jason can no more free himself from the burden of remembering and dwelling upon Caddy and compulsively reënacting his childhood relationship to her than Benjy and Quentin can, and in so doing he bears witness to that blood tie with all the Compsons that he continually attempts to ignore or to use for his own benefit. His mother, his niece, Dilsey, and his own thoughts continually remind him throughout the day of the duties and responsibilities owed to "flesh and blood." In an ironic way, his actions bear eloquent testimony to his own statement that "blood is blood and you cant get around it" (Modern Library edition, p. 260).

The heritage of blood shows preëminently in the way Jason conducts his business and practical affairs. He considers himself a resolutely self-

*Reprinted, with permission, from *Mississippi Quarterly*, 21, No. 3 (Summer 1968), 211–18.

reliant and independent fellow, convinced that the only way to get ahead in the world is to trust no man and to take heed of nobody's feelings. He sees human life as subject to no absolute and eternal powers but only to the endless permutations of chance and change. In a universe governed by *luck*, each man is worth as much as his hands and brains can get for him. This doctrine is a debased version of his father's philosophy, as it is recalled by Quentin just before his monologue ends and Jason's begins. Mr. Compson mocks Quentin's concern with infinitude, with apotheosis, and urges him to keep his mind on "the sequence of natural events and their causes which shadows every mans brow" (p. 195). Every human act, every gesture, every feeling can be characterized by the single adjective "temporary," and life to Quentin's father is a game of chance presided over by the "dark diceman" (pp. 196–7). Faulkner elaborates Mr. Compson's fatalism at this point in the novel not only to suggest the compelling force behind Quentin's suicide, but to provide an ironic framework for Jason's behavior. Jason unwittingly lives his life according to the system of values believed in by his father, for whom he holds nothing but contempt.[2]

Yet Jason would not be a Compson if he did not turn his code of behavior into an inflexible and unmanageable rule. He converts a philosophy of extreme relativism into absolutism, makes temporality eternal. In a hilarious passage at the height of his maniacal determination to catch his fleeing niece, he imagines himself speeding past "the rear guards of Circumstance" and "dragging Omnipotence down from His throne, if necessary" (p. 322). This is apotheosis, of a kind, the ultimate triumph of the private-enterprise system. Yet the rear guards of Circumstance are, cruelly, not far behind. A moment later, when Jason discovers he has forgotten to carry a camphor-soaked handkerchief on his journey toward the Almighty, he sees himself "mocked by his own triumphing." This, indeed, is the keynote of Jason's whole day, being beaten by his own cleverness, or, as Job puts it, "You fools a man whut so smart he cant even keep up wid hisself . . . Mr. Jason Compson" (p. 267). Jason consistently fails to reach his specific, pragmatic goals because of his devotion to unrealities and abstractions.[3] His business sense is seriously impaired by his reliance on personal whims and prejudices for the sake of demonstrating his independence. A nice example is his refusal to bet on the Yankees, the team that won not only the American League pennant in 1928 but the World Series in four straight games. Jason's argument against them is characteristic: "You think a team can be that lucky forever?" (p. 269). Even in the face of logic and sense, he insists on reducing all experience to temporary status, as if he were his father.

While Jason considers all human events to be subject to endless change, he views the human personality itself as inalterably fixed and frozen. This conviction provides Jason with one constant factor in a world of variables; having observed an individual's behavior, one can predict his actions in the future. The fine irony of Jason's monologue is that he can articulate such a belief about everyone he knows, without realizing the ways in which he is fated to obey the very same law. He is frequently incorrect in his predictions about other people, but he manifests his own inescapable obsessions in every move he makes. His ignorance of himself is most clearly and amusingly revealed at the very moments when he expresses his sharp awareness that his behavior is ludicrous. He is so completely concerned with the way his actions appear to other people that he never considers the impulses that drive him from within. When he first catches sight of Quentin with the showman, he says of his following them: "Me, without any hat in the middle of the afternoon, having to chase up and down back alleys because of my mother's good name. Like I say you cant do anything with a woman like that, if she's got it in her. If it's in her blood, you cant do anything with her. . . . And there I was, without any hat, looking like I was crazy too" (p. 250). The point, of course, is that he is *acting* as if he were crazy, not just appearing to be so. He has the madness in his blood, no less than Quentin, and all of his clever awareness of his own and other people's follies and incapacities is no help to him in checking his irrationality. "Like I say blood always tells. If you've got blood like that in you, you'll do anything. [!] I says whatever claim you believe she has on you has already been discharged; I says from now on you have only yourself to blame because you know what any sensible person would do" (p. 256). Jason's pronouns are delightfully ambiguous, suggesting the confusion in his mind between his own and other people's actions, but the "you" in the last sentence can certainly refer to himself. He cannot possibly be considered a "sensible person," and his lack of sense is especially pointed in his inability to learn from his own experience.

Jason's static and unyielding character as well as his similarity to his brothers is emphasized by the structure of his monologue. He announces his conviction about the human personality in his very first statement, "Once a bitch always a bitch, what I say" (p. 198), and then returns to it at the very end of his narrative: "Like I say once a bitch always a bitch" (p. 280).[4] Over and over again during the day he introduces his remarks with the nagging refrain "Like I say," and the tag suggests how incapable Jason is of freeing himself from his own formulas and simplifications. Yet the one supremely important subject that he cannot keep away from is the promiscuity of Caddy and her daughter. He begins and ends with it; his mind revolves and endlessly around and around this one track. His monologue, like Benjy's and Quentin's, moves in a circle, but Jason's has the smallest radius. Benjy circles back through time to his earliest memory of Caddy's kindness, concluding with the pleasure of being put to bed by her as a tiny child. The progression is backwards, but the circle has passed through a great variety of images and impressions, all of which Benjy still actually possesses as part of his tangible enjoyment of the present instant. Quentin traces a smaller, spatial circle, returning at the end to his starting-point in his Harvard room. His aimless, compulsive wandering and the scrupulous attention to petty detail on which his monologue closes mock his desire for a confrontation with eternity, a way out of the circle. But the scope of his journeying seems enormous compared to the infinitesimal area covered by Jason, for all his frantic scrambling around the Mississippi countryside.[5]

Jason resembles Quentin not only in his obsessive concern with his relative's promiscuity, but in his extravagant view of the seriousness of the crimes he must punish and the lengths to which he must go to avenge himself. Quentin visualizes an eternity of suffering with Caddy as an answer to the meaninglessness and impermanence to which he and she are doomed. Jason's pursuit of his niece is a ludicrous parody of Quentin's teleological concern. He asserts an indifference to her fate at one moment: ". . . I says far as I'm concerned, let her go to hell as fast as she pleases and the sooner the better" (p. 256), yet he qualifies this almost immediately when he addresses his niece in his mind: "These damn little slick haired squirts, thinking they are raising so much hell, I'll show them something about hell I says, and you too. I'll make him think that damn red tie is the latch string to hell . . ." (pp. 258-9). Like his brother, Jason will not be happy until he can assure himself that he has tracked his prey to her final, eternal resting place. Such a concern with ultimates and absolutes obscures for both brothers the extent of their actual and literal complicity in the corruption for which they seek revenge. Just as Quentin is shown smearing mud over Caddy's body in a symbolic prefiguration of her sexual impurity (p. 156), so Jason is accused by his niece of making her act the way she does (pp. 276-7). Jason is not wholly responsible for his niece's misconduct, nor did Quentin alone stain his sister's honor, but the brothers' extravagant and unnatural preoccupations—Jason's with respectability, Quentin's with virginity—place intolerable demands upon the young lives they should be protecting.

Jason's devotion to much the same kind of unreal, hopeless, and abstract upholding of "honor" as Quentin believes in is appropriately concluded in a burlesque scene that might have come straight out of Quentin's day. Jason's preposterous tangle with the old man in a pullman car in Mottson is a clear reminder of Quentin's quixotic attack upon Gerald Bland. In both cases the recollection of dishonor leads to blood at the hands of someone wholly unconnected with the family. Quentin had been unable to distinguish the past from the present, his memories from literal fact, while Jason manifests his delusion by assuming that his private affairs are a subject of universal interest and ridicule. When he arrives at the railroad siding in Mottson, he expresses his fear that "the whole world would know that he, Jason Compson, had been robbed by Quentin, his niece, a bitch" (p. 324). He provokes the old man to attack him by assuming that his fantasy has already come true; he calls the old man a liar for not revealing the whereabouts of people whose names have not even been mentioned. The similarity of this incident to Quentin's irrational behavior is pointed up when Jason's rescuer asks him, "What were you trying to do? Commit suicide? . . . You her—brother?" (p. 327). Jason's perpetual worries about bleeding from the blow of a hatchet also recall Quentin's miserable performance as a fighter. Jason wasn't even struck by the old man; he simply hit his head on the rail when he fell. Quentin, likewise, wasn't hit by Dalton Ames, but "had just passed out like a girl" (p. 181). Shreve embarrassedly reports that Quentin *may* have struck Gerald Bland when no one was looking, but there is no question about the blood streaming from Quentin's nose (p. 183). The two brothers are equally pathetic and inept defenders of the Compson name.

Having been reduced in foolishness and in public humiliation to the level of Quentin, Jason is now ready to experience even further degradation. As he sits completely immobilized in his car waiting for some Negro to drive him home, he assumes the posture of the impotent Benjy on his afternoon rides with T. P. Faulkner concludes the scene in Mottson with a picture of Jason being driven home, his mind empty of all but the thought that relief for his headache awaits him in Jefferson:

> They drove on, along the streets where people were turning peacefully into houses and Sunday dinners, and on out of town. He thought that. He wasn't thinking of home, where Ben and Luster were eating cold dinner at the kitchen table. Something—the absence of disaster, threat, in any constant evil—permitted him to forget Jefferson as any place which he had ever seen before, where his life must resume itself. (p. 329)

The blood is quieted, the recollections still; for the moment there is nothing for Jason to do but to surrender himself to physical sensations in the manner of Ben. With this sight of Jason utterly helpless and unable to think about his responsibilities, the novel swings back to Benjy and completes another circle, returning to the situation of the opening pages. Ben and Luster are again at the fence, watching the golfers in the pasture. Despite Jason's and Quentin's absence, the life of the Compsons has resumed itself, in all its pointless repetitiveness.

Jason's descent through a series of ludicrous misadventures from cocksure man-of-the-world to a state of abject dependency is the most brilliant touch in this masterful portrait. While he likes to think of himself as an uncompromising dispenser of favors and punishments, he is actually as helpless to make any significant or lasting impression upon those around him as is Quentin to perform a permanently meaningful act. Jason might like to think that he is a ruthless villain, but he is incapable of hurting anyone but himself. Because he cannot escape the heritage of his past, his life is quite as pathetic and miserable as Benjy's or Quentin's. His final act, the rescuing of Benjy at the monument, is as meaningless a gesture as any of his others.[6] It is not motivated by kindness or generosity, but by the same compulsive concern for public propriety that has always driven him.

The reader's sense of justice is nicely satisfied by seeing the worldly brother come to the aid of one who is unable to cope with the world, yet there is no consciousness within the novel to record and profit from the irony. The characters themselves are largely ignorant of the patterns and correspondences that tie them together. Their recollections and their blood relationships are no source of joy and strength to them, not aids toward knowledge and growth. The movement of the novel is endlessly circular. The ending represents a kind of triumph for Benjy; but the triumph of mindlessness in a work about the tortures and travail of the human mind is a Pyrrhic victory indeed.

Notes

1. Jason's similarity to his brothers has been suggested by recent critics, but it has been demonstrated only in limited and theoretical ways. Lawrence K. Bowling, for example ("Faulkner and the Theme of Innocence," *Kenyon Review*, XX [Summer 1958], 466–87), examines innocence as a characteristic of all three Compson brothers. He shows Jason to be innocent in a different sense from Benjy and Quentin because "he remains ignorant of basic human principles" (p. 475). Cleanth Brooks (*William Faulkner: The Yoknapatawpha Country* [New Haven: Yale University Press, 1963]) compares attitudes toward the future in the three brothers. He says, "Jason is so committed to preparation for the future that he is almost as enslaved as are his brothers" (p. 330). Brooks also emphasizes, however, Jason's difference from his brothers. He contrasts Quentin's commitment in "the code of honor" with Jason's repudiation of that code (p. 337). John W. Hunt (*William Faulkner: Art in Theological Tension* [Syracuse: Syracuse University Press, 1965]) is concerned with what he calls "the locus and status of meaning" for each of the characters, and he contrasts Jason's "purely personal" meaning and "pragmatic value" system with a meaning that, for Quentin, is "a general one, informing all of life" (p. 69). Quentin's and Jason's value systems are contrasted even more sharply by Lawrance Thompson ("Mirror Analogues in *the Sound and the Fury*." *William Faulkner: Three Decades of Criticism*, ed. Frederick J. Hoffman and Olga Vickery [New York and Burlingame: Harcourt, Brace & World, 1960], pp. 211–225): "Jason's sadistic scale of values is more nearly analogous to the values of Iago than to those of the almost Hamlet-like Quentin" (pp. 224–5). Irving Howe *(William Faulkner* [New York: Vintage Books, 1952, 2nd ed.]) draws sharp contrasts among the three brothers: "Benjy is the past recaptured; Quentin . . . cannot hold the past with the purity Benjy can; Jason violently breaks from the past . . ." (p. 161). Jason might like to think he breaks violently from the past; I hope to show that he is as trapped by it as are Benjy and Quentin.

2. Wendell V. Harris (pp. 139–140 above), has traced the influence of Mr. Compson on each of his children, but he limits Jason's debt to his father to "bitterness" and Jason's "petulantly cynical tone."

3. Contrast the traditional view of Jason as altogether incapable of abstract formulations, as a thoroughgoing pragmatist. See, for example, William R. Mueller ("The Theme of Suffering: William Faulkner's *The Sound and the Fury*," *The Prophetic Voice in Modern Fiction* [New York: Association Press, 1959]): "Jason was almost as incapable as Benjy of conceptual thought and was consequently poles apart from Quentin in this respect" (p. 117). Compare Lawrence E. Bowling ("Faulkner and the Theme of Isolation," *The Georgia Review*, XVIII [Spring 1964], 50–66): "Unlike Quentin, who judges human actions by an abstract ideal, Jason considers an act right or wrong solely on the basis of whether it results in his gain or loss of material goods" (p. 59).

4. Bowling ("Theme of Isolation") calls "bitch" the key word for Jason because it

represents "Jason's naturalistic philosophy of life: he considers the whole human race no better than a pack of dogs, and he does everything he can to 'free' himself from any connection with them" (p. 59).

5. The sense the novel provides of activity severely limited and circumscribed is described in terms of the characters' personal isolation by Bowling ("Theme of Isolation") and by William A. Freedman ("The Technique of Isolation in *The Sound and the Fury,*" *Mississippi Quarterly*, XV [Winter 1961–1962], 21–26). Freedman says: "Jason is forever asserting his own independence, his ability to 'stand on his own two feet.' Yet this is but a hyper-reaction to a strong sense of his own imprisonment" (p. 25).

6. John V. Hagopian ("Nihilism in Faulkner's *The Sound and the Fury,*" (pp. 197–206 above) has accurately analyzed the effect of the closing pages.

Quentin Compson: Self-Portrait of a Young Artist's Emotions

Jackson J. Benson*

The Sound and the Fury is the most personal of Faulkner's novels. No other work engaged him for so long with such intensity. It was written, as the author has stated, out of "anguish"—a "dream" that haunted its dreamer for nearly two decades. A story that is retold five times and yet never told to the author's satisfaction appears very much like a ritual, "a spell to banish evil spirits."[1] And just as Hemingway's "Big Two-Hearted River" (the story which Malcolm Cowley discovered as "a spell") is about one thing, while seeming to be about another, so too *The Sound and the Fury* appears to be about the decline of the Compsons, when in fact this decline of a family is but the haunted vision projected out of the anguish of the novel's central character. The haunted dreamer is Quentin Compson, the oldest son and heir. Sensitive and suffering, he becomes the central moral agent in the novel and bears the burden of the author's anguish. To this end, Faulkner endows him with the equipment of the artist—the awareness, imagination, conscience, and civilized burden—so that Quentin comes to represent both the modern artist in general and also, in many revealing ways, the agony of Faulkner in particular.

Quentin Compson is used by Faulkner more often in the early, great period than any other narrator agent. From a first-person point of view, Quentin narrates two of the stories, "A Justice" and "That Evening Sun," in Faulkner's first collection, *These Thirteen*. In *Absalom, Absalom!* Quentin is used as a third-person, Jamesian "center of consciousness." While technically Quentin controls only a little more than a fourth of *The Sound and the Fury* (still, the longest of the segments), he remains the novel's center of consciousness. In effect, Quentin stands for "consciousness," while the remaining ancillary sections of Benjy, Jason, and Dilsey represent "sense," "brain," and "heart." Just as much as Strether in James's *The Ambassadors*, Quentin is the mirror by which the events which occur are given moral focus and perspective. Yet Quentin as a mirror works not with Strether's constant surveillance, but with a different intensity which becomes particularly apparent when one is aware of the

*Reprinted, with permission, from *Twentieth Century Literature*, 17, No. 3 (July, 1971), 143–59.

special relationship of Quentin to his creator. As the artist surrogate who indeed functions as an artist, Quentin, out of the frame of his monologue, provides an *esthètique du mal* by which the novel's meaning can be discovered. When one understands Quentin's autobiographical origins, this *esthètique* can be seen to provide a new ordering to the novel, as well as a firmer approach to the special problems posed by Quentin's stream of consciousness.

I

Rather than merely an object of the author's scorn, Quentin appears to have been created out of mixed feelings, and the relationship of Faulkner to his central character seems to involve both distance and identification. However, many critics, perhaps even most, have had little sympathy for Quentin. Lawrance Thompson, for example, finds Quentin striking a posture of "self-blinding and self-deafening arrogance." At the same time, critics have either denied, like Peter Swiggart, or ignored the possibility that Quentin may be in part a self-projection and a figure designed to purge the author of certain emotional obsessions. The nearest suggestion of such an author-character relationship is made by Michael H. Cowan, who briefly lists several correspondences between the author's life and the facts and characters of the novel. As Melvin Backman has said, "To write of Quentin Compson is to stir mixed feelings," and most critics seem to have been unable to bring together the obvious importance of this major character in Faulkner's early work with their essentially negative reactions to Quentin's character and role.[2]

Quentin may be physically weak, but he is also heroic; he may be obsessed, but he is also at times the most rational major character in the novel. Some clue to the actual Faulkner-Quentin relationship may lie in the fact that the scorn which has characterized much of the critical reaction to Quentin matches rather well, and for many of the same reasons, the scorn with which "Count No-count," Faulkner himself, was treated as he drifted, lost in his own dreams, through the streets of Oxford. In this regard, we might note that many of the reminiscences recorded in *William Faulkner of Oxford* reveal a picture of Faulkner as a young man who was usually alone and often made fun of by the townspeople and university students. Bramlett Roberts recalls, "It's a shameful thing but the kids used to run around here about the time Bill published *The Marble Faun*, and they called him Count and that sort of thing; somewhat in derision," and Calvin S. Brown confesses that "with the cocksure intolerance of the adolescent, I shared the general contempt of the ineffectual Count Faulkner."[3]

Of course, it would be wrong to argue that Quentin is a close or direct projection by Faulkner of his own condition as he perceived it at the time the novel was written, but it would be equally wrong to overlook these elements in Quentin's character and those aspects of his condition which match Faulkner's. To a limited extent, Quentin is a character who, as an objectification of the self, acts as a purgative for the author's own emotions. To a limited extent, Quentin embodies the writer's complaints against a pragmatic, materialistic, and hypocritical society which smothers genuine concern for others and which destroys the creative and idealistic personality. Thus, I would argue that Quentin Compson is yet another self-portrait of the artist as a young man.

If viewed from this angle, Quentin becomes a rather typical literary creation, reminiscent of Stephen Dedalus, Hugh Selwyn Mauberley, J. Alfred Prufrock, and Nick Adams.[4] Even Quentin's name suggests, like J. Alfred Prufrock, Hugh Selwyn Mauberley, and Stephen Dedalus, a certain self-mockery by the author. "Quentin" brings to mind both "queerness" and "contrariness," as well as that stubborn hero within the romantic tradition, Quentin Durward.[5] The novel itself, on this basis, becomes a more typical representative of its historical context and more in tune with the spirit of rebellion and alienation that dominated the works of such comtemporaries as Joyce, Pound, Eliot, and Hemingway. All of these writers produced protagonists with whom they identified, yet viewed with a certain ironic detachment—self-caricatures, as it were—but the young protagonist with all his faults is portrayed as less guilty in each case than the culture which surrounds him. Whatever faults the author and his young protagonist may have in common are magnified in the literary work, partly so that the author may have sympathy for his character and yet escape an overt expression of self-pity, perhaps, as a form of self-flagellation. Moments filled with anxiety ("dreams" filled with "anguish") are relived in order that they may be, at last, mastered and set aside.

Of particular interest in reference to Quentin Compson's frequently asserted self-destruction, obsessive guilt, and masochism is this passage from John Faulkner's biography:

> When Bill used the word "steal" [in reference to unconsciously borrowing two of his brother's story ideas] it was sort of self-flagellation. He was being hard on himself, leaning over backward to do so. It was like him. He was always harder on himself than on someone else. It was his way of demanding more of himself than of another person. There was no excuse in him for his own mistakes.[6]

At the same time, Faulkner's mother may have influenced Faulkner's use of Quentin as an indirect "purging agent" (suggested in a passage in the biography by his other brother):

> Nothing, to her [Faulkner's mother], was smaller and meaner than for an individual to complain about his own shortcomings and apparent misfortunes. Characteristic of this conviction was a cardboard placard hanging above the stove in her kitchen as long as I can remember, on which she

had written in red paint in her neat, clear brush strokes, "Don't Complain—Don't Explain." It was, in a real sense, her philosophy of life, and she passed it on in full measure to her children.[7]

There are a number of rough parallels between Faulkner's family and early life, and Quentin's family and personal history to suggest what some of the "seeds" of the novel may have been. Although Faulkner's mother was in most aspects the opposite of Caroline Compson (though intolerant in some ways, his mother apparently was also tough-fibered, energetic, and loving), his father, like Jason Compson III, had trouble carrying the burden of his prominent forebears and was, to some extent, an educated failure. He was a man, too, who drank and talked a good deal.[8]

As a boy Faulkner matches rather closely the picture of Quentin that we get in *The Sound and the Fury* as well as "That Evening Sun," a quiet, observant, serious, somewhat introverted, and thoughtful child who had no really close friends outside the family. John Ralph Markette (in Webb and Green) recalls that "Bill was a quiet boy and never had too much to say. He didn't seem to enter into many activities in which the other boys participated. He would roam through the woods with us looking for plums, chestnuts and blackberries. When we piled up leaves to jump in, or made sand houses, he would stand by and observe" (p. 29). Louis Cochran confirms this impression (also in Webb and Green): "As a boy he was moody, and variant, given to solitary walks, and a disinclination to mingle with his fellows which set him strangely apart from the romping, frolicsome youth of the town" (p. 218). Although Murry Falkner comments, "My brothers and I were, by and large, sufficient unto ourselves, in the sense that we had no bosom friends" (p. 83), the impression from inside the family is somewhat different from the outside impressions reported above. Both Murry and John tend to picture their brother William as a combination Tom Sawyer-Tom Swift—a leader in games and often very aggressive. At the same time, both brothers picture him, also, as a boy who could be a determined loner and quietly introspective.

The Falkner's family's Mammy Callie, of course, was the basis for Dilsey, matching Dilsey's endurance, aggressive good-humor, and position as part of the family, but differing from her literary counterpart in that she had "no capacity for detachment and fatalism."[9] The younger Jason IV appears to have been patterned after William's brother John, who, by his own testimony, was both a crybaby and a tattletale.[10] The younger Caddy may have had her seed in the cousin, Sallie Murry Wilkins, who was a frequent companion in the Falkner boys' childhood exploits.[11] Benjy appears to have had his origins in an epileptic boy who, inside his own fenced yard, followed the Falkner and other children on their way to school, on one occasion scaring some children who had teased him.[12] Faulkner's own maternal grandmother was called "Dammudy," and she died, after a long, painful bout with cancer, when Faulkner was ten.

At the age when Quentin is at Harvard, Faulkner was an oddball, considered "very queer" by a number of his contemporaries, and had already become a town and campus character. Like Quentin, he seems to have had few close friends, spent much time in solitary walks and in dreaming absentmindedly, and like Quentin also seems to have gotten on best with children. Calvin S. Brown (Webb and Green) tells of Faulkner as a very young man befriending a group of boys ten to twelve years younger, leading them off into the woods on Sunday afternoons for informal games of "paper chase," "running-through," and "capture the flag" (pp. 40–48). And Carvel Collins draws a picture of a Faulkner, who, when he was abroad in 1925, visited the Luxembourg Gardens frequently and there "for hours . . . helped children sail their boats on the pool."[13] When he was about seventeen, Faulkner began his long philosophical and literary discussions with his mentor, Phil Stone, discussions that may be dimly echoed, in the relationship if not the subject matter, in Quentin's long dialogues with his father.

Like Quentin, too, Faulkner was heavily indoctrinated as a child in the history and legends of the family and community. These legends and heavy reading, which included Romantic poetry and the novels of Scott, Cooper, Dickens, Kipling, and Stevenson, as well as the plays of Shakespeare and the dialogue of Plato, seem to have been responsible for laying the groundwork for that almost fanatical adherence to idealism which so often characterizes the incipient satirist and the disillusioned response to society of the young literary rebel.[14]

Little direct information, of course, can be had regarding the intensity of this idealism, but one indication later in life, certainly, was Faulkner's willingness to alienate his family and community by what he wrote[15] and his willingness to risk a deep rift with his own brothers by supporting the Supreme Court desegregation decision.[16] The most outstanding, earlier manifestation of his idealism can be found in his devotion to Estelle Oldham. He fell in love with her as a young teenager, lost her to another man when he was twenty, waited for her for eleven years, and finally married her after she divorced her first husband. Faulkner had waited for Estelle until he was thirty-two years old.

Indeed, one of the major seeds of *The Sound and the Fury*, the crucial role and image of Caddy, lies, I believe in this marriage of Estelle Oldham to another man and what she came to mean to Faulkner as an emotional symbol in the years after she left Oxford to go with her new husband to the Far East. William's brother John reports the outward reactions of William in response to the loss of his childhood sweetheart:

> Phil [Stone] got Bill a job in a bookstore in New Haven. The shop was run by a friend of his, a Miss Rawls or Miss Rawlings, I forget which. That's where Bill went so as to get as far away as possible when he found he'd lost Estelle. He must have gone through torment in that strange land with his whole world gone to pot. He counted the days as Estelle's wed-

ding approached, and when that deed was accomplished he joined the
Royal Flying Corps.[17]

John also testifies that it was Estelle's parents who made the selection of
her husband for her, rejecting William (although in John's opinion Estelle
loved him still) as a ne'er-do-well without even a high school diploma and
with no prospects, except perhaps vague, artistic ones. Their choice instead was Cornell Franklin, a graduate of Ole Miss whose "future seemed
assured in his family's business."[18]

There are enough parallels in this traumatic story to show that it
played some part in Faulkner's twenty-year effort to purge his "anguish"
through the writing and rewriting of *The Sound and the Fury*. New
Haven is enough like Cambridge, at least to outsiders, to approximate the
scene of Quentin's estranged self-torture, as he runs over and over again in
his mind the scene of Caddy's wedding, a wedding interrupted by Benjy's
bellowings of pain after a bout of drinking "sassprillah" (we can only
speculate about Faulkner's drinking during this period in New Haven, but
as a teenager he was in the habit of carrying a hip flask to college
dances[19]).

The Cornell Franklin-Faulkner rivalry is suggested by the story of an
early manuscript. Carvel Collins refers to three unpublished manuscripts
from the early 'twenties which touch on the Quentin Compson theme,
nearly a decade before the writing of *The Sound and the Fury*: a one act
play entitled *Marionettes*, "the story of Sir Galwyn in the unpublished
allegorical booklet titled 'Mayday,' " and a "brief, untitled, one act play
. . . showing how Ruth, an emancipated girl of the prohibition era, ends
her engagement to the more worldly Francis and becomes engaged to
pusillanimous Jim."[20] This latter story, although it can be only doubtfully
attributed to Faulkner, suggests a reversal, a more romantic earlier treatment, of the Franklin-Oldham-Faulkner story.

We know enough of Cornell Franklin to see that he was the very opposite of Faulkner, practical and established in a family business, and, in
general, somewhat like Herbert Head, who in turn is the very opposite of
Quentin. Certainly whatever Franklin's actual faults may have been,
Faulkner was ready to cast him as a villain. Estelle, like Caddy, has her
marriage arranged for her on a practical basis in relation to Franklin's
prospects. In *The Sound and the Fury* it is Head's business prospects (con-
taminated by dishonesty and cheap, slap-on-the-back Babbittry) which
become a central poison in the destruction of the family. Benjy's name
underlines the selling of the family soul to commercialism and must also
have represented Faulkner's own reaction to Estelle's parents' choice and
their apparent reasons for it.

In Faulkner's bitterly satirical portrait of Caroline Compson and her
obsessive need for respectability, we may have Faulkner's emotional reaction to the kind of climate which made Cornell Franklin's success with

Estelle and the Oldham family possible. In *The Sound and the Fury* Benjy's pasture becomes the means to finance the unfertile and futile marriage of respectability to Herbert Head, a plan devised and engineered by Caroline, whose dominant anxiety is that her family be recognized as being as good as her husband's. Quentin's year at Harvard, another product of Benjy's pasture, which brings to Quentin a deep sense of obligation for something that is essentially useless, is also a product of Caroline's pride. Her insensitivity is constantly contrasted with Quentin's over-sensitivity, and the forces that Caroline and her son Jason represent together are those that traditionally defeat the artist and destroy beauty and love, just as Caroline and Jason's victims, Quentin and Caddy, are twisted and destroyed. Caroline cares only, of course, for appearances. Whereas Quentin cares about the act itself and its moral implications, Caroline is concerned about the "talk." As the father states it to Quentin, "You are confusing sin and morality women dont do that your Mother is thinking of morality whether it be sin or not has not occurred to her."[22] ("Morality" in this context can be read as "respectability.")

Many of the basic appositions of theme, symbol, and character in *The Sound and the Fury* can be seen to have their origins in the Faulkner-Oldham-Franklin triangle, and it might not be too much to suggest that much of Faulkner's basic emotional and philosophical apparatus was forged in the heat of the internal conflict that apparently possessed him for so long. For one thing, the novel can be viewed as Faulkner's "growing-up" work wherein the ways of the world, its commercialism (Head, Jason IV) and common sense (Jason III, Spoade), are painfully discovered and are seen to overcome the spirit of youthful idealism. Much of the novel records the battle between cynical age (Jason III, Dalton Ames) and impractical youth (Quentin). The Romantic (a world patterned after the novels of Sir Walter Scott) and the heroic expectations of a young Faulkner are tarnished by the scorn of the worldly and refuted by the hard practicality of an older generation. This, of course, explains why *The Sound and the Fury* is essentially a novel of disillusionment. Faulkner, through Quentin, expresses a disillusionment with himself, mocking many of his own characteristics—particularly, his inability to act effectively. But bitterness pervades the fabric of the entire novel and underlies almost every human action and every human relationship. This is a very hard novel, even a nasty novel, filled with a brutality much more horrifying in its impact than anything Popeye does or anything that a Snopes can do (only in the brutalization of Joe Christmas is there anything really in Faulkner's work to match it). In the center of it all, of course, is Caddy, who is not so much a character in her own right as she is a surrogate for Quentin's spirit—the heroic past once believed in, the absolute idealism of youth, the poetic vision of love and beauty—which is crushed, victimized, and exploited.

Estelle Oldham, who in no literal sense is Caddy Compson, is translated out of her particular identity into the array of emotions which surround Caddy—jealousy, physical desire, romantic idolatry, frustration, self-pity, wounded pride, tarnished honor and shame, and impotency—all of which may well have haunted Faulkner after his loss. The intensity of the Faulkner's devotion for Estelle as well as its duration under what must have certainly seemed hopeless circumstances could be called an "obsession." The important thing is that for some time Estelle was the central emotional generating force for Faulkner, as well as the object of emotional speculation for an extremely fertile and well-schooled imagination. As in the sonnet tradition, the beloved leads her poet-lover into a hell of suffering, while at the same time becoming the source of his inspiration. The elements of Faulkner's "poem," however, are more in tune with the Romantic tradition: the relationship between the lovers is both exotic and impossible (Byron's incestuous relationship with his sister is even suggested in the text as a parallel); the hero and heroine are doomed; the oversensitive protagonist suffers from a curse and thinks constantly of death; the hero meets a mysterious and shadowy death vaguely caused by his emotional torture; the protagonist's doom is frequently foreshadowed by signs; the hero speaks in a literary tongue and sees himself in literary terms; and decadence and world-weariness permeate the atmosphere.

Faulkner, of course, began his writing career as a poet, writing "thousands of lines" of verse in his early years.[22] Much of the earliest verse was apparently written in self-conscious imitation of Renaissance and Romantic poetry, with conventional language, imagery, and allusion. One such poem, a variation of the Petrarchan sonnet, entitled rather prosaically "To A Co-ed," was published in *Ole Miss* two years following the loss of Estelle. This poem (the sestet of which I have reproduced below) suggests that Faulkner's thinking about Estelle may well have been couched in traditional poetic imagery and structured by a consciousness of the courtly-love tradition:

> I could have turned unmoved from Helen's brow.
> Who found no beauty in their Beatrice;
> Their Thais seemed less lovely then as now,
> Though some had bartered Athens for her kiss.
> For down Time's arras, faint and fair and far,
> Your face still beckons like a lonely star.[23]

All of the above-named women in the sonnet lead their lovers to an irrational devotion to the ideal that they represent—Helen, Thais, and Beatrice. "Like a lonely star," Caddy too leads her poet-lover into various levels of hell-like experience. In the novel Caddy is implicitly compared to several women in literature and myth who lead their lovers, figuratively or literally, into hell: Eve, Eurydice, Ophelia, and Persephone (who is carried off by her lover into hell).[24]

As many readers of the novel have pointed out, Quentin, like his creator, has a poetic imagination and his thoughts are often drawn to literary parallels, his perception guided by literary imagery.[25] At the same time, he demonstrates those personal characteristics that we associate with the poet stereotype: weak physically, impractical, sensitive, visionary, introspective, self-conscious, tortured, and perhaps most important of all, mad. Caddy is more than a sexual obsession with him, more than the haunting dream of a sick puritan mind; she is also a dream evoked by poetic "madness"—a symbol of truth, beauty, and perfect love.

This "mad" devotion to the poetic ideal is the Don Quixote-like complexion of Quentin which may well be overlooked or underestimated until one is aware of Faulkner's intense personal investment in Quentin's condition.[26] One may recall Faulkner's story "The Bear" where McCaslin Edmonds tries to explain the meaning of young Ike McCaslin's experiences by reading aloud a poem ("Ode on a Grecian Urn") by Keats:

> She cannot fade, though thou has not thy bliss,
> Forever wilt thou love, and she be fair.

At this point the boy objects and says, "He's talking about a girl." Edmonds says in reply, "He had to talk about something. . . . He was talking about truth. Truth is one."[27] This is what both Faulkner and Quentin are talking about in *The Sound and the Fury.* They, too, talk about a girl. Although Quentin's devotion to beauty is flawed and his search for truth faulty, "All men," in the words of Yeats ("Lapus Lazuli"), "have aimed at, found and lost," and few men have aimed as hard or lost so badly as Quentin Compson.

The relationship of Faulkner to his self-caricature is rather typical of the artist-as-a-young-man treatment in that he both despises Quentin and seeks to justify him. If we consider Quentin only on the basis of his morbid internal drama, his Raskolnikov side, we find it difficult to be anything more than distantly sympathetic with his dilemma. However, Quentin is also involved in another drama, in the conflict between himself and the "sane" world that surrounds him. It is his part in this outside drama wherein his role becomes admirable—his Don Quixote side. The terror implicit in Quentin's part in this outside drama is that his paranoia, if one wishes to call it that, is true and justified. He finds himself, as the sensitive young artist frequently does, in a world that rewards callousness, mean-spiritedness, and self-absorption. Although the Negro mammy Dilsey survives, as an outside observer her survival is almost irrelevant. The only Compson that survives is Jason. The pessimistic alternatives to Quentin's destruction seem to be limited to not understanding (Benjy), not feeling (Jason), or killing the inner self and allowing the shell to live (Caddy).

To the "sunny, normal world," Quentin's world is simply overdone.

It is far too ingenious and melodramatic. One hears America's mother saying, "Aren't you making a fuss over nothing?" Or in the novel itself, one can hear the same outrageous voice of normality as Dalton Ames puts his cigarette out carefully (while Quentin is shaking): "listen no good taking it so hard its not your fault kid it would have been some other fellow" (p. 199). It is ironic that so many readers have, in effect, agreed with Dalton Ames, have agreed that there is a lot of fuss, but it doesn't add up to much. Only ironically does Quentin's pain "signify nothing"—such a sentiment says as much about our indifference and high threshold of awareness as it does about Quentin's overreaction. Every Hamlet or Nick Adams needs a Dalton Ames to put his arm around his shoulder and tell him, "Listen Buddy, there's no use in taking things so hard."

II

Faulkner thus uses Quentin to expiate the emotional excesses of his own frustration and depression, creating an "extreme Faulkner" who operates largely out of the same value system and with the same skills as the author himself. We are presented with "a work of art within a work of art" situation: like the artist, Quentin Compson is trying to say an ideal world into being that can liberate him from the sound and fury of the present world. As an artist within the Romantic tradition, Quentin's tools of narration are very often impressionistic—imaginative substitution and distortion, symbolic magnification, and self-dramatization.

Quentin's creation operates between two extremes: at one extreme is a rhetoric deliberate or voluntary, and at the other, a rhetoric which tends to be involuntary or spasmodic. As in the case of the writer who finds that part of his novel is written in deliberate application and part in the frenzy of inspiration, the rhetoric of Quentin's monologue is guided by the emotional intensities of his subject matter. There are a number of very coherent passages of recollection in the monologue, which, because of their clear ordering, normal punctuation, and freedom from fragmentation, suggest a deliberate, voluntary creative effort. One such passage is the recollection of waiting for the final bell to ring in elementary school (pp. 108–9). The transition into this passage is achieved through a clear series of associations, from thinking about going home during Christmas vacation, to the thought of home, and to the emotion ("my insides would move") at the thought of home which is similar to the emotion he had at the end of school. Here, despite Quentin's general state of agitation, we have a recollection achieved with a certain amount of tranquility.

However, at the end of the memory, there is a sudden shift into an inspired, emotional passage in italics. Whereas the story of waiting for the bell is *about* emotion, this passage is in itself delivered with emotion. Typical of most of the italicized "outbursts," as we might term them, this one is fragmented, fast-paced, and opaque. Also, like most, it is about or connected to Caddy (and usually, as here, to the wedding to Herbert Head as well), and like many, it is exclamatory in tone:

> *Moving sitting still. One minute she was standing in the door, Benjy. Bellowing. Benjamin the child of mine old age bellowing. Caddy! Caddy!*
> (p. 109)

Such italicized passages do indicate a time change, of course, but the time change is ancillary to the moment of inspiration. What is more important for the reader to see is that a hierarchy of values is exposed through the changes in rhetorical patterns.

It is extremely important to understand, however, that these rhetorical levels do not signal a difference between "created" and "non-created" memory; that is, we are not to assume that the more tranquil a passage is, the more artificial it is. All of Quentin's monologue is created, composing an *esthétique* of pain expressed on various levels of intensity. To verify this, we can look briefly at these levels in more detail. Between the extremes described above, the ordered and coherent memory and the italicized outburst, are a range of passages which are more or less intense, depending on the rhetorical framework.

In the Dalton Ames section, for example (pp. 186–203), the narrative is brought close to the intensity of the italicized passages through the complete lack of punctuation (omitting even the apostrophes in contractions) and the omission of capitals, except for proper names and the pronoun "I," increasing the pace and giving the impression of fragmentation. At the same time, the passage has the earmarks of a set piece, a dramatization, in that its narrative is as coherent and well-ordered as the school room scene described above. On a higher level of creative intensity and closer yet to the italicized passages is the father-son dialogue at the end of Quentin's section (pp. 219–222). Here, not only are capitals not used to begin sentences, but capitals are not used for proper names ("benjy"), or the first person pronoun, "i." Not only is punctuation omitted, but unlike the dramatization of the Dalton Ames encounter, the dialogue is not even paragraphed. The clues to change of speaker are "and i" and "and he" which are run into the prose without any break or mark. The pace, at this climactic point in Quentin's work of art, is increased immensely, rushing the reader to the coda, "The last note sounded," and the narrator-guided banalities of Quentin's last rituals of cleansing.

Seldom noticed, but of great significance to our perceiving Quentin's role as surrogate artist and judging the nature and intensity of his *esthétique du mal*, is the assertion by Faulkner that the dialogues with the father are not flashbacks (narrator presented), never in fact occurred, and that they are composed by Quentin.[28] That these dialogues are created by Quentin provides an important clue to the basis on which his testimony should be judged: we are being asked to consider Quentin's created reality *as* creation and not to attempt to separate Quentin from it. Appropriately, in regard to Quentin's own Romantic frame of reference, we are asked to judge him (to use M. H. Abram's terminology) as a "lamp" (a creative artist), rather than as a "mirror" (a tool of the narrator by which memories can be presented for themselves), making our decisions on the quality and nature of his heat and light, rather than on the basis of his literal accuracy. It is Benjy, of course, who is in this sense the "mirror."

The Sound and the Fury, as we noted earlier, was written out of a deep sense of personal rejection. Faulkner's own love had been turned away because he was an insignificant, beginning artist. By contrast, Cornell Franklin was a successful, active, man of the world. Faulkner had no direct means of redress; there was no means by which he could compete with Franklin on Franklin's own grounds. Faulkner had been judged wanting by a set of values he despised, so as a writer he took the only course open to him and retaliated by writing, attacking not only those values by which he had been judged, but those which he had absorbed himself and which had shaped the nature of his internal suffering.

In much the same way, Quentin Compson is deprived of any active, direct means of handling the burden of caring he has assumed, and so he turns to those two resources with which he has already had some success—language and imagination.

Although the following statement is applied by Quentin to the three boys at the bridge who are arguing about the twenty-five dollars they might get for catching the old trout in the pool below, the description applies very well, perhaps intentionally so, to the intensity and progress of Quentin's rhetoric:

> They all talked at once, their voices insistent and contradictory and impatient, making of unreality a possibility, then a probability, then an incontrovertible fact, as people will when their desires become words. (p. 145)

It is traditionally through the magic of words that man is able to approach the infinite. Together with sacrifice, words are an integral part of any ritual to transcend the temporal. In the very significant last dialogue between Quentin and his "father" (wherein Quentin splits himself into parts), these two components are explored directly and in some detail:

> And he you wanted to *sublimate* a piece of natural human folly into a horror and then *exorcise* it with truth and i it was to isolate her out of the loud world so that it would have to flee us of necessity and then *the sound of it would be as though it had never been* and he did you try to make her do it and i i was afraid to i was afraid she might and then it wouldnt have done any good *but if i could tell you we did it would have been so* and *then the others wouldnt be so and then the world would roar away* and he and now this other you are not lying now either but you are still blind to what is in yourself to that part of general truth the sequence of natural events and their causes which shadows every mans brow even benjys you are not thinking of *finitude* you are comtemplating an *apotheosis* in which a *tem-*

porary state of mind will become symmetrical above the flesh and aware both of itself and of the flesh it will not quite discard you will not even be dead and i temporary and he you cannot bear to think that someday it will no longer hurt you like this now (p. 220—my italics)

Here it is clear that Quentin is going to try to restore the virgin, Caddy, as well as try to achieve his own fertility by the power of incantation and the sacrifice, temporarily, of his body. In this context, the father becomes the Father, or perhaps more accurately Satan, who, if he accepts Quentin's "prayer," has the power to make it so.

At the same time, the passage suggests, through the repetition of "sound," and the use of "loud" and "roar," that Quentin's conflict can be seen in terms of his voice in rhetorical opposition to the voices of others—those constant, involuntary explosions of sound in his consciousness that torture him. The voices of Caroline, of Mrs. Bland (Caroline's Cambridge surrogate), Dalton Ames, Gerald Bland (Dalton Ames's Cambridge surrogate), and Herbert Head—as well as the bellowing of Benjy caused by Herbert Head—can only be stilled by saying something (*not* doing something: "I was afraid she might") so powerful that it will make their sound and fury "roar away." Since all, even Dalton Ames in his silk shirts, are interested in status, the magic word becomes "incest." Before turning to such black magic, Quentin has tried the Christian spell, "Did you ever have a sister?" but that didn't work. Tragically, the question was irrelevant.

The metaphor of Caddy, which, as Faulkner has repeatedly said, stands at the center of the novel, and which finds expression repeatedly in the most rhetorically intense passages of Quentin's monologue, extends beyond the double standard of caring, as applied simply to my sister or yours, to a major theme in Faulkner's work. The theme is complex and Quentin's condition, as it is contrasted to the lives of other characters throughout the novel, illustrates it very well. On the one hand, while most of the other characters find it impossible to feel any deep responsibility for others, Quentin finds that his very salvation or damnation depends upon the conditions of others. What other people say or do, in other words, is fundamental to his very existence. Quentin's condition, as well as Caddy's relation to it, becomes clear "On the instant when we come to realize that tragedy is second-hand" (p. 143). Although his father may insist that men are just dolls filled with sawdust and argue that what bothers Quentin is simply nature, not Caddy, Quentin insists that men do bleed. He cannot accept the picture implicit in his father's doctrine of the "sawdust flowing from what wound in what side that not for me died not" (p. 218). Christ did bleed and die; good and evil do exist, and Quentin is prepared to die for that belief, for he, like Christ, is caught in the trap of caring.

In part, Quentin commits suicide so as to preserve this emotional intensity, not allowing it to be dissipated by time so that his father's detachment will at last become his own through the process of aging.[29] All suicides find themselves within what appears to them to be an insolvable dilemma, and part of Quentin's dilemma seems to be his perception that to stay in this world will inevitably bring him into a state of amorality, and the reader, as well as Quentin, perceives that the father's position in all its amorality is profoundly immoral. To stay alive appears to Quentin to be akin to embracing his father's point of view, an anti-idealistic, anti-heroic, and detached cynicism he feels impelled to fight "to the death." The father insists that what Quentin must do is accept "finitude," and in regard to Quentin's fantasy of incest and isolation declares, "You are contemplating an apotheosis in which a temporary state of mind will become symmetrical above the flesh" (p. 220). The word that stings Quentin is "temporary," and he repeats it four times, interjecting it with increasing frequency into the remembered or imagined statement by the father who, in the next to last paragraph of the section, tells Quentin why he won't commit suicide. But as the beginning of the last paragraph states, "The last note sounded," and the last note is "was," the temporariness that Quentin cannot tolerate for it denies that his caring has had any meaning. If it were simply a matter of nature, or as the father puts it, "the sequence of natural events and their causes which shadows every mans brow" (p. 220), then, as Quentin says earlier, "If it wasn't anything, what was I?"

What Quentin is trying to do on the day of his death and through his death was perhaps best explained by Faulkner himself when, during an interview, he discussed what it is the artist tries to do: "The aim of every artist is to arrest motion, which is life, by artificial means and hold it fixed."[30] And so it is that Quentin, when he smashes his watch and later jumps into the water to embrace the shadow-emblem of his caring, is an artist attempting to create a work of art. "To arrest motion, which is life, by artificial means and hold it fixed" is precisely Quentin's aim and summarizes as well as any brief phrase could the central theme of Quentin's monologue. Unfortunately, rather than patterning art after life, Quentin is trying to pattern life after art, attempting, through the magic of words, to make his life itself a work of art.

III

Much of *The Sound and the Fury* is a satirical attack mounted in a spirit of outrage against a society, which like Horace Benbow's in *Sanctuary*, is totally corrupt in its "normality." But the author's fury is modified by a deep sense of futility, and it may be that the novel's title is, in part, a bit of self-directed irony. For the artist, historically, as seer and prophet has found himself often in the helpless position of being able to interpret events, but being able to do very little about altering their course. In this sense, the position of the author matches the position of the "artist" Quentin (and all the other visionary, sensitive characters who approximate Quentin in the other novels). Caddy is the main victim of the family disintegration and of the false values expressed by her environment, whereas Quentin is essentially a secondary victim, not so much of the family and environment itself, as of the keen perception of Caddy's inevitable destruction. By putting his hand to Caddy's throat, he can feel the pulse of life as Caddy pronounces the name of Dalton Ames, and he can emotionally detect the consequences, but he cannot alter the course of the doom that he can foresee. The self thus perceived as Quixotic is the frustration of the author who attempts to expiate both his personal anguish as well as his general rage against a corrupt society. The author's tragedy, like Quentin's, is always (in the words of Quentin's father) "second hand."

Faulkner said of Don Quixote, one of his favorite literary characters, that he was "constantly choosing between good and evil, but then he was choosing in his dream state. He was mad. He entered reality only when he was so busy trying to cope with people that he had no time to distinguish between good and evil."[31] This, too, describes Quentin Compson rather well and points to an aspect of his character too often overlooked. Quixote, like Quentin, is "sick" and feels that he must act to help others according to a set of circumstances we see as "unreal" and code of chivalry we see as inappropriate. But if this were all there were to it, then Don Quixote would be a farce—a silly collection of slap-stick blunders. If Quixote were only trying to force the world to conform to his expectations and his own needs, then he would be vicious. What makes both Quentin and Quixote different from the fool and the tyrant is that both really do care about people, and the principles that they both espouse, as inappropriate as they may seem to the "normal" world, are to a large extent fundamentally moral and sound. Their radicalism is beautiful as well as ludicrous, and truth speaks through their wrong-headedness.[32] The point of *The Sound and the Fury* lies not just in its central emblem of a brave and beautiful girl in a tree with muddy pants—the inevitable and tragic flawing of beauty and truth in human experience—but lies also, and perhaps primarily, in the personal working out of that emblem in the internal conflict and death of Quentin Compson, the "extreme Faulkner."

Notes

1. Malcolm Cowley, "Nightmare and Ritual in Hemingway," in *Hemingway: A Collection of Critical Essays*, ed. Robert P. Weeks (Englewood Cliffs, N.J., 1962) p. 48. (Originally published as the Introduction to *The Portable Hemingway*, ed. Malcolm Cowley [New York, 1945]). Olga Vickery, in *The Novels of William Faulkner* (Baton Rouge, 1964), sees the Quentin section as ritual: "His section is filled with echoes, both literary and Biblical, phrases, names quoted out of context but falling neatly into the pattern of thought. These echoes assume the quality of a *ritual by which he attempts to conjure experience into conformity*

with his wishes" (p. 31—my emphasis). See also Lawrance Thompson, *William Faulkner: An Introduction and Interpretation* (New York, 1967), p. 39.

2. Thompson, p. 40; Peter Swiggart, *The Art of Faulkner's Novels* (Austin, 1962), p. 93; Michael H. Cowan, "Introduction," *Twentieth Century Interpretations of The Sound and the Fury* (Englewood Cliffs, N.J. 1968), pp. 4–5; Melvin Backman, "Faulkner's Sick Heroes: Bayard Sartoris and Quentin Compson," *Modern Fiction Studies*, 2 (Autumn, 1956), 100.

3. *William Faulkner of Oxford*, ed. James W. Webb and A. Wigfall Green (Baton Rouge, 1965), pp. 151, 47. In later references, "Webb and Green."

4. Dedalus and Prufrock are frequently cited parallels. In regard to James Joyce's Stephen Dedalus, see Carvel Collins, "The Interior Monologues of *The Sound and the Fury*, *English Institute Essays: 1952* (New York, 1965), pp. 30–31. In regard to the parallel with T. S. Eliot's Prufrock, see Hyatt H. Waggoner, *William Faulkner: From Jefferson to the World* (Lexington, Ky., 1959), pp. 49 and 53; the Backman article, cited above, p. 106; and Frederick L. Gwynn, "Faulkner's Prufrock—and Other Observations," *Journal of English and Germanic Philology*, 52 (January, 1953), 63–70.

Robert M. Slabey in "Quentin as Romantic," *Twentieth Century Interpretations of The Sound and the Fury*, ed. Michael H. Cowan (Englewood Cliffs, N.J., 1968), pp. 81–82, calls attention to the fact that Prufrock and Dedalus, as well as a number of other literary characters who have been compared to Quentin, have in common a "Romantic sensibility."

5. See Carvel Collins, "Faulkner's *The Sound and the Fury*," *Explicator*, 17, No. 3 (Dec., 1958), Item 19.

6. *My Brother Bill: An Affectionate Reminiscence* (New York, 1964), p. 186.

7. Murry C. Falkner, *The Falkners of Mississippi* (Baton Rouge, 1967), p. 9 See Peter Swiggart's discussion of Quentin's "self-destructive puritanism," pp. 15, 92–93.

8. Murry C. Falkner, pp. 10–12.

9. Lewis P. Simpson, "Yoknapatawpha and the World of Murry Faulkner," Foreword to Murry C. Falkner (cited above), pp. x–xi. See also pp. 13–15, 33–34, 43, 84–86, 103–104; and John Faulkner, pp. 42–47, 192–194.

10. John Faulkner, pp. 16–17.

11. John Faulkner, pp. 65–66, and 87. See also Murry C. Falkner, pp. 32, 35, 54, 61, 69. Another possibility is the tomboy sister of Estelle, Victoria ("Touchie") Oldham—see John Faulkner, pp. 76, 78–80.

12. John Faulkner, pp. 244–245. See also *Faulkner at West Point*, ed. Joseph L. Fant, III, and Robert Ashley (New York, 1964), p. 116.

13. "About the Sketches," introduction to *William Faulkner: New Orleans Sketches* (New Brunswick, N.J., 1958), p. 32.

14. Murry C. Falkner, p. 17; John Faulkner, p. 116.

15. William West in "Remembering William Faulkner" (*Gourmet* [January, 1969]. 22–23, 74–75) tells of an incident wherein two of Faulkner's kinswomen, who had never forgiven him for writing and publishing *Sanctuary*, stole the manuscript of *As I Lay Dying* from his writing and took it home with them.

16. See Murry C. Falkner, p. 241.

17. John Faulkner, p. 118. Carvel Collins in his introduction to *William Faulkner: Early Prose and Poetry* (Boston, 1962), p. 4, says that on April 10, 1918, Faulkner "began work as a ledger clerk at an armanent company in Connecticut." Phil Stone, in Webb and Green, also testifies that it was a job in a munitions factory.

18. John Faulkner, p. 144.

19. John E. Fontaine, Webb and Green, p. 34. See also Claude Maxwell Smith, Webb and Green, p. 63, and John Faulkner, pp. 133–134.

20. Introduction to *Early Prose and Poetry*, pp. 18–19.

21. p. 126. This and other quotations from William Faulkner's *The Sound and the Fury* are taken from the new Vintage Book edition which is photographically reproduced from a copy of the first printing. The early Vintage and Modern Library (1946) editions are corrupt as demonstrated by James B. Meriwether, "Notes on the Textual History of *The Sound and the Fury*," *Papers of the Bibliographical Society of America*, 56 (Third Quarter 1962), pp. 312–315.

22. Phil Stone, Webb and Green, p. 226.

23. Quoted by Louis Cochran, Webb and Green, p. 219. Also reproduced in *Early Prose and Poetry*, p. 70.

24. See Harry M. Campbell and Ruel E. Foster, *William Faulkner: A Critical Appraisal* (Norman, Okla., 1951), p. 57. There is also a parallel between Dante's Paolo and Francesca—see Campbell and Foster, pp. 126–127; and William M. Gibson, "Faulkner's *The Sound and the Fury*," *Explicator*, 22 (January, 1964), Item 33.

25. See Backman, *Faulkner: The Major Years* (Bloomington, 1966), p. 29; Backman, "Faulkner's Sick Heroes," 106; Vickery, p. 40; Waggoner, p. 49; Irving Howe, *William Faulkner: A Critical Study* (New York, 1962), p. 169; Cowan, p. 10; and Walter Brylowski, *Faulkner's Olympian Laugh* (Detroit, 1968), pp. 65, 72–85 *passim*.

26. As I point out later in this essay, Faulkner on one occasion said, "I can see myself in Don Quixote."

27. *Go Down, Moses* (New York, 1955), p. 297.

28. One of the major dualities expressed in Quentin's consciousness is that between reason and emotion, and this duality is most conspicuously articulated as a self-argument between his own position and that which he attributes to his father, made up, apparently, of bits and scraps of his father's conversational mannerisms and favorite aphorisms which Quentin recalls and pieces together and which he often interpolates into hypothetical dialogue. Most commentators on the novel have ignored or chosen to discount the fact that Faulkner explicitly denied that major dialogues actually occurred. (See, for example, Cowan's note, p. 23.) When asked whether Quentin actually had the conversation with his father about incest with Caddy. Faulkner replied, "He never did. . . . No, they were imaginary. [Here, I assume he refers with "they" to all the conversations.] He just said, Suppose I say this to my father, would it help me, would it clarify, would I see clearer what it is that I anguish over" (from *Faulkner in the University*, ed. Frederick L. Gwynn and Joseph L. Blotner [New York, 1965], pp. 262–263).

29. A number of critics make a similar point. See, for example, Swiggart, p. 39: "Quentin's suicide is presented as less a reaction to Caddy's dishonor than a futile attempt to preserve his moral pride in the face of an unknown future that might rob him even of despair."

30. From the Jean Stein interview in *William Faulkner: Three Decades of Criticism*, ed. Frederick J. Hoffman and Olga Vickery (New York, 1963), p. 80.

31. Stein, p. 80.

32. In *Faulkner at West Point* (cited above), Faulkner was asked, "Could you tell us, Mr. Faulkner, exactly what qualities Don Quixote has that make him one of your favorite characters?" Faulkner replied, "It's admiration and pity and amusement—that's what I get from him . . . He has ideals which are by our—the pharisaical standards are nonsensical. His method of trying to put them into practice is tragic and comic. I can see myself in Don Quixote" (p. 94).

Profane Time, Sacred Time, and Confederate Time in *The Sound and the Fury*

Arthur Geffen*

George Stewart and Joseph Backus' contention that William Faulkner intentionally places Quentin Compson's death in *The Sound and the Fury* on June 3, the anniversary of Jefferson Davis' birthday, is summarily dismissed by Cleanth Brooks as an extreme case of symbol-hunting.[1] Brooks rejects Stewart and Backus' theory for two reasons: Faulkner, though he does not depict Quentin's suicide, never suggests (as he easily could have) that it happens after midnight of June 2, the dated heading of the second section of the book; and Faulkner does not indicate that Quentin knows the birthdate of the president of the Confederacy. Furthermore, Brooks implies that Stewart and Backus inadequately relate the "alleged symbol" to the "total fictional context" of the novel; they merely suggest that young Compson's "downfall is somehow tied to the downfall of the Old South."

Whether Brooks treats Stewart and Backus' argument justly is debatable, however. June 3, as the two critics point out, is not only Davis' birthday, but also Confederate Memorial Day in several Southern states including Tennessee, a prominent locality in the novel.[2] Since Memphis is close to Jefferson-Oxford and dominates the region commercially, one can assume that even if Quentin is unaware of Davis' birthday, he probably knows June 3 as a Confederate holiday.[3] Moreover, the date of Quentin's death is not the isolated symbol Brooks would have one believe. As Stewart and Backus demonstrate, it is linked to the date of his father's death which they convincingly fix on April 25, 1912, the anniversary of Caddy's failed marriage, and, significantly, the day before still another Confederate Memorial Day, this time the one celebrated in Mississippi.[4] This is as far as Stewart and Backus carry the pattern of Confederate chronology in the novel, but there are two more critical dates which extend the design. Despite his failure to treat Stewart and Backus' case fully, Brooks's complaints about the dating of Quentin's death and the inadequacy of the critics' relation of the symbols to the larger themes of the novel do present genuine obstacles to the advancement of the proposition

*Reprinted, with permission, from *Studies in American Fiction*, 2, No. 2 (Autumn 1974), 175–97.

that Faulkner uses the dates in *The Sound and the Fury* with strong symbolic meaning.

Stewart and Backus' almost desperate efforts to confirm the possibility that Quentin dies on June 3 reveal one of the major difficulties involving symbolic dating in the novel.[5] In general, a fictional event must fall on the anniversary of the historical, religious, or commemorative date to which it refers in order for the writer to gain his symbolic parallel or irony. However, in this novel, Faulkner sometimes rejects the normal anniversary pattern for one in which the fictional event falls on the day or night before the event to which he is alluding. In the Appendix he reveals this unusual strategy by placing Quentin's robbery of her uncle and elopement with the pitchman "on the one thousand eight hundred ninetyfifth anniversary of the day before the resurrection of Our Lord" (p. 424).

The day-before pattern operates in Quentin's death, in his father's death, in Caddy's marriage, and also with regard to still another date in the novel. Its four sections can be chronologically reduced to two: June 2, 1910, and a sequence moving from April 6, 1928 through April 7 to its conclusion on April 8, Easter Sunday. April 8 is a critical day in the book. Jason's discovery of young Quentin's theft and disappearance, his unsuccessful attempt to recapture her and the money, the black Easter Sunday service, Dilsey's recognition that she has seen the end of the Compson line, and Benjy's traumatic experience at the Confederate monument, all occur on this day. If Faulkner actually adheres to the day-before pattern, April 9 should be an equally significant and conclusive date in Confederate history. As it turns out, this is the day in 1865 when General Robert E. Lee surrendered his army at Appomattox—the single event which popularly marks the death of the Confederacy and the end of the Civil War.

To understand both what one can call Confederate time in the novel and Faulkner's use of the day-before pattern, several kinds of time which surround Confederate time must be first examined. Two of these are, to use Mircea Eliade's terms, profane and sacred time.[6] Confederate time, it shall be later demonstrated, is actually failed sacred time.

As Faulkner indicates in his allusive title, the meaninglessness of profane time—evanescent temporal duration which leads irremediably to death—haunts the minds of a number of key characters.[7] Though Jason, whom Faulkner ironically terms the sole sane modern Compson (p. 420), accepts this secularized conception of time with a vengeance, he succeeds only in maintaining an existence which is devoid of all human spirituality. Furthermore, as shall be later shown, he cannot avoid entrapment in his familial and cultural past. His less sane father and brother are even more unsuccessful in coming to terms with profane time.

Mr. Compson repeatedly exhibits his obsession with the inadequacy of life conceived in profanely temporal terms. In transmitting the legacy of his own father's watch to Quentin, he calls the gift "the mausoleum of all hope and desire," and hopes his son will use it "to gain the reducto absurdum of all human experience" (p. 93). He further expresses the desire that the watch may enable Quentin to forget time occasionally rather than wasting his life in the futile effort to conquer it. However, Mr. Compson—and this foreshadows his son's eventual defeat—fails to resolve his own problem with time. In part, his failure occurs because the problem is not an exclusively philosophical one. His overpowering recognition of the absurdity of chronological time has historical and personal roots as well. The historical present in which he unwillingly lives constantly reminds him of the steadily diminishing power and stature of his family and of his position as a lesser Compson than his forebears. Denied religious ways of transcending temporality because of his skepticism, he attempts desperate and specious escapes from mundane existence: a pathetic self-immersion in a golden Roman past, and the anodyne of alcohol. The first of these ends in ludicrous anachronism with the devotee of Horace, Livy, and Catullus tearing off "caustic and satiric eulogies on both his dead and his living fellow-townsmen" (p. 410). The second concludes with dipsomania and death.

Mr. Compson's delineation of the erosive and paralytic power of temporality and his futile efforts to transcend his condition help to destroy his son. Quentin, on the last day of his life, remembers his father's rejection of man's obsession with time and his depiction of it as mere "mind-function"—an excremental activity (p. 94). He further recalls his father's remarks about his grandfather's watch. And his own attempts to escape sterile time are as ill-fated as his predecessors'. Wrenching the hands off the watch proves ineffectual since it continues to tick. His efforts to flee time temporarily by cheating his shadow (the constant reminder of the sun's passage), and by escaping to a place where other reminders of time like clocks and factory whistles are absent, collapse utterly. Finally he is left with suicide as his only way of moving out of time.

His acceptance of his father's religious cynicism closes off the possibility of his reaching, through ritual experience, a sacred time which might make profane time bearable. Like his father, he rejects the Christian world. Although Christ and St. Francis appear in his thoughts, they are ultimately discarded. Francis becomes important only for his association of death with the sister he never had, and Christ is transformed first into a man not crucified but worn down and out by time (p. 94), and later into a sawdust doll "that not for me died not" (p. 218). Again affected by Mr. Compson, Quentin can find no solace in the idea of an afterlife in which time can be redeemed. He reiterates his father's remark about Christian heaven: "Then the wings are bigger Father said only who can play a harp" (p. 129). Almost the sole meaningful vision of an existence after death that he can summon up is his transitory desire for a private two-person hell with Caddy (pp. 97, 144). Augmenting the pathos of Quentin's condition is his awareness of others, unlike himself, who possess the capacity for mystical religious experience and who can still value ongoing life. He recognizes that Dilsey will call his suicide a "sinful waste," and he recalls—perhaps with mixed envy and contempt—that a brothel full of blacks in Memphis ran, in a "religious trance," out into the street crying " 'Yes Jesus O good man Jesus O that good man' " (pp. 211–12).

Quentin's extreme difficulties with time are also not wholly the product of terrifying philosophical insight. They have strong personal origins as well. He is more aware than Mr. Compson of the moribundity of the family line, and he cannot accept his father's easy evasions of this fact. Quentin mentions the Compsons as a family which formerly produced one governor and three generals (p. 125). Furthermore, thoughts of the last important Compson recur to Quentin throughout the final day of his life. This man is, of course, Quentin's grandfather whose military failures in the Civil War signal the future downfall of the family. Significantly, Brigadier General Compson's greatest defeat occurred at the battle of Shiloh on April 6 and 7, 1862 (p. 408).[8] Needless to say, these two days are the dates of the first and third sections of *The Sound and the Fury*.

Quentin associates his grandfather with the War and even incorporates the defeated general into an early (but later discarded) idea of death. He and Shreve, his Harvard roommate, refer to the liberation of the blacks—the crafty Deacon, in particular—as the work of his grandfather (p. 101). And when Quentin reveals his rejected vision of death, he suggests that the contemplation of death is desirable because in it one can vindicate the past by wiping away the seemingly ineradicable fact of familial and cultural defeat. In this vision, Quentin sees his grandfather both in and out of historical time. The general wears his old uniform but is somehow transformed from the failed brigadier to a man who, in an unspecified conversation with death and his fellow Confederate officer, Colonel Sartoris, is "always right" (pp. 218–19).

The vision and its attempt to transcend time by transforming and sanctifying the historical experience of defeat fail, however. Quentin is left with no way to win out over temporality except to remove himself physically from it.

Though Quentin and his father are haunted and ultimately destroyed by profane time, there are figures in *The Sound and the Fury* who can move out of tormenting temporality to a plane of sacred existence. The most notable of these are Benjy and Dilsey. Undeniably an idiot whose inability to separate time into past, present, and future anchors him in a perpetual present, Benjy is nevertheless not something out of an abnormal psychology textbook. Faulkner presents him as a person who can be viewed as a holy idiot, one touched by divine force and capable of intuitive acts and knowledge denied to far more "intelligent" people. Benjy's capacities are attested to by the most intelligent and the wisest figures in the book—Quentin and Dilsey. Quentin affirms Dilsey's belief that Benjy can smell disaster and loss (pp. 109, 111). Smelling them is to perceive them by the sense least associated with intellectual perception and the sense which, in common belief, is seen as a mysterious means which gifted people use to pierce through appearances to truth.[9]

Dilsey's opinion of Benjy is still higher than Quentin's. She argues powerfully for his inclusion in her black congregation, the community of believers who can reevoke sacred time by participating in the life-giving ritual of the Easter Sunday service. In defending Benjy's inclusion to Frony, Dilsey claims that his place in the Lord's estimation is not based on his intelligence: " 'Tell um de good Lawd dont keer whether he smart er not' " (p. 362). Later, when she is readying Benjy for his trip to the cemetery, she makes the following highly significant statement: " 'You's de Lawd's chile, anyway. En I be His'n too, fo long, praise Jesus' " (p. 396). Here her description of Benjy mirrors the attitude of several societies in the Middle Ages: "In certain localities, they [the feebleminded] unwittingly received homage and reverence through the superstitious belief that they were 'les enfants du bon Dieu,' sacred beings having some mysterious connection with the unknown."[10] On first reading, one might imagine that Dilsey's use of the term "de Lawd's chile" refers to all human beings, all God's children. However, closer inspection proves this false, for she refers to herself as one who is not yet the Lord's child; this reward will come to her only in the afterlife. Benjy then achieves a condition on earth which she can achieve only in the other world. Clearly, Benjy's capacity for transcending profane time is a primary manifestation of his special condition.

There is yet more evidence that Faulkner portrays Benjy as a holy idiot. On Benjy's walk to church, several black children dare each other to touch him (pp. 363–64). One says he is unafraid to do so, claiming that Ben is just a "loony" and therefore not dangerous. Nevertheless, this boy does not touch him. This otherwise gratuitous banter establishes that, in the black "primitive" mind, Benjy—a special kind of idiot—possesses dangerous, possibly benevolent but also possibly destructive, supernatural powers.[11] This all may be taken as Faulkner's mockery of childish black superstition, but such an easy dismissal of black folk beliefs is dubious since the black community in the novel can accomplish what the white one cannot—the transcendence of profane time and the recapture of sacred existence.

If Dilsey sees Benjy as a man-child able to achieve the sacred state of living in an eternal present, she also recognizes that she is neither this gifted nor this lucky. Her escape from the attrition of purely temporal life must be accomplished through festivals embodying mystical belief and ritual experience. Such a festival occurs in the novel on Easter Sunday, or April 8, 1928—its designation in profane time.

In *The Sacred and the Profane*, Mircea Eliade contends that certain sacred celebrations have a unique mission (pp. 68–72, 81). They provide a way of religious communities to pass from profane time to the sacred plane of existence—"a sort of eternal mythical present" associated with the primordial creation of the world and time itself. Sacred time, unlike profane, is inexhaustible; it is circular, reversible, and periodically recoverable. Though the rites which comprise the festival allow the community to reactualize the time of the primordial event, this cannot be done in a merely commemorative way. Religious man must participate in the festival to recreate the primordial time and event in the present. Vital to this reactualization is memory; in fact, the active remembrance of the sacred event is both the means and end of the festival:

> The memory reactualized by the rites . . . plays a decisive role; what happened *in illo tempore* must never be forgotten. The true sin is forgetting. . . . Personal memory is not involved; what matters is to remember the mythical event, the only event worth considering because the only creative event (pp. 101–02).

After the festival, religious man can return to profane existence knowing that he can periodically come back to sacred being by reevoking the "sources of the sacred and the real" (p. 107).

Faulkner presents the time surrounding the black Easter Sunday service as a time out of time. Even Luster, whose religious feelings have been modified by the white community, recognizes this when he shoos away some jaybirds, saying " 'Git on back to hell, whar you belong at. 'Taint Monday yit' " (p. 335).[12] By this he implies that this Sunday is temporarily controlled by the holy forces whose reign ends the next day. Faulkner further emphasizes the antihistorical and timeless quality of the black service in his description of the environment in which it takes place:

> The road rose again, to a scene like a painted backdrop. Notched into a cut of red clay crowned with oaks the road appeared to stop short off, like a cut ribbon. Beside it a weathered church lifted its crazy steeple like a painted church, and the whole scene was as flat and without perspective as a painted cardboard set upon the ultimate edge of the flat earth, against the windy sunlight of space and April and a midmorning filled with bells (p. 364).

This passage establishes a frozen, flat conjunction of space and time which is obviously reminiscent of the perspectiveless art of primitive societies, those cultures which still possess the capacity for reevoking sacred time and existence through ritual. Its antihistoricity is apparent in the return to a pre-Columbian vision of the earth, and its evocation of spatial and temporal uniformity is evident in the calculated vagueness of "space and April."

The striking unity of sacred place with sacred activity and time which is strongly implied by Faulkner is mentioned also by Eliade:

Just as a church constitutes a break in plane in the profane space of a modern city, the service celebrated inside it marks a break in profane temporal duration. It is no longer today's historical time that is present—the time that is experienced, for example, in the adjacent streets—but the time in which the historical existence of Jesus Christ occurred, the time sanctified by his preaching, by his passion, death, and resurrection (p. 72).

This cancellation of present historical time and its replacement by reactualized mythic time is integral to the black service in the novel. Faulkner conveys the negation of the world immediately outside the church initially in the absolute severance of the road from the church, and again in statements which describe the increasing dominance of the churchly activity over the sights and sound of the external universe: "As the scudding day passed overhead the dingy windows glowed and faded in ghostly retrograde. A car passed along the road outside, labouring in the sand, died away" (p. 368).

Far more important, however, is the establishment in the congregation's mind of Christ's time as something not occurring exclusively in the past, but as an entity which lives now and forever. At the heart of the Easter Sunday service is the remarkable sermon delivered by the physically inauspicious Reverend Shegog. By its technique and structure, this sermon asserts the immediacy and perpetual presentness of Christ's life, sacrifice, and redemptive power. It is delivered heavily in the present tense, and bears the stamp of a personal vision seen and communicated spontaneously:

'Listen, breddren! I sees de day. Ma'y settin in de do' wid Jesus on her lap, de little Jesus. Like dem chillen dar, de little Jesus. I hears de angels singin de peaceful songs en de glory; I sees de closin eyes; sees Mary jump up, sees de sojer face: We gwine to kill! We gwine to kill! We gwine to kill yo little Jesus! I hears de weepin en de lamentation of de po mammy widout de salvation en de word of God!' (p. 369).

The success of Shegog's oratory is made plain when members of the congregation affirm the presentness, the eternality of the reactualized vision by crying " 'I sees, O Jesus! Oh I sees!' " (p. 370). Their seeing, it must be noted, is not seeing for the first time. It is a sight born of memory, for remembrance—as was earlier mentioned—is supremely important to the sacred festival. And this is a truth known not only by Eliade, but also by Reverend Shegog and William Faulkner. Repeatedly, though in various forms, Shegog cries " 'I got de ricklickshun en de blood of de Lamb!' " (pp. 367, 368, 369). In fact, this statement, equating sacred memory with salvation, emerges as the dominant theme of his sermon. Furthermore, Faulkner picks up this motif when he describes Dilsey at the moment when she feels the full force of Shegog's power as "crying rigidly and quietly in the annealment and the blood of the remembered Lamb" (p. 371).

The construction of Shegog's sermon is brilliantly shaped to its end—the eradication of profane existence in his congregation's mind and the substitution of the sacred universe of memory and time. The white world in the novel is obviously imprisoned in modernity, secularity, and profanity, and the blacks are not impervious to the blandishments of this world. Luster, for example, is attracted to the tawdry white carnival which threatens the rich black festival.[13] With this in mind, Shegog divides his performance into three sections, each marked by a different dialect. First he speaks like a white man, then in a modified accent, and finally in full black speech. "Recollection" becomes "ricklickshun," "Brethren" becomes "Breddren and sistuhn" (pp. 366, 367, 368). By these changes, the Reverend leads his people away from an alien and profane world, and back into their own universe—in a sense, a "primitive" one, but perhaps for that reason also one in which sacrality is possible.

Since it is Christianity in some form which is being practised in the black Easter service, one may doubt whether the congregation can fully transcend historical time. Eliade contends that Christianity, in contradistinction to other religions, accepts, even "valorizes," historicity (pp. 110–12). The essential Christian myth is not a cosmogonic one; the creation becomes less important than the events of Christ's life and sacrifice, and the display of his redemptive power. Following upon Judaism's rejection of cyclical time, the Christian God manifests himself in historical time, a time having beginning and end which now becomes capable of sanctification. Although Eliade insists that there is a sort of cosmogonic myth residual in Christ's acts—"for the Christian, time begins anew with the birth of Christ, for the Incarnation establishes a new situation of man in the cosmos" (p. 111)—he still maintains that Christianity is bound to historical time, however sanctified, rather than the mythic time of other palaeo-agricultural religions. This is particularly true of modern Christianity: "When a Christian of our day participates in liturgical time, he recovers the *illud tempus* in which Christ lived, suffered, and rose again—but it is no longer a mythical time, it is the time when Pontius Pilate governed Judaea" (p. 111).

However, the church service in Faulkner's novel is as black as it is Christian, and its mixture of cultural traits undercuts a strong dependence on historicity. Shegog employs anachronisms which not only assert the presentness of the past but also collapse his audience's ability to place the Christian experience in a specific historical period. For example, the Roman soldier of Pilate's time becomes "de Roman police" (p. 369). The Reverend also juxtaposes religious events, and shifts from one time to another so rapidly and wildly that his listeners cannot order happenings chronologically and causally. He does not permit the events of sacred history to unfold narratively; rather he bombards his people with a battery of discrete episodes, images, and moral and theological interpretations. Opening with the escape from Egyptian bondage, he quickly switches to a hint of a parable about the rich and the poor. This is rapidly abandoned for a depiction of Mary's terror when the Roman soldiers are coming to kill her first-born. Suddenly Shegog shifts the scene to Calvary, and then counterposes God's justifiable wrath to Christ's gentle guarantee—the promise of salvation to those who have suffered and believed made by one who has shared their suffering. This gives way to the concluding episode of the sermon—judgment day (pp. 368–70). Though the serman always presses forward chronologically, its intensely episodic nature eradicates the causally important interstices between the crucial events which Shegog reactualizes for his brothers and sisters. The entire sacred experience becomes a panoramic flow in which times and events are connected emotionally and mythically rather than causally, and in which the endpoints of sacred history are blended and fused. The beginning and the end—an open end with its glimpse of heavenly glory—are but seconds apart in Shegog's performance, and they are milliseconds apart in his people's consciousness. This unusual but essential aspect of Faulkner's vision of black Christianity as opposed to white is accentuated by the presence of the Christmas decorations in the black church at Easter (pp. 364–65). For the blacks, Christmas and Easter are not two separate festivals, each renewing and reactualizing a separate section of sacred time, but one long unified one.

The undeniable effectiveness of Shegog's sermon is most apparent with regard to three figures or groups in the novel: Benjy, the black congregation, and—most important of all—Dilsey. By his receptivity to the sermon and the communal experience it evokes, Ben justifies Dilsey's inclusion of him in the black congregation. Whereas he has been whimpering and snivelling before the sermon, at the height of Shegog's oration he is tranquil and transfixed: "In the midst of the voices and the hands Ben sat, rapt in his sweet blue gaze" (p. 370). Previously, Faulkner has associated this blueness with a type of pastoral innocence—"His eyes were clear, of the pale sweet blue cornflowers" (p. 342)—and here he may well be suggesting an intense purity within Benjy as well as a pure state of being into which he enters as a result of the service.

The black congregation is marvelously moved by the sermon. Despite their shared secular experience and common religious belief, they are not a true community until Shegog works his magic upon them. Frony, for example, argues with Dilsey about Benjy's inclusion, and she is initially contemptuous of the physically unprepossessing Shegog: " 'En dey brung dat all de way from Saint Looey' " (p. 366). First winning their approval as a religious performer in the white style, and then using the call-and-response technique of black preaching, the Reverend reevokes the black congregation's communal consciousness and finally makes his people vital participants in the sacred service. At several points, Faulkner directly portrays the intense communality and the attendant loss of self which Shegog creates: "the congregation sighed as if it waked from a collective dream;"

"And the congregation seemed to watch with its own eyes while the voice consumed him, until he was nothing and they were nothing and there was not even a voice but instead their hearts were speaking to one another in chanting measures beyond the need for words" (pp. 366, 367). After the sermon is over, and the congregation has moved out of the church into a day formerly gray and rainy but now bright and sunny, several unnamed members of the congregation register their enthusiastic approval:

> "He sho a preacher, mon! He didn't look like much at first,
> but hush!"
> "He seed de power en de glory."
> "Yes, suh. He seed hit. Face to face he seed hit" (p. 371).

Virtually at this point in the novel, Dilsey utters what is to be one of her key statements: "I've seed de first en de last." She immediately repeats this remark in slightly altered form as "I seed de beginnin, en now I sees de endin," and later reiterates it twice in nearly its original form (pp. 371, 375). The statement has multiple meanings. It surely refers to the vision she has shared with Shegog of the beginning and end of Christ's life on earth and of two of the endpoints of Christian sacred history—the crucifixion and the judgment. Also her language duplicates that of the Book of Revelation: "I am Alpha and Omega, the beginning and the ending"; "I am Alpha and Omega . . . the first and the last."[14] Her words may then indicate that she, like Shegog, has seen God face to face. However, the statements, particularly when taken in the context in which they are later uttered, appear also to be comments on the doom of the family she has served all her life. That Dilsey is a seeress possessing intense awareness that the Compson line is dead has been commonly observed, but why does her prophetic insight emerge from the church service? Perhaps Dilsey, having moved for a time into the sacred plane of existence, can now see with utter clarity the fate of those condemned to inescapable profanity. Her statement, interpreted in this light, indicates a boon which can come to those capable of reactualizing sacred existence—the ability to see profane life in all its moribundity and spiritlessness.

Actually, Dilsey's possession of the prophetic gift is not surprising. Of all the major black figures in the novel, she is the one most capable of moving to the sacred plane of existence, and, because of this, the one most incapable of becoming trapped in the profane wasteland. Just as Shegog can spiritually transcend his otherwise grotesque physical appearance, so Dilsey's inner self can rise above the ravages of time and deprivation. In his first description of her in the last section of the novel, Faulkner pointedly dresses her in queenly garb which asserts its regality above its rattiness: "She wore . . . a maroon velvet cape with a border of mangy and anonymous fur above a dress of purple silk" (p. 330). He goes on to depict the triumph of her essential nature over her general bodily decay:

She had been a big woman once but now her skeleton rose, draped loosely in unpadded skin that tightened again upon a paunch almost dropsical, as though muscle and tissue had been courage or fortitude which the days or the years had consumed until only the indomitable skeleton was left rising like a ruin or a landmark above the somnolent and impervious guts, and above that the collapsed face that gave the impression of the bones themselves being outside the flesh, . . . (p. 331).

Moreover, in Dilsey's early response to Shegog's sermon, Faulkner suggests that her strange crying which reflects her participation in Christ's agony, her joy at the hope of deliverance, and her pity for the doomed Compsons, indicates her victory over the attrition of profane existence: "Two tears slid down her fallen cheeks, in and out of the myriad coruscations of immolation and abnegation and time" (p. 368). Her tears reappear at the moment of her entry into the world of sacred time; now possessing the purifying memory of Christ's saving acts and promises, she cries "rigidly and quietly" (p. 371).

Dilsey's ability to transcend time largely results from her periodic renewals of vision and faith as she moves into the sacred time offered by the festival. Furthermore, she—almost alone among the major figures of the book—can handle profane time too. Unlike Quentin who must prove that all clocks lie, Dilsey accepts the fraudulence of profane time in the shape of the one-handed kitchen clock which is always three hours off (pp. 341–42).[15] Her reaction to the "enigmatically profound" clock is a simple one: she merely augments its false time, thereby setting it relatively right in her own mind. For her, profane time is a burden to be endured, not the be-all and end-all of existence; she can therefore accept its practical necessity, even its value. She well knows that real time lies far above and beyond superficial clock time.

Earlier Dilsey's vision of the Compson doom was presented as an outgrowth of her mystical excursion into sacred time. She receives still another reward from her Easter Sunday experience. Before the service, she sings a song first to herself and then aloud. It is described as "something without particular tune or words, repetitive, mournful and plaintive, austere" (p. 336). Though its wordlessness and lack of perceivable melody are not pejorative qualities, Dilsey's song is nevertheless incomplete at this point; it undergoes important transformation during and after the church service. First it is subsumed into the mixture of sound and silence in which the preacher's voice merges with the inner feelings of the congregation—a fusion which Faulkner describes as occurring "in chanting measures beyond the need for words" (p. 367). Then, in the Compson house following the service, immediately after the faulty clock has struck and Dilsey has spoken in one breath of Jason's not returning and of having "seed de first en de last," she sings again. This time, however, the song possesses both words and melody, although in odd combination: "As she moved back and forth she sang a hymn. She sang the first two lines over and over to the complete tune" (p. 375). Growing as it does out of the service, the prophetic vision, and Dilsey's adaptation to profane time, the new song represents not only the culmination of Dilsey's search for cosmic harmony, but also a musical metaphor for sacred time. It is melodically complete and endlessly cyclical in its lyrics. Because of its simplicity and perfection, it is also easily recoverable.

Dilsey and her black community's ability to disengage themselves from profane time obviously enhances their capacity to endure a profane world, and Faulkner underscores endurance of the secular universe and its time as the finest trait of the blacks in the novel. In the Appendix, the sole comment on Dilsey's character is that, along with TP, Frony, and Luster, she "endured" (p. 427). Moreover, the novelist associates the Negroes' power to endure with their blackness and their separation from their white "masters"—the Compsons: "These others were not Compsons. They were black" (p. 426).

But why, if the blacks can employ the rituals of Christianity to renew themselves and survive, cannot the whites—principally the Compsons—do the same thing? Why is this avenue to enduring existence closed off to them? Much of the answer lies in the fact that Christianity holds no more sacred possibilities for the whites.

Quentin and his father's cynical rejection of Christianity has already been discussed, but they are not the only lapsed Christians in the family or the novel. Jason's bitterness toward the old faith exceeds his brother's and his father's. Sunday, even Easter Sunday, has become for him simply the day one can sleep late; he grumbles to his mother about her allowing the Compson blacks to attend the special Easter service:

"Which means we'll eat cold dinner," Jason said, "or none at all."
"I know it's my fault," Mrs. Compson said. "I know you blame me."
"For what?" Jason said. "You never resurrected Christ, did you?" (p. 348).

Mrs. Compson's brand of Christianity is even deadlier than Jason's wisecracking skepticism since her acts and professions of faith are shallow and hypocritical to the point of self-mockery. Though she protests that she has tried "so hard to raise [her family] as Christians" (p. 351), she has acceded to Jason's secularization of the Sabbath, even the holiest of Sabbaths. In one scene, Faulkner contrasts Dilsey's genuine religious feeling with Mrs. Compson's false religiousity (pp. 374–75). Here Mrs. Compson, who has allowed her Bible to fall face down from her bed, blames this on Dilsey and asks Dilsey to hand her the Book. Dilsey smoothes its bent pages, replaces it on her mistress' bed and offers to raise the shade so that Mrs. Compson will have enough light to read. Mrs. Compson declines her offer. Faulkner completes this devastation of Mrs. Compson's pretended Christianity by mockingly comparing the neurasthenic and hypochondriacal woman to "an old nun praying" "beneath the wimple of her medicated cloth" (p. 375).

Whether the Compsons' loss of the Christian possibilities for sacrality is indicative of a similar loss on the part of all white society in the novel is questionable. Nevertheless, the reader is given no examples of anything approaching living faith and ritual in the white community. True, he sees whites going to church, he hears the white church bells ring, but there is the persistent feeling that these people who apparently attend sacred activities out of habit rather than passionate commitment are merely going through the motions. Certainly there is no shred of white religious behavior to compare in intensity or power with the black Easter Sunday service or the fervid actions of the Memphis whores which Quentin puzzles over.

The loss of the Christian path to sacrality does not necessarily condemn the Compsons to an utterly profane existence. As Robert N. Bellah and W. Lloyd Warner have shown, the United States possesses a civil religion capable of imparting some form of sacred meaning to life through national rituals and ceremonies.[16] This religion may be said to furnish its believers with a sacred history as well. The signing of the Declaration of Independence is the cosmogonic event by which a new world or society is formed out of the destruction of the old, and the Civil War is the redefinitive experience whereby the failings of the originally created society are corrected and that society is changed and preserved. These events, roughly comparable to the Christian creation of the world and the redemptive martyrdom of Jesus Christ, are annually reevoked in the celebrations of Independence Day and Memorial Day. The latter holy day in the American civil religious calendar is particularly heavy with Christian borrowings. Abraham Lincoln assumes Christ's position as holy sacrifice, and the theme of death and rebirth—in this case, involving the martyred dead of the War and the collapse and revivification of the Union and its ideals—is monumentally asserted.[17]

Obviously, however, the American civil religion presented by Warner and Bellah is not a fully national religion, but a sectional one—that of the victorious North. Bellah and Warner almost openly admit that Southern experience and ideals are, in effect, excluded from this civil religion. Commenting on the establishment of national cemeteries—like Memorial Day, an outgrowth of the Civil War—Bellah allows that Arlington, the holiest of these burying grounds, was "begun somewhat vindictively on the Lee estate . . . partly with the end that the Lee family could never reclaim it" (pp. 178–79). And though he claims that the setting aside of a section of this cemetery for the Confederate dead mitigates the originally acrimonious motive for its establishment and binds the heretofore warring sections of the land in a new national religious unity, this according of separate but equal status to the fallen of the South is flimsy proof of real reconciliation and common religio-patriotic feeling. This point is amplified by the fact—ignored by Bellah—that the South has never observed a single, uniform date for

Memorial Day and that its days have rarely coincided with the date of the annual celebration in the North. Nor was Lincoln's birthday (when it had a separate existence in the North) even celebrated in most Southern states. Warner, although he calls Memorial Day "an American sacred ceremony," admits that it is a legal holiday only "over most of the United States" (p. 5). Still more indicative of Warner's muted awareness of the difficulty of extending this observance of the national religion to the South is his comment that "in the South only now are they beginning to use it [Memorial Day] to express southern respect and obligation to the nation's soldier dead" (p. 6). This statement which originally appeared in the 1953 edition of Warner's book remained unchanged in the revised edition of 1962. The exclusion of the South from the national religion was obviously still more severe during the period from 1898 to 1928, the approximate time-span of Faulkner's novel.

At least one of the Compsons, Quentin, recognizes and rejects some of the primary assumptions, ceremonies, and deified figures of the national civil religion. Immediately after breaking his watch to destroy his oppressive awareness of temporality, he dismisses the legendary dimensions of Washington—the hero of the earlier phase of American sacred history—along with the miraculous powers of Christ (p. 99). Shortly thereafter, he recalls the last time he saw Deacon: "It was on Decoration Day, in a G.A.R. uniform, in the middle of the parade" (p. 101). This recollection threatens Brooks's position regarding Quentin's knowledge of the symbolic significance of the day *on* which, or—more accurately—*before* which, he dies. Quentin is certain that he saw Deacon on Decoration Day, although he is not sure of the other ceremonial occasions on which he saw the black parading. If he knows Northern Decoration Day, why is he unlikely to be aware of the dates of the corresponding holidays in his homeland? Quentin's remembrance extends yet further. He recalls Shreve's comment about Deacon's presence in the parade: " 'There now. Just look at what your grandpa did to that poor old nigger.' " And his response to this remark of Shreve's indicates Quentin's rejection of the simplistic Northern stance toward emancipation, the War, and his grandfather's guilt with respect to the blacks: " 'Yes . . . Now he can spend day after day marching in parades. If it hadn't been for my grandfather, he'd have to work like whitefolks' " (p. 101). Two more things are noteworthy here. As a Southern bystander and commentator watching a Northern victory celebration, Quentin's position as a perpetual outsider is strongly confirmed. This is further emphasized when one realizes that Quentin's attention is on Deacon, who is masquerading in the uniform of a Northern Civil War veteran; in Quentin's eyes, the black becomes a usurper reaping the benefits of a war in which he never participated. Also, Quentin, picking up Shreve's cue, singles out his grandfather as the prototype of Southern failure and the inadvertent agent of black emancipation. Surely, much of this is cynical joking, but Quentin is also "kidding on the square."[18] As mentioned before, his grandfather appears in Quentin's beatific vision of death, and he is also the failed brigadier of Shiloh, the Southern disaster whose dates mirror those of the first and third sections of the book. Nowhere in the novel do Quentin's feelings of cultural and familial failure coalesce as powerfully as they do here.

The regularity with which twentieth-century Compson losses fall on days associated with Civil War Compson and Southern defeats forces the all-too-obvious conclusion that a retributive justice of the most exact and inexorable kind is being worked on the family and the South. This is incontestable, but it may unfortunately obscure a far subtler point. Though the Compsons are in some ways the unwitting and helpless fools of fortune, their doom is also accomplished by their entrapment in a Southern civil religion just as concerned as its Northern counterpart with sanctifying the culture's exploits in the Civil War and imparting a sacred dimension to the South's great time through ceremony and ritual. In *The Sound and the Fury*, this Southern civil religion is evoked by Faulkner's implicit references to the beginning and end of Southern sacred history—the birth of Jefferson Davis and Lee's surrender, his repeated allusions to Confederate Memorial Days, and his powerful employment of the sacred monument of the Confederate soldier in the last scene of the novel.

Modern civil religions cannot compete with older supernatural systems of belief in terms of psychological and emotional affect and temporal transcendence. They substitute commemoration for intense reactualization of sacred time; no parade, pageant, or historical reenactment can fully transport civil religionists into the old time or make the old time eternally new. Those who participate in civil ceremonies which glorify the past do so as actors rather than as transformed members of the old society. Moreover, even in this diluted fashion, Southern civil religion and the Confederate time it promotes are inferior to Northern religion and Federal time, since the former are powerless to endow their believers with the strength to escape profane time and endure. Assuredly, there can be no powerful sense of community and cultural participation in a society which celebrates its sacred memorial observance on four days which vary from locality to locality. Also, Southern civil religion and the old time and society it glorifies tend markedly toward empty sentimentalization and the pursuit of nostalgia for its own sake. This is borne out in the novel by Quentin and Shreve's mockery of Mrs. Bland's professional Southernizing and her evocation of a "julep-and-darkey" world (pp. 112, 131, 181). Still more important in this regard is the unavoidable truth that the Southern civil religionist is mired in an experience which culminates in utter, irredeemable defeat. Memory, a wholly beneficial entity in the religious festivals which Eliade describes, becomes an instrument of torture rather than redemption. The remembrance of times past haunts Quentin; it hardly liberates him. Whereas Northern religion possesses the possibility of rebirth arising from death, the South can worship only death.

Denuded of the possibility of rebirth, Southern civil religion can make little effective use of Christian borrowings. Jefferson Davis cannot assume the Christ-like proportions of his Northern adversary; Davis' birthday and its celebration are mocking shadows of the Northern reverence for Lincoln. God the Redeemer is replaced in the Southern civil religious sensibility by God the Avenger. The people of the South who enjoyed chosen status under Washington are reduced to the position of the doomed inhabitants of the Cities of the Plain. Moreover, in Faulkner's world, they cannot—should they mistakenly desire to—reintegrate themselves with the values of the triumphant North.[19] Caddy's marriage with Herbert Head ends predictably with her abandonment, while Jason's repeated attempts to succeed in Northern dominated commercial society are disastrous failures.[20] It is therefore appropriate that Caddy's wedding is linked to the sterile celebration of Confederate Memorial Day, and that young Quentin's robbery of Jason's embezzled money as well as her ill-fated elopement with the pitchman are joined to Lee's surrender of his troops and to her great-grandfather's defeat at Shiloh.[21]

Southern civil religion is a religion, then, but finally a terribly unrewarding one. Though it provides a sacred history and ceremonies commemorating the old time, it fails to give its believers deep human satisfaction. In short, it is at once an inescapable and deadly trap. The communication of these ideas perhaps lies behind Faulkner's repeated use of the day-before pattern, a sequence which suggests the persistence of recurring events without imparting the satisfaction one might derive if these events symmetrically recurred on anniversaries. Ultimately, Faulkner seems to say that Confederate time in *The Sound and the Fury* fails because it presents an order which promises but never delivers fulfillment.

Although nearly all the Compsons are somehow imprisoned in Confederate time, their awareness of this varies. Jason and young Quentin exhibit no cognizance that critical moments in their lives are "wired" to the Southern Civil War experience. However, Caddy, Mrs. Compson, and especially Mr. Compson, may possess knowledge (probably subconscious) that they are locked into this inexorable pattern. Allowing that the selection of the date of Caddy's wedding is partly influenced by her pregnancy, the specific choice of Monday, April 25 is an odd one, if only because formal marriages rarely occur on Mondays.[22] Logically, the Compsons rather than the bridegroom and his family would choose the date; witness the language of the wedding invitation sent to Quentin (p. 115). Nevertheless, the reader cannot know whether the bride, her father, her mother, or all three picked this day. The same ambiguity surrounds the matter of how influential the day's proximity to Confederate

Memorial Day is in its selection. April 25, as Stewart and Backus show, is also the day on which Mr. Compson dies. Again, whether he exercises any choice about when he will depart from a world he hates is, to say the least, uncertain. Clearly his death is linked to his accelerating alcoholism, but one does not know whether he employs his ability to force the moment of his death, dipsomaniacally or otherwise.[23] If he does not, his role is entirely passive and the conjunction of the date of his death with Caddy's marriage (and Quentin's death, via the day-before pattern) is a matter of pure fate.

No such ambiguity, however, clouds Quentin's death. In all likelihood, he carefully picks the date of his suicide, recognizing full well its familial and cultural significance. He arises on the morning of June 2 wholly determined to end his life, and thus to escape not only the attrition of profane time but also his entrapment in failed sacred Confederate time. He prepares for his death and winds up his affairs most methodically. Conscious choice animates many of the minutest of his activities on his last day: his choice of clothing, purchase of the flatirons to weigh his body down, disposal of his effects, transmission of the key to his trunk and the two notes which he writes almost upon rising, etc. (pp. 99–100, 105, 122, 213–14, 222). A man who expends this kind of deliberate care on all aspects of the manner of his death could reasonably be expected to give some consideration to the date of this event.[24]

The probability that Quentin consciously selects the date of his death is heightened by a close examination of one key occurrence on his last day. Edmond Volpe suggests that Quentin chooses the time of his suicide and implies that his choice is tied to his fascination with the time on one of the watches in the window of the jewelry store which he visits early on June 2 (pp. 104–05).[25] Volpe's suggestion is compelling, and still more compelling is the way in which Quentin picks his moment. He responds to his attraction to a watch whose hands are extended "slightly off the horizontal at a faint angle, like a gull tilting into the wind," by saying "And so I told myself to take that one." These words indicate an important decision, yet they are ones which, taken in context, cannot refer to the purchase of a watch.[26] Since the horizontal would be either 2:45 or 9:15, Quentin picks out a time either shortly before or after these positions on the dial.[27] The horizontal indicates a symmetric visualization of time, dividing, as it does, the clock face into two equal sections; therefore, the slightly angled position Quentin takes becomes visually analogous to the day-off pattern. This correspondence is probably instrumental in his choice. Given the intensity of his feeling for his sister, his recognition that her marriage separates them forever, and his awareness of the crass shallowness of her husband as well as the forced circumstances of her wedding, Quentin regards her marriage as a virtual death.[28] Remembering, in all probability, that the day after her wedding was a Confederate Memorial Day, he imposes the same pattern on his own death, making it occur a day before another Southern Memorial Day. One must recognize that Quentin is uniquely sensitive to patterns that fail to complete themselves; his life is made up of them. For example, he remembers how, as a schoolboy, he could never make his internal time equal the external time measured by the school bell, and he mentally equates the proprietor of the bakery he visits late on June 2 with a schoolteacher standing before a blackboard on which is written "2 x 2 e 5" (pp. 108–09, 156). If Quentin does in fact calculatedly choose the moment of his death—and the evidence surely points this way—it becomes enormously probable that, operating by highly similar principles, he picks the date of his suicide, with total knowledge of its symbolic meanings for himself, his family, and his culture. Tormented by the inescapability of profane time, incapable of transcending this time for sacred temporality as Benjy and Dilsey can, knowing he is trapped in and doomed by failed sacred time, he accepts the latter pattern in his final act.[29]

The Sound and the Fury contains a number of visual representations of time, of which the watch in the jeweler's window is but one. Another, which has been overlooked in this regard, is the pattern Benjy demands when he goes around the Confederate monument at the end of the novel (pp. 399–401). When Luster attempts to take him to the left, Benjy rebels and starts to bellow. Jason forcibly corrects Luster and makes him take Benjy's path around the monument to the right. The point of reference here is the memorial of the Confederate soldier, suggestive of fixation in Confederate time, and the pattern Benjy insists on is a counter-clockwise rather than a clockwise one. If this is not simply regarded as an idiot's pathological reaction to a violation of accustomed order—and Benjy's possible position as a holy idiot should prevent so uncritical an interpretation—his act may be seen as a truly meaningful one. He refuses to become paralyzed by the monument and all it stands for, though he recognizes its vital importance as a reference point; he refuses to submit to the shape by which profane time is measured; and he resolutely maintains a path counterposed to the clockwise movement. Intuitively, he keeps the pattern which negates the conventional, for only by so doing can he perceive reality in a genuinely orderly and satisfactory fashion. Of course, his transcendence of time is unique and personal. It cannot apply to anyone else or to any community. In contrast, however, the black congregation retains a mode of transcendence which is communal, though the modernization and Northernization of the younger blacks in the novel may presage the loss of this cultural capability.[30] For the Compsons, however, any possibility of communal or individual transcendence is gone. Faulkner has powerfully underscored this latter point by linking—via the anniversary and the day-before patterns—the dates and critical events of each section of the novel to the Confederate experience of defeat, surrender, and ineradicable remembrance of failure.

Notes

1. Cleanth Brooks, *William Faulkner: The Yoknapatawpha Country* (New Haven: Yale Univ. Press, 1963), p. 8; George R. Stewart and Joseph M. Backus, " 'Each in Its Ordered Place': Structure and Narrative in 'Benjy's Section' of *The Sound and the Fury*," *AL*, 29 (1958), 453, n. 10.

2. Stewart and Backus, p. 453, n. 10. References to Tennessee, more particularly to Memphis, abound in Faulkner's novel. See *The Sound and the Fury* (1929, [Appendix, 1946]; rpt. Random House, 1966), pp. 211–12, 305, 417, 421–22, 426. All subsequent references are to this edition.

3. Oxford and Memphis lie about seventy road miles apart. Jason hints at Memphis' mercantile importance when he mentions that there is a board in the city which posts the prices on the cotton exchange every ten seconds (p. 305). Also see n. 21.

4. Stewart and Backus, p. 453. Confederate Memorial Day is celebrated in the South on four different dates: May 30 in Virginia, June 3 in Louisiana, Tennessee, and Arkansas, April 26 in Alabama, Florida, Georgia, and Mississippi, and May 10 in North and South Carolina (Alexander MacQueen, "Memorial Day," *Encyclopaedia Britannica* [Chicago, 1969]).

5. Stewart and Backus, p. 453, n. 10.

6. Mircea Eliade, *The Sacred and the Profane: The Nature of Religion*, trans. Willard R. Trask (New York: Harcourt, Brace, & World, 1959), pp. 68–113. All subsequent references are to this edition.

7. See Jean-Paul Sartre, "Time in Faulkner: *The Sound and the Fury*," trans. Martine Darmon, in *William Faulkner: Three Decades of Criticism*, ed. Frederick J. Hoffman and Olga W. Vickery (1960; rpt. New York: Harcourt, Brace, & World, 1963), pp. 225–32; Brooks, *Faulkner*, pp. 327–31; Perrin Lowrey, "Concepts of Time in *The Sound and the Fury*," in *English Institute Essays, 1952*, ed. Alan S. Downer (New York: Columbia Univ. Press, 1954), pp. 57–82. Sartre's essay, which first appeared in 1939, is at once brilliant and distortive of Faulkner's novel. Persistently Sartre imposes the views of Quentin and Mr. Compson on the author, a point well noted by Brooks (pp. 328–29). Moreover, in depicting what he feels to be Faulkner's vision of man as a creature deprived of the ability to comprehend the present or conceive of the future, Sartre totally ignores the experience of the blacks—especially Dilsey—in the novel.

8. Frederick L. Gwynn and Joseph L. Blotner, eds., *Faulkner in the University* (1959; rpt. New York: Random House, 1965), p. 3; Charlton W. Tebeau, "Shiloh," *Encyclopaedia Britannica* (Chicago, 1969).

9. Divination through one's olfactory sense appears both in sophisticated literature and common discourse. Witness the references to this sense in *Hamlet* and *King Lear* as well as the stereotypical bigot's claim that he can smell out jews, niggers, communists, etc.

10. Stanley Davies, *Social Control of the Mentally Deficient* (New York: Thomas Y. Crowell, 1930), p. 16.

11. While it is possible that the boys are fearful of touching Benjy because he is white, it seems their fear of his magical power is paramount. As anthropologists have repeatedly observed, the possession of destructive *mana* is often inseparable from the possession of beneficient *mana*.

12. Luster's attraction to the carnival, the way he is impressed by the musical saw player there, and his attempts to show off and imitate "quality" which cause him to violate Benjy's ritual at the end of the novel are all indications that he is influenced by shoddy white values.

13. See n. 12. Frony's concern for the opinions of the white community, her marriage to a pullman porter and removal to St. Louis, and TP's donning of the cheap clothes made in

New York and Chicago sweatshops are further examples of the Northernizing and vulgarizing of the blacks. See pp. 362, 426.

14. Rev. 1.8, 22.13.

15. See Lowrey, pp. 78–81.

16. Robert N. Bellah, "Civil Religion in America," in *Beyond Belief: Essays on Religion in a Post-Traditional World* (New York: Harper & Row, 1970), pp. 168–86; W. Lloyd Warner, "An American Sacred Ceremony," in *American Life: Dream and Reality*, rev. ed. (1953; rpt. Chicago: Univ. of Chicago Press, 1962), pp. 5–34. All subsequent references are to these editions.

17. Bellah, pp. 176–79; Warner, pp. 7–8, 14, 20–23, 30, 34.

18. Quentin also sees Deacon as a usurper of his grandfather's position; he claims the black ought to be made a general (p. 121). He also refers to Lincoln somewhat disparagingly when speaking of Deacon's firm conviction that the black possesses part of "Abe Lincoln's military sash" (p. 120). This rejection of Lincoln as culture hero contrasts strongly with the assimilationist Jason's humorous emulation of Lincoln: " 'In 1865,' he would say, 'Abe Lincoln freed the niggers from the Compsons. In 1933, Jason Compson freed the Compsons from the niggers' " (p. 422).

19. The superior viability of Northern civil religion does not indicate that Faulkner believed in its moral superiority. The matter is simply one of cultural survival.

20. See, for example, his bitter experiences with the cotton market (pp. 303–05, 329).

21. Faulkner's personal awareness of Southern Memorial Day is documented on p. 249 of *Faulkner in the University:* "But I can remember the old men, and they would get out the old shabby grey uniforms and get out the old battleflag on Decoration, Memorial Day." See also the rather satiric picture of Decoration Day in North Mississippi which Quentin gives to Shreve and Shreve repeats on pp. 327–28 of *Absalom, Absalom!* (1936; rpt. New York: Random House, 1964). Note also that this celebration takes place on the Tennessee date in June rather than the Mississippi date in April.

22. Stewart and Backus forcefully argue that Faulkner's dates are calendrically accurate (pp. 452–53).

23. Though Caddy tells Quentin (p. 154) that the doctors say Mr. Compson will not live more than a year if he does not stop drinking, he actually lasts slightly over two years from the time of this conversation.

24. Faulkner's statement (p. 411) that Quentin commits suicide in June because he wants "first to complete the current academic year and so get the full value of his paid-in-advance tuition"—part of the money realized from the sale of Benjy's beloved pasture—does not explain why he chooses this day in June. In fact, the comment is not wholly accurate. The text reveals that the school year is not over on June 2: on that day Shreve asks Quentin whether he has gone to his psychology class (p. 125). Moreover, if the boat race mentioned on pp. 75 and 104 is the concluding event of the year, the academic year is a week short of completion on June 2.

25. Volpe, *A Reader's Guide to William Faulkner* (New York: Farrar, Straus, & Giroux, 1964), p. 371.

26. Since he has already left the store, never to return, there is no possibility that the decision refers to buying a watch in the window. Though the chance exists that his choice of "that one" merely reflects his arbitrary acceptance of one particular time as the present moment, his language indicates a more momentous decision, particularly in view of the fact that his next move is the purchase of the flatirons which will weigh down his drowned body.

27. Even allowing that this section is somewhat open-ended, the high likelihood exists that Quentin kills himself around 9:15 on the evening of June 2. This time has almost certainly not passed when Quentin leaves his room. It has been dark a relatively short time, and

people are still on the streets around the post office (p. 222). For psychological reasons, Quentin has been simply "killing time" all day, aware that he can only accomplish his final act at night. Now that darkness has come, there is no reason for him to delay his suicide until around 2:45 in the morning.

28. As Volpe notes (p. 369), Quentin envisions the wedding announcement as a bier. See *Sound*, p. 115. Moreover, Caddy's influence upon all aspects of Quentin's death is considerably heightened if one accepts the hypothesis that Quentin intends to have Shreve relay his last and most important letter to Caddy. One of Quentin's last acts is to check the address on this letter (p. 222), something he would not have to do if it were being sent to his own dormitory room. Though it is conceivable that Quentin sends the letter—for some unimaginable reason—to Shreve's Canadian home address, it is much more probable that the letter is finally intended to reach Caddy who is at this point on her extended honeymoon, and whose future address (after August 1) is dimly etched on Quentin's memory (p. 115).

29. Patricia Tobin, in "The Time of Myth and History in *Absalom, Absalom!*" AL, 45 (1973), 252–70, posits a different set of reasons for Quentin's suicide. However, her argument dominantly concerns Quentin's experiences in *Absalom, Absalom!* rather than the things he undergoes in *The Sound and the Fury*.

30. See p. 182 and n. 13.

"The Magician's Wand":
Faulkner's Compson Appendix

Mary Jane Dickerson*

I

Faulkner's "Appendix: Compson: 1699–1945," written in 1945 for Malcolm Cowley's anthology, *The Portable Faulkner* (1946), deserves more critical attention as a discrete piece of fiction. Recent research by Professor James B. Meriwether and the publication of *The Faulkner-Cowley File* (1966) provide the necessary material for a serious examination of the Compson Appendix's relationship to *The Sound and the Fury*, its particular thematic associations with the fiction Faulkner wrote between 1929 and 1945, and its singular influence on certain pieces of his fiction after 1945. And most of all, the Compson Appendix's ingenious narrative structure merits study for what it tells us about Faulkner's fluid and individual fictional technique and the enduring role of the Compson material in the shaping of his art. As soon as he had finished the piece, Faulkner himself recognized its individual worth in a near-jubilant letter to Malcolm Cowley: "I should have done this when I wrote the book. Then the whole thing would have fallen into pattern like a jigsaw puzzle when the magician's wand touched it. . . . I think it is really pretty good, to stand as it is, as a piece without implications."[1]

Faulkner's provocative comments about writing "a Golden Book or Doomsday Book" about Yoknapatawpha, in which the genealogical strands would be worked out more completely, have stimulated interesting speculation, but I believe Mr. Meriwether's claim that the Compson Appendix is the closest Faulkner came to realizing this ambition to be the soundest.[2] But while we do not have this projected final novel, there is enough evidence in the Compson Appendix concerning the writer's developing insights about the implications of his material to add considerably to our understanding of what that longer work might have represented, thematically and structurally. And, because of the major concern of Cowley's project—to select that material most representative of the writer's genius and most central to the larger scope of his fiction—Michael Millgate has suggested that "Faulkner himself may have

*Reprinted, with permission, from *Mississippi Quarterly*, 28, No. 3 (Summer 1975), 317–37.

252

gained something from the opportunity to review in a fresh light the whole body of his work."[3] Out of this endeavor came a new piece of writing which marks the culmination of a major phase in Faulkner's development as an artist and anticipates certain salient characteristics in the fiction of the final period of his career.

After its initial publication in *The Portable Faulkner* in the spring of 1946, the Compson Appendix appeared later that same year in the Modern Library double volume of *The Sound and the Fury* and *As I Lay Dying*, which contained, on the title page, the misleading statement "With A New Appendix As A Forward By The Author." But it was not until late in 1962, in the Vintage paperback (P-5) reissue of the 1929 text of *The Sound and the Fury*, that the "Appendix" was more properly placed at the end of the novel.[4] This relationship to the novel—one made by editors and publishers rather than the author—has tended to obscure the Compson Appendix's transcendence of its ties to *The Sound and the Fury*. As Meriwether says, "Just what Faulkner meant by 'a piece without implications' is not entirely clear."[5] In the whole passage from his letter to Cowley cited earlier, Faulkner seems to be purposefully ambiguous: the Compson Appendix clarifies the material of the novel, especially the excerpt from the fourth section chosen for *The Portable Faulkner*, but, at the same time, the piece can stand alone as an integral and independent work of fiction in its own right. And it should also be emphasized that the Compson Appendix was surely different in 1945 than it would have been in 1928. In another letter to Cowley, Faulkner speaks to this crucial difference: "The inconsistencies in the appendix prove to me the book is still alive after 15 years; and being still alive is growing changing; the appendix was done at the same heat as the book, even though 15 years later, and so it is the book itself which is inconsistent: not the appendix. That is, at the age of 30 I did not know these people as at 45 I now do; that I was even wrong now and then in the very conclusion I drew from watching them, and the information I once believed. (I believe I was 28 when I first wrote the book. That's almost 20 years.)"[6] The Compson Appendix, therefore, cannot be examined solely as an extension of the text of *The Sound and the Fury*, as it usually is if mentioned at all, though its initial relationship to the novel must be considered carefully. This unique piece must also be read with regard to the time lapse Faulkner mentioned and in the light of what he wrote during that time interval if one is to see clearly its special place in his writing career.

Two important pieces that contribute significantly to the Faulkner canon and to a consideration of the seminal importance of the Compson material have been recently published, though written earlier: a 1933 Introduction to *The Sound and the Fury*, and a prefatory note to the Compson Appendix, apparently written in 1946. The complete Introduction had disappeared from sight after being prepared for a new edition of the novel which was never published, and the prefatory note probably was intended for the Modern Library volume described above. In the Introduction Faulkner revealed the special affinity he felt for this novel: "But when I finished The Sound and The Fury I discovered that there is actually something to which the shabby term Art not only can, but must, be applied."[7] One of the most illuminating comments about *The Sound and the Fury* emerges from Faulkner's comparison of the very act of writing this novel with the experience of writing *As I Lay Dying:* "So when I finished it the cold satisfaction was there, as I had expected, but as I had also expected that other quality which The Sound and The Fury had given me was absent: that emotion definite and physical and yet nebulous to describe: that ecstasy, that eager and joyous faith and anticipation of surprise which the yet unmarred sheet beneath my hand held inviolate and unfailing, waiting for release."[8] And he ended the Introduction with the statement: ". . . in The Sound and The Fury I had already put perhaps the only thing in literature which would ever move me very much: Caddy climbing the pear tree to look in the window at her grandmother's funeral while Quentin and Jason and Benjy and the negroes looked up at the muddy seat of her drawers. . . . Now I can make myself a vase like that which the old Roman kept at his bedside and wore the rim slowly away with kissing it."[9] Since Faulkner said later to Cowley that he had written the Compson Appendix "at the same heat as the book," presumably he was able to recapture some of the original "anticipation" and "ecstasy" he experienced so vividly while writing the novel seventeen years earlier.

The Compson Appendix, then, caught Faulkner's imagination again about the novel he claimed as his favorite and further reveals its meaning as it was enriched for the author by the perspective of writing other stories and novels—and profoundly affects those yet to come. In the prefatory note written shortly after the Compson Appendix itself, he refers to *The Sound and the Fury* as "last year's maidenhead now."[10] We will see later in this discussion that to refer to the novel by that particular image is inextricably wedded to the enduring effect of the Compson material on his creativity. Cowley sees that "Like a tree the Compson story had continued to grow, striking roots into the past—as deep as the battle of Culloden—and raising branches into what had been the future when the published novel ended on Easter morning, 1928."[11] These ties between *The Sound and the Fury* in 1929, the 1933 Introduction, the Compson Appendix in 1945, and the prefatory note in 1946 afford an unusual glimpse into the prominent role of the Compson material in the shaping of William Faulkner's achievement from 1929 to 1946 and allow an assessment of the influence of this material on his later works.

II

By tracing the chronological history of the Compson Mile in the Compson Appendix, Faulkner enlarges the fictional world that is presented on the Yoknapatawpha map that appears as the end papers of *The Portable Faulkner*. Michael Millgate has briefly discussed one of the functions of the Compson Appendix: "It seems possible that Faulkner felt that he had created the social context of the action in insufficient detail, that the book did not clearly evoke the patterns of manners and customs within which his characters moved: the Compson 'Appendix' he wrote for *The Portable Faulkner* is devoted . . . primarily to the elaboration of the Compsons' family history and to the further definition of their place in the social and economic life of Jefferson."[12] The past and the present mesh in a comprehensive manner in the Compson Appendix, a method Faulkner probably deliberately eschewed in the novel, instinctively realizing the primary necessity of concentrating on the inner lives of his characters and achieving the mastery of a technique that serves so richly in later years. It is as if he had to explore their inner selves fully before being able to create their outer world in clearer detail. *Sartoris* represents that earlier groping and struggling for form in its use of genealogy to fuse the past and the present, but the very experience of tackling *Sartoris* no doubt also helped to clarify the possibilities inherent in genealogy that resulted finally in the Compson Appendix.

The image of Caddy, that "beautiful and tragic little girl," remains central to the action of the Compson Appendix just as it had been a controlling focus of the novel. Andrew Jackson, who figures as an historical personage active in the push westward and the subsequent fated displacement of the Indians by the white man and whose portrait adds a depth and authenticity to the historical and social context of the beginnings of the Compson saga in America, also functions, through his passionate concern for his wife, to contribute subtly to the contemporary implications of Caddy's image in his determination to forge "the principle that honor must be defended whether it was or not because defended it was whether or not."[13] And this rough-edged frontier soldier with a chivalric streak helps to create an oblique context for Quentin III "Who loved not his sister's body but some concept of Compson honor precariously and (he knew well) only temporarily supported by the minute fragile membrane of her maidenhead as a miniature replica of all the whole vast globy earth may be poised on the nose of a trained seal" (p. 9).

And finally, there is the sustained episode centered on the picture of Caddy in 1945 "ageless and beautiful, cold serene and damned" (p. 12). Faulkner continues to portray Caddy indirectly—is the woman in the picture really Caddy?—and through her impact on Jason and Melissa Meek. She appears in a faded photograph from a magazine, but Faulkner again manages to create her passionate presence. Jason, after initially recognizing her—" 'It's Cad, all right' " (p. 13)—then adamantly refuses to acknowledge that the beautiful woman in the picture—"a picture filled with luxury and money and sunlight" (p. 12)—could be his sister Caddy because, even now, he is not free of the obsessive jealousy and rage for vengeance that prompted him to steal from her and ultimately to deprive her daughter, Quentin, of love and family. Outward recognition would enmesh him again in the past he had so methodically cut himself away from. To see Caddy rich and still beautiful, even in the most damning and compromising of circumstances ("beside her a handsome lean man of middleage in the ribbon and tabs of a German staff-general" [pp. 12–13]) is enough to raise Jason's galling frustration to hysterical pitch and cause him to refuse to try to save Caddy from whatever "doom" might await her. Jason bragged that "He was emancipated now. He was free. 'In 1865,' he would say, 'Abe Lincoln freed the niggers from the Compsons. In 1933, Jason Compson freed the Compsons from the niggers' " (p. 18). But an added dimension of the Compson Appendix is that Jason would never be completely rid of his past. Faulkner has said, ". . . to me, no man is himself, he is the sum of his past. It is a part of every man, every woman, and every moment. All of his and her ancestry, background, is all a part of himself and herself at any moment. And so a man, a character in a story at any moment of action is not just himself as he is then, he is all that made him. . . ."[14]

Melissa Meek's perceptive consciousness is the vehicle Faulkner uses throughout this central scene to draw the town of Jefferson into the immediacy of the Compson saga. Her condemnation of Jason's role in the family's final disintegration reinforces what the reader has felt in the novel: "—and the mousesized mousecolored spinster trembling and aghast at her own temerity, staring across it [Caddy's picture] at the childless bachelor in whom ended that long line of men who had had something in them of decency and pride even after they had begun to fail at the integrity and the pride had become mostly vanity and selfpity" (p. 13). The town comes vividly into this final scene in the last stage of the family's tragedy for, like Dilsey in the novel, Melissa Meek cares: "*Yes* she thought, crying quietly *that was it she* [Dilsey] *didn't want to see it know whether it was Caddy or not because she knows Caddy doesn't want to be saved hasn't anything anymore worth being saved for nothing worth being lost that she can lose*" (p. 16). Again, the final statement on the tragic implications in the Compson chronicle comes from one who is not a Compson, and Faulkner has surely shown us the first and the last for a more complete tragic recognition. Melissa Meek, the tears streaming down her face, wends her way home from the futile mission for Dilsey's help in the midst of teeming figures of servicemen, many of them doomed as well, to return to Jefferson "where life [is] lived too with all its incomprehensible passion and turmoil and grief and fury and despair" (p. 16). The center has deliberately widened from the family to the town to include finally the larger world through "soldiers and sailors enroute either to leave or to death and the homeless young women" (p. 15). The action has come full circle, beginning with the disintegration of a way of life at Culloden in April of 1746 to end with the battle sounds of World War II echoing in the distance. Further, since, as Meriwether has stressed, Faulkner was working on *A Fable* at the time he wrote the prefatory note to the Compson Appendix in 1946,[15] the beginning and the ending of the piece within the outer framework of war, spanning centuries, would appear to be a clue to its influence on the creative imagination at work on *A Fable*.

Through the genealogical tracery, Faulkner enlarges and illuminates the actions and characters of the present-day Compsons by his selective delineation of their ancestry. He gives us the tantalizing figure of Charles Stuart Compson, who thought he wanted to be a teacher of classics rather than the soldier and opportunist he turned out to be. This portrait sharpens our understanding of Jason III who "sat all day long with a decanter of whiskey and a litter of dogeared Horaces and Livys and Catulluses, composing (it was said) caustic and satiric eulogies on both his dead and his living fellowtownsmen . . ." (p. 8). He was trained as a lawyer but his inclinations and temperament made him a philosophic spectator rather than a man disposed to action. He could only offer words to his son and fragmented understanding to his daughter, but he could not actively alter the doom awaiting a family trying to exist without the necessary measures of love and compassion. The ambivalence in the earlier Compson between the roles of the active man and the contemplative man works itself out in extremes through two of Jason III's sons: to its ultimate paralysis of the will to live in Quentin III, "who loved death above all, who loved only death, loved and lived in a deliberate and almost perverted anticipation of death" (p. 9), and to its opposite in Jason IV, for whom survival becomes paramount and who lives only in the most egotistical way, divorcing his emotions completely from his family and "fellowtownsmen," voluntarily dispossessing himself of the remnants of the Compson Mile to invest his money in cotton and other marketable "futures"—an opportunist like the first Jason but more akin to Flem Snopes, as many have observed, in his single-minded plodding without a ray of vision to transform his actions.

Even the Compson names assume greater meaning through successive generations. The first Compson was Quentin MacLachan, orphaned early (to be motherless either literally or figuratively is part of both the Compson and the McCaslin legacies) and dispossessed at the Battle of Culloden. Sir Walter Scott's *Quentin Durward* was in Faulkner's library and in the one he was building for his grandsons.[16] Faulkner wrote that his grandfather "had a moderate though reasonably diffuse and catholic library; I realize now that I got most of my early education in it. It was a little limited in its fiction content, since his taste was for simple straightforward romantic excitement like Scott or Dumas."[17] Perhaps it is not too far-fetched to speculate that the name "Quentin" came from an early impression of that other young man, Quentin Durward, who left Scotland after his home was laid waste and his family slaughtered to go to France to make his fortune with his ability at arms. At the very least, the name "Quentin," with its reverberations of Scott's romantic hero, suits that first Quentin MacLachan Compson who came to the New World to avenge his dispossession after Culloden, bringing with him the claymore and the tartan, the national symbols of manhood and family. And he, more significantly, stubbornly calls his son Charles Stuart, "attainted and proscribed by name," after the romantic but ill-fated Bonnie Prince Charles Stuart. This son, in his turn and perhaps to reverse the tide of fortune, gives his son "the flamboyant name" of Jason Lycurgus, which functions defiantly to evoke a grander time, to recapture the legendary era when men dared attempt the heroic and quest the unknown. The trial at glory on Culloden Moor, when Prince Charles Stuart compelled men by the force of his personality and insistent vision of a revitalized and independent Scotland, and the remote glory of Greece have come at last to rest in a Jason firmly tied to the present with no imagination, with only the instinct for survival based on dealings with a present-day golden fleece, cotton. Faulkner often uses names and images to effect a reversal which can charge his fiction with a nearly palpable tension. The earlier Quentins and Jasons, through their actions, exhibited more qualities that linked them to the backgrounds splendidly evoked by their names. But the last male descendants—Quentin, who has a twisted and fatalistic conception of his family's history with its tradition of glory and honor, and Jason, who approaches the image of the sterile modern man, devoid of all concerns except making money and steering clear of any emotional entanglements—are the antitheses in temperament of their namesakes, or rather, they have evolved into the absurd extremes of qualities incipient in their namesakes.

Beyond providing the immediate social context of Jefferson through Melissa Meek's viewpoint and the extended historical context and greater understanding of the Compsons through the characterizations of their namesakes, Faulkner makes a distinctive use of the controlling genealogical structure as his major narrative device and extended symbol in the Compson Appendix. Infusing genealogy with the force and function of symbol had been an important innovation in *Go Down, Moses*, chiefly in "The Bear." Indeed, there are obvious parallels in Faulkner's treatment of the symbolic through genealogy in the Compson Appendix and "The Bear": the transferral of the land, Compson's Mile, from the loose ownership of Ikkemotubbe ("a dispossessed American king") to the white man, from the first Jason Lycurgus, avenging an earlier dispossession, to the ultimately dispossessed Jason IV; in "The Bear," the original ownership of the land spawns the miscegenation and incest forever staining the Mc-

Caslin tenure so that Ike refuses his inheritance, becoming by his own volition the dispossessed McCaslin and, like Jason IV, childless, hence the end of the family lineage. Ike discovers the McCaslin family guilt through his perusal of the dusty ledgers containing the genealogy and economic records of the McCaslins and the Beauchamps, black and white. He believes his actual inheritance to be the land tainted with the tragic suffering caused by the sins of his grandfather: *"Eunice Bought by Father in New Orleans 1807 $650 dolars. Marrid to Thucydus 1809 Drownd in Crick Cristmas Day 1832"* followed by *"Tomasina called Tomy Daughter of Thucydus @ Eunice Born 1810 dide in Child bed June 1833 and Burd. Yr stars fell,"* and finally, *"Turl Son of Thucydus @ Eunice Tomy born Jun 1833 yr stars fell Fathers will."*[18] These brief entries, like the genealogical Compson entries, do not elaborate, but they spare nothing. The reader experiences the same process of dawning recognition of the awful truth at the same moment Ike does. Faulkner also refers to the year 1833 in the Compson Appendix when he describes the older time on the land that eventually became the Compson Mile and how that land began to undergo irreversible changes: "forested then because these were the old days before 1833 when the stars fell" (p. 3).

In both works, the year 1833, "when the stars fell," becomes a portentous turning point and solemnly separates the era of the unviolated wilderness from the time when the white man's possession accompanies the desecration of the land so that the natural wilderness is transformed into the denuded and ravaged countryside by the progressive encroachment of the sawmill, the railroad and the monotonous rows of bungalows. The probable incest revealed in the McCaslin genealogical records in "The Bear" and the imagined incest in the Compson Appendix are equally traumatic, causing death by drowning for both Eunice and Quentin. The despoiling of the Virgin Wilderness parallels the physical violation of the female. Through genealogy as symbol, then, the larger stories of the McCaslins and the Compsons emerge and each family history is permeated by an inability to experience love and compassion with any degree of fulfillment, so that human relationships, with few exceptions, are twisted and sterile, and each family is finally unable to transcend the old sins, to reconcile its historical reality and the glow of legend.

In the Compson Appendix Faulkner, as well as chronicling the origin of the white man's ownership and his desecration of the land, also traces his coming from the Old World to the New, a journey shrouded in strife and anguish and motivated by his fierce need to avenge himself upon the misfortune and suffering in his past. The Compson Appendix, then, serves as an effective analogy of the tumultuous settling of America, the Revolution, the Civil War, and, through the faded picture of Caddy, the wars of the twentieth century. But the particular chronicle of the Compsons reveals a story with a decided twist. The Compsons were on the losing side in each war, from the doomed Scottish uprising in 1745 to the conjecture surrounding Caddy's apparent liaison with the German military officer of World War II.[19] Jason III has perhaps explained this fated propensity of the Compsons to be on the losing side to his son Quentin: "Because no battle is ever won he said. They are not even fought. The field only reveals to man his own folly and despair, and victory is an illusion of philosophers and fools."[20] And Caddy first seals her doom with the khaki-clad Dalton Ames and later becomes the mistress of another man in uniform, the German officer; her search for love seems to draw her to men who ostensibly represent an aggressive strength to take the place of the security of the love that has forever eluded her. Better the illusion than total emptiness and despair.

Three Indian stories, written in the 'thirties, and *Absalom, Absalom!*, published in 1936, contributed substantially to the texture and meaning of the Compson Appendix. In *Absalom*, Faulkner interweaves the social context, the psychological exploration, and the deepening preoccupation with the implications of the historical, both the real and the legendary. This complex and subtle novel pulls together what Faulkner achieves independently in *The Sound and the Fury* and the Compson Appendix. Certainly *Absalom*, with its inexorable probing of the past filtered through Quentin Compson's receptivity to pain, added to the scope that would be remarkably implied in the highly condensed Compson Appendix. Quentin's involvement with the Sutpen story in this novel and his similar role in the 1931 story "A Justice," when he first hears about Doom, become explorations into and revelations about the mystery of origins, bound to affect Faulkner's later conception of the Compson Appendix, which is essentially a story of origins, extending beyond the genealogy of the Compson family to distil much of the original historical and legendary experience of a region and of a nation. In his essay " 'The Firmament of Man's History': Faulkner's Treatment of the Past," Michael Millgate views *Absalom, Absalom!* and *Go Down, Moses* as central works of the ongoing creation of the historical autonomy of Yoknapatawpha County, with the narrative prologues in *Requiem for a Nun* functioning later in the same manner to fill in "that whole richly and profoundly imagined world of Yoknapatawpha as it had grown progressively and organically out of a single original conception."[21] The Compson Appendix deserves a place with these works as an integral part of the filling in of historical detail and the embodying of the symbolic function of the past through the genealogy of the Compson family.

In *Absalom, Absalom!* the genealogical and the chronological interweave as the process of the interpretation of the Sutpen tragedy takes place to provide an almost intolerably heightened atmosphere of suspense in which the story of an irretrievable loss of illusion occurs. The Compson Appendix also embodies, in a highly concentrated form, this same account of the loss of time-honored concepts, metaphorically described through the spoiling of the Virgin Wilderness and the ravishing of the female. The image of the grand domain wrested from the Wilderness is also present in *Absalom*. Quentin asks his father, " 'What is it to me that the land . . . or whatever it was got tired of him at last and turned and destroyed him [Sutpen]? . . . It's going to turn and destroy us all some day, whether our name happens to be Sutpen or Coldfield or not.' "[22] And Quentin's intense questions prophesy the ultimate fate of the Compsons as well. When the man approaches the land in order to exact a vengeful recompense, the design is doomed to failure, whether it be Sutpen's Hundred or the Compson Domain. And nowhere is the failure more powerfully imagined than in the similar descriptions of the decay of the once splendid Sutpen and Compson mansions: in *Absalom*, *"You have seen the rotting shell of the house with its sagging portico and scaling walls, its sagging blinds and plank-shuttered windows, set in the middle of the domain which had reverted to the state and had been bought and sold and bought and sold again and again and again"* (p. 213); in the Compson Appendix, "—the weedchoked traces of the old ruined lawns and promenades, the house which had needed painting too long already, the scaling columns of the portico" (p. 8).

The stories "Red Leaves," "A Justice," and "Lo," grouped in the "Wilderness" section in Faulkner's 1950 *Collected Stories*, explore that earlier time on the land before the dominance of the white man in Yoknapatawpha, and though they do not tell specifically about the acquisition of the Compson Mile, they do enhance the perspective of the history of the region that Faulkner draws on so richly in the Compson Appendix. "Red Leaves" is well described in the words Faulkner used for the force of the Wilderness in "The Bear": it is about "the past, which could be the old evils, the old forces, which were by their own standards right and correct, ruthless, but they lived and died by their own code—they asked nothing."[23] "A Justice" concerns mixed blood and the birth of the complex interrelationships of the Indian and the black man, with implications about the white man's relationship with both. And Quentin is the boy-narrator who becomes a participant in this relationship too, much as he does in the later experience of hearing the Sutpen story—not by blood but by the inevitable interrelationships of all of them on the land which he instinctively recognizes pertains to his own birthright and origins: "I was just twelve then, and I would have to wait until I had passed on and through and beyond the suspension of twilight. Then I knew that I would know. But then Sam Fathers would be dead."[24] When he includes the Indian material in the genealogical structure of the Compson Appendix, Faulkner seems to be remembering Quentin's prophetic thoughts in "A Justice," when he pondered what Sam Fathers had entrusted to his keeping. "Lo" (1934) presents Andrew Jackson in a wryly humorous role, active in the gradual displacement of the Indians' vast lands by the white man, and emphasizes the frustrating impossibility of man ever really being able to possess the land: the white man always trying to make the ownership yield a profit and the Indian's innate knowledge of the futility of the white man's effort. And the Indian, in turn, exacts a measure of justice from his basic intuition of what the white man is always up to.

These stories contribute to the underlying implications of the opening sections of the Compson Appendix and are necessary to Faulkner's exploration of the legendary and historical sources of the region he is charting with such care. Moreover, Ikkemotubbe emerges from these stories as a major character conscious of a sense of destiny that gives him, like the early Compsons and Andrew Jackson, stature, complexity and the aura of legend. Since Ikkemotubbe too stole the land from the one in line for the Manship, he comes to share in the white man's guilt in all but stealing the Indians' land and using the black man in slavery. He poisons the members of his own family for the power of the Manship after an extended sojourn among white men. His name "Doom" gains increasing significance in the context of the Compson Appendix, and his doom is entwined in the individual and collective doom of the Compson family. The word "doom" is one that Faulkner repeats throughout the Compson Appendix, expecially to describe Caddy and Quentin; along with "virgin" and "honor" it is one of the key words of the piece.

In the Compson Appendix, then, Faulkner put into final shape an essential part of the design and meaning of the Indian stories, *Absalom, Absalom!* and *Go Down, Moses.* I do not agree with those critics who consider the Compson Appendix a violation of the integrity and art of *The Sound and the Fury.*[25] On the contrary, I believe that, like *Absalom*, it instead reveals the enduring role of the Compson family in shaping a major portion of Faulkner's art. In the portrayal of the Compsons generation by generation, Faulkner goes far to trace the development of the concept of the American hero: the independent frontiersman, the man of action possessing a past he wants to avenge, the introspective man aware of the psychologically crippling forces in his environment and way of life yet capable of initiating action on a grand scale, the torturously introverted man who sees freedom and definition of self and will through self-annihilation, and finally the character who manages to survive under the devastating illusion that he has achieved freedom through rejection of the past and who helps to create a wasted landscape without love and compassion.

III

As the Compson Appendix exhibits direct influences of its predecessors—the Indian stories, the novels *Absalom, Absalom!* and *Go Down, Moses*—in its narrative and symbolic design, so it also helps shape the narrative prologues in its successor *Requiem for a Nun* (1951), which Michael Millgate characterizes as "perhaps foreshadowings of that 'Doomsday Book', that genealogical survey of all the Yoknapatawpha families, which

Faulkner never lived to write,"[26] and in the fictionalized essay "Mississippi" (1954). The prologues deliberately juxtapose the past with the present, rendering the past into the immediacy of the present of each set of *Requiem;* "Mississippi" makes use of the fictional and actual to evoke a rich panorama of the American experience embodied within the geographical confines of a state.

The *Requiem* prologues present a chronicle of the history of Jefferson and of the region itself as an appropriate background to the resolution of Temple's moral struggle. Temple has to acknowledge her past and to accept its reality; she has to move outside herself and identify with the suffering of Nancy and others whose lives touch hers. With our heightened perception of the history of the town and region, Temple's actions and dilemma become more significant. Temple, along with Nancy and Caddy, is the violated female who reinforces the symbolic image of the profaned landscape that can never revert to its original state. The naming of places in the prologues, like the naming of people and a piece of land in the Compson Appendix, becomes a part of that search for origins and meaning for both the individual and the community.

More concretely, however, there are exact parallels that point to a thematic relationship between the Compson Appendix and the three prologues, suggesting strongly that the earlier piece seriously affected Faulkner's handling of the historical material in *Requiem.* The prologue to Act I contains a reference to Jason Lycurgus Compson "who had come to the settlement a few years ago with a race-horse, which he swapped to Ikkemotubbe, Issetibbeha's successor in the chiefship, for a square mile of what was to be the most valuable land in the future town of Jefferson."[27] In the prologue to the second act Faulkner draws a portrait of Andrew Jackson that is very close to that in the Jackson entry in the Compson Appendix. Jackson is shown to be an appropriate namesake for the capitol, especially for a region peopled by the energetic and shrewd early Sartorises, McCaslins, Compsons and Sutpens: "the old duellist, the brawling lean fierce mangy durable old lion who set the well-being of the Nation above the White House, and the health of his new political party above either, and above them all set, not his wife's honor but the principle that honor must be defended whether it was or not since, defended, it was, whether or not" (p. 107). In the Compson Appendix, Faulkner had described Jackson, in his early connection with the "simple dispossession" of the Indians' land, as "JACKSON. A Great White Father with a sword. (An old duellist, a brawling lean fierce mangy durable imperishable old lion who set the wellbeing of the nation above the White House, and the health of his new political party above either and above them all set not his wife's honor but the principle that honor must be defended whether it was or not because defended it was whether or not)" (pp. 3-4). Except for the wry paternalistic description of Jackson as "A Great White Father with a sword" and the additional adjective "imperishable" the two passages are the same. The placing of the Jackson entry in the Compson Appendix after the Indian material and immediately preceding the chronicle of the individual Compsons emphasizes the era in American history of the ruthlessly expanding frontier in which the white man is busy pushing the Indian off the land and attempting to conquer the wilderness, "changing the face of the earth: felling a tree which took two hundred years to grow, in order to extract from it a bear or a cupful of wild honey" (*Requiem*, p. 102). Jackson accurately epitomizes the frontier period. These passages illustrate how Faulkner drew directly on the Compson Appendix for material for the prologues; but more important, the various echoes of the earlier piece in the novel emphasize the impact of a richly integrated past on the action of the present.

The image of the "Compson Mile," "a solid square mile of virgin North Mississippi dirt as truly angled as the four corners of a cardtable top" (p. 3), acts as a leitmotif in the Compson Appendix as Caddy's muddy drawers do in *The Sound and the Fury*. The "Compson Mile" becomes the "Compson Domain" and finally the "Old Compson Place" to reflect the rise and fall of the family. We have already noted that the physical changes on the land record the deteriorating and fluctuating emotional stresses and fortunes in the Compson family in much the same manner that the diminishing Wilderness reinforces the action in *Go Down, Moses* and then foreshadows the treatment of the land in the prologues in *Requiem for a Nun*. There is a distinct thematic statement in the change of the "Compson Mile" from Ikkemotubbe's tenure, when it was still forested and virgin, to 1945 when "the old square mile was even intact again in row after row of small crowded jerrybuilt individuallyowned demiurban bungalows" (p. 9). Only the land itself and the Negroes endure; both bear the scars of heedless exploitation. The eroding landscape mirrors what takes place in the family from the time of the vibrant Jason Lycurgus "driven perhaps by the compulsion of the flamboyant name given him" to Jason IV, who was "The first sane Compson since before Culloden and (a childless bachelor) hence the last . . . . who as soon as his mother died . . . committed his idiot younger brother to the state and vacated the old house, first chopping up the vast oncesplendid rooms into what he called apartments and selling the whole thing to a countryman who opened a boardinghouse in it" (p. 16–17).

In the fictionalized essay "Mississippi," published in *Holiday* in 1954, Faulkner pursues his method of condensing the broad historical sweep into the single, sustained but richly diverse image of the land mirroring the lives of its inhabitants. He says, "In the beginning it was virgin—to the west, along the Big River, the alluvial swamps threaded by black almost motionless bayous and impenetrable with cane and buckvine and cypress and ash and oak and gum; to the east, the hardwood ridges and the prairies where the Appalachian mountains died and the buffalo grazed; to the south, the pine barrens and the moss-hung liveoaks and the greater swamps less of earth than water and lurking with alligators and water moccasins, where Louisiana in its time would begin."[28] The thematic design of the essay echoes the design of the Compson Appendix which presents first the original and virginal forests and then the open and denuded landscape. And the people Faulkner describes in the essay are kin to Andrew Jackson and Jason Lycurgus Compson: "This was the hills now: Jones County which old Newt Knight, its principal proprietor and first citizen or denizen, whichever you liked, seceded from the Confederacy in 1862, establishing still a third republic within the boundaries of the United States until a Confederate military force subdued him in his embattled log-castle capital; and Sullivan's Hollow: a long narrow glen where a few clans or families with North Ireland and Highland names feuded and slew one another in the old pre-Culloden fashion yet banding together immediately and always to resist any outsider in the pre-Culloden fashion too" (pp. 32–33). Charles Stuart Compson got himself into trouble in Kentucky where he was an instigator in a foolish but defiant effort to secede a portion of land from the new United States in order to join Spain. Again, in this essay, Faulkner has evoked the Scots' heritage of pride and defiance to describe these early settlers trying to tame a New World and find a way to preserve an independent spirit while accommodating the growing pains of a new nation.

James B. Meriwether has called attention to four major themes in "Mississippi" which he demonstrates are consistent with the major themes in Faulkner's fiction: racial injustice, the relationship of man to nature, the question of evil, and the necessity of adjusting to change.[29] We have already observed that the Compson Appendix also touches each of these major themes. Through his spare, concise genealogical compilation in the Compson Appendix, Faulkner accomplished in part what the ancient Doomsday Book attempted to do and what he had intended to do later in his life. In the Doomsday Book, there is a definite relationship between the tenantship of the land and its use and the rendering to the overlord his dues or payment in the form of taxes. But this ancient Book reveals more than its fiscal purposes: it gives an account of the power structure and the total resources, both material and human, of the land. In "Mississippi" Faulkner's concern is not for the actual events of the past as much as it is for what Meriwether discusses in terms of how the implications of the historical dimension unfold the "world of fictional truth."[30] And Faulkner's creation of a "world of fictional truth" through the revelation of the historical dimension in the Compson Appendix becomes active in shaping the material in "Mississippi" as it had also subtly informed the three prologues in *Requiem for a Nun*. The Compson Appendix is an artistic source book for the historical dimension of Yoknapatawpha as the Doomsday Book is a historical source book revealing far more than the ostensible facts and figures of the ownership of the land.

William Faulkner said in 1956 that "There is no such thing as *was*—only *is*. If *was* existed there would be no grief or sorrow. I like to think of the world I created as being a kind of keystone in the Universe; that, as small as that keystone is, if it were ever taken away, the Universe itself would collapse."[31] The Compson Appendix is an emblem of that "keystone to the Universe," as it transforms *was* into *is*. Quentin's perception of the meaning of Caddy's virginity for his self-image captures and defines the effect and importance of the Compson Appendix's central relationship to Faulkner's "world of fictional truth": a "miniature replica of all the whole vast globy earth . . . poised on the nose of a trained seal." The Compson Appendix is not only the chronicle of the Compson family; it also embodies the essential meaning of Yoknapatawpha County and the story of the human condition inherent in the violent history of America, stretching from obscure origins across the ocean to the New World, and ultimately delineates a mid-twentieth-century image of America. The piece that was begun as synopsis to help explain a part of one section of *The Sound and the Fury* emerged as a synthesized work of art that represented the major aspects of Yoknapatawpha County. In its unique design and far-reaching implications, the Compson Appendix is a carefully created metaphor controlling the world of Yoknapatawpha County—that "miniature replica of all the vast globy earth"—and a close study reveals the power of the Compson material on Faulkner's imagination and overall achievement, so that the Compson Appendix can indeed become "the magician's wand."

Notes

1. Malcolm Cowley, *The Faulkner–Cowley File: Letters and Memories 1944–1962* (New York: Viking Press, 1966), pp. 36–37.

2. James B. Meriwether, "The Novel Faulkner Never Wrote: His *Golden Book* or *Doomsday Book*," *American Literature*, 42 (March 1970), 96. Faulkner said to Jean Stein in 1956: "My last book will be the Doomsday Book, the Golden Book, of Yoknapatawpha County" (*Lion in the Garden*, ed. James B. Meriwether and Michael Millgate [New York: Random House, 1968], p. 255).

3. Michael Millgate, *The Achievement of William Faulkner* (New York: Random House, 1966), p. 46.

4. Information supplied by Mr. Meriwether.

5. James B. Meriwether, "A Prefatory Note by Faulkner for the Compson Appendix," *American Literature*, 43 (May 1971), 282.

6. *Faulkner–Cowley File*, p. 90.

7. James B. Meriwether, "Faulkner, Lost and Found," *Southern Review*, N. S. 8 (Autumn 1972), 708; rep. above, p. 75.

8. "Lost and found", p. 709; rep. above, p. 76.

9. "Lost and found", p. 710; rep. above, p. 77.

10. Meriwether, "A Prefatory Note," p. 284.

11. *Faulkner–Cowley File*, p. 41.

12. Millgate, p. 99.

13. William Faulkner, *The Sound and the Fury* and *As I Lay Dying* (New York: Modern Library, 1946), p. 4. Subsequent references will appear in the text.

14. *Faulkner in the University*, ed. Frederick L. Gwynn and Joseph L. Blotner (New York: Vintage, 1965), p. 84.

15. Meriwether, "Prefatory Note," pp. 282–283.

16. Joseph Blotner, *William Faulkner's Library—A Catalogue* (Charlottesville: Univ. Press of Virginia, 1964), p. 71.

17. James B. Meriwether, ed., *Essays, Speeches & Public Letters by William Faulkner* (New York: Random House, 1966), p. 179.

18. William Faulkner, *Go Down, Moses* (New York: Random House, 1942), pp. 267, 269.

19. See Elmo Howell, "Faulkner and Scott and the Legacy of the Lost Cause," *Georgia Review*, 27 (1972), 314–325.

20. William Faulkner, *The Sound and the Fury* (New York: Cape and Smith, 1929), p. 93.

21. *Mississippi Quarterly*, 25 (Spring 1972 Supplement), 34–35.

22. William Faulkner, *Absalom, Absalom!* (New York: Random House, 1936), p. 12. Subsequent references will appear in the text.

23. *Lion in the Garden*, p. 115.

24. William Faulkner, *Collected Stories* (New York: Random House, 1950), p. 360.

25. See, for example, Joseph Reed, *Faulkner's Narrative* (New Haven: Yale Univ. Press, 1973), pp. 75, 209–210.

26. Millgate, "The Firmament of Man's History," p. 34.

27. William Faulkner, *Requiem for a Nun* (New York: Random House, 1951), p. 13. Subsequent references will appear in the text.

28. William Faulkner, "Mississippi," in *Essays, Speeches & Public Letters*, p. 11. Subsequent references will appear in the text.

29. James B. Meriwether, "Faulkner's 'Mississippi,' " *Mississippi Quarterly*, 25 (Spring 1972 Supplement), 20.

30. "Faulkner's Mississippi," pp. 15, 16.

31. *Lion in the Garden*, p. 255.

[Faulkner's Most Splendid Failure]

André Bleikasten*

I: BENJY, OR THE AGONY OF DISPOSSESSION

On close inspection, Benjy's speech appears to follow a carefully modulated dramatic curve. The section begins at an almost leisurely pace with extended narrative units devoted to relatively minor incidents (3–15: the delivery of Uncle Maury's message to Mrs. Patterson on December 23, 1900; a trip to the cemetery in 1912).[1] After reverting to the present (15–19), it then moves on to a fairly detailed account of the day of Damuddy's death in 1898 (19–47), interrupted with increasing frequency by memories of Caddy's wedding (23–26, 44–45, 45–46, 47–48) and of three other deaths in the family (33–35: Quentin; 35–38, 40–42: Mr. Compson; 39–40: Roskus). There follows a sequence of thematically related episodes centering on the process of Caddy's growing alienation from Benjy: Caddy uses perfume (48–51); Benjy must sleep alone at thirteen (51–52, 53–54); Caddy with Charlie in the swing (56, 57–58), the latter incident leading up to the parallel present scene with her daughter Quentin (58–62). Benjy's memories then focus more and more sharply on the agony of loss: the episode of his assault on the Burgess girl (62–64) is associated with his desire for Caddy's return as well as with the nightmare of his subsequent castration; the long scene of his renaming (68–88), on the other hand, is above all a poignant reminder of his sister's love and kindness. Moreover, the quick alternation of past and present scenes emphasizes the magnitude of his losses: Quentin's treatment of Benjy is contrasted with Caddy's; the happy memories linked with the name-change scene are set over against the atmosphere of nasty bickering prevailing in the Compson family under Jason's reign. As the past erupts into the present with ever-increasing urgency, Benjy's mind is set spinning. The feverish shuttling back and forth between his memories suggests an emotional crescendo, climaxing eventually in what is to Benjy as much as to

*Reprinted, with permission, from *The Most Splendid Failure: Faulkner's "The Sound and the Fury"* (Bloomington: Indiana University Press, 1976), pp. 70–71, 78–79, 84–85, 89–91, 98–101, 103–07, 108–09, 110–11, 114–15, 118–19, 150–52, 153–54, 158–61, 192–94.

Quentin the most unbearable of all memories: Caddy's loss of sexual innocence (84–85).

Beneath the still surface of Benjy's speech we can thus detect a wild undercurrent of emotional intensities, and its presence is intermittently felt in the very texture of his language. Whenever moments of extreme affective tension or utter mental confusion are recorded, the blank and rigid orderliness of Benjy's syntax breaks down. Words then begin to dash and crash into one another; ellipsis combines with staccato repetition to produce the kind of breathless and pathetic stammering we find, for example, in Benjy's account of his drunkenness on the day of Caddy's wedding (24), or in his recalling of the fateful incident with the schoolgirls (63–64). . . .

What the first section makes obvious, too, is the extent to which the brother-sister relationship is patterned on that of child and mother. For Benjy, Caddy is definitely a mother surrogate; it is she who replaced Mrs. Compson, the failing mother, and of all the family she alone appears to have cared for his well-being and to have given him genuine love. But for Caddy he would never have escaped from autistic isolation. As Faulkner himself put it:

> . . . the only thing that held him into any sort of reality, into the world at all, was the trust that he had for his sister . . . he knew that she loved him and would defend him, and so she was the whole world to him. . . .[2]

Benjy's love for his sister-mother is absolute, but, to forestall any sentimentalizing, let us add immediately that it is absolute only in its need and demand: the infantile dependence on which it is based precludes any authentic reciprocity. Benjy does not love Caddy so much as Caddy's love and in his fierce narcissism he would like this love to be given to nobody else. His keen jealousy, when Caddy begins to be "unfaithful" to him, leaves no doubt about the possessive character of his attachment. And his "love" is far from being innocent if by innocence we mean the absence of any sexual component in his relationship with her. Benjy would not be so extraordinarily alert to his sister's sexual development nor so preoccupied with her virginity if sexuality played no part in his own desire. His desire is innocent only inasmuch as, unlike Quentin's, it is free from any sense of inner conflict and guilt.

Further evidence of this is provided by the Burgess girl episode. It is surely no accident that the scene of Benjy's unique attempt at sexual intercourse occurs at the very place where he used to meet Caddy when she too came back from school. Benjy once again confuses past and present, mistaking today's girl with yesterday's Caddy. The implications of his error should not be overlooked; if the Burgess girl functions as a substitute for Caddy, then Benjy's sexual aggression must be viewed as an attempt at incest. And the following castration then also assumes a new symbolic significance in that it becomes the inescapable punishment for the violation of the primal taboo. In the second section, we shall be told about another incident with a young girl, likewise equated with Caddy (Quentin calls her "sister"), and Quentin will be similarly accused of sexual misconduct. The parallelism, both dramatic and thematic, of the two scenes points to the many interconnections between the first and the second section, and it is interesting to note that the incest motif, so central to Quentin's monologue, already emerges here with its usual correlate, castration.

With Benjy, incestuous desire is not restricted to the field of fantasy as it is with Quentin. If left free to act, he would yield to his urges without the slightest sense of guilt. Is he then to be seen as a fictional embodiment of the Freudian id? Carvel Collins has argued that each of the first three sections of *The Sound and the Fury* may be viewed as a dramatization of one of the agencies of Freud's second "topography," the monologues of Benjy, Quentin and Jason corresponding respectively to the id, the ego and the superego.[3] It seems highly improbable that any such psychoanalytical allegorizing was in Faulkner's mind when he wrote the novel, and it would be preposterous to reduce his characters to dressed up Freudian concepts. Yet if handled with due caution, the parallel proves enlightening, especially with reference to the first section. Benjy's protracted infancy, his self-lessness, his utter amorality, and the uninhibited urgency of his sexual impulse in the Bugess girl episode are assuredly features relating him to the reservoir of drive energy which Freud designated as the id. Even more interestingly perhaps, his monologue recalls in many ways what Freud termed the "primary processes" of the unconscious. In contrast to verbalized, logically ordered conscious thinking, psychoanalysis describes these processes as nondiscursive, iconic, and illogical. . . .

In Benjy's monologue sex and death are never far away and are always seen in close conjunction. Thus in Benjy's memory the Burgess girl scene (sexual aggression) and the castration scene (sexual death) are significantly juxtaposed. Furthermore, the operation depriving Benjy of his manhood is itself suggested through extremely ambiguous imagery. Everywhere else in the section "the smooth, bright shapes" are associated with euphoric sensations: the fast flow of houses and trees during his drives to the cemetery (11, 13), the sight of fire that Benjy so loves (69, 78), and above all the memory of going to sleep with Caddy (83, 92). Here the luminous shapes also herald sleep, but a sleep that is suffocation ("I couldn't breathe out again"), falling ("I fell off the hill into the bright whirling shapes"), descent into death.[4]

This ambiguous interweaving of images of life and death is typical of Benjy's section. Throughout, without ever being named, death is a haunting presence. Thus, the earliest episode, the water splashing incident at the branch, which Benjy harks back to more frequently and lengthily than to any other,[5] is overshadowed by the event of Damuddy's death.

From the memory of this death Benjy's mind slips imperceptibly to all the other deaths that have occurred in the family: the return of Quentin's body after his suicide at Cambridge (33–35), Mr. Compson's death and funeral (35–38, 40–41), the death of Roskus, Dilsey's husband (39–40). In his chaotic memory, these successive deaths are so entangled as to resemble an obsessive harping on a single occurrence, a ritual homage to Death. To this must be added the macabre image of Nancy, the mare shot by Roskus and devoured by the vultures, whose carcass Benjy glimpsed in a ditch one moonlit night (40, 42). Benjy's mind is of course not death-ridden in the same way as Quentin's is; death is something that he cannot comprehend, no more than little Vardaman can understand his mother's death in *As I Lay Dying*, but there is ample evidence that its mystery weighs very heavily on his mind. Moreover, Benjy senses the imminence and presence of death with an infallible animal instinct. When Mr. Compson dies, he howls at death like Dan, the dog, and even before his father dies, he "smells" his impending end (40–42). Benjy's uncanny divination powers in this field are indeed as keen as in the sexual one.

Lastly, there is Benjy's curious penchant for graveyards. The visit to the family cemetery is one of the first scenes recalled in his monologue (9–13), and it is on another of these funeral trips that the novel ends. The cemetery is invariably the goal of the only outings allowed Benjy; ironically, his contacts with the external world are restricted to the immutable Sunday ritual of the pilgrimage to the family dead. The special significance that the place has for him is further emphasized by the fact that one of his favorite games is playing with what Dilsey and Luster call his "graveyard" (67–68)—a blue bottle, perched on a little mound, into which he sticks stalks of jimson weed. As Edmond Volpe notes, Benjy's private graveyard may be taken as a derisory symbol of all his losses.[6] The nasty smell of jimson weed has come to replace the clean smell of trees associated with Caddy. Considering that the weed was used by Southern Negroes in contraception and abortion, and that it was given obscene names by the hill people of Mississippi because of its phallic form,[7] it is tempting to regard it also as an ironic symbol of lost manhood. Benjy's game is a mourning rite, a primitive commemoration of loss and death. The miniature graveyard and its fetid flowers condense all the ambiguities of his crippled and shrunken world—a world as close to its beginning as to its end, forever arrested in its blind innocence, no sooner born than dead. . . .

The first section—the story of the miserable child-man—may thus be said to represent the whole Compson drama in reduced form. It tells us almost all there is to know, but it does so with a deceptive mixture of opaqueness and transparency. To yield its rich harvest of ambiguities and ironies, the prologue must be read again—as an epilogue.

II: THE YOUNG MAN, DESIRE, AND DEATH

If Benjy's monologue serves as a prologue to the whole novel, it is obviously with the section immediately following it that it has its closest affinities. Again Caddy is "the center on the horizon," the remote and haunting figure in which death and desire meet and merge; again everything revolves around the brother-sister relationship, and one may well wonder whether, fundamentally, its function and significance are not much the same as in the previous section: like his retarded brother's, Quentin's love for Caddy is jealous, exclusive, excessive; like his, it can only be described in terms of lack and loss. Yet, while Benjy's desire barely emerges from the primitive demands of need and can be stilled by specific objects, Quentin's is desire in its fullest, or rather emptiest, sense: a desire never to be satisfied, incommensurate with any real object, gliding from substitute to substitute down to the very last—death. In Benjy's childish attachment to his sister there is little more than an indiscriminate hunger for love; Quentin's feelings are rooted in the same archaic soil, but they are refracted through the deceptive prism of an adult or at least adolescent mind, and must be traced through a far more devious discourse. His monologue does not so readily reveal the hidden pattern of its disorder.

To switch from section 1 to section 2 is to pass from the simple to the complex; it means leaving the limbo of blank innocence to be thrust into a private hell of anguish and guilt. Quentin certainly remains an innocent inasmuch as innocence may be equated with "blind self-centeredness." But in opposition to the all but mindless Benjy, he suffers rather from an excess of consciousness and conscience, and although he eventually proves incapable of making an ethical choice, he does possess an extremely keen sense of good and evil. As a consequence, his relationship to Caddy is a much more intricate affair, raising psychological and moral issues totally alien to Benjy's world. The idiot's helpless dependency on his sister is just an aspect of his stunted growth, the result of blocked mental development. With Quentin the blockage is of a subtler kind, and it is only toward the end of his adolescence that its negative implications come to be fully felt. Benjy's love for Caddy hardly strikes us as abnormal once we know that he is fated to perpetual childhood; Quentin's on the other hand, develops into a morbid passion whose outcome can only be death. . . .

There is scarcely a detail in this childhood scene that does not in some way anticipate Quentin's future actions and attitudes. His leap into the hog wallow is the enactment of an old Puritan metaphor, the symbolic performance of what his first and no doubt last sexual experiment means to him: yielding to the urges of the flesh equals wallowing in filth.[8] Mud becomes quite literally the substance of sin: it is water (and as such related to the whole complex of water symbolism pervading the novel), but with its transparency gone, its fluidity thickened into sticky stinking matter—a concrete image of sexual nausea. Just as in *Light in August,* where it is associated with the thick, black, putrid water in the sewers, sexuality here is linked with the unclean and the viscous, and, through the implicit reference to pigs, with loathsome animality. . . .[9]

At once a confession of guilt, an act of penance, and a purification rite, Quentin's gesture foreshadows the magical actions through which he will attempt time and again to ward off the threats of the world, not only during his childhood and adolescence, but up to and even *in* his suicide. Magical too is the code by which he lives and acts: in the last analysis all his perception of good and evil comes down to that of the pure and the impure. The summum bonum is equated in his mind with his sister's intact virginity; his nostalgia for lost innocence is above all the dream of a sexless life. In his monologue Quentin recalls Versh's story about a self-castrated man (143). But castration—an idea which haunts him and a possibility he must have envisaged for himself—does not appear to him as a satisfactory alternative. Castration would simply be a *pis aller,* so to speak, for it would not obliterate the memory of having had a sex:

> But that's not it. It's not not having them. It's never to have had them then
> I could say O That That's Chinese I dont know Chinese (143).

The correlate of this deep aversion to sex is misogyny. Quentin's is the Puritan version of the Fall: Eve was the beginning of evil; it was through her that the innocence of Eden was lost. Although he clings to the Southern myth of Sacred Womanhood, and will defend Woman's honor to the last (as is shown by his fight with Gerald Bland a few hours before his suicide), Quentin's faith in her purity has been shattered by his sister's sexual misconduct. His monologue reverberates with Mr. Compson's cynical remarks on women, and for all his protests and denials he has apparently come to acknowledge the bitter truth that "women are never virgins" (143), that they are by nature impure, that is, impure like Nature herself. One quickly senses that the revered and radiant image of the Immaculate Virgin screens a darker one—not very far removed, in fact, from Jason's definition of women as bitches. Quentin shrinks from so much candor, yet womanhood, in his monologue, is constantly linked to suspect images and sensations—softness, warmth, wetness, darkness—and particularly to dirt. As with other male characters in Faulkner's fiction, we find in Quentin a morbid concern with the physiological evidence of woman's "impurity," menstruation:

> Because women so delicate so mysterious Father said. Delicate equilibrium of periodical filth between two moons balanced. Moons he said full and yellow as harvest moons her hips thighs. Outside outside of them always but. Yellow. Feet soles with walking like. Then know that some man that all those mysterious and imperious concealed. With all that inside of them shapes an outward suavity waiting for a touch to. Liquid putrefaction like drowned things floating like pale rubber flabbily filled getting the odour of honeysuckle all mixed up (159).

Woman's delicacy and suavity are a decoy; the sanctuary of her body hides an ignoble secret: the filth of sex, at once the periodically renewed promise of fecundity (hinted at by the references to the moon and to harvests, and by the symbolism of yellow) and the threat of mortal engulfment. In Quentin's diseased imagination, the menstrual flow and "liquid putrefaction" are confused in the same obscene streaming.

"*Templum aedificatum super cloacam*": Tertullian's horrible definition of woman perfectly sums up Quentin's view. The equation of woman with dirt in his mind is confirmed, moreover, by at least three of the female figures evoked in the second section: Caddy, Natalie, and the little Italian girl whom Quentin meets at Cambridge on the day of his suicide. Caddy is the girl with the "muddy drawers,"[10] and in Quentin's memory, Natalie too is a "dirty girl": twice he recalls Caddy's sarcastic remark when he teased and taunted her about her first kiss: "I didnt kiss a dirty girl like Natalie anyway" (166). As to the "present" episode with the Italian girl, it alternates significantly with the account of the Natalie scene and one of the links between the two scenes is precisely the "dirty girl" motif: Quentin's new "sister" is also "a dirty little child" (155), and in his descriptions of her there are references to "her dirty dress" (158), her "dirty hand" (163), and "her filthy little dress" (165). The dirt is made even more repellent by moisture and warmth. "She extended her fist, it uncurled upon a nickel, moist and dirty, moist dirt ridged into her flesh" (157). And the suggestion of disgust is further strengthened by animal similes: "Her fingers closed about [the two coppers], damp and hot, like worms" (159); "She had a funny looking thing in her hand, she carried it sort of like it might have been a dead pet rat" (159).[11] All these touches lend the scene of Quentin's encounter with the girl a faintly nauseous atmosphere, and emphasize the eerie, almost ominous effect of her silent presence at his side. The girl is an echo of the past and a prefiguration of the future; while taking Quentin back to his childhood as the ironically rediscovered sister, she is also, in her uncanny silence, her dark stare, and her inexplicable stubbornness in following him everywhere, a symbol of Fate, an avatar of "little sister Death," and she is finally another metaphor for soiled innocence, a reminder of the defilement whose unbearable memory is soon to be washed away by the waters of the Charles River. . . .

To grasp its deeper significance [Quentin's suicide], it is necessary to retrace the long and complex process that has led Quentin to choose death. Let us return for a moment to the prophetic hog wallow scene. Quentin's game with Natalie was the beginning of his initiation into sex. Now it is worth noting that *before* Caddy's return to the barn he enjoys the game and apparently feels no compunction about his pleasure. Only when Caddy comes back and surprises him hugging the girl, does the love game make him feel guilty and distraught. Then he begins to panic, for then he suddenly realizes (although his realization remains subliminal) that the intrusion of sex into his life threatens to compromise forever his unique relationship to Caddy. In order to stave off this menace, it becomes indispensable that his sister should acknowledge its seriousness by a firm disavowal of what she has seen. As Caddy does not react in the expected way, he smears her body with mud. Symbolically he thus drags her down with him into the mire of sin, forcing her to share his assumed guilt and so reestablishing—in evil—the intimacy that his game with Natalie had put in jeopardy. After that, quits, they can both go to the branch and purify themselves in its water: the illusion of innocence is provisionally restored.

Quentin's puzzling behavior in the course of this ritual defilement and purgation clearly shows that what most matters to him—at this point as well as later on—is not so much the preservation of sexual innocence, whether his own or Caddy's, as the safekeeping at any cost of the absolute mutuality of a dual relationship. Innocence to him is a means rather than an end, and if he is so anxious to preserve it, it is firstly because it is a token of isolation, safety, and peace. Conversely, if he distrusts sexuality and recoils from it, it is primarily because it imperils his exclusive bond to his sister. Even at this early stage Quentin is virtually prepared to go to any lengths to keep her out of the world's clutches; no price seems too high, and he is quite willing to pay even that of sin provided that the sin committed is a common sin and that they suffer common punishment. In this childhood scene, he compels his sister to share his mudbath. When, later, Caddy is "soiled" by the loss of her virginity, he insists no less on restoring their intimacy, but it is his turn then to join the fallen virgin in the filthy waters of sin.

From the sex game in the barn to the ritual cleansing in the branch, the episode is also prophetic and paradigmatic in that it involves a *triangular* relationship. It foreshadows situation patterns with which Quentin is confronted time and again—except that in the later scenes the roles are ironically reversed. Here the triad consists of Quentin, Natalie, and Caddy, and tension arises as soon as it is formed, that is, from the moment when Caddy appears in the doorway of the barn. The little drama for three characters which then takes place curiously resembles a banal adultery story: Quentin, Natalie, and Caddy virtually play the parts of husband, mistress, and betrayed wife. At least it is along these lines that Quentin seems to interpret the situation. Expecting Caddy to be jealous of her rival and shower reproaches on her faithless partner, he stands ready to go into the dock and plead guilty. The actors, however, do not play the roles they had been given in his private script. In hoping that his sister would play the outraged partner, he has in fact cast her for his own role, one which was already to some extent his in the first branch scene (the splashing incident), and which he will play with ever more pointed jealousy in his subsequent encounters with Caddy: the quarrel after her first flirtation with a "darn town squirt" (166), the long pathetic colloquy about her affair with Dalton Ames (185–203), and the last meeting in her room on the eve of her wedding (151–54). In all those scenes, just as in the early Natalie scene, there are three persons involved, but sex is no longer a childish game and the actors have been allocated different roles: Caddy has replaced Natalie in the part of the "dirty girl," her lovers have supplanted Quentin, and it is he who now plays the thankless role of the *terzo incommodo*.[12]

Insofar as it proceeds from concurrent desires with Caddy at stake, this triangular relationship is bound to generate conflict. In point of fact, from the yet harmless squabbles of childhood to the poignant confrontation before Caddy's wedding, all the scenes just referred to are scenes of potential or overt violence, and each time Quentin turns out to be its agent or its cause.

Most often Quentin's aggressiveness is aimed at Caddy herself: he slaps her, at fifteen, for having kissed a boy, just as he did, at seven, after she had taken off her dress in the branch; he smears her with mud after the incident with Natalie, and in the climatic scene about Ames, he even takes out his jackknife and points it at Caddy's throat.[13] On the other hand, he shows persistent hostility to his sister's lovers: he tries to hit Dalton Ames when he meets him near the bridge (200), and during his interview with Herbert Head, he deliberately antagonizes his future brother-in-law (133–37). The same conflictual pattern reemerges ironically in the two major episodes of Quentin's last day. The episode with the Italian girl culminates in a grotesque inversion of roles. Charged with "meditated criminal assault" (174), Quentin is willy-nilly cast in the role of the seducer, while Julio, the girl's older brother, successfully assumes the part that Quentin could not play—that of defender of his sister's honor: small wonder that Quentin is convulsed with hysterical laughter on realizing the irony of the situation. As to the second episode, the fight with Gerald Bland, it is likewise based on a tragicomic quid pro quo, since it arises from Quentin's unconscious identification of Bland with Caddy's first lover.

The targets of Quentin's aggressiveness do not change, and what it constantly aims at is either the elimination of the hated rival or the punishment of the beloved sister. To recapture the object of his love, he will try anything, from physical intimidation to the subtler stratgems of persuasion. His are in fact all the desperate ruses of the frustrated lover. One of his favorite tactics is vilifying his rivals: *"that blackguard Caddy. . . . A liar and a scoundrel Caddy was dropped from his club for cheating at cards got sent to Coventry caught cheating at midterm exams and expelled"* (152). By exposing Head's disreputable past, Quentin hopes he can induce Caddy not to marry him, and there are similar motives to his caustic comments on Caddy's first boyfriends (166) and on Dalton Ames (113). The point is of course that none is more dishonest here than Quentin himself: what worries him is not so much that Ames and Head are no gentlemen as the threat they pose to his love, and he objects to them as he would to any other man taking Caddy away from him. . . .

Hence [too] the extreme ambivalence of Quentin's attitudes toward his rivals. He hates them as Caddy's seducers; he admires and envies them for the virile potency and daring he lacks. Dalton Ames and Herbert Head realize by proxy his unavowed and unavowable wish: the sexual possession of his sister. No wonder then that he should be such a poor avenger of her outraged honor. His weakness vis-à-vis Caddy's lovers is of the same order as Hamlet's hesitation to kill the usurper of the royal bed:[14] unconscious identification with the successful competitor prevents his wreaking vengeance for the insult.

Quentin's two contradictory wishes—disposing of the rival while becoming like him and taking over his role and prerogatives—thus come to merge in the fantasy of complete substitution, that is, the fantasy of consummated incest:

> . . . it was I it was not Dalton Ames (97–98).
> . . . you thought it was them but it was me (185).

Quentin's desire at this point becomes an imitation of his rival's, just as in the oedipal situation the son's desire is patterned on the father's. It is noteworthy too that the two male figures who most excite his animosity and admiration—Dalton Ames and Gerald Bland[15]—are to some extent father images: in their ability to seduce and dominate, their sexual potency, physical strength, and sporting prowess (shooting in Ames's case; shooting, rowing, and boxing in Bland's), they embody alike the ideal of *mastery* which Quentin pretends to despise because it is out of his reach.[16]

The most amazing thing about this father image is that it never coincides with the image of the real father. Not that the latter's role is marginal. Far from it. It is to his father that Quentin addresses himself at the beginning and end of his monologue, as though he (had) expected of him an answer to his questions, an alleviation of his anguish. If Caddy is the primary object of his discourse, Mr. Compson is to a very large extent its implied *receiver*. The whole of the monologue, frequently punctuated with "Father said," could almost be defined as an imaginary conversation between Quentin and Mr. Compson, a running debate between father and son. In his function of interlocutor *in absentia*, the figure of the father occupies indeed a key position, and it is significant that when Faulkner revised the manuscript of *The Sound and the Fury*, he saw fit to give him an even greater role.[17]

Quentin, Caddy, Mr. Compson: another triad comes to light, and it is without any doubt the most crucial in the second section, the one that brings us closest to the young man's complex and tragic fate. . . .

What Mr. Compson represents to his son is all this past, and through this past he has a hold over him. Mr. Compson is weak, and yet, regardless of what he is or does, he has power—a power originating in his *priority.* And because he comes *after* his father, Quentin is inevitably caught up in a test of fidelity. Through his father, he is heir to the Southern tradition, to its code of honor with all the aristocratic and puritanical standards it implies. When this pattern of values is passed on, however, it has already lost its authority, the more so in this case as the appointed transmitter of the Southern creed is an inveterate skeptic. Quentin clings to it with desperate obstinacy, because to him it is the only available recourse against absurdity, and because its very rigidity seems a safeguard of order and integrity. Yet while transmitting the code, his father's voice has taught him its inanity. Quentin's fidelity is an allegiance to values long dead, and in making them his he chooses defeat. The Southern code has failed; the failure of tradition has become a tradition of failure. In refusing to break with it (as some later Faulkner heroes do), Quentin can only repeat the fatal errors of his fathers. . . .

Quentin's incest fantasy testifies to this entrapment, but one should note that in his circuitous strategies it serves several purposes. To interpret it as a resurgence of a repressed wish is plainly not enough. For the point about the incest with Caddy is that it is at once conceived as *confessed* to the father, and what Quentin secretly intends by confessing it to him is to challenge paternal authority, to provoke Mr. Compson into acting at last as the punishing father. The gamble which Quentin considers is a desperate one, but it is not without hope: the hope that the flagrant transgression of the primal taboo would entail a reaffirmation and restoration of the Law, that the very scandal of his sin would set its dialectic into motion again.

Or, to put it into more specifically Freudian terms, in attempting to provoke paternal retaliation. Quentin may be said to seek the symbolic castration which would free him from his bondage to the incestuous wish. Yet here again one must beware of over-simplification: there are as many reasons to construe his fantasy as an unconscious ruse to be spared castration. For it is certainly noteworthy too that the fantasy is conjugated in a past tense, that incest is referred to as an accomplished fact: "*I have committed incest I said Father it was I* . . ." (97–98). Quentin's is actually "the fantasy of having acted out the fantasy,"[18] typical of the obsessional neurotic: "[For him] it is a question of composing his oedipal fantasy *as if it had already been enacted:* the father already killed, the mother already possessed. In return for which castration need no longer be considered; only guilt persists; this is the reason why it can be so intense with him."[19] If we retain this hypothesis in Quentin's case, our first reading of his fantasy has to be reversed, not to be invalidated but rather to allow for a new contradiction: the imaginary confession of incest should then be interpreted as *both* defiance and escape—castration simultaneously sought after and fled from.[20]

Quentin's death completes the destructive work of his relentless superego.[21] In ending his days, he expunges his guilty desire and appeases his need for self-punishment. Water delivers him from his "shad(from the curse of being burdened with a body and a sex; it dissolve: foulness of the flesh and returns his bones to the mineral chastity of sand:

> And I will look down and see my murmuring bones and the deep water like wind, like a roof of wind, and after a long time they cannot distinguish even bones upon the lonely and inviolate sand (98).

In trying to imagine afterlife, Quentin reverts spontaneously to the water imagery associated with the ritual cleansings of his childhood and adolescence. What he expects from his suicide is a final purgation, washing him of the sin of existence, effacing the very trace of his having been alive. Only then will his guilt be absolved, the debt paid, the Law restored. . . .

III: JASON, OR THE POISON OF RESENTMENT

Thematically there is no major break between section 3 and the preceding sections. But the treatment of themes is set in a very different key and undergoes radical changes. It almost looks as if they had been turned inside out. Thus in Jason's monologue, the brother-sister relationship, though hardly less central than in Benjy's or Quentin's, changes its sign from plus to minus: what Jason feels for Caddy is hatred, a hatred as intense and uncontrollable as Benjy's love or Quentin's love-hate. To him as to them she is a rankling memory; for him as for them she has been the instrument of disaster. Not that he misses his sister as his brothers do, but the loss he has suffered is directly related to her: Herbert Head, Caddy's fiancé, had promised him a job in a bank—a promise broken because of her misconduct. The child she had to leave him as a hostage has therefore become in his eyes "the symbol of the lost job itself" (383–84), and it is on his niece that he will take out his hatred. What differentiates Jason from his brothers is essentially his response to loss: Benjy howls in blind protest; Quentin commits suicide; Jason, on the contrary, carefully nurses his resentment and is determined to take revenge.

Yet the differences are perhaps less significant than the resemblances. "Because like I say blood is blood and you can't get around it" (303): when Jason invokes the family heritage to account for his niece's promiscuity, he is ironically unaware of how much his statement also applies to him. In his monologue he poses as the only sane and sensible man in a world of fools and lunatics, and prides himself on his worldly wisdom and his capacity to cope with reality. He believes and would have us believe that he has nothing in common with the other Compsons. This belief, however, is given the lie by his behavior and is just one of his many delusions about himself. In a sense, it is true, Jason is indeed an outsider and has been one since his early childhood. His mother considers him a true Bascomb (225, 244, 249), and seemingly cherishes him as her only child.

Not unlike Jewel, Addie Bundren's favorite son in *As I Lay Dying*, Jason has been deeply marked by his mother's preferential treatment, but as Mrs. Compson is incapable of loving any one except herself, he has been little more than a pawn in the destructive game she has been playing with the family.[22] All she has accomplished is to mold Jason in her likeness, and, by not allowing him to think of himself as a Compson, she has been quite successful, too, in alienating him from his father, his brothers, and his sister. Of all her children he is undeniably the one most like her in his mean-spirited egoism, his imperturbable smugness, and his petit bourgeois concern for propriety. On closer examination, however, it becomes clear that Jason has inherited as much from his father as from his mother. Mr. Compson's cynical philosophy has left its mark upon his mind as it has upon Quentin's: in spite of his undisguised contempt for his father, Jason has adopted his principles and erected them into a rigid rule of conduct. His inflexible logic is Mr. Compson's skepticism hardened into dogma, and by pushing it to preposterous lengths, he unwittingly exposes its contradictions and provides the final proof, *per absurdum,* of its impracticality.[23]

Even more surprising: Jason turns out to be in many ways Quentin's homologue. On the face of it, the two characters are of course poles apart, and it seems safe to assume that Jason was originally conceived to serve as a foil to his brother. Beside Quentin, Jason is no doubt a buoyant extrovert. Whereas Quentin, in his adolescent romanticism, flees from "the loud, harsh world," Jason, even though he does not feel at home in it, is bustling about with pugnacious energy and desperately scrambling for success. Most critics have noted the contrast between Quentin's quixotic idealism and Jason's hard-nosed pragmatism. What has been less often noted is that the former's idealism and the latter's pragmatism are equally spurious, and that behind these deceptive façades one finds the same amount of self-centeredness and the same capacity for self-delusion, or, to use again Faulkner's more ambiguous term, the same irreducible "innocence." Jason is in fact merely the negative of his brother—a tougher Quentin who, instead of becoming a suicide, has turned sour.

They do not fly together, but birds of a feather they surely are. Throughout, their actions and attitudes reveal startlingly similar patterns. With both there is a persistent refusal of the Other, an unfailingly hostile response to anything or anyone likely to threaten the closure of their narcissistic world. Only—and it is here that the differences show—while Quentin's aggressiveness turns finally against his ego and ends in self-destruction, Jason's strikes out in sadism. . . .

If Quentin's divided self is close to schizophrenia, Jason's conspiracy and persecution fantasies belong with the symptoms of paranoia.[24] The world, as seen and experienced by him, is—in much the same way as for Quentin—the mirror image of his own neurotic self; it is full of hostility and malice, and his relationship to it is one of permanent warfare. As

Jason describes the conflict, one might think that he only fights for survival in an unfriendly environment, and that his aggressive behavior is dictated by the necessities of self-defense. It soon appears, however, that Jason himself writes the script and stages the show, albeit unconsciously, and it becomes quite evident too that his behavior patterns are determined beforehand by the contradictory demands of his paranoid condition. By using every opportunity to antagonize his family and his acquaintances, Jason, while finding release for his pent-up rage, also provokes retaliation from those he abuses and assaults. The expected counterattacks of his opponents are indeed an integral part of his singular game, and they serve in fact several purposes: (1) they provide him with a posteriori justifications for his own aggressions; (2) supply new food for self-pity by confirming him in the role of victim, and (3) gratify as well an obscure need for punishment, as can be seen from the way he courts disaster in the final pursuit episode. To Jason, then, persecuting and being persecuted are complementary, and the compulsive pattern of his internal drives requires that he be alternately agent and sufferer. Which is to say that his bellicose behavior is not just unmitigated sadism. Although Jason may seem to be a simpler character than his brother Quentin (an impression ironically reinforced by Jason's image of himself in the monologue), his antagonistic relationship to others involves likewise complex processes of exchange and transference, and points to the devious workings of a residual sense of guilt. True, with Quentin masochism and self-destruction prevail while with Jason the emphasis is on aggressiveness, yet in both cases one has to make allowances for the intricate play of displacements, reversals, and occultations from which each character derives his many-layered ambiguities. . . .

It is most remarkable, too, that Jason's relationship to his niece parallels Quentin's relationship to his sister in such a way as to become its parodical reenactment. Jason is indeed as compulsively preoccupied with his niece's promiscuity as Quentin was with Caddy's. The reasons given are no doubt different, yet between Quentin's sense of honor and Jason's concern for respectability there is only a difference of degree. Furthermore, Jason is so sincerely outraged by the girl's escapades that a hypocritical care for propriety will hardly do for an explanation. Here again Jason's attitudes are extremely inconsistent, and once more his actual behavior gives the lie to the thoughts and feelings he professes. At one moment he pretends to be indifferent to Quentin's fate:

> Like I say, let her lay out all day and all night with everything in town that wears pants, what do I care (300).

But immediately after his indignation and anger explode:

> These damn little slick-haired squirts, thinking they are raising so much hell, I'll show them something about hell I says, and you too. I'll make

him think that damn red tie is the latch string to hell, if he thinks he can run the woods with my niece (301).

Jason rails at "those damn town squirts" (243) just as Quentin did, and it is revealing that both should use the same colloquial phrase of abuse (see section 2, 166: "It's for letting it be some damn town squirt I slapped you"). His fury here is strongly reminiscent of his brother's resentment of Caddy's early dates. Similarly, in the scene where he confronts his niece at the beginning of section 3 (227–35), his brutality parallels—even in particular gestures such as grabbing her arm—Quentin's aggressiveness toward Caddy in many of the scenes described in section 2. The parallel is further emphasized by the girl's defiant attitude, and when she threatens to tear her dress in front of Jason, one is irresistibly reminded of the scene at the branch on the day of Damuddy's death, when young Caddy took hers off as a challenge to Quentin. In both scenes the gesture of undressing is felt as a provocation, and its effrontery maddens Jason just as it outraged Quentin's prudery. Their being both scandalized by the sight of naked female flesh is a clear index to their puritanical recoil from sex. To Jason as to Quentin, sex is associated with the darkness of sin, and in his monologue woods—the bewitched area that haunted Hawthorne's Puritan sinners—become once again the secret abode of shameful lust: "Are you hiding out in the woods with one of those damn slick-headed jellybeans? Is that where you go?" (229). Significantly too, sexual obsession and ethnic prejudice overlap in the image of the promiscuous Negro girl: ". . . I'm not going to have any member of my family going on like a nigger wench" (234). And it is precisely the same puritan and racist imagery that expresses Quentin's anxiety over his sister's lost honor: "*Why must you do like nigger women do in the pasture the ditches the dark woods hot hidden in the dark woods*" (113–14).

The ambiguity of such attitudes and such language need hardly be stressed again. While professing to be shocked and disgusted by his niece's outrageous make-up[25] and slovenly deshabilles, Jason feels secretly titillated and barely manages to conceal his lecherous thoughts:

> . . . if a woman had come out doors even on Gayoso or Beale street when I was a young fellow with no more than that to cover her legs and behind, she'd been thrown in jail. I'll be damned if they dont dress like they were trying to make every man they passed on the street want to reach out and clasp his hand on it (289).

There is an unmistakable touch of prurience and voyeurism about Jason's constant spying on his niece (again reminiscent of Quentin's attitudes toward Caddy), and what impels him to chase her around the countryside through ditches and poison oak is not only the desire to get his money back but also the hope to catch her in the act. In Jason's relationship to Quentin IV hatred prevails, but its sheer intensity points to the depth of his emotional involvement, and it is probably not going too far, as one critic suggested, to relate it to a "deeply repressed incestuous attraction."[26]

The recurrence of similar if not identical situations, attitudes, gestures, as well as the many verbal echoes of section 2 in section 3, provide conclusive evidence of the very close affinities between Quentin and Jason. Yet they also emphasize the contrast between past and present. Instead of the pathetic confrontations recalled in Quentin's monologue, we find here scenes of harsh vulgarity which show how deep the Compsons have sunk under Jason's rule. In the third section everything takes on a more sordid color. Perhaps too a truer color, revealing Quentin as well as Jason in a clearer light. For after all, Quentin's influence upon his sister was no less damaging than Jason's on his niece. More insidiously, his perverted love produced the same results as outspoken hatred. "If I'm bad," says Caddy's daughter to Jason, "it's because I had to be. You made me. I wish I was dead. I wish we were all dead" (324). Before her, Caddy voiced the same resigned despair, the same awareness of being "bad" (196), and instead of invoking destiny, she could well have accused Quentin of corrupting her. The victims, one of a jealous brother, the other of a vindictive uncle, Caddy and her daughter both recognize themselves eventually as damned in the maleficent mirrors held up to them by their pitiless judges. Quentin and Jason are doubtless not alone in working their wretched fates, but as prosecutors and persecutors they are undeniably instrumental in turning them into "lost women." In the last resort the novel pits the two brothers back to back: Jason is Quentin the censor become torturer; Quentin is Jason with the alibi of high-minded idealism. The third section, in this respect, is not simply a grating repetition of the second; it is also a radical demystification of Quentin's fevered romanticizing. . . .

IV: AN EASTER WITHOUT RESURRECTION?

In the face of the whining or heinous egoism of the Compsons, Dilsey embodies the generosity of total selflessness; in contrast to Quentin's tortured idealism and Jason's sordid pragmatism, she also represents the active wisdom of simple hearts. Without fostering the slightest illusion about her exploiters, expecting no gratitude for her devotion, Dilsey accepts the world as it is, while striving as best she can to make it somewhat more habitable. Unlike the Compsons, she does not abdicate before reality nor does she refuse time, which she alone is capable of gauging and interpreting correctly:

> On the wall above a cupboard, invisible save at night, by lamp light and even then evincing an enigmatic profundity because it had but one hand, a cabinet clock ticked, then with a preliminary sound as if it cleared its throat, struck five times.
> "Eight oclock," Dilsey said . . . (342).

In his rage against time, Quentin tore off the hands of his watch. The Compsons' old kitchen clock has but one left and its chime is out of order. Yet Dilsey does not take offense at its "lying" and automatically corrects its errors. To her, time is no matter of obsession. Not that she adjusts to it out of mere habit. Her time is not simply a "natural" phenomenon, any more than her moral qualities are "natural" virtues. Faulkner describes her as a Christian, and no analysis of the character can afford to discount the deep religious convictions attributed to her. As Brooks again judiciously notes, "Dilsey does not believe in man; she believes in God."[27] Her capacity for endurance and power for loving are sustained and inspirited by the ardor of her faith. Hers is a seemingly naïve piety, a simple faith unencumbered by theological subtleties, but it gives her the courage to be and persevere which her masters lack, and provides her existence with a definite meaning and purpose. Dilsey envisions everything in the light of the threefold mystery of the Incarnation, Passion, and Resurrection of Christ. In Benjy she sees "de Lawd's chile" (396), one of the poor in spirit promised the Kingdom of God, and for her all human suffering is justified and redeemed in the divine sacrifice commemorated during Holy Week. Her attitude toward time proceeds quite logically from the tenets of her Christian faith. Whereas for Quentin, the incurable idealist, time is the hell of immanence, the *reductio ad absurdum* of all human endeavor, it is transfused with eternity for Dilsey. Not "a tale full of sound and fury signifying nothing," but the history of God's people. The Christ of her belief has not been "worn away by the minute clicking of little wheels" (94); his crucifixion was not a victory by time but a victory over time. Guaranteed in the past by the death and resurrection of the Son of God, and in the future by the promise of His return, bounded by the Passion and the Second Coming, time regains a meaning and a direction, and each man's existence becomes again the free and responsible adventure of an individual destiny. Dilsey's Christ-centered faith allows her to adhere fully to all of time's dimensions: her answer to the past is fidelity; the present she endures with patience and humility, and armed with the theologal virtue of hope, she is also able to face the future without alarm. While for Quentin there is an unbridgeable gap between the temporal and the timeless, Dilsey's eternity, instead of being an immobile splendor *above* the flux of time, is already present and at work *in* time, embodied in it just as the word was made flesh. Time, then, is no longer felt as endless and senseless repetition; nor is it experienced as an inexorable process of decay. It does have a pattern, since history has been informed from its beginnings by God's design. And it can be redeemed and vanquished, but, as T. S. Eliot puts it in the *Four Quartets*, "Only through time time is conquered." Which is to say that the hour of its final defeat will be the hour of its fulfillment and reabsorption into eternity.

Firmly rooted in the eschatological doctrine of Christianity, Dilsey's concept of time is theo-logical, not chrono-logical. The assumptions on

which it rests remain of course implicit, but it is in this orthodoxly Christian perspective that we are asked to interpret Dilsey's comment after
Reverend Shegog's sermon: "I've seed de first en de last. . . . I seed de
beginning, en now I sees de ending" (371; see also 375). Given the
religious context of Easter where they occur, her words obviously refer to
the beginning and end of time, to the Alpha and Omega of Christ. But it
goes without saying that they apply as well to the downfall of the Compsons which Dilsey has been witnessing all along. The implication is certainly not that after all the Compsons may be saved, but what the oblique
connection between the Passion Week and the family tragedy suggests is
that for Dilsey the drama of the Compsons is above all one of redemption
denied.

Notes

1. All quotations from *The Sound and the Fury* are to the first edition (New York, 1929)
photographically reproduced in the Modern Library text (New York, 1967) and the Vintage
edition (New York: Random House, 1966).

2. See "The Interior Monologues of *The Sound and the Fury*," in *Merrill Studies in The
Sound and the Fury*, comp. James B. Meriwether (Columbus, Ohio: Charles E. Merrill,
1970), pp. 59–79. The original version of this essay appeared in *English Institute Essays, 1952*
(New York: Columbia University Press, 1954), pp. 29–56.

3. These image associations are echoed in the second monologue: Quentin links death
and sleep (see 144, 215), and several times invokes hell-fire. Moreover, his suicide at the end of
section 2 is symmetrical with Benjy's going to sleep at the end of section 1.

4. 17 narrative units are devoted to the day of Damuddy's death. See 19–22, 22–23, 23,
26–33, 38–39, 39, 40, 42–44, 45 (2 units), 46–47, 54–55, 75, 76, 89, 90, 91–92.

5. See Edmond L. Volpe, *A Reader's Guide to William Faulkner* (New York: Farrar,
Straus, & Giroux, 1964), pp. 103–04.

6. See Volpe. For a fuller discussion, see Charles D. Peavy, "Faulkner's Use of Folklore
in *The Sound and the Fury*," *Journal of American Folklore*, 79 (July–September, 1966),
437–38.

7. Read in Freudian terms, the equation *sex = dirt* might be considered an index of
regression to the anal-sadistic stage of psycho-sexual development. The Natalie scene would
then represent an abortive attempt to accede to genitality, and the hog wallow scene a return
to pregenital sexuality. The traits associated with anal fixation are extremely numerous in the
Quentin section: obsession with the pure/impure, sadistic impulses, compulsive orderliness
and cleanliness, ablution rites, phobia of stains and soiled objects. In this respect as in others
Quentin closely resembles his brother Jason: both are related to what Freud calls the "anal
character" through their emphasis on orderliness, their extreme obstinacy, and their strong
sense of ownership (plain avarice with Jason, emotional possessiveness with Quentin). See S.
Freud, "Character and Anal Eroticism" (1908), *Standard Edition*, 9, 167–75.

8. The hog wallow scene points forward to Quentin's allusion to Euboelus (184), the
swineherd who plunged with his herd into the chasm formed in the earth when Pluto
emerged to rape Persephone. The sexual implications of the mythic reference are reinforced
by the Rabelaisian and Shakespearean image of "the beast with two backs." Fusing these two
references with a third one (the Gadarene swine described by Mark and Luke in the New
Testament), Quentin resumes the image at the end of his monologue in the startling evocation
of "swine untethered in pairs rushing coupled into the sea" (219)—a vision of apocalyptic sexuality, but also a significant prefiguration of Quentin's death in the Charles River.

9. Here again one is reminded of the anal phase, during which the concepts of *dirt* and *property* polarize infantile behavior. Since this is also the time of separation from the mother, dirt, excrement—what is expelled from the body—becomes symbolically linked with the bivalent feelings generated by the child's (re)expulsion from the mother's body. Caddy has become a "dirty girl" to Quentin insofar as he is no longer an extension of himself, i.e., his property. The dirt motif is thus directly related to the central experience of loss.

10. Faulkner himself pointed to the symbolism of the muddy drawers in his interviews with Jean Stein. See Faulkner, *Lion in the Garden* (New York: Random House, 1968), p. 245.

11. Rats often appear in scenes with sexual overtones. In the barn scene Quentin and Natalie hear a rat in the crib. The image of the rat is also associated with Caddy: after she has lost her virginity, her eyes are compared to "cornered rats" (185). In Faulkner's unfinished novel "Elmer" the same image occurs; it also figures in the closing section of *Mosquitoes* and in the rape scene in *Sanctuary*.

12. Quentin thus reverts to the position of the infant within the oedipal triangle. In this respect it should be noted that Caddy later gives her brother's name to her own daughter: symbolically, Quentin II is both the fruit of the imaginary incest and Quentin's homologue as Caddy's child.

13. A number of critics assume that there is a "suicide pact" between Quentin and his sister. The assumption has been questioned by Charles D. Peavy, *ELN*, 5 (March 1968), 207–09. There is no final proof in these matters, but Quentin is obviously not meant to be taken as a reliable narrator of his past, and in his monologue it is often difficult to distinguish fact from fancy.

14. See Ernest Jones, *Hamlet and Oedipus* (New York: Norton, 1949). Critics have often noted the affinities between Quentin and Shakespeare's hero. See, for example, Cleanth Brooks, "Primitivism in *The Sound and the Fury*," *English Institute Essays*, 1952, pp. 13–14. See also William R. Taylor, *Cavalier and Yankee* (New York: Doubleday Anchor Books, 1963), pp. 137–40. As Taylor points out, Quentin is one among many "Southern Hamlets": "The introverted gentleman has a long history in Southern fiction which runs the gamut from Poe's neurasthenic Roderick Usher to Faulkner's Quentin Compson III and includes along the way contributions by Simms, Harriet Beecher Stowe and practically all the talents large and small that have examined Southern life" (p. 138).

15. Bland's symbolic function is further emphasized by imagery assimilating him to a royal personage (112, 130, 149), and it is interesting to note that his mother is likewise compared to a queen. No doubt irony plays its part in these similes, but to Quentin this regal couple is also a mythicized image of the parental couple. Moreover, through the superimposition of the husband-wife relationship on the son-mother relationship one can see the incest motif emerge once again. The ambiguous intimacy between Mrs. Bland and her son, her wide-eyed admiration for his amorous exploits, her ecstatic marveling at his handsomeness (130–31) are in themselves suggestive of near-incestuous relations.

16. In the confrontation scenes between Quentin and his sister's lovers the contrast between his impotence and their manliness is underscored by the ironic use of phallic symbols: Ames' revolver, Head's cigar. One recalls that Ames offers to lend Quentin his revolver, and Head offers him a cigar, both of which are refused. His attitude confirms the denial of sexuality in which his impotence originates. It seems safe to assume that this symbolism was intentional: similar phallic imagery is to be found in Faulkner's uncompleted early novel "Elmer," whose immature hero to some extent prefigures Quentin. The contrast between Quentin and his rivals is further suggested on the symbolic level through their respective relations to the elements of water and fire. For Quentin water means both death and desire, and one of the last memories in his monologue is significantly a remote childhood memory about the nights when he would get up to go to the bathroom, "seeking water" (215). Ames and Bland, his surrogates, on the other hand, possess what Quentin at once desires and dreads; they have both gained mastery over the female element. Bland is an accomplished oarsman; as to Ames,

Caddy tells Quentin that "he's crossed all the oceans all around the world" (187). At the same time these two figures are related to fire (a traditional symbol of male potency): Bland through his association with the sun, Ames through his remarkable markmanship and through his association with bronze and asbestos.

17. See Michael Millgate, p. 163 above. Mr. Compson's reflections upon time in the opening of the second section (93) as well as his speculations about virginity (143) are missing from the manuscript. It is most significant, too, that while many of the references to "Father said" were added upon revision, Faulkner removed "said" from Quentin's final (imagined) conversation with Mr. Compson (219-22). In the manuscript, Faulkner followed the normal pattern of reported speech ("He said . . . and I said . . ."); in the published version, the only clues to change of speaker are the pronouns which are run into the prose without any punctuation mark. Moreover, to suggest the shrinking of Quentin's self, Faulkner substituted "i" for "I." On this point, see Faulkner's comments in *Faulkner in the University*, ed. Frederick L. Gwynn and Joseph L. Blotner (Charlottesville, Va.: University of Virginia Press, 1959), p. 18.

18. The phrase is from Guy Rosolato, "Du Père," in *Essais sur le Symbolique* (Paris: Gallimard, 1969), p. 49. My translation.

19. Rosolato, p. 48. My translation.

20. Quentin's desire to avoid oedipal involvement is also attested by the fantasy of being his father's father, i.e., unfathered: *"Say it to Father will you I will my fathers Progenitive I invented him created I him Say it to him it will not be for he will say I was not and then you and I since philoprogenitive"* (152). In Faulkner's fiction being fatherless is considered alternately a positive privilege and a fatal flaw. It means total self-possession for Lucas Beauchamp, "who fathered himself, intact and complete" (*Go Down, Moses*, p. 118); for Joe Christmas, the protagonist of *Light in August*, it is a source of anguish and alienation. Incidentally, the fantasy of self-generation is also that of the writer—both son and father to his work.

21. Freud notes that in the condition of melancholia the superego is transformed into "a pure culture of the death instinct." See "The Dependent Relationships of the Ego" (1923), *Standard Edition*, 19:53.

22. Between Mrs. Compson and Addie Bundren, Jason and Jewel (of *As I Lay Dying*) there are striking similarities. Though Addie is much more sympathetically drawn than Mrs. Compson, she is also a self-centered mother, and her influence on her children is also largely negative. Jewel, on the other hand, while being capable of abnegation and heroism, resembles Jason in his uncontrollable rage and in his estrangement from the rest of the family.

23. On Jason's indebtedness to his father's philosophy, see Duncan Aswell's perceptive essay, pp. 207-213 above. It is noteworthy too that Mr. Compson (as quoted by Quentin) occasionally makes reflections which would not be out of place in Jason's speech: "pennies has healed more scars than jesus" (221).

24. At times Jason even seems to derive a masochistic pleasure from his humiliations, especially during his frustrated pursuit of Miss Quentin. When the sheriff refuses to help him catch his niece, "he [repeats] his story, harshly recapitulant, seeming to get an actual pleasure out of his outrage and impotence" (378).

25. In Faulkner cosmetic habits are often an index to sexual promiscuity. See, for example, the emphasis on Temple Drake's outrageously scarlet lips in *Sanctuary*.

26. John L. Longley, *The Tragic Mask: A Study of Faulkner's Heroes* (Chapel Hill: University of North Carolina Press, 1963), p. 147.

27. Cleanth Brooks, *Faulkner: The Yoknapatawpha Country* (New Haven, Conn.: Yale University Press, 1963), p. 343.

Voice in "That Evening Sun":
A Study of Quentin Compson

May Cameron Brown*

Although scholars have recognized *The Sound and the Fury* as an important experimental novel, they have failed to remark the similar experimentation exhibited in Faulkner's short story "That Evening Sun," written approximately two years after *The Sound and the Fury*.[1] Some of the major themes of the novel—the deteriorating aristocracy, sexual promiscuity, injustice, pain, death, and the destructiveness of time—appear also in the story, and it too shows Faulkner's interest in experimentation with form. Perhaps the most notable aspect of these two works is Faulkner's attempt to find a voice appropriate to the expression of his ideas; and this with the unity of theme and technique doubtless led to his decision to use Quentin Compson, in spite of his suicide in *The Sound and the Fury*, as the central consciousness of another story of ruthlessness and disorder.[2] In "That Evening Sun," as in section two of *The Sound and the Fury*, Quentin's voice—the diction, syntax, imagery, and ideas unique to him—serves as the primary device for conveying the meaning and value.

The story is narrated by Quentin in first person and in retrospect. It is partly, if not centrally, the story of the child's initiation into the fear, injustice, and death which characterize the adult world, a world which the child can only partially understand. The central events are framed by the activities of the Compson children, a device which creates the irony and hence emphasizes the racial tension of the story. Although Quentin is involved in the central action of "That Evening Sun," he maintains sufficient detachment for the reader to accept him as a reliable narrator who accurately reports what he sees and hears. By modifying the simple syntax of the generic child through the imagery and consciousness which is unmistakably the adult Quentin's,[3] Faulkner creates the double perspective of two Quentins—adult and child—which, as Robert M. Slabey observes, establishes the two "temporal planes" of the story, *is* and *was*,[4] a perspective which was fully developed in *The Sound and the Fury*.

"That Evening Sun" is the story of the Compsons' Negro laundress, Nancy, a woman victimized by her prostitution to white men and ter-

*Reprinted, with permission, from *Mississippi Quarterly*, 29, No. 3 (Summer 1976), 347–60.

rified by her belief—real or imagined—that she will be killed by her Negro husband.[5] It is a study of fear and isolation, narrated appropriately by one of Faulkner's most isolated characters. Like *The Sound and the Fury* and like *Absalom, Absalom!*, "That Evening Sun" is, at least on one level, an attempt by the adult Quentin to examine events from his childhood in order to explain and reconcile himself to that past.

The story exists in three versions: an early manuscript entitled "Never Done No Weeping When You Wanted to Laugh"; the version which appeared in *American Mercury* in March 1931 under the title "That Evening Sun Go Down";[6] and the final version, which was included in *These 13* in the fall of 1931. The differences among these versions have been studied by Norman Holmes Pearson and Leo M. J. Manglaviti,[7] but no one has yet remarked on the implications of the changes between the versions as they affect the voice of the narrator, Quentin Compson.

Faulkner's modifications of the *Mercury* version for the final text reveal a number of insights into his conception of Quentin. As a character in the story, Quentin is a child and must sound like one, but because he is also the twenty-four-year-old narrator, he may have sensitivity and perceptions beyond those of his brother and sister and even those of the adults in the story. As narrator, he is the adult Quentin, recalling a frightening incident from his childhood; and the very fact that he chooses to tell this particular tale indicates much about his adult concerns, just as his memories of his childhood in *The Sound and the Fury*, especially those concerning Caddy, reveal his obsessions and his suffering which culminate in suicide. Although Quentin is the central consciousness in all of the extant versions of "That Evening Sun," the final version shows the indirection and increased ambiguity crucial to the meaning and effect of the story. Faulkner has made Quentin essentially an observer of the action, who conveys emotion and meaning largely through remembered dialogue. He need say very little directly, and the few comments he does make are clear indications of his awareness of Nancy's plight.

Leonard H. Frey has argued that the details of Nancy's situation seem "perfectly matter-of-fact to Quentin"[8] and that as the family leaves Nancy in her cabin, Quentin simply assumes that "Nancy will no longer be available for laundry-duty."[9] Frey tentatively suggests that he may be misreading Quentin's final question: " 'Who will do our washing now, Father?' "[10] It seems likely that he misreads Quentin's character altogether. Unquestionably the story displays brilliant irony, but the irony is hardly the result of Quentin's insensitivity as Frey implies.[11] One of the achievements of the story is that the reader feels precisely what Quentin does about Nancy's plight even though Quentin's communication of his emotions is indirect. A study of Faulkner's careful technique and revisions in relation to Quentin's role in the story and to the voice in which he tells it supports the view that Quentin, whatever his age, is the same as

the sensitive character who narrates Section II of *The Sound and the Fury*.

The opening paragraph of the story is a description of the dehumanization caused by modernity, a description which parallels the dehumanization of Nancy by the white inhabitants of Jefferson. Quentin, in the complex imagery and syntax of the twenty-four-year-old narrator,[12] describes the new electric lights as "ghostly and bloodless grapes" and the laundry which disappears "apparitionlike" into the laundry trucks. The ghost image, a common one in Quentin's vocabulary, differs from the ghosts which haunt his mind in *The Sound and the Fury* in that here it represents the sterility of the modern world; but it is related to the images of the novel in that it suggests the lost past, the inability to act meaningfully, the warm remembered relationships with Negroes, and, taken in conjunction with Nancy's illegitimate pregnancy, the unchaste condition of Caddy, with which Quentin is obsessed in *The Sound and the Fury*. The parallels between the story and the novel are demonstrated repeatedly in his concern with chastity, miscegenation, despair, and death. In keeping with the tight structuring of the story, the evidence of Nancy's dehumanization—the treatment by Mr. Stovall, the jailer, and, to some extent, the children—immediately follows Quentin's introduction of the principal characters in Section I. The story is shaped, at least in part, by the associative aspects of Quentin's consciousness which characterize him in *The Sound and the Fury*. For example, his description of Nancy's face leads to his relation of the actions which have created her appearance. At the same time, in contrast to the spiraling complexity of *The Sound and the Fury*, the narrative is straightforward and simple, a structure befitting the voice of the child, which Quentin carefully recreates.

As Quentin begins his story in retrospect, he introduces other images which are important both to the development of the story and to his own peculiar narration: the "dusty, shady streets" (p. 289) of the past, the ditch through which Nancy carries her laundry and beyond which the children are not allowed to pass alone (p. 290),[13] the balloon-like steadiness of the bundle of laundry on Nancy's head (p. 290). Frey accurately observes that the "balloon is an image natural to a child" and suggests that the incongruity of Quentin's description of the laundry as "steady as a rock or a balloon" is evidence of his childishness.[14] The oxymoronic effect, however, may also be an example of Faulkner's intentional contradictions which create the tension so prevalent in his work.[15] The balloon-laundry image relates directly to Quentin's description of Nancy's pregnancy, "her belly already swelling out a little, like a little balloon" (p. 292), and also suggests the opening laundry reference. The innocent associations thus reflect the adult ones, leading Quentin to recall inhumanity and death. For Quentin, images in the present recall related images from the past which, in turn, reflect on and help to explain the original thoughts that have led to the associations. As one such image the

balloon may represent, among other possibilities, miscegenation, sexual promiscuity, and the changes resulting from the passage of time—the primary causes of Quentin's suffering in all of his narrative roles.

With the introduction of the balloon image, the language in "That Evening Sun" becomes almost imperceptibly that of the nine-year-old child who will relate the details of the events as he remembers them. As the dialogue begins, the sentences become less complex, characterized especially by the use of the *and* connective; introductory words change to "and then" and "so"; and repetition becomes characteristic: "Dilsey was sick" (p. 290); "Dilsey was still sick in her cabin. Father told Jesus to stay off our place. Dilsey was still sick. It was a long time. We were in the library after supper" (p. 292).

In addition, there are rapid time shifts:

> "Maybe she's waiting for Jesus to come and take her home," Caddy said.
> "Jesus is gone," I said. Nancy told us how one morning she woke up and Jesus was gone.
> "He quit me," Nancy said. "Done gone to Memphis, I reckon. Dodging them city *po*-lice for a while, I reckon."
> "And a good riddance," father said. "I hope he stays there."
> "Nancy's scaired of the dark," Jason said. (p. 293)[16]

Further indication of childlike comprehension is the repeated pattern of a statement or question in dialogue followed by "mother said," "I said," or "father said" and the repetition of the proper name. The overall effect is the child's emphasis on proper names and a simple perception which does not perceive tone or value in the speech of others.

As the vocabulary and syntax become childlike, the reader becomes less and less aware that the story is being told in retrospect and becomes, as Quentin is, absorbed into the past which is the heart of the story. Yet we never completely lose sight of the young man who is the initial teller of the tale. Although Quentin in a sense becomes the nine-year-old boy again, his insights are colored and modified by the older Quentin, for whom the story of Nancy's plight has much personal significance.

Quentin's insights are perhaps best recognized through contrast with those of the other children and the adults, who appear in the story much as they do in *The Sound and the Fury*. Caddy, who is seven, is the same curious little girl who climbs the tree to observe Damuddy's death in the novel. She questions every adult statement and interprets everything she hears literally. For example, when Nancy, lying in the dark of the children's room, whispers "Jesus," Caddy asks, " 'Was it Jesus? . . . Did he try to come into the kitchen?' " (p. 296). Quentin explains " 'It's the other Jesus she means' " (p. 297). Characteristically, it is Caddy who persuades the other children to go with Nancy to her cabin. When Quentin, in his usual prohibitive manner with her, objects that their mother has not

given them permission, Caddy responds, " 'She didn't say we couldn't go' " (p. 300). In her goading of Jason, it is Caddy who introduces the childish fear which ironically parallels the real terror of Nancy: "I'm not afraid to go . . . . Jason is the one that's afraid" (p. 300). Her repeated "Scairy cat" (pp. 293, 309) sets up the contrast on which the tension of the story builds. She only vaguely understands Nancy's fear; " 'Why is Nancy afraid of Jesus? . . . Are you afraid of father, mother?' " (p. 299). Since her parents ignore her questions, she can only surmise that Nancy's fear is related to her blackness, an assumption which is, of course, partially correct: " 'If something was to jump out, you'd be scairder than a nigger' " (p. 309).

Just as Caddy is the same curious, adventuresome, determined little girl who is the center of *The Sound and the Fury*, so Jason is a portrait in miniature of the character in the novel.[17] He is a wilful five-year-old, who threatens the adults with tears to get his own way: " 'I'll stop [crying] if Dilsey will make a chocolate cake' " (p. 299). Further, he is a cruel, totally self-centered tattletale. " 'You hurt me,' " he tells Nancy. " 'You put smoke in my eyes. I'm going to tell' " (p. 306). His primary concern is determining what a "nigger" is: " 'Jesus is a nigger . . . . Dilsey's a nigger too . . . . I aint a nigger . . . . Am I, Dilsey?' " (pp. 297–298).[18] Along with Caddy, Jason helps to set the irony of the story and to expose the racial issues which are developed by the adults; and their two uncomprehending and, in Jason's case, insensitive voices provide a contrast to Quentin's understanding but seemingly objective narration. As in *The Sound and the Fury*, where he cries because he understands that Damuddy is dead, Quentin, unlike his brother and sister, is able to infer truth from adult behavior. The significance of the characterizations of Caddy and Jason as well as those of the adult Compsons is that these are Quentin's memories of his family. A less acute observer or one with different sensibilities would recall a different version of the story and of the behavior of the characters. What we learn of Mr. and Mrs. Compson, for example, is Quentin's impression, one consistent with his memories in *The Sound and the Fury*.

Jason's egocentricity is skillfully reflected in Mrs. Compson, whose sole concern is for her own safety and convenience: " 'You'll leave me alone, to take Nancy home? . . . Is her safety more precious to you than mine?' " (p. 293). " 'You'll leave these children unprotected, with that Negro [Jesus] about?' " (p. 294). Like her Bascomb son, she has only a literal and self-centered concept of the events and a clear awareness of her position as a white woman. Although she is revealed primarily through her dialogue, Quentin indirectly characterizes her in the opening scene when Nancy comes late to cook breakfast and as a result it is "too late for [him] to go to school" (p. 291). The fact that Mrs. Compson does not prepare his breakfast reinforces our impression of her as the complaining, self-pitying mother who is incapable of motherhood, and underlies the

distinction between master and servant, black and white which the story so forcefully presents.

Another aspect of the master-servant relationship is exhibited in Mr. Compson's behavior. Unlike his wife, he at least accepts Nancy's fear as real to her, but he believes that her behavior is foolish. Even though he agrees to walk home with her for a time, considering this to be his duty to his servants, his attitude toward Nancy is condescending: " 'And if you'd just let white men alone. . . . If you'd behave yourself, you'd have kept out of this' " (p. 295). He serves as protector of the children, silencing any specific reference to Nancy's situation, and he insensitively tries to comfort Nancy by telling her that Jesus probably has taken another wife. In his assumed gallantry, he is clearly callous. Nancy is really less than human to him, and he becomes irritated by her seemingly unwarranted fears. His standard reply to the uneasiness of both his wife and Nancy is "Nonsense" (pp. 294, 307, 308): " 'When yawl go home, I gone,' Nancy said. . . . 'Nonsense,' father said. 'You'll be the first thing I'll see in the kitchen tomorrow morning' " (p. 308). It is significant that Mr. Compson calls Nancy a "thing."[19]

Quentin's emphasis on these particular aspects of his father's behavior indicates his awareness of the discrepancy between blacks and whites and of the cruelty of the actions and attitudes of the adult whites. In contrast to the other members of his family, he shows an unusual sensitivity to Nancy's situation. Their voices serve as a sort of dissonant orchestration through which we hear the terrified moans of Nancy and the understated comprehension of Quentin's consciousness. In keeping with the introversion characteristic of him in other works which he narrates, most of his perceptions are presented to us indirectly through descriptions or records of conversations. At the beginning of the story proper, he describes Nancy as "tall, with a high, sad face sunken a little where her teeth were missing" (p. 290). The introduction of the missing teeth prepares us for the scene in which Nancy confronts the white bank cashier Mr. Stovall, asking for her payment. Quentin makes two significant observations in his scene: "So we thought it was whisky until that day they arrested her again" (p. 291) and "her belly already swelling out a little, like a little balloon" (p. 292). The first statement refers to Jason's accusation (as he parrots his father) that Nancy is drunk when she tells the children that she is " 'going to get [her] sleep out' " (p. 290) instead of cooking breakfast for the family. It is possible that Quentin recognizes that Nancy's illness is early pregnancy; and his recollection of the words of the jailer who discovers Nancy during her attempted suicide may indicate his own ironic view of the jailer's trustworthiness: ". . . it was cocaine and not whisky, because no nigger would try to commit suicide unless he was full of cocaine, because a nigger full of cocaine wasn't a nigger any longer" (p. 291). The reference to Nancy's swelling belly concludes this scene and is followed immediately by the vine metaphor, which refers to Nancy's un-

born child and Quentin's observation that "we could see her apron swelling out" (p. 292). By the very juxtaposition of these images we may well assume that Quentin understands what is happening.

His comprehension of Nancy's fear is another aspect of Quentin's character and voice which distinguishes him from the other children and the adults in the story. His feeling that something is wrong is stated as clearly as his initial description of Nancy's face. The first direct statement which Quentin makes in the story occurs during the one time he is alone with Nancy. He finds her in the kitchen, sitting by the cold stove:

> "Mother wants to know if you are through," I said.
> "Yes," Nancy said. She looked at me. "I done finished." She looked at me.
> "What is it?" I said. "What is it?"
> "I aint nothing but a nigger," Nancy said. "It aint none of my fault."
> She looked at me, sitting in the chair before the cold stove, the sailor hat on her head. I went back to the library. It was the cold stove and all, when you think of a kitchen being warm and busy and cheerful. And with a cold stove and the dishes all put away, and nobody wanting to eat at that hour. (pp. 292–293)

The cold stove parallels the fire in Nancy's cabin at the end of the story, the fire which is too hot and too bright, the burning lamp on which Nancy puts her hand without noticing. It is an unnatural light which Nancy feels will prevent the murder from occurring in the dark. In this scene, too, Quentin is perceptive of her fear: "There was something about Nancy's house; something you could smell besides Nancy and the house. Jason smelled it, even" (p. 302). When the children hear someone coming, Quentin looks at Nancy's sweating face and says, " 'She's not crying' " (p. 306). The sweat is symptomatic of her terror.

Throughout the story Quentin reports each detail with characteristic insight. He has seen Nancy's shaking hands and sweating face; he has heard the sound that Nancy makes which is "not singing and not unsinging" (p. 300). He has heard references to cutting down vines (p. 292), slitting bellies (p. 295), blood (p. 307), and coffin money (p. 308). It thus seems highly unlikely, as Frey would believe, that he merely thinks Nancy is going away.[20] It is, after all, Quentin who, after Nancy mentions her coffin money, relates the brief story of Mr. Lovelady and his suicide wife.[21] It is Quentin who makes the connection between Nancy's plight and that of the Loveladys, and only Quentin who really believes that Nancy will not be "the first thing [they'll] see in the kitchen tomorrow morning" (p. 308). His final question " 'Who will do our washing now, Father?' " (p. 309) is not then a callous query about Nancy's replacement as laundress. It is a typically understated and perhaps even fatalistic perception of the situation. Had Faulkner allowed a nine-year-old child the ability to verbalize everything which he instinctively perceives, the

story would be entirely implausible. Rather it is one aspect of Faulkner's craft that Quentin communicates his sensibility indirectly in this story. It is essentially Quentin's unconsciousness, what he knows, but cannot directly state, that is the voice of "That Evening Sun."

Quentin's awareness of sights, sounds, and smells is a key to the identification of his narrative voice in "That Evening Sun." The odors of Nancy's cabin and of her fear pervade his consciousness as does the silence, interrupted by Nancy's loud talking and her moaning, signaling her fear and, for Quentin, her death. While Quentin's consciousness centers on twilight in *The Sound and the Fury*, in "That Evening Sun" there is darkness, a darkness which is emphasized by the incongruous blazing fire in the cabin and a darkness in which Nancy's eyes "looked like cat's eyes do, like a big cat against the wall" (p. 296), so dark that in the children's room Quentin cannot even tell that Nancy is there. It is the key image of the story, pervading the children's room, the ominous ditch, and Nancy's cabin just as the terrors of the adult world threaten the children's innocence.

The ghost image which opens the story and prepares us for the ghostlike quality of the tale is repeated indirectly on two occasions. When Nancy is in the children's room, Quentin feels that her eyes have been "printed on [his] eyeballs" (p. 296) though he cannot see her, and he describes the sound of her voice as if "nobody had made it, like it came from nowhere and went nowhere, until it was like Nancy was not there at all" (p. 296). At the end of the story, as the children cross the ditch with their father for the last time, Quentin describes the scene: "We went down into the ditch. I looked at it, quiet. I couldn't see much where the moonlight and the shadows tangled" (p. 309). The shadow, one of the most common images in Quentin's imagination (and conspicuously missing from all but the final version of the story), is both literal and figurative. It is an accurate description of what Quentin sees as well as a metaphoric representation of the world of fear and death where Nancy resides. Perhaps more than any other of Faulkner's characters Quentin lives in a shadow world, between reality and illusion, sanity and madness, life and death. It is entirely fitting that the last visual image he gives us in "That Evening Sun" is the shadow juxtaposed against the reflection of the fire from Nancy's open doorway as she waits for death.

Although the shadow does not recur as an obsessive image in this story, through his choice of the title Faulkner establishes it as a key to Quentin's consciousness. Taken from the opening line of W. C. Handy's "St. Louis Blues," "I hate to see de ev'nin' sun go down," the title reveals much about Nancy's situation—her loss of Jesus, her fear, and her loneliness. Equally important is its application to Quentin, whose isolation and unhappiness—generally associated with shadows and twilight—parallel Nancy's unbearable misery. The racial problem and his

responsibility as a white gentleman are aspects of his heritage which torment him in *The Sound and the Fury* and in his later narrative role in *Absalom, Absalom!*

In an essay on Faulkner's technique, Robert Penn Warren lists three narrative types: the objective or impersonal presentation of character; the personal narrative in which the character unfolds in his own language; and the episodic narrative, in which a "voice" is the index of sensibility.[22] "That Evening Sun" encompasses all three types to some degree. The presentation seems to be objective, in that Quentin makes no direct judgments. Yet his voice is clearly not impersonal: it is distinctively his, and Quentin Compson is incapable of detachment, as the interrelationship of past and present images clearly indicates. As the adult narrator, he is re-experiencing a significant event from his past, unconsciously shaping and modifying his memories of Nancy and his family through his adult consciousness. Finally, the story is episodic as a child would tell it, and Quentin's voice becomes the index of sensibility. The story is both an examination of the evil and fear of the adult world and a study of a young man's initiation into that world. It portrays the sense of doom and despair which surrounds the Compsons in the rest of the cycle of stories which concern them, and it provides us with additional insights into the nature and voice of Quentin. The events which he narrates here, along with his involvement in the Sutpen story in *Absalom, Absalom!*, help to clarify his role in the canon and may help to explain the reasons for his suicide in *The Sound and the Fury.*

If we recall that the working title of *The Sound and the Fury* was "Twilight" and consider this title along with the principal images of "That Evening Sun," sunset and darkness, we can see that these images refer consistently to Quentin, who, like Nancy, hates to see "that evening sun go down" and who remains caught in "the suspension of twilight"[23] created by his heritage and his own consciousness. Voice, the vision of experience that Quentin represents, provides the unity and meaning of the story, and Faulkner's decision to use him as the central narrator testifies not only to Faulkner's fascination with Quentin but also to his early success with narrative experimentation.

Notes

1. "That Evening Sun" was written in the fall of 1930, and there is sufficient internal evidence to suggest a strong relationship to the novel, completed in the fall of 1928.

2. "Justice," also written in the fall of 1930 and narrated by Quentin, is further evidence of Faulkner's interest in Quentin as a central consciousness.

3. Quentin's unusual perceptions of fear and death and the corresponding images of ghosts, shadows, twilight, and darkness as well as his characteristically rigid behavior with Caddy are key aspects of his consciousness as Faulkner had created it in *The Sound and the Fury.*

4. Robert M. Slabey, "Quentin Compson's 'Lost Childhood,' " *Studies in Short Fiction*, 1 (Spring 1964), 174.

5. In his examination of the story, Cleanth Brooks argues that "That Evening Sun" is Nancy's story, that our sympathies are focused on her, and that the other characters "serve finally as mere foils to her" (*A Shaping Joy: Studies in the Writer's Craft* [London: Methuen & Co. Ltd., 1971], p. 234). Nancy is, of course, the subject of the story, but I wish to suggest that Faulkner was equally concerned with Quentin, not only as the narrator of the story but also as the young initiate. Quentin is the only character who does not serve as a "mere foil" to Nancy because he can intuitively identify with her suffering, and it is precisely this sensitivity that makes him the only appropriate narrating agency. "That Evening Sun" is not a story narrated by an unnamed third person, but one which Quentin chooses from his own past to tell. Brooks's comments seem not to take into account Faulkner's conscious artistry in his selection of Quentin.

6. Faulkner first tried to place the story with *Scribner's* in October 1930. James B. Meriwether, *The Literary Career of William Faulkner: A Bibliographical Study*, Princeton: Princeton University Library, 1961, p. 175.

7. Pearson, "Faulkner's Three 'Evening Suns,' " *Yale University Library Gazette*, 29 (October 1954), 61–70; and Manglaviti, "Faulkner's 'That Evening Sun' and Mencken's 'Best Editorial Judgment,' " *American Literature*, 43 (January 1972), 649–654.

8. "Irony and Point of View in 'That Evening Sun,' " *Faulkner Studies*, 2 (Autumn 1953), 35.

9. Frey, p. 37.

10. *Collected Stories of William Faulkner* (New York: Random House), 1950, p. 309.

11. Frey, p. 37.

12. The opening paragraphs contain the longest sentences of the story, sentences which consist of several appended clauses of the type which are representative of Quentin's voice in *The Sound and the Fury*.

13. In addition to its implications of fear and death, the ditch represents a racial boundary, the dividing line between the white and black worlds. Appropriately, it is Caddy who takes the initiative to cross the ditch to Nancy's cabin just as it is Caddy who climbs the tree to observe Damuddy's death. The ditch, which represents a kind of bridge between the two worlds and which appears in Quentin's section of *The Sound and the Fury* as he recalls the night when Caddy loses her virginity, is reminiscent of the bridge in the novel where Quentin fails to kill Dalton Ames and the bridge from which he commits suicide. Although Quentin crosses the ditch to Nancy's cabin, he is helpless to save her just as he is incapable of saving his sister.

14. Frey, p. 38.

15. For a full discussion see Walter J. Slatoff, *Quest for Failure: A Study of William Faulkner* (Ithaca, New York: Cornell University Press, 1960), pp. 53–76.

16. This passage provides strong support for Faulkner's choice of the name Jesus. The religious pun emphasizes Nancy's concern with death and, through Mr. Compson's comment, indicates the rejection of religion by the Compson family. In addition it provides another parallel with *The Sound and the Fury*, in which the religious underpinning is an important motif. It is significant that Quentin, who on Maundy Thursday participates in a Last Supper and is put on trial, is the observer of Nancy's trial and her preparations for death at the hands of Jesus.

17. In the conclusion of the story, Quentin observes Jason on their father's back, "the tallest of all of us" (*Collected Stories*, p. 309). The image may reflect the fact that Jason is the only member of the Compson family who survives to function in the real world. The terrible irony, of course, is that he survives principally because of his viciousness and insensitivity.

18. Jason's non-sequitur logic, characteristic of the child's comprehension, is not unlike

that of Vardaman Bundren in *As I Lay Dying:* "My mother is a fish." Evans B. Harrington, "Technical Aspects of William Faulkner's 'That Evening Sun,' " *Faulkner Studies,* 1 (Winter 1952), 57, notes that Jason's comments, which interrupt Nancy and Dilsey's conversation about Jesus, are perfectly timed and advance the intensity of the story through contrast with the adult discussion.

19. Cleanth Brooks accurately suggests that Mr. Compson behaves as anyone else in his position would behave (*A Shaping Joy,* p. 234). That is not, however, sufficient reason to excuse his treatment of Nancy. It is, I think, crucial to Faulkner's conception of Quentin and his role in the story that he is the only character who perceives Nancy as a human being.

20. Frey, "Irony," p. 37.

21. The story contains an attempted suicide and an actual one, significant incidents for the young narrator who will himself be a suicide.

22. Robert Penn Warren, "William Faulkner," in *Forms of Modern Fiction,* ed. William Van O'Connor (Minneapolis: The University of Minnesota Press, 1948), p. 141.

23. "A Justice," *Collected Stories,* p. 360.

[Faulkner's Narrative Poetics in *The Sound and the Fury*]

Arthur F. Kinney*

The Sound and the Fury is Benjy's book: *his* consciousness begins and closes the novel, and it is to his memorialization of death at the small graveyard alongside the golf course and at the family plot in the Jefferson cemetery that we first and last attend. From the very beginning, Benjy transforms the significance of loss—the lost Caddy which our constitutive consciousness will make analogous to Luster's lost quarter, the lost golf ball, and Benjy's emasculation—into something greater, something which transcends clock time and allows Benjy to fuse both a memorable past and a painful present, joy and grief, love and death. Such equations tend to cancel out permanent anguish and provide for Benjy a compromise with existence. He locates the same solutions that the other Compsons do, more or less successfully, but with greater concentration. His perceptions consequently provide us with the basic epistemological question in the novel: is the idiocy of this tale told by an idiot in the tale itself or in the telling of the tale?

Benjy's narrative consciousness supplies discrete episodes linked in ways both seen and unseen which in turn demand our own constitutive consciousness to connect them. Benjy's world is grounded in a trust based on familiarity. His direct responses are to stimuli he has long since learned—the sound "Caddy," his sister's slipper, the smell of trees, the sight and warmth of fire, even a new wheel on the old family carriage—and he has built from them a neat and safe world of patterned structures. He has, at these moments of configuration, an integrated consciousness. Only when there are no known things for him to assimilate—only when order is deliberately interrupted or dismissed—does he know anxiety and terror; his only fear is a fear of removal, never a fear of encounter. Benjy's stability, then, is from within; his world is organized by the centrifugal forces of his own self and the power of his stubborn and continual will. Conversely, he is helpless when the support of tradition is withdrawn, when his trust is betrayed. Thus his personal tragedy—with widening implications through the remainder of the novel—is an enlarg-

*Reprinted, with permission, from *Faulkner's Narrative Poetics: Style As Vision* (Amherst: University of Massachusetts Press, 1978), pp. 139–61.

ing sense of loss, for he makes correlations among the deaths of Damuddy, of Jason III his father, and of Quentin III his brother; the departure of Caddy his sister; and the loss of his masculinity. Through this progressive demise of the Compsons, he can share the emotions of others, even strangers, from the outset of the novel: his identity, like theirs, is stripped from him bit by bit. His perceptions have become so acute by training that when Benjy bellows in the first scene, it is not only to the sound of a call for "Caddy" but also to the voice of someone who like himself has found something missing and whose entire being is concentrated on its recovery.

Not merely Caddy but Caddy and Benjy are at the center of Benjy's perceptual life; his memories revolve not around her, but around his relations with her and her absence from him; and much of his effort goes into willing her presence, her return, or in finding simulations of it in others: in the behavior of Quentin IV, in the maternalism of Dilsey, and in the companionship of T. P. and Luster. When he is attracted to mirrors (as he always is, for they increase his perceptual range), he does not see himself but Caddy or metonymies of her in a slipper, firelight, or the cushion she would hand him from his mother's chair; for Benjy, even the mirrors become Caddy's surrogate. Moreover, at the heart of his recollections of his sister is one day in particular which he recalls in eighteen distinct episodes (including most of the longest), the day he played with her and with Versh and Quentin in the branch and Caddy got her drawers muddy; significantly, it is also the day of Damuddy's funeral. It is in fact this juxtaposition that filters his perspective on life. " 'I dont care whether they see or not,' " Caddy says of her dirty drawers to Quentin, " 'I'm going to tell, myself,' " but she does not tell because the house itself is shut off to the children—their father meets them on the back steps, hustles them into the kitchen, locks Benjy into a high chair, and leaves Dilsey in charge. Dilsey will explain neither the crowd in the front parlor nor the great hush and their mother's tears. " 'You'll know in the Lawd's own time,' " is all that Dilsey will say. So Caddy never explains the fight at the branch, and this secret, which is also Benjy's secret, correlates with the secret in the front room—how, Benjy is not quite certain. To this he adds one final secret which also seems to him correlative, because it too brings a crowd to the front room of their house, it too is not explained, and it too sees Caddy in trouble (or so he feels and so Quentin intimates). It is Caddy's wedding: "Caddy put her arms around me, and her shining veil, and I couldn't smell trees anymore and I began to cry." These three troublesome visions of Caddy—Quentin angry with her and hitting her when she is in dirty clothes, his father keeping her from the front room, the family ridding themselves of her to a man he does not know—coalesce at the core of his consciousness and shape his visual thinking.

The force of Benjy's narrative consciousness comes in the narrow sharpness of his focus and in his ability to see certain discrete moments as reduplicative. The opening series is indicative of the whole first chapter. We first see Benjy and Luster walking along the fence that separates Compson land from the golf course; they turn and head for the branch, and for Benjy this change in direction triggers a memory of Caddy, when she was cold like Benjy, but when she befriended him, when their cold was privately shared and no one came between them; this in turn reminds him of Caddy and the out-of-doors, and he recalls that she smells like trees; he next thinks of his own connection with nature in the jimson weed which he puts on graves. He apparently does not wish to recall Caddy's naturalness and his own in connection with death, however, a sign of permanent loss, so he rejects this memory and returns instead to the thoughts of the cold day when he and Caddy were alone. Unfortunately, this memory is interrupted when Luster leads him by the carriage house and he sees the carriage that took them all to his father's burial. No matter how hard he tries to concentrate on the present, on objects, on nature itself, Benjy's thoughts return constantly to Caddy and this in turn leads him to impressions of privation and of death. The branch scene juxtaposed to Damuddy's death and to Caddy's wedding, his repeated attempts to find an associative parallel with Caddy's several losses, consumes most of his attention and response, his sight and hearing; only at night, when his analogizing memory turns persistently to a fusion of Caddy and Quentin IV, is he able, however tentatively, to forget about death.

It is by their boyfriends' dismissal of him that he first links Caddy with Quentin IV.

> "Send him away." Charles said.
> "I will." Caddy said. "Let me go."
> "Will you send him away." Charlie said.
> "Yes." Caddy said. "Let me go." Charlie went away. "Hush." Caddy said. "He's gone." I hushed. I could hear her and feel her chest going.
> "I'll have to take him to the house." she said. She took my hand. "I'm coming." she whispered.
> "Wait." Charlie said. "Call the nigger."
> "No." Caddy said. "I'll come back. Come on, Benjy." . . .
> *You old crazy loon, Quentin said. I'm going to tell Dilsey about the way you let him follow everywhere I go. I'm going to make her whip you good.*

The assimilation of Caddy and Quentin IV in their effect of removing him from watching them—his visual thinking here seems not to distinguish their markedly differing tones—allows him to recognize Quentin's escape down the pear tree at the end of the present day in April 1928 as the completion of the analogy, for one of his last memories of the day at the branch is Dilsey pulling Caddy down from that same tree, where she climbed to see what was going on in the Compson parlor. Thus Benjy's present day ends as it began: it is totally enclosed, and he is back, comfortably at last, to the day in the past of a happier childhood that he knows best, the day he knows as much of as can now be known. It contains its mysteries for him still, but it also has his secrets. It is his day, he *possesses* it, and his perceptions are confirmed by present patterns of behavior, so he can sleep.

Benjy recalls and visualizes not in single concrete images but in associative clusters of images. His fluid consciousness seems to fasten on two primary groupings, those that represent Caddy or accompany her—rain, trees, slipper, fire—and those that are associated with privation, loss, and death. His jimson weed, for example, *Datura stramonium*, native to Mississippi, is ill scented and is said to have been fatal to children; the squinch owl like the blue jay is a superstitious sign of death as are the jars of poison that decorate his homemade grave; even the narcissus he holds at the end of the novel is associated with Nemesis because its scent was so sweet it was supposed to have made the Furies mad and frenzied. The farther reaches of allusion are beyond the boundaries of Benjy's consciousness but are meant to signal our own: they reinforce Benjy's fundamental analogy which makes the branch scene, Damuddy's death, and Caddy's wedding not merely correlative *but identical*. With Benjy sin, death, and promiscuity are interchangeable, are made one— and it is this felt impression that will govern not only his perception of life but Quentin's, Jason's, and Dilsey's as well. It is because he fastens in memory on these common themes which join episodes of his past into a seamless coherence that his mind moves so freely from one time and place to another, for it also insists on the linkages of sex, promiscuity, and death. It is instructive that on the holograph, Faulkner has *Twilight* as the working title of this novel.

Not only the absence of Caddy but the enforced synonymity of copulation and death is fundamental, too, to Quentin's outlook: " 'Is it a wedding or a wake?' " Shreve asks him as he dresses in his suit for a death that will marry him to Caddy for eternity, marry them in the clean flames of hell. It is a conjunction Caddy had also made for him; bewildered by her promiscuity and fearful of the sexual act itself, he asks Caddy if she enjoys it. She does not; *"When they touched me I died."* It is important that our constitutive consciousness recognize that at the deepest levels of their experience Benjy and Quentin, in their separately voiced threnodies, are true doubles, brothers in the Dostoyevskian sense.

Like Benjy, Quentin absorbs into his morbid celebrations fundamental concrete images of the past which they share—the pasture, the swing under the cedars, Caddy's treelike smell, her wedding veil—and like Benjy when he looks in the mirror he too sees Caddy, although for him it is, significantly, an image of her wedding day and she is running *away* from him:

> In the mirror she was running before I knew what it was. That quick, her
> train caught up over her arm she ran out of the mirror like a cloud, her

*veil swirling in long glints her heels brittle and fast clutching her dress on-
to her shoulder with the other hand, running out of the mirror the smells
roses roses the voice that breathed o'er Eden. Then she was across the
porch I couldn't hear her heels then in the moonlight like a cloud, the
floating shadow of the veil running across the grass, into the bellowing.*

We can recognize the similarity of vocabulary here as well as the similarity of statement—Caddy resembles flight, privation, loss; the distance
between them, from Quentin's view, widens irrevocably, as in a dream.
Where Benjy buries one memory in another, blurring the roughest and
most anguishing edges in the final mystery of the day at the branch,
Quentin tries to cover grief over with abstractions. He claims his father
rather than Benjy as his conscious model: his opening remarks (like
Benjy's) serve as an index to the operation of his thoughts.

> When the shadow of the sash appeared on the curtains it was between
> seven and eight o'clock and then I was in time again, hearing the watch.
> It was Grandfather's and when Father gave it to me he said, Quentin, I
> give you the mausoleum of all hope and desire; it's rather excrutiating-ly
> apt that you will use it to gain the reducto absurdum of all human ex-
> perience which can fit your individual needs no better than it fitted his or
> his father's. I give it to you not that you may remember time, but that you
> might forget it now and then for a moment and not spend all your breath
> trying to conquer it. Because no battle is ever won he said. They are not
> even fought. The field only reveals to man his own folly and despair, and
> victory is an illusion of philosophers and fools. . . .
> If it had been cloudy I could have looked at the window, thinking
> what he said about idle habits. Thinking it would be nice for them down
> at New London if the weather held up like this. Why shouldn't it? The
> month of brides, the voice that breathed *She ran right out of the mirror,
> out of the banked scent. Roses. Roses. Mr and Mrs Jason Richmond
> Compson announce the marriage of.* Roses. Not virgins like dogwood,
> milkweed. I said I have committed incest, Father I said. Roses. Cunning
> and serene. If you attend Harvard one year, but dont see the boat-race,
> there should be a refund. Let Jason have it. Give Jason a year at Harvard.

As with Benjy, the clustering here and the linkages that remain unspoken
are extraordinary and revealing. The conceptual—time, marriage, virginity, incest—are aligned so as to make them all susceptible to foolishness
and despair, but also to make their conquering power equally foolish.
Quentin is struggling here toward a life philosophy, not a death philosophy; the sunlight and Jason's renewal of the Compson legacy at Harvard frame for him those troublesome thoughts of sin, promiscuity, and
death that will not stay down. In addition, beneath these conscious attempts, Quentin must know that as his father dismisses the story of incest
so he dismisses the power Quentin assigns to virginity and to time. What
then of the loss of Caddy? Can this be truly tragic? Is it possible—the
thought occurs to Quentin several times in chapter 2—that, as Caddy

once remarks, Mr. Compson will die within the year, his philosophy pos-sibily disappearing with him? Does this make him the final proof or the final victim of his own views of triumph and of time? Quentin's conscious-ness is governed by abstractions, but, like Benjy's, it is primarily reflexive, his morbid intellection really the equivalent of the idiot's memorial reconstruction as both spend their day searching for Caddy and reconsti-tuting her in their own dimensions. Quentin shares with Benjy a deep trust in the world and an extreme self-centeredness which produce in him his father's despair and his brother's sense of progressive loss: Benjy's stream of consciousness from Damuddy's funeral through Caddy's wedding to the imminent loss of Quentin IV is mirrored by Quentin in the movement from Caddy's wedding through an attempted substitute in the little Italian girl to Little Sister Death as the last and final reality. Cor-relative to Benjy's, Quentin's day is also circular; it moves from the mutilation of the watch (of time) to self-mutilation (the stopping of human time, of human life *in* time); although he is attracted to water as Benjy is to fire, both end their days by submitting themselves to the ele-ment that most attracts them only to assure themselves of its destructive properties.

But there is also a significant difference between the two brothers. Benjy *wills* Caddy back; Quentin tries to *win* her back. From the moment he awakens, he makes his day a response, by replication, of the day he fought Dalton Ames, for this time he means to earn possession of his sister, to *deserve* Caddy. His elaborate plans for suicide reflect his elaborate stance the day he told Dalton Ames to get out of town—it is just as unreal, just as sentimental—and he images the day through the same visual prisms of birds, water, shadow, and broken sunlight. When he takes the train from Cambridge to find a suitable place to hide the flatirons until later that day, he chooses a bridge reminiscent of the site where he fought Dalton and lost. As he looks in the water, the morbidity of his plan fuses sex and death as they swell up in his consciousness.

> Where the shadow of the bridge fell I could see down for a long way, but not as far as the bottom. When you leave a leaf in water a long time after awhile the tissue will be gone and the delicate fibers waving slow as the motion of sleep. They dont touch one another, no matter how knotted up they once were, no matter how close they lay once to the bones. And maybe when He says Rise the eyes will come floating up too, out of the deep quiet and the sleep, to look on glory. And after awhile the flat irons would come floating up. I hid them under the end of the bridge and went back and leaned on the rail.

Again he feels the imminence of an earned death, for he did not save his sister. Yet now as then his plans for self-immolation are purifying and restorative; the water gives him once more that vision of the *"clean flame the two of us more than dead."* Even when a trout appears, commanding and killing mayflies, he subjects it to his willed reenactment, for, after darting about, it "hung, delicate and motionless among the wavering shadows." Three young boys come along, resembling the Compson boys, and talk idly of winning a prize by catching the fish. "They all talked at once, their voices insistent and contradictory and impatient, making of unreality a possibility, then a probability, then an incontrovertible fact, as people will when their desires become words." Even the unfamiliar children have been absorbed into his mind to reflect himself: their pattern is a paradigm for his own mental processes and they talk, too, of violation as death.

Like Benjy, Quentin wants to possess Caddy; he is jealous of her sexual attractiveness, her men, and her promiscuity. His real enemies, then, are as basic as human nature and as wide as the world, but in his own mind they are all embodied in Dalton Ames, whom—despite his attractiveness to Caddy—Quentin knows to be slippery, thoughtless, crude, and selfish, a meddler. He finds it easy, then, to see Dalton Ames in Gerald Bland.

> Bland came out, with the sculls. He wore flannels, a grey jacket and a stiff straw hat. Either he or his mother had read somewhere that Oxford students pulled in flannels and stiff hats, so early one March they bought Gerald a one pair shell and in his flannels and stiff hat he went on the river. The folks at the boathouses threatened to call a policeman, but he went anyway. His mother came down in a hired auto, in a fur suit like an arctic explorer's, and saw him off in a twenty-five mile wind and a steady drove of ice floes like dirty sheep. Ever since then I have believed that God is not only a gentleman and a sport; He is a Kentuckian too.

By means of Quentin's sardonic humor, we learn that Gerald rows on top of the water; he never goes below the surface, never achieves depth. Perhaps what galls Quentin additionally is that Mrs. Bland in her " 'eight yards of apricot silk,' " protects and supports her son in a way that Caroline Compson never supported Quentin. But the chief thing that Quentin envies is "Gerald's horses and Gerald's niggers and Gerald's women"—his attractiveness and his sexual exploits.

Quentin no sooner sees Gerald than he juxtaposes him, in his mind, to Dalton—

> Dalton Ames. Dalton Ames. Dalton Shirts. I thought all the time they were khaki, army issue khaki, until I saw they were of heavy Chinese silk or finest flannel because they made his face so brown his eyes so blue. Dalton Ames. It just missed gentility. Theatrical fixture. Just papier-mache, then touch. Oh. Asbestos. Not quite bronze.

—and then both blend, in his mind, into Sydney Herbert Head, "Hearty, celluloid like a drummer. Face full of teeth white but not smiling." Herbert, like Gerald, went to Harvard; like Dalton, he is "*A liar and a scoundrel Caddy was dropped from his club for cheating at cards got sent to Coventry caught cheating at midterm exams and expelled."* Later in the day, Gerald and Mrs. Bland save Quentin from arrest by a marshal, much as Dalton tried to save Quentin by giving him an excuse to avoid their duel, but Quentin is provoked by a remark Gerald makes and they fight. Since we do not hear the remark—since no one hears it—it was likely never made: Quentin has projected his memorial anticipation onto present reality stimulated by Bland's boasts of exploiting women successfully, like Dalton Ames. But like Benjy, Quentin makes present reality serve him as an analogue—once again he is bloodied, and Shreve, whom Spoade was "Calling . . . my husband," reifies Caddy in helping him to clean up. In fact, the only period of the day when Quentin's mind is not analogously fixed on Dalton Ames in one surrogate or another is the time he spends with the Italian girl. She is dark like Natalie, a girl he used to arouse Caddy's envy, but even here he is served by his myopic intellection, for Julio's attack on him for stealing his sister is a more humiliating fight than the one with Bland or Ames or the argument with Head. Throughout his final day in what he insists is an antagonistic world, Quentin can amuse himself best by stepping on shadows, by cheating time, by gazing into water: by the known acts of simulated suicide. Conceptually, he projects his own death to join a dead Caddy. *"When they touched me I died."*

Much of Quentin's effort is spent reaffirming scenes of his past in which Caddy is absent, not, as with Benjy, scenes where she is an active participant. The reason emerges in the course of his monologue: although Caddy always shows affection for Benjy, she finally found Quentin too unrealistic. She becomes as cruel to him as Ames, Bland, or even (verbally) Spoade. "You're meddling in my business again didn't you get enough of that last summer"; *"I dont give a goddam what you do."* His consciousness screens this actual Caddy out with discomfort. What he remembers best are the scenes he sentimentalizes: the dirty drawers, the elaborate suicide pact, his arrangements to meet Dalton Ames. Other memories, such as the knife at Caddie's throat and Dalton's gun, are phallic images that both attract and repel him, so his thoughts then move to mirror images: the reflections of loneliness ("murmuring bones"; "roof of wind"; "lonely and inviolate sand"); the sense of inevitability ("Spoade was in the middle of them like a terrapin in a street full of scuttering dead leaves, his collar about his ears, moving at his customary unhurried walk"); the movement toward death that will reunite them. In self-fulfilling images of an abstracted sentimentalism, Quentin reemerges as Caddy's hero and as his own best champion.

Quentin's chapter also charts a spreading sense of loss and decay paralleled by the underplot of his father's morbid vision and death; his stilted college rhetoric can only meld into his father's grandiose philosophizing, can only return him to thoughts of decay and meaninglessness.

Like his mother, Quentin can handle—indeed, cannot escape—the concrete images of his past: Caddy's men, her pregnancy, her veil. But he cannot accommodate his father's abstractions of these because they are meant to criticize and correct his self-indulgence.

> and he every man is the arbiter of his own virtues whether or not you consider it courageous is of more importance than the act itself than any act otherwise you could not be in earnest and i you dont believe i am serious and he i think you are too serious to give me any cause for alarm you wouldn't have felt driven to the expedient of telling me you have committed incest otherwise and i i wasnt lying i wasnt lying and he you wanted to sublimate a piece of natural human folly into a horror and then exorcise it with truth and i it was to isolate her out of the loud world so that it would have to flee us of necessity and then the sound of it would be as though it had never been and he did you try to make her do it and i i was afraid to i was afraid she might and then it wouldnt have done any good but if i could tell you we did it would have been so and then the others wouldnt be so and then the world would roar away and he and now this other you are not lying now either but you are still blind to what is in yourself

It is in this final montage that we come to know Quentin best. In this reconstructed conversation with his father (whether actual or contrived, we cannot be sure) it is his father who drives Quentin to commit suicide, for it is his father who trusts most that he cannot do it—*who challenges him*, in the end, *as Dalton and Head and Bland had*. The abstraction that Quentin supplies and clings to—incest—is significantly an abstraction of restoration: he means to reunite the family. That his father will have none of it suggests that his own basic value—that of the family and of Caddy herself—is now jeopardized. In a nearly incoherent rush of words Quentin admits, for the first and last time, that she was pregnant when she was married; he finally surrenders temporarily to his father's insistent (but morbid) superiority. But he restores himself, too, in the last lines of his chapter; in brushing his teeth in preparation to meet Caddy, he reinstates his dream of a cohesive family, and in his imagery and his linked concerns he also wills Benjy's world back into his own.

Neither Benjy nor Quentin lives in the world of actuality; to them, the real world is composed of memories and voices wholly subjective and internal. The external world is composed only of stimuli which awaken and confirm the foregone conclusions of their recollected pasts. This activity of perception and conception proclaims the idiocy in one, leads to suicide in the other: both are analogous and both are radically correlative to Caddy's flight, to Jason III's alcoholism, and to Caroline's hypochondria, all versions of willed self-destruction. It is a bleak picture—bleaker even than similar portraits in Balzac and Flaubert—and we are tempted to ask if there is no alternative. Could the Compsons survive by escaping from the claustrophobic atmosphere of the family and these self-indulgent revisitings of their past? It is at precisely this point that we are supplied with the narrative consciousness of Jason.

The middle son, Jason IV, moves in the wider world of Jefferson. He works at the hardware store, he does a certain amount of bank business, and he visits the Western Union regularly; on the day we see him, he gets two letters and receives and sends a number of telegrams. He has a woman in Memphis. By his varied activities, he manages to keep the Compsons going by keeping one foot in the mercantile world of Jefferson, one foot in the antebellum Compson household. But Jason's narrative consciousness tells us that he finds Jefferson and his home both sources of humiliation, analogous trials where he is put upon by those who refuse to accord him the proper respect. For him, values are easily transferred from one environment to the other because the two are correlative. Neither exercises his imagination or his true talents because both demand only that he contribute to situations established prior to his time. His profoundest interpretation of the Compson dilemma is his ability to see that, like the Bascombs, like business generally, appearances are more important than realities where they happen to differ, and that, if one is skillful and persistent enough, in time appearance can bring reality up to its own standards, substance up to form. Jason finds an articulate, even insistent supporter in his mother, much as Benjy and Quentin found support in Caddy and Jason III. Caroline Compson's own myth, that Jason is a Bascomb not a Compson (although to our constitutive consciousness the names seem similar), underscores Jason's sense of his business acumen and reinforces his sense of superiority to Earl, to Job (whom he correlates with Dilsey), and to the men who hang around the Western Union office; it also reinforces the necessary lies about Caddy's support of Quentin IV, the thousand dollars he withdrew from the hardware business for a car and his own diligence and shrewdness.

From all this we might conclude that Jason is free of much of the Compson morbidity, their thoughts displaced by his action. We should have thought so if we had been introduced to him first. Now, however, we see ways in which he resembles Benjy and Quentin. He is as self-centered and self-indulgent as they are, caught up by his memory of the past and haunted by a sense of persistent personal loss. Jason, too, has trusted to the Compson name and been betrayed in that trust. Now his central fantasy is that he is victimized by everyone. It makes a strangely acute analogue to Quentin's own fantasy of virginity and incest, for both accommodations to fact—Quentin's of the past, Jason's of the present—build on real truths. Quentin is virgin and he and Caddy did contemplate, however briefly and with whatever aimlessness, an act of incest. Jason is victimized—by Quentin IV, by the man with the red tie, and by himself. His excited movements, his constant action, his spiteful tyranny at home, his real nastiness, pettiness, and meanness are all deliberate attempts to hide his sense of humiliation and failure from his family and from himself. But his perpetual frenzy and his series of incompleted actions show us that beneath his anxiety and his acts of deliberate cruelty are self-hatred and despair, for he is more Quentin's brother than he knows.

Yet Jason is not so confused that he does not dimly recognize this himself. Where Quentin III is hounded by thoughts of Dalton Ames, Jason IV cannot help but compare himself to his older brother. References to Quentin's year at Harvard are choric. "Selling land to send him to Harvard and paying taxes to support a state University all the time that I never saw except twice at a baseball game"; "I says no I never had university advantages because at Harvard they teach you how to go for a swim at night without knowing how to swim and at Sewanee they dont even teach you what water is." This sardonic humor is grounded in hatred and runs as deep as envy, for it too is essentially as self-accusatory as Quentin's recollections of Dalton Ames have been. Jason sees his own double in Quentin: they both stand on ideals, and both are aware of their own defeats long before defeat arrives. Jason is as much concerned as Quentin with managing time (both make constant references to clocks), with worrying about personal honor and family position, and with leaning, for final judgment, on public opinion: to be governed by inner and outer senses of respectability. Jason also shares with Quentin and with Benjy an analogizing consciousness. He continually measures the present state of the Compson household against its past and sees the present as a poor parody. He sees Quentin IV as another Caddy, she who first betrayed him when her marriage broke up and Sydney Head withdrew his promise of a position in the bank for Jason. Caddy once said to Quentin, "Im bad anyway you cant help it"; significantly, Quentin IV modifies this when she tells Jason, " 'If I'm bad, it's because I had to be. You made me.' " Quentin IV's provocative behavior in dress and manner, her continual acts of promiscuity, her secret dates and her flaunting of boyfriends while walking down the alley behind Earl's hardware store are all analogous to Caddy for Jason, and all promise to him a repetition of loss, this time the real loss of financial support.

Like his father and like Quentin, Jason tries to abstract his position. Jason's own terms are financial: investments, projected income, hoarded savings, and Wall Street speculations. The philosophy he builds on such a shaky foundation—that one must deal shrewdly to stay alive, that victory belongs to the greedy and to the clever—is at once a debasement of his father's sense of decadence and a vulgar parody of Quentin's musings on morality. Yet it also parallels them, for at the center of his corruption is Jason's yearning to re-create the past. Jason bolsters himself, as his brothers do, by living in a world of self-projections. Benjy replaces his uncomfortable present with correlative moments in the past; Quentin lives the fantasy of incest and of challenging Dalton Ames successfully; Jason lives with his fantasies of his cleverness at business dealings—in his quips on the market, his high-handedness with Earl and Job, his affair with Lorraine, and his treatment of his niece. But such fantasies display meanness rather than shrewdness, disproportionate meanness rather than common sense. Lorraine's letter mocks him even more than he realizes. Dilsey's efficiency is seen by him (significantly) as a constant affront. In chasing Quentin IV through Jefferson and out the back roads onto Ab Russell's lot, Jason reifies his own frenzy, his own needless secrecy and confusion, and his summary of the chase—"Like I say it's not that I object to so much; maybe she cant help that, it's because she hasn't even got enough consideration for her own family to have any discretion"—is for us a pathetic *self*-condemnation.

This like all else Jason proclaims—and he talks largely in declarative sentences—has the hollow ring of self-defeatism. He too builds his own defenses. He reorders the world by his ideal form of logic and his imposed sense of business, of clever acquisition and the shrewd deployment of resources. His thoughts constantly turn on logical connectives, on *because, when, where,* and *if.* He maintains authority by withholding some of the facts, such as the forged checks he gives Caroline to burn and the amount of the money order Caddy sends her daughter. Where he cannot maintain this kind of absolute control, where he is at the mercy of others, he turns uncertainty itself into virtue by presuming to understand it: " 'Cotton is a speculator's crop. They fill the farmer full of hot air and get him to raise a big crop for them to whipsaw on the market, to trim the suckers with.' " He does not converse with others but talks *at* them, in incomplete sentences and in clichés. In apposition to his mother's platitudes and his Uncle Maury's written circumlocutions, he manages to retain authority by using his cruel and embittered wit; his images are not from nature, as Benjy's and Quentin's are, but from man-made objects: Quentin IV's face looks "like she had polished it with a gun rag"; her nose, puffed from crying, "looked like a porcelain insulator." All these defenses are obviously strained, for Jason is also essentially suicidal: in seeking confirmation of his own self-deprecation from the outside world, he willfully insults others; he provides for his family in a way he knows may collapse at any moment; he even risks his uncertain position at the store. " 'I dont know why you are trying to make me fire you,' " Earl tells him.

Fearfully competitive to survive, Jason also becomes, in his decline, merely contentious. He quarrels over trivialities. His notion of life as a contest replaces Benjy's notion of life as family love and Quentin's view of life as chivalric adventure. Jason is very much of the present century, yet he argues from nothing to nothing; his narrative consciousness itself, like his arguments and actions, is largely a sham, and his conclusion, that one gesture is as good as another, forces Lorraine, Quentin IV, Caroline Compson, Dilsey, and Caddy into an unfortunate and misleading equivalency. Jason's final torrent of words functions for us precisely as Benjy's last perceptions of the early fall of 1898, the day of the scene at the branch, and Quentin's kaleidoscopic jumble of facts, ideas, and delusions just before his suicide.

> When I finished my cigar and went up, the light was still on. I could see the empty keyhole, but I couldn't hear a sound. She studied quiet. Maybe she learned that in school. I told Mother goodnight and went on to my room and got the box out and counted it again. I could hear the Great American Gelding snoring away like a planing mill. I read somewhere they'd fix men that way to give them women's voices. But maybe he didn't know what they'd done to him. I dont reckon he even knew what he had been trying to do, or why Mr Burgess knocked him out with the fence picket. And if they'd just sent him on to Jackson while he was under the ether, he'd never have known the difference. But that would have been too simple for a Compson to think of. Not half complex enough. Having to wait to do it at all until he broke out and tried to run a little girl down on the street with her own father looking at him. Well, like I say they never started soon enough with their cutting, and they quit too quick. I know at least two more that needed something like that, and one of them not over a mile away, either. But then I dont reckon even that would do any good. Like I say once a bitch always a bitch. And just let me have twenty-four hours without any damn New York jew to advise me what it's going to do. I dont want to make a killing; save that to suck in the smart gamblers with. I just want an even chance to get my money back. And once I've done that they can bring all Beale Street and all bedlam in here and two of them can sleep in my bed and another one can have my place at the table too.

It is all there with Jason as with Benjy and Quentin—the inescapable past, the deep sorrow over the family's loss of pride and honor, the self-justifications and rationalizations strongly argued, the lack of self-confidence, and—most of all—the overwhelming self-pity. His day, like theirs, has been circular, and his consciousness ends too where it began: "Once a bitch always a bitch, what I say." Although Jason has been considerably more active, he has accomplished less and told us less about the Compsons and himself: he is distinctively Benjy's and Quentin's brother, but he is also the least of them.

No matter how thoroughly and painfully the events of Jason's crowded but empty day mirror his consciousness, his inner self, we cannot tell at the close of his chapter whether his debasement is the result of his character or whether his character is the result of the Compsons' own decline. Chapter 4 is meant to answer this essential question of our constitutive consciousness in its more fluid and multiple perspective on the present-day Compson household.

We have seen contradictory images of Dilsey; while Quentin's view of her as a devoted and loving surrogate mother confirms Benjy's attitude, Jason sees her as meddling, old, and inefficient, now more of a burden than a contribution to the Compsons. At last we meet her directly; and the passage surprises.

> The day dawned bleak and chill, a moving wall of grey light out of the northeast which, instead of dissolving into moisture, seemed to disintegrate into minute and venomous particles, like dust that, when Dilsey opened the door of the cabin and emerged, needled laterally into her flesh, precipitating not so much a moisture as a substance partaking of the quality of thin, not quite congealed oil. She wore a stiff black straw hat perched upon her turban, and a maroon velvet cape with a border of mangy and anonymous fur above a dress of purple silk, and she stood in the door for awhile with her myriad and sunken face lifted to the weather, and one gaunt hand flac-soled as the belly of a fish, then she moved the cape aside and examined the bosom of her gown.
>
> The gown fell gauntly from her shoulders, across her fallen breasts, then tightened upon her paunch and fell again, ballooning a little above the nether garments which she would remove layer by layer as the spring accomplished and the warm days, in colour regal and moribund. She had been a big woman once but now her skeleton rose, draped loosely in unpadded skin that tightened again upon a paunch almost dropsical, as though muscle and tissue had been courage or fortitude which the days or the years had consumed until only the indomitable skeleton was left rising like a ruin or a landmark above the somnolent and impervious guts, and above that the collapsed face that gave the impression of the bones themselves being outside the flesh, lifted into the driving day with an expression at once fatalistic and of a child's astonished disappointment, until she turned and entered the house again and closed the door.

What we are given is not so much a person as an emblem passage of the Compsons, *The Sound and the Fury* in miniature. "Regal and moribund": her weakened attempts to don the splendid garments of the past and the regal purple associated with Christ on Easter Sunday upon her own body, no longer large and splendid enough to hold them, is correlative to the condition of the family itself; hers is a collection of worn ornaments from a tired and long-ago time. She has been "consumed" by the past, "the days" such as we have been given in the first three chapters "or the years" which have witnessed her decline. She is as "fatalistic" in her expression as Benjy, Quentin, or Jason, and like them she has apparently fought against the inevitable; she too has "a child's astonished disappointment." Her one gesture in response to the "bleak and chill" world is to examine "the bosom of her gown," to look inward. But she resembles her environment in what she sees; there we find an indomitable "skeleton." Her movement, correlative to those we have seen, is circular; she steps out of her house only to return into it once again.

Beyond all this her resemblance is a resemblance to death; she has declined almost beyond recognition. In her barren landscape there are no alternatives: no postures for continuing save by willful endurance. What we have, then, is a description of doom. We are further startled to find her double, physically, in Benjy: "His skin was dead looking and hairless; dropsical too, he moved with a shambling gait." Dilsey like Benjy retains the strength of her own fortitude. " 'En who gwine eat yo messin?' " she says to Caroline, scoffing at her offer to make breakfast (for it is not, we may be sure, a genuine offer), yet she continues to do her chores "with a sort of painful and terrific slowness." Dilsey's faith, like that of Benjy and Quentin, is self-generated, trusting, and futile, working through its own persistent sense of charity against her husband Roskus's choric comment, repeated by her children, that " *'Taint no luck on this place.'* "

The cause for Dilsey's exhaustion is not far to seek. Like Benjy, Quentin, and Jason, she has persisted in her loyalty to the Compsons and to the Compson past. She is the retainer, the perennial house servant whose source of authority, compassion, and self-possession come from Christianity now ignored by Caroline, Jason, and Quentin IV, and from an antebellum tradition that has long since passed its usefulness. She too would perpetuate the myth of former Compson grandeur. As we move outward, however, we see that Dilsey is indirectly described by her surroundings. She is an older version of Luster: while he feeds Benjy with assurance and compassion, his "other hand lay on the back of the chair and upon that dead surface it moved tentatively, delicately, as if he were picking an inaudible tune out of the dead void." The cause for demise— the combination of sin, promiscuity, and death—is figured upstairs, where Quentin IV's room has "that dead and stereotyped transcience of rooms in assignation houses." The entire house, seen full and from the outside, not only reinforces our new view of Dilsey's limitations but undercuts Jason's pathetic attempts at preserving the past by sheer effort of will: it is now only a "square, paintless house with its rotting portico." If there is any large resemblance to the Compson household in chapter 4, it is (tellingly) in the description of Nigger Hollow, where "What growth there was consisted of rank weeds and the trees were mulberries and locusts and sycamores—trees that partook also of the foul desiccation which surrounded the houses." Although we may first hope for order, what we are presented with is the shabby and decadent, the consequence of a long erosion of past life into something like the prescience—even the presence—of death. Caroline Compson's reaction to the departure of Quentin IV—" 'Find the note,' she said. "Quentin left a note when he did it' "—is neither the confusion of senility nor a poor joke, but a summing up of the mood, the inner awareness and weariness of them all.

Against the weight of this signification of attrition, Faulkner juxtaposes the sound and the fury of the Easter service at Nigger Hollow. The church itself, like the landscape before it, seems unreal.

> The road rose again, to a scene like a painted backdrop. Notched into a cut of red clay crowned with oaks the road appeared to stop short off, like a cut ribbon. Beside it a weathered church lifted its crazy steeple like a

painted church, and the whole scene was as flat and without perspective as a painted cardboard set upon the ultimate edge of the flat earth, against the windy sunlight of space and April and a midmorning filled with bells.

The emphasis is on the simulation of authenticity which reflects other simulations: Dilsey's of the past, Jason's of success, Quentin's of Dalton Ames, and Benjy's of Caddy. The inside of the church mirrors the outside; it is another attempt to create a cause for celebration.

> The church had been decorated, with sparse flowers from kitchen gardens and hedgerows, and with streamers of coloured crepe paper. Above the pulpit hung a battered Christmas bell, the accordion sort that collapses. The pulpit was empty, though the choir was already in place, fanning themselves although it was not warm.

The Christmas bell at Easter—perhaps a deliberate linkage by those faithful who serve the church—strikes also at the theatricality of the event, and this is personified in the Reverend Shegog himself, a traveling show " 'fum Saint Looey.' " " 'Dat big preacher' " does not match local expectations either.

> The visitor was undersized, in a shabby alpaca coat. He had a wizened black face like a small, aged monkey. And all the while that the choir sang again and while the six children rose and sang in thin, frightened, tuneless whispers, they watched the insignificant looking man sitting dwarfed and countrified by the minister's imposing bulk, with something like consternation. They were still looking at him with consternation and unbelief when the minister rose and introduced him in rich, rolling tones whose very unction served to increase the visitor's insignificance.
> "En dey brung dat all de way fum Saint Looey," Frony whispered.

Yet what follows is the spectacle they had hoped for, the act they came to see. "He tramped steadily back and forth beneath the twisted paper and the Christmas bell, hunched, his hands clasped behind him. He was like a worn small rock whelmed by the successive waves of his voice." He moves the audience to compassion, to communal anguish, "so that when he came to rest against the reading desk, his monkey face lifted and his whole attitude that of a serene, tortured crucifix that transcended its shabbiness and insignificance and made it of no moment, a long moaning expulsion of breath rose from them, and a woman's single soprano: 'Yes, Jesus!' " The brief description of Reverend Shegog deliberately recalls the description of Dilsey which opens the chapter, and this scene isolated and given us anywhere else might be, in its pitiful meagerness transformed to joy, a moving testament to faith, a transportation into tongues. But it cannot be so here, in chapter 4 of *The Sound and the Fury*, where it is charged with the burden of all that has gone before it and all that is hinted to come; here it is almost unbearably tragic. The congregation at Nigger Hollow reflects the Compson family, working at their own hope, living on their own faith, communally and spiritually willing to themselves the belief in a glorious past and the promise of a glorious future. They, too, see life as a trial which anticipates a resurrection after death. Although Quentin III sees spilled blood as useless when cleaning up after his fight with Gerald Bland while the Nigger Hollow congregation sees the blood of the Lamb, the blood of possibility, both views are self-fulfilling prophecies. Just as the Compsons re-form life to their own expectations, so the worshipers at Nigger Hollow see what they came to see, find what they planned to find. So the power of Shegog's Word—in a novel so concerned with the power of words—does not, finally, convert anyone previously unconverted. Everyone and everything return to what they were before. Frony leaves church still worried about their appearance, their respectability, as Caroline Compson might worry (" 'Whyn't you quit dat, mammy?' . . . Wid all des people lookin. We be passin white folks soon.' "); Dilsey has confirmed what she knew with her sacred sense of time and history (" 'He seed de power en de glory' . . . 'I've seed de first en de last' "); and Benjy, who has "sat, rapt in his sweet blue gaze" throughout the service, is still actively engaged in his separate and interior world.

Juxtaposed to this climatic scene is Jason's bloody fight with the old circus hand, sound and fury without *any* religious signification. It is no accident and no sly parody, but the secular parallel to what goes on in Nigger Hollow. Jason enters Mottstown with the reputation worthy of a Shegog, "his file of soldiers with the manacled sheriff in the rear, dragging Omnipotence down from His throne, if necessary." His fight is the good fight, too, for he defends (if only ironically, interested as he is in appearances) the pride and honor and decency—the moral uprightness—of his family line. But the tinsel trappings of the church have no parallel in a circus tent; he finds only unloaded boxcars as earlier he had found Quentin IV's room empty. The joy at the church service is countered and seriously modified in his total frustration, his overwhelming despair. He has from the outset of his day been witness to the most serious progressive loss of all, for no one has understood or befriended him—not his mother or Dilsey, whose income is gone; not the sheriff, who exposes at last his own legal and economic corruption; and not the old man at the circus, who, with his butcher knife, would disclose Jason's essential ineffectualness. The smell of gasoline which overcomes him is analogous to the smell of trees for Benjy and the smell of honeysuckle for Quentin, but this time there is no love or salvation in the most mundane (and mechanically produced) sensation. " 'What were you trying to do?' " asks a man who intervenes in his behalf, a stranger. " 'Commit suicide?' "

Dilsey herself, returned to the Compson household, is refreshed, but as for Jason there is no permanent relief for her among the Compsons. Christ may have risen, but he has not harrowed Jefferson on his way. In her routine round of resumed duties—the meal; Caroline's Bible and hot-water bottle; the supervision of Luster, who is twanging on the saw; and

Benjy, who is moaning—she lives her own diminished present, her kitchen as limited an environment as Quentin's private hell and Quentin IV's upper room. In this mundane and repetitive existence, her activities are caught up in the same clop-clop rhythm as Queenie's, soon to be harnessed and taken to the graveyard. Both echo the inherent lines of the title: "Tomorrow and tomorrow and tomorrow" creeping in its petty, repetitive, unrelieved pace. This becomes the final irony for the Reverend Shegog's sermon, and for the insistent but futile dreams, sacred and secular, that barely sustain the still-living Compsons.

The confusion of names in *The Sound and the Fury*—the Quentins, Jasons, Maurys—suggests the essential unity of the family's vision: its agreement on purpose, its strident devotion to a reliance on appearances, and its compulsive and obsessive need to look inward and backward, its steady myopia. Benjy's castration like his idiocy seem outer images for them all: on Holy Saturday they have only the idiot's birthday to celebrate, and a circus is in town; on Easter Sunday Quentin IV has escaped her tomb, but the novel implies that she will only follow Caddy's path into an inevitable promiscuity and despair of her own (as well as her world's) making. Dilsey's spiritual and spirited opposition to the selfish, secular Jason remains futile. There is no resurrection here, no reconciliation; there is only resignation.

Each chapter of the novel circles around and back into itself; each ends in its beginning, like the narrative consciousness in *Light in August*, or the brooding tale of Conrad's Marlow on a barge at Gravesend. Despite the unique perspective and mental geography of each of the Compsons, we are given an essential unity in the emptiness of their present lives, in the lost vitality of their visions, and in the hopelessness of their dreams. Even the novel ends, as it began, with Benjy, for everyone comes, at last, to meet him on his own terms. They are the terms that correlate Damuddy, his father, Quentin, and Caddy, the terms of loss and of death. In a short time we find him "squatting before a small mound of earth. At either end of it an empty bottle of blue glass that once contained posion was fixed in the ground. In one was a withered stalk of jimson weed." This is a memorial celebration to all that he holds dear—to his family now gone, to his childhood, to the past generally. His Sunday ride to the larger graveyard, the family and community memorial to the past, is also just such a tribute. His insistence on the primacy of the past—of *their* past—is maintained even when Luster disrupts Benjy's careful construction of eternal time by driving old Queenie clockwise around the town square. Powerfully, fatefully we learn with Benjy that the establishment of peace and eternity by limited and mundane routine—Dilsey's means of survival too—is harrowingly, tragically vulnerable. Jason races out to confirm Benjy's patterning of events, to preserve appearances and secure the preservation of the Compsons. So they pass backward now, physically as well as mentally and spiritually, back over the ground they have just covered. Above them and behind, the Confederate soldier looks out, facing south, facing in the direction of the Compson home. Nothing has changed—"Ben's fist and his eyes were empty and blue and serene again as cornice and façade flowed smoothly once more from left to right; post and tree, window and doorway, and signboard, each in its ordered place"—except for one thing. Benjy is holding a flower, significantly a narcissus and significantly one that is broken. It has been straightened and mended, however, with twigs and a bit of string, by the black servant. Benjy does not see that. But we do.

The circle around the courthouse is a reduced replica of the circularity of the largest hopes and fantasies of *The Sound and the Fury*. It is fitting that, a quarter century later in the 1945 Appendix to this novel, the larger chronology of the Compsons begins with the heroism of Andrew Jackson ("who set the wellbeing of the nation above the White House and the health of his new political party above either and above them all set not his wife's honor but the principle that honor must be defended whether it was or not because defended it was whether or not"), and the line ends with Benjy's dishonorable incarceration in the state asylum at Jackson, Mississippi. From Jackson to Jackson; from insistence on abstract honor and glory to concrete idiocy; from dust unto dust. *The Sound and the Fury* is life itself; it draws its final terms beyond what the Compsons find at either end. In that sense, our constitutive consciousness alone draws its most comprehensive circle and we are invited, in this last analysis, to include ourselves.

Narration as Creative Act: The Role of Quentin Compson in *Absalom, Absalom!*

Thomas Daniel Young*

Many commentators have pointed out that Faulkner devoted a great deal of time—to some even a disproportionate amount—to the Judith-Henry-Charles love triangle in a story that is ostensibly about the rise and fall of Thomas Sutpen. Despite the fact, too, that Faulkner exerts considerable artistic energy in pointing out that Shreve McCannon and Quentin are both unreliable narrators, their version is usually considered the reliable one—not only of what Thomas Sutpen and his family did (and even the actions of some persons who might not have belonged to the family) but *why* they did what they did. The credibility of Shreve and Quentin to most readers is not diminished by Quentin's deep emotional involvement in the tale he is telling or by Shreve's insatiable desire to make every detail of the story he creates (with Quentin's urging) fit neatly into a preconceived pattern. This desire for artistic unity is so great that Shreve ignores any facts that he considers unnecessary to his sense of structure, and, as Brooks and others have pointed out, he creates new ones as he thinks they are needed. Even Faulkner's insistence that "nobody saw the truth intact"[1] has not affected the view of many critics. They still insist that the conclusions drawn by Quentin and Shreve are more nearly correct than are those of the other narrators. Faulkner even indicates, in a latter to Malcolm Cowley, that it is Quentin's story, not his, that Quentin is responsible for—whatever symbolic overtones the story may contain. Another statement by Faulkner, however, has not been ignored. When the reader has read all the different versions of what happened in *Absalom, Absalom!*, Faulkner says, he should offer his own view. With this encouragement, perhaps, this work of art, one of the most evocative and imaginatively designed novel ever written in America, has also become one of the most written about. Faulkner even goes on to say that the reader's view—"this fourteenth image" of the blackbird—might be the "truth."

The reading I offer of this much interpreted novel—feeling a little

*Reprinted, with permission, from *Faulkner: Modernism, and Film: Faulkner and Yoknapatawpha 1978*, ed. Evans Harrington and Ann J. Abadie (Jackson: University Press of Mississippi, 1979), pp. 82–102.

like Fra Lippo Lippi from Browning's poem as I do so—is based on the following hypotheses: (1) that the Quentin Compson who appears as character and narrator in *Absalom, Absalom!* is the same youth who had the disturbing and destroying experiences related in *The Sound and the Fury,* and (2) that the narrative he creates in *Absalom, Absalom!* is vastly influenced by the impact these experiences had on him. Given the opportunity and the motivation of Mr. Compson's letter announcing Rosa Coldfield's death, he and Shreve attempt to supply missing details of the Sutpen legend and to furnish plausible motivations for some of the improbable actions of the participants in that story. Quentin is the principal agent, therefore, in the creation of a story that gives temporary relief to powerful emotional disturbances that will ultimately destroy him. The story Quentin creates assuages momentarily the deep feelings of frustration and despair produced by his unmanly and ineffectual behavior before Dalton Ames, a seducer of Quentin's sister Caddy. The story he and Shreve piece together out of the few facts Quentin has learned from his father and Rosa Coldfield help Quentin to accept momentarily the incestuous love he suspects he feels for Caddy. As narrator of much of the action of *Absalom, Absalom!,* Quentin creates a story in which he can participate vicariously as both brother-seducer and brother-avenger.

In August, 1909, Quentin Compson discovers that his sister Caddy is having an affair with Dalton Ames, a young construction worker who has recently moved with his company into Jefferson. (It was not the first time Quentin had known or suspected that Caddy was giving herself to men, and each incident as it occurred had left Quentin more confused, less certain of exactly how he felt toward Caddy.) His confusion is confounded by the fact that he can neither control her behavior nor punish those who participate with Caddy in her improper acts. Once he throws coal at the pimply faced boy who is necking with Caddy among the trees outside their front door. On another afternoon Caddy comes home and as soon as Benjy, her younger, idiot brother, sees her (or smells her), he begins "pulling at her dress," and they go in the house, with him yelling at her and pushing her up the stairs to the bathroom door. There he stops her and backs her against the door, putting his arm across her face, "yelling and trying to shove her into the bathroom" (SF85).[2] By making her scrub with soap, Benjy is trying to remove from her the scent she has applied to attract the boys. Quentin says later that Benjy can smell death, that he knew by how Caddy smelled exactly when Caddy committed her first sex act. On that evening soap will not remove the scent, and when Caddy comes into the kitchen where T. P. is feeding Benjy, Benjy begins to howl. Caddy rushes out of the house; Quentin follows her down to the branch where she lies with "her head on the sand spit the water flowing about her hips there was a little more light in the water her shirt half saturated flopped along her flanks" (SF186). When Caddy sees Quentin standing on the bank, she asks if Benjy is still crying. Quentin says he is and tells her to get out of the water, but she does not move. He tells her again and she comes out on the bank, and he asks her if she loves the man to whom she has given herself. She takes his hand and puts it on her breast, under which he can feel her heart thudding. She answers "No," and he asks if *he* made her do it, but before she can answer, Quentin promises to kill the boy before Mr. Compson can find out about it. Then, he says, they will take the money with which he is supposed to pay his Harvard tuition and run away together. Still lying on her back, she places his hand on her throat and says "Poor Quentin. . . . You've never done that, have you?" (SF188). She lies there with his head against her chest, and he asks if she remembers the day she muddied her drawers in the branch when their grandmother died. (This crucial scene will be examined in some detail later.) She tells him good night and asks him to meet her later at the branch, saying now she must meet someone. He sees her and some man with their heads close together. She tells Quentin to go on home, but he says he is going to take a walk. He goes close enough to town to see the courthouse clock and circles back by the Compson house and notes as he passes that the light is out in Benjy's room. He goes back to the branch and lies on the bank with his face close to the ground so he cannot smell the honeysuckle. After a while Caddy comes back from her date and offers herself to him twice. He tells her to shut up and asks her, "do you love him now?" She can only answer, "I don't know," and urges him not to cry because, she says, "I'm bad and you can't help it."

But Quentin has found out what he wants to know. No longer is the source of his distress a nameless, faceless quality whom he knows only as man. He is a distinct, separate, human creature, an individualized man named Dalton Ames. For two or three days Quentin seeks out Dalton before seeing him going into the barbershop, where he confronts him. But Dalton says they can't talk there and promises to meet Quentin at one o'clock on the bridge outside of town. When they meet at the barbershop, Dalton's only concern seems to be for Caddy, asking two or three times: "Is she all right? Does she need me for anything?" Quentin does not respond but assures him he will meet him at the bridge at one o'clock.

As one would expect from a brother who loves his sister, Quentin is determined to defend her honor in the respected tradition of the culture to which he belongs. He tells T. P. to saddle Prince and have him at the side door, but when Caddy keeps asking him where he is going he decides to walk. He leaves the house walking slowly down the drive, but he begins to run as soon as he thinks he is out of sight. As he approaches the bridge, he sees Dalton leaning on the rail with a piece of bark in his hand, from which he is breaking pieces and dropping them into the water. Quentin comes up to him and says, "I came to tell you to leave town." Dalton doesn't seem to hear him and continues to drop the pieces of bark into the water and watch them float downstream. Quentin repeats his ultimatum and Dalton asks quietly, "Did she send you to me?" Quentin responds that nobody sent him, not her, not even his father; "I'll give you to sundown to leave town." Dalton lays the bark on the railing and with three swift motions, rolls a cigarette, lights it, and flicks the match over the rail. Again he speaks quietly: "What if I don't leave town?"

"I'll kill you," Quentin responds; "don't think just because I look like a kid to you." Quentin's hands begin to shake on the rail and he is afraid to try to hide them for fear Dalton will see how excited he is. Then Dalton asks him his name, saying "Benjy's the natural isn't he?" Again Quentin says, "I'll give you until sundown." Then Dalton asks him not to take it so hard, that if it had not been him "it would have been someone else." To Quentin's question "Did you ever have a sister did you?" Dalton responds, "No but they're all bitches." Quentin can no longer control himself and strikes out at Dalton: "I hit him my open hand beat the impulse to shut it to his face his hand moved as fast as mine the cigarette went over the rail I swung with the other hand he caught it too before the cigarette reached the water he held both my wrists in the same hand his other hand flicked to his armpit under his coat behind him the sun slanted and a bird singing somewhere beyond the sun we looked at one another while the bird singing he turned my hand loose" (SF199). Taking the bark from the rail, Dalton tosses it into the water and lets it float almost out of sight. Without aiming the pistol he hits the large piece of bark, and then two smaller ones, no larger than a silver dollar. He hands the pistol to Quentin saying, "You'll need it from what you said I'm giving you this one because you've seen what it will do." "Again," Quentin remembers, "I hit him I was still trying to hit him long after he was holding my wrists but I still tried then it was like I was looking at him through a piece of coloured glass I could hear my blood and then I could see the sky again and branches against it and the sun slanting through them and he holding me on my feet." Quentin doesn't realize immediately what is happening to him—he does not know he has fainted—so he asks Dalton if he had hit him. Dalton lies and answers, "Yes how do you feel?" Then he offers Quentin his horse to get back home on. Dalton leaves and Quentin, utterly crushed, leans against a tree, his mind completely filled with one emasculating thought: "I . . . just passed out like a girl." When Caddy comes up, having heard the shots and thinking Dalton might have killed Quentin, she says she has told Dalton never to speak to her again. Quentin asks her if she loves him, and she takes his hand and puts it against her throat and when he says, at her request, "Dalton Ames," he feels the blood surging "in strong accelerating beats."

Soon after this confrontation with Dalton Ames, Quentin tells his father that he has committed incest with Caddy. But Mr. Compson knows his son, or thinks he does, and recognizes Quentin's terrible confession for the lie it is. He tells Quentin he should not be upset over his sister's promiscuity, that only a man would put much value on a woman's chastity. What Quentin should do, he remembers Mr. Compson's saying, is to leave early and take a month's vacation in Maine before the fall term at Harvard begins. We know, however, that Quentin does not take his father's advice; instead he spends September, 1909, in Jefferson, because there on one afternoon and evening he hears from his father and Miss Rosa Coldfield, the old maid daughter of a deceased local merchant, the details of the most fascinating and bewildering tale that legend-rich Jefferson can boast of. Like all the other residents of the town, Quentin is aware of the legend of Thomas Sutpen and his family, but in these conversations in September, 1909, with Rosa Coldfield, Sutpen's sister-in-law, and Mr. Compson, whose father was Sutpen's best friend in Jefferson, Quentin must have had his memory jogged; surely he learned some new details.

Miss Coldfield tells Quentin her view of the Sutpen legend because she thinks he might become a literary man and reveal the facts of this tragic story to the world. What she doesn't know is that four months later in a dormitory room at Harvard, Quentin and his roommate will "create" a harrowing tale of revenge, incest, miscegenation, and fratricide out of the few details he garners from Rosa and Mr. Compson. She has concluded, she insists to Quentin that hot summer afternoon, that someone besides Clytie and the idiot Jim Bond, the grandson of Judith Sutpen's fiancé, Charles Bon, might be out at the ruins of Sutpen's Hundred, and she wants Quentin to go with her to investigate. The truth is that Miss Rosa has little to tell Quentin that is not already common knowledge around town. Thomas Sutpen came out of nowhere, without warning, brought with him a band of strange Negroes, and built the largest plantation in the county on land he had acquired from some Indians. When the plantation was barely completed he married Ellen Coldfield, Rosa's older sister, upon whom he begat a son and a daughter. When Judith became engaged to Charles Bon, a law student from the university, Sutpen for no apparent reason forbade the marriage. Then the war came and Thomas, his son Henry, and Charles Bon went off to serve in the Confederate army.

Rosa can never understand, she tells Quentin, why her father allowed Ellen to marry Sutpen, who to her is an ogre; and his children, her niece and nephew, are far from normal. Just before Ellen dies, soon after the war began, Rosa promises her that she will care for her niece, although the niece is four years her senior. A year later, at her father's death, she moves out to the Sutpen place. After the war when Sutpen returns to the ruined plantation—the son Henry has already killed his sister's fiancé at the front gate—Rosa agrees to marry him but leaves abruptly one evening after he has made an unspeakable proposition to her. She returns to her little house in Jefferson, dons black, and lives the next forty-three years on the charity of her neighbors.

It is extremely doubtful, as I have said, that Quentin learns any new facts from Miss Rosa's version of the Sutpens. Most of the details of the legend that she knows—although she is the only narrator in the novel who had a personal acquaintance with Sutpen—must have been common knowledge around Jefferson. But Quentin must have been impressed with the highly subjective nature of Miss Rosa's account. She takes a few simple facts and creates a legend that gives some solace to the devastating wound she feels. Her only possible explanation for the insult Sutpen had given her—he says let's mate and if the issue is male, "I'll marry you"—is that he was a demon, a monster, a devil that rose out of the ground. She shapes the facts to make them meet her own emotional needs, a device Quentin will use later in his own behalf.

Later the same evening, while Quentin is waiting until it is time for him and Miss Rosa to go out to the old Sutpen place, Quentin hears other facts about Sutpen, some which Mr. Compson had learned from his father. Most of these facts are also well-known and need not be rehearsed in detail here. Because he had been turned away from the front door of a Virginia plantation when he was thirteen or fourteen, Sutpen formulated a design. This "design" required that he have his own plantation, complete with manor house, servants, slaves, family, and respectability. First he went to the West Indies, where because of an act of personal valor and a long period of recuperation he came to know and was allowed to marry the daughter of the owner of the sugar plantation he was managing. When the first child was born, it became apparent to Sutpen (for some reason never fully explained in the novel) that this woman, through no fault of her own, could never fit into his "design." Consequently he divorced her, giving her far more than a fair share of their common property, and left. Then in June, 1833, he showed up in Jefferson, remained a few days and disappeared, to return a short time later with a wagon filled with wild Negroes (two of whom were female) and a French architect. Out on the ten square miles he had acquired from Ikkemotubbe, Sutpen, his Negroes, and the French architect set about building the largest house in the county. After the house was built, though it had no windows, doors, or furniture, Sutpen began to invite citizens of the town to come out to drink and hunt or to watch the fights he had arranged between the Negroes or between himself and one of the Negroes. Finally after the house had stood in its unfinished state for three years, Sutpen appeared in Jefferson again, this time with four wagons filled with mahogany, crystal, rugs, and chandeliers. Again, nobody was ever to know where the goods had come from. Immediately after the house was completed, he acquired the last piece of property he needed to be a respectable planter. He married the daughter of a poor but honest and devout small merchant of the town. Then, almost as if he were following his preconceived notion of the perfect plan, Sutpen had the son, to inherit and carry along the family name, and the daughter, to grace his household, to help her mother entertain, and in due time to allow him to enjoy the love and companionship of grandchildren.

His would seem the ideal family, and one which was the result of his own tenacious desire to mold his personal affairs exactly as he would have them be. In 1857 Henry, the son, enrolled at the University of Mississippi, and his second Christmas there he brought a friend, Charles Bon, home to spend the holidays; Bon was a sophisticated young man from New Orleans, several years older than Henry, and a man of mystery, worldy elegant, apparently wealthy, with an ease of manners and a swaggering gallant air completely out of keeping with the atmosphere of a small provincial university less than ten years old. (Mr. Compson wondered how Bon got there in the first place.) When Henry brought Bon home again for a few days at the beginning of the summer of 1859, any casual observer could see that he was attempting to model himself after Charles in every respect, and immediately after the two boys left, Ellen Sutpen announced her daughter's engagement to Charles. Soon after Charles departed for New Orleans, Thomas Sutpen followed him.

The next Christmas Henry brought Charles home with him again, but this time Henry and his father had a quarrel and both boys rode away. Soon thereafter war was declared, Thomas Sutpen became second in command of the regiment Colonel Sartoris raised in Jefferson, and Henry and Charles joined a company formed at the university.

Mr. Compson speculates on what Henry found, when he accompanied Charles to New Orleans, that disturbed him so deeply. "It would not have been the mistress," Mr. Compson says, "or even the child, nor even the Negro mistress or even less the child because . . . Henry and Judith had grown up with a Negro half-sister of their own. . . . No it would be the ceremony, a ceremony entered into, to be sure, with a Negro, yet a ceremony" (AA117).[3] Mr. Compson thinks that Henry waited for Bon to denounce the woman and dissolve the marriage, that Henry objected not to bigamy but to the fact that Bon was making Judith a part of a harem.

As Mr. Compson recalls the facts of the war experience, Bon was commissioned shortly after the war began but Henry remained a private. At Pittsburg Landing Charles was wounded and Henry carried him back to safety. For four years, Mr. Compson insists, Henry gave Charles the opportunity to renounce the New Orleans mistress and child or, as Mr. Compson expresses Charles's thoughts, "For four years now I have given chance the opportunity to renounce for me but it seems that I am doomed to live, that she and I are both doomed to live" (AA119). Both Henry and Charles thought that one or both of them would be killed, Mr. Compson says, thus making unnecessary a decision from either (Bon's is, will he marry a woman who he thinks to be his half-sister and Henry's is, will he kill his own brother to keep the marriage from occurring?). When the war ended, both men were still alive, and the decision was still not made. As Mr. Compson describes the two men riding up to the gate of the Sutpen house, it seems to Quentin that he can almost see them: "facing one another at the gate. Inside the gate what was once a park now spread unkempt, in shaggy desolation, with an air dreamy, remote, and aghast

. . . up to a huge house where a young girl waited in a wedding dress made from stolen scraps. . . . They faced one another on the two gaunt horses, two men, young not yet in the world . . . with unkempt hair and faces gaunt and weathered." Quentin imagines Henry saying: "Don't you pass the shadow of this post"; and Charles replying: "I am going to pass it, Henry" (AA132). Afterwards, Wash Jones rode up to Miss Rosa's door and yelled until she opened it and then announced in the same tone: "Henry has done shot down that durn French fellow. Kilt him dead as a beef."

A week after Judith buried Bon she brought to Quentin's grandmother a letter which she said she had received from Bon just before he returned from the war. Although the letter was not addressed to Judith and was not signed by Bon—Ellen Schoenberg argues it was probably intended for the mistress in New Orleans—Mr. Compson believes that this letter, unlike the flowery formal effusions sent from Oxford before the war, proves that Bon loved Judith. Mr. Compson is convinced that Henry saw the letter, and its sincere tone was all the proof he needed to persuade him that Bon was going through with the wedding.

These are the essential facts Quentin has of the Sutpen story when he accompanies Rosa Coldfield out to the old decayed mansion on that September evening of 1909. On their journey out that evening Miss Rosa says that when she learned that Henry had killed Charles, she went immediately to the Sutpen place. She brushed past Clytie (Judith's black half-sister) and found Judith standing in the door holding in her hand a photograph that she had given Bon. (She also says that she never saw Bon alive.) Seven months later Sutpen returned and three months after his return, he and Rosa were engaged. Then one day there was the "death of hope and love, of pride and principle, the death of everything" (AA168). Sutpen returned to the house and spoke the "outrageous words exactly as if he were consulting with Jones . . . about a bitch dog or cow or mare." As Shreve will summarize Sutpen's conversation later: "He suggested that they breed together for test and sample and if it was a boy they would marry." As already indicated, after this conversation Miss Rosa returned to Jefferson, not to see Sutpen's Hundred again for more than forty years. Nearly sixty at the time Rosa left, Sutpen made one last desperate effort to save his design. He seduced Wash Jones's granddaughter, but when she bore him a girl he insulted her—saying to the girl that if she were a mare he could give her a warm stall in the barn. Jones killed Sutpen, his grandchild, and her baby, and was later killed by the sheriff's posse.

These final details of Sutpen's career—the authorial presence breaks his customary pattern of not intruding into his narrative to tell us that most of Rosa's remarks on Sutpen are highly subjective—are lost on Quentin because he can't get beyond "that door" behind which Bon lay. He imagines Henry "with his shaggy bayonet-trimmed hair, his gaunt worn unshaven face, his patched and faded gray tunic, the pistol still hanging against his flank: the two of them, brother and sister curiously alike as if the difference in sex had merely sharpened the common blood to a terrific, and almost unbearable similarity" (AA172). Always active, Quentin's fertile imagination allows him to hear Henry's remark to his sister: "You cannot marry him now because I've killed him."

We have few facts relating the manner in which Quentin spent his time at Harvard during the fall of 1909. Indeed we next see him on a railway siding in Virginia on his way home for Christmas. He gives an old Negro a quarter as a Christmas gift and tells him he'll be back that way "two days after New Years" (SF107). We don't even get the details of Quentin's and Miss Rosa's visit to Sutpen's Hundred until January, 1910, when Shreve and Quentin are discussing a letter from Mr. Compson, in which he relates that Miss Rosa was buried on January 10, after having lain in a coma for two weeks. Knowing Quentin's highly emotional state, however, we can well imagine that during that fall he might have done considerable brooding over what happened to the Sutpen family and why. In fact some of the highly suggestive conclusions he urges on Shreve regarding the strange behavior of the Sutpens suggest that by January, 1910, he has already arrived at solutions to some of that family's problems that are considerably different from those which Mr. Compson had offered. A young man who is utterly confused about his feelings toward his own sister must have found Mr. Compson's speculations about the Bon-Judith-Henry triangle very provocative indeed. For example there is Mr. Compson's attempt to understand the precise nature of the Judith-Bon relationship: "You see? there they are: this girl . . . who sees a man for an average of one hour a day for twelve days during his life and that over a period of a year and a half, yet is bent on marrying him to the extent of forcing her brother to the last resort of homicide" (AA99). Mr. Compson can no more understand this relationship than Quentin can those Caddy had with Dalton Ames and her other lovers. "Did you love them?" Quentin asked her. "When they touched me," she replied, "I died." Mr. Compson can only offer an explanation which he himself would not accept from Quentin. He would not believe Quentin had had an incestuous affair with Caddy; yet he says, "It was Henry who seduced Judith, not Bon." We know, of course, that Mr. Compson is not speaking literally in his reference to Judith and Henry, but in his highly distraught emotional state Quentin cannot be expected to make the necessary figurative leap. Later, as we know, he does confuse Gerald Bland, an acquaintance at Harvard, and Dalton Ames, Caddy's lover.

Mr. Compson's comments about Judith and Henry sound remarkably similar to those he makes in his discussion with Quentin regarding Caddy's promiscuity. To Quentin, referring to Caddy, he says: "it was men invented virginity . . . . women are so delicate so mysterious. . . . Delicate equilibrium of periodical filth between two moons balanced . . . . People . . . cannot do anything very dreadful at all they cannot even remember tomorrow what seemed dreadful today" (SF96). Referring to Henry's attitude toward Judith, he says: Henry may have known "that his fierce provincial's pride in his sister's virginity was a false quality which must incorporate in itself an inability to endure in order to be precious, to exist, and so much depend upon its loss, absence, to have existed at all. In fact, perhaps this is the pure and perfect incest: the brother realizing that the sister's virginity must be destroyed in order to have existed at all, taking that virginity in the person of the brother-in-law, the man he would be if he could become, metamorphose into, the lover, the husband" (AA96).

Quentin and Shreve are motivated by Mr. Compson's letter announcing Rosa's death to attempt to flesh out the skeleton of the Sutpen legend that they know. Shreve is having to do the job with less than Quentin's complete participation because Quentin still cannot pass the door where Judith was standing when Henry came to tell her that he had killed Charles Bon. His mind is filled with an image of "the brother and sister slashing at each other with twelve or fourteen words and most of these the same words repeated two or three times so that when you boiled it down they did it with eight or ten." Quentin's fatally wounded psyche is totally involved in the story of the Sutpen children because it includes both parts of his divided self. In his confused emotional state—one in which he cannot define exactly his feelings toward his sister Caddy—he is attracted to Charles Bon, the brother-seducer. And living always with the knowledge of his shameful behavior when he attempted to defend the family's honor by confronting Dalton Ames on the bridge, he must find much to admire in Henry Sutpen, the brother-avenger. In his attempt to bring his sister's seducer to justice, Quentin has been completely humiliated. First Dalton Ames intercepted the blows which Quentin had aimed at his chin—he had held both of Quentin's hands in one of his—then Quentin fainted, and Dalton had lied to him and Caddy, saying he had struck Quentin, in order to help Quentin save face. Surely Quentin's interest in the Sutpen family is partially motivated by his subconscious search for self-respect.

In this mood, then, Quentin tells Shreve on that cold January night in Cambridge, Massachusetts, of his visit to the Sutpen home the previous September and of how he had met Henry Sutpen, who had come home to die. Shreve and Quentin consider Mr. Compson's account of Miss Rosa's visit to the old plantation with an ambulance to bring Henry into town for medical attention. They are aware, too, that Clytie has mistaken the purpose of this visit, thinking the sheriff is coming for Henry; therefore she has set fire to the decayed old house, she and Henry perishing in the flames. The only thing left, then, of Sutpen's design is an idiot black boy "to lurk around those ashes and those four gutted chimneys and howl" until someone comes and drives him away.

Together Shreve and Quentin—Faulkner says it might have been either of them speaking and was in a sense both—try to supply some of the missing details in the Sutpen story and to give rational explanations for some of the actions that seem on the surface inexplicable. Quentin's interest in the Judith-Charles-Henry triangle has already been referred to and Shreve apparently would like to tie up some of those loose ends of a fabulous legend that could have occurred only in that faraway Southland that never existed anywhere at anytime except in his imagination. His view of art is that of the classicist; he is seeking artistic unity, to make all of the details fit a preconceived pattern. Among the many missing details that he and Quentin supply through pure speculation are: that Sutpen told Henry that Charles was his brother but that Charles was not aware of this fact; that there was a lawyer in New Orleans maneuvering events so that Charles went to school at the University of Mississippi in order to meet Henry and through him, Sutpen; that the lawyer wrote Henry, Henry showed the letter to Bon, and Bon guessed that they were brothers; that Charles merely wanted a hint of recognition from his father; that Henry wrestled with the problem of incest and asked Bon "must you marry our sister?"; that Sutpen told Henry that Charles Bon's mother was part Negro.

This last point is a very important one. In spite of the arguments by Olga Vickery, Cleanth Brooks, and others, there is nowhere in the novel convincing evidence that Bon was part Negro. As Ellen Shoenberg has suggested, the conviction that Charles Bon is part Negro is based on the belief that if this supposition were true it would logically explain why Sutpen put aside his first wife. A southern white man wanting to be an aristocratic planter in the 1830s would know that a woman of mixed blood could not possibly fit into his "design." But as reasonable as this explanation for Sutpen's action is, the truth of the matter is that this supposition usually accepted as truth was created in Quentin's imagination. If indeed it is a fact, it is one that only Quentin knows, and there is no place he could have learned it—not from his father because his father does not know it; not from his grandfather because there is no evidence that Quentin ever spoke to his grandfather about the Sutpen family; not from Henry Sutpen because, despite Cleanth Brooks's insistence, it is highly unlikely that Quentin's one brief meeting with Henry occurred under conditions that would have made the passing of such information possible. One can only conclude that this bit of crucial information came from the disturbed imagination of Quentin Compson, and the inevitable question, therefore, is why?

In his confused state—one, as I have already said, in which he is both Charles Bon and Henry Sutpen—he can well understand the Charles Bon side of his personality. Unable to understand his own feeling toward his sister—his apparent impotence will not allow him to know for certain the nature of his love for Caddy—he can easily entertain the possibility that one might want to marry his own sister. But why would he kill a brother whom he loves more than anyone else in the world, except to protect the honor of this beloved sister?

To put this matter in proper perspective, one should look again at the famous branch scene of *The Sound and the Fury*. In this, perhaps the central episode in the novel, Caddy wet her dress playing in the branch, and Versh, a young Negro boy a few years older than Caddy, says, "Your mommer going to whip you for getting your dress wet." Caddy replies, "She's not going to do any such thing." And in the ensuing argument, she says she will pull her dress off and let it dry. Quentin tells her she had better not; "You just take your dress off," he warns her. Caddy makes Versh unbutton the dress and she draws it over her head and throws it on the bank to dry, leaving her wearing only her "bodice and drawers." Quentin is so infuriated that Caddy has exposed her body to Versh, a black man, that he "slapped her and she fell down in the water."

Shreve is closer than he knows to expressing Quentin's deepest concerns, therefore, when he says that maybe one day in the spring following the Christmas visit Bon merely concluded, "All right I want to go to bed with a girl who might be my sister." After the four years in the war have settled nothing, Bon must have decided, Shreve and Quentin conclude, definitely to go back and marry Judith. In a scene much like that with Dalton Ames at the bridge—and one created by Quentin's disturbed imagination—Charles hands Henry a pistol and tells him to shoot him if he wishes to prevent the wedding. In Quentin's version Henry is as inept as he was himself at the bridge; Henry's hand trembles as he looks at the pistol: "You are my brother," he says. "No, I'm not," Bon responds, "I'm the nigger that's going to sleep with your sister. Unless you stop me." This remarks arouses Henry. In terms of Quentin's own psychic dilemma, the part of him that is the brother-seducer (Charles Bon) is opposed by the part that is the brother-avenger (Henry Sutpen). In the tale he is concocting, Quentin is able at one stroke to chastise the sister who would expose herself to a black man and to bring to justice the man who would despoil that sister. This remark—"I'm the nigger that's going to sleep with your sister"—provokes immediate action: The boys propose that Henry grabs the pistol from Bon, flings it away, grabs Bon by the shoulder and says, "You shall not! You shall not! Do you hear me?" Bon responds, "You will have to stop me Henry"; and they begin the long ride back to Sutpen's Hundred. When they arrive at the gate and Charles still has not changed his mind, Quentin imagines Henry, with his pistol lying unaimed across his saddle bow, saying: *"Don't you pass the shadow of this post."* (Quentin's ultimatum to Dalton Ames: "Be out of town before sundown.") When Bon passes the shadow, Henry, as Wash Jones says, shoots him "dead as a beef." Then the boy who cannot bear to see his sister strip before their black companion imagines Henry rushing up to his sister, who is threatened with ravishment by a Negro, yelling, "You can't marry him now because I killed him!"

To comprehend the harrowing tale Quentin and Shreve have created out of the sparse set of facts at their disposal, one must always be mindful of Shreve's lack of knowledge of the South. To him it is a not-quite-real kind of place, one in which the fantastic, Gothic legend he and Quentin have concocted could have and probably did occur. But for Quentin the tale is of another quality and serves a different function. A highly disturbed, psychotic personality desperately seeking a solution to the psychic dilemma that threatens to strangle him, he is, I repeat, mentally ill, and like all persons similarly affected, he cannot escape his own set of mental facts. Quentin can relate to Henry Sutpen, however, because Henry is able to avenge a great wrong that threatens his sister. We must realize, however, that the Henry Sutpen of fact, the one who lived near Jefferson and attended the University of Mississippi, is not the Henry Sutpen that Quentin has created. The real Henry Sutpen undoubtedly was able to place in proper perspective and accept, therefore, an escalating series of Old South taboos: bigamy, bigotry, miscegenation, and maybe even incest. He is sane, if somewhat naïve, and is consequently intensely affected by the attitudes of his society. Quentin, on the other hand, is deeply disturbed and therefore is not rational. Because of the ambiguous nature of his own feeling toward Caddy, he can understand why a man might have erotic desires for his own sister. In his disturbed state, however, he associates promiscuity with miscegenation, which to many in the Old South was promiscuity carried to its most horrible extreme. To fulfill his deepest need, therefore, Quentin creates a Henry who is able to tolerate Bon's marrying his own sister but who is unable to accept the overt promiscuity of a black man sleeping with that beloved sister.

Shreve has fashioned a tale with enough suspense and melodrama to do justice to his conception of the South, a land in which as he expressed it, "it takes two niggers to get rid of one Sutpen." And in the fullness of time he says the Jim Bonds "are going to conquer the western hemisphere." Quentin is not listening too closely, for his interest is not really in Jim Bond, except maybe as his irrational howling reminds him of the sound his brother Benjy makes. When Shreve asks, however, "Why do you hate the South?" Quentin responds in utter frustration, "I don't hate it! I don't hate it! I don't hate it!" For the story Quentin creates and assists Shreve in articulating is only indirectly about the South, and he thinks Shreve has missed the point of his tale. What Quentin is really trying to sort out is precisely how he feels about his sister Caddy and what kind of response his confused emotional state will permit him to make. His is a tale born of desperation. Perhaps his opportunity to create a story detailing the circumstances under which an incestuous love of brother for sister is at least quasi-acceptable—and at the same time to create his alter ego, a character powerful enough to punish his sister's would-be seducer—provides Quentin strength to get through the last torturous year of his life. We see him only twice more: in April, when he returns to Jefferson to attend Caddy's wedding (when he is a rather assertive, effective young man, getting T. P and Benjy, who have had too much champagne, out of the front yard and into the barn); and on June 2 as he executes a careful, meticulously prepared plan for his own death by leaping from a bridge much like the one upon which he had humiliated himself before Dalton Ames. His vicarious experience as hero, apparently, could sustain him no longer.

Notes

1. Frederick L. Gwynn and Joseph L. Blotner (eds.), *Faulkner in the University: Class Conferences at the University of Virginia, 1957–1958* (New York: Random House, 1965), 273.

2. All references are to the Vintage Edition (New York: Random House, 1954). Pages cited will be given in the text.

3. References to *Abaslom, Absalom!* are to the Modern Library College edition (New York: Random House, 1965). Page numbers are given in the text.

Candace

Alan Cheuse*

> *'It's Caddy!' the librarian whispered. 'We must save her!'*
> Appendix to *The Sound and the Fury*

I

1

Hooray for Hollywood! The palms and sea mist, they knocked her for a loop! Flattening her hand against the front fender of the car, she tugged at her broken heel as if her touch alone might fix it. The driver, having deposited her worn valises onto the sidewalk in front of the hotel entrance stood sulking, nursing his hand, just a few paces behind her.

"Mis' Aitkins," the driver muttered.

"Goddman, you still here? I thought you'd be heading back for the Rockies by now . . ."

"I'm supposed to see you settled in . . ." Again, his voice trailed away, subsumed into the strangest sound, the murmur of the nearby ocean and the rattle of automobiles passing to and fro with a frequency known only in the wealthiest of districts.

"Settled in? You'd love to see me settled, and you'd love to settle in me . . ."

The driver punched the side of the car.

"Don't get so dramatic, Johnny-Bonny, you can't cure your cut and bleeding with a metal massage."

The driver might have said something else but she couldn't have heard it. A large open car roared past, spitting smoke and the shouts of its cheerful occupants. The driver leered at her, looking back long enough to make his passengers fear for their lives. And they screamed all the louder, some it appeared, in fright, others in amazement.

"How come I didn't get here sooner?" She addressed her question now to the rising spires of the exotic buildings some dozen yards away which bore the name *Nice Plaza*. Leafy plants formed a border separating

*Reprinted, with permission, from *Candace & Other Stories* (Cambridge/Newton, Massachusetts: Apple-wood Books, Inc., 1980), pp. 57–100.

the pavement from the grounds. Either she knew the answer or knew none was possible since she didn't pause to listen for any reply. "Goddman, I don't even know *how* I got here!" She turned and again addressed the sulking driver. 'With you driving, Johnny-Bonny . . .''

A little fellow dressed in a sky-blue coat and cap came running up the path from the entrance.

"Good afternoon, Ma'am," he chirped, and smiled servilely.

"You have a shoemaker in your hotel?"

"A shoe repair service, Ma'am?"

"A shoe repair service, yes?"

"Why, yes, we do."

"Then pick up my bags and show me the way to it."

"Good-bye, *Madam*," said the sulking driver.

She did not look back. Somewhere around Sacramento he had pulled the car over and tried to kiss her and she had yanked off her shoe and hit him in the hand. That had calmed him down quite a bit, but now he was acting snarly again. I'd have given you rabies if I could have, she had told him, and if I could have I wouldn't have wasted a good heel on your hand. They had not spoken for the remainder of the trip, not even to exchange good mornings when she had emerged from the hotel in that town whatever it was called the day's drive north of where they now stood.

"Could you please mail this for me," she said to the bellhop, removing from her bag one of the letters she had written to occupy her time during the silent part of the drive. He accepted her request with a smile.

Hooray! She'd biffed and sneaked and slinked and scraped for the last decade. Sometimes she had followed men like dogs, sometimes men had followed her. But she'd never walked with as much smartness and stiff-necked strut as she did the twenty yards or so up the path—broken heel and all—to the entrance of the stucco castle by the sea.

Colors, shapes, a gush of people flowed around in the lobby. More palms, brittle-leaved and healthy, spread their limbs in welcome. Other trees unnameable to a Mississippian stretched to the balcony of the second floor where gentlemen in sport caps and steel spectacles looked down with great interest upon her arrival. If the hotel had a mind it would be thinking: who is this woman? what men will try to woo her? If the scene were in the movies as she imagined it could have been, the viewer would have all eyes focused on her flashy figure. But it was more like a ball at the Judge's house in French Lick, more like a stage play, most like a musical. The air glistened with the glint of silver candle holders, and dabs of color emanated from pots of fresh flowers on tables here and there about the lobby. Whirling about in the presence of, she might even call what she felt, despite her halting gait caused by her broken heel, a life as best she lived it.

"Chippy? Where are you, Chippy?"

A frail voice broke through the crowd's chatter.

"Chippy? Chipper?"

A mother had lost her child! Only God could make such accidents happen and still let you live . . .

"Chiiiipy?" Shrill now, her cry turned to purer pain.

Then up trotted a dog no bigger than a delta mosquito and it barked at her mistress' ankles until the woman, now smiling broadly, lifted the little beast in her arms.

"Ah, Chiiipy . . . Mam's is missed you where you been a dog too mischiefy . . ."

Candace felt her heart sputter, burst, and then something fell heavily through space, like a daredevil she once loved up in Memphis whose parachute failed him one Fourth of July.

"Boy!" she called to the bellhop when sighting him at last through the torn curtains of the palms. "You see if that driver of mine is still outside. Tell him I got to speak to him right away 'bout some bags I left in the car! And I want you to be sure my room looks out on the water!"

"The Ocean, ma'am?"

"*The* Ocean!"

2

. . . *Beautiful dreamer* . . .

It was worth her last penny. The music shimmered in the air, the curtain dissolved into layers of light, thick and luscious you could cut them with a knife. On stage, a swing flew riderless through space, then picked up a woman at the far right and swung back and the woman faded away mysteriously into the rainbow mist of music.

. . . *wake unto me* . . .

How many times she'd seen this show? Candace held her breath as the woman swung out once more over the orchestra pit, revealing garters, gauze pants, sly glances from her large harlequin eyes. She clenched her teeth, touched her knees together, took another breath.

"A dying art," sighed a bald man sitting next to her.

"I've done it and I'd do it again if they let me," she said, but the man had addressed his comment to another man on his right.

Two baggy-trousered comedians appeared near the lip of the stage.

". . . said it was alright. So I took *two* bites!"

She thought of her room, its view of rough surf, hidden rocks. Soon she'd leave it. But not the ocean, never.

"Well what *is* so different about the carpenter's daughter?"

"Oh, you ought to see her *anvil* down the street!"

Her tower room protruded through the mist. She could see its turret windows. She fingered her purse.

"Pardon me." When she bumped knees with the bald man, he laughed so hard he sweated.

"My pleasure. Pardon me." He wiped his eyes with his coat sleeve. "You sat here last week, didn't you? I watched you from the other side of the aisle. You really enjoy this dying art."

"I used to be an entertainer myself."

"And where was that?"

"On the southern circuit."

"I know it well. Did you play the *Ruby* in—"

"*Who was that wife I saw you with last night?*"

"That's flattering of you to say."

"*That was no wife!*"

"Certainly, I could."

"*That was my lady!*"

"Why'n't you tell me your name so I don't feel out of place talking to you this way?"

3

Squatting in a stream bed
red tie

She woke up shivering. Stale cigar smoke filled the turret spaces, misted her windows.

4

She posted a letter and this is what she imagined: a clerk would pick it up and read the address; then he would place it in a special box for mail for that section of the country; minutes later another clerk would pick up the pile of mail accumulated there and tie them together for faster passage toward the south; then a train would speed them toward Memphis (?) or Little Rock (?) or New Orleans (?).

She watched through the slot but no one appeared. She turned away, smoked a cigarette, read a wanted poster. No one appeared.

"Excuse me," a voice came from behind her.

"I'm sorry," she said, standing aside so that a slender dark-haired woman her own age (or perhaps slightly older) could slide her letter into the slot.

"They don't come running to fetch them," she said.

"What's that?" The woman smiled. "You speaking to me, honey?"

"I said they don't bust their tails rushing to grab up the letters."

5

"That's enough. You sound like a nigger mammy at a funeral but you look terrific. We might have something for you coming up soon."

Candace smiled at the man as she slipped behind the wall of ladders and empty barrels. Her chest ached.

"How long they been keeping you down on the farm, honey?" asked the wardrobe lady when she turned the costume back. "You got a real nice future if you stay out of the light."

"What the hell you mean by that?"

"They do a lot with make-up but you stay out of the light."

Standing there before the mirror wearing nothing but high-heeled shoes and a kerchief, Candace wanted to punch the old woman in the face. But she resisted.

"I was more afraid about my voice."

"You should be. I heard you sing. But he likes 'em like you look so he don't tell the real truth."

"What's the real truth?"

"You're a lot like ten dozen others. But less pale, more lines."

Candace shivered, caught in a cold draft from the stage beyond the ladders.

"Will he use me?"

"God, will he!" the old wardrobe woman cackled.

6

One day Maeve followed her from the hotel. Candace visited a dress shop, her hairdresser, a tea shop, a palmist, and then the post office. In the post office, she wrote a letter and mailed it right there. Then she went to the Sisters of the Bleeding Wound Orphanage. Maeve waited for her outside for an hour and then gave up and went home.

7

Squatting in the stream bed

8

My country tis of thee
Sweet land of liberty
Of thee I sing . . .

She stood between two of the oldest girls, holding their frail hands tightly while the nun held up large photographs of famous places: The Lincoln Memorial . . . the Jefferson Memorial . . . the Washington Monument . . .

Your bodies are like these temples. Never forget that.

A photograph of New York City as seen from a ferry boat.

This land . . .

One of the little girls squeezed her hand.

"I got to go."

"Can't you hold out just a minute, darlin'!"

"I got to go."

"Well . . . if you got to go, you got to go."

"So do I," said the other little girl. One was white, the other swarthy. Each of them smiled alike, as though trained before the mirror at such matters.

"Well, kin I take you, honies? Show me the way."

"It's like Alice through the rabbit hole," said the darker girl.

"What's that?"

"It's a secret way. You're too big to come."

"I could try."

"All right," said the light-skinned girl. "Come along."

9

"Where'd you meet this one? In a post office?"

"I met him at the studio. He saw me once from a car."

"You're so lucky, Caddy. I meet bellboys and cops and you meet producers."

"We'll see what he can produce. I'm tired of vaudeville, I'm tired of running around looking for something I know I won't like when I get it! I'm tired of . . . everything I have to do. I once had a life!"

"Not much from what you told me about it."

"I'm a mother . . ."

"Are you drunk?"

"I am *not* drunk."

"Let me smell your . . . Candace *Ait*kins!"

"Oh, go'n Maeve, I'll crown you. It was just a little goofing with some of the ladies in the wardrobe department."

"What fluid they give you to drink while you was talking?"

"Told you I drink nothing. That's a habit I give up when I stopped living with my husband. And it's a good thing I did you know I was never one to hold my liquor."

"Candace, I'm worried about what you're doing to yourself . . ."

"Don't you worry 'cause I done most of it already."

"Yeah, honey, but the trouble may be you don't understand that even after you give yourself what you think you deserve there's a lot more to go on living after that. You figure you done everything you wanted to do and get everything by the time you're twenty-five that's swell. But what about the next forty years or so you got to live? People in the books, in the moving pictures, they end when the story ends but real people go on waking up every day after their tragedies happen and they have to make up their faces and eat their breakfast and catch a street car for work."

"I'm as real as all that. I do those things. I eat, I sleep everyday."

Candace sank down onto the rug and stretched her arms above her head. "I'm so human in fact, Maeve, I think I'm going to be sick."

Maeve kneeled alongside her, stroked her forehead.

10

Candace lay on her back, felt him thought about pear blossoms a tree she'd never see

11

The ocean writhed on the horizon and now and again leaped as though it were in tune with the moon's pulse. Foam and moon glitter gathered at wave top when the surf rolled. A scent of salt and rich cigar smoke curled above her.

"What's this place called, Mister Herman?"

"It's just a beach."

"I like it." She stroked the back of his hand, aware of his thigh against hers.

"My house lies just down the way, dearie. Care to stroll in that direction?"

"And leave this big old car all by its lonesome on the beach?"

"We could drive then." His body twitched, as though he sensed something might roll in on the surf's rough curl. There was something odd about him; she could sense it but not say the name.

"Or stay right here."

"As you wish."

"I like you."

"Because I'm funny."

"You don't agree with me, do you?"

"I've always known I've been funny, Miss Compson."

"For Chris'. Mister Herman, please call me Caddy. That's what they called me back home." She rebelled against saying more. But her body went slack at the thought of all that. "Perhaps we *should* walk."

"Will you tell me about yourself, Caddy, if we do?"

"I'd tell you anyway, Mister Herman."

"And now you call me 'Herm.' "

"Herm . . ." She then told him only part of her story, but that was enough to make him gasp, sigh, and then, with the sound washed out by the waves, but because he was sitting so close to her with enough force to shake her as he shook, he wept. Lifting herself ever so slightly off the seat, she eased out a bubble whose sputter was so faint she only felt its gently dying vibrations beneath her panties as the ocean's growl drowned whatever noise it might have made before he heard it. "I shouldn't have said anything about my daughter . . ." Who opened the door next to her? She must have, and yet she did not recall the act.

"Come back, Candace." Herm called to her. He caught up with her, but not soon enough to keep her from soaking her dress in the high-blown spume from the breakers.

"I grew up in Coney Island and I know dangerous water when I see it," he murmured to her as he led her by the elbow back toward the car. "Once a little boy, a real young-un, from our very own block . . ."

She broke free and ran a few paces toward the blackness behind the car. Then she stopped, as though she found herself at the end of a taut leash, and she screamed: "*You* know dangerous water when you see it? You know dangerous water? I've been to hell in a washtub full of water and still don't know the difference between plain and complicated! I still don't know the difference! So come here, come closer, you dare? I dare you! Come closer and I'll show you what I mean. I wish I could show you what's like to be me and live like this, day in, day out, all these years that seem too brief and still fill up each day with so many hours I could run off into that world's washtub ocean and show my face no more—"

"You come home and *wash* your face, you'll be all right, then, you'll feel better."

She squirmed in his rough grip, he had a surprisingly strong grip for a man his size, but anyway she didn't want him to let her go and so she cursed only a short time longer and then let him subdue her.

"You caught me in the dark," she said. "You found me out."

"I saw you."

"You saw me? You saw the lines of it shooting out from me?"

"I make movies that have to show people those things. My movies make people laugh *or* cry depending on, if we know enough tricks, what we want from them, which means really what we think they want. There, there." He petted her as though she were the cat she never owned as a little girl. "You come home with me now, I'll make you happy. There, there . . ."

"Even if'n I don't wanna be?"

"There, there . . ."

12

Watching the pale fellow with the face as round as a full moon, she imagined that he didn't even come up to her breasts: Now what would he be like, she mused, waiting for him to reach the top of the ladder. Why he'd be like my big baby, all tender and moony and moany. That gave her a chill. She squirmed in her chair. Pay attention, she commanded herself.

The man fell backward off the ladder and she roared in laughter along with everyone else except for the sour little man in the golf cap behind the megaphone. Later he came over and introduced himself.

"I'm Frank," he said.

"And I'm earnest," she said.

"Save that for the vaudeville," he said, showing her that his sour expression was all an act itself. "You're Herm's friend, ain't you?"

"I'm a friend of the arts," she heard herself declare and thought she was as funny as the moon-faced man on the ladder. God, I don't know what I am till I find myself saying it.

"You ever do any vaudeville?"

"A lot," she lied.

"Where?"

"In . . . Memphis."

"You want a be in a moving picture?"

"Don't you think I'm a little too old for that?" she asked, feeling her voice go all girlish in spite of herself.

13

So hot in this room I could melt.
Dear Mama
Strips off a stocking.
I arrived here not too long ago
Another.
So damn hot.
Raises an arm. Sweat runs like a creek down a hillside.
Brother, it is hot!
Peels off panties.
This hotel cools me off. Never thought I'd see more sea than the gulf.
Oh
Mama this ocean at evening time the colors of the sun settling like a liquid egg of flamish organe organe o-r-a-n-g-e over near the palms of beaches that stretch beneath the ocean toward Japan.

Summers at home, with dark squatting down on us so quick you'd think some scrappy child'd caught the bugger sun in a with a fishhook near its eye and yanked it down to bleed elsewhere over some other folk's horizons

Mama
I will write this if it kills me I am going to learn to express these things
Papa's health
Dresses for my beloved quickbeautied girl
Read a book with words strung together in it last week and have finally settled
brother!

overhead in oasis deseter film scratch that out
desert revue I hope to find a part in perhaps it will work out that I might
work as an assistant to a movie producer who knows

"Thought you was getting dressed?"

"Too hot to do that yet."

"Why'n't you just go like that? Bound to give you a part."

"*You're* a bitch."

"You don't have to share my room with me, Miss Mississippi Moss or
whatever you got down there."

"Down where?"

"Don't get touchy, love. I meant down there in Mississippi."

"Back East, you should say."

"Where I grew up, it was down below. If not beneath us."

"You know, Maeve, you are getting kind of snippy like. Keep it up
and I will move out."

14

"And sedge a fadda nistic! Take that that and that!"

The large round moon slicked swiftly through the air and bits of
cream scudded from its sides.

"Missed! Well, here a bell mad house! I'll just stick it right in there!"
The fat man loped towards her, frightening her a little with his squeaky
voice and the mad gleam in his eye. He loomed above her, fatter than
taller but bigger than she. An illusion? That didn't matter.

"Oh, now, heavens!" She threw up her hands. "Could you do that to
a little girl like—"

Muff! The creamy pie slugged into her mouth, and her eyes stuck
together. Slop, slippy lickity, it tasted awful and delicious at the same
time. Whirling about, she could hear the fat man's breathing. Then he
grabbed her breasts and hugged on for dear leer . . .

"Enuf!" came the director's cry somewhere outside her cream-sight.
"This is the worst I've ever seen! Get the hell out of here, all of you!
Everybody get ready for the second scene. Where's Herman? I got a bone
to pick wid him!"

15

She used a typewriter now.
DEAr MAMA,
    YOU OUGHT TO SEE ME

16

The dream returned.

17

"Ladies and Gentleman, I would like to introduce to you my new business associate and beloved wife, Miss Candace Aitkins, formerly of Indiana and Mississippi."

"To the new Mrs. Freed!"

"A toast!"

"Speech! speech!"

"I hope my vaudeville experience . . ."

18

squatting in a water

19

He threw her onto the bed and her slip rose up over her knees. Without a sound, he tore away the cotton panties, leaving her naked to his rough and probing fingers. Someone watching might have told her that his unsheathed cock spewed sperm across her belly but all she noticed was the cross dangling from his neck chain. He forced her to touch her tongue to it. She nipped a piece of skin from his shoulder and his outcry burst her eardrums. Blood ran down the bedstead to the sea.

20

She went to a doctor and he gave her a powder to help her sleep.

21

      black

My father.

My brothers.

      My daughter

My mother.

22

I screwed him good that day.

23

She'd wear the fanciest dress that fifty bucks could buy. Her hair all golden in that summer sun the best cocks in town'd stand and crow for her attention. Music of ocean at her window, this vision dispersed. I am not she, she not me, or her us him at when. Useless wandering.

These damned headaches goin' to drive me out of my own brain if I can get away somehow! The wind whacks at my temples like it was a hurricane, I look around and the lightest weed ain't stirring but a frazzle . . .

"Your bodies are like temples . . ."

24

"I want you to turn out the light now, Candace. If you want to keep on writing, you can go to the study. You may have noticed we have a few extra rooms in this shit house . . ."

"I'd rather sit here with you, Herm."

"I have to be at the studio at five. Which is in exactly four hours. We've been drinking six hours with your friend Maeve and her low-class boyfriend. Need I say more?"

"So she likes bellhops. Chacun a son gout."

"And shacunt a son goo to you too Miss Assippi. I would you to turn out the light and come to bed."

"I'm sorry that my pleasures turn out to give you pain, Herm."

"That's a wonderful line, darling. You should write it down quickly before it melts. Except for two reasons. One, the stage is a dead form of entertainment, and two, people don't talk that way."

"I do. I always did, and I do now."

"You do, that's true. But if you heard that line on stage you wouldn't believe it. So it doesn't matter what's real or not but what you believe when you're in the audience. And I wouldn't believe it if it hit me in the face with all its curlycues and Southern drool. So turn out the light."

"Would you like *this*, Herm?"

"You're a temptress, another Vonda Vambling. But I have to be at the studio in three hours and fifty-seven minutes."

"Come out on the terrace a minute then and look at the ocean with me."

"Open the door. I'll listen from here."

"I want you to listen with me."

"What do you hear in that ocean, Candace? Mermaids? All I ever hear is crashing and gnashing. It reminds me of my gut."

"Same here, Herm. But I guess we got different insides."

"And outsides in case you think I don't have eyes. I see what you're showing me, honey. But I got to get to sleep."

"Perchance to dream . . ."

"That's a good line. You write that down."

"Don't be snide, honey."

"I'd rather be snide than sleepy. Good night, my little delta flower. Turn off the light."

"You'll say goodnight to all this?"

"You're the mermaid trying to lure me to the rocks. But I can't see through my eyelids so you can't lure me too far."

"Life is just one long joke to you, isn't it, Herm?"

"Life is the saddest thing I ever discovered I couldn't escape from, darling, so's I make movies to make people laugh a little and forget about it all."

"Why do I live here with you, Herm?"

"Because you like the terrace overlooking the beach . . ."

"What if I leap from that terrace, what'd you do then?"

"Leap? You'd jump. Please, don't use lines like that . . . not credible . . . Candace, I'm sinking fast . . ."

"Sink, you faggot kike. I'm going to throw myself off the terrace and make such a scene like you'd never believe but the whole world'll know—"

Faster than she thought he could move he threw aside the covers, leaped from the bed, crossed the space between them in one bound and slapped her so hard across the mouth that she staggered backward through the space between the open doors and only the waist-high railing kept her from falling. The light went out and she was left with the roar of the surf and her heart beating faster than she had ever felt before. Something in her life had changed and whether for better or for worse didn't matter since the sense of flux itself terrified her beyond her wildest imaginings.

25

Damuddy, can you hear me? Can you hear? I'm moving water. Turds in running stream. I climbed a tree and saw you lying there. From that time forward, I loved you.

26

"If you have dreams like that, you should see a reader. You never know what they could be trying to say to you."

"Maeve, I can't help but think I should come back and live with you. I'm so unhappy."

"Have another drink, Caddy. That'll make you feel better. Say, why'n't we trade places I'll go live in that big house of yours and you can have all my clients."

"You're joking, honey. I'd give anything to come back and live this life again. I just may do it."

"It's not so bad, is it? Why, see this necklace? A big producer over at Vita-Pix gave it to me last week. And you know what? I'm going to see that old friend of yours in Palm Springs *next* week. It's not so bad, is it?"

"No, not at all, Maeve. Herm's been wonderful to me but I just can't stand it any longer. He's . . . he's not normal, you know."

"What's he make you do? He make you do things with . . . you know, like that Frenchie we used to hear about over at the Wilshire?"

"He doesn't do anything but work and sleep. Course, he takes me to the best restaurants, God, we love to eat. He's let me write a script for a new movie they're making. But, God, I'm all written out and want to play a little and he's never there or when he is he can't do it."

"Caddy, honey," said Maeve, sliding next to her on the sofa. "How'd you like to write a part for me in that new movie of yours?"

"It's serious, Maeve," said Candace. "No pie throwing or that silliness."

Maeve gave Candace a squeeze and lay her head against her breast.

"Bet you could write something in for an old war horse like me?"

"Sure, I could, Maeve," said Candace, sliding her hand along Maeve's waist. "I think you'll like it. It's about a young southern girl who's abandoned by her boyfriend and then turned out of her family 'cause of that. She carries her baby to term and then leaves it at an or- phanage . . ."

Maeve made a quiet assenting noise and nuzzled her cheek against Candace's breasts.

"Wonder who that could be about?"

"She's a wild, wild girl, smokes cigarettes, and drinks whiskey in places no girl her age's ever allowed into without some kind of special beau."

Maeve eased her hand inside Candace's bodice and raised her nipple with her touch.

"Herm says it's like nothing they've ever done before 'cause she's wild and free and all the goodie-goodies are goin' to be shocked by her but he thinks that we can do it if we just suggest things, you know, without showin' them directly."

She squirmed and gave Maeve a friendly squeeze. "Darlin', I can't talk when you're giving me the chills like that."

"Honey, I'm going to fix you another drink."

"Why'n't we smoke this reefer instead? One of the camera boys gave it to me, said it was the best in Hollywood."

"I'll try anything once."

"There's the difference 'tween you and me, honey. I just keep on counting."

II

Dear Mama,

Now we can call it two. You may be shocked at that, me writing about it the way I might be telling you about the score of a baseball game or the number of guests we had for tea, but that's the way I am and by now you ought to know. A daughter who's been married twice and divorced twice and quite a shame to her family. But not to herself. But if you're going to read any further in this letter and hear about what a beautiful place this is down here, a place you've never been but would love to hear about and perhaps someday soon your health and finances permitting even come down to visit then you will have to accept the fact that I came down here for that reason. So there's the only ugly thing that you'll find in this letter and I'm glad I said it and now I will tell you about all things bright and beautiful and gay and frolicky and the colors Mama the colors you have never seen them until you come down this way south of the border, the purple of the jacaranda just like home, the oranges of the flowers we never see even though we were nearly tropic, dark mountains that flash silver at you in the first light of morning, green so green it *defines* the color, Mama, and a sky that stretches so far around you when you stand on this central plain of the plateau of the state of Jalisco—none of those dirty old border towns for me, I'll tell you, I want deep south, Mama, south of south, our South, to this place which is nearly a thousand miles south of where you're sitting and reading this letter—Mama, so far south Jefferson is *north!*

Oh, Mama, I married a hick and then I married a Jew and I deserve to be here celebrating after a divorce. The first time, you remember I wrote to you about it, I mourned as though someone I knew well had died.

Well, I lost the train there, didn't I? And you know why? Because I was biting into a mango, and the juice rolled down my lips and over the bodice of a lovely white lace dress I had made for me the week I was waiting around for Herm's lawyer to finish up doing his business, which was mainly talking to people and paying bribes. You've never tasted a mango, I'll reckon, Mama, and let me describe it to you. The fruit is shaped like a sweet potato but the skin is greenish orange and smooth, and you've got to prick the skin with a knife or a fingernail but not so deeply that you can't just lift up a flap of skin and peel it back in strips. The edible part is pulpy, overbrimming with juices, and you've got to bite quick and suck the meat into your mouth and savor it there. Try to nibble at it and you'll end up the way I did, with a soiled bodice and a need for a napkin and a bowl of water.

The waiter, a dandy little boy about fourteen, slender, dark, and somewhat undernourished, quite unlike the way our brother looked at that age, muscley, even mealy-muscley looking, Mama, if you know what I mean, as though somebody had sprayed his arms with grit you could see the shape of underneath the bulgy skin, this waiter just helped me clean myself up. I can't tell you how much help the men down here offer me. Ha, Mama, that was a joke. They're impolite, shall we say, in the extreme, and I have to every now and then give them a smack the way you do mosquitoes back home at night after the lights go down. They are plain

fresh and nasty. Primitive is what an English friend I have made the acquaintance of at a pretty whitish-colored lake called Chapala calls them.
He says that they are not like niggers but that they are more like Indians, a
different race, and that their art and culture as he calls it is a grade above
the Africans who made their best art three thousand years ago and the
Egyptians who made their best art four and five thousand years ago.

The other day, just on the day I met this man (who is travelling with
his overweight German wife who has a sharp tongue and is always making
eyes at the waiters even if they are fourteen, Mama, I must tell the truth),
we took a rickety bus ride for nearly two hours to the other side of the lake
and then we discovered that the bus didn't go back to our hotel and we
had to rent a boat and get ourselves rowed for miles back to the other side.
A great rainstorm came up out of the west and we had to row to the
nearest island which the owner of the little bar in the shack on the center
of it said was called Scorpion Island. Because of the shape? my English
friend asked. Because of the scorpions, the bartender said back to him,
and the Englishman nearly jumped out of his shoes. LOOK OUT for
them! he shouted to his wife, and to me, and he stood up on the little pic-
nic table the bar owner had set up for people to sip their beers at, and he
wouldn't come down for nearly ten minutes after the bartender explained
in broken English that he was only making a joke, that it was the shape of
the island. Oh, Mama, we had a good time as good as any time I'd had
since you and I went to French Lick together that summer what seems
such a long time ago . . . I laughed so hard myself I had to pee, and so I
went around to the back of the only trees nearby on this tiny place (Oh,
Mama, will I ever send this dirty letter to you or shall I rub out these nasty
little lines with mango juice or ink) and there I was with my then quite
new white dress raised up over my knees, me squatting there, my little
new white undies slid down to my ankles, and just as I was feeling on the
verge of peeing I saw—yes, you guessed it, if you're reading this letter
Mama, you guessed it, a creepy crawly scorpion tiny as my little finger
and looking more monstrous than a dinosaur. And you know what I did,
Mama? So scared and all as I was? I watched him crawl toward me as
though I was the London Bridge or a giant redwood and then when he
was under me and God knows what he was about to do then crawl on or
sting me in the place of places when he was under me yes I gushed down
on him the way the heavens gushed down on us. May the Scorpion God
have mercy on Its Soul!

Dear Maeve,
    I am disconsulate.

Dear Herm,
    Your deelightful check arrived and I thank you my ex and my
why. It is just simply so beautiful here that I'm not sure just how much

longer I can stand it. Isn't that queer? Sullied—is that the word?—as I am by my past experiences, even the beautiful shapes and shades of this land

Dear Maeve,
Mexico is a place for us bad-uns. I have had the naughtiest of naughties and all of it to the tune of the strings and fat bass fiddles crossed with guitars they call mariachees. Picture a lake the color of fresh cream with not a cloud in the sky to reflect on its surface. Plunk down next to it green mountains and a hotel or hacienda here or there with only the wind off the water to tell their inhabitants that a boat may be approaching from the other shore. In early morning, all is still. By noon, the servants have awakened and clean houses, patios, beaches, whole skyfronts with their funny brooms they call trapeadors or "husbands" because they sling them around with such glee but never seem to get much done with them. We take a wee drink or two at lunch and by late afternoon we sway to music not yet begun to be played, the chirpy, brassy, punchy, twangy mariachee. Ee-ee!

Mostly I drink and take a bite to eat with the British couple (actually he's British and she's German) who've taken such a liking to me. I will tell you about him in a moment, poor dear that he is. But I ought to say something about what happened to the other

You see
I tried early mass at the tiny cathedral near the lakeside. It has a small altar of simple silver service, and a dark Indian lady and I were the only creatures kneeling. I didn't know exactly what to do.

Dear Lord,
I feel as though I were a creature in a story, my fate as far out of my hands as the clouds drifting off the shore of Scorpion Island. I have talked to friends about this. Some say that we all feel this way as if to dismiss it. Others say, yes, they have had the same feeling but the only thing to do is laugh it away. Lord, I can no longer laugh. Once, I could. Once, kneeling in a stream bed home, I felt the surging waters clean me free of filth. But Lord this pain no longer leaves. It is with me day and night, day or night, night or morning. Sweet and pungent orders odors no longer please me. The taste of all your good things leaves my mouth bitter. I am a slut and a whore and all terrible monstrosities of woman being. I have allowed men to touch me all over, and to pierce me all over, and to saturate me all over, and to torture me all over, and taste me all over, and to show me all over, and Lord I no longer no which is myself, my own parts, and which are the parts of the world. Lord, if you told me even this pain that pierces down into the root of me, as though a sliver of sharpest wood had pierced me, were nothing but words on a page that would only increase the pain. Lord, if you told me that I had no being except what others thought of me that would only deepen the terrible loneliness I feel. Lord, if you told me that my dear dead father and my

sick mother, and my dear, and dead, and damned brothers, mad and maimed by their own hands or by others each of them, if you told me that all of us or any of us had no being except what you told me that would only turn the screw tighter, twist the vine tighter around that part of me, how can I use any single word to describe it, that part of me, is it my heart, my soul, my spirit, my feeling, my nerves, my womb, my liver, my spine, my brain, my tongue, Lord, I have let men put themselves into me in the hope that would make the hell go away. And it did not. Lord, I have let men put other men into me in the hope that it would make the hell go away. And it did not. Lord, Lord, I have let other women put things inside of me in the hope that the hell would go away. And it stayed. Lord, I have let men and women Lord you have seen it I cannot say it but the hell stayed with me. Why did I get sent to hell before I died, Lord? Does that mean that I can go to heaven when I die because I am already in hell? Dear Lord, God, creator of the scorpion, have mercy on me.

Dear Maeve,

Have you ever tasted a mango? a papaya? a guava? The wonderful fruits they have here ain't no joke, darling, at all. Last night a dark devilish looking Mexican in a tuxedo took me for a carriage ride around the wonderful city of Guadalajara, and I ate mangos and threw the seeds out of the carriage and dark Indian boys rushed to catch the seeds because of the magical powers I must have put into them.

Dear Herm,

The check arrived and I am so grateful. Did you know what a wonderful time I could have here when you suggested that we do it this way? You are a wonderful person yourself to have suggested this to old me.

How is the picture going I have tried to read about it in the Los Angeles paper that drifts down here every now and then but find no news about it. Is Vonda still going to be the lead? And that deep voiced old cracker from near my old home town, what's his name?

Dear Mama,

I am having a fine time here, squired about as I am by every respectable tourist in sight. You would love this place except you can't drink the water. Perhaps some time I will come back up home and tell you face to face about what a good thing has happened to me.

How is She? You hardly ever say more than a few words about her when you write at all. I know how it is when you're ailing, but you must as a mother know how much the simplest phrases mean to me. Do you think you could get a picture taken? I would love that so much. Separated from her, I feel like part of my body itself has been taken from me. You do know yourself, Mama, what I mean.

Dear Lover,

You have gone back to Italy in such a huff that I don't even know what or why I'm writing this to you. But I did want to tell you that I miss your talk terribly, and that I have since you left gotten so tan myself that you might mistake me for a native. But the main thing I wanted to write to you about is my internal conversion and the things that it is changing in the outside part of my life. That night when we walked all the way to Ajijic and back and you told me about your writing and your own family and your illnesses and your special reasons for wanting me to come with you, I never could put in to words the feelings that I had then building up inside of me like rain clouds on the mountains in Michoacan. When you touched my hand with the back of yours, something electric went charging through me, and—remember!!—I fell back against the palm and you caught me, and you said that you had never known a woman whose voice in any language magnetized you as much as my own. You talked about my accent, and I was so surprised whenever anyone mentions that I never heard it I am surprised and tickled by it. You held my arm so tight I could feel the blood damming up at my shoulder and in my throat. I told you that I knew what you wanted. You said I didn't. I told you that I did. But first I had to ask you. I had to ask you, what does my life mean? I have tried love, and I have tried marriage, and I have tried love without marriage, and I have tried crimes and I have tried praying, I have tried smoking marijuana and drinking alcohol and eating the button of the peyote cactus, I have tried being a mother, I have tried, but it is so hard over this distance . . . Last night I tried to kill myself by walking into the lake and I could not go all the way. Does that surprise you? You knew I was that kind of person or you would not have held my arm so tight. Only men with serious intentions hold a woman's arm that way. Didn't you know our custom here? Calm, you said, and wait for the rhythm to come upon you. Calm, you said, and let the thing flow through you and out again into the soil. Christ, I told you all those things about me, all those things I never have spoken to anyone about, not even my two husbands. Calm, I am calm . . . I had waded out into the lake up to my waist. That gentle tide that you noticed for us the other day at the water-side lapped at my bosoms. Why, I might have been stepping into a bath the water seemed so warm. And then I remembered your words, and calm kept me steady, living, and I thought to myself, why, how can you do this, Caddy, your story's not over yet! And I laughed to myself, and I remembered your words, calm, and how your wife's eyes glistened when you kissed my hand at the casino, and how the mariachee band played all night, and I thought I was drowning in air, I didn't need water, because at that moment a thunderbolt slapped against the mountains on the Michoacan shore, and the music of the band drifted over the waters from the Casino, and I felt nothing less than just one big silly at the thought that I could kill myself when my story had not yet ended. I missed your accent all of a sudden, and the odd taste of your mouth when you kissed me under that palm tree. Can you really tell whether it's male or female from the smell of it?

How could that be? I waded back to shore, thinking that I must live on long enough to ask you that trick. Does a female palm tree have the monthlies? Does a male palm tree stand erect at the sight of a lady palm? Can you read your lady's palm when you're erect? Oh, isn't that a nasty thing for a lady to write when she knows a man only just a short time! Lover, I know this sounds perfectly insane but I must see you again soon, and since I have the cash ready for my ticket I'm going to buy a boat ticket as soon as I reach Veracruz, and sail for Europe. Will you stand still in your little house as you described it to me so lovely until my arrival? Will your wife hate me for writing this if she sees this? You're the only man who has ever made me think that I might want to live again with someone. I'm not like those silly young things—I'm just not young no more—you read about in novels and so I won't follow you to the ends of the earth. But I'll come, I'm coming, I'm already on my way, as you read this, to Italy. Ah, E-Tahl-Ya! as you shouted it. That night when the music drifted out upon the waters and you played me . . . I've never written anything like this before and I certainly don't expect to ever read it from someone else's hand—when you showed me what you needed and that was what I needed to . . . I've just heard a rumor that two Americans died on the road to Guadalajara, killed by bandits while riding in their motor car.

III

So I, who had never had a sister and was fated to lose my daughter, set out to make myself a beautiful and tragic little girl. I returned to Memphis in a state of shock so deep and profoundly disruptive of the normal responses to the world that I did not know how disturbed I was until I was nearly well again.

Gone.

She was gone, when I arrived that April afternoon, and so I did everything within my power to absent myself from felicity a while. Compared to the life I took up on Beale Street and Yahnahmee and Gayoso, pain was the gift of beings who had once had pleasures to compare it to.

Gone. Disappeared. Vanished. (   ) Years spilled from my life, like milk from an overtuned pitcher.

'28, '29, '30, '31, '32, '33. I hear these were hard years for Yankees, but where I sprawled most of it didn't mean all that much to me. You with your European disposition ought to know something about what I mean when I say that. I knew and I didn't, I cared and I didn't care, I was there and yet at the same time I was absent. I was the impression absence leaves when it's getting gone from a place where it's never been before and never will be.

I myself had known what disappearing meant ever since the day I departed for Memphis in Herbert's fine car, my belly filled with the seed of that child who would grow to disappear on the day that I returned full circle from the west to the place I departed from. Herbert, my husband-to-be, was driving while I sat suffering the pains and pangs and shakes and trembles of a separation I never willed but found myself innured to. Jefferson faded away into the greenery behind us and ahead lay Eudora, a town not on the direct route to Memphis but through which we rolled, just as splendid as if we'd planned it, because Herbert, in his excitement had taken a wrong turn.

Herbert, I said, I need a cool drink real bad. I was perspiring, I'll tell you, and not just because of the extra weight I had been carrying those last few weeks but because of the ordeal of the farewells. Or nonfarewells, since no one but mother came to see me climb into that car and depart, Papa and Jason being of one mind about my condition, and Quentin being . . . being . . . just a moment . . . I'm sorry, Doctor . . .

Now, I says, I need that soda pop.

Honey, I want to reach Memphis by dark, says Herbert. I got a real nice dinner planned for us at the hotel restaurant.

Which hotel? I asked.

He told me, and secretly I gave a cheer. It was the biggest and best, but I wasn't going to have that hotel and miss my drink so I told him that I would die and never reach that hotel and that room and that dinner he had his heart set on if I didn't have a drink of soda pop, and then I just leaned over and lay my head against his shoulder and let my hand drop into his lap and he gave a yelp like a pup with his nose caught in a doorway and nearly drove off the road into the porch of the country store just on the outskirts of Eudora. He never gave me any more trouble after that. That night he let me do what I liked and never asked more than once for me to do for him things that I told him I'd never do and that was that.

Gone. I left him alone in the room that night, walking by myself for about an hour through strange Memphis streets, and finding myself taunted and tempted but not attacked by men with obvious intentions. I wanted to stay with him but found I could not. He had been so handsome in his white suit at French Lick that for months after he courted me I couldn't think of him in any way but that. But in the hotel room, with his white suit on the bed and his turkey neck hanging limply between his balding knees he was a sight to behold. For a few minutes. And then flee from, as I did.

Gone. Whatever feeling I had for him and for the life that we would make together left me almost as quick as we ourselves packed my things into the shiny new automobile and left the home county.

Gone. Like the years that flowed from my life after I returned to Memphis.

Like Herbert himself.

He never forgave me for that night. I know that for a fact, because he wrote to me now and then letters that always turned back to that one evening, and how much it hurt him to discover my true nature. Doctor, is this what this talk's supposed to do? bring back those words, those moments when the pain came on so strongly that I want to forget about them forever but can't? *Gone.* But he wrote before he died the other month of a heart attack that he still remembered the way I looked at him after we got undressed. I was a bit silly from the champagne but from the look in *his* eye he was stone sober and not about to think of anything else but what he wanted to happen next.

You hep me off with this dress now Herbert, I teased him, seeing him standing there in his underdrawers. He reminded me of Daddy on nights when he came upstairs so drunk he forgot that we could see him if he left his bedroom door open too wide. I'm rambling. I should tell you what happened then. You're right, this ain't no story this is my life and I do want things to get better, 'though I know better than you do that they can always take a turn for the worse. And then another turn. Like the one we took to Eudora instead of continuing on straight north toward Memphis.

You hep me off with this dress. Like that, that's right. God, I kissed him until I thought my lips were going to bleed, that's right. And then I guided his hands here I don't mind shame no longer applies in my life I've seen the worst turns downward toward Hell and its countryside, which are located somewhere northwest of Memphis but you can't find them on the map. So I stepped out of my dress and he stepped out of his drawers and we were playing statue of a nude to each other's gazes when it came to me that I was truly thirsty and I asked him to fetch me another cool drink. He laughed and took me in his arms but I told him that nothing was going to happen until I had that cool drink and so he went into the bathroom and ran the tap and filled me a glass of water and I told him that wasn't cool enough I wanted a real drink and so he went into his suitcase and came out with a bottle of whiskey and I told him I wanted soda pop and he called me a goose and I told him I wasn't kidding and that if he didn't get it for me that I'd go out and fetch it myself. Well, me. You should have seen his face.

Candace, he said. I'm taking you away to marry you and give your child a father.

My child has a father, I said. Just 'cause it ain't you don't give you reason to be so mean to me. I want a soda pop.

Candace, you get over here, he said.

No!

Candace, you step over here or I'll come spank you.

No! You get that soda pop and you can do what you like but you get nothing until then.

His mouth turned sour-like, and he suddenly seemed to know that if I didn't want him to strip his shoes and socks off real quick that I must think he ought to cover himself up instead. I am going to marry you, I'm taking you away from the troubles you got at home because you lived so badly, I'm going to give you a house all your own big enough to keep you happy and I'm going to make your brother a treasurer of a company and you tell me you won't do nothing for me until I fetch you some soda pop?

Thass right.

You're talking like a nigger, he said. Stop that nigger talk and you come here.

Don' cho lahk me to tawk lahk dis here, Hehbet, spooning on nigger like chocolate onto a ice cream sundae. Whass wrong, honee? You don't want to held yo-sef in check til you gets de sodee pop for Mis' Candace?

You stop that and come on over here.

No! I stamped my foot and stood my ground. You fetch me that pop.

You talking like you're drunk.

I ain't drunk now, you should hear me talk when I'm drunk, I don't need to be drunk to talk this way 'cause I watch my father and mother talk like this all my life. Now you go and fetch me that pop, Herbert, or you just ain't going to use that thing of yours tonight.

He blushed, looked down quick at it, and laughed.

God, you're a nasty bit, aren't you? I didn't know how nasty you were when I proposed to you.

I felt my belly, real casual-like. It felt good and taut and smooth, as though nothing was inside it but the thought of what I was thinking about in my head. Nothing alive that is, just thoughts positive and beautiful. Nothing at all to do with life.

Hell with the soda pop, Herbert, I said. I was just testing you to see how loyal you were to me your new little wife. And you just failed. I'm going home.

He was furious all of a sudden, now he realized I was playing games.

You're not going any further than that bed there, he said.

Ooooo! Herbert, I cooed, you're talking tough enough for me to feel real frightened. And I don't know what I'd do if I got scared. I pretended to look around for a way out.

You just get right over there, he said, advancing toward me. You just talked yourself into a real pretty pickle.

You got the pickle, Herbert honey, 'cept it ain't so pretty. Except like we say, pretty ugly.

God, you are a foul mouthed little thing you are, he said. I didn't know this much about you when I said I'd do all those things for you. You think I ought to do them now?

Herbert, I said, rushing to the window. I'm going to jump out on the fire escape and scream for help if you lay a hand on me.

No, you won't. You're my wife.

Not yet. I tried to open the window but it was locked.

Don't you do that. We're getting married tomorrow so you might as well be now.

If you can catch me we will, I said, unfastening the window lock and reaching up to pull the window open.

Don't you, hey!

Help! I shouted out into the street. No one looked up. Help, Papa!

Stop that. He grabbed my wrists and tried to wrestle me away from the window.

Help me, Papa Papa, help!

Now someone called up to the window, hey, what's going on up there?

Man and wife! Herbert called down, holding me by the wrist.

Rape! I screamed.

Hey, hey, you, you, shouts drifted up from the streets.

Goddamn you, bitch, he said, twirling me about as though he was trying out a new dance step. Doctor . . . he was all swolled up down there, his pretty pickle, and the lights went out, I remember, though the window stayed open the entire time, and I let him push me over to the bed, and he did a few things to me, and then just as I had to decide what I wanted to do we heard a lot of feet running about in the hall, and loud voices, but though people came racing by our door no one actually knocked on it. Herbert was sweating, God, he was, and it was running down on to me since by now he was hovering over me like a old bear of the woods. His body was smooth and mostly hairless, but he had a funny way of sniffling that made me want to giggle as though he had a lot of hair and was tickling me with it. Then, just like the Catholics do sometimes, I heard a voice, it was a voice from inside me, crying, Mama, I'm alive, you be careful, be tender with the load you're carrying, you know who it is, and Doctor, as though it were for the twenty-ninth, instead of the fourth or fifth time I rolled over gently on my side and helped him in the sideways style so that my baby would not have to bear the weight of a man was not her father.

Poor Herbert! You ever been in Memphis when the lights went out? You never been any place in our country! You never been in the south, you never knew what it was like in a city like Memphis when the sun went down and all the country people go into hiding, just as Herbert was having us do, and all the city people (and southern city folk are strange, let me tell you), all the high divers come out and do their stuff on the dark. You known what we do? We take a long drink of some sweet tasting whiskey the way a diver takes a deep breath and then we plunge in over our heads into black light in dark alleys where you can wiggle your behind to your soul's contempt and never no one know the difference between penitence and penny toss 'cause it's always too dark to see. Why it's a sea so black and awful that the man who hears you cry rape one moment and rushes to your rescue will grab you from behind the next.

These boys out in the country they'll just grab hold of you. That's how they live, how they love to live. And you get one of these country lovers in the city and he'll do just about anything because he doesn't know how to act. He's a fish out of water. Fish. A real varmit, I mean, collecting the injuries of others as though they were cash in his bank account and he was counting the interest. And what the women do comes out of your case books too, what they do in the City of Dreadful Night. That's a title of a poem my dear dead brother sent me in a letter. I have the letter with me. I want to read it to you before I go.

Going, going. I left Herbert in the room and I descended into what some of my family thought I was from the beginning and into what others thought I was driven by my element to become. I took my time walking to the stairs, but Herbert didn't bother to call after me. He knew I wouldn't come back. I wanted him to call out to me, I'll admit, but I didn't want to come back. I didn't even want to look back not because I was afraid I'd turn into a pillar of salt because I was heading down the stairs towards rather than away from the cities of the plain—how my brother helped me to talk! I have to admit, since he wrote me that long letter, here, you see, I still carry it with me, since I am the recipient of letters rarely and the writer of many I carry it with me as a token of his love for me, and I write letters as the true act of love for my departed daughter who now has disappeared from the face of the earth as though an autumn tornado picked her up and carried her away into some never-never land that you might see in a movie made by some imaginative producer with a lot of cash and very few guts, my childish Herm maybe, I was descending the stairs and he did not call out, or if he did I didn't hear him, and by the time I reached the street three men had approached me. Dutiful dark inhabitants of the lobby of twilight, they leaped from their seats to catch me before I went out the door and into the street fearing that some infectious whim might strike me and prevent my return to their hotel where they made it their businesses to keep track of all the available women. Guided by one of them, the first one to reach me, (and that was all that mattered), I went to a cafe, drank my fill of whiskey, and allowed him to consider all of the possibilities which might have brought a girl as young as I was then to such a pass. Though I was going, I was not yet gone (and won't be until I finish my story) since what I realized just before deciding to come and speak to you, if only this once, was how long I had let others determine my ways and how little I had told about myself, and how small a part of my own life I had actually created myself, and for good or for evil or for both or neither (for if God made me this way, if anything could plan a mind such as mine, and feelings such as mine, and a life such as mine, then all things are possible).

Where you headed when I saw you? this tall slim jim with a cowboy tie and a glassy head of dark hair asks me.

To hell in a handbasket. Want to come along?

Where'd you learn to talk like that? You go up the university or something?

Don't need to do that, I said. My brother, he says, we're going to hell just fine without all of us getting our education.

Who's your brother, what's his name?

Jason.

I know him?

If you do, you're a bastard like him and I don't want to drink your money.

Well I don't know him. But I sure do like to know you. What's your name?

Besides.

That's right?

That's my name. Its a funny name but it's mine. Besides.

Besides what. Shit. You want another drink. It makes you into a real comedy star. You ought to drink more milk though, besides, because you're looking mighty skinny for a girl wants to attract real men.

Feel this, I say, taking his hand by the wrist and touching it to my belly. This going to require a lot of milk.

God, you are drunk.

Besides.

Drunk besides!

What do you call this place?

Ted Mooney's.

And this town?

Memphis, don't you know it's Memphis?

I don't know much but I know you got to give this town another name if I'm going to talk to you for more than one second more. I turned to the man at the left of me at the bar and he didn't seem surprised that he wanted to talk more to me. I was putting his hand on my belly when Cowboy Tie turned me around.

Hot City! he exclaims.

Hot damn! I scream back at him.

What you doing to this pretty thing? asks the man on the left of me. You fixing to fuck up her life?

You keep out her life, Bean Dog, says Cowboy Tie.

Or what? says Bean Dog.

Or I'll slice you up and feed you to nigger pups for breakfast.

Haw! haw! what the hell's a nigger pup? O! you mean what you and your family raise in your backyard and call them roses? Haw!

You stand behind me here, says Cowboy Tie to me, and with one motion which includes treating me rather tender-like since he knows I am going to be a mother and treating the situation rather seriously he swings me behind him and steps up to face Bean Dog. Except that Bean Dog isn't there. A knife is. And Cowboy Tie squints hard as the knife sweeps past his face.

Blood gushed across the bar, and I fainted.

When I awoke it was a lady standing over me, and no men in sight.

How'd you come here? she asks. She's about fifty, with lines that run rouge like water in irrigation ditches. Her dress is about as old as she is, least the style makes me think so. And she smells of outlandish perfume, Eau de Ham Sandwich or some such scent, until I realize that it's me I smell.

I don't know, I say squeezing or trying to squeeze up into a ball. I'm tired, sick to godman, I want to go home. Herbert? Where's Herbert? I ask her. I'm feeling just awful, like a bitty baby done done it in her pants and wants a Mama.

You wait here, I'll help you, she says. Temple?

I thought I was in some church.

Come help this girl clean herself up.

Yes, ma'am.

A younger woman brought me clean clothes. But they were a strange style and I told her I couldn't wear them.

You'll wear them, she says in a voice I didn't dare challenge.

How'd you get here? the girl dressing me asks.

I don't know, I said. I described the fight and all that and she says, oh. That's all.

You tell me the name of your hotel, the old lady says when she comes back into the room. I could hear laughing and piano music coming from somewhere on the same floor. I told her where we are staying and she laughs and says it ain't all that far from here. And she takes me by the hand and leads me out of the room, down a long flight of stairs, the piano music growing louder as we descend, and finally to a large green door leading, I correctly figured, to the street. I wish I could have stayed inside a while longer. The laughing and the music called out to me. I looked at the greenness of the outer door, my stomach felt awful and I wanted to sleep. I'll take you part way home, says the old lady, and we leave the house and walk a few blocks toward what became the center of the city and then she left me only a couple of yards from the hotel door.

This time was Herbert was gone. The room was locked, no one answered my knock, and when I went back down to the lobby to ask for the key the man at the desk told me that my husband had checked out. I cried all of a sudden, tears running down my cheeks like in a big home-style rainstorm. I pounded the desk top with my fists. The clerk tried to calm me down but I couldn't stop wailing. Then of a sudden across the lobby my name gets called.

Who's that? I spin around.

Lean long-faced man chewing on a pipe, newspaper across his knees.

He went up to Indiana, you got to follow him, this man says.

Damn if I do.

And if you don't, he says, flicking his eyes across me so friendly-like that I figured he didn't want me in any danger.

He give you the message? I inquire, still standing at the desk. I'm afraid to get too close to him so I won't be disappointed when I discover that his interest in me turns out to be like all the others in this state.

The man shrugs, which I take to mean, of course.

Your bag, Missus, says the clerk just then, sliding my only suitcase across the top of the desk. I asked him to hold it for a minute more, went to use the powder room on the ground floor, counted my money, and came back out to find the man with the pipe had disappeared, and my suitcase standing by the potted palm just at the door. Without looking back, I picked it up and hiked out the door to the bus station and caught the first bus to Indianapolis.

Herbert wasn't too happy to see me.

I thought you'd go back home, he said, standing in the living room of his folks' house, the place where he first told me how much he wanted to marry me.

Back there? I laughed as I unpacked. Your jokes just kill me, I said. Now I want to take a hot bath. It's not good for a woman in my condition to get so tired out.

I heard him arguing with his folks while I was running water in the tub. That argument didn't end until three months later when I left for good.

I don't know that I can explain just by talking to you. Gone, gone, gone, is the way it keeps saying over and over in my head, as what I felt and where I went and how I must have appeared to other people. I returned to Memphis, had my baby, gave it home, watched my father buried. I took up the theatre as a profession, which allowed me from time to time to return to the state. I watched my baby as she grew from nothing to a full-sized girl—there's many things involved in this that can't be said now or perhaps even ever. I thought for a time that I would be an actress who could make these bad feelings come out in my work but that didn't seem to mean much after a while I gave up on that and settled down to trying to stay alive minute by hour by day by month by year after year after year. Up to Denver; down to Salt Lake City; up to Omaha; down to Houston; over to Albuquerque; east to St. Louis; and then to the west. Doctor, I have travelled. So much since that time it has been hard for me to give myself time to think and study the parts of my life that hurt me the most the parts that I need to study so I can make the present good for me, the past is never past for me it is always present my mind sometimes seems to me like the grand opera house I played in so large the casts of three grand events performed in it at the same time and I was in the audience sitting near the rear, listening, nodding, praying, crying, laughing, oh, always with a sense of humor, waiting for the rehearsal to end. The last act means only another run-through from the beginning. The music. The lights. The jokes. The tintinabulation of the cymbals of the belles . . .

Oh, there's story after story to tell. The night would have to stop disappearing to the other side of the world before I could finish. Up in Salt Lake, a driver, two months on the run with the proceeds of . . .

or, There was once this man opened up a little theatre in a small town in the Northwest thought he could hire a troupe of . . .

or, That in Aleppo once . . .

or, Now Benson was a high shade of yellow and sported a mind like a fancy new car. And when we left for the I'll tell you about Herm at least. He was the best of a weak lot. Which speaks well for none of them; but not poorly for him. All of them, many things to say about the

Nights in Albuquerque hang in the high part of the sky, like the stars. You try to catch their passage but you fail . . .

Three miles west of the edge of a small town near the northeast pocket of . . .

Here is a woman. Do you know her? She has come a . . .

Two men could be seen walking along a stretch of gravel path . . .

It was in the year 1920 on a quiet April day

Inside the bar, the noises of the crowd subsided

. . . My father gave me a piece of advice . . .

Gifford married Karen on June 6, 196

"Number, please," said the operator.

I could say anything, I could say carry me along taddy like you done through the toy fair and what difference would it make. There is no question about what will happen next, no question whatsoever and because there is no question there need be no reason. No, I don't think that I'll take my own life. We have in my family a number of things that we have already accomplished, one of them being suicide, the other being idiocy, the next being alcoholism, the other being miserliness, and, godman, you might think that that was enough to boast about but then you will have to add to the list, which tacks on a number of venal sins, several mortal sins—sometime I'll tell you how Clarsworth and I raised the money for the vaudeville troupe—sometime—social disgraces, iniquities, as Dis Dilsey we used to call her our Mama used to call what we did to each other, dis dat and d'other, a barnfull of just plain disgusting behavior down to and including the night when Jason came bursting into my room and caught me sitting with my legs up on the table and I wasn't wearing any pants and he caught a look at me and started shouting and jumping up and down and screaming so loud you'd think it had a flashing-neon eye winking at him . . .

Now you have said nothing to me but that you think that I want to make my life a living Hell . . .

Now you have asked me to write down for you what I can remember about my past

Which to me is like a declaration of undependance from the present which is fine with me since the moment I'm living in gives me pain why not live in the past.

And so I thought that I would copy out for you part of a letter which

(I'm stopping everything now because I just remember sitting on a swing with the first man to put his finger inside me, is that the kind of thing you need to hear)

part of this letter which my brother a educated boy sent to me from college the one who killed himself

"*Noi siam ventui al luogo ov'io t'ho detto/ che tu vedrai le genti dolorose,/ ch'hanno perduto il ben dello intelletto.*"

Dear Candace,

I am speaking to you across all these miles and thinking how much I would like to hear the sound of your voice, hear you laugh. Here he quotes a lot of poetry which I cannot remember. And goes on. I raised that shade and looked out over the mountains of home, and saw that nigger on a mule as big as a rabbit, a sign, a landmark . . . I heard a bell of pure reverberation and it called me back to myself and I knew that purity lay beneath the water, was the water itself, remember the time in the stream bed how I could ever forget when we baptized each other with our own noneternal self-affection, and you said that you would run away and you ran.

I returned to Memphis once more before leaving behind forever that place where I couldn't live and yet couldn't live without. I knew how I felt about it because I made an abortive trip to Europe just after returning there as I said I did as I described to you the next to the last time when I found her gone, my mother ill, my family mostly dead and the ones left alive better off dead or ought to be dead and my husbands dead and I went to Italy to visit friends and they had died or gone away and only their empty house was there to greet me. And I left the doorstep of that house in Italy and turned right around and returned to Memphis because I knew in that moment when I didn't walk in the door of that villa because there was no one left to greet me there I knew then where she was. Yes.

Forgotten but not gone. I had known for a while but could not bring myself to understand as we sometimes do the things we know all along are real and I went from Italy to Memphis, strange route, and I reached the country on a boat loaded with people like yourself of your persuasion religion whatever and they were kind to me telling me that I was pretty as they had always imagined American girls to be and I said Oh, American, am I American? and then understood that that was so although for all these years I imagined myself as something particular to one part of the country only and found the rest of the country as odd and curious and unfamiliar as I found Italy, although when I travelled abroad on that brief trip I was less aware of my surroundings than I had been when I went north or west. They liked to talk about their families they were going to see when the boat docked and asked me where I was going and I told them the truth.

I'm going to see my daughter.

How nice, how nice, the women chanted. How nice that you're going to see your daughter. Why, I overheard them talk among themselves, she looks so young, she looks like a little girl herself, her light hair, so pretty, she no wrinkles has at all, a skin of a little girl

Whenever we saw each other on deck they asked are you getting nervous you'll see your daughter soon? So soon how getting nervous she is from the thought of seeing her daughter walking the deck or shivering in my room

It is a far piece from New Orleans to Memphis. And yet I didn't remember the trip up the Old Trace, passing passing red leaves trees fields of such powerful recollections that I might have read all about their attractions before I had even lived it and then lived it and the land seemed to draw all the force and feeling out of me as though itself recognized what I would have to not feel in the day ahead

It was a warm evening towards the end of September when I entered the city for the last time. I had ridden the entire way in a private car a Buick then it was quite the style you know and we drove past the same hotel since I knew that I did not need a bed for the night and even if I did I would not have given my custom to a place such as that with memories of Herbert in the window well in the doorways halls. We rolled past we made the necessary turns I retraced my route quite accurately to the driver and he said

Are you sure you want to go to this place accent on this time he was trying to tell me something he thought I didn't already know and I said

Yes, indeed, that is my destination

And he said,

You're the he hesitated wanted to say boss then substituted lady in charge

Madam you might call me I said

What he said what you sure have a sense of humor ma'am

Do I I said I did once I know I used to dance in vaudeville and play in the moving pictures just bit parts but they required that I have a sense of humor Here we are I said recognizing the house by its door

He pulled the car over to the curb and turned around to face me where I sat without feeling much of the thing in that moment in the rear of the car

Could I know you he said.

IV

The sea gave off the color of blood, as though it were somehow conscious of the plan.

"I don't like the scene tonight," said Bergère, plucking at his tie. "It's too pretty . . ." He shook his head, suffering privately at the cruelty of their plot and the deep and resonant shades of the water, hills, sky. Veins bulged in his arms, his own blood surging through his brain as though the tide called sooner to him than to the sea. No older than eighteen, his dark eyes showed his lack of sleep and his skin the years he had spent in dimly-lit caverns. I should put my feet up on the bench and smoke a cigarette or two. But instead I'm afraid that I may pee.

"Here they come," said his companion. It was as if they existed each in different spheres until the moment for action arrived. It had been that way before. I am tall, he is short. My bowels. Stubby little fucker who would murder his granny if she tweaked his nose. He dislikes my proletarian origins and I think he smells like the rest of the people of his province whatever their social class. "Time to play magician."

"What's that?" Bergère said, looking up at the couple smiling for the photographer on the beach front. Their black limousine sat at the entrance to the Sandborn-Nice. The man looked quite ordinary in his carefully-pressed blue uniform. The death's head caught the light of the late spring sun. Sprightly walk. Something special there. His teeth would be perfect, and he could do more pushups than anyone in their own unit, of that one could be sure. ". . . pushup!" Dac's voice broke into his thoughts. He was reading my mind! But no, look at her, she brings out the thought in all men. Her hair nearly the color of the bay, her legs as trim as my baby sister's. And she must be nearly forty!

". . . quite a number," Dac finished, speaking through his own clenched teeth as she turned her back to the driver.

"She's American." "She's been with him a year now."

"I don't think I've ever seen an American woman before," said Bergère.

"You must be joking," said Dac as he watched the couple disappear up the hotel steps and through the arches that led into the lobby.

"Why, man, do you think we run a tourist colony up our way? Who wants to swim in our coal mines?"

Dac spat onto the roadway, barely missing Bergère's left shoe. "Well, come on," he said before Bergère could respond to his challenge. "We've got a war to fight. You have your papers?"

"Yes," said Bergère. "But I have to piss something awful."

"Christ, man, at a time like this! What kind of softie are you?"

"Softie? I've got to piss."

"Okay, okay, do it in the hotel. There's a WC just off the kitchen."

"We have to go up to the second floor anyway. I'll find one on the second floor."

"Maybe you'd like to use the one in their room."

Bergère laughed, in spite of himself. Now he recalled why he enjoyed working with the little florist's son. Both of them lived far from home, both of them made the most of it.

"I'd like to use her," he said, patting Dac on the shoulder as they walked to the path which led to the kitchen's underground entryway. "I wonder what she's like." He touched the knot of his fat red tie.

"We should fuck her," said Dac. "I wouldn't mind that."

"And behave like those animals? I was only joking."

"The war's on. I have no illusions." Dac lowered his voice as they passed the gendarme on duty at the door. "Good afternoon, how you doin'?"

The gendarme raised his eyebrows at Bergère's appearance.

"Who's he?"

"My cousin. He has to pee before he goes to work up the beach."

"He looks tender. Do you have to hold his hand? Or something else?"

Dac showed the gendarme that he thoroughly enjoyed his remark by patting Bergère on the buttocks and shooing him in the door.

"He'll be out in a moment, officer."

"And you too perhaps," the gendarme said, "when they find that you're bringing your entire family in to piss."

"I wish you'd piss on his shoes," Dac said as they climbed the stairwell to the ground floor and then continued on to the second. "There's the little WC at the end of the hall. Do it quickly. We have only a few minutes before the truck leaves the city."

Bergère nodded and walked swiftly down the end of the hall. The room lay in the opposite direction. I could have only a few minutes to live myself, he considered, why do I want to make the time go by so fast? He counted the number of doors he passed, found the water closet and yanked on the door. Locked.

"What?" came a gruff female voice from within.

He did not reply but instead hurried back to where Dac was waiting for him.

"You didn't go in."

"Someone was using it."

"But you still have to piss."

"Don't make me feel like a child. I'll hold out till later."

Dac touched his arm.

"Good, lad. I knew you could do it."

Bergère grew angry, feeling the hard metal piece inside his coat.

"No more jokes."

"Jokes keep my mind off things."

"I don't live that way myself."

"You haven't lived that long, kid, that you know how to live. Make the most of it." He talked through his teeth. "And make it short."

"The job, you mean?"

Dac did not have time to reply.

Footsteps behind them. They turned nervously to see a wide-hipped middle-aged woman in a nurse's costume following them down the hall.

"Young man!"

Bergère stopped suddenly while Dac kept on moving a few paces further down the hall.

"Yes, Madame," he said as calmly as he could.

"Was that you outside the door?"

"Come on," Dac said in a voice louder than normal. "Come along."

"Good-bye, Madame."

"I was only trying to inquire—"

"Come on!" Dac insisted, herding his companion down the hall.

Bergère bowed his head, feeling he did not know why quite embarrassed. I am rude to old ladies and I don't know why I'm here. What is this thing in my pocket? What are we doing here? Who are the enemies? What are these questions? How can I walk? Will we make it to the end? My breath, why does it hurt me to breathe? My mother never lived as long as that old bitch but she once worked as a matron at a movie theatre . . .

"Here it is," Dac said, his voice almost sunk to a whisper. "Are you alright? You're trembling."

"My bladder."

"Steady now. Time to play magician."

Dac looked both ways down the hall, then knocked on the door.

The American woman opened it. A voice barked in German behind her, but she moved as though she were walking under water, caressing the door with her right hand even as they forced her back into the dimly-lighted room whose windows lay muffled in thick, purple draperies. The voice barked again from a corner at the bed and they shouted at him and at the woman.

Something in the way she looked at him drew from Bergère a long shiver. Her wide blue eyes, the awareness in that glance, seemed to mate with a wish now revealed to him as she finally released her grip on the door and had they the time he would happily have emptied his aching bladder across the front of her creamy-white silky garment with pearl buttons lying open down the front to show her freckled breasts. Her hands upraised not so much in surprise as recognition, her posture in that instant impossible, fantastic, demanding witness. It would haunt him for the rest of his life.

The Disappearance of
Quentin Compson

John W. Hunt*

I

One of the many pleasures of reading William Faulkner comes from his mastery of the impressionist technique of presenting an effect prior to its cause. The reader's peripheral vision is often so circumscribed while in the presence of a character's limited consciousness that to him, as to the character, an event will become suddenly there, without antecedent, without warning, and, because of this, with tremendous force. In "furious immobility" the reader stops, and time stops—or seems to. More accurately, for the reader as for the character, time stretches, expands into a specious present full of meaning and rich in incident. Often exploration of that expanded moment then becomes the focus of what follows.

Something akin to this characteristic experience can happen to one who examines Faulkner's literary career in the last half of the 1920s. Suddenly and unexplained *The Sound and the Fury* is there. Few, I suspect, first read Faulkner in sequence of publication, but when his novels are read in any sequence the mystery is still there. *The Sound and the Fury*, to borrow Sartre's metaphor, seems to "pounce upon us like a thief."[1] What we now know, after the work of Meriwether and Millgate and Blotner and others, is that the mystery remained there for Faulkner too.

The incidents surrounding the writing of *The Sound and the Fury* are familiar to most Faulknerians. When Horace Liveright wrote Faulkner in late November of 1927 that he would not publish his first Yoknapatawpha novel, *Flags in the Dust*, Faulkner's reply, dated five days later, was restrained and confident: "It's too bad you dont like Flags in the Dust. . . . I'd like for you to fire it on back to me, as I shall try it on someone else. . . . Regards to everyone."[2] Inside, however, he was churning: " 'I was shocked: my first emotion was blind protest.' "[3] He had had rejections before, but this was "THE book," he had boasted earlier to Liveright, "of which those other things were but foals."[4] As David Minter puts it, "to Faulkner it seemed that he had discovered an inexhaustible

*This essay was written specifically for this volume and is published here for the first time by permission of the author.

kingdom; to his publisher it seemed that he did not even 'have any story to tell.' "[5] And so, he quit thinking about writing for others and wrote for himself. What he wrote was the story of Candace Compson, "a beautiful and tragic little girl."[6]

As we know, it was not all that simple, although essentially the story is true. Four years after *The Sound and the Fury* was published, Faulkner looked back upon his writing of it as a moment of epiphany when the door clapped shut between him and the commercial world and he said to himself, "Now I can write. Now I can just write."[7] It became the novel at once closest to him personally—he had fallen in love with Caddy—and the most removed, as though the experience of "that first ecstasy"[8] in which it was written released it to become its own enigmatic and self-contained entity—fixed, timeless, forever beautiful. By the 1950s he was speaking of the novel in interviews with the special tenderness a mother feels for her child. Sensing in 1953 that his powers were diminishing, and confessing in a letter to Joan Williams that he was "getting toward the end," Faulkner claimed, "at last, . . . some perspective" on all he had done. His response to a backward view was "simply amazement": "now I realise for the first time what an amazing gift I had" (*Letters*, p. 348). He was speaking of the whole body of work he had produced, but when we set his words against his earlier consistent claims about the importance of *The Sound and the Fury*, it is clear that for him his amazing gift was first fully realized in the writing of that novel.

Liveright's letter on *Flags in the Dust* was almost a clichéd rejection notice, as though he were going down a check list:

> Soldier's Pay was a very fine book and should have done better. Then Mosquitoes wasn't quite as good, showed little development in your spiritual growth and I think none in your art of writing. Now comes Flags in the Dust and we're frankly very much disappointed by it. It is diffuse and non-integral with neither very much plot development nor character development. We think it lacks plot, dimension and projection. The story really doesn't get anywhere and has a thousand loose ends. If the book had plot and structure, we might suggest shortening and revisions but it is so diffuse that I don't think this would be any use. My chief objection is that you don't seem to have any story to tell and I contend that a novel should tell a story and tell it well.[9]

Although Liveright's letter seems singularly imperceptive now that Faulkner's career is complete, it is hard to fault him greatly for missing what Faulkner had accomplished. Faulkner's shock and blind protest came from knowledge Liveright could not possibly have shared. Beginning with *Sartoris/Flags in the Dust*, as he told Jean Stein almost thirty years later, he had discovered that in his own native soil he did have a story worth writing about and had created from it his apocryphal world, a mixture of fiction and fact, uncanonical but also "a kind of keystone in the Universe."[10] With *Flags in the Dust* he had moved beyond writing other people's books, the "youngly glamorous" *Soldiers' Pay* and the "trashily smart" *Mosquitoes*.[11] Bypassing *Mosquitoes* and reaching back to *Soldiers' Pay*, as Millgate has observed, he picked up thematic materials and elements of situation for his first Yoknapatawpha novel, treating them in a less self-consciously literary and more integrated way.[12] Yet for all that we can now see in it from the perspective of what followed, *Flags in the Dust* belongs more to the apprentice period than to Faulkner's great period initiated by *The Sound and the Fury*. Faulkner had a story, many stories, to tell, but his authorial voice still too much betrayed the romantic posturing of his earlier novels. The townspeople, hill people, and families, living and dead, were there, and the houses and rivers and woods and fields and seasons, yet although he had discovered Yoknapatawpha County, Faulkner had not taken full possession of it.

When Faulkner closed the door and started writing for himself, he discovered in Quentin Compson a character whose voice would allow him to take full possession of his apocryphal world. *The Sound and the Fury* is Quentin's novel in a special way. It is also Caddy's story (certainly it was at its inception), just as *Absalom, Absalom!* is Sutpen's story, but in significant measure Caddy's and Sutpen's stories become what they are for us because of Quentin's controlling and defining presence. There are many differences, of course, and the point should not be labored. Quentin's presence controls in only one of the four narrations making up *The Sound and the Fury*, while in *Absalom, Absalom!* he is present throughout either as listener or as teller. Caddy is his contemporary, his very sister, while Sutpen is from "old ghost-times" and is known to him only from stories and legends and a few relics and surviving artifacts. Quentin's special place in the Faulkner corpus is not simply a function of his having been the first major character-narrator; rather, in him Faulkner found his first powerful way of telling the story of Yoknapatawpha County. Quentin's consciousness so dominates *The Sound and the Fury*, once we have read his section, that all events of the other sections are qualified by his anxieties about Caddy. All present meaning for him is entrapped in the sexuality of a sister who cares not a biblical fig for it. By use of a narrator thus carefully defined, Faulkner tells two stories which develop in relation to one another, the one the subject of the narrator's focus, the other the story of the focusing narrator.

One need not be exclusive about this. The power of Benjy's section and of Jason's, and of the section told in Dilsey's dominating presence, arises from the same narrative strategy and is also to be insisted upon. Within the novel, each narration works, achieves a complete dramatic statement, although there is truth in Faulkner's repeated claim that he told the story of Caddy four times and never finished it. But key to the sum's being more than its parts is Quentin, not because his section is more true than the others, which it is not, but because his character allows it to be more serious, more resonant across time with meaning and implication about what Caddy's story is—within the novel, in the Yoknapatawpha apocrypha, and for the world of which the apocryphal world is the microcosm. One reason for the more resonant quality of Quentin's section, I suspect, is that fewer people would admit to a closer identification with Benjy or Jason than with Quentin. Once defined in *The Sound and the Fury*, Quentin's character was at hand for another powerful telling of a Yoknapatawpha tale, Sutpen's story in *Absalom, Absalom!*

II

Biographers and textual critics point to some evidence which allows reasonable speculation about Faulkner's first discovery of Quentin, or at least his earliest use of him. He appears as narrator in both "A Justice" and "That Evening Sun Go Down," both of which, Blotner suggests, although he says he cannot prove, were probably written between Liveright's rejection of *Flags in the Dust* and the inception in writing of *The Sound and the Fury* in the early months of 1928. If "Never Done No Weeping When You Wanted to Laugh" preceded the writing of "A Justice," probably Quentin first went down on paper in that unpublished early try at "That Evening Sun Go Down."[13] At whatever time Quentin first emerged in Faulkner's writing, it is clear that once conceived he emerged quickly. Noel Polk speculates that the last revision of Quentin's section, a major one, may have been in July of 1929 when Faulkner received the book's galleys from the publisher. If so, he argues, it is probable that Quentin's character in *The Sound and the Fury* was sharpened finally in relation to Faulkner's development of Horace Benbow in *Sanctuary*, which he worked on in the early months of 1929.[14]

The history of Quentin's appearances and disappearances in the Faulkner corpus tells us something important about the way Faulkner worked as an artist developing his apocryphal world. If "A Justice" and what Norman Holmes Pearson calls Faulkner's "Three 'Evening Suns' " were written prior to the writing of the unfinished story "Twilight," which became *The Sound and the Fury*, it is highly probable that Quentin entered the Faulkner corpus as a narrator.[15] Facts curious in retrospect trigger questions. There is no mention of Benjy at all in "A Justice" and the three "Evening Suns." The first published reference to Quentin is in Benjy's section of *The Sound and the Fury*, narrated eighteen years after Quentin's death. In his own voice, Quentin survives only 129 pages, and he commits suicide at the age of twenty on the first day he is introduced as a narrator. As narrator of "That Evening Sun Go Down," Quentin is twenty-four years old, and in "A Justice" his point of view is roughly equivalent in maturity though his age cannot be so precisely calculated. Both stories were first published in 1931, the former revised and published again the same year as "That Evening Sun."[16] In all subsequent publications of the two stories, Quentin of the same age remains narrator, although the narrator is not identified in that portion of "A Justice" compressed as a prelude to "A Bear Hunt" in *Big Woods* (1955).

Elements of several stories, one published and others completed but not published, took their final form in *Absalom, Absalom!* (1936) where Quentin was made narrator of them only when they became part of that novel. Neither "The Big Shot," written prior to late January 1930, nor its re-worked version, "Dull Tale," was published during Faulkner's lifetime, but elements of "The Big Shot" can be found in "Wash," written probably in 1933, published in 1934, and related by an omniscient narrator. The final version of Wash's story appears in *Absalom, Absalom!* where Quentin, with some help from Shreve, narrates it as a story he had heard from his father. As Faulkner labored in 1934 on *A Dark House*, the working title for *Absalom, Absalom!*, he wrote Harrison Smith about his use of Quentin to tell Sutpen's story, or to tie it together.[17] He was working from "Evangeline," an unpublished story he had written in 1931 in which Sutpen's story first took a completed form. It too has elements in it originating at least as far back as "The Big Shot." In one story, unrelated to *Absalom, Absalom!*, Quentin appears as narrator only in the story's final form. He narrates the *Big Woods* version of "A Bear Hunt," from which he was absent when the story was first published in 1934.

Quentin is the narrator of the original versions of "Lion" and "The Old People" and probably narrated the first version of "Fool About a Horse"; in each case, however, he is not the narrator of their final versions. When "Lion," written and published in 1935, became part of "The Bear" of *Go Down, Moses* of 1942, it was narrated in the third person with Isaac McCaslin as the protagonist. In the other two stories Quentin did not survive to the first stage of publication. Blotner conjectures that he was the narrator of the earliest version of "Fool About a Horse," also written in 1935, but was eliminated when the story was revised before publication in *Scribner's* in 1936. The narrator of the version in *Scribner's* is unnamed, and revisions of 1938–39 integrated the story into *The Hamlet* of 1940 with V. K. Ratliff as narrator. In mid-1939 Faulkner wrote "The Old People" with Quentin as narrator, but when it was first published, in *Harper's* in 1940, an unidentified narrator told the story and direct links of the narrator to the character of Quentin were obscured, although indirect links can be found. For example, "our farm four miles from Jefferson" is similar to a phrase used in "A Justice."[18] In the story's final form, published as part of *Go Down, Moses*, it is narrated in the third person with Isaac McCaslin as "the boy."

At the time of Faulkner's death in 1962, then, Quentin remained as a narrator in the final printed form of only three stories not integrated into novels—"A Justice," "That Evening Sun," "A Bear Hunt." He was made narrator of "Wash" when it became part of *Absalom, Absalom!* He was probably the narrator, but eliminated before publication, in "Fool About a Horse," and before publication he was also the narrator of "The Old

People." Although he narrated the first published version of "Lion," he was eliminated from that story too when it was integrated into "The Bear" of *Go Down, Moses*. Ratliff replaced him as narrator in the final form of "Fool About a Horse" which appeared in *The Hamlet*, and Isaac McCaslin replaced him as the protagonist when "Lion" and "The Old People" were told in the third person as a part of *Go Down, Moses*.

III

In getting at some of the reasons for Faulkner's decisions to bring Quentin into and out of various texts and to make certain substitutions for him, one can be helped by biographical studies correlating what was happening in Faulkner's life at the time such decisions were made.[19] There is an inner logic in the corpus itself, however, which does not require heavy reference to Faulkner's person and situation, and to understand it is to learn something useful about how Faulkner worked as an artist. Our brief look at Quentin's movement in and out of some Faulkner texts shows that although Faulkner had to let manifestations of his Yoknapatawpha imagination go into print from time to time, he was rarely satisfied that he had gotten them right. He gave his very best to his novels. The record of *Absalom, Absalom!* revisions is tortuous and demonstrates an uncompromising ambition. In his introduction to the first Modern Library edition of *Sanctuary* in 1932, he even craftily created a public scandal in boasting of his extensive revisions. In interviews he freely confessed that sometimes his decisions to release stories were influenced by the need for money, a fact borne out in his letters and in Blotner's biography.

The pattern of Quentin's entrances into and exits from Faulkner's novels and stories between 1928 and 1941 suggests that his usefulness to Faulkner was both crucial and limited as the Yoknapatawpha cycle developed. He entered when Faulkner sought a way of accounting morally for the deterioration of an aristocratic family, and he exited when Faulkner felt he needed to present other and wider perceptions of the forces and currents in Yoknapatawpha County. Many of Quentin's concerns and a version of his function in the corpus were given to Isaac McCaslin in a different context, but Isaac quickly reached his limits of usefulness as well.

The story about Sam Fathers' parentage which Quentin hears at the age of twelve in "A Justice" could not have been told with the same effect by Quentin directly, for it is too full of humor, too much the tall tale, for his treatment. By shifting the burden of the narration to Sam, who has the story secondhand from Herman Basket, Faulkner assigns it to an adult temperament, to one who can relate it in a style beyond the ability of a twentieth-century young educated townsman who has no black or Indian blood. But by framing the story with Quentin at a much more mature age than the age he was when he first heard it, Faulkner allows the qualities of Quentin most useful to him to set the final tone. In the story's frame,

Quentin reluctantly acknowledges that he has glimpsed the formative role of violence and sexuality in historical societies.

At the age of twenty-four Quentin tells about Nancy in "That Evening Sun," like "A Justice" a tale of violence and sexual betrayal. In this case, however, the story is related directly by Quentin who begins it with the posture of a detached social historian. Gradually, as the story moves toward the last evening the Compson children spend with Nancy, the distanced stance of the social historian fades and the action of the story makes its own implied commentary about its import. By the time the children and their father leave Nancy in her cabin waiting for Jesus, the tone of the story has completely changed and the burden of Nancy's despair and doom hangs heavy. This, then, becomes Quentin's kind of story—sex, betrayal, impending violence, doom, and despair.

Similarly, the story of Wash in *Absalom, Absalom!* is appropriate for Quentin to narrate. He relates the story as his father's, conveying with it his father's speculations about Wash's thoughts and feelings and motives. Nonetheless, Mr. Compson's interpretations speak to Quentin's distress at Sutpen's story, weakening his resistance to a conclusion condemning himself. The vitality displayed by the originless Sutpen, although rapacious, was not at odds with the true tradition which has formed the present in which Quentin has to live. For all their differences in class, Quentin can share Wash's incredulity at Sutpen's treatment of Milly when she fails to give him a colt instead of a filly. Because of Sutpen's stature in the culture, as he hears and reconstructs Sutpen's story Quentin is more devastated by its elements of violence and sexual domination than he is by the same elements in "A Justice" and "That Evening Sun." Quentin's heritage as a white southerner includes direct knowledge of landed aristocracy but only indirectly the experiences of blacks and Indians.

After finishing *The Sound and the Fury* Faulkner dropped Quentin from his writing for many years, although he collected "A Justice" and "That Evening Sun," the latter revised, in *These 13* (1931). Extending Polk's suggestion, we may say that Horace Benbow, "in effect, a forty-three-year-old and completely jaded Quentin," took over his place and function for a period (p. 299). Not until he had written *As I Lay Dying* (1930), *Sanctuary* (1931), and *Light in August* (1932) did Faulkner take up Quentin again—that is, when he began *Absalom, Absalom!* in 1934. Perhaps because Quentin was very much on his mind when he laid that novel aside, he used him in "Lion" and probably in "Fool About a Horse." (We are comfortable with 1935 as the date for the writing of "Lion," while the first composition of "Fool About a Horse" can be assigned to that date only tentatively.)

If Quentin was the first narrator of "Fool About a Horse," then it is the only story we know about which, originally his, ended as Ratliff's. It is perfectly appropriate that it should, for Ratliff's storytelling posture is characteristically aesthetic rather than moral. The story of how Pap (later, Ab Snopes) was led on, caught, and made a fool of by the legendary Pat Stamper would become a tale of outrage were it to remain in the hands of the humorless Quentin. There is a good deal of humor in "A Justice" too, of course, and Faulkner successfully removed Quentin from the direct telling of its central tale, but the tale itself was sufficiently full of poisonous politics and sexual competition to interest a person of Quentin's character. Nor would Quentin be capable of the storytelling style demanded by "A Fool About a Horse," a tale of plain country folk. Such a story must be told lightly and for enjoyment, for if the incidents and people are looked at too long it becomes a story of cruelty. Ratliff holds the tale at arm's length, letting the point of the tale be as much the twists and turns and surprises of its telling as it is of the qualities of its characters. His remove from the action makes the story a spectacle, just as Shreve's distance from Sutpen's tale allows him to make a marvel of it. In response to his own bawdy creations, Shreve blurts out, " 'Jesus, the South is fine, isn't it. It's better than the theatre, isn't it. It's better than Ben Hur, isn't it.' "[20] It does not matter to Shreve how the story comes out, just so it is a good theatre and is good fun to tell. For Quentin all telling, if it is worth telling at all, requires pain.

The final disposition of "Lion," however, and of "The Old People," both clearly stories originally narrated by Quentin, was made as Faulkner finished the last phase of his great period from 1928–1942. When they became Isaac's stories in *Go Down, Moses*, the settings of both were pushed back to the time of Isaac's boyhood and changes were required too in the group frequenting the hunting camps. In more fundamental ways both stories were transformed by integration into the overall strategy of the new novel. They were re-written to contribute to the development of another protagonist who grew to share many of Quentin's concerns about the tradition, but who responded, however ineffectively, in a much different way. Yet, working with the *Scribner's* and *Harper's* versions of these stories, we can say that though transformed, what was essential in their earlier forms was kept, for both remained stories of the out-of-doors, of wisdom of the wilderness, and of initiation into manhood. By reason of these essential qualities, and Faulkner must have felt this, they were never properly Quentin's kind of stories. Nothing shown of his character in *The Sound and the Fury* and *Absalom, Absalom!* makes it appropriate for Quentin to say, "So the instant came; I pulled the trigger and ceased to be a child forever and became a hunter and a man."[21]

Miss Rosa in *Absalom, Absalom!* makes canny inference about Quentin's character when she appeals to his "literary" temperament. Precisely because this young man of 1909 headed for Harvard, this young Southern man practiced as a listener in the presence of his father, has, as his heritage, heard about Sutpen all his life, she knows he will be caught up once again in a family history of power, adultery (she does not know about the threat of incest), and violence explaining why God let loose the War. As a literary young man of Southern heritage Quentin has every day to confront the past intimately, personally, because it is always with him lodged and honored in family memory. Miss Rosa's ghosts are Quentin's, and they live indoors in her "dim hot airless room with the blinds all closed and fastened for forty-three summers" (p. 7). Quentin finds one of them to be real when he enters another "bare, stale room," this one in Sutpen's decaying mansion, "whose shutters were closed too" (p. 373).

Only twenty-six years earlier, while poring over the plantation commissary records in the same December month in which Old Ben and Lion were killed, Isaac too, at the age of sixteen, discovers racism, violence, and adultery and incest—in his own family lineage. But his listening had been in the hunting camp located on what was once old Thomas Sutpen's land, and his ghosts—Lion, Old Ben, and Sam Fathers—live there, outdoors in the wilderness, "myriad yet undiffused of every myriad part."[22] He believes that Sam Fathers had set him free from the failure of humanity in the tradition that allowed Sutpen's kind of civilization to exist. It was Sutpen's and old Carothers McCaslin's desire to possess, to own the land and the other people on it, that made God let loose the War.

Common to Quentin's distress with Sutpen and Isaac's with old Carothers was each man's refusal to acknowledge kinship with his black progeny. Like Quentin, Isaac is a moral historian, but unlike him he does not assume history's force to be unyielding. Freed by Sam Fathers, he believes he can, not repudiate, but relinquish legally inherited possession of the land and thereby keep himself free of the taint of possession.

As he is with Quentin, Faulkner is merciless in his judgment of Isaac. Quentin, the abstracter who twists the hands off his watch, escapes history; Isaac escapes it too, re-writing it as myth, relinquishing his watch to catch a vision, out of time, of an old bear. Quentin fixes upon a rigid moral code, never unambiguously operative in the tradition, which when broken breaks him; Isaac fixes upon a buck that "still and forever leaped, . . . forever immortal," and in that vision stops time (p. 178). Quentin is sick with the honeysuckle sweet smell of sex, obsessed with Caddy whose free spirit unnerves him, whose vitality makes him frantic, whose sexuality becomes all of her for him. Isaac experiences a time of "brief unsubstanced glory" (p. 326) when he marries, but quickly routed by his wife's sexuality and his own lust, promises her the farm, which she then rejects, and for the rest of his life tries to escape periodically to the ever-receding and sexless world of the wilderness. When the sin of old Carothers is shown to be repeated by his great-great-great-grandson Roth Edmonds in "Delta Autumn," over half a century after being set free Isaac is a sterile and pitiable old man crying "We will have to wait" and offering money and the old hunting horn to the great-great-great-granddaughter (who is also his great-great-granddaughter) of old Carothers, the black mother of Roth's child. " 'Old man,' " she says when he tells her to go North and marry her own kind, " 'have you lived so long and forgotten so much that you dont remember anything you ever knew or felt or even heard about love?' " (p. 363). Cass Edmonds articulates the judgment which the events of Isaac's life dramatize: no man is ever free, " 'not now nor ever' " (p. 299).

IV

Faulkner was essentially finished with Quentin by the time he had used him to tell Sutpen's story in *Absalom, Absalom!* Quentin's story had been told, not in the usual way but by his telling of the stories of others. In effect, he had become something of a specialist, and once his task was accomplished he was out of work. Faulkner tried to employ him again in a few stories written after *Absalom, Absalom!*, but in every case cut him when those stories reached their final form. One story, which is not an exception but which does stand curiously alone, is "A Bear Hunt." Faulkner inserted Quentin as narrator when it was made a part of *Big Woods* in 1955. Within the logic of Faulkner's developing corpus I can find no good reason why he should have done this; perhaps in his imperial manner as creator of his kingdom he was simply giving a final salute to an old friend who had done so much for him when he needed him most.

Quentin's special task had been to give a moral and historical account of Yoknapatawpha County with the sensibility of a young and vulnerable aristocrat who suffers from the diminishment of meaning in his time. At first, in telling the stories of Sam Fathers and Nancy of the Compson household, Faulkner showed Quentin to be extraordinarily sensitive to the power of sexuality displayed in the violence which attended it. When Faulkner next used Quentin, to tell Caddy's story, he found in Quentin's sensibility a way of taking full possession of his whole apocryphal county; Quentin's obsession with Caddy's sexuality allowed for historical explanation of his own aristrocratic family's deterioration and, by extension, the deterioration of the tradition from which it came. As an aristocrat Quentin inevitably looks to his family heritage to verify his own worth.

Although successful reading of *Absalom, Absalom!* requires no prior knowledge of Quentin's character in *The Sound and the Fury*, one can understand why Faulkner saw him as the right instrument for telling Sutpen's story. "I use him," he wrote to Harrison Smith while in the early phase of the novel's composition, "because it is just before he is to commit suicide because of his sister."[23] The reconstruction of Sutpen's history quickens when Shreve forces it to an exploration of the relationship among Sutpen's children. Quentin the brooding moral historian resists the moral of the history, but cannot ignore the conclusions to which his special obsessions lead him: the low-born Sutpen's vitality and ambition, his sexuality and drive for power, were of the tradition. The tradition itself as interpreted through his sensibility therefore fails Quentin in his quest for the moral purity that would have assured him of his own worth. Since for Quentin the past binds the present, it can only destroy him.

As he moved outdoors, as it were, still pursuing the relationship of a diminished present to the past in Yoknapatawpha County, Faulkner developed many of Quentin's concerns in Isaac. Although he shows enormous sympathy for Isaac's desire to invoke a time when and a place where, to escape to an untainted world, Faulker neither believes in such a time and place nor sees that Isaac's belief in it can allow him to live where he must, in nature, time, and history. He shows him taking a positive action, but in a negative direction, out of history: he does not relinquish, he repudiates.

In developing Cass Edmonds as a character sympathetic to Isaac, but one who acknowledges experience as historical, Faulkner accomplished something similar in *Go Down, Moses* to the balancing effect he achieved by countering Quentin with Dilsey in *The Sound and the Fury*. Edmonds is no saint, and I do not believe that Dilsey is either (although I am not so sure), but like Dilsey he does accept his humanity and try to cope. In him Faulkner continued to lay the basis, present in his novels from the beginning, for what he would accomplish in the next cycle of Yoknapatawpha. In later novels Quentin's function as moral historian was taken over by Faulkner's other great Yoknapatawpha narrators, Ratliff, Stevens, and Chick Mallison. Increasingly there was more lightness of touch in the Yoknapatawpha novels, though the material remained as heavy, as Faulkner's narrators took an increasingly ironic stance. All of the novels about the Snopeses were published after Faulkner had essentially finished with Quentin. Indeed, before he handed Quentin's role to Isaac in *Go Down, Moses*, in the publication of the *The Hamlet* (1940) Faulkner had moved to the countryside with the first Snopeses, whose worse case was already moving toward the town.

V

Faulkner took one more intensely creative look at Quentin, along with all the Compsons, when he wrote the "Appendix" for inclusion in *The Portable Faulkner* (1946). The letter to Malcolm Cowley accompanying the Appendix shows that he was pleased with what he had done. "I think this is all right," he wrote, "it took me about a week to get Hollywood out of my lungs, but I am still writing all right, I believe." And, again, "Let me know what you think of this. I think it is really pretty good, to stand as it is, as a piece without implications."[24] Cowley was filled with admiration. Sixteen years after the publication of *The Sound and the Fury* the story was still alive in Faulkner's imagination, for in the Appendix Faulkner had added to the story of Caddy. But "without implications"? "The more I admired his Appendix, the more I found that some of the changes raised perplexing questions," Cowley recalled (p. 41). In fact, Faulkner's boldness was somewhat unnerving:

> His creative power was so unflagging that he could not tell a story twice without transforming one detail after another. He waved his magician's wand, and a pear tree in blossom was metamorphosed into a rainspout. He waved the wand again, and four thousand additional dollars appeared in Jason's strongbox, while the box itself, after vanishing from a closet, materialized in a locked bureau drawer. That was easy for him, but I was merely an editor, not a magician, and what was I to say about his text (pp. 45–46).

Cowley was merely an editor, but he had a job to do, decisions to make, closure to achieve. What *are* we to say about his text? Cowley queried Quentin's age in "That Evening Sun"; "Don't worry either about chrn. in EVENING SUN," Faulkner wrote back (p. 55). He queried *"du homme."* "I know it's *de l'homme*," Faulkner responded, but he had reasons; still, "Change it as you see fit" (p. 43). Then he queried the rainspout (though Faulkner had written "rainpipe"). Faulkner did not want it changed, and obliquely suggested it should really be "gutter" (p. 57). The text had already been sent to Viking, so Cowley instructed Viking to tell the copy editor or proofreader or printer that where he had pencilled in "plum tree" in the Appendix (Cowley had meant "pear tree") to let the original stand. By an oversight, when the *Portable* was printed, the pear tree remained in. When the Appendix returned later to Faulkner's own hands, the rainpipe was restored, and so it remains in *The Mansion* (1959), the last reference in the Faulkner corpus to Miss Quentin's escape.

Pear tree, plum tree, rainspout (rain spout), gutter, rainpipe? Why did it all become such a "sempiternal question," as Cowley calls it, such "a high comedy of misunderstanding" (pp. 64, 46)? Did it really matter to Faulkner? Cowley decided that it did, but not in the way he had at first thought. Faulkner later explained:

> I dont want to read TSAF again. Would rather let the appendix stand with the inconsistencies, perhaps make a statement (quotable) at the end of the introduction, viz.: The inconsistencies in the appendix prove that to me the book is still alive after 15 years, and being still alive is growing, changing; the appendix was done at the same heat as the book, even though 15 years later, and so it is the book itself which is inconsistent: not the appendix. That is, at the age of 30 I did not know these people as at 45 I now do; that I was even wrong now and then in the very conclusion I drew from watching them, and the information in which I once believed (p. 90).

Reflecting on Faulkner's explanation, Cowley concluded:

> If I had offered to change everything in the published novel that did not agree with the Appendix, I suspect that Faulkner would have encouraged

me in the undertaking. It was vastly different, however, when I urged him to change the Appendix and make it agree with the published book, for that would have meant going back to an earlier time when he had known or invented much less about the Compson family (p. 47).

I have never been much impressed with the reasons Faulkner gave for letting all of his inconsistencies stand, although one cannot help but enjoy the fancy footwork of some of his attempts to make them acceptable. I suspect that at times he was simply stubborn—it was *his* property—and we must respect that. Sometimes he probably did not want to bother, especially since the task if pursued could be endless. At other times he knew it really did not matter, and if editors insisted enough, he would let him have their way. Why not "pear tree" instead of "rainpipe"? Cowley's question was not answered. But sometimes it did matter and Faulkner could then be adamant. "That Evening Sun" dealt with the tragic consequences of a dilemma specific to Quentin's kind of family. His kind of sensibility was required to move the story with power toward a fated end inherent in his family's condition, but that sensibility needed to be at a more mature stage than Quentin had reached in *The Sound and the Fury*. Probably there was stubbornness in this instance too, and perhaps a little nostalgia, gratitude that in the early formation of Quentin's character he had first discovered how to enter Yoknapatawpha County with a power to possess it completely. There is no reason why there must be only one reason.

More, however, is involved, for when Faulkner wrote the Appendix he was "making . . . fiction out of his own fictions," as Minter has said (p. 209), which is to say he was treating his fiction as part of the past and writing history about it. As part of history his own fictions were no more sacred than any other facts. They were only useful, and if the truth he was attempting to embody demanded that fiction be mixed with the history of his fiction, he did not hesitate to make the mix. His trust was in the imagination where there was movement and therefore life. To that imagination Faulkner gave his trust because from it his art derived. It required work, however, not just transcribing his muse. As we have seen, Faulkner wrote, re-wrote, and wrote again; he combined, recombined, and moved characters and events around, sometimes replacing characters with others and sometimes opening up new aspects of a character he had used before. He laid work aside and took it up once more. When he finally let work go, for whatever reason—money, humility, a sense of having reached his limits—he did not always keep a copy of what had gone into print. What he needed of it was still in his imagination.

Faulkner told Cowley that it was Quentin who was doing the brooding, not Faulkner.[25] It was also Quentin who believed that history determines the present inexorably, not Faulkner. For Faulkner the past is dead, but history is not; it is what the imagination can continue to make of it. As Noel Polk insists, history was "essentially just one more of the tools of his trade."[26] Art, his trade, derived from his imagination, which often worked historically because it was very much focused on the present. When Faulkner wrote the Appendix, Quentin was part of Faulkner's past. Coldly, he looked at him one more time, and found him unchanged. Quentin's epitaph took less than three hundred words. To Caddy, however, he devoted a third of his Appendix. She was still in motion.

Notes

1. Jean-Paul Sartre, "Time in Faulkner: *The Sound and the Fury*," trans. Martin Darmon, in *William Faulkner: Three Decades of Criticism*, ed. Frederick J. Hoffman and Olga W. Vickery (East Lansing: Michigan State University Press, 1960), p. 232.

2. Letter dated 30 November 1927, in *Selected Letters of William Faulkner*, ed. Joseph Blotner (New York: Random House, 1977), p. 39.

3. Joseph Blotner, *Faulkner: A Biography* (New York: Random House, 1974) p. 560.

4. Undated letter, probably 16 October 1927, in *Selected Letters*, p. 38.

5. David Minter, *William Faulkner: His Life and Work* (Baltimore: The Johns Hopkins University Press, 1980), p. 88.

6. From "An Introduction for *The Sound and the Fury*," ed. James B. Meriwether. *Southern Review*, 8 (N:S., Autumn 1972), 710. Meriwether, p. 707, says it is almost certain that Faulkner wrote the introduction in the late summer of 1933. The full text is reprinted here on pp. 75–77.

7. From "An Introduction to *The Sound and the Fury*," ed. James B. Meriwether, *Mississippi Quarterly*, 26 (Summer 1973), 412–13. Meriwether believes this introduction was also written in 1933, and probably is an earlier form of the one referred to in n. 6. The full text is reprinted here on pp. 70–74.

8. "An Introduction for *The Sound and the Fury*," *Southern Review*, p. 710.

9. Quoted in *Faulkner: A Biography*, p. 560.

10. "Interview with Jean Stein vanden Heuvel," in *Lion in the Garden: Interviews with William Faulkner, 1926–1962*, ed. James B. Meriwether and Michael Millgate (New York: Random House, 1968), p. 255.

11. Letter to Liveright dated mid or late February 1928, in *Selected Letters*, p. 40.

12. Michael Millgate, *The Achievement of William Faulkner* (New York: Random House, 1966), pp. 76–77.

13. One can infer from Blotner that it might have; see *Faulkner: A Biography*, pp. 565–66 and p. 82 note for line 2 of p. 566. See pp. 565–69 for Blotner's discussion of the Quentin-narrated stories probably written prior to the writing of *The Sound and the Fury*.

14. "*Afterword*," in *Sanctuary: The Original Text*, ed. Noel Polk (New York: Random House, 1981), p. 298.

15. Pearson's essay on the various versions is entitled "Faulkner's Three 'Evening Suns,' " *Yale University Library Gazette*, 29 (October 1954), 61–70.

16. All dates of first composition and publication in this and the following two paragraphs have been confirmed by inspection of five sources: Joseph Blotner's *Faulkner: A Biography*, *Selected Letters*, and "Notes" in *Uncollected Stories of William Faulkner* (New York: Random House, 1979) for which Blotner is the editor; and James B. Meriwether's *The Literary Career of William Faulkner* (Princenton: Princeton University Library, 1961) and his "William Faulkner: A Check List," *Princeton University Library Chronicle*, 18 (Spring 1957), 1–23.

17 Letter probably dated February 1934, in *Selected Letters*, p. 79.

18. *Uncollected Stories*, p. 203.

19. Minter's *William Faulkner: His Life and Work* and Karl Zender's "Faulkner at Forty: The Artist at Home" in the *Southern Review*, 17 (N.S., Spring 1981), 288–302, are notable recent examples.

20. William Faulkner, *Absalom, Absalom!* (New York: The Modern Library, 1951), p. 217.

21. "The Old People," in *Uncollected Stories*, p. 207.

22. William Faulkner, *Go Down, Moses* (New York: The Modern Library, 1955), p. 328.

23. Letter probably dated February 1934, in *Selected Letters*, p. 79.

24. Letter dated 18 October 1945, in Malcolm Cowley, *The Faulkner-Cowley File: Letters and Memories, 1944–1962* (New York: The Viking Press, 1966), p. 37. All subsequent references to Cowley are to this text.

25. *The Faulkner-Cowley File*, p. 15.

26. *Faulkner's "Requiem for a Nun": A Critical Study* (Bloomington: Indiana University Press, 1981), p. 3.

Quentin Compson and Faulkner's Drama of the Generations

Donald M. Kartiganer*

I

More perhaps than the chronicler of a mythic corner of Mississippi, Faulkner is the premier American novelist of family. His people, however uniquely and memorably portrayed, invariably trail behind them clouds of familial qualifiers: the grandparents, parents, and siblings whose cumulative identity is the indispensable context of individual character. The bulk of Faulkner's people are not so much single, separate persons as collective enterprises, the products and processes of family dramas apart from which the individual actor is scarcely intelligible. Confronting the single member of the Sartoris, Compson, McCaslin, or Snopes lines, or even of the less amply elaborated lines such as Bundren, Hightower, Sutpen, or Varner, we soon find ourselves addressing family complexes, synchronic and diachronic systems whose individual units take their meanings from their transactions with each other.

In the novels concerning the families most fully described by Faulkner—the Sartorises, Compsons, and McCaslins—the historical dimension of these transactions takes on a special richness and significance. The central setting for character and action becomes the dynamic space between the generations of family, as plot and personality complete themselves only as a process of several lifetimes. The exchanges of father and son, of past and present, become an essential imagery in Faulkner's portrayal of the modern world.

To focus on Faulkner's drama of generations is to see his work in a context much with us these days; namely, the idea of the burden of the past on the present. As much as any modern writer, Faulkner understood this burden; a modernist, a Southerner, and a Falkner, he may be said to have arrived on the twentieth-century literary scene infected with a triple dose of the anxiety of influence. The condition Shreve McCannon is trying to understand in *Absalom, Absalom!* was Faulkner's as well as Quentin Compson's: " 'What is it? something you live and breathe in like air? a

*This essay was written specifically for this volume and is published here for the first time by permission of the author.

kind of vacuum filled with wraithlike and indomitable anger and pride and glory at and in happenings that occurred and ceased fifty years ago? . . . so that forevermore as long as your childrens' children produce children you wont be anything but a descendant of a long line of colonels killed in Pickett's charge at Manassas?' " (p. 361).

Belatedness for Faulkner is more than a matter of literary latecoming, a need to compete for priority with Hawthorne and Keats and Conrad; it is a latecoming to the world and to his region. What does one do when the deeds have already been done, the wars fought; when the great moments, as well as the most violent and shocking, have sealed themselves into an untouchable past one can only revere—and dream, futilely, of matching?

Initially, Faulkner's vision of the generation tells a story of steady decline. Steeped in the collective nostalgia of the South for its antebellum past and his own personal nostalgia for the past of his great-grandfather William Clark Falkner, he saw himself emphatically at the wrong end of a decline in power and potential achievement. As David Minter has recently put it, "With the sense of place and family pressing on him from all sides . . . [and] [d]eeply exposed to the play of associations with creatures living and dead, he became acutely aware of the force of human heredity and the flow of human generations." It is likely that there is much of the young Faulkner in those characters of his who "feel themselves less individuals than commonwealths," whose "ancestors appear as gigantic heroes, larger and more admirable than they have any hope of becoming . . . [or] as sinister shadows associated with injustice, violence, and lust."[1] Given his regular visits to his father's livery stable, where men drank whiskey and swapped yarns, or to his grandfather's house, or to Mammy Caroline Barr's cabin, Faulkner's early years must have been a long immersion in recollection and anecdote, much of it no doubt indifferent to pure fact, assuming, like Aunt Jenny's tale of her brother Bayard's death in *Flags in the Dust*, "a mellow splendor like wine," until the commonplace or the merely reckless could "become a gallant and finely tragical focal-point" (p. 14).

Faulkner's fiction is a full account of the dynamics of decline, always attentive to the remorseless pull of the past toward repetition: the inability of the present to escape its own memory, its destiny not to achieve a comparable grandeur but only to live over again, in the minor keys of reminiscence and gesture, the over-weening past. Present action issues forth as an irrevocable dependency, marked with the implicit impotence of latecoming.

But if the meaning of decline is the preoccupation of such early novels as *Flags in the Dust* and *The Sound and the Fury*, this is by no means the extent of Faulkner's understanding of the generations. In subsequent works—*Absalom, Absalom!, The Unvanquished, Go Down, Moses*—he tries to articulate not only the meaning of entrapment in a regressive pattern, moving backward to the mythologized Fathers, but also the possibilities of converting decline into something else: as if time might be a medium of creative interaction as well as simply a medium of doom. Faulkner explores the human capacity to expand the processes of exchange, to reverse or re-invent the seemingly fatal momentum of a generational pattern. His hope is to transform mere dependency into a kind of partnership with the past that allows the self to participate in its own self-engendering, to become integral to its history so that it is more than a pre-determined result. Faulkner's dream of belatedness, in other words, is the imagination of a self as organic force within the whole evolving pattern: the past as perceptually modified by a creative present.[2]

If we examine Faulkner's major families as they develop through his fiction we can see emerging something like a three-tiered pattern of generational relationships.[3] Frequently this pattern will be a neat father-son-grandson lineage, but this is not always the case, as we will find with the Compsons. The first tier is an originating force usually vested, as in the Sartorises and McCaslins, in a single powerful figure, a kind of fountainhead from whom the entire family line flows. This is the founder who haunts everything that is future to his own present, a condition brought home by the fact that we usually see this first level not directly but in the responses of the other levels to it. In the first Sartoris novel, *Flags in the Dust*, for example, John Sartoris is only a shared memory, yet through that memory powerful enough to be "a far more definite presence in the room than the two of them [Old Bayard and old man Falls] cemented by deafness to a dead time and drawn thin by the slow attenuation of days" (p. 5). To Old Bayard and Falls, to Aunt Jenny and Simon, Sartoris is a "glamorous fatality" (p. 433) exhumed from the real man they once knew; for the young Bayard Sartoris, he is invisible endowment of codes of daring and violence which Bayard tries vainly to emulate in the deflated circumstances of a post-war world.

Despite—or rather because of—the founder's ghost-like fictional representation, and regardless of whatever modifications or shifts may occur, the line will always in some sense belong to him. Even the most striking reversals and/or re-creations will acknowledge his abiding force because they can be carried out only in the language and form of action which he has fathered. To that extent, then, there is a necessary fatality in the condition of being successor to him.

The second tier, the son of the originator, manifests itself as a moral reversal. This generation is not as impressive as the first in terms of sheer size and power (partly owing to the responses of the third tier), but it nevertheless is capable of seriously undermining the fundamental principles of the father and reversing them into an entirely new direction. In comparison with the generation to follow, at least, this son is relatively unhaunted—and undaunted—by his powerful predecessor. He struggles successfully to create an identity of his own, and he usually does so at the level of action within the real social world. He is, in fact, the last of the line capable of carrying out his reaction to the past largely, although not entirely, in real life terms.

In *Flags in the Dust* this middle term is missing, but it receives vivid treatment in *The Unvanquished*, in both the McCaslin and Sartoris families. Uncle Buck and Uncle Buddy turn the manor house their father built over to the slaves, and devise a system by which those slaves can earn their freedom. John Sartoris' son Bayard, a younger and much transformed edition of the character in *Flags in the Dust*, performs a comparable reversal. Through much of *The Unvanquished* Bayard finds himself seeking as well as being forced into his father's heroic mold: " 'Ain't I told you he is John Sartoris' boy? Hey? Ain't I told you?' " (p. 213). But in "An Odor of Verbena" he reverses that mold by meeting his father's murderer unarmed, replacing violent revenge with a purely moral confrontation. Bayard's form of heroism clearly undermines that of his father, and comprises a thorough criticism and reappraisal of the Sartoris heritage; yet the reversal itself pays homage to the father. Bayard's act, after all, is hardly free of Sartoris bravado; nor can he escape the *confirmation* of his act as that of a Sartoris. Upon his return home, Aunt Jenny takes his face in her hands and cries, " 'Oh, damn you Sartorises! . . . Damn you! Damn you!' " (p. 292). There is even the confirmation by Drusilla, the character-become-caricature in her obsession with the Sartoris code: the sprig of verbena she has placed on his pillow, "filling the room, the dusk, the evening with that odor which she said you could smell alone above the smell of horses" (p. 293).[4]

The third tier—the grandson—is the turn to the aesthetic: an attempt to repeat or re-create the first generation in some form of imaginative venture that is more fantasy than act, more gesture than real irrevocable deed. It is a shift from the possibilities of content to those of form. This is the generation that confronts what it takes to be definitive evidence of a declining world. Its act of initiation—perhaps as early as consciousness—is to enter the awareness of its own impotence, to recognize its possibilities solely as aesthetic ones that can engage the world at levels inherently inferior to those of the founding generation. The third generation answers the call to repetition in two ways. The first is to build an alternate structure that is either conventionally aesthetic—such as a vase or narrative fantasy—or is some "act," equally indifferent to reality, that emulates the first generation in form but not in substance. The second way is to re-create the very history in which the third generation has found its impoverished location: reconstituting that history so as to alter both its meaning and the role of the third generation within it. In Faulkner's major families Bayard Sartoris of *Flags in the Dust* and the Quentin Compson of *The Sound and the Fury* are versions of the first alternative; the Quentin of *Absalom, Absalom!* and Ike McCaslin of *Go Down, Moses* are versions of the second.[5]

Despite his frantic pursuit of bold action, Bayard Sartoris of *Flags in the Dust* is a third-generation aesthete in that he performs nothing but a series of pointless exercises in pure recklessness. It is as if he were trying to experience the style of Sartoris daring without the substance of adequate occasion. The novel's conventional aesthete, Horace Benbow—unburdened with generational pressures—only echoes Bayard's aimlessness. An enthusiast of blown glass, "Macabre and inviolate; purged and purified as bronze, yet fragile as soap bubbles" (p. 180), and a practicing lawyer whose time is spent largely in "conferences which wended their endless courses without threat of consummation or of advantage or detriment to anyone involved" (p. 194), Horace makes clear how Bayard is conducting his life in a comparable aesthetic dimension, however violent its rhetoric or the serious "detriment" it eventually causes Old Bayard.

Oddly paired returnees from the War—one a flyer, the other a YMCA worker—Bayard and Horace are, as Cleanth Brooks has noted, "neatly reversed images of each other. Neither of them has a life purpose; neither has a true vocation. Both are somehow cut off and lost."[6]

Bayard is the third generation hopelessly imprisoned in and paralyzed by a cycle of repetition. The Sartoris myth subsumes the future, as Olga Vickery points out, with "all the force of a categorical imperative": action is reduced to a set of "imitative rituals in which form becomes more important than meaning."[7] Bayard's act of irrelevant courage which finally results in the death of Old Bayard is carried out under the very eye of the first generation: "directly over them John Sartoris' effigy lifted its florid stone gesture, and from among motionless cedars gazed out upon the valley where for two miles the railroad he had built ran beneath his carven eyes" (p. 351). The image of stone suggests eloquently the fixed fate which Bayard has been able to challenge only with the deeds that risk accomplishing it.

One of the interesting characteristics—and difficulties—of the third generation is that it responds not to the second but to the first generation. It is not the tier of moral reversal (when it exists) that evokes or challenges the aesthetic nerve of the "grandson," but the tier of originating force. In fact, one of the immediate effects of the aesthetic turn is that it aggrandizes that force, transforming it from a merely powerful presence into myth.

The tales of the first generation are passed to the third by such raconteurs as Aunt Jenny who, knowing the men themselves, embroider those tales without risk of forgetting the realities. For Young Bayard, however, the tales he imbibes are free to assume a paralyzing force, at once emasculating him and arousing his own aesthetic tendencies. Elevating into myth, memories seep backwards into the origins themselves, with the effect of reducing the "son" in size (although without

negating his moral reversal) and imposing themselves even more powerfully on the "grandson."

The largest question Faulkner raises in his dramas of the generations
is whether this grandson—almost always the last of the line—can find in
the aesthetic realm a genuine power which will enable him to do more
than succumb to that myth to which he is at once father and sacrifice. Out
of this web of inter-relations, in which the aesthete's original sense of
decline is strengthened by his own mythologizing response to the first
generation, the aesthete chooses among a series of options: whether, like
young Bayard Sartoris, to complete his act of mythologizing in a total
abandonment of his own life and ego; or, like Ike McCaslin in "The
Bear," to complete the myth by inventing it *forward*, into a future that
only now, in an act more "imaginative" than socially effective, becomes
possible; or, from within the solid structure of a history that seems ended,
to re-create, and thus give birth to, the fundamental meaning which
history has not known.

II

Before moving to a discussion of the Compsons, I want to look in
some detail at the Hightower family in *Light in August* as a concise and
vivid model, completed virtually within a single chapter (20) of the novel,
of how these levels of generation frequently engage each other. Insofar as
we can separate Gail Hightower I from the mythologizing of his grandson, we find a formidable enough originating force: a self-taught lawyer,
a slave holder, a drinker, a principal non-churchgoer who once turned an
outdoor church revival "into a week of amateur horse racing" (p. 447),
and a man who, when the time came, went to war as a cavalryman. All in
all, he seems well summarized in this phrase: "a hale, bluff, rednosed man
with the moustache of a brigand chief" (p. 446).

As for his son, not accorded a name in this novel, he methodically
reverses the life of his predecessor in fashioning his own. Before the war he
is a minister, a strict teetotaler, above all an abolitionist "almost before
the sentiment had become a word to percolate down from the North"
(p. 447). Living in the same house with a slave holder, he will not eat
food grown or cooked by a slave.

And yet there is a remarkable lack of strife between father and son,
and no apparent anxiety on either side. In fact the two seem curiously to
accept each other, as if each deeply respects without in any degree sharing
the principles and practices of the other: "it would [n]ever have occurred
to either of them to wish mutually that he had been given a different son
or a different father" (p. 445). There is a sense in which Faulkner idealizes
this relationship—as he will elsewhere idealize the transactions of reversal—partly I suspect from a tendency to over-simplify the problems of being a son to a powerful if not entirely admirable father. It was not of

course his own particular problem. What seems to save the son from the dangers that threaten the grandson is his first-hand knowledge of the father, a knowledge that prevents mythologization and its potentially crippling effects. Whatever Gail Hightower I may be for his son—slave holder, drinker, religious skeptic, man of violence—he remains a man in the real world, a world in which the son too can act and implement an identity.

It is important to note, however, that although the son's identity is a full one, it is by no means an independent one, for the son has really distanced himself no further from the father than a mirror does from the object it reflects. He has literally reversed his father, and thus the father's identity is unmistakable in his own. The father "was a lawyer, who had learned law somewhat as his son was to learn medicine, 'by main strength and the devil's grace and luck' as he put it" (p. 446). The defining quality of both men is precisely what the son's wife admires most in the father: a "simple adherence to a simple code" (p. 446). The fact that the son has not been free to choose a life *irrelevant* to his father's is evidence enough of the strain of fatality in Faulkner's view of the generations, but fatality here in no sense precludes the son's ability to act forcefully and effectively in the world.

In addition to the curtailment of freedom implicit in the very idea of generation, there is also in the son a first glimmering of an aestheticism that will become so prominent in the grandson. When the son goes to war, a gap opens between his purposes and his deeds, coloring those purposes with just a tint of indifference to the real world in which he expects to carry them out. The fact that the son took his place on the Confederate side in the conflict, "the very side whose principles opposed his own, was proof enough that he was two separate and complete people, one of whom dwelled by serene rules in a world where reality did not exist" (p. 448). He goes to war unarmed, initially as a chaplain, then as a self-trained surgeon. When the war is over, he practices surgery as a vocation. But even in this—although hardly the kind of action that would get him killed, like his father, in a henhouse—he remains his father's son: "This probably of all the son's doing the father would have enjoyed the most: that the son had taught himself a profession on the invader and devastator of his country" (pp. 447–48).

It remains for Gail Hightower II to endure the full anxiety of the generations, and to form the aesthetic mode that simultaneously enhances and designs to alleviate that anxiety. To begin with, as is always the case with the third generation, Hightower is never to know directly the originary being who haunts him—which is of course a primary factor in the haunting. Gail Hightower I becomes a romantic hero through the ornamentation of his former black cook, Cinthy, and timeless legend through the aesthetic adoration of his grandson. Horrified by the coat his father wore during the Civil War (apparently because it is real), and by its patch of Yankee blue which implies for Hightower an actual Northern soldier dead at his father's hands, Hightower turns in relief to the terror-free violence of his grandfather, who "had killed men 'by the hundreds' " (p. 452), but wholly within the harmless confines of Cinthy's tales.

The story of his grandfather being shot in a henhouse trying to steal a chicken, following a dramatic raid on Jefferson, becomes for Hightower the invincible art object that paralyzes his own life before it can begin. Hightower confronts his future like one already deceased, a latecomer to the world who finds such perfection in his inheritance that it is "as though the seed which his grandfather had transmitted to him had been on the horse too that night and had been killed too and time had stopped there and then for the seed and nothing had happened in time since, not even him" (p. 59).[8]

Hightower's response to this situation is one of total capitulation to the invented past, marked by his attempt to find for himself an aesthetic existence somehow parallel to that of his grandfather. Hightower turns to the Church as the parallel structure he seeks, the embodiment of a life "like a classic and serene vase, where the spirit could be born anew sheltered from the harsh gale of living and die so, peacefully, with only the far sound of the circumvented wind, with scarce even a handful of rotting dust to be disposed of" (p. 453). He learns, however, that parallels will not do—because *people*, their "faces full of bafflement and hunger and eagerness" (p. 461) intrude: his congregation, his wife, ultimately Byron, Lena, and Joe Christmas. These are the impediments that must be uprooted—although basic to his commitment to the aesthetic is the necessity that they must uproot *themselves*, must abandon *him*, leaving him with the most powerful illusion of all, which is his guiltlessness. It is the freedom from guilt, from responsibility—"*I dont want to think this. I must not think this. I dare not think this*" (p. 464)—that is crucial to his dream of inhabiting a world suspended above the real one. The apex of that dream, and of his final abandonment of self, is his account of his wife's debauchery and death as the act of his grandfather, Hightower's murderer by virtue of the myth that has enveloped his life: "And if I am my dead grandfather on the instant of his death, then my wife, his grandson's wife . . . the debaucher and murderer of my grandson's wife" (p. 465, ellipsis in text).

Hightower is the aesthete who can conceive of no different dream than a perfect repetition of, and within, the fable of his grandfather's death. He is the exemplar of repetition-as-doom: the life lived in the present as nothing more than the necessary fragments of human passion and suffering with which "to pant with" (p. 466), as if only to fuel his perpetual journey back into the past. Not to reverse, revise, re-create, but in fact to give up creativity: to indulge an imagination-less aestheticism, losing himself in his repetitions of the single unchanging scene: "the wild bugles and the clashing sabres and the dying thunder of hooves" (p. 467).

III

The Sound and the Fury and *Absalom, Absalom!* are Faulkner's two most powerful versions of the drama of generations. Although only one of several focal points, Quentin Compson is, in terms of the problems of inheritance, the key figure of both novels: the one who is most profoundly effected by the fact of generation and is forced to the most extreme measures by way of confronting it, the one who is closest to his creator, and thus representative of the crisis of the modern imagination itself in its encounter with the past.[9] In the transaction between Quentin and the various grandfathers and fathers who precede him we find something like Faulkner's definitive account of the tragedy and potential triumph of the latecomer.

Unlike *Flags in the Dust*, *The Sound and the Fury* (minus its 1946 Appendix) presents its founding generation obliquely, not in the form of detailed memories, tales of old grandeur, but as a prevailing mood, a kind of double vision within Compson consciousness, white and black, that rounds the present with a past, producing a paradoxical condition of pessimism and yet perpetual surprise at the disparities of decline: as, for example, Dilsey looks out on an unpromising Easter Sunday "with an expression at once fatalistic and of a child's astonished disappointment" (p. 331). As with the Sartorises, the essential action of the Compsons is to bear witness to their own fall; the important difference is that as readers we encounter the fall, and glimpse the traces of high origin, solely from within that consciousness as it pursues its daily activities—always aware of the past, yet seldom pausing to admire or even wonder at it.

There is no family folklore, then, mellowing with age, no statues with their overbearing epitaphs, no contemporary revivals of old-time heroics—such as the young John Sartoris leaping from his bullet-riddled plane with a gallant thumb of the nose to brother Bayard—to remind the living of their inadequacy. The founding Compsons are not even named, and none of their exploits (except an occasional reference to high offices held) is given concrete formulation. Compson glory, rather, is written only in the little that is left of it, embedded in the residue of a downward history.

We watch this history unfold itself in Benjy's juxtaposed glimpses of present and past, a barn in which "The big cow and the little one were standing in the door, and we could hear Prince and Queenie and Fancy stomping inside" and a barn in which *"The stalls were all open. . . . The roof was falling. The slanting holes were full of spinning yellow"* (p. 13); in Jason's assertion of dignity through invocation of a past he is elsewhere quick to mock (but never to forget): "you dont hear the talk that I hear and you can just bet I shut them up too. I says my people owned slaves here when you all were running little shirt tail country stores and farming land no nigger would look at on shares" (p. 298); in Luster's charge to his idiot passenger in the old surrey, immediately prior to the wild outburst that concludes the novel: " 'Les show dem niggers how quality does, Benjy' " (p. 399); or in the outside narrator's description of Dilsey: "She had been a big woman once but now her skeleton rose . . . as though muscle and tissue had been courage or fortitude which the days or the years had consumed until only the indomitable skeleton was left rising like a ruin or a landmark. . . ." (p. 331).[10]

Chiefly we see the pressure of former greatness on Quentin, although he almost never specifically refers to events prior to his own past. Instead, he is a living museum of Compson relics, in every action and attitude alluding implicitly to a past he needn't bother to remember. He is essentially a performer of gestures, a third-generation aesthete who, by the strength of his mythological aggrandizement of a tradition already formidable enough to challenge the future, fosters his own paralysis. His actions always have a touch of decadence to them, as if they were deliberate parodies of their usual purposes: like flowers which, at first bloom, are already pressed between the pages of a book.

Our first views of Quentin at age nine in Benjy's monologue present him as a youngster schooled in the rules of moral rectitude and social propriety, from his assault on Caddy for taking her dress off at the branch to his concern later that day first with Damuddy—" 'How can they have a party when Damuddy's sick' "—and then with his mother—" 'Mother was crying . . . Wasn't she crying, Dilsey' " (p. 31). At age ten he already displays a gift for futile, if fervent valor, by fighting with a boy who threatened to " 'put a frog in her desk.' " He makes sure that the boy " 'was as big as me' " but fails to calculate the chances of anyone's finding a frog in November (p. 83). We need not accuse Quentin in any of these instances of an indifference to real pain and genuine threat in order to note his obsession with the *forms* of gentlemanliness: the desire to groom himself as the proper heir to a Southern aristocratic birthright.

In his own monologue, focusing on the adolescent years that culminate in his suicide, Quentin's character is a tissue of gestures reflecting the duties of that birthright. Whatever their success or relevance as deed, as gestures they are performed by Quentin with all the adroitness of the actor who knows his part perfectly. His behavior in the bakery with the little Italian girl is typical: a display of easy generosity to a child—which is also a bit of tactful charity to one of the less fortunate—a polite compliment to the baker, and just a hint of rebuke to her for suspecting the child's intentions:

> "You're going to give her that bun?" the woman said.
> "Yessum," I said. "I expect your cooking smells as good to her as it does to me." (p. 157)

That the upshot of this bit of graceful patronage from one of the well-born should be an enraged brother accusing Quentin of child-molesting is only a bit of backstage business that should not completely obscure a skillful performance. Quentin has executed his gestures properly, as he has a score of previous ones: the gesture of moral outrage to an ex-Harvard card cheater—"I dont know but one way to consider cheating I dont think I'm likely to learn different at Harvard" (p. 134); the gesture of admonishment to a sister stooping beneath her station: *"It's not for kissing I slapped you. . . . It's for letting it be some darn town squirt"* (p. 166); the gesture of protection for a sister deflowered by a sophisticated rake: "I'll give you until sundown to leave town" (p. 198).

It is not only Quentin's effectiveness that is dubious in these cases; there is also the deeper question of whether he ever *intends* these gestures to "succeed," or whether Quentin even has a vision of what success in these affairs might amount to. Michael Millgate has observed, "Whenever Quentin acts, his concern is for the act's significance as a gesture rather than for its practical efficacy."[11] Quentin's attraction to gesture is based on its aesthetic quality: gesture as purely an exercise in style, the "fine dead sound" (p. 217) of pure form.

The confrontation with the little girl's brother Julio, which concludes Quentin's attempts to escort her home, serves to point up both Quentin's failure to play a similar brotherly role and the distance between his performances and any interest he might have in their attendant realities. Julio does not bother with the protocol of serving at least a day's notice on his foe, and is indifferent to the more gentlemanly forms of physical combat: "he sprang upon me. We went down. His hands were jabbing at my face and he was saying something and trying to bite me, I reckon, and then they hauled him off and held him heaving and thrashing and yelling and they held his arms and he tried to kick me until they dragged him back" (pp. 172–73). As for the sister, who may have in some way enticed Quentin, Julio is equally ungallant: " 'Git on home . . . I beat hell outa you!' " (p. 176). For Julio, protecting one's sister is not a piece of theater.

In Quentin's later scuffle, if giving Gerald Bland a sound thrashing for his verbal abuse of women were the chief object, he might have " 'grabbed up her damn hamper of wine and done it' " (p. 207)—as Shreve insists he would have—rather than try to slug it out with a trained boxer. But for Quentin the traditions of gallantry are not susceptible, or even relevant, to criteria of success or failure. His inheritance is one he sublimates in his reception of it, transforming it into an unreality "symmetrical above the flesh" (p. 220). Since it is more artifact than existential code, Quentin can no more "enact" his tradition in the real world than Hightower can repeat his grandfather's destiny in a hen-house. To the third generation aesthete, tradition is supreme gesture, and his single option is parallel gesture. Such a response is both an appreciation of the past—ennobling it into an art object immune to time—and a protection against it: against the likelihood, more fearful than art, that the past has some grounding in reality. As a result, Faulkner's third generation para-lyzes itself at the level of action, seeks to be indifferent to the results of ac-tion, substituting the criteria of an isolated, willfully irrelevant art.

Yet reality intrudes: at best as an inconvenience, such as blood stains on one's vest; at worst, as an insupportable contradiction, such as the younger sister, vessel of purity, going to her wedding with one man (a blackguard) as the pregnant mistress of another (also a blackguard). Quentin's gestures, masterful in inception, complete themselves as prat-falls: a Hamlet not altogether distinguishable from the fool.

Quentin's most extreme efforts at finding aesthetic arenas that are beyond the impertinent testings of reality are his attempts to claim in-cestuous relations with Caddy and his suicide. In the first of these Quentin predictably is indifferent to Caddy's body and literal incest. The incest he seeks is the purely poetic one he tries to impose on Caddy through verbal pressure alone—an engagement not of flesh but of metaphor:

> *we did how can you not know it if youll just wait I'll tell you how it was it*
> *was a crime we did a terrible crime it cannot be hid you think it can but*
> *wait . . . and I'll tell you how it was I'll tell Father then itll have to be*
> *because you love Father then we'll have to go away amid the pointing and*
> *the horror the clean flame I'll make you say we did I'm stronger than you*
> *I'll make you know we did you thought it was them but it was me listen I*
> *fooled you all the time it was me* (pp. 184–85)

Quentin vacillates from his desire to have Caddy literally believe that somehow it was he, not Dalton Ames or the others, who had intercourse with her, to his deeper hope that Caddy will accede to his poetic fantasy, to recognize and thus confirm the power of the *word*; and in the word, beyond the questionings of the loud world, to incarnate a hell purer and more permanent than any earth-bound pleasure could possibly be. But Caddy—whose very pulse beats with the spoken name of her real lover, who is ready to have real incest with Quentin—can no more understand Quentin's plea for belief in poetic truth than can their father.

Mr. Compson responds to Quentin's claim to have committed incest as if it were another first-generation example of misplaced heroics—or the threat of such heroics—rather than the purely *aesthetic* assertion it is, calling not for belief but for the suspension of disbelief, as in the service of any poetic utterance: *"and he did you try to make her do it and i i was afraid to i was afraid she might and then it wouldnt have done any good but if i could tell you we did it would have been so and then the others wouldnt be so and then the world would roar away"* (p. 220).

More successful than Quentin's desire to convince his sister and father of the meaning and power of imagined incest is his carrying out of suicide as the basic plot of his June 2, 1910 monologue. The whole tenor of Quentin's elaborate preparations is that of one who is imitating the gestures of suicide without seriously intending to realize them. Neatly packing his things in a trunk and handbag, stacking up books, writing notes to his father and roommate, Quentin behaves like someone who is nothing if not well-practiced at the niceties of suicide, yet his very efficiency colors his conduct with a decidedly theatrical tint. Moreover, some of his subsequent actions, such as applying iodine to a cut in order to prevent infection, and cleaning the blood stains from a vest he plans to wear to the bottom of the Charles River, seem to be those of an actor who expects to play this part still another time.

The serious point of Quentin's procedure is that for the first time in his life he has found a style perfectly consistent with its content. It is a style that is at once "decadent"—completely remote from any content—*and*, by virtue of that very remoteness, consistent with this particular act of the undoing of life, of self-annihilation: the purely negative gesture equivalent to an art that asserts its uselessness as its supremacy. Quentin carries out a *real* suicide as if it were the *performance* of suicide. This is not the hypocrisy of the one hand ignorant of what the other hand is doing, but the pure aestheticism of suicide genuinely "one-handed." Existence within art is always the dream of Faulkner's aesthetes, a dream of existence as non-existence: not to wear the rim of the bed-side vase away with kissing, but to *be* that vase. Quentin's suicide—which ends for us not at the bank of the Charles but with his plans to borrow Shreve's clothes brush for last-minute grooming—is the "making real" of that dream: non-existence in the form of the human action that knows itself as art.

As André Bleikasten has eloquently put it: "Quentin's suicide is the ending of an elaborate play performed from first to last in a mock theater, among shadows and reflections, and staged by a Narcissus enthralled by his own image. . . . Quentin's encounter with death is . . . [t]he last of his fictions."[12]

Toward the end of his monologue Quentin makes explicit the connection between death and that tradition whose flesh-and-blood dimensions he has never understood:

> It used to be I thought of death as a man something like Grandfather a friend of his a kind of private and particular friend. . . . I always thought of them as being together somewhere all the time waiting for old Colonel Sartoris to come down and sit with them. . . . Grandfather wore his uniform and we could hear the murmur of their voices from beyond the cedars they were always talking and Grandfather was always right (pp. 218–19).

Between Quentin and the founding generation he repeats in his aesthetic key is the figure of his father. Mr. Compson is the "middle term" in *The Sound and the Fury*, as he will be in *Absalom, Absalom!*: the generation of moral reversal. He is obviously to be distinguished from Bayard Sartoris of *The Unvanquished* or Buck and Buddy McCaslin of that novel or *Go Down, Moses*, yet his reaction to the first generation is, like theirs, a principled rejection of its fundamental attitudes and assumptions. The major legacy of the founders is a belief that, for good or ill, human beings can act, can engender permanent effects in the world, can cause differences. Mr. Compson's response to that legacy is a deep skepticism, a relentless insistence on the futility of action:

> Because no battle is ever won he said. They are not even fought. The field only reveals to man his own folly and despair, and victory is an illusion of philosophers and fools. (p. 93)

> she couldnt see that Father was teaching us that all men are just accumulations dolls stuffed with sawdust swept up from the trash heaps where all previous dolls had been thrown away (p. 218)

Mr. Compson is partially responsible for passing along the traditions Quentin feels compelled to repeat—"for you to go to harvard has been your mothers dream since you were born and no compson has ever disappointed a lady" (p. 221)—but primarily he functions as a critic of those traditions, exposing their absurd presumptuousness: "any live man is better than any dead man but no live or dead man is very much better than any other live or dead man" (p. 125).

In this role of critic—implicit to the second generation's reversal of the first—Mr. Compson acts as a challenge to Quentin, for whom the only reversal available is the rejection of his father's position. In the act of suicide Quentin confirms "aesthetically" precisely the capacity for bold, irrevocable action Mr. Compson has tried to uproot: "he we must just stay awake and see evil done for a little while its not always and i it doesnt have to be even that long for a man of courage and he do you consider that courage and i yes sir dont you" (p. 219).

In suicide Quentin reverses reversal, returns to the founding generation. Despite everything, he has remained faithful to the central commitment of his life, which is to sacrifice himself to a repetition of the past. He is Faulkner's most pathetic and most moving image of a compulsive, uncreative repetition; with terrible irony he corroborates past glory only by subverting it in the chilling wastefulness of self-annihilation.

The other members of the Compson third generation are alternatives (not necessarily attractive or feasible ones) to that drama of inheritance of which Quentin is the center. Benjy, through his idiocy, is immune to the burden of a prior generation, even as he is immune to most of the ravages of time: his life is a series of re-entries into the key moments of his past. Jason, unlike Quentin, has made serious efforts to remove himself from generational pressure, even as his mother has tried to link him with the less lofty Bascombs rather than the Compsons. Jason scoffs at his heritage "Blood, I says, governors and generals. It's a damn good thing we never had any kings and presidents; we'd all be down there at Jackson chasing butterflies" (p. 286). By no means completely free of the pride of ancestory—" 'I've got a position in this town, and I'm not going to have any member of my family going on like a nigger wench' " (p. 234)—Jason escapes Quentin's compulsion to repeat; yet his attempts to involve himself in the real world of stock markets and forgery are hardly more satisfactory. As for Caddy, she may well be driven to her own tragedy of abandoning the family and her daughter by the failure of the male third generation to handle its inheritance effectively.

Dilsey is the novel's vision of what a life sensitive to history, but not paralyzed by generational conflict, might look like. She subsumes the whole generational question into the larger frame of all known history: " 'I've seed de first en de last,' Dilsey said. 'Never you mind me'. . . . I seed de beginnin, en now I sees de endin' " (p. 371). It is not just the Compson family, first generation through third, she holds in her encompassing vision; it is all history as viewed through the Christian understanding of history, leading from a beginning to a God-chosen end.

In the context of that belief, to which the Compsons have lost access, the pressures of generation so prominent among Faulkner's white aristocratic families become close to irrelevant. Dilsey's past is larger and more forgiving than Quentin Compson's. She does not repeat it, but takes her place as part of its continuation and redemption.

> [My name will] *be in the Book, honey, Dilsey said. Writ out.*
> *Can you read it, Caddy said.*
> *Wont have to, Dilsey said. They'll read it for me. All I got to do is say*
> *Ise here.* (p. 71)

IV

From a position in *The Sound and the Fury* that is at least arguably marginal (in the sense that each speaker is only one voice in Faulkner's four-fold narrative) Quentin Compson moves to centrality in *Absalom, Absalom!* For the most part silent, since it is largely the voices of Miss Rosa, Mr. Compson, and Shreve that we hear, he is yet the vortex of all their talking: the one whose corroboration each narrator seeks, as he is the one whose single, all-inclusive imagination is the force that impels those narratives into unified form.

As in *The Sound and the Fury*, Quentin is still a museum of the past: "his very body was an empty hall echoing with sonorous defeated names; he was not a being an entity, he was a commonwealth" (p. 12). At first glance he seems purely passive, no longer active enough even to be humiliated by the contradictions of gesture and reality. For much of the time he merely listens: "the listening, the hearing in 1909 mostly about that which he already knew" (p. 31), a listening that at times can scarcely be borne—"*Yes. I have heard too much, I have been told too much; I have had to listen to too much, too long*" (p. 207).

But Quentin's passivity is not so much submission to the narrative power of others as it is the patience of the priest to whom all others must come with their narrative offerings. For he is the only one in the novel who is able through his own aesthetic courage and insight to coordinate the partial and conflicting narratives of *Absalom, Absalom!* into the completed tale. Quentin remains the third-generation aesthete, whose sole function in life can only be to repeat a past apart from which he is inconceivable. But in *Absalom, Absalom!* he turns on that past a powerful creative eye, capable of finding—or inventing—the meanings and moral pattern that persuasively interpret it. In doing so Quentin elevates himself, the paralyzed aesthete, to a new status with regard to the events which have preceded him. He reconciles the condition of repetition with that of creative authority; he is at once the victim of the past as well as the originator and bearer of its awful responsibility.

In this second creation of Quentin, Faulkner expands his notion of third-generation possibility. He does not relieve Quentin of his destiny, since the Quentin we conclude with is still on the brink of suicide; but he seriously alters the *quality* of that suicide. It is no longer in the realm of gesture, the aesthetic parallel of a past sublimated into a "classic and serene vase" untouched by time, but a fitting climax of the creation and acceptance of an authentic tragic history. The first Quentin is the latecomer committed to an aestheticism indifferent to reality; the second is the tragic hero who has deliberately invented a Southern history he is convinced is *true*—despite the fact that it is the single history he cannot bear to live with.[13]

In *Absalom, Absalom!* the three tiers of generation exist with a richness unparalleled elsewhere in Faulkner's fiction. Particularly striking is the presence of the fathers, who come to the foreground in the figure of Thomas Sutpen—at once larger and more concrete than the heroes and ghosts of sentimentalized fable. Mythologized, vilified, even mocked in the clashing memories of contemporaries, "sons," and "grandsons," Sutpen ultimately emerges as a fully human character. A curious aspect of the generational drama in this novel, however, is that it unfolds outside the usual blood lines, with Sutpen as the founding father not only to Henry and Judith but to Mr. Compson and Quentin, who repeat the structural roles of son and grandson they play in *The Sound and the Fury,* projecting them into the Sutpen story. The Sutpen dynasty itself ends abruptly when Henry, by murdering Charles Bon in 1865, fails to complete the moral reversal he has begun in 1860 with the renunciation of his birthright. Abandoning the son's necessary identity in Faulkner's generational scheme, Henry effectively ends the Sutpen line. There is no unequivocal third-generation Sutpen—which from one perspective is the tragedy of the family. Absent of blood successors to fulfill itself, the house of Sutpen enlists for its successor generations the entire South, with Quentin Compson as the chief spokesman, responding to Sutpen as the founder of all: as if *"it took Father and me both to make Shreve or Shreve and me both to make Father or maybe Thomas Sutpen to make all of us"* (p. 262).

The major narrators of *Absalom, Absalom!*, as I have described elsewhere in some detail, re-tell the story of Sutpen and his children as a means of understanding and justifying their own lives: the past becomes for them an imagery for self-examination.[14] My concern here is strictly with the contribution each of these narrators makes towards Quentin's understanding of the story, which finally embraces all the others, combining them in the final version which—with his own vital additions—becomes the account of the past we believe in.

Common to the narrative of Miss Rosa, Mr. Compson, and Shreve is the fact that Quentin receives little new information from them as to the motive behind the murder of Charles Bon, which is the mystery on which all previous versions founder. What Quentin derives from these narratives are the subjective moods of the various tellers: the mythic demonism of Miss Rosa, the fatalism of Mr. Compson, the Byronic romanticism of Shreve—all of which interpret the heritage of the Sutpen story that has come down to Quentin.

From Miss Rosa, the contemporary of Sutpen, Quentin absorbs a tale of dark grandeur that, for all its obvious mythologization, will always remain with Quentin as an image of the striking size and lethal power of the first generation. Here is a drama of cosmic sin and retribution, with Sutpen as the Satanic center of a series of events, meaningless except in the context of demonic influence: " 'I saw Judith's marriage forbidden without rhyme or reason or shadow or excuse' " (p. 18). Sutpen becomes a figure of colossal force, "creating the Sutpen's Hundred, the *Be Sutpen's Hundred* like the oldtime *Be Light*" (p. 9), enacting what amounts to an unfathomable, irrational crime—but in a world in which *"justice . . . presides over human events"* (p. 134).

Mr. Compson is the one who speaks of Sutpen's generation as " 'people too as we are, and victims too as we are, but victims of a different circumstance, simpler and therefore, integer for integer, larger, more heroic and the figures therefore more heroic too' " (p. 89); but the fundamental thrust of his narrative, as it is in *The Sound and the Fury*, is to reverse the father's legacy from its claim, at the very least, to the performance of deliberate, purposive and effective *action* into a history that is only another sorry example " 'of a horrible and bloody mischancing of human affairs' " (p. 101). Charles, Henry, Judith—even Sutpen—are all equally victims "of the same folly and mischance" (p. 87), all equally participants in events they implement without really understanding them. Our own inability to fathom motive and design is simply our awareness of a fatality the founding generation was too blind to recognize: " 'It's just incredible. It just does not explain. Or perhaps that's it: they dont explain and we are not supposed to know.' " (p. 100). The result of Mr. Compson's reversal is not only a continued mystery with regard to the murder—the threat of bigamy, he admits, is hardly an adequate motive for Henry to kill Bon—but also a substantial reduction of all the ancestors. Even the Civil War shrinks to " 'a stupid and bloody aberration in the high (and impossible) destiny of the United States' "—perhaps caused merely by this family squabble with " 'that curious lack of economy between cause and effect which is always a characteristic of fate when reduced to using human beings for tools, material' " (p. 118–19).

Shreve is difficult to separate from Quentin, since much of what he says is reiteration of what presumably he has heard earlier from Quentin, and who also—as Faulkner reminds us repeatedly—often speaks cooperatively with Quentin. Nevertheless Shreve is a distinct character who contributes to Quentin's final understanding, but is not wholly at one with that understanding despite his necessary participation in it. In a sense Shreve is in the curious position of viewing Quentin's role of third-generation aesthete as a kind of privilege he wishes to share. For he recognizes not only the burden of that position but its special honor and richness: " 'Because it's something my people haven't got. Or if we have got it, it all happened long ago across the water and so now there aint anything to look at every day to remind us of it" (p. 361). Shreve's aspiration, however, for brotherhood with Quentin in third-generation repetition of the past, is one that Quentin himself finally will not allow: " 'You cant understand it. You would have to be born there' " (p. 361).

Shreve's special contribution to the totality of narrative that Quentin absorbs is his romantic interpretation of the past: an emphasis on Sutpen children caught in a star-crossed network of fraternal and incestuous love, with Charles Bon, the outcast son, as the special hero of the tale. In at least one instance—the attempt to exonerate Charles Bon from a charge of exploiting his half-sister Judith as a means of gaining recognition from his father Sutpen—Shreve takes a position which becomes convincing to Quentin only after a long and impassioned effort on Shreve's part.

This emphasis by Shreve is the version Quentin is instinctively closest to, but finally that romantic re-telling takes its place with the previous ones that Quentin has been listening to all his life: the cosmic mythologizing of Miss Rosa, the cynical reductions of Mr. Compson, even the naked re-telling of Sutpen himself (presumably heard from Grandfather)—the most puzzled of all the narrators. All these versions combine to become part of a general development in Quentin's own interpretation of the story, an interpretation that breaks through the subjective colorings and distortions into a completely humanized and plausible Sutpen history: the fully realized account that, according to the novel, *only* the third generation narrator can devise.

Solely from Quentin come the two "facts" which persuasively unravel the mystery of why Henry shot Charles Bon, and convert the whole Sutpen history from implausible or unfathomable event into intelligible form. These are the facts of Charles Bon's origin as the partially black son of Thomas Sutpen and his first wife. The question of *how* Quentin discovered Bon's origin is one which Faulkner has chosen not to answer. We are left at the end of the novel simply with the conviction that Quentin is right, that he has somehow come upon or invented the clue that finally explains the history he has grown up with. The result is the sudden bursting of the entire story—in all its diverse tellings and re-tellings—into its most profound meaning, the tragic history of generations ruptured from each other, unable to accept the conditions of their very being.

Ironically enough, the completion of *Absalom, Absalom!* is dependent on the retrospect of the third generation—broken away from its own history, as it were, by virtue of the very murder it seeks to understand. The triumph of Quentin Compson is that, operating within his given aesthetic role, he has re-established or created an organic relationship with a past of which, in *The Sound and the Fury*, he was but a pathetic imposter. From the status of paralyzed grandson, absorbed entirely in the death-repetition of events he scarcely comprehends, Quentin emerges in *Absalom, Absalom!* as the one who finally confers meaning on the past. It is a meaning whose content and form—his intense identification with Henry Sutpen—completely implicates him in the past. Yet Quentin transforms the prison of repetition in which he functions by bestowing a new intelligence on the history that has engendered him. He creates what the past *does not know about itself*, what the past has been waiting for the present to remember. He creates the history that culminates, however tragically, in his own identity.[15]

Notes

I have used the following editions of Faulkner's novels (page numbers are cited in the text): *Absalom, Absalom!* (New York: Random House, Modern Library, 1951); *Flags in the Dust* (New York: Random House, Vintage Books, 1974); *Light in August* (New York: Random House, Vintage Books, 1972); *The Unvanquished* (New York: Random House, Vintage Books, n.d.); and *The Sound and the Fury* (New York: Random House, Vintage Books, 1954).

1. Minter, *William Faulkner: His Life and Work* (Baltimore: The Johns Hopkins University Press, 1980), p. 3.

2. For a different approach to Faulkner's treatment of the generations, and a different understanding of the limits of repetition, see John T. Irwin, *Doubling and Incest/Repetition and Revenge* (Baltimore: The Johns Hopkins University Press, 1975). Irwin writes, "For Faulkner, doubling and incest are both images of the self-enclosed—the inability of the age to break out of the circle of the self and of the individual to break out of the ring of the family. . . . Thus, the temporal aspects of doubling and incest evoke the way in which the circle of the self-enclosed repeats itself through time as a cycle, the way that the inability to break out of the ring of the self and the family becomes the inability of successive generations to break out of the cyclic repetition of self-enclosure" (p. 59). "This sense of a cyclic repetition within whose grip individual free will is helpless presents itself in Faulkner's novels as the image of the fate or doom that lies upon a family" (p. 60).

3. Faulkner's interest in the generations is largely in its male, white, "aristocratic" manifestations. Within black and poor-white families he does not portray the kind of genera-

tional conflict I describe in this essay; nor does he seem to regard women as particularly subject to the pressures of inheritance.

4. Although the tier of reversal is missing from *Flags in the Dust*, there are some approximations to it in Old Bayard, though for the most part he continues to exist within the given Sartoris traditions, as evidenced in his treatment of Caspey, his coming to the aid of Simon when the latter is in debt, and in his resolute loyalty to old man Falls' form of medicine. Hints of a reversal come, however, in Old Bayard's criticism of his father's generation: " 'They were all pretty good men in those days,' Old Bayard agreed. 'But you damn fellers quit fighting and went home too often.' " (p. 249). And perhaps most tellingly in this exchange with Falls:

"Will," he said, "what the devil were you folks fighting about, anyhow?"

"Bayard," old man Falls answered, "damned if I ever did know." (p. 252).

The absence of a reversal in *Flags in the Dust* may be owing, given the dependence of the novel on the Falkner family for its generational patterns, to Faulkner's inability to find any sign of such reversal in that family. His grandfather, J. W. T. Falkner, was hardly an appropriate candidate; while Old Bayard owes much to him, the Bayard of "An Odor of Verbena" owes little. According to Joseph Blotner's biography, J. W. T. had to be "talked out of" taking vengeance on his father's murderer; and his behavior following the shooting of his son Murry was hardly a departure from the ways of the Old Colonel (except perhaps in skill of execution: J. W. T.'s gun failed to fire seven times, at which point the potential victim shot him in the hand). See Blotner, *Faulkner: A Biography* (New York: Random House, 1974), pp. 51, 54.

5. For a complete discussion of Faulkner's life and work in terms of his attempts as an artist to bridge a gap between the imaginative and real worlds, the world he created and the world he lived in, see Minter, *passim*.

6. Brooks, *William Faulkner, The Yoknapatawpha Country* (New Haven: Yale University Press, 1963), p. 106.

7. Vickery, *The Novels of William Faulkner*, second ed. rev. (Baton Rouge: Louisiana State University Press, 1964), p. 19.

8. The story of the grandfather's death is inconsistently told: at one point he is shot from his horse in Jefferson, at another he is killed in a henhouse. Hightower seems unconscious of the contradiction, but given his indifference to truth in general—" 'A negro might have invented it. And if Cinthy did, I still believe. Because even fact cannot stand with it' " (p. 458)—one imagines he would not care.

9. A number of commentators have noted the link between Faulkner and Quentin; see for example Lewis P. Simpson, "Faulkner and the Legend of the Artist," in *Faulkner: Fifty Years After 'The Marble Faun'*, ed. George H. Wolfe (University, Alabama: The University of Alabama Press, 1976), who writes, "Faulkner discovered in Quentin the first profound portrayal of his own imagination—a fiction yet a symbol of a deep inner reality, a powerful apprehension of modern existence" (p. 97). See also Jackson J. Benson, "Quentin Compson: Self-Portrait of a Young Artist's Emotions," *Twentieth Century Literature*, 17 (July 1971), reprinted above, pp. 214–230.

10. Since the founding generation of the Compsons is not specified, its identity is more or less a collective one, including Grandfather. Mr. Compson, to all intents and purposes, is the second generation, Quentin—as his eldest male son—the third. The Appendix of 1946, filling in the details of five generations of Compsons, locates General Compson as the turning point in the history; his father, Quentin MacLachan II, "was the last Compson who would not fail at everything he touched save longevity or suicide" (p. 408). In the novel proper the reversal of Compson destiny resides in Mr. Compson.

11. Millgate, *The Achievement of William Faulkner* (New York: Random House, 1966), p. 96. In creating Quentin, Faulkner probably drew upon his earlier reading in nineteenth-century English and French poetry, particularly Gautier, Swinburne, and Wilde, whose theories of romanticism and aestheticism Quentin partially exemplifies.

12. Bleikasten, *The Most Splendid Failure: Faulkner's "The Sound and the Fury"* (Bloomington: Indiana University Press, 1976), pp. 141–42.

13. Critics of the two Compson novels occasionally assume a consistent identity in Quentin, particularly John T. Irwin and Estella Schoenberg, *Old Tales and Talking: Quentin Compson in William Faulkner's "Absalom, Absalom!" and Related Works* (Jackson: University Press of Mississippi, 1977), who for example asserts that "Quentin knows that he is projecting Caddy's affair with Dalton Ames and his own jealous despair onto the young Sutpens and Charles Bon" (p. 87). My own reading is to see Quentin's specific family problems—particularly his relationship with Caddy—as largely irrelevant to *Absalom, Absalom!* Not only is Caddy not mentioned in the second novel, but it is Mr. Compson, not Quentin, who stresses the incestuous desires of Henry for Judith, and Shreve who emphasizes the love of Bon for his alleged half-sister. More important, however, is the great difference in character between the two Quentins, not to mention their narrative skill which, as Schoenberg points out, Quentin shows no evidence of in *The Sound and the Fury* (p. 23). Minter speculates that it was Faulkner's writing in 1933 of two introductions for a possible re-issue of *The Sound and the Fury* that "provided the occasion for his discovery of Quentin Compson as a narrator of Thomas Sutpen's story." (p. 157).

14. See my *The Fragile Thread: The Meaning of Form in Faulkner's Novels* (Amherst: The University of Massachusetts Press, 1979), pp. 69–106.

15. Faulkner's last full portrayal of the third-generation aesthete is Ike McCaslin in *Go Down, Moses*. Ike carries his interpretation of the founding generation as guilty of a mortal crime into a social action—forfeiting his land; yet his recognition of that act as primarily a symbolic gesture preserves his aesthetic role, as does his childlessness. Unlike Quentin, Ike does not introduce new facts into his interpretation of the past; rather, he sets that past against a larger background of sin and future redemption, thus *continuing* the past, projecting it forward to a conclusion that only Ike can envision.

In Defense of Caroline Compson

Joan Williams*

Caroline Compson is frequently dismissed as a whiner and complainer by readers of *The Sound and the Fury* who consider her responsible for the downfall of the Compson family. But the people of Jefferson do not feel this way. There is a discrepancy between the ways Caroline impresses the reader and the impressions she makes on her own townspeople. Take the storekeeper Earl, Jason's employer, for example. In section four Jason is disagreeable to Earl over time he has taken off for lunch. If Earl doesn't like it, Jason tells him, he knows what he can do. Earl replies that he has known for a long time, meaning fire Jason. But, a successful businessman, he does not. He supplies a good reason. "If it hadn't been for your Mother I'd have done it before now, too. She's a lady I've got a lot of sympathy for, Jason. Too bad some other folks I know can't say as much." There is also the incident when Jason's niece Quentin takes money from him and he rushes to the Sheriff. As usual, he is short-tempered and quarrelsome, even when asking for help. The Sheriff asks quickly, "Did your Mother know you had that much on the place?" In his response, there is more concern for Caroline than for Jason, and the suggestion that he considers Mrs. Compson more responsible than her son. When alone with his mother, Jason often speaks roughly to her. Yet he is quite aware of the respect with which she is held in the community, and he in his turn respects that. He is fiercely protective of her reputation. He threatens Quentin if she misbehaves on the place "where my mother lives." Being temperate toward his mother is the only softening effect Jason has; it is the only emotion which turns him into a human being. Otherwise, he is thoroughly dislikeable. Reviewing the novel now in light of these various scenes, and from a different perspective since I read it first at nineteen, there seem to be reasons to admire Caroline Compson.

She may have been misunderstood because the reader is swayed against her when she is first introduced. What is it now? she is saying, and we think: what an irritable woman. But what mother in a household with four active children has not cried out the same—Oh, what is it

*This essay was written specifically for this volume and is published here for the first time by permission of the author.

402

now?—longing for respite from noise and fussing, longing for a moment's peace. Something always is happening among the Compsons, and Caroline is justified in thinking that something now has, if only another childish quarrel. Mothers will sympathize with the bodiless voice asking its tired question. Having raised two active boys a year and a half apart, I now find humor in the passage, too. I have experienced the traumas of boisterous children, while possessing myself a quiet nature, given to solitude. I imagine Faulkner's lips twitching as he wrote the words. Since he grew up in a household of four boys, surely he echoed his mother. In his thirties when he wrote this novel, Faulkner might have seen Caroline with more objectivity later in his life. After bringing up a child of his own and several step-children, having been grandfather to three boys, he might have felt compassion for her as, older, I do.

In the first pages, Caroline is fearful about riding in the carriage with the young black T. P. driving. We are put off by her, again. In actuality she is right. Roads were not smooth but rough country roads then as I recall them, either gravel or dirt. The ride is likely dangerous. The horse is old. At the novel's end, another young black, Luster, drives Benjy and shows off recklessly. Mrs. Compson sensibly knew her young black servants, and was right in feeling she was safe only with the older Roskus. Now, at the present time of the novel, so much has happened to Caroline Compson that she rightly lives with a sense of doom. When her granddaughter disappears, there looms up what always lies under the surface of her mind. "Quentin left a note." She refers of course to her son's suicide. Her agonies seem to me justified and not of her own making. She is, rather, a victim.

For life has taken a heavy toll. She is described in 1928 as having white hair and pouched eyes; by 1933, she is dead. If Mrs. Compson followed conventional Southern behavior, which seems likely, she would have married in her late teens, as Caddy does, or in her early twenties—and it was not uncommon to marry as early as sixteen. She should have been in her sixties in 1928, yet the mind's eye conjures up a much older woman from the text. Did she have four children within a four-year time span rather late in life? Medical expertise was not great in those days, and certainly not in the rural South of northern Mississippi. Mrs. Compson's headaches and frail health might not be hypochondria—she does not run from doctor to doctor the way true hypochondriacs do—but a more serious physical disorder never diagnosed. And she surely has other worries. She comes from a less important family than the Compsons. In the South the caste system was particularly rigid and formative in one's life. Once, she was a starry-eyed bride marrying upward into the Compson family. Then everything turned to dust. Still, Mr. Compson holds over her head his supposed superiority, fostering her own insecurity—there is nothing but disillusionment in this marriage. Mrs. Compson often remarks that all that has happened to the family is a judgment on her.

The desire to marry above herself is the only thing she has done that I can see to make her feel guilt. In viewing her life, Mrs. Compson can only know she'd have been much better off with a stable, hard-working man from her own class. In her secret heart, Mrs. Compson knows she is stronger than her husband, and that she must pretensively live as if she did not know it.

If blame is to be laid on a family member for what happened to the Compsons, it belongs on the head of the household, Mr. Compson. It was his name and his bloodline which were to be upheld. Mrs. Compson did her part and provided heirs. Mr. Compson failed the family. He appears not to work but to live off inheritance which is fast going. We know Benjy's pasture was the last land that could be sold. Many of Quentin's confused thoughts before suicide are remembrances of his father's conversations about time. Time, Mr. Compson preaches, is absurdity when carried to its logical conclusion. Everything is illusion and there is nothing worth fighting for. These are hardly words of inspiration for a sensitive young man setting out for college, and particularly one who will already have trouble adjusting from a small town in Mississippi to an Eastern establishment like Harvard. Guilt-ridden like most alcoholics, Mr. Compson advises that everything is nothing. Why then bother to struggle, or advance, or to live at all? Mr. Compson's own life is a destructive model for those of his children who are competent to understand it.

But Caroline Compson contends not only with her husband. As was often customary, three generations lived under the Compson roof. Caroline's mother-in-law has been in residence. Conflicts inherent in that situation are legendary, but harmony seems to have existed; Mrs. Compson is distraught when her mother-in-law dies. Furthermore, Damuddy has spoiled her favorite grandchild, Jason. In that situation the parent pays, and must endure or undo the spoiling. Still, Mrs. Compson seems not to have caused trouble by challenging Damuddy's authority. The reverse is true: as a young mother, Caroline is the sensible one in the family. Seeing Jason and what happens to him, she begs the others not to spoil the retarded Benjy. "He must learn to mind." Her own instinct as a mother must have been to treat him differently too, to overprotect him, but she has the fortitude to do what is best for Benjy, as she tries to do what is best for all her children, unlike Damuddy. Mrs. Compson's brother Maury sees his sister as competently playing the role assigned her, as if she were an actress and had to take a part given by some omnipotent director, whether she wanted it or not. As a Southern woman, Mrs. Compson was trained to be submissive; having married into the Compsons, she is doubly defensive. She is apparently able to train her black household servants what all white women taught them about the management of homes, the use of silver and crystal and linen; she endures her husband's drinking, and her brother's, and the interference of Damuddy.

Further, her strength, like any mother's, is sapped by raising four children close in age.

The Compson children are pictured as fighting, kicking, and tearing up one another's toys; active siblings. But Caroline at all times possesses a mother's instinct for them. When we meet her, this is quickly apparent. She wants to keep Benjy from the cold at the beginning of *The Sound and the Fury*—and it is clear that his memory of her is positive about this. Maury overrules her. "Let him go, Caroline." The implication is that she should let him go altogether. But she cannot desert her son; rather, she tries to make him as independent as possible. Before Benjy goes outdoors, Caroline cups his face with her hands and holds him to her. "My poor baby," she says and then speaks to Caddy with similar endearment: "take good care of him, honey." It is Caddy that interrupts this show of affection and challenges her mother, claiming that Benjy is not a poor baby, that he has his Caddy. She seems as competitive as Damuddy. Detractors of Caroline feel that this remark shows Caddy's dislike for her mother. But who has been the role-model for Caddy to learn to love Benjy but Caroline? It is Caroline's expression of love and warmth for him, her touching him as equally as the others, that has taught Caddy to love Benjy too. Caddy is playing the way little girls do with dolls—Benjy only happens to be her live one. She is play-acting at being mother, wife and housekeeper—at being the responsible one—as she later bosses the children the day of Damuddy's funeral.

Caroline's detractors further argue that the Compson children learned love and motherhood from Damuddy. But nowhere in the novel does Damuddy have connection with any of them except Jason. The children do not seem to mourn her, but to regard her death with a mixture of curiosity and awe as the household routine is interrupted. In contrast, Mrs. Compson is involved with all the children, and always she is warm and loving and supportive, teaching them to love one another, something parents can fail to do. It is something Mr. Compson fails to do. This love is not only active; it can be a passive enduring. Her son Quentin, for instance, confusedly thinks of his sister in incestuous terms, or thinks he does. This is not unusual for boys his age. He would have straightened out in time, and Mrs. Compson seems to know that. But when his self-questioning seems to get the better of him, his impassioned cry is for his mother. *If I could say Mother, Mother.* Could Quentin possibly be bemoaning his inability to call for her, meaning that he cannot rush backward in time, flinging himself on his mother as he must have once, to have consoled a cut or a childhood trauma? Now, too old to do that, Quentin regrets the loss of childhood in the loss of her.

But Caroline shows unusual concern for all her children. She alone respects Caddy's need for privacy as a young girl and assures it when the others attempt to spy on her. When Caddy becomes pregnant out of wedlock, Mrs. Compson singlehandedly arranges for the girl's marriage. Caddy's condition in those days in Mississippi was a scandal. Although then many young women could never have faced the shame of telling a parent, she has confided in her mother; that she did so shows a bond of love, understanding, and trust. By the same token, many others would have scarred their daughters with reproaches, emphasizing their own embarrassment rather than concern for the girl. Mrs. Compson did not do that. Instead, she did the expedient and practical thing. Caddy could have been sent away to have the baby, left to return home to gossipy townspeople with her baby lost to her. Caroline knows that, married, Caddy could hold up her head and so could her daughter. When Caddy's marriage fails, Caroline admits the baby to her own home. Admitting the illegitimate granddaughter, Caroline puts the child's welfare above her own and deprives herself of her daughter in order to give the baby a new life. Had Caddy been as willing to put her child's welfare above her own, she would have remained with Head and made a home for Quentin IV, at least until the girl was older.

Mrs. Compson shows great patience with Jason, too, out of maternal concern. As the other child, Jason is often crying, seems almost a sissy as a tattle-tale, and shows tenderness only in wanting to cuddle up with Damuddy at night. Mean, stern, and cold as a man, he remarks bitterly to his mother about his father drinking himself to death. Jason is left with his father's responsibilities, with his debts, and Jason's character is formed by his chip-on-the-shoulder attitude. Perhaps not being able to get his way, as he could at first with Damuddy, he is ill-formed for life. Yet Mrs. Compson tries to respect and obey him as the new head of the house while also trying to uphold her husband's memory and trying to make Jason respect him. She tries to teach Jason to love Benjy too, to forget his handicaps, remarking that he must do so because Benjy is his brother. She is an active model of love, and urges her children to love one another. So if she is "baffled" by her children as they grow older, she has every right to be. They instill in her a sense of displacement and loss. Who is she? By her husband, her father, her son, and even the black servant she taught, she is stripped of authority in all the aspects of her present narrow life. If she sounds piteous, there is really only longing for some affirmation of love from her family.

Caroline Compson, then, is a pure product of her time and place, as Faulkner was. Faulkner was not an aggressively virile man; long past the time when courtliness was over he remained courtly to women. He may have been hindered from understanding women because of this. Men and women had strongly defined traditional roles in his Mississippi, which led to a certain apartness between the sexes. This may have kept Faulkner from defining Caroline's heart. What he knew was that women should not interfere in certain affairs of household; there they were to look pretty and to keep their mouths shut. It was not uncommon for them to be told that, and to be physically punished if they had "run their mouths." By 1928, when the novel begins, Caroline has lived a long time with these limitations, with this sense of imposed inferiority, as well as with two facts which might have totally shattered another woman. Her oldest son has committed suicide, her youngest is an idiot. She had possessed dreams for them both; now daily she confronts Benjy's hopeless condition and his physically unappealing presence. State asylums were then places of horror, and she is much too compassionate to send Benjy to one, even though his removal might have allowed her to be a happier person. She alone keeps him out, living in the knowledge that when she dies, Jason will commit him. She can easily guess that. She lives with debilitating sorrow over many things. The house is falling down around her and Caroline Compson cannot prevent it. But given her instincts, her past actions, and her present punishment, I can understand why the people of Jefferson maintain their respect for her.

Family Conflict in
The Sound and the Fury

John Earl Bassett*

Although *The Sound and the Fury* represented for Faulkner a major creative breakthrough, it does have much in common with his previous novel, *Sartoris*. Both describe the decline of an established Mississippi family and the discrepancy between the family's self-myth and its middle-class actuality. In each a house, with its attendant black servants, is the setting; and loss of home and childhood are central themes. In both one finds a "sick" protagonist, crippled by his inability to live in a changing world, one character incestuously attached to a sister, parents either dead or tragically incompetent. In each novel one main character dies while another survives, badly flawed but better able to adapt to the modern world and less suicidal in his tendencies. Each novel, while affirming the need to adjust to change and modernity, also condones grief and regret for what has been lost.

The differences between the novels are more obvious and, because of the later book's intensity, more significant. Though there is nothing theoretically original about his treatment of time, consciousness, and symbolic form not found in Mann, Joyce, or Proust, Faulkner was able to use what he had learned from his great predecessors to create out of his own experience a cast of characters with vivid reality and complex personal conflicts. *The Sound and the Fury* achieves much of its resonance from its confinement to a single family whose incestuous sterility and lack of love suggest both their own decay and a broader social malaise. Both in theme and method *The Sound and the Fury* is the prime example in American fiction of bourgeois collapse. Yet it was as well Faulkner's own means of working through a set of deep-seated personal anxieties that had kept him from developing as an artist. For the first time he opened himself up to his most profound concerns, particularly those involving parental betrayal, fraternal conflict, and his own literary career.

The Sound and the Fury is emotionally grounded in maternal betrayal and paternal inadequacy. It deals with attempts to retrieve a lost world in which a loving, nurturing mother and strong father provide a

*Reprinted, with permission, from *Studies in American Fiction*, 9, No. 1 (Spring 1981), 1–20.

408

stable home and family environment. In a series of sibling conflicts, through which Quentin as eldest son most clearly reflects the author's dilemmas, all the characters also become parts of a larger whole and reflect aspects of the personality of the author. While dramatizing the collapse of this single Southern family, moreover, *The Sound and the Fury* suggests the fragmentation and aloneness of the sensitive twentieth-century American lacking religion, traditional myths, and coherent community, and living in a world where individualism in its ultimate extensions has become narcissism. The repeated presence of motherless homes, weak or perverse parents, and family conflict in Faulkner's fiction suggests not only that he imaginatively connected familial decline with Southern history and with modern alienation—as so many have argued—but also that the loss of the mother and the ineffectuality of the father had important personal implications for him. In *The Sound and the Fury* he transforms such personal anxieties into a fiction with profound cultural implications.

The biographical circumstances of Faulkner's creative break-through in this novel are interesting to recall. His recovery of Estelle Oldham Franklin was enormously important to him, even though their marriage was to be a sad one. For ten years her loss had rankled him and damaged his self-esteem. In this period Faulkner's fragile poetry and fiction were not only decadent but often self-pitying. He avoided the deep psychological thematics that characterize his later writing, even though such images as ruined gardens and epicene maidens anticipate important later motifs.[1] Then, as his fiction matured rather rapidly, in the late 1920s—just when Estelle was returning to him—certain themes and patterns became dominant: sibling rivalry for love of the mother; bad mothering and ineffectual fathers; homes from which young people seem excluded or homes to which they have a hard time returning; pathologically alienated young men; and incestuous connections between brothers and sisters that suggest a displacement of love for the mother. Some of these, notably the last, had appeared in earlier manuscripts, composed when Faulkner was unable or unready to develop them fully.

His severe reaction to losing Estelle in 1918, combined not only with the conjunction of his artistic maturity and her return but also with the thematics of his first major novels, suggests that the loss of Estelle was identified with an earlier loss of maternal affection. It is not known whether Maud Faulkner ever wilfully neglected her eldest son; their later relationship was certainly a close one. More likely such events as the birth of his younger brother Jack and then a severe bout with scarlet fever the year of John's birth contributed to a childhood trauma in which he feared he was losing his mother's love. He did suffer frequent spells of loneliness then, and the one time a psychiatrist later examined Faulkner his diagnosis was that Faulkner "might not have received enough love from his mother."[2]

In 1907, when Faulkner was nine, his "Damuddy," Lelia Butler, died. The novelist has Quentin at about the same age when his Damuddy dies. Although it is not certain that the actual event was particularly traumatic for Faulkner, at that time Maud Faulkner was preparing to give birth to another son. Consequently, as Joseph Blotner shows, the "children were left more often to their own devices." That summer Faulkner and Estelle Oldham played much together for the first time and decided "they would get married and have a chicken farm."[3] The connections among these events help explain the events in the novel. The birth of younger brothers was the occasion of feelings of loneliness. Both a severe illness and the death of Damuddy occurred simultaneously with such births. Estelle Oldham was part of a childhood romance that compensated for a perceived loss of maternal affection. The recovery of Estelle around 1927, which removed Faulkner's obsession with the events around 1918, in effect enabled him to deal with the earlier loss in fiction. At the same time Faulkner may have anticipated the problems of his coming marriage, as *Flags in the Dust* implies. He was by his own admission severely upset by personal anxieties and problems during the writing of *The Sound and the Fury*.[4]

Faulkner often said that he began the novel as an attempt to capture lost innocence. He gave several versions of its genesis, and three images are central.[5] First, the exclusion of the children from the house was at the center of the book's genesis. Second, the image of Caddy's soiled drawers is directly related to that exclusion. Third, Benjy, the only one who can really be called "innocent," very soon became for Faulkner the best way to begin telling the story of lost innocence, the drama of the human mind's grief and longing for a fantasied state of childhood bliss.

Benjy's section, establishing the major conflicts and characters in the novel, reveals a family both physically and mentally sick.[6] Benjy's fragmented associations portray a fragmented family in which the lack of sustaining relationships is reflected in his disassociated thoughts and images. Deaths, funerals, and illness are prevalent. The central episode is Damuddy's funeral, linked to later funerals for Mr. Compson and Quentin. The sick adults—two parents and Uncle Maury—are unable to care for the children. Faulkner, moreover, connects Caroline's poor mothering to her being bed-ridden and depicts her giving birth to a second son as a betrayal of the first.[7]

The children are raised by substitute mothers—Dilsey, Damuddy, Caddy. The nurturing Dilsey manages the house, but as a black woman can never socially be a satisfactory mother-substitute. Even at age seven Caddy insists on replacing her as boss. Damuddy, with whom Jason has slept, has been a mother for him; and her death grieves Jason the most even as it provides another incentive for Caddy to become the mother. Before doing so, she must soil her drawers, the act which so enrages Quentin. Her soiled drawers not only suggest her later loss of virginity, traumatic to both, but more specifically connect anal soiling with the common childhood fantasy of anal birth.

Caddy, of course, is not merely a mother-substitute but a girl and young woman growing as a separate person. While the rest of the family remain frozen in time like Quentin, or ensnared in a self-centered past like her parents, or outside time like Benjy, Caddy is an attractively rebellious individual, the one Compson to assert her own independence from the stultifying environment of her youth. As such she is not only Faulkner's "heart's darling" but a projection of that part of Faulkner himself which he saw liberating itself from its past. As surely as each of the brothers reflects an aspect of the author so does she; and she asserts herself by an act of creation, a birth and an illegitimate one at that.

On the other hand, Caddy suffers as much as anyone from the lack of maternal care. Like Dewey Dell Bundren's, her fall into promiscuous sexuality seems related to the lack of an adequate mother. She must become her own mother not only by giving birth to a child but by assuming at an early age responsibilities at which her mother has failed. Just after she inquires about her mother's illness, her own father asks, "Are you going to take good care of Maury" (p. 92). She feeds Benjy and prepares him for bed. When Damuddy is dying, she must also unbutton Jason for bed as "he began to cry." In her individuality Caddy is an attractive character for Faulkner, a foil to the self-indulgent Caroline. Her concern for others, however, is not returned. Jason exploits her. Quentin perceives her only as a narcissistic reflection of himself. Benjy depends mostly on images associated with her; he later attacks the Burgess girl mostly because her bright colors remind him of Caddy.

Each of these three brothers suffers from a different character pathology and set of fixations that govern his relationship with Caddy and others. For the infantile Benjy love is Caddy offering him a bowl of porridge or Dilsey feeding him a birthday cake. He responds to the simplest recognitions only—the flickering of a fire, the mirror, and finally the sound of "Caddy" from a nearby golf course. His usual reactions are to moan, slobber, or bellow. Still, this moron who has never developed beyond an infantile oral-incorporative stage does embody the novel's theme of yearning for simple love and oneness with the mother. As Benjy seems arrested at this stage, Jason has an anal personality. The fat sniffling crybaby always has his hands, perhaps onanistically, in his pockets, a gesture that signals his retentive character. Versh infers, "Jason going to be a rich man. . . . He holding his money all the time" (p. 43). As a tattletale, moreover, he holds his secrets inside him until he can release them as a perverse gift to his parent. Quentin meanwhile really yearns for a primitive symbiosis with a nurturant maternal figure. With all three brothers Faulkner also suggests an inability of the male character to outgrow a fear of castration; Benjy is actually gelded; Jason is associated with sterility; and Quentin's whole story is marked by suggestions of emasculation.

Their fixations, moreover, are tied to a single point in time, the death of Damuddy, which is directly connected to the exclusion of the children from the house and from the mother whose own illness is several times confused with Damuddy's (pp. 75–76, 87, 91–92). The loss of Damuddy is, literally for Jason and figuratively for the others, related to the loss of maternal love and care. They must even sleep in a different room than usual, the one where they "have the measles" (p. 89). Finally Caddy takes over the maternal role. Benjy makes the adjustment more or less naturally. Jason cries, and tattles on the others. Quentin's response is more complicated. Frustrated in his wish for his mother, he transfers his attachment to Caddy, not erotically but masochistically. In a later "Appendix," Faulkner wrote that Quentin "loved not his sister's body but some concept of Compson honor . . . not the idea of incest which he would not commit, but some presbyterian concept of its eternal punishment," that he "loved death above all, who loved only death, loved and lived in a deliberate and almost perverted anticipation of death" (p. 411).

The brothers' problems, however, have not only a sexual basis. At the center also lies a first acquaintance with death. They are not allowed to be part of the family at a time of death, but are encouraged to play out a fantasy that a party is going on in the parlor. Sheltered from death, they are isolated from time and change, life and sexuality. The Compson world is one of deception and hiding, covering unpleasant reality with false names. Caroline Compson covers up her own self in bed, but blankets her sick character as if physical weakness were her only problem. She averts her eyes from the sexual growth of her daughter and granddaughter. She blurs the reality of mental illness in the family by changing a son's name, hides the facts of her granddaughter's illegitimacy by not allowing mention of her own daughter's name, and generally covers her own failures by a wordgame in which "Bascomb" identifies the good and "Compson" the bad. Because she never looks at the checks Jason burns in her presence, she does not have to recognize they are specious. Her fantasies of gentility protect her from reality and involvement. Her husband's defenses are also crippling. He isolates himself not in the bedroom but the office, resorts not to hypochondria but alcoholism, plays not with family names but with ancient philosophers and comforting abstractions. Similarly Uncle Maury carries on his romance by means of furtive deception, lives off the family while boasting of delusory plans. It is no surprise that Jason, who prides himself on being candid and outspoken, deceives his mother, his sister, and himself, or that Quentin wraps himself in an elaborate incestuous fantasy that terminates in a suicide which suggests a final pathetic attempt to achieve fusion with the lost mother.

Quentin feels the loss of his mother most poignantly. He repeatedly laments, "If I'd just had a mother so I could say Mother Mother" (p. 213), or "If I could say Mother. Mother" (p. 117). In Quentin's final moments, however, he confronts images of both parents, his mother in a complex fantasy and his father in a remembered conversation. He recalls a childhood storybook with a picture of "a dark place into which a single weak ray of light came slanting." The picture, which at some point he "jagged out," obsessed him "until the dungeon was Mother herself she and Father upward into weak light holding hands and us lost somewhere below even them without even a ray of light" (p. 215). The image suggests parental betrayal and withdrawal. In another passage implying a similar dungeon-womb, Quentin is a King replacing his father and wreaking vengeance on his siblings: "I'd break that place open and drag them out and I'd whip them good" (p. 215). Quentin's fantasy, however, is troubled by two other images of his mother—the realistic one of her self-indulgently lying "back in her chair, the camphor handkerchief to her mouth" (p. 214), and the metaphorical one of a masculine woman who "was never a queen or a fairy" but "always a king or a giant or a general" (p. 215). This aggressive mother seems the greatest threat to Quentin's identity.

Quentin's condition illustrates two aspects of the threat: Caroline is a maternal failure, and Caddy, although Faulkner's "heart's darling," is both betrayer and castrater. Quentin feels he lost Caddy not only to her lovers but also to Benjy, who is her greatest concern, as he lost Caroline to Jason. Caroline wanted to take Jason off with her, to leave the others with Father:

> I can take Jason and go where we are not known
> I'll go down on my knees and pray for the
> absolution of my sins that he may escape this
> curse try to forget that the others ever were (p. 128).

Her fantasy is simply an inversion of Quentin's. Jason is her favorite son, "the only one who isn't a reproach." "You are all I have," she reminds him, for Caddy and Quentin "were always conspiring against me. Against you too, though you were too young to realise it." Caroline's paranoia is accompanied by an inverse jealousy. A mother reproaches her son for aligning with the daughter who is herself the object of his displaced love for the mother. She then accepts by default the other son, who is as selfish and self-pitying as she, and imagines a world where they two alone can escape the damages of time and their own imperfections. Quentin meanwhile has tried to recoup his loss by displacing his love onto Caddy. The pathos of his attempt is dramatized in scenes with Caddy, in the sequence with a little Italian girl in Boston, and in his quixotic efforts to tilt against three young men—Dalton Ames, Herbert Head, and Gerald Bland.

Quentin spends his final afternoon as big brother to a young girl who has lost her way home. They first meet at the bakery door, where a cruel proprietess, one of several false mothers in the book, would throw out "the little wretch" as a thief.[8] Quentin provides her with cake and ice cream, then searches for her home; but mother after mother denies her at the door. By the time her brother Julio assaults Quentin for stealing his sister, she has adopted Quentin; and as his own sister indirectly costs him his life, the "little sister" almost costs him a brutal beating by a "brother."[9] The whole sequence with Julio and the sheriff, in fact, is a parody of Quentin's own honorable attempts to protect his sister. Julio even has as little success defending his sister as Quentin does with Caddy. As a literal alien he finds his threats as empty as those of the figuratively alienated Quentin; he is, to Marshall Anse, a foreigner who should probably be arrested himself.

Quentin's memories lead from the smell of honeysuckle, always associated with Caddy's downfall, into the slap he gave her at fifteen for kissing a man, to his interrupted petting with Natalie in the barn. Caddy, considering Natalie "a dirty girl," had pushed her down a ladder, terminating what she perceived as a sexual situation. After Natalie left in a pique, Quentin did not wash himself but plunged into the hog-wallow. Trying to force Caddy to care whether he had been bad, he smeared mud all over her. Caddy ripped his face with fingernails, drawing blood, in an attempt to scratch his eyes out. For Quentin the entire memory signals thwarted sexuality and his own emasculation. Progressively he has lost his manhood. He cannot fight Dalton Ames, can only slap him like a girl. He goes unconscious not because Ames hits him but because he "had just passed out like a girl" (p. 201). With Ames's pistol he is ineffective against Herbert Head. His hand is as tender as one "just out of the convent" (pp. 135–36). In both cases Caddy must come to protect him. Their roles keep inverting; he is the passive one, and by the end his name belongs to a girl.

The loss of manhood culminates in two scenes near the end—the abortive suicide pact with Caddy and the fight with Gerald Bland, a snobbish Kentucky youth with a stable full of horses, Negro servants, and women. Gerald is an ironic image of Quentin's own wish-fulfillment. When he went off to Harvard, his mother came along, just as Caddy had originally gone to school because Quentin had. Mrs. Bland took "an apartment in town, and Gerald had one there too, besides his rooms in college" (p. 112). When he sails in the college races she rides along beside the river "in a hired auto . . . parallel with him, the car in low gear . . . like a King and a Queen . . . on parallel courses like a couple of planets." In Quentin's final reverie he and his own mother are the King and Queen. Mrs. Bland has the same snobbish concern for caste and name that Caroline Compson has, but with more justification. Her first introduction, moreover, is inclosed between two memories of Caddy's marriage, the latter including Quentin's introduction to Herbert, who presumes to be his big brother. Thereby Herbert would not only take the beloved sister but also usurp the role of eldest brother. The longer scene between Quentin and Herbert (pp. 130–39) is preceded by another reference to Gerald's women and to the letter Mrs. Bland has sent Quentin. She tries to become a mother also to Quentin, for he has the proper Southern credentials for her affection. She twice tries to change his roommates, to move out that barbaric fat Shreve McKenzie, with whom Quentin has an incipient homosexual relationship. Quentin remains unseduced, because Mrs. Bland already has a chosen son. Quentin requires nothing less than exclusive possession of the mother, but he loses each mother-figure to a "fraternal" rival.

On Quentin's final day, Mrs. Bland and Gerald drive by just as he is arrested and return him to Cambridge. While in the car, just as he passes the little girl for the final time, he "couldn't stop" the obsessive memories of Caddy and virginity—his own blurred with hers (p. 183). Italic and roman print are not distinct here, and images of Gerald with his "cap made for motoring in England" and "Oar blades winking" are conflated with Dalton Ames and Caddy's many lovers, "they two blurred with the other forever more."[10] This combination incites Quentin's rage. Gerald and Dalton have Mother and Caddy, as from childhood Jason and Benjy seem to have shut him out. Caddy's attempts to comfort him ("Poor Quentin you've never done that have you") become taunts, to which his only reply is the vain attempt to replace the lovers with himself by means of words:

> I'll tell Father then it'll have to be because you love Father then we'll have to go away amid the pointing and the horror and the clean flame I'll make you say we did I'm stronger than you I'll make you know we did you thought it was them but it was me listen I fooled you all the time it was me you thought I was in the house where that damn honeysuckle (p. 185).

When Caddy is deflowered Benjy bawls and bellows. Quentin goes with her to the creek, where she cleanses herself. She praises Dalton (as Mrs. Bland is praising Gerald), who has been in the army and around the world. Quentin tries to make Caddy say she was forced into sex, that she hates Ames. Her condescending avowal that she really hates him is as false as are both Quentin's boasts that he has fornicated "lots of times with lots of girls" and his plan for mutual suicide. Caddy, like Addie Bundren, will not substitute false words for true experience. By the end of the scene, which directly precedes Quentin's pathetic confrontations with Gerald and Dalton, his fantasies have been destroyed and he has been emasculated. The language is implicitly sexual:

> it wont take but a second Ill try not to hurt
> all right
> will you close your eyes
> no like this youll have to push it harder
> touch your hand to it

> but she didn't move her eyes were wide open looking past my
> head at the sky
> Caddy do you remember how Dilsey fussed at you because
> your drawers were muddy
>> dont cry
>> Im not crying Caddy
>> push it are you going to
>> do you want me to
>> yes push it
>> touch your hand to it
>> dont cry poor Quentin (p. 189).

Quentin sobs, Caddy gets up and straightens her clothes, Quentin had dropped his knife. His searching for the missing instrument recalls Benjy's looking down for his missing testicles.[11]

Meanwhile the honeysuckle is overwhelming—April in Mississippi, June in Massachusetts (p. 210)—but for Quentin it is "the saddest odour of all" just as "was" is "the saddest word of all." Again time and sex fuse in Quentin's mind as reminders of his own most profound loss, that of his mother. To stop experience at the happiest moment would mean to deny the passage of time and sex from the time Quentin was an only child. It was actually births that had to be stopped. Quentin's futile attempts to deny Caddy's sexual activity, and to transport her to a timeless world in hell or beyond, are unsatisfactory substitutes even in his own mind. At the moment when he first imagines his own suicide, and even the Day of Judgment when "only the flat-iron would come floating up," he is curiously obsessed with Dalton Ames. His one wish is, "If I could have been his mother lying with open body lifted laughing, holding his father with my hand refraining, seeing, watching him die before he lived" (p. 98). To have prevented Ames's birth might satisfy Quentin. Since Ames is the one to possess the sister/mother, he also suggests the brothers of whom Quentin was jealous. To have prevented their birth, and retained exclusive possession of the mother, only that would completely satisfy Quentin.

The ineffectual father, found in so much of Faulkner's fiction, also contributes to Quentin's malaise; and the crucial image in his final fantasy (p. 215) suggests equal betrayal by both parents. "Bred for a lawyer," Mr. Compson keeps an office without clients, does little all day but drink, write satiric eulogies, and daydream of the past. Like Quentin he acts only in words, not the high-sounding words of honor and courage and virginity, but the fictions of a cynical resignation. He has two other traits Quentin lacks—alcoholism, which finally kills him but may have helped him survive for years, and misogyny, which precludes the self-destructive concern with virginity paralyzing Quentin. He bequeaths that, along with his name, to a younger son who combines it not with alcohol—Jason will not drink—but with miserliness.

Father's obsession with words, and Quentin's, points more directly at the significance in this novel of Faulkner's underlying concern for his own artistic career, a concern even clearer in *As I Lay Dying*, which revolves around a dialectic over the failure of words. It also seems likely that Faulkner connected, even if unconsciously, his literary career with the loss of childhood happiness. Those novels most concerned with the process of fiction-making and epistemology (*The Sound and the Fury, As I Lay Dying, Light in August, Absalom, Absalom!*) all revolve around characters terribly alienated from or exiled from the home and vainly trying either to escape time and reality or to verbalize a fiction to accommodate that reality. Faulkner's comments on art and literature invariably alluded to Keats's "Ode on a Grecian Urn" and the continual attempt of the writer to stop time while keeping the experience behind the writing alive, an attempt foredoomed to failure. Even his often discussed device of the "frozen moment" suggests that for Faulkner art depended paradoxically on being both something that stopped time and something that remained alive forever. Life is motion, ever changing; art is a means both to enshrine and to take revenge on life for changing. Quentin Compson's frustration is learning that words do not control reality, that they cannot reify what never existed, that his words can determine his sister's past or future no more than breaking a watch crystal can stop time.

Quentin's chapter both begins and ends with words between father and son, referring to Time and the Sister. Father calls the family-heirloom watch, passed on to his son, a "mausoleum of all hope and desire," an aid not to remember time "but that you might forget it now and then for a moment and not spend all your breath trying to conquer it" (p. 93). Time and the Sister are central concerns throughout this chapter, but also parts of more complex patterns of imagery that come together by the end. Two separate strands are clear. One, consisting of honeysuckle, gasoline, and water, links the mother Caroline to the sister Caddy, to sexuality, and also to Quentin's infatuation with death. The other, consisting of shadows and mirrors, clocks, and "words," symbolizes Quentin's futile attempt to order and control experience. Honeysuckle is a reminder of Caddy's sexuality and the scenes of her promiscuity, though at times it is replaced by roses or wistaria, recalling youth or the past. In Quentin's final "dungeon dream" the honeysuckle got "into the room in waves building and building up until I would have to pant to get any air at all out of it until I would have to get up and feel my way like when I was a little boy" (p. 215). It gives way to gasoline, a reminder of Caddy's wedding. Herbert Head's wedding present to Caddy was one of the first cars in Jefferson, and the smell of gasoline remains important for both Quentin and Jason, who associates it with Caddy's subsequent dismissal by Herbert and his own loss of a bank position. On this day Quentin insists on using gasoline to remove a bloodstain from his clothes, the stain resulting from his fight with Gerald Bland over what he chose to regard as an insult to his sister. At the same time he is obsessed with sleep, getting through a door, and "the sad generations seeking water." Thoughts of gasoline, Gerald, and Mrs. Bland, moreover, then give way to a memory of his mother and her vanity in sending a son to Harvard, described as "the caverns and the grottoes of the sea tumbling peacefully to the wavering tides because Harvard is such a fine sound forty acres is no high price for a fine sound" (p. 217). Death by water becomes his only means to escape time and to reunite himself with Mother or Caddy.

Time and consciousness remained an important theme for Faulkner, whether he focused on man's necessary fictions about the past (*Absalom, Absalom!*), life as change and motion (*The Hamlet* and *Go Down, Moses*), or comic continuity amid tragic terminations (*Light in August*). By the end of his own career he had returned in time to the setting of his early fiction and the commencement of his own career (World War I and *A Fable*); to the time of his youth (*The Reivers*); and to retelling and reworking stories from earlier books (as in *The Mansion*). For Quentin Compson time is the crucial enemy of his own aesthetic apotheosis. The shadow, into which he often retreats, would seem to represent for him that paler self, lacking the mortality of the flesh-and-blood self, in his desired state. Throughout the chapter Quentin's shadow haunts him at moments of greatest consciousness about Caddy. He continually tramples it, in an action as absurdly ineffective as breaking a watch. Quentin depends on as many illusions and deceptions as the rest of his family; but for him the stakes are higher, the game more serious, the consequences fatal.

Quentin seeks eternity, and words are his and Faulkner's means of achieving it. Quixotic Quentin tells his father that a man of courage can strike down evil. Father flippantly replies that the verbal confession of incest obviates the need for further action, that words are a sufficient defense mechanism. In his Latinate manner he argues that the lie was an attempt "to sublimate a piece of natural human folly into a horror and then exorcise it with truth." Quentin, whose simultaneous dependence on and dissatisfaction with words does reflect Faulkner's dilemma as developing artist, confesses a desire to flee the world with Caddy and a belief that the verbal disclosure reifies the act and blocks out other people. Father responds that "you are not thinking of finitude you are contemplating an apotheosis in which a temporary state of mind will become symmetrical above the flesh and aware both of itself and of the flesh it will not quite discard you will not even be dead" (p. 220). Quentin retaliates against only one word—"temporary." He grants Father everything except permanence. To stop change would be worth all the rest; but Quentin's secular eschatology is even more futile than Dilsey's religious salvation. If one of Father's final lines seems apt advice for Jason— "watching pennies has healed more scars than Jesus"—his last words are Quentin's epitaph: "was the saddest word of all there is nothing else in the world its not despair until time its not even time until it was" (p. 222).

Throughout the chapter Father seems less a parent than a priest, for

Quentin comes to him as a false penitent whose attempts to confess an imaginary incest begin "Father I have committed incest." Quentin's impulse seems almost religious, and in Faulkner's novels fiction-making as either flight from reality or adjustment to reality often has a religious dimension.[12] Quentin, like a good Southerner haunted by Pickett's fatal charge spelling the downfall of an idyllically envisioned world, longs for this edenic bliss. But he also, like the poet, believes words can go a long way toward a remedy for the loss. Reverend Whitfield in *As I Lay Dying* is comically reminiscent of Quentin when, on arriving at Anse's house in fear that Addie before dying has confessed their adultery, learns his fears are groundless. He concludes that God, satisfied with the words and the will, would not ask for a real confession. Quentin will offer the real confession, even if only of imagined deeds. The confession like poetry is verbal, and he vainly hopes it will reify the illusion.[13]

Jason IV reflects the familial conflicts of *The Sound and the Fury* as fully as and more subtly than does Quentin. He is also an original creation. No American novelist before 1929 had presented such a villain, inaccurate as the term may be, realistically from the inside and in his own voice.[14] Jason is, of course, narcissistic, cruel, dishonest, and self-destructive. His control of the narrative and his frequently candid speech, however, make it harder for the reader to distance himself from Jason than from Uriah Heep or other literary villains. Even Faulkner never managed such a realistic villain again; with Popeye and Flem Snopes, for example, he resorts to the grotesque and other distancing devices.

Faulkner stands in the same relationship to Jason that he does to Horace Benbow in *Sartoris*, though ironic distance is measured by cruelty rather than dreamy idealism. Traits have been inverted. Quentin, the romantic idealist, dies. Jason, who has some of the hard, violent cruelty of Bayard, survives. His more superficial relationship to Faulkner is clearer only in retrospect. Faulkner came to see himself, especially after his own father's death in 1932, as the sole supporter of a widowed mother, a house full of servants, assorted relatives, and (as much as he loved them) another man's children. Later letters to Hal Smith and Robert Haas sound, if less extreme, like Jason's protests about his financial responsibilities.[15] Jason's misogyny is also of a piece with aspects of such later novels as *Sanctuary*, *Light in August*, and *The Wild Palms*, reflecting not Faulkner's overall attitude toward women but one part of it, a streak suggesting both a feeling that women had caused him his greatest problems and a projection of his own frustrated desires. Jason respects a good honest Memphis whore more than any respectable woman, and indeed in Faulkner's novels only brothels seem to provide happy homes. Finally Jason's cruelty to his brothers is quite close to the behavior of William when he was a boy.

Jason is in both contrast and conflict with his brother Quentin. His opening lines and one of his defining motifs—"Once a bitch always a bitch, what I say"—establish a tension with Quentin's idolatry of the

virgin sister; but his refusal to treat women as equal human beings is finally as self-destructive as Quentin's. His first concern is his niece's truancy
(both the second and third sections open with "Quentin" skipping classes).
The niece, as symbolic presence of the deed which cost Jason his bank
position, becomes a scapegoat. As namesake of the dead brother, for
whose education the family's land was sold, she also objectifies a continual threat to Jason. She is, of course, a burlesque of everything which
obsessed Quentin, since even if her mother "placed no value whatever" on
her virginity she at least cared for the implications of its loss to Benjy and
Quentin, whereas Miss Quentin scarcely admits there is a moral issue involved in her promiscuity.[16] Having been denied like Quentin the love of
her mother, she has a deprecatory self-image. At seventeen she cakes
"paint on her face" to hide herself even in the mirror, confesses "I'm bad
and I'm going to hell," gives scant attention to any kind of self-
development or self-protection, and finally vanishes as permanently as
Jim Bond. Like Caddy she gives herself sexually but without either affection for others or personal strength. Like Quentin she is self-destructive
but without any romantic idealism or attachment. As with Jason money
becomes her only weapon but without any familial center or personal
ambition.

Money is the key to Jason's character as time and the sister are to
Quentin's. In *The Sound and the Fury* sex and money interweave, as they
do more comically in *The Hamlet*. Money is Jason's substitute for sex, and
his only sex is what he purchases from Lorraine. Similarly his protection
of his money—or rather what he steals from Quentin as well as what he
saves of his own—is comparable to his brother's attempt to hoard Caddy's
virginity and finally just as futile. The sexuality of Caddy and her daughter in each case destroys the preservation. In Jason's case all of his losses
are tallied in financial terms as in Quentin's they are in sexual terms; and
in both cases it is the loss of masculinity and the expected masculine role
that results.[17] Jason does not interrupt his monologue with past obsessions
as Quentin does. Only two scenes from the past play an important
part—the return of baby Quentin to be supported by the Compsons (not
the wedding or fall of Caddy) and the death and funeral of Father (not
any other relationship with him). The first reminds Jason not only of his
personal loss but also of what he self-pityingly sees as an added responsibility. In truth it means a financial windfall for him, and he has saved as
much from Caddy's checks as he would likely have made from his bank
job. The second may have made him the primary support of a decadent
family and a passel of servants, but it also puts him in a position of un-
challenged power. That is represented by his exploitation of Caddy, when
he cheats her out of a hundred dollars for a fleeting glimpse of her
daughter, by his subsequent gelding of brother Benjy, and by his having
power of attorney for his mother. It also means that Jason figuratively
marries his mother, for in effect the two of them raise Quentin, badly, as

her father and mother. By being able to avenge himself, moreover, through Miss Quentin he exercises his hostility against the siblings who are her mother and namesake.

Jason is also the only Compson who goes to work, though he keeps his job only because of Earl's respect for his mother. His failure at work is a measure of his inability to establish viable personal relationships. Unless a clear financial bargain can be struck, Jason cannot function. His thousand dollars is no longer in Earl's business, and their connection is strained. He retains Lorraine with periodic subsidies, making him not a lover but her "daddy" or keeper. The servants he can suffer only by seeing himself as an abused provider. To Luster he cruelly denies tickets to the show for want of a mere nickel. To his mother he can show his feelings only by depositing checks in her account and by managing her finances. Maury, his major threat for her affections once, is now defined as a financial threat. Caddy, the sister who for Quentin is the object of his transferred maternal idealization, is for Jason a source of dishonestly appropriated money; and Miss Quentin, defined as a financial burden, is really a capital investment with regular returns. At the end Jason chases futilely after her. He tries to restore her to the home, as his brother Quentin would restore first Caddy and then the little Italian girl to the home. Whereas for Quentin the restoration implies a return to an earlier state of perfection in the relationship to mother/sister, for Jason it implies a lost state of dignity, masculine respectability, and positive self-esteem.[18] Money becomes the key to his personality less because of a basic anal trait than because he associates it with the bank he was promised. Hoarding money becomes his only means to retrieve what was lost. He becomes a pseudo-banker, vaulting others' money like his own, handling forged checks drawn on banks from St. Louis or Indianapolis, and pretentiously playing the stock market.

The personal relationships keep circling back on themselves so that Caddy, for example, to whom Quentin transfers his maternal attachment, then becomes in the year of his death the mother of Quentin, and must herself fail in that. Jason becomes his own father, but in doing so he must also be father both to Benjy, nee Maury, namesake of Caroline's own brother, and to (Miss) Quentin, thus the seeds of his own destruction. Even harmless Benjy is a threat to Quentin's incest and to Jason's respectability, is perceived as a primitive innocent but a symbol of familial decay, a mute victim but a screaming prophet of chaos. While Quentin's romance suggests a desire to return to a primitive fusion with the mother, a self-enclosed world, and a childhood free of competition for love, Jason's vision suggests the converse. In a cruelly ironic way Jason is the man, not unlike Faulkner, responsible for supporting other men's children; the person losing his position because of an unwanted birth; the man forced to work for dollars in a world where the romantic Quentins are destroyed like serious writers in the marketplace; and the man pro-

tecting his own interests against rival siblings. This does not mean that
either Jason or Quentin is a direct autobiographical image of Faulkner,
but rather that the complicated family conflicts, parental failures, and
sibling jealousies are reflected in the stories of both Quentin and Jason,
and that both brothers incorporate projections of Faulkner's own personality even as in less complex ways Horace and Bayard do in *Flags in
the Dust.*

The final chapter confirms the implications of the first three. It seems
to offer an alternative to the chaos—Dilsey—but does so only in a limited
way. Faulkner's comment that "They endured" was written during a period when he was much more concerned with the condition of black people
in Mississippi. Dilsey in *The Sound and the Fury* is a gaunt, old woman
with dropsical paunch and collapsed face, barely struggling in her "painful and terrific slowness." She does have a healthy attitude toward time
and change that none of the whites have, and she is the only good mother
in the book. If a conventionalized mammy whose almost exclusive concern with her white folks reveals Faulkner's own blindness, she also by
virtue of the sympathetic and accurate surface portrayal becomes his best
black character in the early fiction, a significant development from
Caspey, Isom, and Simon. Until around 1940 Faulkner used black
characters mostly as tools in the development of white conflicts, though as
much from a sense of his own incapacity as anything else. Certainly by the
early 1930s the tragic implications of slavery and racism bore heavily on
his mind. Dilsey has a cohesive personality, and with her religion a cohesive world-view. As even Reverend Shegog's sermon implies, however, it is
an undependable fiction. Only by theatrics can he stir up his congregation. He begins his sermon rationally and in the voice of a white man.
Waxing eloquent he then shifts to the black idiom, is himself consumed by
his voice as he moves "in and out of the myriad corruscation of immolation and abnegation and time" to bring sinners "the ricklickshun en de
Blood of de Lamb." But even if it provides comfort to Dilsey on a bleak
Easter Sunday, the service's sheer theatricality confirms the doubtfulness
of its wider relevance. There is no indication that it brings salvation to
others: Frony, embarrassed at Benjy accompanying Dilsey, is as concerned as a Compson with public appearance; Luster can tease Benjy as
cruelly as Jason teases Luster.

Dilsey has "seed de fust en de last," and her Easter religion is another
version of one of the novel's central themes, the desire to recover a lost innocence. Benjy, Quentin, Jason, Dilsey, Caroline all search futilely for a
past that is unattainable. For Dilsey the religious presence does provide a
comfort available to no one else. The ceremony of innocence, however,
has been drowned with Quentin; and if his niece's flight from the tomb of
her house is a parodic Easter resurrection (as her namesake's death was a
parodic sacrifice), it is also a final irony directed against vain attempts to
restore the past and the mother.[19] Quentin does not rise; she descends

down a tree, like Jack fleeing the giant, with a treasure wrongfully stolen from the parent. But she does not return it to the needy mother. Rather if she departs as her mother had, Quentin vanishes and "whatever occupation overtook her would have arrived in no chromium Mercedes; whatever snapshot would have contained no general of staff" (p. 426). Jason the giant meanwhile futilely chases after her in quest of his own restoration, almost at the cost of his own life.[20] The only recapturing of the past is one that comes at the cemetery, and even Benjy's attempt to go there is unsuccessful.[21]

Notes

1. Certainly the choice of subject matter in *The Marble Faun, A Green Bough, New Orleans Sketches, Soldiers' Pay, Mosquitoes,* and the early short stories was partly governed by literary fashions, imitated models, and the episodes of Faulkner's postwar experience. That there was a blockage of the material from his childhood becomes clear when the rapid development to *The Sound and the Fury* is considered. The early unpublished material, moreover, includes the germs of later novels, but he was then unable to complete them. Consider "The Big Shot," "Evangeline," and "Elmer." The comments on Estelle Oldham are not intended to deny the influence of Helen Baird on Faulkner's early work.

2. Joseph Blotner, *Faulkner: A Biography* (New York: Random House, 1974), II, 1453–54. It seems that John's not Jack's birth was particularly unsettling. A first child commonly feels more anxiety at age three upon the birth of a younger sibling than at age one, when he is too young to feel the threat seriously. According to Blotner, Faulkner's cruel pranks were directed against John. He once lured John into jumping from a window with paper wings. He once tied a rope to a fire hydrant and to John, played horse, pulled one end off the hydrant and sent John falling on his face. He once substituted gunpowder for flash powder, so that John had an unpleasant experience with a camera.

3. Blotner, I, 110.

4. Blotner, I, 571.

5. See, for example, James B. Meriwether and Michael Millgate, eds., *Lion in the Garden* (New York: Random House, 1968), pp. 145, 245; Frederick L. Gwynn and Joseph L. Blotner, eds., *Faulkner in the University* (1959; rpt. New York: Vintage Books, 1965), pp. 32–32; and a previously unpublished introduction to the novel by Faulkner printed in *MissQ,* 26 (1973), 410–15.

6. William Faulkner, *The Sound and the Fury* (1929; rpt. New York: Random House, 1954). References in the text are to the Vintage Books edition, "reproduced photographically from a copy of the first printing."

7. On Faulkner's psychological portrait of a family see Lois Gordon, "Meaning and Myth in *The Sound and the Fury* and *The Wasteland,*" in *The Twenties,* ed. Warren French (Deland: Everett/Edwards, 1975), pp. 269–302. On Caddy as the mythic center of a false Eden see Boyd Davis, "Caddy Compson's Eden," *MissQ,* 30 (1977), 382–94. Several critics have argued from the same specifics as I do, but in quite different directions. See John L. Longley, Jr. " 'Who Never Had a Sister': A Reading of *The Sound and the Fury,*" *Mosaic,* 7 (1973), 35–54. An original psychoanalytical reading of the novel is provided by M. D. Faber in "Faulkner's *The Sound and the Fury*: Object Relations and Narrative Structure," *AI,* 34 (1977), 327–50. A recent article using biographical information well is David Minter, "Faulkner, Childhood, and His Making of *The Sound and the Fury,*" *AL,* 51 (1979), 376–93.

8. Her wedding ring is emphasized (p. 156).

9. The sequence recalls the "little sister death" motif in Faulkner's early prose.

10. See p. 184, where Quentin jumbles Caddy's and his words in *"I dont know too many there was something terrible in me terrible in me Father I have committed Have you ever done that We didnt we didnt do that did we do that."*

11. John Irwin, in his stimulating study *Doubling and Incest/Repetition and Revenge* (Baltimore: Johns Hopkins Univ. Press, 1975), has explicated this passage rather fully. The best study of Quentin's voice in the novel is Stephen M. Ross, "The 'Loud' World of Quentin Compson," *SNNTS*, 7 (1975), 245–57.

12. Major examples are Reverend Hightower, Reverend Whitfield (comically in *As I Lay Dying*), *A Fable*, and *Requiem for a Nun*, and they go back to Reverend Mahon in *Soldiers' Pay*.

13. Quentin confesses primarily to his father; but his roommate at Harvard is named Shreve, a derivative of "shrive," to take confession and prescribe penance. Quentin's final confession is actually a written note to Shreve. Moreover, Spoade's crude jokes about Quentin's marriage to Shreve, when he will not visit Cambridge whores, connect his roommate to his long preserved virginity and indirectly back to the Sister, in addition to the father. What is remarkable about Quentin's Cambridge experience is the way in which he envisions so many people as substitutes for relations at home: Mrs. Bland as the mother, Gerald as a brother as well as the self, a little Italian as the sister, and Shreve at different times as father or brother. When upset at Estelle Oldham's marriage, Faulkner had fled to New England, then to Canada. Quentin's not-really-desired departure is for New England and is inseparable in the novel from a beloved's wedding, but the Canadian meets him there. Faulkner went to one Ivy League city, New Haven, Quentin to another, Cambridge.

14. Defenses of Jason as a semi-sympathetic character are based not only on the weaknesses of his relatives but also on the attribution of some of Faulkner's own personality features to him. See, for example, Linda W. Wagner, "Jason Compson: The Demands of Honor," *SR*, 79 (1971), 554–75; and David Aiken, "The 'Sojer Face' Defiance of Jason Compson," *Thought*, 52 (1977), 188–203. Also see James Mellard, "Type and Archetype: Jason Compson as Satirist," *Genre*, 4 (1971), 173–88; and Stephen M. Ross, "Jason Compson and Sut Lovingood: Southwestern Humor as Stream of Consciousness," *SNNTS*, 8 (1976), 278–90.

15. Joseph Blotner, ed., *Selected Letters of William Faulkner* (New York: Random House, 1976), pp. 78, 122. For a discussion of Faulkner's artistic utilization of his own misogyny see Albert Guerard, "The Misogynous Vision as High Art: Faulkner's *Sanctuary*," *SoR*, 12 (1976), 215–31.

16. For insightful discussion of Caddy, and Miss Quentin, see Eileen Gregory, "Caddy Compson's World," in *The Merrill Studies in* The Sound and the Fury (Columbus: Merrill, 1970), pp. 89–101; Gladys Milliner, "The Third Eve: Caddy Compson," *MQ*, 16 (1975), 268–75; and Douglas B. Hill, Jr., "Faulkner's Caddy," *CRevAS*, 7 (1976), 26–38.

17. See Irwin, p. 47.

18. It is appropriately coincidental that although *The Sound and the Fury* was written in 1928, and Jason's personal financial collapse occurred in April of that year, it was published in October 1929, the month of the Stock Market Crash, which to many signified the collapse of an economic and social order. By the way, the name of Jason's prostitute is noteworthy. Caroline's name seems a curious combination of Candace and Lorraine. The desired mother is sought by the two brothers in the paired forms of the whore and the virgin.

19. See Irwin, pp. 154–55.

20. The ogre follows Quentin, is almost killed by a hatchet (in Mottstown), but as the money is not returned to the mother's home neither is the ogre killed.

21. This article is written with the help of a leave of absence from Wayne State University. I wish to thank the several colleagues, especially Arthur F. Marotti, who helpfully criticized earlier drafts.

INDEX

Works and characters appear under the author's name except in the case of Faulkner where characters are listed separately *in italics*. Only notes of substance or of important bibliographical concern are included.